MCTS: Microsoft Exchange Se
Configuration Study Guide, 2n

MW00675327

Exam 70-236

OBJECTIVE	CHAPTER
Installing and Configuring Microsoft Exchange Servers	
Prepare the infrastructure for Exchange installation	1
Prepare the servers for Exchange installation	2
Install Exchange	2, 8
Configure Exchange server roles	3, 4
Configuring Recipients and Public Folders	
Implement bulk management of mail-enabled objects	5
Configure recipients	5
Configure mail-enabled groups	5
Configure resource mailboxes	5
Configure public folders	5
Move mailboxes	5
Configuring the Exchange Infrastructure	
Configure connectors	4
Configure the antivirus and anti-spam system	7
Configure transport rules and message compliance	7
Configure policies	7
Configure public folders	6
Configure client connectivity	4
Monitoring and Reporting	
Monitor mail queues	9
Monitor system performance	9
Perform message tracking	9
Monitor client connectivity	9
Create server reports	9
Create usage reports	9

Sybex®
An Imprint of
 WILEY

Exam objectives are subject to change at any time without prior notice and at (ISC)²'s sole discretion. Please visit (ISC)²'s website (www.isc2.com) for the most current listing of exam objectives.

Sybex®
An Imprint of
WILEY

MCTS
Microsoft® Exchange Server 2007 Configuration
Study Guide
Second Edition

Joel Stidley

Wiley Publishing, Inc.

Acquisitions Editor: Jeff Kellum
Development Editor: Gary Schwartz
Technical Editors: Nagesh Mahadev and Jeff Guillet
Production Editor: Eric Charbonneau
Copy Editor: Judy Flynn
Production Manager: Tim Tate
Vice President and Executive Group Publisher: Richard Swadley
Vice President and Publisher: Neil Edde
Media Assistant Project Manager: Jenny Swisher
Media Associate Producer: Shawn Patrick
Media Quality Assurance: Josh Frank
Book Designers: Judy Fung and Bill Gibson
Compositor: Craig Johnson, Happenstance Type-O-Rama
Proofreader: Candace English
Indexer: Ted Laux
Project Coordinator, Cover: Lynsey Stanford
Cover Designer: Ryan Sneed

Library of Congress Cataloging-in-Publication Data

Stidley, Joel, 1976-
  MCTS : Microsoft Exchange server 2007 configuration study guide (Exam 70-236) / Joel Stidley.—2nd ed.
    p. cm.
  ISBN 978-0-470-45852-5 (paper/cd-rom)
  1. Electronic data processing personnel—Certification. 2. Microsoft software—Examinations—Study guides. 3. Microsoft Exchange server. I. Title.
  QA76.3.S749826 2009
  005.7'1376—dc22
                         2009013305

Dear Reader,

Thank you for choosing *MCTS: Microsoft Exchange Server 2007 Configuration Study Guide, Second Edition (Exam 70-236).* This book is part of a family of premium-quality Sybex books, all of which are written by outstanding authors who combine practical experience with a gift for teaching.

Sybex was founded in 1976. More than thirty years later, we're still committed to producing consistently exceptional books. With each of our titles we're working hard to set a new standard for the industry. From the paper we print on to the authors we work with, our goal is to bring you the best books available.

I hope you see all that reflected in these pages. I'd be very interested to hear your comments and get your feedback on how we're doing. Feel free to let me know what you think about this or any other Sybex book by sending me an email at `nedde@wiley.com`, or if you think you've found a technical error in this book, please visit `http://sybex.custhelp.com`. Customer feedback is critical to our efforts at Sybex.

Best regards,

Neil Edde
Vice President and Publisher
Sybex, an Imprint of Wiley

To my loving and patient wife and children

Acknowledgments

This book, like all publications, took a lot of hard work and patience on many levels. First, thanks go out to the entire Exchange team at Microsoft for making a truly awesome product. Second, a thank-you to Will Schmied and Kevin Miller for creating the foundation for this book when they wrote the first edition. Although the book looks drastically different from that earlier edition, a portion of the original content has been distilled and refined to make this edition a great composition.

Next, I'd like to thank Jeff Kellum, Pete Gaughan, Jenni Housh, and Connor O'Brien at Sybex for doing all of the back-office work to get this project done. Of course, I'd also like to thank both Eric Charbonneau and Gary Schwartz, who worked closely with me to mold the raw product into something much more valuable.

Two of the most critical pieces of a successful technical book are technical and grammatical accuracy. Thankfully, I had three of the best editors that I've worked with; Judy Flynn, Nagesh Mahadev and Jeff Guillet, to make this book accurate both technically and grammatically.

I'm also indebted to a number of other people who were crucial for providing honest and direct guidance and assistance along the way: Siegfried Jagott, Erik Gustafson, and Andy Schan.

About the Author

Joel Stidley has been working in the IT field for over 13 years, and he has been a computer fanatic for much longer. He obtained his first Microsoft certification in 1999 and is currently an MCSE, MCTS, and Exchange MVP. At the beginning of his IT career, he was supporting MS-DOS and Windows for Workgroups clients on a Novell NetWare network at a small manufacturing company. Shortly thereafter, he discovered the joys of Windows NT Server. Joel worked with Microsoft Exchange on the Exchange Server 5.0 beta releases. Since that time, he has done migrations from legacy messaging systems such as Lotus cc:Mail to Exchange as well as numerous Exchange 5.5 to 2000 and 2003 versions. He also led an engineering team to create a shared Exchange 2000 hosting platform before Microsoft released guidance on how to do so. Since then, he has been working extensively with Exchange 2000, 2003, and 2007 in a variety of environments.

In 2004, Joel founded ExchangeExchange.com, a Microsoft Exchange–focused community website, where he blogs and provides forums for discussing Exchange, PowerShell, certification, and general Windows information. In the last few years, he has also been writing extensively. He contributed content to *MCITP: Microsoft Exchange Server 2007 Messaging Design and Deployment Study Guide: Exams 70-237 and 70-238* (Sybex, 2007) and served as lead author on *Professional PowerShell for Exchange Server 2007 SP1* (Wrox, 2008) as well as *MCTS: Windows Server 2008 Applications Infrastructure Configuration Study Guide* (Sybex, 2008). Currently, he is the principal systems architect at Terremark Worldwide, Inc., where he works with a variety of directory, storage, virtualization, and messaging technologies.

He currently lives in the Dallas, Texas, area with his wife and two children. You can contact him at joel@exchangeexchange.com or read his blog at http://exchangeexchange.com/blogs/joel.stidley/.

Contents at a Glance

Contents

Chapter 5   **Working with Recipients, Groups, and Mailboxes   253**

Table of Exercises

Introduction

A few years ago, Microsoft changed its certification program to contain four primary series: Technology, Professional, Master, and Architect. The Technology series of certifications is intended to allow candidates to target specific technologies and is the basis for obtaining the Professional, Master, and Architect series of certifications. The certifications contained within the Technology series consist of one to three exams focused on a specific technology and do not include job-role skills. By contrast, the Professional series of certifications concentrates on a job role and is not necessarily focused on a single technology but rather on a comprehensive set of skills for performing the job role being tested. The Master series of certifications requires three weeks of sessions and up to three written and lab exams. The Architect certifications are premier certifications that consist of passing a review board consisting of previously certified Architects. To apply for the Architect series of certifications, you must have a minimum of 10 years of industry experience.

When obtaining a Technology series certification, you are recognized as a Microsoft Certified Technology Specialist (MCTS) on the specific technology or technologies on which you test. The Professional series certifications include Microsoft Certified IT Professional (MCITP) and Microsoft Certified Professional Developer (MCPD). Upon meeting the entry requirements, attending all of the training sessions, and passing the exams, you can achieve a Microsoft Certified Master (MCM) series certification. Attending additional training sessions and passing a board review for an Architect series certification will allow you to become a Microsoft Certified Architect (MCA).

This book has been developed to give you the critical skills and knowledge you need to prepare for the 70-236 exam requirements for obtaining the MCTS: Configuring Exchange Server 2007.

The Microsoft Certified Professional Program

Since the inception of its certification program, Microsoft has certified more than two million people. As the computer network industry continues to increase in both size and complexity, this number is sure to grow—and the need for *proven* ability will also increase. Certifications can help companies verify the skills of prospective employees and contractors.

Microsoft has developed its Microsoft Certified Professional (MCP) program to give you credentials that verify your ability to work with Microsoft products effectively and professionally. Several levels of certification are available based on specific suites of exams. Microsoft has recently created a new generation of certification programs:

Microsoft Certified Technology Specialist (MCTS)   The MCTS certification is considered the entry-level certification for the new generation of Microsoft certifications. The MCTS certification program targets specific technologies instead of specific job roles. You must take and pass one to three exams.

Microsoft Certified IT Professional (MCITP)   The MCITP certification is a Professional series certification that tests network and system administrators on job roles rather than only on a specific technology. Obtaining the MCITP certification generally consists of passing one to three exams in addition to obtaining an MCTS-level certification.

Microsoft Certified Professional Developer (MCPD)   The MCPD certification is a Professional series certification for application developers. Similar to the MCITP, the MCPD certification focuses on a job role rather than on a single technology. Obtaining the MCPD certification generally consists of passing one to three exams in addition to obtaining an MCTS-level certification.

Microsoft Certified Master (MCM)   MCM is the elite certification series. Obtaining an MCM requires a candidate to demonstrate senior-level technical and business expertise. The qualified candidate will have several years of experience designing, deploying, and managing the certified technology as well as an MCITP certification in the same technology track.

Microsoft Certified Architect (MCA)   MCA is Microsoft's premier certification series. Obtaining the MCA requires a minimum of 10 years of experience and passing a review board consisting of peer Architects.

How Do You Become Certified on Exchange Server 2007?

Attaining Microsoft certification has always been a challenge. In the past, students have been able to acquire detailed exam information—even most of the exam questions—from online "brain dumps" and third-party "cram" books or software products. For the new generation of exams, this is simply not the case.

Microsoft has taken strong steps to protect the security and integrity of its new certification tracks. Now prospective candidates must complete a course of study that develops detailed knowledge about a wide range of topics. It supplies them with the true skills needed, derived from working with the technology being tested.

The new generations of Microsoft certification programs are heavily weighted toward hands-on skills and experience. It is recommended that candidates have troubleshooting skills acquired through hands-on experience and working knowledge.

Fortunately, if you are willing to dedicate the time and effort to learn Exchange Server 2007, you can prepare yourself well for the exam by using the proper tools. By working through this book, you can successfully meet the exam requirements to pass the Configuring Exchange Server 2007 exam.

This book is part of a complete series of Microsoft certification study guides published by Sybex that together cover the new MCTS, MCITP, and MCPD exams as well as the core MCSA and MCSE operating-system requirements. Please visit the Sybex website at www.sybex.com for complete program and product details.

MCTS Exam Requirements

Candidates for MCTS certification on Exchange Server 2007 must pass one Exchange Server 2007 exam. Other MCTS certifications may require up to three exams. For a more detailed description of the Microsoft certification programs, including a list of all the exams, visit the Microsoft Learning website at www.microsoft.com/learning/mcp.

The Configuring Exchange Server 2007 Exam

The Configuring Exchange Server 2007 exam covers concepts and skills related to installing, configuring, and managing Exchange Server 2007 in the enterprise. It emphasizes the following elements of Exchange Server 2007 support and administration:

- Installing and configuring Microsoft Exchange servers
- Configuring recipients and public folders
- Configuring the Exchange infrastructure
- Monitoring and reporting
- Configuring disaster recovery

This exam is quite specific regarding Exchange Server 2007 requirements and operational settings, and it can be particular about how administrative tasks are performed within the operating system. It also focuses on fundamental concepts of Exchange Server 2007 operation. Careful study of this book, along with hands-on experience, will help you prepare for this exam.

 Microsoft provides exam objectives to give you a general overview of possible areas of coverage on the Microsoft exams. Keep in mind, however, that exam objectives are subject to change at any time without prior notice and at Microsoft's sole discretion. Please visit the Microsoft Learning website (www.microsoft.com/learning) for the most current listing of exam objectives.

Types of Exam Questions

In an effort to both refine the testing process and protect the quality of its certifications, Microsoft has focused its newer certification exams on real experience and hands-on proficiency. There is a greater emphasis on your past working environments and responsibilities and less emphasis on how well you can memorize. In fact, Microsoft says that certification candidates should have hands-on experience before attempting to pass any certification exams.

 Microsoft will accomplish its goal of protecting the exams' integrity by regularly adding and removing exam questions, limiting the number of questions that any individual sees in a beta exam, limiting the number of questions delivered to an individual by using adaptive testing, and adding new exam elements.

Exam questions may be in a variety of formats. Depending on which exam you take, you'll see multiple-choice questions as well as select-and-place questions. Simulations and case study–based formats are included as well. You may also find yourself taking what's called an *adaptive format exam*. Let's take a look at the types of exam questions and examine the simulated testing technique so that you'll be prepared for all of the possibilities.

With the release of Windows 2000, Microsoft stopped providing a detailed score breakdown. This is mostly because of the various and complex question formats. Previously, each question focused on one objective. However, recent exams, such as the Windows Server 2008 Active Directory exam, contain questions that may be tied to one or more objectives from one or more objective sets. Therefore, grading by objective is almost impossible. Also, Microsoft no longer offers a score. Now you will be told only if you pass or fail.

Multiple-Choice Questions

Multiple-choice questions come in two main forms. One is a straightforward question followed by several possible answers, one or more of which is correct. The other type of multiple-choice question is more complex and based on a specific scenario. The scenario may focus on several areas or objectives.

Select-and-Place Questions

Select-and-place exam questions involve graphical elements that you must manipulate to answer the question successfully. For example, you might see a diagram of a computer network, as shown in the following graphic taken from the select-and-place demo downloaded from Microsoft's website.

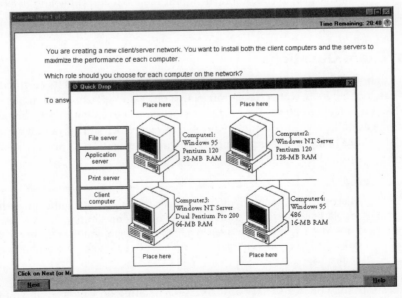

A typical diagram will show computers and other components next to boxes that contain the text "Place here." The labels for the boxes represent various computer roles on a network, such as a print server and a file server. Based on information given for each computer, you are asked to select each label and place it in the correct box. You need to place *all* of the labels correctly. No credit is given for the question if you correctly label only some of the boxes.

In another select-and-place problem you might be asked to put a series of steps in order by dragging items from boxes on the left to boxes on the right and placing them in the correct order. One other type requires that you drag an item from the left and place it under an item in a column on the right.

For more information on the various exam question types, go to www
.microsoft.com/learning/mcpexams/policies/innovations.asp.

Simulations

Simulations are the kinds of questions that most closely represent actual situations and test the skills you use while working with Microsoft software interfaces. These exam questions include a mock interface on which you are asked to perform certain actions according to a given scenario. The simulated interfaces look nearly identical to what you see in the actual product, as shown in this example.

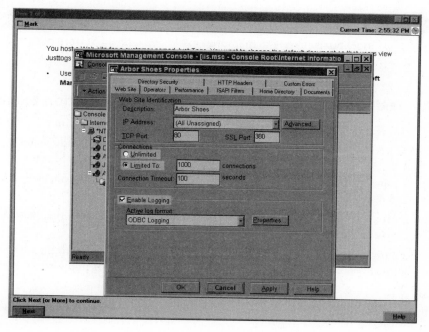

Because of the number of possible errors that can be made on simulations, be sure to consider the following recommendations from Microsoft:

- Do not change any simulation settings that don't pertain to the solution directly.
- When related information has not been provided, assume that the default settings are used.
- Make sure that your entries are spelled correctly.
- Close all the simulation application windows after completing the set of tasks in the simulation.

The best way to prepare for simulation questions is to spend time working with the graphical interface of the product on which you will be tested.

Case Study–Based Questions

Case study–based questions first appeared in the MCSD program. These questions present a scenario with a range of requirements. Based on the information provided, you answer a series of multiple-choice and select-and-place questions. The interface for case study–based questions has a number of tabs, each of which contains information about the scenario. At present, this type of question appears only in most of the design exams.

 Microsoft will regularly add and remove questions from the exams. This is called *item seeding*. It is part of the effort to make it more difficult for individuals merely to memorize exam questions that were passed along by previous test-takers.

Tips for Taking the Exchange Server 2007 Configuration Exam

Here are some general tips for achieving success on your certification exam:

- Arrive early at the exam center so you can relax and review your study materials. During this final review, you can look over tables and lists of exam-related information.
- Read the questions carefully. Don't be tempted to jump to an early conclusion. Make sure you know *exactly* what the question is asking.
- Answer all questions. If you are unsure about a question, then mark the question for review and come back to it at a later time.
- On simulations, do not change settings that are not directly related to the question. Also, assume default settings if the question does not specify or imply which settings are used.

- For questions you're not sure about, use a process of elimination to get rid of the obviously incorrect answers first. This improves your odds of selecting the correct answer when you need to make an educated guess.

Exam Registration

You may take the Microsoft exams at any of more than 1,000 Authorized Prometric Testing Centers (APTCs) around the world. For the location of a testing center near you, call Prometric at 800-755-EXAM (755-3926). Outside the United States and Canada, contact your local Prometric registration center.

Find out the number of the exam you want to take, and then register with the Prometric registration center nearest to you. At this point, you will be asked for advance payment for the exam. The exams cost $125 each, and you must take them within one year of payment. You can schedule exams up to six weeks in advance or as late as one working day prior to the date of the exam. You can cancel or reschedule your exam if you contact the center at least two working days prior to the exam. Same-day registration is available in some locations, subject to space availability. Where same-day registration is available, you must register a minimum of two hours before test time.

 You may also register for your exams online at www.prometric.com.

When you schedule the exam, you will be provided with instructions regarding appointment and cancellation procedures, ID requirements, and information about the testing center location. In addition, you will receive a registration and payment confirmation letter from Prometric.

Microsoft requires certification candidates to accept the terms of a nondisclosure agreement before taking certification exams.

Is This Book for You?

If you want to acquire a solid foundation in Exchange Server 2007, and your goal is to prepare for the exam by learning how to use and manage the new operating system, this book is for you. You'll find clear explanations of the fundamental concepts you need to grasp and plenty of help to achieve the high level of professional competency you need to succeed in your chosen field.

If you want to become certified as an MCTS, this book is definitely for you. However, if you just want to attempt to pass the exam without really understanding Exchange Server 2007, this study guide is *not* for you. It is written for people who want to acquire hands-on skills and in-depth knowledge of Exchange Server 2007.

What's in the Book?

What makes a Sybex study guide the book of choice for hundreds of thousands of MCPs? We took into account not only what you need to know to pass the exam but also what you need to know to take what you've learned and apply it in the real world. Each book contains the following:

Objective-by-objective coverage of the topics you need to know   Each chapter includes a list of the objectives it covers.

 The topics covered in this study guide map directly to Microsoft's official exam objectives. Each exam objective is covered completely.

Assessment test   Directly following this introduction is an assessment test that you should take. It is designed to help you determine how much you already know about Exchange Server 2007. Each question is tied to a topic discussed in the book. Using the results of the assessment test, you can figure out the areas where you need to focus your study. Of course, we do recommend you read the entire book.

Exam essentials   To highlight what you learn, you'll find a list of exam essentials at the end of each chapter. The exam essentials sections briefly highlight the topics that need your particular attention as you prepare for the exam.

Glossary   Throughout each chapter, you will be introduced to important terms and concepts that you will need to know for the exam. These terms appear in italics within the chapters. At the end of the book, a detailed glossary defines these terms, as well as other general terms you should know.

Review questions, complete with detailed explanations   Each chapter is followed by a set of review questions that test what you learned in the chapter. The questions are written with the exam in mind, meaning that they are designed to have the same look and feel as the questions you'll see on the exam. Just as on the exam, there are multiple-choice questions, and select-and-place questions.

Hands-on exercises   In each chapter, you'll find exercises designed to give you the important hands-on experience that is critical for your exam preparation. The exercises support the topics of the chapter, and they walk you through the steps necessary to perform a particular function.

Real-world scenarios   Because reading a book isn't enough for you to learn how to apply these topics in your everyday duties, we have provided real-world scenarios in special sidebars. These explain when and why a particular solution would make sense, in a working environment you'd actually encounter.

Interactive CD   Every Sybex study guide comes with a CD complete with additional questions, flashcards for use with an interactive device, a Windows simulation program, and the book in electronic format. Details are in the following section.

What's on the CD?

With this new member of our best-selling Study Guide series, we are including quite an array of training resources. The CD offers numerous simulations, bonus exams, and flashcards to help you study for the exam. We have also included the complete contents of the study guide in electronic form. The CD's resources are described here:

The Sybex e-book for Exchange Server 2007   Many people like the convenience of being able to carry their whole study guide on a CD. They also like being able to search the text electronically to find specific information quickly and easily. For these reasons, we've supplied the entire contents of this study guide on the CD in PDF format. We've also included Adobe Acrobat Reader, which allows you to view the PDF contents as well as use the search capabilities.

The Sybex test engine   This is a collection of multiple-choice questions that will help you prepare for your exam. There are four sets of questions:

- Two bonus exams designed to simulate the actual live exam.
- All the questions from the study guide, presented in a test engine for your review. You can review questions by chapter or by objective, or you can take a random test.
- The assessment test.

Here is a sample screen from the Sybex test engine.

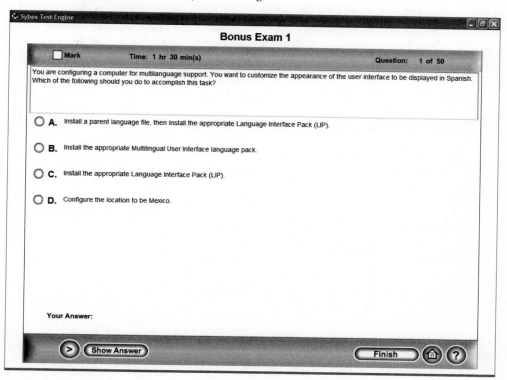

Sybex flashcards for PCs and handheld devices   The flashcard-style question offers an effective way to test your understanding of the fundamental concepts covered in the exam quickly and efficiently. The Sybex flashcards set consists of over 100 questions presented in a special engine developed specifically for this study guide. Here's what the Sybex flashcards interface looks like:

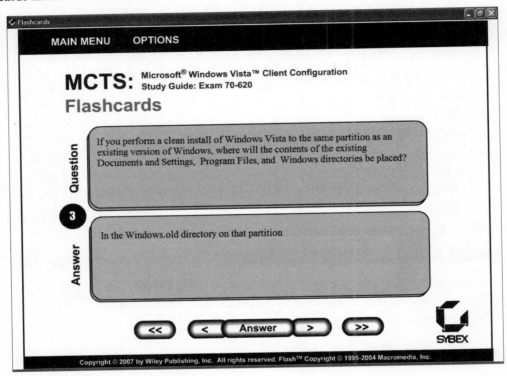

Because of the high demand for a product that will run on handheld devices, we have also developed, in conjunction with Land-J Technologies, a version of the flashcard questions that you can take with you on your Palm OS PDA.

Hardware and Software Requirements

You should verify that your computer meets the minimum requirements for installing Exchange Server 2007 as listed in Tables 2.2 through 2.4 in Chapter 2. We suggest that your computer meet or exceed the requirements for a more enjoyable experience.

The exercises in this book assume, in every chapter except Chapter 7, that you have performed a clean installation of Exchange Server 2007 into an empty forest. Chapter 7 assumes you have Exchange Server 2003 in your organization before installing Exchange Server 2007. Neither of these assumptions, if not met, should impact your ability to perform the exercises.

Contacts and Resources

To find out more about Microsoft Education and Certification materials and programs, to register with Prometric, or to obtain other useful certification information and additional study resources, check the following resources:

Microsoft Learning Home Page

www.microsoft.com/learning

This website provides information about the MCP program and exams. You can also order the latest Microsoft Roadmap to Education and Certification.

Microsoft TechNet Technical Information Network

www.microsoft.com/technet

800-344-2121

Use this website or phone number to contact support professionals and system administrators. Outside the United States and Canada, contact your local Microsoft subsidiary for information.

Prometric

www.prometric.com

800-755-3936

Contact Prometric to register to take an MCP exam at any of more than 1,000 Prometric Testing Centers around the world.

MCP Magazine Online

www.mcpmag.com

Microsoft Certified Professional Magazine is a well-respected publication that focuses on Windows certification. This site hosts chats and discussion forums and tracks news related to the MCSE program. Some of the services cost a fee, but they are well worth it.

Assessment Test

1. Which Exchange Server 2007 server roles provide Outlook Web Access (OWA) functionality to clients?

   A. Mailbox

   B. Hub Transport

   C. Client Access

   D. Edge Transport

2. You are the Exchange administrator for a large network and are about to install the first Exchange server in the organization. Before you do that, however, you must prepare your forest. To which of the following groups must you belong in order to prepare the forest for an installation of Exchange Server 2007? (Choose all that apply.)

   A. Server Admins

   B. Domain Admins

   C. Schema Admins

   D. Enterprise Admins

3. What Exchange-related service is found only on mailbox servers?

   A. Microsoft Exchange EdgeSync

   B. Microsoft Exchange Active Directory Topology

   C. Microsoft Exchange Information Store

   D. Microsoft Exchange POP3

4. What is the function of the checkpoint file within each storage group?

   A. It stores the contents of the mailboxes in the storage group.

   B. It stores the contents of transactions that are not committed to the database.

   C. It stores configuration information about the mailbox databases.

   D. It contains information about which transaction logs have been committed to the database already.

5. What is the name of the Microsoft antivirus and antispam product that has been released for Exchange Server 2007?

   A. Client Security Suite

   B. Forefront Security for Exchange Server

   C. Microsoft Exchange Antivirus

   D. Windows Defender

6. Your company has hired an outside agency to provide accounting services. Many of your employees need to email messages to people in this agency using the Internet. You want to set it up so that the people in the agency appear in the Exchange global address list. What type of recipient object do you need to configure for each person in the outside agency?

   A. Mailbox

   B. Mail-enabled user

   C. Contact

   D. A mailbox with a foreign owner

7. Your manager comes to you and asks you to archive every email in every folder that is older than 60 days to your new archive solution. You don't think that this is the good idea to do right now, so what arguments might you be able to use so you can put it off until off-hours?

   A. Processing this many messages will put a tremendous load on the server and might cause it to become unresponsive.

   B. You can't control the contents of every folder with MRM.

   C. FCC regulations say that you cannot archive all the emails and that some of them need to be maintained online for more than a year.

   D. Both A and B are correct.

8. You are taking a long-overdue vacation and want system notifications regarding public folders to be sent to one of your assistants while you are away. What permission would you assign the assistant on each of the folders?

   A. Folder Owner

   B. Folder Manager

   C. Folder Contact

   D. Folder Notification

9. Where are messages in routing held before they arrive at their final destination?

   A. A queue

   B. A transaction log

   C. A checkpoint file

   D. A storage group

10. Which type of clustering in Exchange Server 2007 has a single point of failure for its disk?

   A. Cluster continuous replication

   B. Network load balancing

   C. Volume shadow copy

   D. Single copy clustering

11. Why would you want to restore a database to a recovery storage group and not to the production storage group?

   A. Because that is the only way you can restore a database in Exchange 2007.

   B. So you don't overwrite the production database because you might want to recover data from it later.

   C. The production database is not damaged. You are trying to recover a single mailbox, and this is the best way to do it.

   D. You can't restore a database to a recovery storage group.

12. What Exchange tool can you use to quickly check performance statistics on your Exchange Server 2007 servers?

   A. Exchange Performance Manager

   B. Exchange Event Viewer

   C. Exchange Server Performance Monitor

   D. Exchange Performance Console

13. A hierarchical arrangement of one or more Windows Server 2003 domains that share a common namespace is referred to as a _____ .

   A. Windows Server 2003 site

   B. domain site

   C. domain tree

   D. domain forest

14. What Exchange Server 2007 server role would you place in the DMZ of your company's network to accept and process SMTP messages?

   A. Hub Transport

   B. Unified Messaging

   C. Client Access

   D. Edge Transport

15. What utility will you need to use to configure security settings on your Exchange Server 2007 servers that are specific to their roles as Exchange servers?

   A. Security Configuration Wizard

   B. Exchange Security Wizard

   C. Exchange Configuration Manager

   D. Exchange Management Console

16. When a database is taken offline, the process is called what?

   A. Mounting

   B. Dismounting

   C. Stopping

   D. Suspending

17. What is responsible for updating recipient information in the Edge Transport servers' ADAM database?

  A. ADAMUpdate

  B. EdgeSync

  C. RecipientUpdate

  D. EdgeUpdate

18. From where can you create mailboxes in Exchange Server 2007? (Choose all that apply.)

  A. The Exchange Management Shell

  B. The Exchange Management Console

  C. The Active Directory Users and Computers console

  D. The Exchange System Manager

19. It is not a good idea to allow users to store email in PST files if you are implementing an MRM plan. Why?

  A. It takes more server resources for the server to attach to a workstation, mount the PST file, and then scan it for records that meet content settings.

  B. Users can turn off their computers, and if a server cannot connect to a user's computer, it cannot manage the records.

  C. PST files cannot be managed.

  D. Storing messages in a PST file breaks single instance storage.

20. A user named Mary is the owner of a public folder. Mary leaves your company, and the former administrator deletes her user account. As the current administrator, you now need to modify the client permissions on the public folder. What will you have to do?

  A. Create a new account with the same user information as the deleted account.

  B. Restore a backup tape of the server that was created before the user was deleted.

  C. Designate your account as the owner of the folder.

  D. Create a new public folder and move the contents of the old folder to it.

21. What tool can you use to determine the delivery status of a message sent from one user in your Exchange organization to another?

  A. Message tracking

  B. Exchange Best Practices Analyzer

  C. Microsoft Operations Manager

  D. Queue Viewer

22. In a cluster, what kind of traffic is sent over the private network?

  A. Mailbox database access requests

  B. Heartbeat traffic

  C. Client access requests

  D. DNS query requests

23. If an Exchange 2007 Enterprise server can have 50 storage groups, how many recovery storage groups can it have?

    A. It can have 49, because you are required to have one in production.

    B. It can have 1, because that's all you get.

    C. It can have 5, because this is based on the standard limit that also applies to the Enterprise server.

    D. It can have 50, because it's configurable with a Registry key.

24. Into what Exchange Management Shell cmdlet can you pipe input to create CSV reports?

    A. Export-CSV

    B. Create-CSV

    C. Make-CSV

    D. Import-CSV

25. What administrative console is used to configure the link costs that Exchange Server 2007 uses when routing messages?

    A. Exchange System Manager

    B. Active Directory Users and Computers

    C. Active Directory Sites and Services

    D. Active Directory Domains and Trusts

Answers to Assessment Test

1. C. The Client Access server role provides all non-MAPI and RPC connectivity for clients, such as HTTP, POP3, and IMAP4. See Chapter 2 for more information.

2. C, D. To prepare the forest for Exchange installation, a user must belong to both the Schema Admins and Enterprise Admins global groups. The user must also belong to the local Administrators group on the computer on which the process is actually run. See Chapter 1 for more information.

3. C. Only the Microsoft Exchange Information Store service is found just on Mailbox servers. The other services listed are found on other server roles or multiple server roles. See Chapter 3 for more information.

4. D. The checkpoint file contains information about which transaction logs have been committed to the database and which transaction logs have not been committed to the database. There is one checkpoint file per storage group. See Chapter 3 for more information.

5. B. Forefront Security for Exchange Server, a product previously known as Antigen by Sybari, is now part of Microsoft. See Chapter 7 for more information.

6. C. A contact (or mail contact) holds the address of a non-Exchange mail recipient. Contacts are made visible in the global address list. See Chapter 5 for more information.

7. D. It would be better to establish custom managed folders, have users move mail into those folders, and then start to manage the default folders. Also, user-created folders are not manageable with MRM; only default and custom managed folders are manageable with MRM. See Chapter 7 for more information.

8. C. A person with the Folder Contact permissions can receive email notifications relating to a folder. Notifications include replication conflicts, folder design conflicts, and storage limit notifications. See Chapter 6 for more information.

9. A. A queue is a temporary staging location for those messages in transit that are between processing steps. There are multiple queues found on each Hub Transport server, and each one represents a set of messages to be processed in a specific way. See Chapter 4 for more information.

10. D. A single copy cluster is susceptible to a lost disk. See Chapter 8 for more information.

11. C. In the past you had to restore the database to an out-of-organization server and then merge the mailbox out with `Exmerge` and deal with it. With the recovery storage group, you don't have to do this anymore. When you restore a database to a recovery storage group, the database is not linked to any mailboxes. If the mailbox is no longer in the dumpster, restoring from backup to the recovery storage group is the best way to get access to the mailbox. See Chapter 10 for more information.

12. C. Although the Performance console has always been available to you in Windows Server 2003, Exchange Server 2007 gives you a customized Performance console called the Exchange Server Performance Monitor that can be accessed from the Toolbox node of the Exchange Management Console. See Chapter 9 for more information.

13. C. A domain tree is a hierarchical arrangement of one or more Windows Active Directory domains that share a common namespace. Domain Name Service (DNS) domain names represent the tree structure. The first domain in a tree is called the *root domain*. See Chapter 1 for more information.

14. D. Of the new server roles in Exchange Server 2007, only the Edge Transport is designed to be placed in the DMZ, outside the Active Directory domain. See Chapter 2 for more information.

15. A. You will need to use the Security Configuration Wizard, a new addition in Windows Server 2003, to configure the security configuration on an Exchange Server 2007 server. See Chapter 2 for more information.

16. B. When you dismount a database, you take it offline and prevent clients from accessing it. See Chapter 3 for more information.

17. B. The EdgeSync process is responsible for updating the ADAM database on Edge Transport servers with configuration and recipient information. See Chapter 4 for more information.

18. A, B. In Exchange Server 2007, you can create mailboxes from the Exchange Management Shell or the Exchange Management Console. See Chapter 5 for more information.

19. C. MRM works only on folders that are stored in an Exchange database mounted on an Exchange server. See Chapter 7 for more information.

20. C. An administrator has the permission to change the owner of a folder. Once the administrator takes ownership of the folder, they can then perform administrative tasks, such as configuring client permissions. See Chapter 6 for more information.

21. A. You can search the message tracking logs to determine whether a message was delivered to a user's mailbox. See Chapter 9 for more information.

22. B. The private network of a cluster is used to pass heartbeat traffic, which is used to determine the status of the cluster nodes. See Chapter 8 for more information.

23. B. One is all you get per server. The recovery storage group should be mounted only when it is needed, so there is no reason to have more than one. See Chapter 10 for more information.

24. A. You will use the Export-CSV cmdlet to take piped input and create CSV files. See Chapter 9 for more information.

25. C. The Hub Transport server, which is responsible for routing all messages in Exchange Server 2007, computes the lowest-cost route to the site containing the destination Mailbox server based on the site-link costs configured on site links between the sites. Sites (and site-link costs) are created and configured using the Active Directory Sites and Services tool. See Chapter 1 for more information.

Chapter 1

Preparing for the Exchange Installation

MICROSOFT EXAM OBJECTIVES COVERED IN THIS CHAPTER:

✓ **Installing and Configuring Microsoft Exchange Servers**

✓ **Prepare the infrastructure for Exchange installation.**

If it isn't already clear from the title, the primary goal of this book is to prepare you to pass the 70-236 exam. This being the case, we'll spend most of our time together ensuring that you acquire the required knowledge and skills to help you achieve that goal. As someone who has a great deal of passion for messaging, I also hope not only to help you to be successful on the exam, but also to be successful as a messaging professional.

In this chapter, we will start with some of the basics of Exchange and Active Directory. Later on in this chapter, we will look at what's new in Exchange Server 2007. This should help those who have used previous versions of Exchange Server ramp up on key new features. As part of that discussion, we will also cover what is no longer included in or supported by Exchange Server 2007. In later chapters in the book, you'll dig deeper into key concepts and core skills that will prove to be important in your day-to-day administration of Exchange Server 2007 and, of course, important to you on exam day.

This chapter provides you with a good conceptual background of the topics covered in the remainder of the book. Specifically, we will address the following:

- Overview of Exchange Server

- What is new and what has been removed in Exchange Server 2007

- Active Directory and its integration with Exchange Server 2007

What Is Exchange Server 2007?

The fact that you are reading this book means that you probably have a basic understanding of what Exchange Server is about and what it is used for. To set the stage for the remainder of the book, let's review a little bit of the history of Exchange Server.

Exchange was introduced as a Microsoft product in 1996, as the eventual full replacement of Microsoft Mail. Exchange 4.0, as it was called, was an X.400-based messaging system that introduced us to features such as public folders and calendaring functions. It didn't fully embrace the Internet until 1997, however, when Exchange 5.5 was released and we were able to use Outlook Web Access and send and receive SMTP email.

The next version, Exchange 2000, maintained most of the features from the previous releases except for the built-in directory service, which contained configuration and information about mailboxes and recipients. What filled this void? A descendant of the Exchange 4.0 directory was reworked into a more powerful version that was then built into Windows 2000 and called Active Directory or, as the service is called in Windows Server 2008, Active Directory Domain Services (AD DS). Although this was a painful transition for many organizations due to the complexity of the migration, it turned out to be the right direction for Exchange as a product. This change allowed Exchange to become more flexible and more scalable.

Exchange 2003 was released three years later with improved scalability, stability, and mobility. Features like RPC over HTTP, Recovery storage groups, Exchange ActiveSync, and the Exchange migration tools made it one of the most compelling yet easiest versions to deploy to date.

Even with the improvements found in Exchange 2003, there were areas that needed work. Exchange 2007 was released as a 64-bit-only application, requiring the use of 64-bit-capable hardware with a 64-bit edition of Windows Server. It also introduced the concept of server roles, allowing specific features of Exchange to be installed on separate servers. Two of these five new roles are the Unified Messaging role, which provides for integrating voicemail and fax features, and the Edge Transport role, which is designed as an Internet-facing mail-processing engine.

What is Exchange Server 2007? Simply put, it is an enterprise-class messaging system that provides the best-in-class email delivery, unified messaging, and electronic calendaring functionality.

Active Directory for Exchange Server 2007

As briefly discussed in the last section, *Active Directory* is one of the most important components of Exchange Server. Although a full discussion of Active Directory is outside the scope of this book, the nature of Exchange Server's tight integration with Active Directory warrants a brief discussion of the technology and an examination of how it affects the Exchange messaging environment.

Active Directory

To understand Active Directory, it is first necessary to understand what a directory is. Put simply, a *directory* contains a hierarchy that stores information about objects in a system. This is similar to how a phone directory stores information about a person, their phone number, and their home address.

Windows Server 2008 introduced Active Directory Domain Services (AD DS). This is essentially a rebranding of Active Directory to describe the feature better and to be able to incorporate related products with Active Directory branding in Windows Server 2008. These products include Active Directory Certificate Services (AD CS), Active Directory Lightweight Directory Services (AD LDS), Active Directory Federation Services (AD FS), and Active Directory Rights Management Services (AD RMS). Since Active Directory for Exchange Server 2007 works with both Windows Server 2003 and 2008 and the core functionality is the same, this book will generically refer to it either as Active Directory or AD.

A *directory service* is the service that manages the directory and makes it available to users on the network. Active Directory stores information about objects on a Windows Server network and makes it easy for administrators and users to find and use it. Active Directory uses a structured data store as the basis for a hierarchical organization of directory information.

You can use Active Directory to design a directory structure tailored to your organization's administrative needs. For example, you can scale Active Directory from a single computer network all the way to many networks. Active Directory can include every object, server, and domain in a network.

What makes Active Directory so powerful and so scalable is that it separates the logical structure of the Windows Server domain hierarchy from the physical structure of the network.

Logical Components

In Exchange 5.5 Server and prior versions, resources were organized separately in Windows and in Exchange. Now the organization you set up in Active Directory and the organization you set up in Exchange Server 2007 are the same. In Active Directory, the domain hierarchy is organized using a number of constructs to make administration simpler and more logical. These logical constructs, which are described in the following sections, allow you to define and group resources so that they can be located and administered by name rather than by physical location.

Objects

An *object* is the basic unit in Active Directory. It is a distinct named set of attributes that represents something concrete, such as a user, printer, computer, or application. *Attributes* are the characteristics of the object; for example, a computer is an object and its attributes include its name and location. A user is also an object. In Exchange, a user's attributes include the user's first name, last name, and email address. User attributes also include Exchange-related features, such as whether the object can receive email, the formatting of email it receives, and the location where it can receive email.

Organizational Units

An *organizational unit (OU)* is a container in which you can place objects such as user accounts, groups, computers, printers, applications, file shares, and other organizational units. You can use organizational units to hold groups of objects, such as users and printers, and you can assign specific permissions to them. An organizational unit cannot contain objects from other domains, and it is the smallest unit to which you can assign or delegate administrative authority. Organizational units are provided strictly for administrative purposes and convenience. They are transparent to the end user but can be extremely useful to an administrator when segmenting users and computers within an organization.

You can use organizational units to create containers within a domain that represents the hierarchical and logical structures within your organization. This enables you to manage how accounts and resources are configured and used.

You can also use organizational units to create departmental or geographical boundaries. In addition, you can use them to delegate administrative authority over particular tasks to particular users. For instance, you can create an OU for all your printers and then assign full control over the printers to your printer administrator.

Domains

A *domain* is a group of computers and other resources that are part of a network and share a common directory database. A domain is organized in levels and is administered as a unit with common rules and procedures. All objects and organizational units exist within a domain. Also, all domains are part of a forest, which is a collection of domains.

You create a domain by installing the first domain controller inside it. In Windows Server 2008, a domain controller is created first by installing the Active Directory Domain Services role. Once the role has been installed, you can use the Active Directory Domain Services Installation Wizard to install Active Directory. To install Active Directory on the first server on a network, that server must have access to a server running as a *Domain Name System (DNS)* server. If it does not, the installation wizard will install and configure the DNS service for you.

A domain can exist in one of five possible domain functional levels, as outlined in the following list:

- *Windows 2000 mixed*: The default domain functional level for all new domains. It allows for Windows NT 4.0 backup domain controllers (BDCs), Windows 2000 Server domain controllers, and Windows Server 2003 domain controllers. Local and global groups are supported, but universal groups are not. Global catalog servers are supported. Exchange Server 2007 cannot be installed into a domain with this functional level.

- *Windows 2000 native*: The minimum domain functional level at which universal groups become available, along with several other Active Directory features. It allows for Windows 2000 Server, Windows Server 2003, and Windows Server 2008 domain controllers. Exchange Server 2007 can be installed in a domain with this functional level, but some advanced cross-forest features are not available.

- *Windows Server 2003 interim*: This supports only Windows NT 4.0 and Windows Server 2003 domain controllers. This mode is only used when you upgrade domain controllers in Windows NT 4.0 domains to Windows Server 2003 domain controllers. The domains in a forest are raised to this functional level; the forest level has been increased to interim.

- *Windows Server 2003*: This level provides all Windows Server 2003 features and functionality such as domain rename. This allows for only Windows Server 2003 and higher domain controllers. All cross-forest Exchange Server 2007 features are supported at this functional level.

- *Windows Server 2008*: This provides the highest level of features, such as fine-grained password policies. This level allows for only Windows Server 2008 and higher domain controllers.

WARNING The move from a lower functional level to a higher one is irreversible, so be sure that all domain controllers running previous versions of Windows Server have been retired or upgraded before you change the functional level.

Domain Trees

A *domain tree* is a hierarchical arrangement of one or more Windows Active Directory domains that share a common namespace. DNS domain names represent the tree structure. The first domain in a tree is called the *root domain*. For example, a company named Wiley Publishing (that has the Internet domain name wiley.com) might use the root domain wiley.com in its primary domain tree. Additional domains in the tree under the root domain are called *child domains*. For example, the domain sales.wiley.com would be a child domain of the wiley.com domain. Figure 1.1 shows an example of a domain tree.

FIGURE 1.1 A domain tree is a hierarchical grouping of one or more domains.

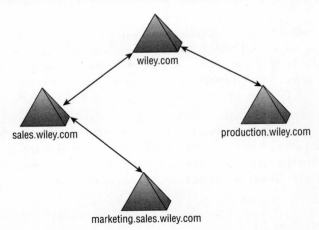

Domains establish trust relationships with one another that allow objects in a trusted domain to access resources in a trusting domain. Since Windows Server 2003, Active Directory has supported transitive, two-way trusts between domains. When a child domain is created, a trust relationship is automatically configured between that child domain and the parent domain. This is a two-way trust, meaning that resource access requests can flow from either domain to the other. The trust is also transitive, meaning that any domains trusted by one domain are automatically trusted by the other domain. For example, in Figure 1.1, consider the three domains named wiley.com, sales.wiley.com, and marketing.sales.wiley.com. When sales.wiley.com was created as a child domain of wiley.com, a two-way trust was formed between the two. When marketing.sales.wiley.com was created as a child of sales. wiley.com, another two-way trust was formed between those two domains. Though no explicit trust relationship was ever defined directly between the marketing.sales.wiley.com and wiley.com domains, the two domains trust each other anyway because of the transitive nature of trust relationships.

Domain Forests

A *domain forest* is a group of one or more domain trees that do not form a contiguous namespace but might share a common schema and global catalog. There is always at least one forest on the network, and it is created when the first Active Directory–enabled computer (domain controller) on a network is installed. This first domain in a forest is called the *forest root domain*, and it is special because it is really the basis for naming the entire forest. It cannot be removed from the forest without removing the entire forest. Finally, no other domain can ever be created above the forest root domain in the forest domain hierarchy. Figure 1.2 shows an example of a domain forest with multiple domain trees.

FIGURE 1.2   A domain forest consists of one or more domain trees.

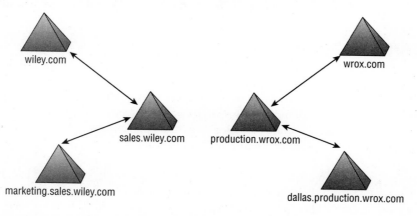

A forest defines the outermost boundary of Active Directory; the directory cannot be larger than the forest. You can create multiple forests and then create trust relationships between specific domains in those forests; this would let you grant access to resources and accounts that are outside a particular forest. However, an Exchange organization cannot span multiple forests.

Physical Components

The physical side of Active Directory is primarily represented by domain controllers and sites. These enable organizations to optimize replication traffic across their networks and to assist client workstations in finding the closest domain controller to validate logon credentials.

Domain Controllers

Every domain must have at least one *domain controller*, a computer running Windows Server that validates user network access and manages Active Directory. During the process of configuring Active Directory, you have the option of creating a new domain or joining an existing domain. If you create a new domain, you also have the option of creating or joining an existing domain tree or forest. A domain controller stores a complete copy of all Active Directory information for that domain, manages changes to that information, and replicates those changes to other domain controllers in the same domain. Schema and infrastructure configuration information are replicated between all domain controllers in a forest.

In Windows Server NT 4.0, a distinction was drawn between primary and backup domain controllers. This distinctions meant that the primary domain controller was the only server that changes to objects in the directory. Since Windows 2000 Server was released, all domain controllers are considered peers, and each holds a writable copy of Active Directory. As you talk to people in the IT industry, you may hear them improperly refer to additional Active Directory domain controllers as backup domain controllers (BDCs). Usually when they say this they mean that an additional domain controller is required. Introduced with Windows Server 2008 was a new option similar to BDCs called read-only domain controllers (RODC).

Global Catalog

In a single-domain environment, users can rely on Active Directory to provide all of the necessary information about the resources on the network. In a multiple-domain environment, however, users often need to access resources outside their domain—resources that might be more difficult to find. For this, a *global catalog* holds information about all objects in a forest. The global catalog enables users and applications to find objects in an Active Directory domain tree if the user or application knows one or more attributes of the target object.

Through the replication process, Active Directory automatically generates the contents of the global catalog from the domain controllers in the directory. The global catalog holds a partial replica of Active Directory. Even though every object is listed in the global catalog, only a limited set of attributes for those objects is replicated in it. The attributes listed for each object in the global catalog are defined in the schema. A base set of attributes is replicated to the global catalog, but you can specify additional attributes to meet the needs of your organization.

By default, the entire forest has only one global catalog, and that is the first domain controller installed in the first domain of the first tree. All others must be configured manually. It is recommended to always add a second global catalog for backup and load balancing. Furthermore, each domain should have at least one global catalog to provide for more efficient Active Directory searches and network logons.

Active Directory Sites

An Active Directory site is a group of computers that exists on one or more IP subnets. Computers within a site should be connected by a fast, reliable network connection. Using *Active Directory sites* helps maximize network efficiency and provide fault tolerance. DNS also uses Windows sites to help clients find the closest domain controller to validate logon credentials.

Exchange Server 2007 makes extensive use of Active Directory information on global catalog servers. For efficient communication, Exchange Server 2007 requires a local global catalog server.

Sites are created and configured using the Active Directory Sites and Services tool. No direct relationship exists between Windows domains and sites, so a single domain can span multiple sites, and a single site can span multiple domains.

One of the biggest mistakes administrators make is not defining all of the IP subnets and assigning them to the appropriate sites. Failing to do this can block the installation of Exchange Server 2007, causing mail-flow issues and client-connectivity problems.

Before deploying Exchange Server 2007, review the Active Directory site configuration to ensure all IP subnets are defined and assigned properly.

Schema

A *schema* represents the structure of a database system—the tables and fields in that database and how the tables and fields are related to one another. The Active Directory information is also represented by a schema. All objects that can be stored in Active Directory are defined in the schema.

Installing Active Directory on the first domain controller in a network creates a schema that contains definitions of commonly used objects and attributes. The schema also defines objects and attributes that Active Directory uses internally. When Exchange Server 2007 is installed, Exchange setup extends the schema to support information that Exchange needs. Updates to the schema require replication of the schema across the forest and to all domain controllers in the forest. Additional information about how Exchange updates the schema will be presented in Chapter 2, "Installing Exchange Server 2007."

Active Directory Partitions, Masters, and Replication

The information contained within Active Directory is not all stored in a single location, or partition in this case. Actually, five Active Directory partitions contain different pieces of information about the Active Directory forest and domains. Because each partition type contains different information, the domain controllers to which each partition type is replicated within the forest are also different. We'll briefly cover these directory partitions in the following sections.

Domain Partition

The domain partition contains all the objects that you as an administrator are used to working with on a daily basis. These objects include items such as user accounts, computer accounts, and groups. The contents of the domain partition thus are specific to each individual domain within a forest and therefore are replicated only to the domain controllers in that specific domain.

Configuration Partition

The configuration partition contains all the configuration information about the forest, including information about Active Directory and AD-integrated applications such as Exchange Server. As such, the configuration partition is replicated to every domain controller in the entire forest. Applications benefit from storing their configuration data in the configuration partition because no additional work or configuration is needed to ensure that configuration information is available forest-wide.

Schema Partition

The schema partition, true to its name, is the housing location for the information that defines what objects exist within that Active Directory forest. Each object also has multiple attributes that can be configured, and thus they are also defined in the schema. The schema partition, being so critical to Active Directory, is also replicated to every domain controller in the forest. Unlike other data in Active Directory, only one copy of the schema partition is writable; that is to say that only one domain controller can make changes to the schema. This special domain controller is known as the *schema master*. We'll discuss the "roles" that domain controllers hold, including that of the schema master, later in this chapter.

Application Partition

Application partitions were introduced in Windows Server 2003 and were designed for holding data that is specific to an application. By default, no application partitions are created in a fresh installation of Active Directory; however, some are usually created to store Active Directory–integrated DNS zones. Application partitions are not limited to being replicated to only a single domain or the entire forest—replication can occur with any domain controller in the forest, spanning multiple domains.

Global Catalog Partition

The global catalog partition is a special type of Active Directory partition that is replicated to configured domain controllers across the entire forest. The global catalog is a read-only partial representation of all objects in a forest. It is used to locate information about objects from any domain in the forest without having to know in which domain the object is located. Exchange heavily relies on the global catalog server to resolve recipient email addresses.

Active Directory Masters

Within each Active Directory forest, five unique "roles" exist (or more properly, *operations masters*) that reside on certain domain controllers. Active Directory uses a multimaster replication system, which means that all domain controllers are equal. Well, mostly equal. Certain tasks do not lend themselves well to having multiple domain controllers performing them (especially at the same time), so the operations master roles exist. Active Directory has five operations master roles, and initially all five exist on the first domain controller installed in a new forest. You can, and should, move roles around as additional domain controllers are joined to the forest and as subsequent domains are created within the forest.

The operations master roles in Active Directory are as follows:

- *Domain naming master*: Only one domain naming master role exists within an entire forest. The domain controller that holds this role is responsible for creating new domains in the forest and also for removing domains from the forest. These tasks cannot normally be performed if the domain controller holding this role is unavailable.

- *Schema master*: There is only one schema master role within a forest. As we discussed briefly, any changes that need to be made to the schema of the forest must be made on the schema master. Once the changes are made on the domain controller holding this role, they are replicated to the rest of the domain controllers in the forest. A failure of the schema master will prevent any schema modifications from being made in that forest. Exchange Server 2007, specifically, requires schema modifications and thus will fail to install if the schema master cannot be contacted.

- *Infrastructure master*: An infrastructure master role exists in each domain in the forest and is responsible for updating changes made to user account names and group memberships. The domain controller holding this role in the domain maintains the up-to-date copy of this information as it is changed and then replicates it to the other domain controllers in the domain.

- *PDC emulator master*: One primary domain controller (PDC) emulator master role exists in each domain in the forest. The PDC emulator master is required to provide backward interoperability with Windows NT 4.0 backup domain controllers (BDCs). In a mixed environment, the PDC emulator master processes all password changes in the domain. Additionally, failed authentication attempts are forwarded to the PDC emulator to be retried, accounting for changes that might have occurred to the password. The PDC emulator master also typically functions as the Network Time Protocol (NTP) source for the domain and is usually configured to take time input from a trusted internal (that is, atomic or satellite clock) or external NTP time source.

- *RID master*: One RID master role exists in each domain in the forest and is responsible for issuing blocks of relative identifiers (RIDs) to other domain controllers in the domain. This block of RIDs is known as the *RID pool*. When a domain controller runs low on RIDs in its RID pool, it makes a request to the RID master for another block of RIDs for its usage. Each object that exists within a domain has a unique security identifier (SID). This SID is composed of two parts: a domain RID (common throughout the domain) and a unique RID from the RID pool. These are combined to create a globally unique (within the forest) SID for that object. When the pool of RIDs has been exhausted on a domain controller, it will be unable to create new objects in the domain. Exchange Server 2007 creates several security principals during its installation and thus requires the usage of some RIDs from the RID pool of a domain controller.

Replication

Although I've mentioned replication in Active Directory several times, I have not yet properly discussed it. I'll remedy that situation now before moving into the next section of this chapter.

Replication is the process by which all domain controllers in a domain or forest pass changes to other domain controllers and thus update their copies of the specific Active Directory partitions they hold as they themselves receive replication updates from other domain controllers. Because changes occur almost constantly across multiple domain controllers within a forest, the replication used for Active Directory is referred to as *loosely consistent*, meaning that not every domain controller in the forest with a certain partition will have the same information at any time. However, over time, *convergence* occurs as all domain controllers receive and pass replication updates and the partitions that they hold become closer to matching exactly. In a production environment with multiple domain controllers, complete convergence is almost impossible to achieve, but that rarely poses a problem. Administrators with the appropriate permissions can always manually trigger replication to be performed between domain controllers, so important changes can be forced to replicate if normal replication schedules are not appropriate at the time, which is typically a problem only when dealing with *intersite replication*.

Given that Active Directory uses sites to map the Active Directory network to that of the physical network, replication thus occurs differently between sites (intersite replication) than it does between domain controllers in the same site (intrasite replication). Intersite replication is designed to have the minimum possible impact on the typically slower wide area network (WAN) links that commonly separate the physical locations that Active Directory sites represent. As such, the replication traffic is highly compressed and also occurs on a schedule that is configured on the *site link* object that is created to logically connect two Active Directory sites. Thus, changes made on a domain controller in Site A will not be sent to a domain controller in Site B until the next scheduled replication time based on the replication interval and allowable replication times that were configured. Conversely, intrasite replication occurs almost immediately after a change has been made to some bit of Active Directory information. The domain controller that the change is made on will wait 15 seconds (to account for any additional changes) and then will begin replicating its changes to the other domain controllers within that site. After replication has occurred with the first replication partner that domain controller has, it will wait three seconds and then commence replication with its next replication partner, and so forth, until the original domain controller has replicated with all replication partners within that site.

Replication latency occurs when a change made on one domain controller has not been replicated to another domain controller, either in the same site or in a different site. Obviously, the replication latency within a site should always be much lower than that between sites, but should replication problems arise between domain controllers, latency can even exist within a site. On the surface, replication latency is not completely desirable, and it must be dealt with accordingly when using a distributed multimaster replication environment like Active Directory uses. Faster, higher-quality (or cheaper) WAN links will lend themselves to configuration replication occurring more frequently than slower, less reliable (or more expensive) WAN links. The price to be paid for lower replication latency in an Active Directory environment that is otherwise healthy and functioning properly is the cost of pushing more data over these typically congested and high-cost WAN links. The administrator who is ultimately responsible for managing Active Directory across your organization will have to determine what is best to meet their specific needs.

To learn more about Active Directory, start by checking out the Windows Server 2008 product documentation. It provides an overview of the technology and illustrates many of the benefits of using Active Directory.

Active Directory and Exchange Server 2007

In versions prior to Exchange 2000 Server, Exchange maintained a directory of its own through a service known as the Directory Service. The Directory Service maintained a copy of the directory in a database file on each Exchange server and took care of replicating changes in the directory to other Exchange servers.

Since Exchange 2000 Server, Exchange has been totally reliant on Active Directory to provide its directory services. This reliance causes a shift in the way that the Exchange directory is maintained. The section "Forests" examines the effects that boundaries of a forest place on Exchange. Then the section "Domain Name Service (DNS)" looks at the interaction of DNS in an Exchange organization.

Forests

By default, the global catalog shows objects only within a single Active Directory forest, so an Exchange organization must be within the boundaries of a forest. This is different from earlier versions of Windows NT and Exchange 5.5. In previous versions, an Exchange organization could span domains that did not trust one another because Exchange 5.5 did not rely so much on the underlying security structure of Windows NT. With Active Directory and Exchange Server 2007, the security structure is integrated, which means a single

Exchange organization cannot span multiple forests but can span multiple domains within a single forest.

Domain Name Service (DNS)

For Active Directory and Exchange Server 2007 to function, DNS must be properly functioning in your organization. Outlook Web Access, SMTP connectivity, and Internet connectivity all rely on DNS.

Active Directory is often called a *namespace*, which is similar to the directory service in earlier versions of Exchange and means any bounded area in which a given name can be resolved. The DNS name creates a namespace for a tree or forest, such as wiley.com. All child domains of wileypublishing.com, such as sales.wiley.com, share the root namespace. In Exchange Server 2007, Active Directory forms a namespace in which the name of an object in the directory can be resolved to the object. All domains that have a common root domain form a *contiguous namespace*. This means the domain name of a child domain is the child domain name appended to the name of the parent domain.

In Active Directory, a DNS domain name such as exchangeexchange.local does not directly affect the email addresses for Exchange users created in that domain. Although a user's logon name might be user@exchangeexchange.local, you can control how email addresses are generated using email-address-generation policies in the Exchange Management Console.

Active Directory Partitions

Although you've examined briefly already how Exchange Server 2007 uses the different Active Directory partitions, you'll dig a bit deeper in this section. Recall that there can be only one Exchange Server organization within an entire forest. Specific examples of how Exchange Server 2007 uses these Active Directory partitions include the following:

- The configuration partition stores all configuration information about the Exchange organization. This information includes items such as recipient policies, address lists, and Exchange settings. The configuration partition is replicated to every domain controller in the forest; therefore, this critical Exchange configuration information is available to every domain user irrespective of which domain holds their user account.

- The domain partition stores information about the basic blocks of Exchange Server: its recipient objects. Recipient objects include the users, contacts, and groups that have configured email addresses. We'll go into great depth about configuring and managing recipients in Chapter 5, "Working with Recipients, Groups, and Mailboxes."

- The schema partition is modified by the Exchange Server 2007 setup routine to add attributes to existing objects, such as users and groups. Additionally, the schema is extended to include Exchange Server–specific objects that are required for Exchange Server to function properly. We'll cover modifying the schema to support the installation of Exchange Server 2007 in Chapter 2, "Installing Exchange Server 2007."

- The global catalog partition received many new items of information as a result of the installation of Exchange Server 2007 in a forest. Exchange uses the global catalog to generate address lists for usage by Exchange recipients, and Exchange Server also uses it to locate a recipient to aid in the delivery of mail items to that recipient. Exchange Server automatically generates the global address list (GAL) from all recipients listed in the global catalog.

Message Flow

In previous versions of Exchange Server, a complex link-state routing algorithm was used to route messages between geographically separated Exchange servers. Exchange used routing groups that were connected with routing-group connectors to perform this routing. With the elimination of routing groups and link-state routing in Exchange Server 2007, all Exchange message routing is performed by Hub Transport servers using the Active Directory sites and site links that service Active Directory itself. As such, message routing (both within the same site and across site links) is significantly less complex in Exchange Server 2007.

We will cover Exchange Server 2007 routing in Chapter 3, "Configuring the Mailbox and Hub Transport Roles."

Within each Active Directory site that contains a Mailbox server (or Unified Messaging server), you must have at least one Hub Transport server. The Hub Transport server is responsible for routing all messages within a site and between connected sites. Even a message that is sent from a recipient on Server A to another recipient on Server A must first cross through a Hub Transport server for delivery—a big change in message routing from Exchange Server 2003. When messages must be routed between sites, the Hub Transport server in the originating site determines the best route available at that time to the destination server and routes the message accordingly.

Message routing between sites occurs as detailed here:

1. The sending user submits the message to their mailbox on the Mailbox server.

2. The Mailbox server notifies a Hub Transport server in its Active Directory site that it has a message awaiting pickup.

3. A Hub Transport server in the same Active Directory site as the originating Mailbox server picks up (retrieves) the message from the Mailbox server.

4. The Hub Transport server performs a query against Active Directory to determine what Mailbox server the recipient of the message is on.

5. The Hub Transport server then computes the lowest-cost route to the site containing the destination Mailbox server based on the site link costs configured on site links between the sites.

6. The Hub Transport server in the originating Active Directory site then sends the message along the lower-cost route it has computed.

7. If multiple Active Directory sites must be crossed, the message is delivered to a Hub Transport server along the path and then passed along to a Hub Transport server in the destination site.

8. If there are no operating Hub Transport servers in the destination site, the message will be queued on a Hub Transport server in the site closest to the one where the destination Mailbox server resides. The message will not be delivered until a Hub Transport server in the destination site is available to deliver it.

9. When the message reaches the Hub Transport in the destination site, that Hub Transport server assumes responsibility to deliver the message, and the message is sent to the appropriate destination Mailbox server.

What's New in Exchange Server 2007?

With any new release of an established product like Exchange Server, Microsoft includes new (and improved) features that benefit both the administrative side of the product and the end-user experience. I'll briefly highlight some of the key features that are new or improved in Exchange Server 2007 (although this list is certainly not all-inclusive):

- *Exchange Management Console*: The first, and most striking, change that many administrators with Exchange experience will notice is that the familiar Exchange System Manager is gone and has been replaced by the completely redesigned Exchange Management Console (EMC). By examining the ways administrators worked and the tasks they needed to perform, Microsoft designed the EMC to be as intuitive and workflow-oriented as possible. The EMC also takes advantage of the improvements in Microsoft Management Console 3.0. We will spend a good deal of our time together in this book working with the EMC.

- *Exchange Management Shell*: Another dramatic change from an administrative standpoint is the Exchange Management Shell, which is a new command-line shell and scripting environment for Exchange administrators. Any action that can be carried out in the EMC can be performed just as easily in the Exchange Management Shell, and many actions that an Exchange administrator will perform can be performed only from within the Exchange Management Shell. You'll see as you work with Exchange Server 2007 that almost every configuration action you perform in the EMC will present you with the corresponding Exchange Management Shell code that is actually being used to carry out those changes.

- *64-bit*: Exchange Server 2007 is the first messaging platform to utilize the benefits of 64-bit hardware and operating systems fully. In fact, Exchange Server 2007 is available for production use only in 64-bit versions. The amount of RAM available to be used efficiently in 64-bit environments is significantly higher than in 32-bit environments, thus allowing for more mailboxes and storage groups on a single Exchange server.

- *Active Directory (AD) site–based routing*: No longer do you need to plan, implement, and manage an Exchange-specific routing environment with routing groups. Exchange Server 2007 is AD site–aware and will use the existing Active Directory sites configuration to perform routing and to select which Exchange servers it should directly communicate with. This change will allow a closer alignment of the physical network topology with the Exchange routing topology.

- *Server roles*: Gone are the days of every Exchange installation being the same as every other installation. Also gone are the days of a single check box being the determining factor in the role played by an Exchange server. Exchange Server 2007 now allows—in fact, it demands—you to deploy it in one or more of several available roles. The familiar back-end server of old is now referred to as a Mailbox server, although it can certainly still host public folders. The closest role to that of the old front-end server would be that of the Client Access server. You'll examine all the roles, uses, benefits, and limitations of Exchange Server in detail in Chapters 2 and 3.

- *Unified messaging*: Once a popular, complex, and costly third-party add-on for Exchange, unified messaging is now available within Exchange Server 2007 by deploying the Unified Messaging role and using Exchange Server 2007 Enterprise client access licenses (CALs). Unified messaging is outside the scope of the 70-236 exam, so I will not be discussing it in this book.

- *Highly available*: In the past, if you wanted highly available Exchange servers, you had two choices from Microsoft: active/passive clusters or active/active clusters. Both were certainly suitable but complex and costly—a reality that prevented many smaller organizations from providing a highly available Exchange solution. Additionally, there were third-party applications that promised various high-availability solutions for Exchange Server, and many of them were very good products. Seeing the need to revamp the high-availability solutions offered in Exchange and wanting to take advantage of new clustering capabilities, Microsoft introduced three new high-availability solutions in Exchange Server 2007: local continuous replication (LCR), cluster continuous replication (CCR), and standby continuous replication (SCR). Clustering using active/passive nodes has been improved and renamed to single copy clustering (SCC), while support for active/active clustering has been eliminated entirely. You will examine high availability for Exchange Server 2007 in Chapter 8, "Configuring Highly Available Exchange Server Solutions."

- *Compliance and message management*: As email continues to grow and evolve as the number-one means of business-critical communication, the need to manage and enforce certain policies on email content and usage also grows. Exchange Server 2007 presents several novel, and quite useful, methods that allow organizations to control the growth of the messaging stores and also to monitor and control the usage of email, thus protecting the organization from legal or other troubles. You'll examine compliance and message management in Exchange Server 2007 in Chapter 7, "Configuring Security, Compliance, and Policies."

- *Antivirus and antispam controls*: The Edge Transport role, one of the new Exchange Server 2007 server roles, is responsible for preventing spam messages from entering your Exchange organization. The intelligent message filter (IMF) has been removed from the Exchange servers that host mailboxes and public folders or that handle client access requests and moved into the Edge Transport role, which is designed to operate in a demilitarized zone (DMZ) network if desired. Additionally, Sybari's Antigen antivirus product is now a Microsoft product known as Forefront Security for Exchange Server. Forefront is a complete Exchange-aware antivirus application that can be used on the Edge Transport server as a network edge scanner and also on the Hub Transport server to scan messages traversing your internal network. You'll examine antivirus and antispam issues in more detail in Chapter 7.

What's No Longer Supported in Exchange Server 2007?

In any new release of a software product, discontinued or de-emphasized features are inevitable. Such is the case with Exchange Server 2007, although some of these items might surprise experienced Exchange administrators. The items that follow in no way represent every change that has occurred in Exchange Server 2007, but they do represent some of the most interesting ones.

Features That Have Been Removed or Replaced

The following key features and functionality have been removed from Exchange Server 2007:

- *Routing groups*: Link-state routing is no longer used in Exchange Server 2007 and has been replaced by Active Directory site–based routing. This places further importance on the proper planning and design of the Active Directory forest into which Exchange Server 2007 will be installed, but it reduces the overall amount of planning and administration required to maintain an Exchange organization. Now all routing (both AD and Exchange) is controlled and configured from a single location—the Active Directory Sites and Services console—thus providing consistent, predictable results that can be controlled as your physical network dictates. You'll examine Active Directory more as it relates to the installation of Exchange Server 2007 in Chapter 2.

- *Administrative groups*: Administrative groups, which were previously used in Exchange Server to control administrative access to groups of servers, have been replaced by the Exchange Server 2007 split permissions model that emphasizes using universal security groups. We'll cover administrative roles more in Chapter 3.

- *Exchange management via Active Directory Users and Computers*: Management of all recipient objects (discussed more in Chapter 5) is now performed via the Exchange Management Console and Exchange Management Shell. Management of Exchange recipients has been integrated in the Active Directory Users and Computers (ADUC) console in the previous two versions of Exchange Server, but Exchange administrators who've worked with Exchange Server 5.5 will recall this method of management very well.

- *Streaming database*: The streaming database (`*.stm`), first introduced in Exchange 2000 Server, has been removed in Exchange Server 2007.

- *Recipient Update Service*: The Recipient Update Service (RUS) has been removed from Exchange Server 2007. To find out more about how to work with recipients, you will examine email address generation more in Chapter 5.

- *Exchange 5.5 interaction*: Exchange Server 2007 does not interoperate with the Active Directory Connector (ADC) or Site Replication Service (SRS) as in the previous two versions of Exchange. As a result, you cannot directly migrate from Exchange Server 5.5 to Exchange Server 2007. We'll discuss migration briefly in Chapter 2.

- *Network News Transfer Protocol (NNTP)*: This has been removed completely. You'll need to use Exchange Server 2003 or Exchange 2000 Server to provide this protocol to clients.

- *X.400 message transfer agent*: This has been removed completely. You'll need to use Exchange Server 2003 or Exchange 2000 Server if your organization needs this message transfer agent protocol.

- *Novell GroupWise connector*: This has been removed completely. You'll need to use Exchange Server 2003 or Exchange 2000 Server to provide this connector.

- *Lotus Notes connector*: This is no longer available, but Microsoft has provided migration and coexistence tools for Exchange Server 2007 by using the Microsoft Transporter Suite tools.

- *Active/active clustering*: This is no longer supported. You'll need to implement either an active/passive SCC model or consider using the new high-availability features provided by CCR. You'll spend all of Chapter 10, "Disaster Recovery Operations for Exchange Server," looking at highly available Exchange Server 2007 implementations.

- *IMAP4 access to public folders*: You'll need to retain Exchange Server 2003 or Exchange 2000 Server to provide IMAP4 access to public folders to clients.

- *Exchange WebDAV extensions*: Exchange WebDAV has been replaced by the Exchange Web Services.

Features That Have Been De-emphasized

The following key features and functionality have been de-emphasized in Exchange Server 2007:

- *Public folders*: Public folders are no longer required in a clean installation of Exchange Server 2007. In previous versions of Exchange Server, public folders contained critical system data such as the Offline Address Book (OAB) and free/busy calendaring data. This is no longer the case, because no system data is stored in public folders in a pure Exchange 2007 environment. Public folders, however, are still supported in Exchange Server 2007, although Microsoft recommends moving to SharePoint Portal Server or another product for those items that previously were stored in public folders. It's expected that public folders (which were initially advertised as not being supported in Exchange Server 2007) will not be supported in a future release of Exchange Server. Microsoft's official support policy says that they will support Public Folders in Exchange 2007 until 2016. I'll cover public folders in Exchange Server 2007 in Chapter 6, "Configuring and Managing Public Folders."

- *Exchange Server 2003 virus scanning API (VSAPI)*: Although Exchange Server 2007 still supports the VSAPI, its role is being de-emphasized because Microsoft has started to integrate antivirus controls at the transport layer. We'll cover antivirus controls in Exchange Server 2007 in Chapter 7.

You can look at the entire list of new and removed features in Exchange Server 2007 by visiting the TechNet website at http://technet.microsoft .com/en-us/library/aa996018.aspx.

Preparing the Infrastructure for Exchange Server 2007 Deployment

If you are planning to deploy Exchange Server 2007, you need to make sure that all of the requirements are met. We have covered many of these requirements over the last few sections in this chapter. These requirements and limitations encompass much of what you need to know to be successful in preparing to install Exchange Server 2007, and to succeed on the exam.

- The schema master must be running Windows Server 2003 Service Pack 1 or later.

- A global catalog running Windows Server 2003 Service Pack 1 or later must be available in each Active Directory site into which Exchange will be deployed. This cannot be a Windows Server 2008 read-only domain controller.

- The Active Directory forest must be set to at least the Windows Server 2000 functional level; however, if cross-forest free/busy information will be shared or forest-to-forest delegation is used, the forest must be set to at least the Windows Server 2003 functional level.

- The Active Directory domain that Exchange will be installed into or that contains Exchange recipients should use at least the Windows 2000 Server native domain functional level.

- All Exchange Server 5.5 computers must be removed from the domain and the Exchange organization must be set to Exchange 2000 native mode.

- Exchange Server 2007 and Exchange Server 2007 Service Pack 1 do not support renaming of the Active Directory domain. If you are considering performing a domain rename, you must do so before deploying Exchange Server 2007.

- Any Exchange 2000 servers and machines with the Exchange 2000 management tools installed in the environment must have the latest post–Service Pack 3 rollup applied.

- Any Exchange Server 2003 computers and machines with the Exchange 2003 management tools installed must have Service Pack 2 applied.

- Be sure that you have verified that your backup, file-level antivirus, third-party mobile messaging, and alert monitoring systems will support Exchange Server 2007.

 Real World Scenario

Planning an Active Directory Deployment

If you are planning a completely new Active Directory deployment for your organization, then you should be certain to place domain controllers and global catalog servers in locations that make sense for how your company is organized and how it operates. When planning how and where to locate these key servers in your Active Directory environment, there is no absolute answer that works for all scenarios. The saying "the more, the better" is not necessarily true, especially if replication over slow WAN links becomes too much for those links to handle. Conversely, saying "less is more" is almost always untrue when it comes to implementing a solid Active Directory infrastructure. Remember, this will be the foundation of your entire network, so you should take however long you need to get it right the first time.

These are a few general guidelines you should keep in mind as you're working in different scenarios:

- Every domain in the Active Directory forest should have at least two domain controllers. This is for both client load balancing and disaster recovery in case one domain controller should fail.

- You should place additional domain controllers in domains as organizational structures (such as physical location or client groupings) dictate.

- You should be aware that additional domain controllers will cause additional replication traffic, which can be problematic for intersite replication across slow WAN links.

- Every Active Directory site must have at least one domain controller and that one domain controller must be configured as a global catalog if Exchange servers or users are in that site.

- If a site has multiple domain controllers, consider using a Bridgehead server for Active Directory replication to other sites.

- Install the right number of Global Catalog servers in each site to support the applications. When using 32-bit domain controllers, the ratio of Global Catalog processor cores to Exchange Mailbox server processor cores is 1 to 4. When using 64-bit Global Catalogs with enough memory to cache the entire Active Directory, the ratio is 1 to 8.

Summary

The better you understand how the Exchange system works, the better you'll be able to plan a viable network and troubleshoot that network when problems occur. This chapter examined three basic aspects of Exchange Server architecture: how Exchange is integrated with Active Directory, how information is stored and organized in Active Directory, and how messages flow within an Exchange organization.

At the top of the Active Directory hierarchy is the domain forest, which represents the outside boundary that any Exchange organization can reach. A domain tree is a hierarchical arrangement of domains that share a common namespace. The first domain in a tree is the root domain. Domains added under this are child domains. Within the domain tree, domains establish trust relationships with one another that allow objects in a trusted domain to access resources in a trusting domain. A domain is a group of computers and other resources that are part of a network and share a common directory database. Each domain contains at least one domain controller. Multiple domain controllers per domain can be used for load balancing and fault tolerance.

When Exchange is installed, many objects, such as users, are enhanced with Exchange-related features. A global catalog holds information about all the objects in a forest. Objects can be grouped into organizational units that allow administrators to manage large groups of similar objects effectively at the same time.

Within Active Directory, five partitions store certain pieces of the total information that makes up Active Directory. These partitions are the domain partition, configuration partition, schema partition, global catalog partition, and application partition(s). There can be multiple application partitions within the forest and domains.

Although Active Directory uses multimaster replication, there are five specific roles that only one domain controller in a forest or domain can hold at any one time. The five roles are the domain naming master (one per forest), schema master (one per forest), infrastructure master (one per domain), PDC emulator master (one per domain) and RID master (one per domain). The failure of a domain controller holding each role will have different effects on the forest and domain. Exchange Server 2007 must contact the domain controller holding the schema master role during setup to modify and extend the schema.

Active Directory is loosely consistent, meaning that not every domain controller in the forest with a certain partition will have the same information at any time. However, over time, convergence occurs as all domain controllers receive and pass replication updates and the partitions that they hold become closer to matching exactly. In a production environment, complete convergence is almost impossible to achieve, but that rarely poses a problem.

Intersite replication is designed to have the minimum possible impact on the typically slower WAN links that commonly separate the physical locations that Active Directory sites represent. As such, the replication traffic is highly compressed and also occurs on a schedule that is configured on the site link object that is created to connect two Active Directory sites logically. Conversely, intrasite replication occurs almost immediately after a change to some bit of Active Directory information has taken place. The domain controller that the change is made on will wait 15 seconds (to account for any additional changes), and then it will begin replicating its changes to the other domain controllers within that site.

As you prepare to deploy Exchange Server 2007, you must ensure that the schema master for the forest has at least Windows Server 2003 Service Pack 2 applied and that the domain and forest functional level is set to Windows 2000 native at a minimum. Next you will want to check to make sure that at least one global catalog at each site that Exchange Server 2007 will be installed in has Windows Server 2003 Service Pack 1, or later, applied.

Exam Essentials

Understand Active Directory.   Although this book is not trying to prepare you for an exam related to Active Directory design, support, or administration, it is absolutely imperative that you understand how Active Directory is designed and how it functions. With Exchange being completely Active Directory–integrated and –aware, all administrative functions related to users and mailboxes are tied into Active Directory. To that end, ensure that you have a good understanding of both the logical and physical structure of Active Directory. In addition, you should understand the various domain functional levels that are available in Windows Server 2003 and Windows Server 2008 and how they will impact your overall network.

Understand basic message routing.   It is helpful, both in preparing for this exam and in the day-to-day administration of Exchange Server 2007, to understand how messages are routed within the same site and between different sites. All messages are routed through the Hub Transport server, even if the originating and destination recipients reside on the same Mailbox server.

Understand the infrastructure requirements.   Exchange is so tightly integrated with Active Directory that specific requirements need to be met on the versions and placement of domain controllers. Understand the domain and forest functional levels that need to be set to install Exchange Server 2007.

Review Questions

1. You are currently running in the Windows 2000 mixed domain functional level and are considering making the switch to the Windows 2000 native domain functional level. Which of the following would be valid concerns to take into account before making the switch? (Choose all that apply.)

    A. The switch is irreversible.

    B. If you later decide to switch to the Windows 2000 mixed domain functional level, all object configuration will be lost.

    C. Exchange Server 5.5 cannot be run in a Windows 2000 native domain functional level environment.

    D. You must upgrade or retire all Windows NT 4.0 domain controllers.

2. Which of the following statements is true of domains in a single-domain tree?

    A. Domains are not configured with trust relationships by default.

    B. Domains are automatically configured with one-way trust relationships flowing from parent domains to child domains.

    C. Domains are automatically configured with two-way nontransitive trusts.

    D. Domains are automatically configured with two-way transitive trusts.

3. By default, how long will a domain controller wait to initiate replication to its replication partners in the same Active Directory site after a change is made on it?

    A. 3 seconds

    B. 3 minutes

    C. 15 seconds

    D. 15 minutes

4. A hierarchical arrangement of one or more Active Directory domains that share a common namespace is referred to as a _____ .

    A. Windows Server 2003 site

    B. domain site

    C. domain tree

    D. domain forest

5. You have just installed the first Windows Server 2008 server on your network and want to make it a domain controller. How would you do this?

    A. The first Windows Server 2003 server is automatically made a domain controller.

    B. Install Active Directory Domain Services role on the computer.

    C. Install DNS on the computer.

    D. Install the schema on the computer.

6. Which of the following statements about an organizational unit is true?

   A. An organizational unit cannot contain objects from other domains.

   B. An organizational unit can contain objects only from other trusted domains.

   C. An organizational unit can contain objects only from other domains in the same domain tree.

   D. An organizational unit can contain objects only from other domains in the same domain forest.

7. What service is the primary provider of name resolution on a Windows Server 2008 network?

   A. X.400

   B. DNS

   C. WINS

   D. SMTP

8. Messages in Exchange Server 2007 are routed by which server?

   A. The global catalog server

   B. The infrastructure master server

   C. The Hub Transport server

   D. The Mailbox server

9. If Exchange Server 2007 fails to contact a certain operations master role holder during installation, the installation process will fail. Which operations master role is this?

   A. Infrastructure master

   B. Schema master

   C. RID master

   D. Domain naming master

10. Message routing between Exchange Server 2007 Mailbox servers uses what method to determine the best route?

   A. Link-state algorithms

   B. Site link costs

   C. Packet latency

   D. Open-shortest-path-first routing

11. Of the following features available in Exchange Server 2003, which are no longer supported in Exchange Server 2007? (Choose two answers.)

   A. Public folders

   B. The streaming database

   C. Command-line management

   D. Integration with Exchange Server 5.5

12. User account objects are found in which Active Directory partition?

   A. Configuration

   B. Global catalog

   C. Schema

   D. Domain

13. What impact does the failure of the domain controller holding the schema master role have on the normal operations of Active Directory?

   A. Active Directory will cease to function properly until the schema master role has been brought back online.

   B. Active Directory will continue to function normally except that schema modifications cannot be processed until the schema master role has been brought back online.

   C. Active Directory will continue to function normally except that intrasite replication will fail until the schema master role has been brought back online.

   D. Active Directory will continue to function normally except that down-level Windows NT 4.0 BDCs will not be able to interact with the domain of which they are a part.

14. To use universal groups in your Active Directory domain, at what minimum domain functional level must you be running?

   A. Windows Server 2003

   B. Windows 2008

   C. Windows Server 2003 interim

   D. Windows 2000 native

15. Which of the following is the smallest object that other Active Directory objects can be placed within and have authority delegated over them?

   A. Organizational unit

   B. Forest

   C. Domain

   D. Site

16. Which domain controllers in an Active Directory environment maintain a copy of the configuration partition?

   A. Certain domain controllers in all domains

   B. All domain controllers in a single domain

   C. All domain controllers in the forest

   D. Certain domain controllers in the forest

17. *Intersite replication* refers to which of the following?

    A. Replication between domain controllers in the same Active Directory site

    B. Replication between domain controllers in different domains

    C. Replication between domain controllers in different forests

    D. Replication between domain controllers in different Active Directory sites

18. Which Active Directory partition is used to create the Exchange address lists?

    A. Configuration

    B. Global catalog

    C. Schema

    D. Domain

19. If the Hub Transport server in the destination site is unavailable, where will a message in routing be queued up temporarily?

    A. On the Hub Transport server in the source site

    B. On the Mailbox server in the destination site

    C. On the Hub Transport server in the destination site

    D. On the Hub Transport server in the site nearest to the destination site

20. What administrative console is used to configure the link costs that Exchange Server 2007 uses when routing messages?

    A. Exchange System Manager

    B. Active Directory Users and Computers

    C. Active Directory Sites and Services

    D. Active Directory Domains and Trusts

Answers to Review Questions

1. **A, D.** The switch to the Windows 2000 native domain functional level is a one-time, one-way switch and is irreversible. Once you have switched to the Windows 2000 native domain functional level, you will no longer be able to have Windows NT 4.0 domain controllers within the organization.

2. **D.** Windows Server 2003 (along with Windows 2000 Server) and Active Directory support two-way transitive trusts between domains. When a child domain is created, a trust relationship is automatically configured between that child domain and the parent domain. This trust is two-way, meaning that resource access requests can flow from either domain to the other.

3. **C.** The domain controller on which the change is made will wait 15 seconds (to account for any additional changes) and then will begin replicating its changes to the other domain controllers within that site. After replication has occurred with the first replication partner of the domain controller, it will wait 3 seconds and then commence replication with its next replication partner, and so forth, until the original domain controller has replicated with all replication partners within that site.

4. **C.** A domain tree is a hierarchical arrangement of one or more Windows Active Directory domains that share a common namespace. Domain Name Service (DNS) domain names represent the tree structure. The first domain in a tree is called the *root domain*.

5. **B.** To create a Windows Server 2008 domain controller, you first install the Active Directory Domain Services role on it and then run DCPromo. During this process, you have the option of creating a new domain or joining an existing domain. If you create a new domain, you also have the option of creating or joining an existing domain tree or forest.

6. **A.** An organizational unit is a container in which you can place objects such as user accounts, groups, computers, printers, applications, file shares, and other organizational units. An organizational unit cannot contain objects from other domains and is the smallest unit to which you can assign or delegate administrative authority. Organizational units are provided strictly for administrative purposes and convenience.

7. **B.** DNS is the primary provider of name resolution for Windows Server 2003–based networks. In fact, the Windows Server 2003 domain structure is based on DNS structure, and Active Directory requires that DNS be used.

8. **C.** All messages in Exchange Server 2007 are routed to their destination mailbox by the Hub Transport server, even if the message is sent between recipients on the same Exchange Mailbox server.

9. **B.** Any changes that need to be made to the schema of the forest must be made on the schema master. Exchange Server 2007 requires schema modifications and thus will fail to install if the schema master cannot be contacted.

10. **B.** The Hub Transport server, which is responsible for message routing in Exchange Server 2007, computes the lowest-cost route to the site containing the destination Mailbox server based on the site link costs configured on Active Directory site links between the sites.

11. B, D. The streaming database (`*.stm`), first introduced in Exchange 2000 Server, has been removed in Exchange Server 2007. Several other enhancements have been made to storage in Exchange Server 2007. Exchange Server 2007 does not interoperate with the Active Directory Connector (ADC) or Site Replication Service (SRS) as in the previous two versions of Exchange. As a result, you can no longer directly migrate from Exchange Server 5.5 to Exchange Server 2007.

12. D. The domain partition contains all of the objects that you as an administrator are used to working with on a daily basis. These objects include user accounts, computer accounts, and groups. The contents of the domain partition thus are specific to each individual domain within a forest and therefore are replicated to the domain controllers in that specific domain only.

13. B. A failure of the schema master will prevent only schema modifications from being made in that forest.

14. D. The Windows 2000 native domain functional level is the minimum domain functional level at which universal groups become available, along with several other Active Directory features; it allows for Windows 2000 Server and Windows Server 2003 domain controllers only.

15. A. The organizational unit (OU) is a container in which you can place objects such as user accounts, groups, computers, printers, applications, file shares, and other organizational units. An organizational unit cannot contain objects from other domains and is the smallest unit to which you can assign or delegate administrative authority.

16. C. The configuration partition contains all the configuration information about the forest, including information about Active Directory and AD-integrated applications such as Exchange Server. As such, the configuration partition is replicated to every domain controller in the entire forest.

17. D. Intersite replication occurs between domain controllers in different Active Directory sites. Intrasite replication occurs between domain controllers in the same Active Directory site. Sites can span domains, and domains can span sites; thus, no direct relationship must exist between the two. Forests do not replicate.

18. B. Exchange uses a global catalog to generate address lists for usage by Exchange recipients and also uses it to locate a recipient to aid in delivering mail items to that recipient. The global address list (GAL) is automatically generated by Exchange Server from all recipients listed in the global catalog.

19. D. If there are no operating Hub Transport servers in the destination site, the message will be queued on a Hub Transport server in the site closest to the one where the destination Mailbox server resides. The message will not be delivered until a Hub Transport server in the destination site is available to deliver it.

20. C. Sites (and site link costs) are created and configured using the Active Directory Sites and Services tool.

Chapter

2

Installing Exchange Server 2007

MICROSOFT EXAM OBJECTIVE COVERED IN THIS CHAPTER:

✓ **Installing and Configuring Microsoft Exchange Servers**

- Prepare the servers for Exchange installation.
- Install Exchange.

The Exchange Server 2007 installation process is pretty straightforward. However, you still need to address some issues in a careful manner. In this chapter, you will learn the necessary steps to prepare to install Microsoft Exchange Server 2007. Exchange Server 2007 provides plenty of installation flexibility—you'll spend time in this chapter looking at the three methods you can use. After you've done that, you'll spend some time examining the various Exchange Administrator roles available and configuring and assigning them as appropriate.

The main topics of this chapter are as follows:

- Exchange Server 2007 editions and licensing

- Exchange Server 2007 roles

- Preinstallation server and network considerations

- Preinstallation modification of Active Directory

- Modification of existing Exchange organizations to support migration

- Choosing the appropriate role or roles to be installed

- Performing graphical user interface installations

- Performing unattended installations

- Performing command-line installations

- Configuring the Exchange Administrator roles

Exchange Server 2007 Editions and Licensing

There are three main licenses that pertain to the various Microsoft Exchange product packages:

Server license This license provides the legal right to install and operate Microsoft Exchange Server 2007 on a single-server machine. In addition, you can install the Exchange Management Console (the primary utility used to administer an Exchange Server 2007 organization) on additional machines without additional licenses.

Client access license (CAL)   This license provides a user with the legal right to access an Exchange server. An organization designates the number of CALs it needs when Microsoft Exchange server is purchased. Each CAL provides one user with the legal right to access Exchange server. Any client software that has the ability to be a client to Microsoft Exchange Server is legally required to have a CAL purchased for it. Microsoft Exchange Server 2007 uses either the per-user or per-device licensing model, which means that each user or device accessing the server must possess a valid CAL.

Client license   This license provides the right to install client software such as Microsoft Office Outlook 2007 on a client computer.

Since licensing policies can change over time, always check the latest policy to ensure your compliance. You can find the licensing policies for Exchange Server 2007 at www.microsoft.com/exchange/howtobuy/default.aspx.

As mentioned already, Microsoft Exchange Server 2007 is available in two editions: *Standard* and *Enterprise*. The main difference is that the Enterprise Edition supports the advanced features mentioned later. However, it's important to reiterate that both versions of Exchange Server 2007 are 64-bit applications, meaning that they must be installed on a 64-bit version of Windows Server 2003 or Windows Server 2008 and on hardware that provides 64-bit support.

Standard Edition Features

The Standard Edition includes the following features:

- Basic messaging functionality
- Role-based server installation
- Support for volume shadow copy
- Usage of the recovery storage group
- Support for Outlook Anywhere (replaces HTTP over RPC) and Outlook Web Access
- Database size limit of 16 terabytes (new in Exchange Server 2007)
- Maximum of five storage groups per mailbox server
- Maximum of five databases per mailbox server
- Support of local continuous replication
- Support of standby continuous replication

Additional Enterprise Edition Features

The Enterprise Edition includes all the features of the Standard Edition plus the following:

- Allows up to 50 storage groups per Mailbox server
- Allows up to 50 databases per Mailbox server
- Supports all clustering models: single copy clusters, local continuous replication, standby continuous replication, and cluster continuous replication

Exchange Server 2007 Compared to Previous Versions

To allow you to see just how different Exchange Server 2007 is from previous versions, Table 2.1 compares a small subset of features across each version of Exchange Server from 2000 to 2007.

TABLE 2.1 Exchange Server 2007 Compared to Previous Versions

Key Feature	Exchange Server 2007	Exchange Server 2003	Exchange 2000 Server
Exchange Server intelligent message filter (IMF)	Available	Available	Not available
Distribution groups restricted to only authenticated senders	Available	Available	Not available
Attachment stripping	Available	Not available	Not available
Open proxy detection (prevents DoS) and spam	Available	Not available	Not available
Per-user journaling	Available	Not available	Not available
Message retention and expiration policies	Available	Not available	Not available
Transport rules	Available	Not available	Not available
Active/passive clustering	Available	Available	Available
Active/active clustering	Not available	Available	Not available
Continuous replication	Available	Not available	Not available

TABLE 2.1   Exchange Server 2007 Compared to Previous Versions *(continued)*

Key Feature	Exchange Server 2007	Exchange Server 2003	Exchange 2000 Server
Database portability	Available	Not available	Not available
Recovery storage groups	Available	Available	Not available
Different out-of-office messages for internal and external senders	Available	Not available	Not available
Outlook Mobile Access	Not available	Available	Not available
Over-the-air search of mailbox from wireless device	Available	Not available	Not available
Voicemail delivery to mailbox	Available	Not available	Not available
Fax delivery to mailbox	Available	Not available	Not available
Outlook Voice Access	Available	Not available	Not available

Obviously, this is just a small sampling of the overall feature set of each version of Exchange. However, it does give a quick glimpse into some of the newer features that help make Exchange Server 2007 stand out from its predecessors. You can get a complete listing of the feature set of each version of Exchange by visiting the following page on the Microsoft website: www.microsoft.com/exchange/evaluation/features/ex_compare.mspx.

Exchange Server 2007 Roles

As you learned in Chapter 1, "Preparing for the Exchange Installation," Exchange Server 2007 no longer uses the familiar front-end and back-end nomenclature to designate a server's primary function. Exchange Server 2007, much like Windows Server 2008, has moved to a roles-based installation model (and thus increased functionality and security). This offers five distinctly different server roles for deployment. Some, such as the Hub Transport and Mailbox server roles, are mandatory. Others, such as the Client Access, Edge Transport, and Unified Messaging roles, will vary in usage from organization to organization. Let me go into detail on each of these roles and the functions they provide.

Mailbox Server

The Mailbox server role is the first of two required Exchange Server 2007 roles. As its name implies, the primary function of the Mailbox server role is to provide users with mailboxes that can be accessed directly from the Outlook client. The Mailbox server also contains the databases that hold public folders if you are still using them in your organization. As a point of comparison, the Mailbox server is most like the back-end server from previous versions of Exchange.

As noted previously, the Mailbox server can hold up to 50 storage groups per server with a total of 50 databases (stores) per server. Each storage group has its own set of transaction logs, so single-database storage groups do have a place in just about any size of organization from a disaster recovery and business continuity perspective.

The Mailbox server role is also where high availability for mailboxes and public folders comes from. Mailbox servers in Exchange Server 2007 can be made redundant using single-copy clustering (which is similar to the traditional active/passive clustering provided in previous versions of Exchange), cluster continuous replication (CCR), or standby continuous replication (SCR). Additionally, smaller organizations will find significant value in the new local continuous replication (LCR) functionality offered by Mailbox servers.

Unlike previous versions of Exchange Server, in Exchange Server 2007 messages are not actually routed between mailboxes by Mailbox servers. All message routing, even between mailboxes on the same Mailbox server, is now the responsibility of the Hub Transport server, which I'll cover next. Because of the nature of the data contained on Mailbox servers, they do not need to be directly accessible from the Internet. Additionally, Mailbox servers must be members of Active Directory domains that have been prepared for the installation of Exchange Server 2007 and they must have fast, reliable connectivity to global catalog servers and domain controllers in the same Active Directory site.

Hub Transport Server

The Hub Transport server is the second mandatory Exchange Server 2007 role that must be deployed. The primary function of the Hub Transport server is to route messages for delivery within the Exchange organization. Since message routing is performed outside the Mailbox server role, many new and needed features and functions become available. As an example, while messages are being routed through the Hub Transport server, you can apply transport rules and filtering policies that determine where they'll wind up, such as in a compliance mailbox in addition to the recipient's mailbox, or what they'll look like, such as every outbound message having a disclaimer stamped on it.

Along with message routing, all message categorization that used to occur on the originating Mailbox server in previous versions of Exchange is now performed on the Hub Transport server. Hub Transport servers are thus a critical part of your healthy and functioning Exchange Server 2007 organization. Although Hub Transport servers cannot be clustered for high availability, multiple Hub Transport servers can (and should) be placed in each Active Directory site where Exchange Mailbox servers exist. In this arrangement, all Hub Transport servers will distribute load and provide failure redundancy.

Another key role that Hub Transport servers fill is providing antivirus and antispam controls inside your internal network. Although the Edge Transport server (or some other hardware or software third-party device) is intended as the primary defense against virus-infected and spam messages, the Hub Transport server allows you to put internal controls in place to prevent virus-infected messages from being sent from within your Exchange organization. Also, as part of an in-depth defense strategy, it places extra layers of protection around your most critical data.

Hub Transport servers must be members of Active Directory domains and must have fast, reliable connectivity to Mailbox servers. There must also be at least one Hub Transport server in every Active Directory site that contains a Mailbox or Unified Messaging server. If not, messages will never be sent to or from these servers in that site.

Client Access Server

As mentioned in the discussion of the Mailbox server role, Outlook clients can connect directly to the Mailbox server to access mailboxes and public folders. Other non-MAPI clients, such as POP3, IMAP4, mobile, and web-based clients, must connect to the Mailbox servers via a Client Access server. In this way, the Client Access server is most like the front-end servers utilized in previous versions of Exchange Server. One major difference with the Client Access server role is that, rather than proxying most requests from the client to the back end, the CAS server will process the requests directly.

In addition to providing non-MAPI client access to the Exchange databases, the Client Access server provides other features, such as Autodiscover, which allows an Office Outlook 2007 client to configure a user's profile automatically without the need to enter the server and mailbox information as with previous versions of Outlook. Although a Client Access server is not a requirement, it is recommended even in sites that do not have direct Internet access. With the options of using Office Outlook Web Access and Exchange ActiveSync–enabled mobile devices, it's a good bet that not every client in an organization will be a MAPI one.

Client Access servers also need to be members of Active Directory domains and should typically be located on the internal portion of your organization's network. If the Client Access server must be accessible from the Internet, it should be presented to the Internet via some sort of application-layer firewall to secure connections to and from the Client Access server and the Internet.

Edge Transport Server

The Edge Transport server, an optional role, is an entirely new dedicated role in Exchange Server 2007. Designed to be deployed in the DMZ of your network, the Edge Transport server is used to provide a secure SMTP gateway for all messages entering or leaving your

Exchange organization. As such, the Edge Transport server is primarily responsible for antivirus and antispam controls as well as protecting the recipient data held within Active Directory.

When an inbound message is received by the Edge Transport server, it scans the messages and then takes the appropriate actions if it determines that the message is a virus or if it appears to be a spam message. Normal, clean messages are delivered to a Hub Transport server for policy and compliance enforcement as well as for delivery to the final recipients.

Unlike all other Exchange Server 2007 roles, the Edge Transport role cannot be deployed on a server with any other roles—it must be deployed by itself on a completely separate server. This is done to increase Exchange security and the overall security of the internal network. The Edge Transport server, because of its specialized role, is not intended to be a member of the Active Directory domain, or at least the corporate Active Directory. Since the Edge Transport servers are supposed to be placed in the DMZ portion of the network, you would not want to open all of the TCP ports into your Active Directory domain controllers, nor would you want any security compromise of an Edge Transport server to expose your corporate Active Directory. To simplify password management in larger organizations, some have chosen to create a separate Active Directory domain for the servers in the DMZ.

Since recipient information is needed for proper message acceptance and routing, the Edge Transport server uses a specialized instance of Active Directory Application Mode (ADAM) or Active Directory Lightweight Directory Services (AD LDS) in Windows Server 2008 to store its configuration and recipient information. The Hub Transport server then initiates one-way replication from Active Directory to the Edge Transport server to stay up-to-date.

Because of its specialized role, the Edge Transport server requires two-way SMTP access only through the external firewall. This is a radical departure from previous versions of Exchange Server and will increase the security of that server dramatically. Only two-way SMTP and one-way (from the inside) Active Directory synchronization traffic is required through the internal firewall.

Unified Messaging Server

The last of the Exchange Server 2007 server roles is also the most radically changed from any previous version of Exchange Server. Seeing the increased integration with Exchange Server by third-party voice and fax messaging companies, Microsoft raised the bar and built that functionality, and much more, into Exchange Server 2007.

The Unified Messaging server role provides the following functionality to an Exchange Server 2007 organization:

- Fax reception and delivery to Exchange mailboxes
- Voice call answering, voicemail recording, and delivery of voicemail to Exchange mailboxes

- Voicemail access via a phone connection
- Message read back via a phone connection, including replying to the message or forwarding it to another recipient
- Calendar access via a phone connection, including meeting request acceptance
- Out-of-office messages in voicemail via a phone connection

Unified Messaging servers are intended to be deployed only in the internal network and must be deployed in sites that contain at least one Hub Transport server. Additionally, the Unified Messaging server must have reliable, high-speed connectivity to the Mailbox servers, domain controllers, and global catalog servers in the organization. An IP PBX or VoIP gateway device is required to tie the Unified Messaging server to the phone system.

The Unified Messaging server role is outside the scope of the 70-236 exam; therefore, we will not be discussing it any detail throughout the rest of the text.

Preinstallation Server and Network Considerations

You must address several important issues before installing Exchange Server. Having the correct information and making the right decisions about these issues will go a long way toward ensuring a successful installation. These preinstallation issues are covered in the following sections:

- Verifying system requirements
- Verifying Windows services and components
- Installing the Security Configuration Wizard
- Verifying name resolution
- Running network and domain controller diagnostics tests

Verifying System Requirements

I'll now list the minimum requirements for the computer system upon which Exchange is to be installed. These minimums are valid when you install only the core components. Using additional Exchange components, and depending on your particular performance demands, could require more resources than these minimum requirements.

Hardware Requirements

Table 2.2 details the minimum recommended hardware requirements for installing Exchange.

TABLE 2.2   Exchange Server 2007 Hardware Requirements

Item	Minimum Requirements
CPU	Must be an x64 64-bit architecture server system that provides support for the Intel EM64T or AMD64 platform. The Intel Itanium IA64 platform is not supported; 32-bit x86 systems are not supported except in a management station role. See Table 2.3 for specifics on the number of CPU cores recommended.
Operating system	Windows Server 2003 SP1 x64 or Windows Server 2003 R2 x64, Windows Server 2008 x64, Standard or Enterprise Editions. The management tools can be installed on a 32-bit Windows Server 2003 or Windows XP SP2 computer.
Memory	Minimum of 2GB RAM; see Table 2.4 for specifics on the amount of RAM recommended for each server role.
Hard disk space	Minimum of 200MB on the server's system drive. Minimum of 1.2GB on the server drive where the Exchange executables will be installed.
Optical drive	A DVD drive, local or network accessible, is required.

The Microsoft Exchange Server software comes on a DVD, a first for Exchange Server. If the machine intended to be the Exchange server has no DVD drive, the administrator can copy the necessary files from the DVD to a shared hard disk or share a DVD drive on another computer.

Table 2.3 details the recommended processor specifications for installing Exchange. Unlike with previous versions of Exchange Server, it's not really easy to give blanket specifications for processors in Exchange Server 2007. What each server will need depends not only on the role of the server but also on the size of the organization. The values in Table 2.3 are guidelines from Microsoft.

TABLE 2.3 Exchange Server 2007 Processor Recommendations

Server Role	Minimum CPU	Recommended CPU	Recommended Maximum CPU
Edge Transport	1 CPU core	2 CPU cores	4 CPU cores
Hub Transport	1 CPU core	4 CPU cores	8 CPU cores
Client Access	1 CPU core	4 CPU cores	4 CPU cores
Mailbox	1 CPU core	4 CPU cores	8 CPU cores
Unified Messaging	1 CPU core	4 CPU cores	4 CPU cores
Multiple roles	1 CPU core	4 CPU cores	4 CPU cores

You'll notice that Table 2.3 refers to CPU cores instead of CPUs. With six-core CPUs currently shipping in servers, and with even more dense packages expected soon, it's becoming easier and easier to pack a large amount of processing power into size-efficient rack mount servers.

Table 2.4 details the minimum recommended memory specifications for installing Exchange. As with the CPU recommendations given previously in Table 2.3, memory specifications are not easily nailed down to exact values. Table 2.4 presents guidelines established by Microsoft, but you'll see a bit later how you can get some more exact numbers that work for your specific organization.

TABLE 2.4 Exchange Server 2007 Memory Recommendations

Server Role	Minimum RAM	Recommended RAM	Recommended Maximum RAM
Edge Transport	2GB	Not less than 1GB per CPU core; 2GB minimum	16GB
Hub Transport	2GB	Not less than 1GB per CPU core; 2GB minimum	16GB
Client Access	2GB	Not less than 1GB per CPU core; 2GB minimum	16GB
Mailbox	2GB, but depends on number of storage groups	2GB plus 2MB–5MB per mailbox on the server	32GB

TABLE 2.4   Exchange Server 2007 Memory Recommendations *(continued)*

Server Role	Minimum RAM	Recommended RAM	Recommended Maximum RAM
Unified Messaging	2GB	Not less than 1GB per CPU core; 2GB minimum	4GB
Multiple roles	2GB, but depends on number of storage groups	4GB plus 2MB–5MB per mailbox on the server	8GB

As noted in Table 2.4, the minimum recommended memory for a Mailbox server depends on the number of storage groups that the Mailbox server is hosting. Table 2.5 outlines the recommendations for memory based on the number of storage groups.

TABLE 2.5   Exchange Server 2007 Memory Recommendation vs. Storage Groups

Number of Storage Groups	Minimum Memory
1–4	2GB
5–8	2GB
9–12	6GB
13–16	8GB
17–20	10GB
21–24	12GB
25–28	14GB
29–32	16GB
33–36	18GB
37–40	20GB
41–44	22GB
45–48	24GB
49 or 50	26GB

Additionally, the recommended memory for a Mailbox server is specified as a value (as provided in Table 2.5) plus 2MB to 5MB per user with a mailbox on the Mailbox server. Users are broken into four basic groups based on the number of messages they send and receive in an average day. Table 2.6 outlines these profiles and the corresponding amount of RAM to be allocated per user.

TABLE 2.6   Exchange Server 2007 Memory Recommendations vs. User Behavior

User Type	Messages Sent/Received per Day (50KB Each)	RAM per Mailbox
Light	5 sent/20 received	2MB
Average	10 sent/40 received	3.5MB
Heavy	20 sent/80 received	5MB
Very heavy	30 sent/120 received	No value specified

Oddly enough, Microsoft defined the "very heavy" user type but did not provide any recommendations for the amount of RAM to plan for per mailbox of that category. It would be best to plan for at least 5MB of RAM for each mailbox that falls into that category.

So as you can see, determining the amount of memory or even the number of CPU cores you need to plan for in your Exchange Server 2007 servers can be a challenging task.

Storage Requirements

Planning for and configuring storage for Exchange Server 2007 is an immensely large topic, one that could fill an entire book this size. To that end, I'm not going to cover every possible scenario or every technology available. I will, however, touch on some of the basic concepts in this area, including storage technologies, volume (or logical unit number [LUN]) configuration and design, and redundant array of inexpensive disks (RAID) levels.

Storage Technologies

Storage technologies have, much like Exchange Server has, continued to grow and evolve over time. When planning for storage for Exchange Server 2007, you can opt to use four acceptable storage technologies. The correct choice will depend on the needs of your organization and the expense you are prepared to bear.

Fibre Channel   Still the most expensive and most reliable and robust storage solution on the market, Fibre Channel–attached SCSI drives are the best choice for almost any size of organization. With backbone network speeds that range as high as 8Gbit/sec now, Fibre

Channel storage area networks provide many exciting and business-relevant solutions that make placing Exchange databases on them ideal. Many vendors, with the largest being EMC, Cisco, and IBM, have Fibre Channel solutions. Fibre Channel–attached SCSI disks come in 10,000 and 15,000 RPM speeds, although most new installations will use 15,000 RPM exclusively.

Serial-attached SCSI (SAS)   SAS disks are the next step down from Fibre Channel–attached SCSI disk systems. SAS disks can be found both as internal components of most new Intel-based servers and as external disk array cabinets that can be easily attached to the Exchange server. Many SAS arrays have throughput as high as 3Gbit/sec, surpassing many older Fibre Channel systems as well as SATA drives and older SCSI drives. One drawback of SAS drives is that they are currently limited to 10,000 RPM in speed, which might not be fast enough for larger organizations that need both high capacity and high input/output.

Serial ATA (SATA)   Serial ATA is a new serial interface for standard ATA/IDE disk drives. These drives are typically found in workstation computers, not server-class computers. SATA disks are almost always slower than SAS or SCSI disks, with typical speeds of either 5,400 or 7,200 RPM. The upsides to SATA drives are their rather large size and their exceptionally low price. However, with the low mean time between failure (MTBF) of SATA disks and their slow speed, SATA drives are not a solid choice for anything but the smallest Exchange Server 2007 implementation.

Internet SCSI (iSCSI)   iSCSI is the single network-attached storage method that Microsoft supports for Exchange Server 2007. iSCSI connects SCSI disks to servers using standard Ethernet cabling and dedicated Ethernet adapters in servers. Although most new Ethernet adapters have TCP/IP offload engines (TOEs) on them to support iSCSI usage, you won't want to deploy iSCSI using the same network adapters in use for normal network traffic because of the amount of traffic going to and from the storage network. Treat iSCSI as you would Fibre Channel–attached storage systems, and place two to four Ethernet ports in each server dedicated to the iSCSI storage network. iSCSI is somewhat mature now at several years of age, but it is still far behind traditional Fibre Channel SAN systems in many regards. However, iSCSI is typically less expensive than Fibre Channel.

 Other than iSCSI, no network-attached storage transports are supported in Exchange Server 2007.

RAID Levels

Regardless of how you configure your volumes (LUNs), you're likely not going to allocate a single disk drive to a single volume. This is because you need to prevent data loss in the event of drive failure and because you likely won't have the right-sized disks to allocate just one for a volume to Exchange Server 2007. Therefore, you'll likely pool several disks together using a RAID solution that is controlled by a battery-backed RAID controller.

Several types of RAID are available, and many vendors have further modified the basic types of RAID with their own proprietary types.

The most common RAID types in use today are as follows:

RAID-10   RAID-10 arrays are actually a combination of two other RAID types, RAID-0 and RAID-1. In RAID-10, two or more mirrored (RAID 1) sets are striped across one striped (RAID 0) set. Since data is written to all disks simultaneously in the striped set and no striping is done for parity information, the data throughput of a RAID-10 set is very good. A single disk failure in a RAID-10 array does not impact write performance because the other member of the mirror set is still intact. Read performance is excellent because reads are able to be performed against only a single mirror in the set. The RAID-10 array can sustain the loss of disks only from a single mirror in the array; should disks be lost from both mirrors in the array, the array will need to be completely rebuilt from restored data.

RAID-5   RAID-5 arrays take a group of disks and write parity information to them for all data that is written. As an example, if you take five 70GB disks and create a RAID-5 array, approximately 70GB will be taken for parity data and the remaining 280GB of space will be available for data storage. Since parity information is written each time data is written to the array, disk I/O increases dramatically. A single disk failure will not prevent the RAID-5 array from functioning, but it will slow down both reads and writes because data must be reconstructed using the parity information. If a second disk fails before the RAID-5 array has been completely rebuilt, the data is lost and the array will need to be completely rebuilt from restored data.

RAID-6   RAID-6 arrays (also called RAID-5E by IBM) take the RAID-5 concept a single drive further and allocate two drives for parity information; thus, in the example using five 70GB disks, to create a RAID-6 array there would be approximately 140GB of parity space and 210GB for data storage. RAID-6 is exceptionally useful with larger arrays that can have long rebuild times that range from many hours to several days because of the size of the array and the ongoing disk I/O.

Of course, the real trick to the whole RAID situation is figuring out what type of RAID array to configure for your Exchange data. Transaction logs, by their very nature of being critical to Exchange and of needing fast sequential read/write access, should always be placed on RAID-10 (or RAID-1) arrays if possible. These arrays should be controlled by battery-backed cached controllers to prevent data loss. In order to provide the appropriate amount of throughput and space, RAID-10 is also the common choice for Exchange databases. However, with the appropriate number of disks, RAID-5 and RAID-6 can also be viable options.

Volume (LUN) Configuration and Design

In Exchange Server 2003, the basic recommendation was to create a volume (or LUN) for each storage group's databases and another for its transaction logs. Therefore, you'd typically have two volumes per storage group. The same basic recommendation holds true in Exchange Server 2007. However, Microsoft now recommends that only one database be created per storage group for better backup, transaction processing, and high availability. Having one database per storage group is a requirement when using LCR, CCR, and SCR. Thus a single Exchange Server 2003 storage group that contained five databases (such as four mailbox stores and a public folder store) occupied only two volumes in the recommended configuration. In Exchange Server 2007, five databases (stores) would now occupy five times as many volumes, or a total of 10 volumes, since the guidance is to place only one database per storage group. The reasoning behind this change is simple: Exchange disk I/O is mostly random access, and storage systems benefit greatly when a set of disks (a volume) is performing a single task at a time. By isolating a single database on a single volume and placing its transaction logs on a separate single volume, you maximize disk I/O and you simplify recovery when doing volume-based snapshots. This simplifies disk-based snapshots since each database will be on a separate disk so that, when a disk-based snapshot needs to be restored, only one database will be affected.

The catch to this approach is that if you had 50 storage groups configured on your Mailbox server, each with two volumes assigned, you'd need 100 drive letters—far in excess of the 23 drive letters typically available on a server. The solution to this problem is to use NTFS file system mount points. In this way, you can present (for example) three databases to Exchange Server, as outlined here:

- Database1, stored in `e:\database1`, where database1 is an actual directory on that volume, volume1

- Database2, stored in `e:\database2`, where database2 is a mount point from volume2

- Database3, stored in `e:\database3`, where database3 is a mount point from volume3

Of course, you must carefully take into account many other considerations and scenarios when designing an Exchange Server 2007 deployment for anything beyond a few databases. There is a large amount of documentation around storage considerations in Exchange Server 2007 on the Microsoft TechNet website. Also, the Exchange 2007 Mailbox Server Role Storage Requirements Calculator, discussed next, can help you make educated decisions about how much storage you'll need and how it should be configured on your storage subsystems.

Storage Requirements Calculator

In an effort to try to take a lot of the confusion out of the process (and also to help ensure that you get the best possible result), the Exchange team has created the helpful Exchange 2007 Mailbox Server Role Storage Requirements Calculator, a Microsoft Excel file that you can use to plan all aspects of a Mailbox server, including storage, memory, and CPU. You can download the file from the team's blog, You Had Me At EHLO, at the following location: `http://msexchangeteam.com/archive/2007/01/15/432207.aspx`.

The calculator takes into account many parts of the Exchange organization, including the number of mailboxes, types of users, clustering model (if any) in use, and the day-to-day operational and administrative tasks. Figure 2.1 presents some sample output of the calculator for an organization that wants to place 2,000 mailboxes on a server in a CCR model. In this case, two Mailbox servers would need to be configured, as the calculator recommends.

FIGURE 2.1   Sample output from the Exchange 2007 Mailbox Server Role Storage Requirements Calculator

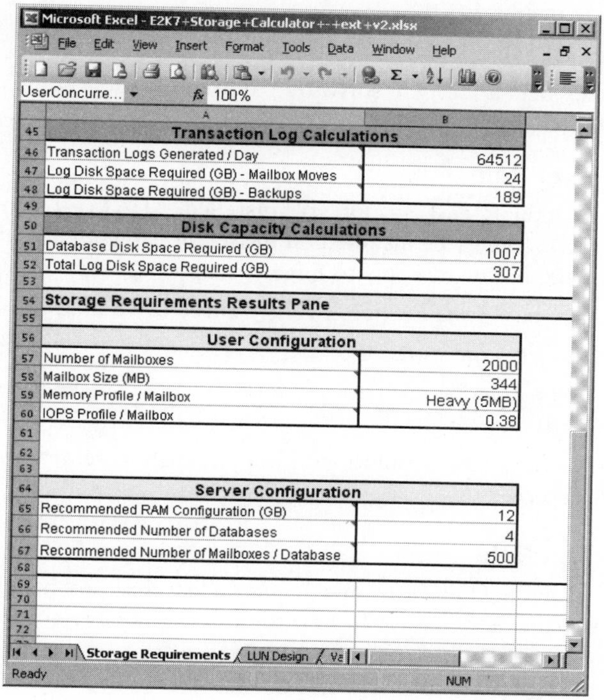

Software Requirements

Exchange Server 2007 Service Pack 1 (SP1) can be installed only on a 64-bit version of Windows Server 2003 SP1 (Standard or Enterprise Edition), Windows Server 2003 R2 (Standard or Enterprise Edition), or Windows Server 2008 (Standard or Enterprise Edition). You cannot install Exchange Server 2007 on a Windows Server 2008 Core installation. The Exchange management tools can be installed on either 32-bit or 64-bit editions of Windows XP Service Pack 2 (SP2), Windows Vista, Windows Server 2003 SP2, and Windows Server 2008.

The other general software requirements you must meet to install any Exchange Server 2007 server roles or management tools on Windows Server 2003 or Windows XP are as follows:

- Microsoft .NET Framework 2.0 (plus applicable updates)
- Windows PowerShell 1.0
- Microsoft Management Console (MMC) 3.0
- Windows Installer 3.1 for 32-bit computers that will have the Exchange management tools installed

The server must also meet the following general software requirements to install any Exchange Server 2007 server roles or management tools on Windows Server 2008 or Windows Vista:

- Microsoft .NET Framework 3.0
- Windows PowerShell 1.0

The server must also meet additional software requirements depending on the specific server role being installed.

Edge Transport Server Role

For servers that will have the Edge Transport role installed, ADAM—or on Windows Server 2008 computers, AD LDS—must be installed on the server using all default options. Additionally, the following requirements apply to Edge Transport servers:

- Should not be a member of the Exchange Active Directory domain
- Must have a DNS suffix configured
- Must be able to perform name resolution of Hub Transport servers successfully from the Edge Transport server
- Must be able to perform name resolution of Edge Transport servers successfully from the Hub Transport server

Hub Transport Server Role

For servers that will have the Hub Transport role installed, there are no additional software requirements; however, the servers must be able to perform name resolution for the Edge Transport server roles successfully.

Client Access Server Role

For servers that will have the Client Access role stalled, the following software requirements apply:

- Internet Information Services (IIS) 6.0 (IIS 7.0 for Windows Server 2008)
- World Wide Web (WWW) publishing component
- ASP.NET
- Remote Procedure Call (RPC) over Hypertext Transfer Protocol (HTTP) Proxy Windows networking component if Outlook Anywhere will be used

Mailbox Server Role

For servers that will have the Mailbox role installed, the following software requirements apply:

- Internet Information Services (IIS) 6.0 (IIS 7.0 for Windows Server 2008).
- Network COM+ access must be enabled.
- Windows Server 2003 x64 requires hotfix 904639 and 918980.
- The Simple Mail Transfer Protocol (SMTP) and Network News Transfer Protocol (NNTP) must not be installed.

Unified Messaging Server Role

For servers that will have the Unified Messaging role installed, the following software requirements apply:

- Microsoft Speech service (Exchange will install this if needed).
- Windows Media Encoder.
- Windows Media Audio Voice codec.
- Microsoft Core XML Services (MSXML) 6.0.
- The Simple Mail Transfer Protocol (SMTP) and Network. News Transfer Protocol (NNTP) must not be installed.

 Windows Server 2008 requires that the Desktop Experience be installed prior to installing the codecs

Client Access Requirements

The last requirements that you'll need to ensure are met are those for client access to Exchange Server 2007. Microsoft has stipulated that only Outlook 2007, Outlook 2003, and Outlook XP (2002) are supported for access to mailboxes and public folders on Exchange Server 2007. If Exchange will be deployed without public folders, only Outlook 2007 is supported; Outlook 2007 with at least Service Pack 1 is recommended due to some important fixes that are included. Also, if auto client configuration is using Autodiscover, Outlook 2007 is also required.

Office Outlook Web Access (OWA) obviously requires a web browser to function on the client end, although only Internet Explorer is supported with OWA Premium. Any other browser will have the OWA Light, which is optimized for lower bandwidth or vision-impaired users. OWA Light also does not have support for tasks, reminders, message flags and categories, printing, spell check, or conversation view.

Mobile devices can also access Exchange Server 2007, but the only supported types are Windows Mobile 2003 Second Edition, Windows Mobile 5.0, Windows Mobile 5.0 with Messaging and Security Feature Pack (MSFP), and other Windows Mobile 6 devices that are compatible with Exchange ActiveSync, such as some Palm OS, Nokia, Sony Ericsson, Motorola, Symbian, Helio, and Apple Computer devices.

 For the latest list of supported Exchange ActiveSync devices, please visit http://www.microsoft.com/exchange/evaluation/features/owa_mobile.mspx.

Verifying Windows Services and Components

Microsoft has made the Exchange Server 2007 setup process easier and more error-proof than ever before. As part of this improved setup process, you are prompted to verify and install, as necessary, those key services that are required to support the installation of Exchange Server 2007. Before you can install Exchange Server 2007 on a server, however, you must install the required services and components (discussed previously). As practice, you'll install and verify the correct services and components for a Windows Server 2003 Mailbox server in Exercise 2.1.

 The steps to verify Windows services, perform network diagnostics, and run /PrepareSchema and /PrepareDomain are all part of the regular installation sequence for a new Exchange Server 2007 organization.

EXERCISE 2.1

Installing Required Services and Components on Windows Server 2003 R2

Follow these steps to prepare a Windows Server 2003 computer with the required services and components:

1. Open the Add or Remove Programs applet, located in the Control Panel.

2. Click the Add/Remove Windows Components button.

3. In the Windows Components dialog box, select the Application Server option and click the Details button.

4. In the Application Server dialog box, shown here, select the Enable Network COM+ Access option.

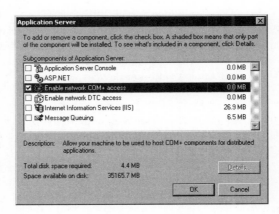

EXERCISE 2.1 *(continued)*

5. Select the Internet Information Services (IIS) option, and click the Details button.

6. In the Internet Information Services (IIS) dialog box, shown here, select the World Wide Web Service option. The Common Files and Internet Information Services Manager options will be selected also.

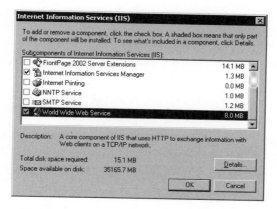

7. Click OK to close the Internet Information Services (IIS) dialog box.

8. Click OK to close the Application Server dialog box.

9. Back in the Windows Components dialog box, scroll down and select the Microsoft .NET Framework 2.0 option, as shown here.

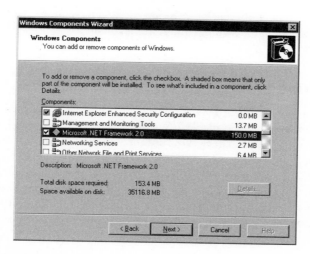

10. Click Next to continue.

EXERCISE 2.1 *(continued)*

11. Click Finish when prompted.

12. Download the Windows PowerShell 1.0 (KB 926139) and the Microsoft Management Console (MMC) 3.0 (KB 907265) installers from the Microsoft website.

13. Start the installation of the PowerShell by double-clicking the downloaded file.

14. When prompted, click Next to dismiss the opening page of the installation wizard.

15. Accept the EULA, and click Next again to continue.

16. Install the MMC 3.0 package using the same steps you used to install the PowerShell package.

17. Download and install the hotfixes for Windows Server 2003 x64 in KB 904639 and KB 918980.

18. Install the Windows Server 2003 SP1 Support Tools package from the Windows CD-ROM. The installer is located in the X:\SUPPORT\TOOLS folder.

You can download the Microsoft .NET Framework 2.0 installer from the Microsoft website if you don't see it in your list of components available to install.

You can verify that services are running by opening the Services console located in the Administrative Tools folder.

Installing the Security Configuration Wizard

The Security Configuration Wizard (SCW) is an advanced role-based security configuration management and hardening tool available in Windows Server 2003 SP1, Windows Server 2003 R2, and Windows Server 2008. The SCW is installed by default on Windows Server 2008; however, it isn't on Windows Server 2003. Installing SCW on Windows Server 2003 is outlined in Exercise 2.2. Exchange Server 2007 provides extensions that can be imported into the Security Configuration Wizard to increase the role-based security of your Exchange Server 2007 servers. Although you cannot utilize this functionality until after one or more Exchange Server 2007 roles are installed on the server, you can install the SCW ahead of time.

EXERCISE 2.2

Installing the Security Configuration Wizard on Windows Server 2003

Use the following steps to run the Security Configuration Wizard on a Windows Server 2003 R2 computer:

1. Open the Add or Remove Programs applet, located in the Control Panel.

2. Click the Add/Remove Windows Components button.

3. Select the Security Configuration Wizard option and then click OK.

4. Back in the Windows Components dialog box, click Next to continue.

5. Click Finish when prompted.

 The Security Configuration Wizard is installed by default in Windows Server 2008 and can be run from the Security Information section of Server Manager.

Verifying Name Resolution

It should go without saying that functional name resolution within an Active Directory forest is absolutely critical. Because Exchange Server 2007 extends the existing foundation provided by Active Directory, functional name resolution is thus absolutely required for the proper operation of the Exchange organization. In short, you're not likely going to be at the stage of deploying Exchange Server 2007 if your name resolution isn't functioning at that time.

All Exchange Server 2007 servers must be able to resolve names and IP addresses for all other Exchange Server 2007 servers, all domain controllers, and all global catalog servers. For organizations using the Edge Transport role in the DMZ, this also means that all Edge Transport servers must be able to contact all Hub Transport servers inside the protected internal network and vice versa. To that end, functional name resolution becomes more than just an issue of making sure that you've done your job within Active Directory; it is also a task in which the network administrator in charge of configuring and maintaining your organizational firewalls and external DNS must be involved.

You can perform quick network resolution testing using the nslookup command from an Exchange Server 2007 server. Figure 2.2 shows how the nslookup command has been used to resolve both internal and external names.

FIGURE 2.2   Using `nslookup` to verify functional name resolution within the network

Running Network and Domain Controller Diagnostics Tests

If you've installed the Windows support tools as discussed in Exercise 2.1, then you'll have the `dcdiag` and `netdiag` diagnostic tools available to you. In Exchange Server 2003, these tools were linked in the setup preparation tasks and running them was recommended. You should run these commands manually before even getting to the setup process of the first Exchange Server 2007 server.

The `dcdiag` command performs the following types of checks (among others):

- Connectivity, to verify proper DNS records and LDAP/RPC connectivity
- Replications, to check for replication errors
- NetLogons, to verify that the proper permissions exist to allow for replication
- RIDManager, to verify that the RID master is accessible and functional
- KCCEvent, to verify that the Knowledge Consistency Checker (KCC) is functional and error-free
- Topology, to verify that an accurate and functional replication topology has been generated by the KCC
- DNS, to verify proper operation and health of DNS services

Figure 2.3 presents some sample output from the dcdiag command.

FIGURE 2.3   Using the dcdiag command to verify domain functionality

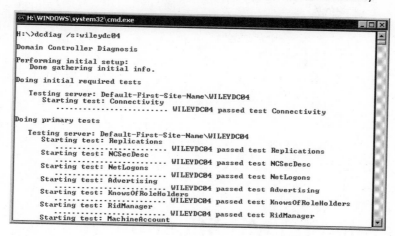

The netdiag command performs the following types of checks (among others):

- Checks for IPConfig on each network adapter
- Checks for automatic private IP addressing (APIPA) on each network adapter
- Checks the domain membership of the server
- Checks the default gateway of the server
- Performs domain controller discovery
- Performs LDAP testing
- Performs Kerberos testing

Figure 2.4 presents some sample output from the netdiag command.

You should resolve any issues noted with either test before installing and configuring Exchange Server 2007.

TIP   You can get more information about the tests performed, usage of dcdiag and netdiag tools, andcorrective actions to perform as a result of the dcdiag and netdiag tools by searching the Microsoft website for "Windows Support Tools."

FIGURE 2.4   Using the netdiag command to verify network functionality

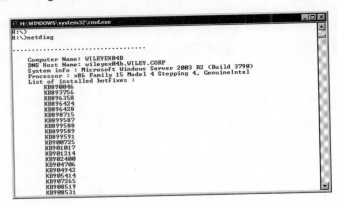

Preinstallation Modification of Active Directory

Because of Exchange Server 2007's involvement with Active Directory, its installation involves a number of Windows Active Directory user and group security accounts. Some of the more pertinent groups are as follows:

Schema Admins   Members of this group have the rights and permissions necessary to modify the schema of Active Directory. To run the setup with the /PrepareSchema or /PrepareAD option, which modifies the schema for Exchange Server 2007 and is described later in this chapter, you must belong to the Schema Admins group, the Enterprise Admins group, and the local Administrators group on the computer on which you actually run the command.

Enterprise Admins   Members of this group have the rights and permissions necessary to administer any domain in a forest. To run setup with the /PrepareSchema, /PrepareLegacyExchangePermissions, /PrepareDomain, or /PrepareAD option, you must be a member of the Enterprise Admins group and the local Administrators group on the computer running the tool.

Domain Admins   Members of this group have the rights and permissions necessary to administer any computer or resource in a domain. You must be a member of this group in order to run setup with the /PrepareDomain option, which prepares each domain for Exchange Server 2007 installation.

Administrators

Members of this local group are given the rights necessary to administer a local computer and install software on it. To install Exchange Server 2007 on a Windows Server 2003 computer, you must be a member of this group. This level of privileges is needed because, during installation, services will be started and files will be copied to the \<%SystemRoot%>\SYSTEM32 directory.

The installation of Exchange Server 2007 will also create several new security groups:

Exchange Organization Administrators

Members of this group have full access to all Exchange Server properties throughout the Exchange organization. By default, the administrative account that is used to install Exchange Server 2007 is placed into this group.

Exchange Recipient Administrators

Members of this group have the required permissions to modify any Exchange-related property on all Exchange recipients. By default, the Exchange Organization Administrators group is placed into this group.

Exchange Server Administrators (servername)

Members of this group have access to the specified Exchange Server configuration data in Active Directory and also have administrative access to the Exchange server. By default, this group contains no members.

Exchange Servers

Members of this group are the computer accounts for all Exchange servers. This security group provides Exchange servers with the permissions necessary to access one another and perform necessary Exchange functions.

Exchange View-Only Administrators (servername)

Members of this group have view-only access permissions to all Exchange Server properties and recipient objects in the Exchange organization. By default, the Exchange Recipient Administrators and Exchange Server Administrators (servername) are members of this group.

Exchange2003Interop

This group is created and utilized only during an upgrade scenario from Exchange Server 2003. This group provides authentication for connections made between Exchange Server 2007 Hub Transport servers and Exchange Server 2003 Bridgehead servers.

Before installing the first Exchange server in an organization, you might need to prepare the forest and each domain into which Exchange will be installed. For these tasks, you will use these commands available within the Exchange Server 2007 setup.exe command: /PrepareSchema, /PrepareAD, /PrepareAllDomains, and /PrepareDomain.

/PrepareSchema must be run once in a forest and should be run on the domain controller that is configured with the schema master role, although this is not a requirement. It extends the Active Directory schema with the objects necessary to run Exchange Server 2007. The /PrepareAD command must also be run within the domain root of the forest and is used to create the global Exchange objects and configuration. If the schema has not yet been extended, the /PrepareAD command will accomplish that. Additionally, the /PrepareAD command accomplishes the tasks performed by the /PrepareDomain command in the domain root. The /PrepareDomain command must be run in each domain where Exchange 2007 will be installed to identify the domain's address list server and to create special domain accounts that Exchange needs in order to run properly. Alternatively, the /PrepareAllDomains command will perform the /PrepareDomain command against each of the domains in the forest provided the account with which you are running the command is a member of the Enterprise Admins group.

In previous versions of Exchange Server, you had to run the ForestPrep and DomainPrep commands. In Exchange Server 2007, these commands have been removed and replaced with other options, allowing greater flexibility in how Exchange Server 2007 is deployed.

Though this seems like a complicated installation routine, it does provide a significant advantage. Many businesses separate the administrative responsibilities of domain management, schema management, and Exchange management. For example, one group might be in charge of administering the schema and the primary domains of the forest, another might be in charge of managing the child domains, and still another group might be in charge of managing Exchange.

These additional setup tools provide the ability for separate administrators to perform their necessary part of the Exchange installation and simplify the Exchange deployment. For example, the group in charge of managing the schema will have the permissions required to run the /PrepareSchema command to extend the schema. Domain administrators will have the permissions required to use the /PrepareDomain command that modifies domains. To run the /PrepareAD command, the administrator will need both Schema Admins and Enterprise Admins permissions because this command is all-encompassing. Once these tasks are completed, Exchange administrators can install and manage Exchange without receiving permissions for the other preparation tasks.

If a single administrator or group runs the network and has all the appropriate permissions (or if there is only one domain in your forest), this simplifies the installation of Exchange. If the account with which you install the first Exchange server belongs to the Schema Admins, Enterprise Admins, and Administrators groups for the local computer, you do not need to run /PrepareAD, /PrepareSchema, or /PrepareDomain manually since you will run them during the regular Exchange setup process.

Verifying Domain and Forest Functional Levels

Before you can move on to the actual preparation of the Active Directory forest and domains for the installation of Exchange Server 2007, you must ensure that they are at the Windows 2000 native functional level or higher. Exercise 2.3 outlines the steps to verify and/or raise the domain and forest functional levels of your Active Directory environment.

EXERCISE 2.3

Verifying the Domain and Forest Functional Levels

To verify the domain and forest functional levels follow these steps:

1. In the root domain of the Active Directory forest, log into a domain controller with Domain Admins credentials.

2. Open the Active Directory Users and Computers console.

3. Right-click the domain name in the console, and select Raise Domain Functional Level. The dialog box shown here opens.

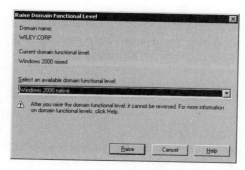

4. If the domain functional level is less than Windows 2000 native, select either Windows 2000 Native (ideally if there are no Windows 2000 domain controllers), Windows Server 2003 level, or Windows Server 2008 level and click the Raise button.

5. When prompted to make the change, click OK. Note that this is a one-way change that cannot be undone.

6. Repeat the steps for every other domain in the forest.

7. To change or verify the forest functional level, open the Active Directory Domains and Trusts console while logged into a root domain controller with Enterprise Admins credentials.

8. In the console, right-click the root of the Active Directory Domains and Trusts node and select Raise Forest Functional Level. The dialog box shown here opens.

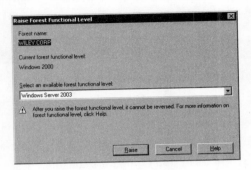

9. Raise the forest functional level to at least the Windows 2000 Native option, and click the Raise button. You'll be prompted to accept the change here as well.

Preparing a Windows Active Directory Forest

To run the /PrepareSchema command, you must belong to the Schema Admins and Enterprise Admins security groups. In addition, you must belong to the local Administrators group on the server on which Exchange will be installed. If you are not a member of these groups, the appropriate administrator will have to run the /PrepareSchema command before you can install Exchange Server 2007.

When the /Prepare Schema command is run, it performs only one task: it extends the Active Directory schema with Exchange-related information.

Exercise 2.4 outlines the steps for running the /PrepareSchema command in a forest that does not have a previous version of Exchange running. We'll discuss the process to prepare a forest and domain for Exchange Server 2007 to coexist with Exchange Server 2003 or Exchange 2000 Server later in this chapter.

WARNING   Do not run the /PrepareSchema command as your first preinstallation step if you have an existing legacy Exchange Server 2003 or Exchange 2000 Server organization. You must run the /PrepareLegacyExchangePermissions command first. See the section "Modifying Existing Exchange Organizations to Support Migration" later in this chapter for additional discussion of this scenario.

EXERCISE 2.4

Running the /PrepareSchema Command

To run the /PrepareSchema command, follow these steps:

1. Logged into a server in the same site as the Schema masters operations role with an account that is a member of both the Schema Admins and Enterprise Admins groups.

2. Insert the Microsoft Exchange Server 2007 DVD into the server's DVD-ROM drive. If the server does not have a DVD-ROM drive, you can copy the files to a network location and then proceed using that location.

3. Open a command interpreter window by selecting Start ➢ Run, entering CMD, and pressing Enter.

4. In the command interpreter window, enter the following command: *X*:\setup /prepareschema, where X represents the location of the Exchange Server 2007 setup files, local or remote. Press Enter to start the schema preparation process as shown here.

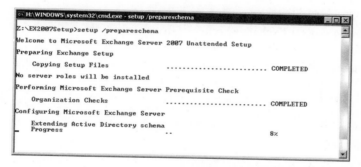

5. If setup finds any errors, they will be displayed and the /PrepareSchema process will fail. You will need to rerun the command after you have corrected the noted errors.

You can run the /PrepareSchema portion of setup while installing the first Exchange Server 2007 computer. This situation is typically encountered only in smaller organizations where only one domain exists within the Active Directory forest.

Preparing the Root Windows Active Directory Domain

Once the forest has been prepared by extending the schema with the /PrepareSchema command, the next step you'll need to perform to ready the forest for an installation of Exchange Server 2007 is to prepare the root-level domain in the forest and create the Exchange global objects in Active Directory. You accomplish this process by issuing the /PrepareAD command, which will also prepare the root domain with the /PrepareDomain command.

When the /PrepareAD command is run, it performs several tasks:

- If the forest contains no existing versions of Exchange Server, /PrepareAD prompts you for an Exchange organization name and then creates the organization object in the Active Directory. The organization is at the top of the Exchange hierarchy. This case-sensitive field can be up to 64 characters in length. The organization name is associated with every object in the Exchange directory, such as mailboxes, public folders, and distribution lists. The organization name cannot be modified after installation.

- It creates the universal security groups that were discussed previously in this chapter.

- Creates the Microsoft Exchange container and organization if they do not already exist

- Verifies that the schema has been updated and that the organization is up-to-date

- Creates the default Accepted Domains entry if it doesn't already exist

- Assigns permissions throughout the configuration partition

- Imports the Rights.ldf file to add the extended rights that are required for Exchange to install into Active Directory

- Creates the Microsoft Exchange Security Groups organizational unit (OU) in the root domain of the forest and assigns permissions on this OU

- Creates the following universal security groups (USGs) in the Microsoft Exchange Security Groups OU:
  - Exchange Organization Administrators
  - Exchange Recipient Administrators
  - Exchange Servers
  - Exchange View-Only Administrators
  - Exchange Public Folder Administrators (new in Exchange Server 2007 Service Pack 1)
  - ExchangeLegacyInterop

- If they don't already exist, creates the Exchange 2007 administrative group called Exchange Administrative Group (FYDIBOHF23SPDLT) and the Exchange 2007 routing group called Exchange Routing Group (DWBGZMFD01QNBJR)

Exercise 2.5 outlines the steps for running the /PrepareAD command.

You can run the /PrepareAD portion of setup while installing the first Exchange Server 2007 computer. This situation is typically encountered only in smaller organizations where only one domain exists within the Active Directory forest.

EXERCISE 2.5

Running the /PrepareAD Command

Follow these steps to run the /PrepareAD command:

1. Log into a domain controller of the root domain with an account that is a member of the Enterprise Admins group.

2. Insert the Microsoft Exchange Server 2007 DVD into the server's DVD-ROM drive. If the server does not have a DVD-ROM drive, you can copy the files to a network location and then proceed using that location.

3. Open a command interpreter window by selecting Start ➢ Run, entering CMD, and pressing Enter.

4. In the command interpreter window, enter the following command: *X*:\setup /preparead /organizationname:*NAME*, where X represents the location of the Exchange Server 2007 setup files, local or remote, and NAME represents the name you want for the Exchange organization. In this example, we'll call the new organization WILEY. Press Enter to start the root domain preparation process as shown here.

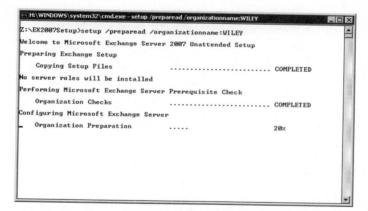

5. If setup finds any errors, they will be displayed and the /PrepareAD process will fail. You will need to rerun the command after you have corrected the noted errors.

After the /PrepareAD command has been completed and replication has occurred between domain controllers, you can check two places to identify changes quickly that have been made within Active Directory. The Active Directory Users and Computers console will contain a new organizational unit named Microsoft Exchange Security Groups, as shown in Figure 2.5, which holds the universal security groups discussed previously.

As shown in Figure 2.6, the Active Directory Sites and Services console (Services node) displays the Exchange organization that was created and several configuration items for it. To enable the Services node, you will need to click the Active Directory Sites and Services root node and then select View ➢ Show Service Node.

FIGURE 2.5 Viewing changes in Active Directory Users and Computers after running the /PrepareAD command

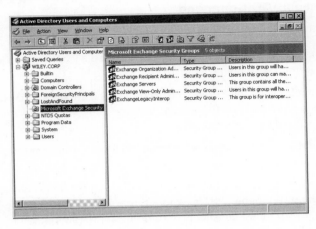

FIGURE 2.6 Viewing changes in Active Directory Sites and Services after running the /PrepareAD command

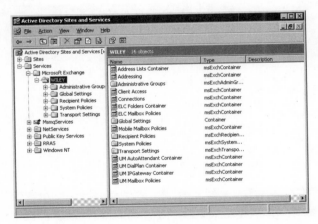

Preparing Other Windows Active Directory Domains

Once you have prepared the Windows Active Directory forest using /PrepareSchema and created the Exchange organization and global objects using the /PrepareAD command, you must also prepare each additional domain in the forest that will run Exchange Server 2007 using the /PrepareDomain command. You must run the /PrepareDomain command in each domain that will contain Exchange Server 2007 servers or recipient objects or that has users or groups that will manage Exchange Server 2007 computers.

To run the /PrepareDomain command, you must be a member of the Domain Admins group for that domain and the Administrators group on the local computer where you will be running DomainPrep. DomainPrep performs the following tasks:

- Configures the required permissions on the domain container for the Exchange Servers group, Exchange Organization Administrators group, Authenticated Users group, and Exchange Recipient Administrators group.

- Creates a new container named Microsoft Exchange System Objects and sets permissions on the container for the Exchange Servers group, Exchange Organization Administrators group, and the Authenticated Users group.

- Creates a domain global group in the domain called Exchange Install Domain Servers. This group is then added to the Exchange Servers universal security group in the root domain.

Exercise 2.6 outlines the steps for running the /PrepareDomain command.

EXERCISE 2.6

Running the /PrepareDomain Command

Follow these steps to run the /PrepareDomain command:

1. Log into a domain controller with an account that is a member of the Domain Admins group.

2. Insert the Microsoft Exchange Server 2007 DVD into the server's DVD-ROM drive. If the server does not have a DVD-ROM drive, you can copy the files to a network location and then proceed using that location.

3. Open a command interpreter window by selecting Start ➤ Run, entering CMD, and pressing Enter.

4. In the command interpreter window, enter the following command: *X:*\setup /PrepareDomain, where X represents the location of the Exchange Server 2007 setup files, local or remote. Press Enter to start the root domain preparation process as shown here.

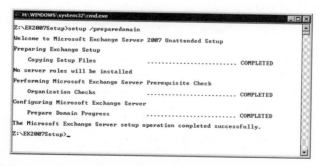

5. If setup finds any errors, they will be displayed and the /PrepareDomain process will fail. You will need to rerun the command after you've corrected the noted errors.

You can run the /PrepareDomain portion of setup while installing the first Exchange Server 2007 computer. This situation is typically encountered only in smaller organizations where only one domain exists within the Active Directory forest.

As shown in Figure 2.7, the Microsoft Exchange System Objects container now exists, although it cannot be clicked and opened like other containers or organizational units. You will need to select View ➢ Advanced Features to enable viewing of advanced objects such as the Microsoft Exchange System Objects container within Active Directory Users and Computers.

FIGURE 2.7   Viewing changes in Active Directory Users and Computers after running the /PrepareDomain command

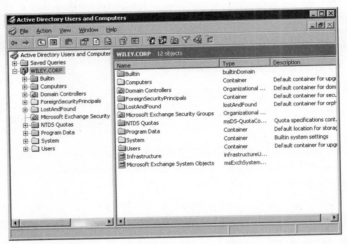

Modifying Existing Exchange Organizations to Support Migration

If you will be installing Exchange Server 2007 into an existing Exchange Server 2003 or Exchange 2000 Server organization, you must make additional configuration changes to Active Directory and the legacy Exchange organization. The /PrepareLegacyExchangePermissions command must be run in every domain in which the Exchange Server 2003 or Exchange 2000 Server DomainPrep has been run previously to ensure that the legacy Recipient Update Service (RUS) continues to operate correctly on the older Exchange servers. The RUS is required in legacy Exchange Server 2003 and Exchange 2000 Server environments to update some attributes on a recipient, such as the proxy address and the email address. If you've ever created a new mailbox-enabled user before in an Exchange Server 2003 or Exchange 2000 Server organization and had to wait a few minutes for an email address to be stamped on it, then you were waiting on RUS to fire.

In these older Exchange environments, RUS runs in the context of the local server account for the Exchange server on which it is running. Each Exchange server's computer account is a member of the Exchange Enterprise Servers security group that is created during the Domain-Prep process. The attributes that RUS needs to be able to modify and update are grouped together into a property set, and DomainPrep grants the Exchange Enterprise Servers security group the required permissions to modify the attributes in question. Since Exchange Server 2007 no longer uses this legacy Exchange Enterprise Servers security group, a solution is needed to allow RUS to continue to operate properly.

As outlined earlier, Exchange Server 2007 now uses a universal security group named Exchange Recipient Administrators. The members of this group have the required permissions to manage the email-related attributes of all recipients. The legacy Exchange Enterprise Servers security group does not provide access, by default, to the property set that is created to allow the Exchange Recipient Administrators group access to these email-related attributes. To that end, when the schema modification is performed as part of the preinstallation of Exchange Server 2007, RUS will no longer have permission to manage recipients' email attributes and stops functioning entirely. The workaround to this problem is to run the setup /PrepareLegacyExchangePermissions command before any other setup steps when integrating Exchange Server 2007 with legacy Exchange organizations.

Exercise 2.7 outlines the steps for running the /PrepareLegacyExchangePermissions command. You will need to be a member of the Domain Admins group and the Exchange Organization Administrators groups in each domain in which this command is run. To run the command as shown in Exercise 2.7, in which it runs against all domains in the forest, you will need to be a member of the Enterprise Admins group as well.

EXERCISE 2.7

Running the /PrepareLegacyExchangePermissions Command

Follow these steps to run the /PrepareLegacyExchangePermissions command:

1. Log into a domain controller in the root domain with an account that is a member of the appropriate groups, as specified above.

2. Insert the Microsoft Exchange Server 2007 DVD into the server's DVD-ROM drive. If the server does not have a DVD-ROM drive, you can copy the files to a network location and then proceed using that location.

3. Open a command interpreter window by selecting Start ➤ Run, entering CMD, and pressing Enter.

4. In the command interpreter window, enter the following command: *X*:\setup **/preparelegacyexchangepermissions**, where X represents the location of the Exchange Server 2007 setup files, local or remote. Press Enter to start the root domain preparation process.

5. If setup finds any errors, they will be displayed and the /PrepareLegacyExchangePermissions process will fail. You will need to rerun the command after you've corrected the noted errors.

Real World Scenario

Deploying Exchange Server 2007 in a Large Organization

You are the lead network administrator for a large manufacturing corporation that has 45 geographical locations within North America. In the past, your company has never had a real company-wide network that spanned all locations and linked all users and resources together. You have just completed installing a new Windows Server 2003 Active Directory network that provides one unified network to all users and all locations within your organization.

Your network consists of a single Active Directory forest and, under the root domain, five domains named canada.manufacturing.com, mexico.manufacturing.com, west .manufacturing.com, central.manufacturing.com, and east.manufacturing.com.

The root domain of manufacturing.com contains no user accounts or member servers. For each of the five child domains, you have two assistant administrators that have the Domain Admins permissions for their applicable child domain. Only your user account has the Enterprise Admins and Schema Admins permissions configured. Also, only your user account has the Domain Admins permissions for the root domain. You have local administrative access on the servers in the root domain, and your assistant administrators have local administrative access on all computers and servers in their child domain. Your office is located within the east.manufacturing.com child domain.

To facilitate the process of installing Exchange Server 2007 on six Windows Server 2003 computers in each child domain, you have provided network shares in each child domain that contain the installation source files. Also, you have run the /PrepareSchema portion of the Exchange setup program to extend the Active Directory schema to support the installation of Exchange Server 2007. After you run the /PrepareSchema command, you will next need to run the /PrepareAD command and specify the Exchange organization name.

Once you've completed these tasks, you should run the /PrepareDomain command for the east.manufacturing.com child domain. You can then start to install Exchange Server 2007 servers in the east.manufacturing.com child domain if desired. Also, your assistant administrators might begin to install the remaining Exchange Server 2007 servers using the installation source files located on their local network shares. As you can see, the Exchange installation process can be quite lengthy and complicated in a large network environment; however, careful planning and execution can lead to first-time success. In reality, this process can actually be simpler than the ForestPrep and DomainPrep process of Exchange Server 2003 that required you to delegate permissions from within the Exchange System Manager before the assistant administrators could start installing Exchange servers.

Installing Exchange Server 2007

As briefly discussed, Exchange Server 2007 gives you several ways to install the product. Most installations will likely be standard graphical user interface (GUI) installations, so you'll examine that method first. However, when you have many Exchange Server 2007 installations to perform or you want to do something besides watch the installation take place, you can perform an unattended installation of Exchange. As you also saw in Chapter 1, you can perform the installation steps from the command line, which you'll examine here as well. Of course, before you start any of the installation methods I'll be discussing in this chapter, make sure you meet all of the requirements outlined in Chapter 1. The order that you deploy the Exchange server roles is important. A simple way to remember the proper order is acronym C.H.M.U.. which stands for Client (Client Access), Hub (Hub transport), Mailbox, and Unifed (Unifed Messaging).

Performing GUI-Based Installations

The most common installation method for Exchange Server 2007 will likely be the standard GUI-based method. This method is especially well suited for smaller organizations that might be installing only a few Exchange Server 2007 servers or for administrators who are not as comfortable or familiar with the other installation methods available. Exercise 2.8 outlines the process to install the first Exchange Server 2007 server into an organization.

For Exercise 2.8, we're not going to prepare the Active Directory forest or domain. This type of installation is well suited for the single-domain forests common in smaller organizations. You'll utilize the Active Directory preparation discussed in Chapter 1 later when we cover command-line-based installation methods.

EXERCISE 2.8

Installing Exchange Server 2007 from the Graphical User Interface

To use the GUI-based method to install Exchange Server 2007, follow these steps:

1. Log into the domain controller in the root domain which holds the Schema role with an account that is a member of both the Schema Admins and Enterprise Admins groups.

2. Insert the Exchange Server 2007 DVD into your server's DVD drive, or browse to the network location that holds the Exchange Server 2007 setup files. The DVD should autostart.

3. If the DVD does not autostart or if you have a network-based installation, double-click the setup.exe file to launch the Exchange Server 2007 installer.

4. If prompted with a security warning when running setup.exe as shown here, click Run to allow the setup program to run.

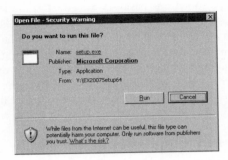

5. If you have installed all the required prerequisites, you will be able to click Step 4 (shown in the following screen shot). If not, you'll need to click the steps before that and install the required software.

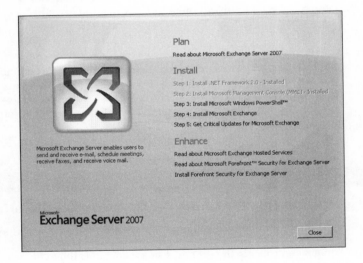

EXERCISE 2.8 *(continued)*

6. The Copying Files dialog box might briefly appear. After a short wait, the Exchange Server 2007 Setup dialog box appears as shown here. Click Next to continue.

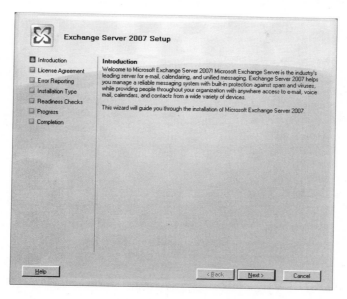

7. In the License Agreement dialog box, accept the terms of the licensing agreement and then click Next to continue.

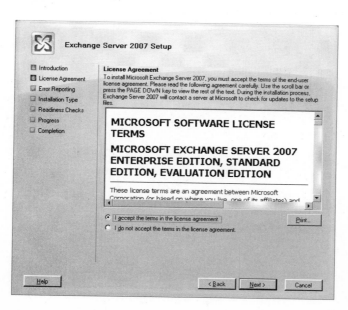

8. In the Error Reporting dialog box, you will need to select whether you want to report errors in the operation of Exchange Server 2007 to Microsoft. After making your choice, click Next to continue.

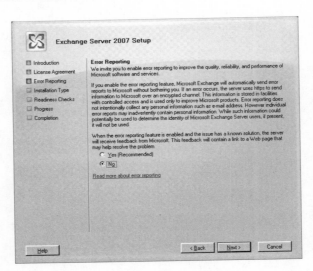

9. In the Installation Type dialog box, you will need to determine what server roles you will want to install. Since this is the first Exchange Server 2007 server you're install-ing, you must install at least the Hub Transport and Mailbox roles. For this exercise, select the Typical Exchange Sever Installation option and click Next.

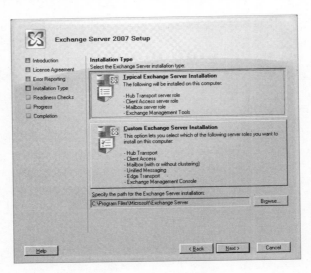

EXERCISE 2.8 *(continued)*

10. In this exercise, no forest or domain preparation has been done previously; thus, in the Exchange Organization dialog box, setup asks you for the name that will be used for the Exchange organization. Specify your organization name, and click Next to continue.

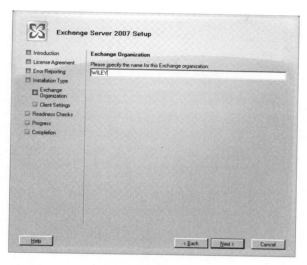

11. In the Client Settings dialog box, Exchange setup asks whether you will be using older versions of the Outlook client or any Entourage (for Macintosh) clients to access the server. The answer to this question determines whether public folders are created during installation. Select Yes (to create the public folders), and then click Next to continue.

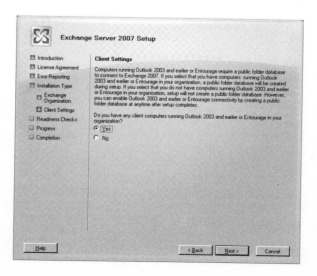

12. If the Readiness Checks dialog box notes any failures, address these items before continuing and click Retry. Once you have no failure items here, you will be able to click Install to continue.

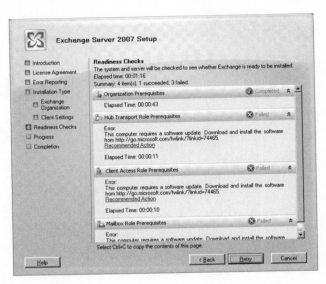

13. The installation process now starts as shown here. Notice how the setup routine configures the forest schema since you did not perform that process manually.

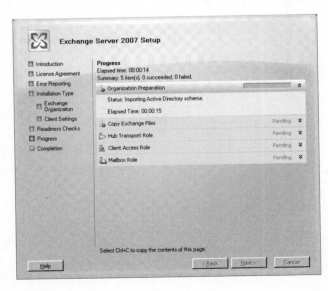

EXERCISE 2.8 *(continued)*

14. After you've installed Exchange Server 2007 on your server, you need to perform some final steps. Select Finalize Installation Using the Exchange Management Console, and click Finish.

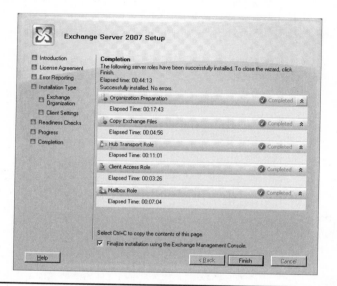

 The Exchange organization name cannot contain any of the following special characters: ~ (tilde), ` (grave accent), ! (exclamation point), @ (at sign), # (number sign), $ (dollar sign), % (percent sign), ^ (caret), & (ampersand), * (asterisk), () (parentheses), _ (underscore), + (plus sign), = (equal sign), {} (braces), [] (brackets), | (vertical bar), \ (backslash), : (colon), ; (semicolon), " (quotation mark), ' (apostrophe), <> (angle brackets), , (comma), . (period), ? (question mark), / (slash), and whitespace at the beginning or end.

With Exchange Server 2007 now installed on your server, we'll move onto the post-installation configuration steps you need to perform to complete the installation process. Exercise 2.9 will examine some of these tasks. You can perform the rest of the tasks at your convenience.

EXERCISE 2.9

Performing Post-installation Configuration of Exchange Server 2007

Perform the following steps once the Exchange installation has completed:

1. As soon as the Exchange Management Console loads, you'll be prompted to enter the product key to license the server on which Exchange Server 2007 was installed, as shown here. Click OK to acknowledge the licensing prompt.

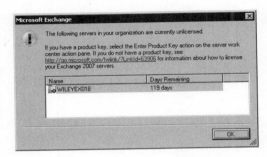

2. The middle pane of the newly redesigned Exchange Management Console displays all of the configuration steps Exchange Server 2007 recommends or requires that you perform after installation has been completed.

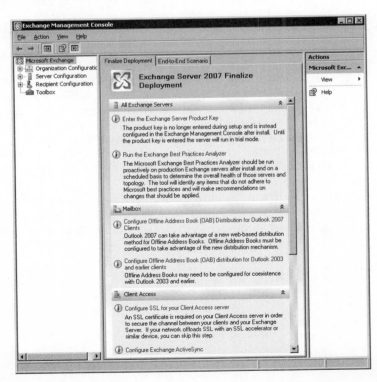

3. To license the Exchange server properly, click the Enter the Exchange Server Product Key link. A new pop-up dialog box tells you how to configure the server with the product key.

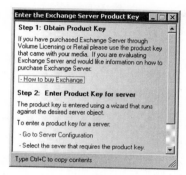

4. Click the Server Configuration node in the left pane of the Exchange Management Console. Select the server to be licensed, as shown here, and then click the Enter Product Key link on the right side of the Exchange Management Console.

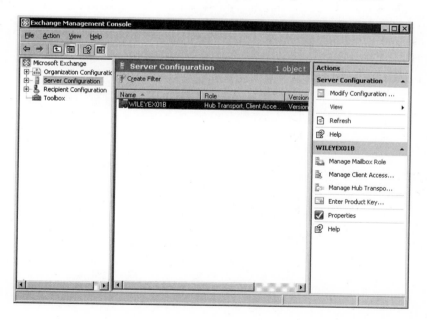

5. Enter your product key in the Enter Product Key dialog box as shown here, and then click Enter.

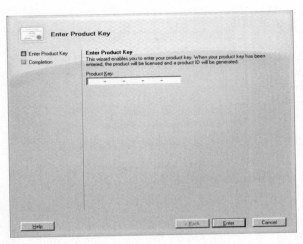

6. The product key will be validated, and the server's licensing status will be updated as indicated. Note the PowerShell code that is displayed. This illustrates how you can license a server from the command line or via a script. Click Finish to complete the licensing process.

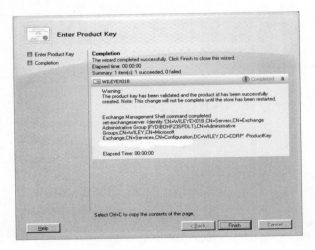

7. You can return to the list of post-installation configuration tasks to be performed by clicking the Microsoft Exchange node at the root of the left display tree. Other common tasks to perform now include running the Exchange Best Practices Analyzer (ExBPA), configuring Offline Address Books (OABs), configuring the SMTP domains that will accept mail, and configuring the postmaster mailbox for the organization.

8. As a last step, check for critical updates that need to be installed after the installation of Exchange Server 2007 by visiting http://update.microsoft.com/microsoftupdate/ or by clicking the Step 5 link in the Exchange setup splash page shown previously.

Performing Command-Line and Unattended Installations of Exchange Server 2007

As with nearly every Exchange Server 2007 task, you can perform the installation of Exchange Server 2007 from the command line fairly easily. The basic syntax of the setup.com command when used from the command line is as follows:

```
Setup.com /mode:<setup mode> /roles:<server roles to install>
[/OrganizationName:<name for the new Exchange organization>]
[/TargetDir:<target directory>]
[/UpdatesDir:<directory from which to install updates>]
[/DomainController <FQDN of domain controller>] [/DoNotStartTransport]
[/EnableLegacyOutlook] [/LegacyRoutingServer]
[/AddUmLanguagePack:<UM language pack name>]
[/RemoveUmLanguagePack:<UM language pack name>] [/NewProvisionedServer]
[/RemoveProvisionedServer] [/ForeignForestFQDN] [/ServerAdmin <user or group>]
[/NewCms] [/RemoveCms] [/RecoverCms] [/CMSName:<name>] [/CMSIPAddress:<IP
address>]
[/CMSSharedStorage] [/CMSDataPath:<CMS data path>] [/AnswerFile <filename>]
[/EnableErrorReporting] [/NoSelfSignedCertificates] [/AdamLdapPort <port>]
[/AdamSslPort <port>]
```

The number of options presented can be overwhelming, but you can examine each of the options available in Table 2.7.

TABLE 2.7 Exchange Server 2007 Setup.exe Options

OPTION	EXPLANATION
/mode:<setup mode>	Tells setup what mode of installation to perform. The default selection if no mode is specified is Install, and the following choices are available: Install, Upgrade, Uninstall, and RecoverServer. The Upgrade option upgrades only a prerelease version of Exchange Server 2007 on the server and cannot be used to upgrade a previous version of Exchange to Exchange Server 2007. The RecoverServer mode is used for Exchange Server recovery operations, which I'll discuss in Chapter 10, "Disaster Recovery Options for Exchange Server."
/roles:<server roles to install>	Specifies what server roles will be installed in a command-separated listing: CA, or ClientAccess; HT, or HubTransport; MB, or Mailbox; ET or EdgeTransport; UM, or UnifiedMessaging; and MT, or Management-Tools. If a server role is specified, you do not need to specify the MT option because the Exchange management tools will automatically be installed at that time. Also, remember that there must be at least one Hub Transport server in each site where a Mailbox server exists, and the Edge Transport server cannot be installed on a domain member server in the Exchange forest.
/OrganizationName:<name for the new Exchange organization>	Specifies the Exchange organization name. This is required only for the first installation being performed in the organization.
/TargetDir:<target directory.>	Specifies the location where Exchange Server 2007 will be installed on the server. The default location is %programfiles%\Microsoft\Exchange Server.
/UpdatesDir:<directory from which to install updates>	Specifies the location from which updates will be installed.
/DomainController <FQDN of domain controller>	Specifies the domain controller to be used to read and write to Active Directory.

TABLE 2.7   Exchange Server 2007 Setup.exe Options *(continued)*

OPTION	EXPLANATION
/DoNotStartTransport	Specifies that the Microsoft Exchange Transport service will not start when setup completes. Use this option if you need to perform additional configuration before the Edge Transport or Hub Transport server accepts messages, such as when configuring antispam agents or transport rules.
/EnableLegacyOutlook	Specifies that older versions of the Outlook client will be used in your organization. This option causes setup to create a public folder database on the Mailbox server. Public folders are optional if all clients are Outlook 2007. Omitting this option will prevent setup from creating a public folder database. This option can be used only on the first Mailbox server installed in the Exchange organization.
/LegacyRoutingServer	Specifies the legacy Exchange Server 2003 or Exchange 2000 Server Bridgehead server that has a routing group connector created for coexistence between Exchange 2007 and either Exchange 2003 or Exchange 2000.
/AddUmLanguagePack <UM language pack name>	Specifies which unified messaging language pack to install.
/RemoveUmLanguagePack: <UM language pack name>	Specifies which unified messaging language pack to remove.
/NewProvisionedServer	Creates a server placeholder object in Active Directory so you can delegate the setup of a server. Grants user permissions on this placeholder server object so the user can install Exchange Server 2007 on the server later.
/RemoveProvisionedServer	Removes a previously created server placeholder object, provided Exchange Server 2007 has not already been installed on the server.
/ForeignForestFQDN	Specifies a user in another Active Directory forest who can administer Exchange Server 2007.
/ServerAdmin <user or group>	Grants permission to a user account or group in Active Directory on a provisioned server object. This option must be used with the /NewProvisionedServer option.

TABLE 2.7   Exchange Server 2007 Setup.exe Options *(continued)*

OPTION	EXPLANATION
/NewCms	Creates a new clustered Exchange 2007 Mailbox server. This option must be used with the /CMSName and the /CMSIPAddress options.
/RemoveCms	Removes an Exchange 2007 clustered Mailbox server. Must be used with the /CMSName option.
/RecoverCms	Specifies recovery of an Exchange 2007 clustered Mailbox server. This option must be used with the /CMSName option.
/CMSName	Specifies the name of the Exchange clustered Mailbox server.
/CMSIPAddress	Specifies the IP address of the Exchange clustered Mailbox server.
/CMSSharedStorage	Specifies that the cluster node will use shared storage. By default, the cluster node will not use shared storage.
/CMSDataPath	Specifies the path for shared disks.
/AnswerFile, or /a <filename>	Specifies an answer file that contains advanced options for setup. You can specify these options in the answer file: /EnableErrorReporting, /NoSelfSignedCertificates, /AdamLdapPort, and /AdamSslPort.
/EnableErrorReporting	Enables error reporting.
/NoSelfSignedCertificates	Specifies that setup should not create self-signed certificates in the case where no other valid certificate is found for Secure Sockets Layer (SSL) or Transport Layer Security (TLS) sessions. You can use this option only if you are installing the Client Access or Unified Messaging roles.
/AdamLdapPort <port>	Specifies which LDAP port the ADAM instance should use. This option is used only when installing the Edge Transport role.
/AdamSslPort <port>	Specifies which DAP SSL port the ADAM instance should use. This option is used only when installing the Edge Transport role.

So, a typical command-line installation might use an entry like the following:

```
Setup.com /mode:Install /roles:HT, CA, MB, MT
/DomainController wileydc01.wiley.corp
```

If this were the first server in the organization to be installed, you might use the following entry:

```
Setup.com /mode:Install /roles:HT, CA, MB , MT
/DomainController wileydc01.wiley.corp
/OrganizationName:WILEY /EnableLegacyOutlook
```

If you wanted to prevent the Microsoft Exchange Transport service from starting so you could perform additional configuration on the Hub Transport server, you might use the following entry:

```
Setup.com /mode:Install /roles:HT, CA, MB
/DomainController wileydc01.wiley.corp
/DoNotStartTransport
```

Figure 2.8 illustrates the installation of a new server in an existing Exchange organization.

FIGURE 2.8   Performing the command-line installation process for Exchange Server 2007

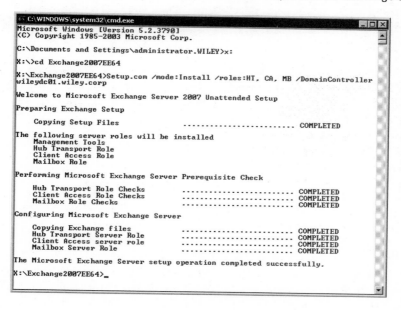

Verifying the Installation of Exchange Server 2007

After you complete the installation process on each Exchange Server 2007 computer in your organization, take some time to ensure that the installation process was completed successfully. If any errors are encountered during installation, the setup routine will alert you. You should review applicable setup logs, services, folder structures, and other items to ensure the success of the installation.

PowerShell

You can verify the list of installed server roles on the Exchange Server 2007 server by using the Get-ExchangeServer servername cmdlet from the Exchange Management Shell. Select Start ➢ Programs ➢ Microsoft Exchange Server 2007 ➢ Exchange Management Shell to open the command shell, shown in Figure 2.9. If you use the cmdlet without specifying a server, all installed servers and their roles are returned.

FIGURE 2.9 Verifying the installation of an Exchange Server 2007 server with PowerShell

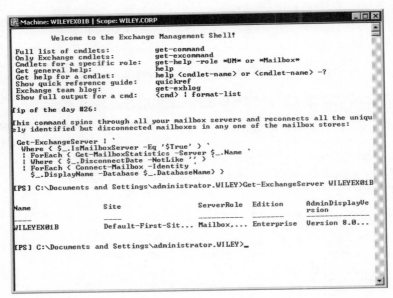

Event Viewer

The Exchange Server 2007 setup process writes several events to the Application log. You should examine these log entries to ensure that no warning or error events were logged that relate to the setup of Exchange Server 2007. Figure 2.10 illustrates a sample Application log event entry indicating the successful installation of the Mailbox server role.

FIGURE 2.10   Verifying the installation of an Exchange Server 2007 server with the
Application log

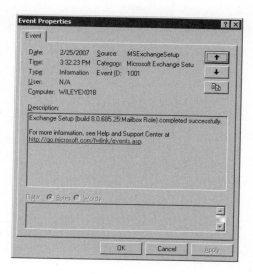

Setup Log Files

As with previous versions of Exchange, Exchange Server 2007 creates a setup log that can
be reviewed for errors or for the successful completion of the setup process. The following
logs will be created during setup:

- C:\ExchangeSetupLogs\ExchangeSetup.log tracks every task performed as part of
  the setup process and contains information about the status of all checks performed,
  installation steps carried out, and changes made to the system. Figure 2.11 provides a
  sample of the information found in this log file.

- C:\ExchangeSetupLogs\ExchangeSetup.msilog contains information about unpacking
  the installation code from the installer MSI file. Figure 2.11 provides a sample of the
  information contained in this log file.

If you installed Windows to a volume letter other than C, substitute that
letter in the log file paths to locate the Exchange setup logs.

FIGURE 2.11 Examining the ExchangeSetup.log log file

```
ExchangeSetup.log - Notepad
File Edit Format View Help
[2/25/2007 2:05:35 PM] [0] **********************************************
[2/25/2007 2:05:35 PM] [0] Starting Microsoft Exchange 2007 Setup
[2/25/2007 2:05:35 PM] [0] **********************************************
[2/25/2007 2:05:35 PM] [0] Setup version: 8.0.685.25.
[2/25/2007 2:05:35 PM] [0] Logged on user: WILEY\administrator.
[2/25/2007 2:05:35 PM] [0] Command Line Parameter Name='mode',
Value='Install'.
[2/25/2007 2:05:35 PM] [0] Command Line Parameter Name='sourcedir',
Value='X:\Exchange2007EE64'.
[2/25/2007 2:05:35 PM] [0] Command Line Parameter Name='fromsetup',
Value=''.
[2/25/2007 2:05:35 PM] [0] ExSetupUI was started with the following
command: '-mode:install -sourcedir:X:\Exchange2007EE64 /FromSetup'.
[2/25/2007 2:05:43 PM] [0] Setup is choosing the domain controller to use
[2/25/2007 2:05:44 PM] [0] Setup is choosing a local domain controller...
[2/25/2007 2:05:48 PM] [0] Setup has chosen the local domain controller
WILEYDC01.WILEY.CORP for initial queries
[2/25/2007 2:05:48 PM] [0] PrepareAD has either not been run or has not
replicated to the domain controller used by Setup. Setup will attempt to
use the Schema Master domain controller WILEYDC01.WILEY.CORP
[2/25/2007 2:05:48 PM] [0] The schema master domain controller is available
[2/25/2007 2:05:48 PM] [0] The schema master domain controller is in the
local domain; setup will use WILEYDC01.WILEY.CORP
[2/25/2007 2:05:48 PM] [0] Setup is choosing a global catalog...
[2/25/2007 2:05:48 PM] [0] Setup has chosen the global catalog server
WILEYDC01.WILEY.CORP.
[2/25/2007 2:05:48 PM] [0] Setup will use the domain controller
'WILEYDC01.WILEY.CORP'.
[2/25/2007 2:05:48 PM] [0] Setup will use the global catalog
'WILEYDC01.WILEY.CORP'.
[2/25/2007 2:05:48 PM] [0] No Exchange configuration container was found
for the organization. Message: 'Could not find the Exchange Configuration
Container.'.
[2/25/2007 2:05:48 PM] [0] The following roles are unpacked:
[2/25/2007 2:05:48 PM] [0] The following roles are installed:
[2/25/2007 2:05:48 PM] [0] The local server does not have any Exchange
files installed.
[2/25/2007 2:05:48 PM] [0] Setup will use the path 'X:\Exchange2007EE64'
```

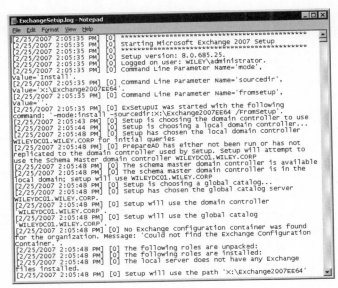

These log files are quite extensive and contain a large quantity of information. The best way to start looking for any issues is to search each log file for the string "error." If the "error" string is found, then you can read the text at that point in the log file to determine the specific error. You can search within most applications, including Notepad, by pressing F3 to open the Find/Search dialog box, The results of a search are shown in Figure 2.12.

FIGURE 2.12 Examining the ExchangeSetup.msilog log file

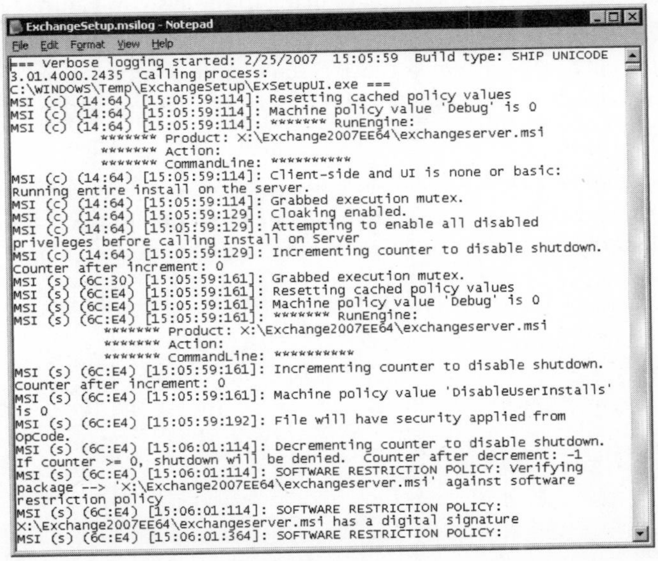

```
ExchangeSetup.msilog - Notepad
File Edit Format View Help
=== Verbose logging started: 2/25/2007  15:05:59  Build type: SHIP UNICODE
3.01.4000.2435  Calling process:
C:\WINDOWS\Temp\ExchangeSetup\ExSetupUI.exe ===
MSI (c) (14:64) [15:05:59:114]: Resetting cached policy values
MSI (c) (14:64) [15:05:59:114]: Machine policy value 'Debug' is 0
MSI (c) (14:64) [15:05:59:114]: ******* RunEngine:
           ******* Product: X:\Exchange2007EE64\exchangeserver.msi
           ******* Action:
           ******* CommandLine: **********
MSI (c) (14:64) [15:05:59:114]: Client-side and UI is none or basic:
Running entire install on the server.
MSI (c) (14:64) [15:05:59:114]: Grabbed execution mutex.
MSI (c) (14:64) [15:05:59:129]: Cloaking enabled.
MSI (c) (14:64) [15:05:59:129]: Attempting to enable all disabled
priveleges before calling Install on Server
MSI (c) (14:64) [15:05:59:129]: Incrementing counter to disable shutdown.
Counter after increment: 0
MSI (s) (6C:30) [15:05:59:161]: Grabbed execution mutex.
MSI (s) (6C:E4) [15:05:59:161]: Resetting cached policy values
MSI (s) (6C:E4) [15:05:59:161]: Machine policy value 'Debug' is 0
MSI (s) (6C:E4) [15:05:59:161]: ******* RunEngine:
           ******* Product: X:\Exchange2007EE64\exchangeserver.msi
           ******* Action:
           ******* CommandLine: **********
MSI (s) (6C:E4) [15:05:59:161]: Incrementing counter to disable shutdown.
Counter after increment: 0
MSI (s) (6C:E4) [15:05:59:161]: Machine policy value 'DisableUserInstalls'
is 0
MSI (s) (6C:E4) [15:05:59:192]: File will have security applied from
OpCode.
MSI (s) (6C:E4) [15:06:01:114]: Decrementing counter to disable shutdown.
If counter >= 0, shutdown will be denied.  Counter after decrement: -1
MSI (s) (6C:E4) [15:06:01:114]: SOFTWARE RESTRICTION POLICY: Verifying
package --> 'X:\Exchange2007EE64\exchangeserver.msi' against software
restriction policy
MSI (s) (6C:E4) [15:06:01:114]: SOFTWARE RESTRICTION POLICY:
X:\Exchange2007EE64\exchangeserver.msi has a digital signature
MSI (s) (6C:E4) [15:06:01:364]: SOFTWARE RESTRICTION POLICY:
```

Additionally, you can use the Exchange Management Shell script `Get-SetupLog.ps1` to parse the setup logs to look for errors. To use the `Get-SetupLog.ps1` script, start the Exchange Management Shell and change directories to the location of the Exchange Server scripts, typically `C:\Program Files\Microsoft\Exchange Server\Scripts` if Exchange Server 2007 was installed on volume C of the server. After changing to the Scripts directory, enter the following command, as shown in Figure 2.13: **Get-SetupLog c:\exchangesetuplogs\exchangesetup.log -error -tree**. Any errors will be brought quickly to your attention. The setup logs are cumulative from all installation attempts, so you should delete or move the files if an installation attempt is abandoned, so as not to confuse troubleshooting later.

FIGURE 2.13   Using `Get-SetupLog.ps1`

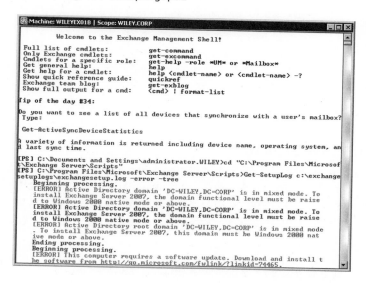

Active Directory

As discussed earlier, several changes are made to the forest and domain level during an installation of Exchange Server 2007. The easiest change to look for is the existence of the Exchange-related universal security groups.

You can also view an advanced change made to Active Directory by opening the Active Directory Sites and Services console. Click the Active Directory Sites and Services node at the root of the left pane, and then select View ➢ Show Services Node to enable the display of the Services node in the tree on the left side. Expand the Services node and you'll see an entry named Microsoft Exchange. If you click that entry in the left pane, you'll see pertinent information displayed on the right side of the window, as shown in Figure 2.14. The amount of information displayed depends on the specific Exchange organization and whether legacy Exchange servers exist.

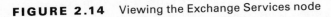

FIGURE 2.14 Viewing the Exchange Services node

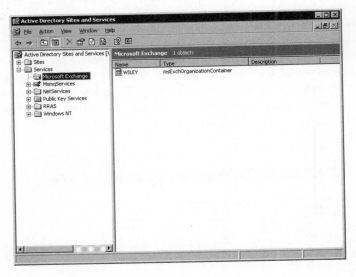

Installation Folder Structure

You can also examine the contents of the installation folder to determine whether all Exchange setup steps have completed properly. In the default installation, Exchange Server 2007 is installed to C:\Program Files\Microsoft\Exchange Server, as shown in Figure 2.15. However, you can modify this during setup.

FIGURE 2.15 Viewing the Exchange installation folder

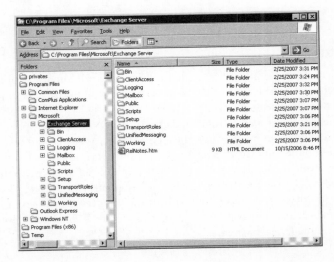

The following folders will be available in this location after the successful installation of Exchange Server 2007:

\bin   Contains all of the executable applications and related files used by Exchange Server 2007. This is created during the installation of any server role.

\ClientAccess   Contains the configuration files needed by the Client Access server role and thus is created only during the installation of a Client Access server. Inside this folder are the following Client Access role–related folders: Autodiscover, Exchweb, Owa, PopImap, and Sync.

\ExchangeOAB   Contains the offline address book data. This folder is found only on the Client Access server role.

\Logging   Contains log files for Exchange Server 2007 and is found on all server roles.

\Mailbox   Contains the schema files, DLL files, database log files, and transaction log files for the mailbox and public folder databases that are created during setup. This folder is found only on the Mailbox server role and contains the following subfolders: Addresses, First Storage Group, MDB Temp, OAB, and Schema. If public folders were installed with the Mailbox server, the Second Storage Group subfolder will also be present here.

\Public   Contains XML files and drivers that are needed for address lookup and header processing during transport operations. This folder is found only on the Hub Transport and Edge Transport server roles.

\Scripts   Contains prewritten Exchange Management Shell scripts that can be used to automate management tasks. This folder is found on all server roles.

\Setup   Contains the subfolders Data and Perf, which contain XML and data files that are used during the configuration of Exchange Server 2007. This folder is found on all server roles.

\TransportRoles   Contains the subfolders Agents, Data, Logs, Pickup, Replay, and Shared. The Pickup and Replay folders are used in certain mail-flow situations. The Logs folder contains all data logged by Hub Transport and Edge Transport servers. The Agents folder contains any binary files that are associated with a transfer agent. The Shared folder contains any agent configuration files, and the Data folder contains the IP filtering database if in use. This folder is found only on the Hub Transport and Edge Transport server roles.

\UnifiedMessaging   Contains several subfolders that hold the configuration and setup files for unified messaging operations and speech recognition. The following subfolders are located here: AdministrativeTools, Badvoicemail, Common, Config, Doc, Grammars, Logs, Prompts, Speech, Voicemail, and WebService. This folder is found on Unified Messaging servers.

Exchange Services

The installation of Exchange Server 2007 creates and configures many services on the server. Figure 2.16 illustrates the services you'll see based on the default installations performed earlier in this chapter, and Table 2.8 outlines the services created for all server roles.

FIGURE 2.16   Viewing Exchange services

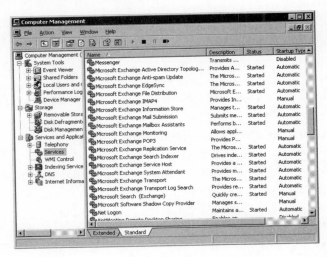

TABLE 2.8   Exchange Server 2007 Services

Service	Server Role Where Found
Microsoft Exchange Active Directory Topology Service	Mailbox, Client Access, Hub Transport, Unified Messaging
Microsoft Exchange ADAM	Edge Transport
Microsoft Exchange Credential Service	Edge Transport
Microsoft Exchange EdgeSync	Hub Transport
Microsoft Exchange File Distribution	Client Access, Unified Messaging
Microsoft Exchange Anti-spam Update	Edge Transport, Hub Transport
Microsoft Exchange IMAP4	Client Access
Microsoft Exchange Information Store	Mailbox
Microsoft Exchange Mail Submission	Mailbox
Microsoft Exchange Mailbox Assistants	Mailbox
Microsoft Exchange Monitoring	Mailbox, Client Access, Hub Transport, Unified Messaging, Edge Transport

TABLE 2.8   Exchange Server 2007 Services *(continued)*

Service	Server Role Where Found
Microsoft Exchange POP3	Client Access
Microsoft Exchange Replication Service	Mailbox
Microsoft Exchange Search Indexer	Mailbox
Microsoft Exchange Service Host	Mailbox, Client Access
Microsoft Exchange Speech Engine	Unified Messaging
Microsoft Exchange System Attendant	Mailbox
Microsoft Exchange Transport	Hub Transport, Edge Transport
Microsoft Exchange Transport Log Search	Mailbox, Hub Transport, Edge Transport
Microsoft Exchange Unified Messaging	Unified Messaging
Microsoft Search (Exchange)	Mailbox

Securing Exchange Server 2007 with the Security Configuration Wizard

As discussed previously, you should run the Security Configuration Wizard shortly after installing any Exchange Server 2007 role on your servers. If you haven't already installed the Security Configuration Wizard on your server, you should follow the steps outlined in Exercise 2.10.

EXERCISE 2.10

Installing the Security Configuration Wizard

Follow these steps to install the Security Configuration Wizard:

1. Open the Add or Remove Programs applet, located in the Control Panel.

2. Click the Add/Remove Windows Components button.

3. Select the Security Configuration Wizard option, and then click OK.

4. Back in the Windows Components dialog box, click Next to continue.

5. Click Finish when prompted.

To perform any of the Security Configuration Wizard–related tasks, you will need to be logged into the Exchange Server 2007 server with an account that has at least the Exchange Server Administrator role and is a member of the local Administrators group on that server. For Edge Transport servers, you'll just need to use an account that is a local administrator on that server. By default, if you're using the same account you used to install Exchange Server 2007, you'll be OK.

Once you have finished the Security Configuration Wizard installation, you'll next need to register the Exchange Server 2007 server role extensions for the Security Configuration Wizard, in effect extending the ability of the wizard to help you secure your Exchange Server 2007 server intelligently. To register the extensions, enter the following command from the command line, as shown in Figure 2.17:

```
scwcmd register/kbname:Ex2007KB /kbfile:"%programfiles%\
Microsoft\Exchange Server\scripts\Exchange2007.xml"
```

FIGURE 2.17   The process for the server you installed in Exercise 2.8

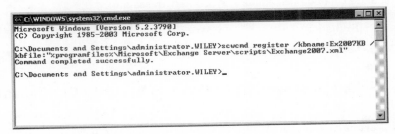

If you're performing the process on an Edge Transport server, use the following command, as shown in Figure 2.18, instead:

```
scwcmd register
/kbname:Ex2007EdgeKB /kbfile:"%programfiles%\
Microsoft\Exchange Server\scripts\Exchange2007Edge.xml"
```

FIGURE 2.18   Registering the Exchange server role extensions for the Security Configuration Wizard

After the extensions for the Exchange Server 2007 server roles are registered, you can then use the Security Configuration Wizard to secure the Exchange server, as detailed in Exercise 2.11.

EXERCISE 2.11

Using the Security Configuration Wizard to Configure Exchange Server Security

Follow these steps to use the Security Configuration wizard to customize security for an Exchange server on Windows Server 2007:

1. Select Start ➤ Programs ➤ Administrative Tools ➤ Security Configuration Wizard.

2. Click Next to dismiss the welcome page of the Security Configuration Wizard.

3. On the Configuration Action page, shown here, select the Create a New Security Policy option and then click Next.

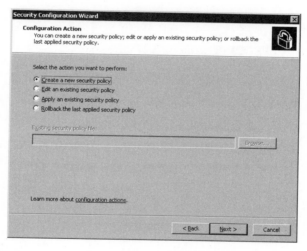

4. On the Select Server page, verify that the correct server name appears or enter the server name or IP address, and click Next to continue.

5. When the progress bar has completed on the Processing Security Configuration Database page, click Next to continue.

6. On the Role-Based Service Configuration page, take the time to read the notice given and then click Next to continue.

7. On the Select Server Roles page, shown here, verify that the Exchange Server 2007 roles you have installed on the server are selected. You'll also notice several other pertinent items depending on the server's configuration, such as Web Server, Middle-Tier Application Server, and so on. Click Next to continue.

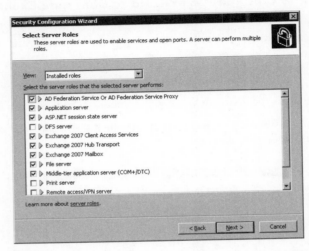

8. On the Select Client Features page, shown here, you need to select each client feature that is required on the Exchange server. Typically the default selections are correct, and no changes need to be made. Click Next to continue.

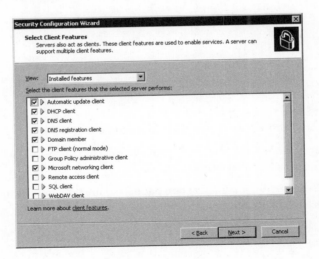

9. On the Select Administration and Other Options page, shown here, you will need to select each administration feature that is required on your Exchange server. The default selections are typically correct, and no changes need to be made in most cases. Click Next to continue.

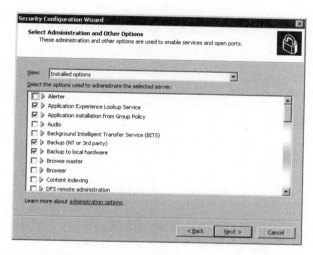

10. On the Select Additional Services page, shown here, you will have the opportunity to select additional services that must be enabled on the Exchange server. This is commonly where you'll see antivirus settings and other third-party application services. Click Next to continue.

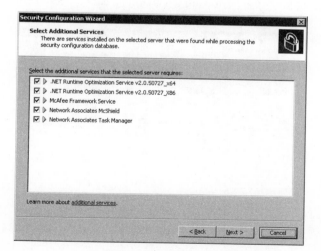

11. On the Handling Unspecified Services page, shown here, you will need to select the action that is performed when a service not currently installed on the local server is found. The default option of Do Not Change the Startup Mode of the Service is recommended in most cases, although selecting to disable new services automatically is a significantly more secure configuration. For this exercise, leave the default selection and click Next to continue.

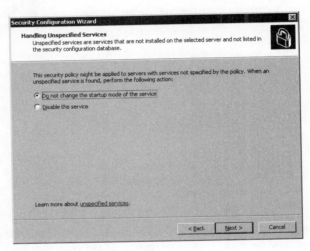

12. On the Confirm Service Changes page, shown here, you will be able to review the changes that the new Security Configuration Wizard policy will make to the current service configuration. After reviewing the changes, click Next to continue.

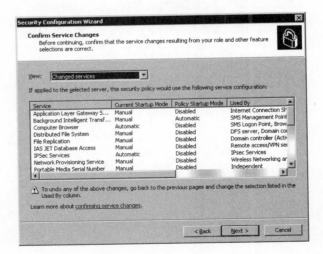

13. Now the Security Configuration Wizard moves into the next phase, network security. On the Network Security page, shown here, ensure that Skip This Section is not selected and then click Next to continue.

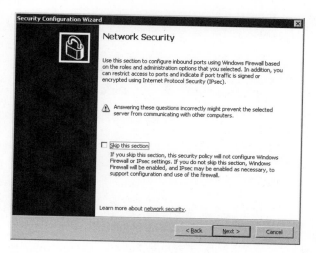

14. On the Open Ports and Approve Applications page, shown here, you will have a chance to verify and add open ports on the Exchange server. If you were running the Security Configuration Wizard on Edge Transport servers, you'd need to add open ports for LDAP communication between ADAM and Active Directory on TCP ports 50389 and 50636. In this exercise, the currently configured ports are acceptable. Click Next to continue.

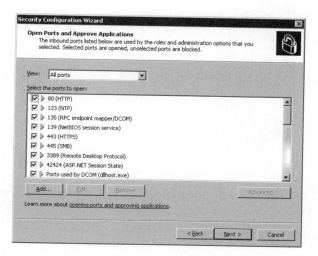

15. On the Confirm Port Configuration page, shown here, you'll get a summary of the open and approved ports on the server. After verifying that everything is acceptable, click Next to continue.

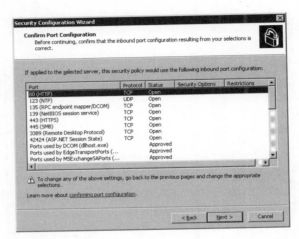

16. You don't need to use the Security Configuration Wizard to configure any additional settings for the Exchange Server 2007 server roles. On the Registry Settings page, shown here, select the Skip This Section check box and then click Next to continue.

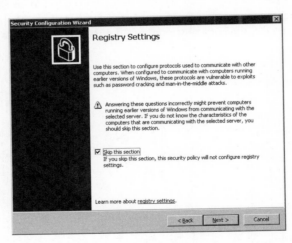

17. On the Audit Policy page and the Internet Information Services (IIS) page, ensure that the Skip This Section check box is selected and then click Next to continue.

18. On the Save Security Policy page, click Next to continue.

EXERCISE 2.11   *(continued)*

19. On the Security Policy File Name page, shown here, you will need to enter a filename for the security policy and an optional description. Click Next to save the policy.

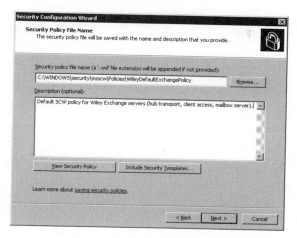

20. If prompted that a reboot of the server is needed, as shown here, click OK to acknowledge the warning.

21. On the Apply Security Policy page, shown here, select the Apply Now option and then click Next to continue.

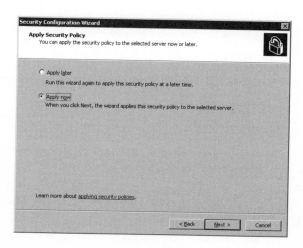

22. The policy might take some time to be applied, as shown here. When it has been applied, click Next to continue.

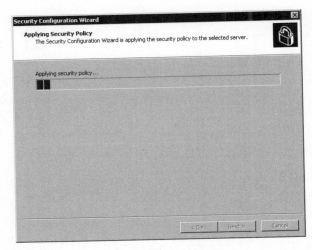

23. When prompted, click Finish to complete the Security Configuration Wizard.

24. Restart the server if you were previously informed that it was necessary to apply the configured policy.

Configuring the Exchange Administrator Roles

In Exchange Server 2003, there was little real separation in permissions between administrators responsible for Active Directory and administrators responsible for Exchange. For changes to be made to messaging-specific properties on a group or user account, the administrator had to be (at a minimum) an Account Operator. By the same token, that administrator could actually manage any account in the domain—certainly not a good separation of administrative responsibilities.

In Exchange Server 2007, the assignment of administrative permissions can be grouped into three scenarios:

- One administrator (or a group of administrators) has the ability to perform administrative tasks for both Active Directory and Exchange Server 2007.

- Different administrators (or groups of administrators) have the ability to perform specific tasks related to Active Directory and Exchange Server 2007.

- All Exchange Server 2007 tasks can be completely isolated from Active Directory by installing Exchange into an Exchange resource forest, although this scenario is less likely to be utilized in many organizations.

A property set is simply a means of grouping together many different Active Directory attributes and then controlling permissions on that group of attributes using a single access control entry (ACE) as opposed to configuring the ACE on each individual property. Exchange Server 2007 uses the property sets model and creates a property set known as email information that is used to control permissions entries on all Exchange-related attributes. Through this model, Exchange Server 2007 administrative roles are better defined and separated from Active Directory administrative roles than was the case in previous versions of Exchange Server.

Introducing the Exchange Server 2007 Administrative Roles

To allow for better separation of administrative duties with Exchange Server 2007, the following roles are implemented and the appropriate security groups are created during the setup of Exchange:

Exchange Organization Administrators role   The members of the Exchange Organization Administrators security group have the highest level of permissions over Exchange-related items within the Exchange organization. This gives members of this group the ability to perform tasks that impact the entire organization, such as creating, modifying, or deleting connectors; creating, modifying, or removing server policies; and changing any global configuration option. Additionally, this group is a member of the Exchange Recipient Administrators group and inherits all the permissions and rights granted to that group.

Exchange Recipient Administrators role   The members of the Exchange Recipient Administrators security group have the permissions they need to modify any Exchange-related property on any Active Directory user, group, public folder contact, or dynamic distribution list. The members of this group also have the ability to manage Client Access mailbox settings and Unified Messaging mailbox settings as applicable to the organization. Additionally, this group is a member of the Exchange View-Only Administrators group and inherits all permissions and rights granted to that group.

Exchange View-Only Administrators role   The members of the Exchange View-Only Administrators security group have read-only access to the Exchange organization and read-only access on all Exchange recipients.

Exchange Server Administrators role   The last role available, and the only one that doesn't have a security group created for it during the /ADPrep phase of setup, allows access to the local server's Exchange configuration data. Users configured with this role have the permissions needed to administer a certain server but cannot make any changes that would globally impact the Exchange organization as a whole.

By default, no Exchange Server Administrators are configured, so you will need to do that on your own, as detailed in the section "Configuring Administrative Roles," if you intend to use that role. As you'll see, you must manually add the selected user or group to the local Administrators group on the Exchange servers in question after you configure the Exchange Server Administrator role within Exchange.

Configuring Administrative Roles

You can configure administrative roles, like most everything else in Exchange Server 2007, from either the Exchange Management Shell or the Exchange Management Console. In Figure 2.19, you can see the administrative role configuration for our Exchange organization in the default (post-installation) state. Notice there is one entry for each of the first three roles we discussed previously.

FIGURE 2.19   Examining configured administrative roles with the Exchange Management Console

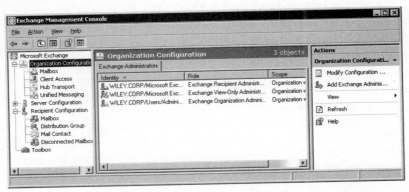

Conversely, you can perform the same task using PowerShell by using the following command in the Exchange Management Shell: Get-ExchangeAdministrator. Figure 2.20 shows the results of this action.

FIGURE 2.20   Examining configured administrative roles with the Exchange Management Shell

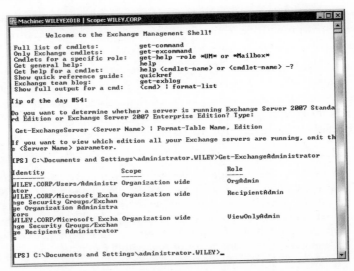

In Exercise 2.12, you'll add an administrative role to a user.

Adding Administrative Roles

To add an administrative role to a user, follow these steps:

1. Open the Exchange Management Console by selecting Start ➢ Programs ➢ Microsoft Exchange Server 2007 ➢ Exchange Management Console.

2. Click the Organization Configuration node.

3. In the action pane on the right side of the window, click the Add Exchange Administrator link. The Add Exchange Administrator Wizard opens, as shown here.

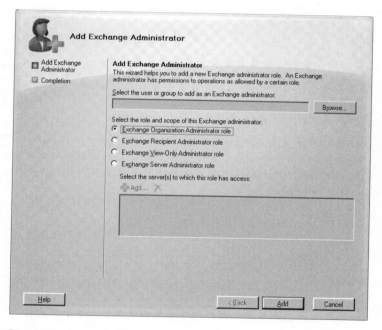

4. Click the Browse button to locate the user or group account to which you want to add the Exchange administrative role.

5. Select the appropriate role you want for the selected user or group account. If you are configuring the Exchange Server Administrator role, you will need to select the specific Exchange servers for the user or group configuration. When you're done, you might have a screen similar to the one shown here.

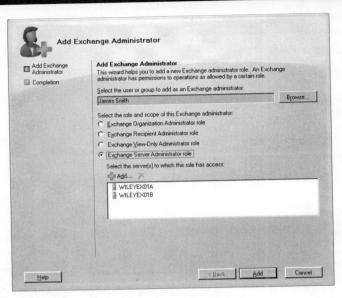

6. Click Add to create the administrative role configuration.

7. If you've configured the Exchange Server Administrator role, you might see results similar to those shown here. Check for any errors, and be sure to note any additional steps you need to complete. When you're done, click Finish to complete the process.

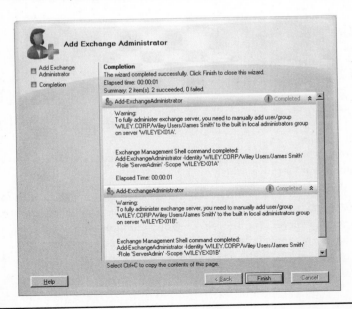

To configure an administrative role using the Exchange Management Shell, you would enter the following command: **Add-ExchangeAdministrator -Role Role -Identity Domain\User**. For example, to add Emily West in the Wiley domain as an Exchange Organization Administrator, your entry would look like this: **Add-ExchangeAdministrator -Role OrgAdmin -Identity Wiley\ewest**, as shown in Figure 2.21.

To remove a user or group that has been configured with an Exchange administrative role, you can simply select the user or group name in the list and then click the Remove link in the right pane of the Exchange Management Console window. When prompted, if you are sure you want to remove the user or group, click Yes. You will next be presented with a summary of the operation that was completed. Click OK, and you have just removed that user or group. You can perform the same task from the Exchange Management Shell using the following command: **Remove-ExchangeAdministrator -Role Role -Identity Domain\User**.

FIGURE 2.21   Configuring Exchange Administrator roles using the Exchange Management Shell

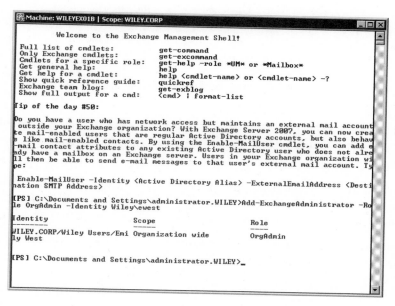

Real World Scenario

Take Command!

One of the best features of Exchange Server 2007 is the wealth of command-line and PowerShell options you have at your disposal. You can now install, configure, administer, and manage an Exchange Server 2007 organization completely from the command line! In fact, some less commonly performed tasks within Exchange Server 2007 can be performed only using the Exchange Management Shell.

To get the most from the power and flexibility that the Exchange Management Shell offers, you will need to learn about PowerShell scripting and start to build your own administrative toolset of scripts and cmdlets. The Exchange setup process will help get you started because it copies several dozen prewritten PowerShell scripts during the setup process to the Scripts directory, which is found on a default installation at `C:\Program Files\Microsoft\Exchange Server\Scripts`.

Beyond that start, you'll want to spend some time learning about PowerShell and how it is used specifically within Exchange Server 2007. You can find a wealth of information about PowerShell at the following locations:

```
http://www.microsoft.com/technet/scriptcenter/hubs/msh.mspx
http://blogs.msdn.com/PowerShell/
http://channel9.msdn.com/wiki/default.aspx/Channel9.WindowsPowerShellWiki
http://www.microsoft.com/windowsserver2003/technologies/management/
powershell/default.mspx
```

You'll likely also want to consider using a professionally written scripting application, moving up a few notches from Notepad. One of my favorites is PrimalScript from SAPIEN Technologies. You can find more information about this product at `http://www.primalscript.com`.

Regardless of how you proceed, you should learn how to maximize the power and control that PowerShell in the Exchange Management Shell gives you—you won't be disappointed with the results and the time you saved!

Summary

Before you even start to install the first Exchange Server 2007 server, many items need your time and consideration. Taking the time to prepare your organization properly for the introduction of Exchange Server 2007 will yield positive results, regardless of whether this is an upgrade/coexistence scenario with legacy versions of Exchange or whether it's a completely new installation of Exchange Server 2007.

One of the most important phases of an installation is preinstallation. Before starting the actual installation, you must make sure that the minimum requirements for Exchange are met. You must obtain the proper licenses to ensure compliance with legal issues. Because Exchange utilizes user accounts from Active Directory, Exchange Server 2007 is tightly integrated with it. Before Exchange can be installed, you will need to ensure that the required Windows services and components are installed and running. To avoid problems during the setup process, you should use the dcdiag and netdiag tools to test your network's connectivity. Finally, you must prepare the Active Directory forest and domains by running the appropriate commands.

Before you actually start to install your new Exchange Server 2007 servers, you should take some time to plan what roles you'll be installing, how many of each role you'll be installing, and, most important, where within your Active Directory forest you'll be installing the servers. Recall that certain requirements and limitations govern how you can install each Exchange Server 2007 server role. As a quick summary, consider the following points:

- Edge Transport servers must not be members of the Exchange forest's Active Directory domain.

- Edge Transport servers should be installed in the portion of your network that is exposed to the Internet, such as the DMZ.

- The Edge Transport server role cannot be installed in combination with any other Exchange Server 2007 server role.

- Each Active Directory site that is to contain a Mailbox server or Unified Messaging server must have at least one Hub Transport server.

- The Hub Transport server is a required server role.

- Hub Transport servers cannot be clustered or use network load balancing.

- The Mailbox server role is no longer responsible for message routing.

- At least one Mailbox server must be installed before you can install a Unified Messaging server.

- The Client Access server role is required for any type of client access other than Outlook MAPI access.

- A Client Access server is required to enable Outlook 2007 Autodiscover.

- Client Access servers must be part of an Active Directory domain and should never be directly exposed to the Internet.

- The Hub Transport, Mailbox, and Client Access server roles will be installed by default on the first Exchange Server 2007 server.

In almost every installation of Exchange Server 2007, you will be using two or more Exchange servers. Perhaps one server will be a Client Access and Mailbox server and the other will be a Hub Transport server. Alternatively, maybe two Mailbox servers are installed in a cluster continuous replication model and two additional servers are installed with the Client Access and Hub Transport roles. Perhaps in the DMZ, there might also be two Edge Transport servers installed for message routing and hygiene controls. The bottom line is that there is no specific number of Exchange Server 2007 servers that you must have as a rule—rather your organization's size, locations, and needs will determine how many you need, where you place them, and what roles you install.

Although installing Exchange Server 2007 is fairly straightforward, you must complete many important tasks correctly beforehand to ensure that the actual installation process will be successful. Planning and analyzing the desired Exchange organization ensures that the correct number of servers and the proper roles are installed where needed. It's just as important to know how to install an Exchange server as it is to know how to plan for the installation of an Exchange server—one cannot create success without the other.

Exam Essentials

Keep your roles straight.   Exchange Server 2007, for the first time ever, actually has specific roles defined that allow you to configure and install only the Exchange components and services you need on each individual server. Remember, not all roles are intended to be installed together, and the Edge Transport role must be installed on a server that is not part of the Active Directory forest. Know which roles are required and which ones are optional and how each role interacts with the others.

Remember CHMU.   If you remember the acronym C.H.M.U., you can remember the order that the Exchange roles should be installed. The acronym stands for Client (Client Access), Hub (Hub Transport), Mailbox, and Unified (Unified Messaging).

Know the Exchange Management Shell.   As you've seen, just about every task performed in Exchange Server 2007 can be performed from both the Exchange Management Console and the Exchange Management Shell. Be sure you understand how to perform basic tasks from the shell. There are actually some more advanced, less frequently performed tasks that can be performed only from the Exchange Management Shell!

Trust but verify.   After you complete the installation of Exchange Server 2007 on each server, take some time to verify that the installation completed successfully by examining the setup logs for errors and verifying that the correct services are installed and running. You can also examine the directory structure created during Exchange setup, check for the Exchange universal security groups in Active Directory, and examine the Event Viewer for indications of how setup really went.

Understand preinstallation setup.exe options. If you're working in single-domain forest, you might never need to work with the /PrepareSchema, /PrepareAD, and /PrepareDomain commands. Even if this is the case, you should still learn what these powerful setup commands do and what permissions are required to use them. Consider the example of a very large, geographically dispersed network where multiple administrators at various levels work together to manage and maintain the network. In this situation, these commands are invaluable tools that can assist you in getting Exchange Server 2007 installed by splitting up the installation tasks according to domain group permissions that have been assigned.

Remember which groups interact with Exchange. Several different security groups interact with Exchange before, during, and after the installation of Exchange is complete. You should keep in mind the basic functions and responsibilities of each of these groups.

Know the limitations of coexisting with older versions of Exchange. There is no direct upgrade path for Exchange Server 2007 as there was with Exchange Server 2003. As such, you'll likely be coexisting with older versions of Exchange for a while if they exist in your organization. If you will be installing Exchange Server 2007 into an Exchange organization that contains Exchange Server 2003 or earlier versions of Exchange, you'll need to keep the following requirements in mind:

- Exchange Server 2007 cannot be installed in an Exchange organization that contains Exchange Server 5.5. You must migrate all mailboxes and public folders to Exchange Server 2003 or Exchange 2000 Server first in this scenario.

- All Exchange Server 2003 servers must have, at a minimum, Exchange Server 2003 SP2 installed.

- All Exchange 2000 Server servers must have, at a minimum, Exchange 2000 Server SP3 installed.

- All Exchange 2000 Server servers must have the most current post-SP3 update rollup installed as well. See MSKB 870540 to obtain the most current post-SP3 update rollup for Exchange 2000 Server.

Remember the requirements to install Exchange Server 2007. Exchange Server 2007 can be installed only on a Windows Server 2003 x64 SP1 or R2 computer. All domain controllers and global catalog servers that the Exchange Server 2007 computer will communicate with must have at least Windows Server 2003 SP1 applied, and the domain and forest functional levels must be at the Windows 2000 native functional level or higher. The hardware and software requirements detailed previously in this chapter must also be met to install and operate an Exchange Server 2007 organization successfully.

Review Questions

1. One of your company's locations contains an Exchange server with 25 users, each using Microsoft Outlook. You have purchased 25 client access licenses (CALs). The company hires 10 new employees who will connect to the site remotely using Outlook Web Access. How many additional CALs must you purchase?

   A. 0

   B. 2

   C. 5

   D. 6

   E. 10

   F. 12

2. You are the Exchange administrator for a large network. You do not have the appropriate permissions to update the Active Directory schema on your network, so you must get another administrator to do this before you can install Exchange Server 2007. To which of the following groups must that person belong in order to run the /PrepareSchema utility? (Choose all that apply.)

   A. Server Admins

   B. Domain Admins

   C. Schema Admins

   D. Enterprise Admins

3. You will have two Exchange Server 2007 computers that provide all messaging access for your 250 network users. If all 250 of your users connect to the Exchange server using Office Outlook 2007 and Outlook Web Access, how many CALs do you need to have?

   A. 1

   B. 2

   C. 250

   D. 500

4. Your company is running a messaging system that consists of four Exchange 2000 Server computers running on Windows 2000 Advanced Server. Which of the following steps must you take to migrate to Exchange Server 2007? (Choose all that apply.)

   A. Upgrade all servers to Exchange 2000 Server Service Pack 3.

   B. Upgrade all servers to Exchange 2000 Server Service Pack 2.

   C. Install Windows Server 2003 on all servers.

   D. Update the legacy permissions for the RUS.

5. In a large organization with thousands of Exchange mailboxes, what storage technology provides the highest performance, although it costs the most to implement?

   A. iSCSI

   B. SAS

   C. SATA

   D. Fibre Channel

6. Exchange Server 2007 breaks from the standard client access license (CAL) model and uses two different CALs that provide different functionality to Exchange clients. What functionalities are available only when using the Enterprise CAL? (Choose all that apply.)

   A. Managed folders

   B. Calendaring

   C. Antivirus controls

   D. Outlook Web Access (OWA)

   E. Outlook usage

7. Your network consists of a single Active Directory forest with three domains: one root domain and two child domains. If Exchange Server is to be installed in only one of the two child domains and not at all in the root domain, how many times must you run the /PrepareSchema command?

   A. None

   B. One time

   C. Two times

   D. Three times

8. What software components must be installed on any server that will have any Exchange Server 2007 role installed? (Choose all that apply.)

   A. Microsoft .NET Framework 2.0

   B. Security Configuration Wizard

   C. Windows PowerShell 1.0

   D. Windows Installer 3.1

   E. Microsoft Management Console (MMC) 3.0

   F. Simple Mail Transfer Protocol (SMTP)

9. Your network consists of a single Active Directory forest with three domains: one root domain and two child domains. If Exchange Server is to be installed in only one of the two child domains and not at all in the root domain, how many times (minimum) must you run the /PrepareDomain tool?

   A. None

   B. One time

   C. Two times

   D. Three times

10. Which of the following Exchange Server 2007–created universal security groups would not be present in a fresh installation of Exchange Server 2007?

    A. Exchange Organization Administrators

    B. Exchange Server Administrators (*servername*)

    C. Exchange Recipient Administrators

    D. Exchange2003Interop

    E. Exchange View-Only Administrators (*servername*)

11. Your Windows Active Directory forest consists of a single domain tree. That tree consists of a single root-level domain and four child domains of that root domain. You are about to prepare the root-level domain for an Exchange Server 2007 installation. After you've prepared the forest schema, what other command must you next run in the root-level domain?

    A. setup /PrepareDomain

    B. setup /PrepareAD

    C. setup /DomainPrep

    D. setup /PrepareLegacyExchangePermissions

12. Which of the following is the only network protocol storage technology approved for usage with Exchange Server 2007?

    A. iSCSI

    B. SAS

    C. SATA

    D. Fibre Channel

13. What listed component is required to support the installation of the Mailbox server role on an Exchange Server 2007 server?

    A. Microsoft Core XML Services (MSXML) 6.0

    B. ASP.NET 2.0

    C. Active Directory Application Mode (ADAM)

    D. Network COM+ access

14. What type of RAID array is recommended for holding the Exchange transaction logs?

    A. RAID-5

    B. RAID-6

    C. RAID-10

    D. RAID-0

15. Exchange Server 2007 uses the concept of role-based server installation, allowing each "role" to be installed separately from the others. What two roles are mandatory in a new Exchange Server 2007 installation?

A. Edge Transport

B. Mailbox

C. Client Access

D. Unified Messaging

E. Hub Transport

16. What Exchange Server 2007 server role do the Edge Transport servers communicate with to ensure proper mail flow and delivery?

A. Hub Transport

B. Unified Messaging

C. Client Access

D. Mailbox

17. When running the `setup /PrepareAD` command, what extra information is required for an installation of Exchange Server 2007 into an organization with no previous Exchange installations?

A. `/CleanInstall`

B. `/OrganizationName:`*NAME*

C. `/CreateOrganization`

D. `/NewOrganization`

18. If you are installing Exchange Server 2007 into a forest that has never had an Exchange organization before and that forest contains only a single domain, which of the following commands must be issued before starting the actual installation of Exchange Server 2007?

A. `setup /PrepareSchema`

B. `setup /PrepareAD`

C. `setup /PrepareDomain`

D. All of the listed commands

E. None of the listed commands

19. Exchange Server 2007 supports which of the following types of clustering? (Choose all that apply.)

A. Active/active

B. Active/passive

C. Cluster continuous replication

D. Partial cluster replication

20. Which of the following Exchange Server 2007–created universal security groups have full access to all Exchange Server properties throughout the Exchange organization?

A. Exchange Organization Administrators

B. Exchange Server Administrators (*servername*)

C. Exchange Recipient Administrators

D. Exchange2003Interop

E. Exchange View-Only Administrators (*servername*)

Answers to Review Questions

1. **E.** Every user who connects to the Exchange server will need a CAL, no matter what method (Outlook, Outlook Web Access, and so on) is used to connect.

2. **C, D.** To run the /PrepareSchema utility, a user must belong to both the Schema Admins and Enterprise Admins global groups. The user must also belong to the local Administrators group on the computer on which the utility is actually run.

3. **C.** Exchange Server 2007 is licensed in the per-user or per-device mode, meaning that each client (user or device) that accesses the server must have a valid CAL. Since you have a total of 250 clients, you need to have 250 CALs for your organization even if the clients access the Exchange server in more than one way, such as Outlook or Outlook Web Access.

4. **A, D.** To migrate Exchange 2000 Server computers to Exchange Server 2007 computers, the Exchange organization must be operating in Exchange native mode. In addition, all Exchange 2000 Server installations must be updated with Exchange 2000 Server Service Pack 3. Additionally, the /PrepareLegacyExchangePermissions setup command will need to be run to ensure that the RUS continues to operate after the Active Directory schema is updated for Exchange Server 2007.

5. **D.** Fibre Channel is still the most expensive and yet is also the most reliable and robust storage solution on the market.

6. **A, C.** The standard CAL provides licensed Exchange Server 2007 functionality such as email, calendaring, and remote access via OWA. The new Exchange Server Enterprise CAL is required to access the advanced features of Exchange Server 2007, such as Forefront Security for Exchange Server (antivirus and antispam), unified messaging, and other desirable features such as compliance controls, managed folders, and per-user journaling. Enterprise CALs are added to existing Standard CALs to make all functionality available.

7. **B.** You must run the /PrepareSchema command one time, and one time only, for each Active Directory forest that will have Exchange Server 2007 installed into it.

8. **A, C, E.** Any server that will have any Exchange Server 2007 role installed on it must have, at a minimum, the following software installed:

   - Microsoft .NET Framework 2.0
   - Windows PowerShell 1.0
   - Microsoft Management Console (MMC) 3.0

   Additional software requirements must be met depending on the specific server role being installed.

9. **C.** Once the Windows Active Directory forest is prepared using the /PrepareSchema command, each domain in the forest that will run Exchange Server 2007 must also be prepared using the /PrepareDomain command. In addition, the forest root domain and each domain that will contain Exchange Server 2007 mailbox-enabled objects, or that has users or groups that will manage Exchange Server 2007 computers, must have the /PrepareDomain command run in it.

10. D. The Exchange2003Interop security group is created and utilized only during an upgrade scenario from Exchange Server 2003. This group provides authentication for connections made between Exchange Server 2007 Hub Transport servers and Exchange Server 2003 Bridgehead servers.

11. B. In the root-level domain, you will need to use only the /PrepareAD command after the /PrepareSchema command has been run. The /PrepareAD command includes the functionality of the /PrepareDomain command. The /PrepareDomain command would then be used in each other domain in which Exchange will be installed.

12. A. Internet SCSI (iSCSI) is the single network-based storage method that Microsoft supports for Exchange Server 2007. iSCSI connects SCSI disks to servers using standard Ethernet cabling and dedicated Ethernet adapters in servers. Although most new Ethernet adapters have TCP/IP offload engines (TOEs) on them to support iSCSI usage, you will not want to deploy iSCSI using the same network adapters in use for normal network traffic. Treat iSCSI as you would Fibre Channel–attached storage systems, and place two to four Ethernet ports in each server dedicated to the iSCSI storage network. iSCSI is somewhat mature now, at several years of age, but is still far behind traditional Fibre Channel SAN systems in many regards. iSCSI, however, is typically less expensive than Fibre Channel.

13. D. For servers that will have the Mailbox role installed, the following software requirements apply:

- Internet Information Services (IIS) 6.0.
- World Wide Web (WWW) publishing component.
- Network COM+ access is enabled.
- Windows Server 2003 x64 hotfix 904639 and 918980.
- The Simple Mail Transfer Protocol (SMTP) and Network News Transfer Protocol (NNTP) must not be installed.

14. C. Transaction logs, by their very nature of being critical to Exchange and needing fast sequential read/write access, should always be placed on RAID-10 (or RAID-1) arrays if at all possible. These arrays should be controlled by battery-backed controllers to prevent data loss.

15. B, E. The Mailbox and Hub Transport roles are mandatory in all Exchange Server 2007 installations. The Client Access role will be used in nearly every Exchange Server 2007 implementation, and usage of the Edge Transport and Unified Messaging roles will vary by organizational needs and comfort.

16. A. When an inbound message is received by the Edge Transport server, it scans the message for viral and spam qualities and then takes the appropriate (as configured) actions if it determines that the message meets the criteria for one or both of these items. Normal, clean messages are delivered to a Hub Transport server for policy and compliance enforcement as well as delivery to the final recipients. All message routing and delivery is accomplished by the Hub Transport servers in Exchange Server 2007.

17. B. When Exchange Server 2007 is being installed and no legacy Exchange organizations exist, you will need to specify the Exchange organization name by running the following command: `setup /PrepareAD /OrganizationName:`*NAME*, where *NAME* is the name you want to call the Exchange organization.

18. E. If there is only one domain in your forest, the installation of Exchange is simplified. If the account with which you install the first Exchange server belongs to the Schema Admins, Enterprise Admins, and Administrators groups for the local computer, you do not need to run /PrepareAD, /PrepareSchema or /PrepareDomain manually since you will run them during the regular Exchange setup process.

19. B, C. Exchange Server 2007 supports two types of true clustering: single-instance clusters (also referred to as *active/passive clusters*) and cluster continuous replication. Active/active clusters, which were supported by Exchange Server 2003 and Exchange 2000 Server, are no longer supported in Exchange Server 2007. Exchange Server 2007 also provides another high-availability solution, known as *local continuous replication,* that creates a second (standby) copy of the databases.

20. A. The members of the Exchange Organization Administrators group have full access to all Exchange Server properties throughout the Exchange organization. By default, the administrative account that is used to install Exchange Server 2007 is placed into this group.

Chapter

3

Configuring the Mailbox and Hub Transport Roles

MICROSOFT EXAM OBJECTIVE COVERED IN THIS CHAPTER:

✓ **Installing and Configuring Microsoft Exchange Servers**

  ▪ Configure Exchange server roles.

With the basic task of installing your first Exchange Server 2007 server behind you, you're now off to the heart and soul of installing an Exchange organization; that is, configuring the server roles. In the next two chapters, we will cover how to configure each of the Exchange server roles for use.

The main topics of this chapter are as follows:

- Configuring the Mailbox server role

- Configuring the Hub Transport server role

- Changing server roles and removing servers from the Exchange organization

Configuring the Mailbox Server

The Mailbox server role is going to be one of the first Exchange Server 2007 roles you'll be configuring in your organization, whether it's on the same server as the Hub Transport server (and possibly the Client Access server) or on a dedicated server. Perhaps your Mailbox servers will be in a highly available configuration (as discussed in Chapter 8, "Configuring Highly Available Exchange Server Solutions," or maybe your organization is smaller and a single Exchange server is all you need. Whatever the case may be, the Mailbox server will require some configuration and management actions before it is ready to perform its function in your organization.

Understanding the Exchange Storage Structure

Before we get to some of the configuration and management tasks you might perform on your Mailbox server, we'll discuss the Exchange storage structure and provide some important fundamentals that we'll build on later in this chapter and throughout the remainder of this book.

Exchange Databases

Mailbox servers contain databases that hold either mailbox or public folder data. Within these databases reside all the messages and other content items that exist within the emails and public folder items of the organization. Each database in Exchange Server 2007 consists of a single *rich-text (EDB)* file. By default, Exchange Server 2007 creates the first database for you in a default storage group. (We'll discuss storage groups in the next section of this chapter.) You can find the `Mailbox Database.edb` file by default in the `C:\Program Files\Microsoft\Exchange Server\Mailbox\First Storage Group` directory, as shown in Figure 3.1.

FIGURE 3.1   The default mailbox database

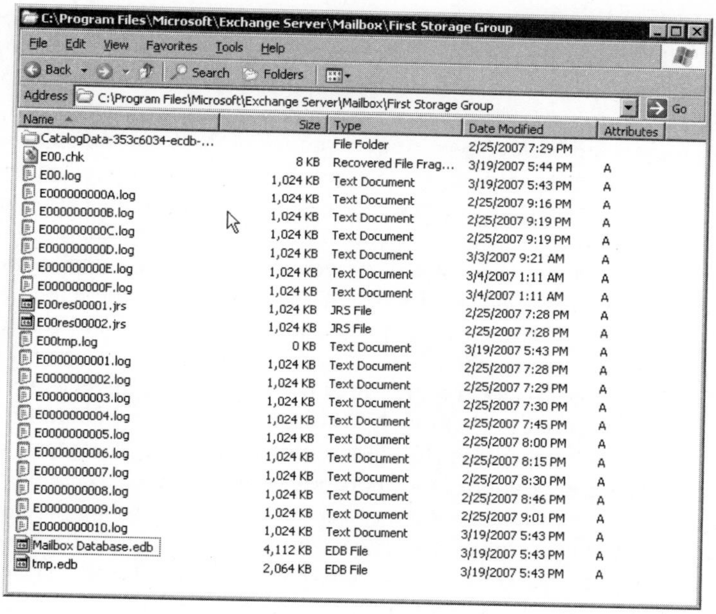

If during the installation of the Exchange Mailbox server role you opted to create a public folder database, it would be created by default at `C:\Program Files\Microsoft\Exchange Server\Mailbox\Second Storage Group` and be named `Public Folder Database.edb`.

> **NOTE**   In Exchange 2000 Server and Exchange Server 2003, the database is made up of two files: a streaming media file (`.stm`) that contains email received in Multipurpose Internet Mail Extensions (MIME) format and the familiar Extensible Storage Engine or ESE (`.edb`) B-tree database file that stores MAPI-formatted messages. Exchange Server 2007 only uses a single ESE file that stores all messages in MAPI format and only converts to and from Internet formats when needed.

Storage Groups and Related Files

A *storage group* is a group of databases on a server that share a set of transaction logs. Backup and restore in Exchange Server 2007 provides support for multiple databases and storage groups on a single server. Since all databases in a storage group share the same transaction logs, backups are typically done at the storage group level. Creating multiple storage groups allows for fewer mailboxes to be affected if an outage for a database is experienced. It also reduces the size of each backup, allowing for quicker restores.

As outlined in Chapter 2, "Installing Exchange Server 2007," Exchange Server 2007 Enterprise Edition allows up to 50 databases and 50 storage groups. Exchange Server 2007 Standard Edition allows for up to five databases and five storage groups. Although you can create multiple databases per storage group, the best practice that Microsoft is promoting is a single database per storage group.

Each storage group is represented by a single instance of the *Extensible Storage Engine (ESE)* and shares a single set of transaction log files. Whenever a transaction occurs on an Exchange server, the responsible service first records the transaction in a *transaction log*. Using transaction logs allows for faster completion of the transaction than if the service had to commit the transaction to a database immediately, because the transaction log structure is much simpler than the database structure. Data is written to these log files sequentially as transactions occur. Later, regular database maintenance routines commit changes in the logs to the actual databases when system processes are idle. Consequently, the most current state of an Exchange service is represented by the EDB file plus the current log files.

The *checkpoint files* are used to keep track of transactions that are committed to the database from a transaction log. Using checkpoint files ensures that transactions cannot be committed to a database more than once. Checkpoint files are named Exx.chk and normally reside in the same directories as the transaction log files. Those transaction logs that have been committed to the database are cleared during a database backup. (We discuss this further in Chapter 10, "Disaster Recovery Operations for Exchange Server"). You can see the checkpoint file, log files, and other storage group files in Figure 3.1.

Using multiple databases and storage groups allows you to plan your organization's data storage by classifying various types of data or assigning separate databases to more important users.

The function of each type of file shown in Figure 3.1 is as follows:

Exx.chk   The checkpoint file is named with the log file prefix, such as E00 for the first storage group, E01 for the second storage group, and so on. The checkpoint file contains a record of which logs have been committed to the Exchange database and which transaction logs still remain to be committed.

Exx.log   This file is the transaction log currently in use (the file to which data is actively being written) by the storage group indicated by the number. When this log is full at 1,024KB, it will be renamed to the next sequential number for the storage group. A new Exx.log file will then be created, and transactions will be written to it until it is full. In previous versions of Exchange, these log files were 5MB in size.

Exxhhhhhhhh.log   These are older transaction log files and are named with the log prefix, such as E01, followed by an eight-character hexadecimal number. Thus, you would have E0100000001.log as the first log file for the second storage group on the server. The numbers 1 through 0 and the letters *A* through *F* are used in hexadecimal numbering system. These files will always be 1,024KB in size.

Exxres00001.jrs and **Exxres00002.jrs**   These two files are reserve transaction log files and serve only as emergency storage if the volume the logs are located on becomes full. If the volume does become full, the transactions currently being processed are written to disk and the databases in the storage group(s) on that volume are dismounted. By having two reserved transaction logs, Exchange can ensure that no transactions are lost during this process. These files will always be 1,024KB in size.

Tmp.edb   This file is a temporary workspace for processing active transactions. This file is typically only a few megabytes in size and will be deleted automatically when all databases in the storage group are dismounted or the server's Microsoft Exchange Information Store process has stopped.

Exxtmp.log   This file serves as the transaction log file for the Tmp.edb workspace. This file will never be larger than 1,024KB in size.

name.edb   This file is the B-tree database file. In Figure 3.1, it was named Mailbox Database (which is a default name), but you will likely see different names in your organization over time for each mailbox and public folder database file.

All of the file locations discussed and shown in Figure 3.1 are the defaults provided by the Exchange setup process. As with any database, however, you will want to have transaction logs and actual database files on different physical volumes if possible. Transactions that occur within Exchange Server 2007 are always first written to the transaction logs and then read and written into the actual database file at a later time depending on the current load being placed on the server. Transaction log access is typically sequential, whereas database access is almost always random. By placing each storage group's transaction logs on one physical volume and the databases for that storage group on another physical volume, you'll increase speed, performance, reliability, and recoverability of that storage group as a whole. With the emphasis in Exchange Server 2007 on one database per storage group, you should effectively be planning for two different physical volumes per server for each storage group on that server.

Configuring Storage Groups and Mailbox Databases

Now that you have a basic understanding of how the Exchange storage structure is designed, let's examine some common storage group tasks and database-related tasks that you'll be performing on Mailbox servers.

   In this chapter, you'll be examining mailbox databases. I discuss public folders in Chapter 6, "Configuring and Managing Public Folders."

Using Storage Groups

Since storage groups are basically containers that hold databases, they are fairly simple to create and they require little management. The following sections describe how to create, configure, and manage storage groups.

> Often naming conventions are created to make working with databases and storage groups easier. The default First Storage Group group may not scale well when you are working in an environment of 25 Exchange servers. Many companies will opt to shorten this name to something without spaces, like SRV01SG01, designating that this storage group is on the computer named SRV01. Removing spaces in storage group and database names also makes them easier to work with in Exchange Management Shell. If there are spaces in the name, you need to encapsulate the name in double or single quotation marks, such as "First Storage Group" or 'First Storage Group.'

Creating a Storage Group

By default, a single storage group is created on each server and is named First Storage Group. Since every storage group is created on and associated with a single server, you will always find storage groups listed on the Database Management tab of the Mailbox server view in the Exchange Management Console, as shown in Figure 3.2.

FIGURE 3.2   Storage groups always belong to a specific server.

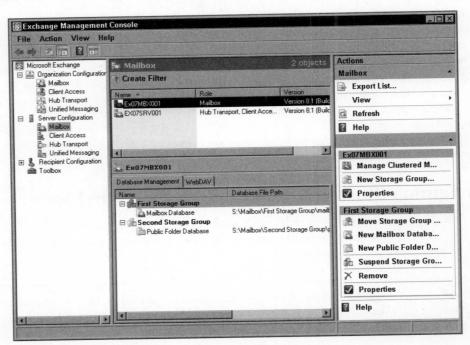

Exercise 3.1 outlines the steps for creating a new storage group.

Creating a New Storage Group

To create a new storage group, follow these steps:

1. Click Start ➤ Programs ➤ Microsoft Exchange Server 2007 and then select Exchange Management Console.

2. Expand the Microsoft Exchange root object, expand the Server Configuration folder, click Mailbox, and then click the server for which you want to add a storage group.

3. In the Actions pane on the right for that Mailbox server, click the New Storage Group link, as shown here.

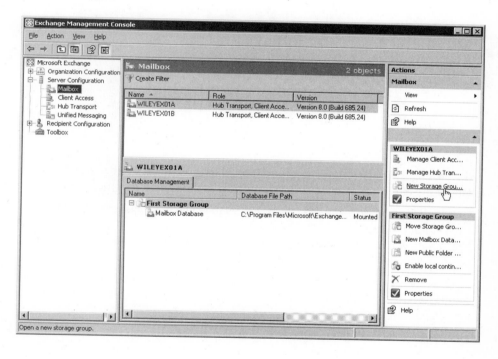

4. The New Storage Group Wizard opens, as shown here.

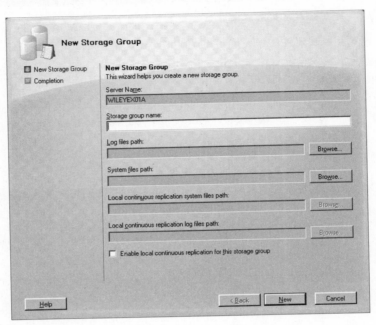

5. Provide a name for the storage group, and then use the Browse buttons to locate the path for the log files and system files associated with the storage group:

   ▪ The transaction log location is the directory in which the transaction log file for the storage group resides. By default, a location is created for the log file based on the name you give the storage group. You can change this location while creating the storage group or at any time after creation.

   ▪ The system path location is where any temporary database files (named tmp.edb) and checkpoint files (named edb.chk) are stored. You can change this location during or after creation.

6. By default, Exchange will place both the log files and the system files in the same location. If you'll be configuring local continuous replication, configure those options as well. Click the New button when you're done configuring options to create the storage group. The results are displayed for you, as shown here.

EXERCISE 3.1 *(continued)*

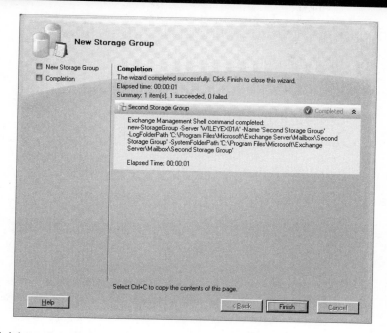

7. Click Finish to close the wizard and complete the storage group creation process.

Notice how the Exchange Management Console always tries to show you the corresponding Exchange Management Shell code you'd need to perform the same task. In most cases, you can copy and paste the code displayed into Notepad, edit it accordingly, and use it to perform the same task again—and that's exactly what you're going to do here by creating the Third Storage Group group on your server. Be sure to create the folder itself first, using Windows Explorer to house the files, and then run the PowerShell script that looks like this from the Exchange Management Shell:

```
new-StorageGroup -Server EX07SRV001 -Name "Third Storage Group"
-LogFolderPath "T:\Mailbox\Third Storage Group"
-SystemFolderPath "T:\Mailbox\Third Storage Group"
```

 You'll find the Exchange Management Shell shortcut in the same folder as the Exchange Management Console. Click Start ➢ Programs ➢ Microsoft Exchange Server 2007 to get there.

Figure 3.3 shows the results of the action.

FIGURE 3.3 Creating a new storage group from the Exchange Management Shell

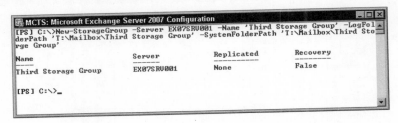

Look at the Exchange Management Console, shown in Figure 3.4. You can now see the Second Storage Group and the Third Storage Group groups we just created, although they do not yet have any databases in them. We'll get to that task shortly.

FIGURE 3.4 Viewing the newly created storage groups

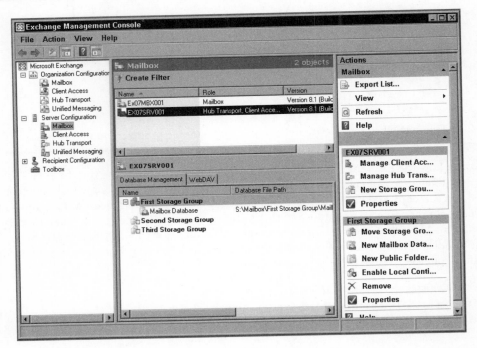

To list all of the storage groups in the Exchange organization from the Exchange Management Shell, you can use the get-StorageGroup cmdlet. To list all of the storage groups on a specific server, use the -Server switch and specify the server name.

Configuring Storage Group Properties

Only one property page is available for storage groups in Exchange Server 2007. You can open the storage group properties by right-clicking a storage group from the view shown in Figure 3.4 and selecting Properties from the context menu. Alternatively, you can click the Properties link under the storage group options in the Actions pane on the right of the Exchange Management Console. In the storage group's Properties dialog box, shown in Figure 3.5, you're given the option to change the storage group name or to enable or disable circular logging. This is quite a far cry from Exchange Server 2003, which allowed you to change storage group paths from this dialog box as well.

FIGURE 3.5   Configuring storage group properties

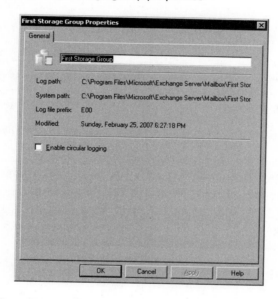

The following information is displayed for you in the storage group's Properties dialog box:

- The storage group name.
- The transaction log location.
- The system path location.
- The log file prefix, which is chosen by the system and cannot be altered. It designates the prefix, such as E00 or E01, attached to the log file for the group.
- The date and time the storage group properties were last modified.
- The status of circular logging for the storage group, which you can opt to enable or disable.

You can configure transaction log files for each storage group to be recycled to prevent accumulation of transaction logs on disk. This process is called *circular logging*. Instead of continually creating new log files and storing the old ones, the database engine "circles back" to the oldest log file that has been fully committed and overwrites that file. Circular logging minimizes the number of transaction log files on the disk at any given time. The downside is that these logs cannot be used to recover a database past the last full backup. These logs contain only the data not yet committed to the database. Another related disadvantage of circular logging is that it does not permit a differential or incremental backup of the databases.

Circular logging is disabled by default and can be enabled or disabled as discussed previously. Table 3.1 summarizes and compares what happens when circular logging is enabled and disabled.

TABLE 3.1   Circular Logging Enabled vs. Disabled

Circular Logging Enabled	Circular Logging Disabled (the Default)
Transaction log files are recycled.	Old transaction log files are stored.
The re-creation of a database is not permitted.	The re-creation of a database is permitted.
Differential or incremental backups are not permitted.	Differential and incremental backups are permitted.
A full or incremental backup will not delete old transaction log files.	A full or incremental backup automatically deletes old transaction log files.

As mentioned earlier, circular logging enables Exchange to conserve disk space by maintaining a fixed number of transaction logs and overwriting those logs as needed. Without circular logging, Exchange creates new log files when old ones fill up. Circular logging is disabled by default, and it is generally recommended that you leave it disabled except possibly for storage groups that contain only public folder databases with noncritical data—if such things exist anymore!

Beyond the configuration choices you have in the storage group's Properties dialog box, you might also need at some point to change the log file and/or system file paths associated with the storage group. Although you can no longer perform these tasks from the Properties dialog box, Exchange Server 2007 still has you covered.

Exercise 3.2 outlines the steps for changing the storage group paths.

EXERCISE 3.2

Changing Storage Group Paths

To change the storage group file paths, follow these steps:

1. Click Start ➤ Programs ➤ Microsoft Exchange Server 2007 and then select Exchange Management Console.

2. Expand the Microsoft Exchange root object, expand the Server Configuration folder, click Mailbox, and then click the server that contains the storage group with the path you want to change.

3. Click the storage group whose path you want to change. In this example, select the First Storage Group group.

4. To change either or both of these paths, simply click the Move Storage Group Path link under the storage group options in the Actions pane on the right side of the Exchange Management Console. Alternatively, you can right-click the storage group and select the Move Storage Group Path menu item from the context menu that appears. Either way, the Move Storage Group Path Wizard opens, as shown here.

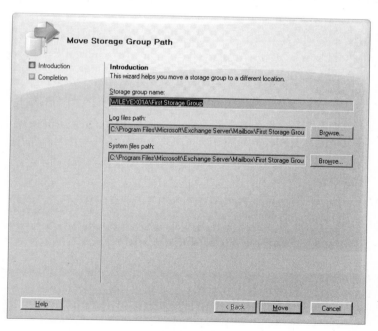

EXERCISE 3.2 *(continued)*

5. The process to change the paths is the same as when you created the storage group in Exercise 3.1. Note that this time the system file path will *not* automatically follow whatever you select for the log file path, so you will need to change both paths manually if you're looking to move both to the same location. When you've configured the desired paths, click the Move button to commit the changes. If the storage group contains any databases, you'll be prompted to allow the dismounting of the databases, as shown here. Click Yes to continue.

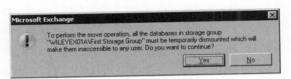

6. As always, Exchange Server 2007 will display a summary page requiring you to click Finish to close the wizard. Again, notice that the code displayed was the code actually used to perform the change.

Remember, all you're actually changing here by altering the storage group paths are the locations of the transaction log files and the location of the system files associated with the storage group. The actual database files associated with the storage groups have their locations configured with the database properties, which will be discussed later in this chapter. As a net result of making the changes discussed here, your default Mailbox Database.edb file will remain in its default location of C:\Program Files\ Microsoft\Exchange Server\Mailbox\First Storage Group, while the transaction logs and system files will be moved to the new location of C:\Program Files\Microsoft\Exchange Server\Mailbox\First Storage Group NEW. Of course, when working on a production system, you would not typically just move the logs and system files to a different location on the same volume; you'd move them to a completely separate physical volume attached to the server.

To change the storage group paths from the Exchange Management Shell, you just need to copy and paste the code and edit it accordingly. As you did when you created a new storage group with PowerShell previously, make sure that you create the appropriate folder(s) with Windows Explorer before running your code, which might look something like this:

```
move-StorageGroupPath -Identity "EX07SRV001\Second Storage Group"
-LogFolderPath "T:\Mailbox\Second Storage Group"
-SystemFolderPath "T:\Mailbox\Second Storage Group"
```

Figure 3.6 shows the results of the action.

FIGURE 3.6   Changing storage group paths from the Exchange Management Shell

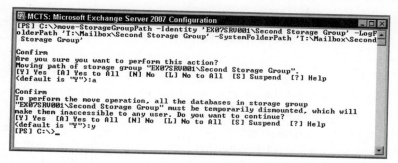

You'll need to have files in the source paths before you can use the move-StorageGroupPath cmdlet to change the storage group paths. In other words, if the storage group is empty and has no databases, this command won't work. The Exchange Management Shell will inform you of this and then present the alternative command to make a configuration-only change. This updates only the configuration information in Active Directory and does not move any files associated with the storage group.

Using Databases

The default storage group, named First Storage Group, is created during Exchange installation. A single database is also created within that storage group, a mailbox database named Mailbox Database.edb.

You can create up to four additional new databases in the First Storage Group group, although the best practice is to limit databases to one per storage group and create additional storage groups for any additional databases. Recall that the limitation of Exchange Server 2007 Enterprise Edition is 50 databases total and 50 storage groups total. The process for creating a mailbox database and a public folder database is functionally identical, and for the most part, so is the configuration of the two different types of databases. In the sections that follow, I'll cover creating, configuring, and managing a new mailbox database. When you're configuring a public folder database, many of the properties you will configure and much of the management is identical. Some differences in the configuration, such as the replication of public folders, are discussed in Chapter 8.

Creating a Database

Creating a new database is a straightforward process. Exercise 3.3 outlines the steps for creating a new mailbox database.

EXERCISE 3.3

Creating a New Mailbox Database

Follow these steps to create a new mailbox database:

1. Click Start ➢ Programs ➢ Microsoft Exchange Server 2007 and then select Exchange Management Console.

2. Expand the Microsoft Exchange root object, expand the Server Configuration folder, click Mailbox, and then click the server that contains the storage group in which you want to create a new database.

3. Right-click the storage group object in which you want to create the database, and select the New Mailbox Database option from the context menu. This opens the New Mailbox Database Wizard, as shown here. Alternatively, you can click the New Mailbox Database link under the storage group options in the Actions pane on the right of the Exchange Management Console.

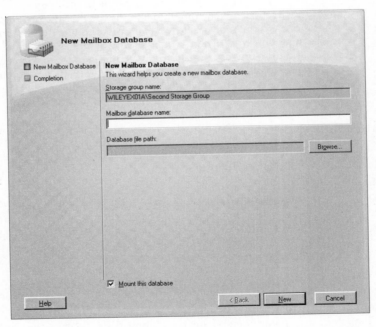

4. Type a name for the new mailbox database, and select the database file path by clicking the Browse button. Remember, the database should be on a different physical volume than its storage group's transaction logs if possible. To ensure that the database is available for immediate use, leave the Mount This Database option checked. Click New to complete the database creation process.

EXERCISE 3.3 *(continued)*

5. As usual, Exchange displays a summary page showing the success or failure of the actions you instructed it to perform. Notice this time, however, that there were two different actions performed: creating the database and mounting the database.

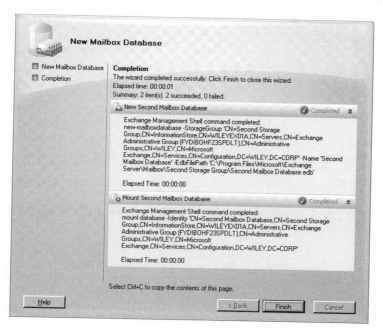

6. Click Finish to close the wizard.

To perform the same process from the Exchange Management Shell, you'll need to ensure that the database path exists by creating the appropriate folder with Windows Explorer. Additionally, you'll need to ensure that you have both PowerShell scripts correctly written: one to create the database and one to mount it. Your code might look similar to the following. Notice how almost all of the text pertains to making an Active Directory configuration.

```
new-MailboxDatabase -StorageGroup "EX07SRV001\Third Storage Group"
-Name "Third Mailbox Database" -EdbFilePath
"S:\Mailbox\Third Storage Group\Third Mailbox Database.edb"

mount-Database -Identity
"EX07SRV001\Third Storage Group\Third Mailbox Database"
```

Figure 3.7 shows the results of the action.

FIGURE 3.7 Creating a new mailbox database from the Exchange Management Shell

Looking at the Exchange Management Console, shown in Figure 3.8, you can see that now you have three storage groups, each of which has a mailbox database within it.

FIGURE 3.8 Examining the results of the mailbox database creation process

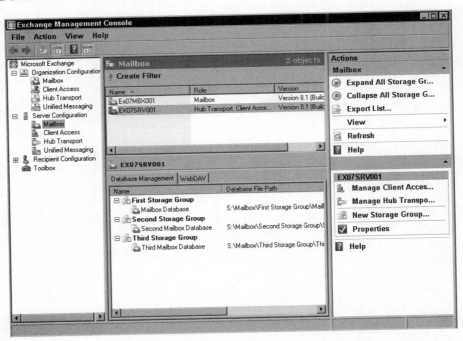

Configuring Database Properties

You use three property pages to configure a mailbox database. Unlike with previous versions of Exchange, you cannot configure any of these properties until after you've created the mailbox database. To access the mailbox database properties, either you can right-click the applicable mailbox database and select Properties from the context menu or you can click the Properties link under the mailbox database options in the Actions pane on the right side of the Exchange Management Console. Either way, the Properties dialog box shown in Figure 3.9 opens for you.

FIGURE 3.9 General properties of a mailbox store

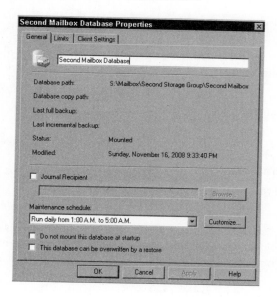

GENERAL

You use the mailbox database's General tab, shown in Figure 3.9, to configure the following properties:

- Naming the database during its creation. As with storage groups, you can change the name of a database after creation as well.

- Selecting the destination mailbox to which messages will be journaled. Depending on your needs and the type of CAL your organization is using (Standard vs. Enterprise), you will be able to journal all communications for an entire mailbox database (Standard) or, on a more granular level, journal only those messages that are sent to recipients outside the organization for certain users on a mailbox database.

Journaling is outside the scope of exam 70-236 but is covered in detail on exam 70-237. You can get more information about that exam by visiting www.microsoft.com/learning/exams/70-237.mspx.

- Choosing the times at which you want the automatic database maintenance routines to run. Select from several preset values using the drop-down list, or click Customize to open a calendar-style interface.
- Deciding whether to mount the store when the Exchange server starts. (If it doesn't, you'll have to do it manually.)
- Deciding whether the store can be overwritten during a restore from backup. See Chapter 10 for more information about backup and recovery.

The following properties are only for display on the General tab of the Properties dialog box and cannot be changed:

- The database path
- The database copy path, if local continuous replication is in use
- The date and time of the last full backup
- The date and time of the last incremental backup
- The status of the database
- The date and time the database was last modified

LIMITS

You use the Limits tab, shown in Figure 3.10, to configure limits values that are applied to all mailboxes within the mailbox database. Values set at this level are automatically applied to all mailboxes, but you can manually configure individual mailboxes as well and thus override these limits.

This tab lets you set configure settings in two areas: storage limits and deletion settings. Settings in the Storage Limits area refer to the limits (in kilobytes) placed on the size to which mailboxes in the store can grow and what happens when that limit is exceeded. Rather large limits are set by default, so you'll likely want to change them soon after creating the mailbox database. You can set limits for when to issue a warning, when to prohibit sending, and when to prohibit sending and receiving. You can also configure the interval when the Information Store checks these values and issues warnings.

The settings in the Deletion Settings area refer to how long (measured in days) deleted items in a mailbox and deleted mailboxes are retained on a server after a user or administrator deletes them. You can also configure the store to keep deleted items and mailboxes until the store has been backed up, regardless of the actual values entered. Items that have been deleted in a mailbox can be recovered during the retention period through the Outlook

Recover Deleted Items function. Deleted mailboxes can be recovered during the retention period by an administrator using the Exchange management tools.

FIGURE 3.10 Limits properties of a mailbox store

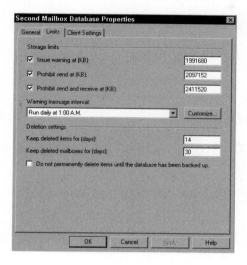

CLIENT SETTINGS

You use the Client Settings tab, shown in Figure 3.11, to configure settings that are applied to the client sessions of users who have mailboxes in the mailbox store. You can configure the following here:

Default public store: Every Exchange user must have a default public store that is used for public folder access. This does not limit access to only the chosen public store but rather provides an entry point—the first place the client will look for public folder content. Click the Browse button to open a list of available public stores from which to choose. We discuss public folders in Chapter 6.

Offline address list: The Offline Address Book field specifies the default offline address list that users of this mailbox store will download when synchronizing the offline address list on their client. Like the public folder setting, this is simply a default value and does not prevent other available offline address lists from being used.

FIGURE 3.11   Client access properties of a mailbox store

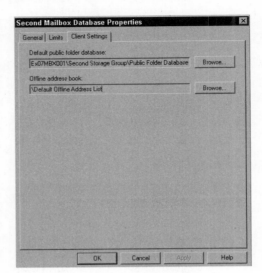

Managing Stores and Storage Groups

Once they are created and properly configured, both storage groups and stores require proper management to keep everything running smoothly. Much of this management is covered elsewhere in this book:

- Backing up and restoring (Chapter 10)
- Managing public folders and replication (Chapter 6)
- Managing individual users and their mailboxes (Chapter 5)
- Tracking messages and monitoring the status of message flow (Chapter 9)

Viewing and Managing Mailbox Information

Unlike Exchange Server 2003, Exchange Server 2007 does not group mailboxes under their mailbox databases by default. You can still get a listing of just those mailboxes that are physically in a specific mailbox database, but you'll have to work a little bit harder to get there. When you look at Exchange Server 2007 mailboxes, which I'll cover in great detail in the next chapter, you'll see the default view of all mailboxes, as shown in Figure 3.12.

If you want to see just the mailboxes located within a specific database on a specific Mailbox server, you'll need to create a filter. To create the filter, click the Create Filter button that appears above the mailbox listing and then select the desired filter items. For example, to filter the display to just those mailboxes in a specific mailbox database, you'd select the Database and Equals options and then browse to select the database whose mailboxes you're interested in seeing. When you have the filter configured, be sure to click the Apply Filter button. Figure 3.13 displays a sample filtered output. Compare this to the listing shown in Figure 3.12.

FIGURE 3.12　Viewing Exchange mailboxes

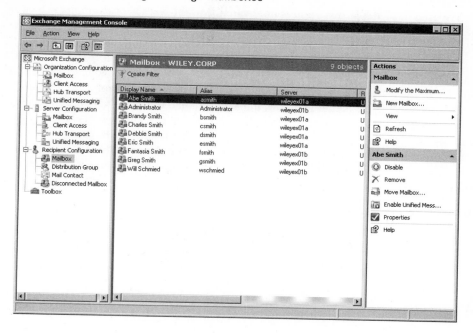

FIGURE 3.13　Using display filters to display mailboxes in a specific mailbox database

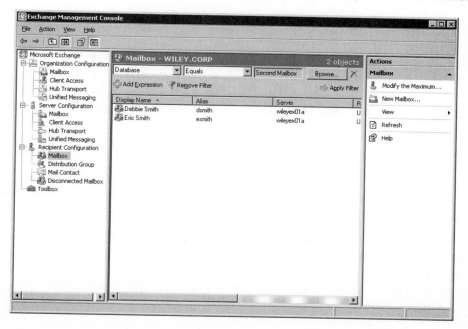

If you've worked with previous versions of Exchange, you'll notice that some information you're used to seeing at this point is not available in this view. For example, you can't see login information about the last date and time a user accessed the mailbox, you can't see information about the client that was used to perform that login, and (perhaps most important) you can't see information about how large the mailbox is within the mailbox database. You can still retrieve this information from the Exchange Management Shell, but it is not one of the features that has, as of yet, made it back into the graphical interface.

Another radical change is that you now, much as you had to do in Exchange Server 5.5, perform recipient management from within the Exchange management tools instead of through Active Directory Users and Computers. Double-clicking a mailbox in a list will open the Properties dialog box for that mailbox, as shown in Figure 3.14. This might be what you are accustomed to seeing in Active Directory Users and Computers, but now it definitely has a messaging feature focus.

FIGURE 3.14   Viewing a mailbox object

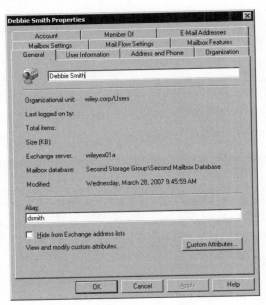

Since managing mailboxes and all mail-related settings is now done within the Exchange management tools, you'll have to delete mailboxes using the Exchange management tools. We discuss all the available configuration and management options for mailboxes in Chapter 6.

Mounting and Dismounting Databases

One of the great advantages of having multiple databases is that you can take individual databases down for maintenance without affecting other databases on the server. Taking a database offline is referred to as *dismounting*; bringing it back online is referred to as *mounting*. To mount or dismount a database, simply right-click the database and choose the appropriate option from the context menu. Alternatively, you can click the appropriate link under the database options in the Actions pane on the right side of the Exchange Management Console.

To perform these tasks from the Exchange Management Shell, you'll need to use a PowerShell script that looks similar to this for dismounting:

```
dismount-Database
-Identity "EX07SRV001\Third Storage Group\Third Mailbox Database"
```

For mounting, your PowerShell script will be similar to this:

```
mount-Database
-Identity "EX07SRV001\Third Storage Group\Third Mailbox Database"
```

Figure 3.15 shows the results of these actions.

FIGURE 3.15 Dismounting and mounting databases using the Exchange Management Shell

Deleting Mailbox Databases

To delete a mailbox database, just right-click it and choose Remove from the context menu. Alternatively, you can click the Remove link under the database options in the Actions pane on the right side of the Exchange Management Console. Before you can delete a mailbox database, you must either delete or move all mailboxes within that database. Exchange will not let you delete a database that contains mailboxes.

To remove a mailbox database using PowerShell from the Exchange Management Shell, you'll execute a script similar to this one:

```
remove-MailboxDatabase -Identity
"EX07SRV001\Third Storage Group\Third Mailbox Database"
```

Figure 3.16 shows the results of this action.

FIGURE 3.16 Deleting a mailbox database using the Exchange Management Shell

Regardless of which method you use to delete a mailbox database, you'll need to remove the database file and some other related files manually from the storage location. You'll be informed of this requirement regardless of which deletion process you use.

Deleting a Storage Group

You can delete any storage group by right-clicking it and choosing Remove from the context menu. Alternatively, you can click the Remove link under the storage group options in the Actions pane on the right side of the Exchange Management Console. However, the storage group must not have any stores associated with it. This means that you must first remove all stores in the storage group before you can delete the group. To remove a storage group using PowerShell from the Exchange Management Shell, you'll execute a script similar to this one:

```
remove-StorageGroup -Identity "EX07SRV001\Third Storage Group"
```

Figure 3.17 shows the results of this action.

FIGURE 3.17 Deleting a storage group from the Exchange Management Shell

Regardless of which method you use to delete a storage group, you'll need to manually remove the folders previously used by the storage group. You'll be informed of this requirement no matter which deletion process you use.

Real World Scenario

Using Databases and Storage Groups

Opinions abound on how you should configure your Exchange organization's storage groups and databases. We'll examine some cold hard facts here and then let you determine the best solution for your organization's needs.

A storage group, regardless of how many databases are in it, uses only one set of transaction logs. This is a good thing until you need to configure circular logging. Circular logging is configured at the storage group level and thus applies to all databases inside that storage group. This can become a large problem if that storage group contains critical email databases. In reality, is there such a thing as a noncritical email database? For databases on which you configure circular logging, consider creating a separate storage group just to hold them.

When performing backups of your Exchange data, you should be aware that you can configure backups only at the storage group level. Thus you have the option to back up only an entire storage group and its databases, not the individual databases within the storage group. However, when performing a restoration, you can opt to restore only specific databases within the storage group. Storage groups are backed up as a whole, and this can impact the length of time required to perform your backups, especially when performing full (normal) backups. I'll cover Exchange backup and restoration more in Chapter 10.

The combination of storage groups and databases that you ultimately configure will depend on the needs of your network. However, with the limitation of 50 databases in 50 storage groups in Exchange Server 2007, it really doesn't make sense to design your Exchange implementation in any other way than with one database per storage group. When we examine highly available solutions in Chapter 9, "Monitoring and Reporting," this design will make even more sense.

Configuring the Hub Transport Server

The Hub Transport server role also will always be one of the first Exchange Server 2007 roles you'll install in your organization (remember CHMU—Client Access, Hub Transport, Mailbox, Unified Messaging, discussed in Chapter 2), whether it's on the same server as the Mailbox server role or on a dedicated server. Perhaps your Hub Transport servers will be highly available by virtue of more than one per Active Directory site being installed, or maybe your organization is smaller and a single Exchange server is all you need. Whatever the case, the Hub Transport server will require that you perform some configuration and management actions before it is ready to perform its function in your organization.

Understanding the Message Routing Process

In previous versions of Exchange Server, a complex link-state routing algorithm was used to route messages between geographically separated Exchange servers. Exchange used routing groups that were connected with routing group connectors to perform this routing. With the elimination of routing groups and link-state routing in Exchange Server 2007, all Exchange message routing is performed by Hub Transport servers using the Active Directory sites and site links that service Active Directory. Therefore, message routing (both within the same site and across site links) is significantly less complex in Exchange Server 2007.

Within each Active Directory site that contains a Mailbox server (or Unified Messaging server), you must have at least one Hub Transport server. The Hub Transport server is responsible for routing all messages within a site and between connected sites. Even when a message is sent from a recipient on Server A to another recipient on Server A, it must first cross through a Hub Transport server for delivery—a big change in message routing from Exchange Server 2003. When messages must be routed between sites, the Hub Transport server in the originating site determines the best route available at that time to the destination server and routes the message accordingly.

Message routing within a single Active Directory site occurs as detailed here:

1. The sending user submits the message to their mailbox on the Mailbox server that contains the mailbox. Using the Outlook client, the message is submitted via MAPI and written directly into the sending user's Outbox.

2. The Microsoft Exchange Mail Submission service, running on the Mailbox server of the sender, detects a message in a user's Outbox and randomly selects an available Hub Transport server in that Active Directory site.

3. The sending Mailbox server then submits a new message notification to the Exchange store driver on the Hub Transport server, which causes the Hub Transport server to retrieve the queued message from the user's Outbox on the Mailbox server via MAPI.

4. The store driver on the Hub Transport server then submits the message to the categorizer queue on the Hub Transport server for the categorizer to process. The categorizer moves a copy of the message from the user's Outbox to the Sent Items folder within the sending mailbox.

5. The Hub Transport server also performs any additional modifications on the message that the configuration of the Exchange organization requires. Such modifications might include stamping a disclaimer, blocking delivery of the message, or stripping undesirable attachments from the message.

6. The Hub Transport server then places a copy of the message into a local delivery queue, where the store driver running on the Hub Transport server delivers the message using an Exchange Data Objects connection to the Mailbox server where the recipient resides.

Configuring Hub Transport

Now that you've got a basic understanding of how the Exchange message routing process works, let's examine some common hub transport configuration tasks that you'll be performing on Hub Transport servers. I'll discuss more advanced configuration of the hub transport, such as managed folders and transport rules, in Chapter 7, "Configuring Security, Compliance, and Policies." To start the hub transport configuration, you'll need to locate the Hub Transport servers within the Exchange Management Console, as shown in Figure 3.18.

FIGURE 3.18   Viewing the Hub Transport servers

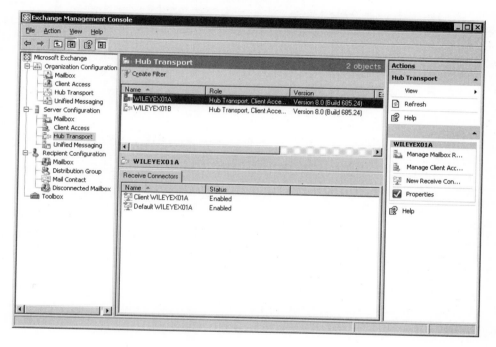

Configuring Server Settings

There are four property pages used to configure a Hub Transport server. To access the Hub Transport server properties, you can either right-click the applicable Hub Transport server and select Properties from the context menu or you can click the Properties link under the server options in the Actions pane on the right side of the Exchange Management Console. Either way, the Properties dialog box shown in Figure 3.19 opens for you.

FIGURE 3.19 The General tab of the Hub Transport server's Properties dialog box

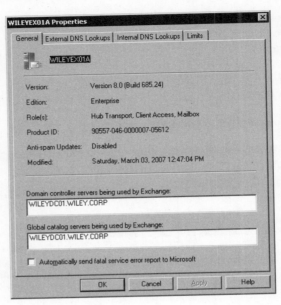

General

A Hub Transport server's General tab, shown in Figure 3.19, contains only one directly configurable option but displays information about many other items. The lone directly configurable option is whether to enable error reporting to Microsoft for this server.

You'll be able to view information about the following items on the General tab:

- The version and edition of Exchange installed on the server
- The roles installed on the Exchange server
- The product ID of the installed version of Exchange
- The status of antispam updates on the server
- The last time the Exchange configuration on the server was modified
- The domain controllers and global catalog servers in use by Exchange

External DNS Lookups

The External DNS Lookups tab, shown in Figure 3.20, allows you to configure how some send connectors perform DNS lookups. You can opt either to use the DNS server settings configured on all adapters (or just one adapter installed in the server) or to enter the DNS servers to be used for external DNS lookups manually. Typically this is changed to offload DNS lookups from your internal DNS servers to another set of DNS servers specifically designed for high-volume DNS queries or if your internal DNS servers are not connected to the Internet, as in the case of servers behind a proxy. Typically, though, the Hub Transport server will use the same DNS servers as configured on the installed network adapters or some other internal DNS server, as they are typically configured to be able to forward unresolved queries to external DNS servers as needed.

FIGURE 3.20   The External DNS Lookups tab of the Hub Transport server's Properties dialog box

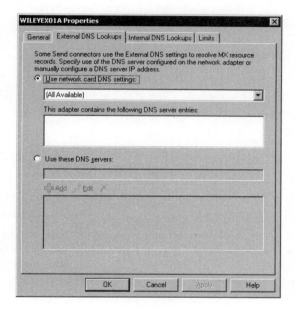

Internal DNS Lookups

The Internal DNS Lookups tab, shown in Figure 3.21, allows you to configure how DNS lookups are performed internally to the organization. You can opt either to use the DNS server settings configured on all adapters (or just one adapter installed in the server) or to enter the DNS servers to be used for internal DNS lookups manually.

FIGURE 3.21   The Internal DNS Lookups tab of the Hub Transport server's Properties dialog box

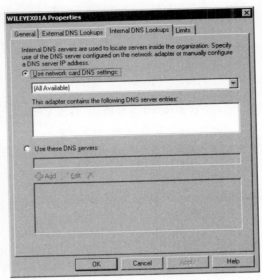

Limits

The Limits tab, shown in Figure 3.22, allows you to configure how the Hub Transport server attempts to deliver messages. The following options are available to configure:

Outbound Connection Failure Retry Interval (Minutes): Specifies the retry interval for subsequent connection attempts to a remote server where earlier connection attempts have failed. The default value is 10 minutes and is not recommended to be changed without guidance from Microsoft Product Support Services (PSS).

Transient Failure Retry Interval (Seconds): Specifies the retry interval between each connection attempt. The default value is 300 seconds (5 minutes).

Transient Failure Retry Attempts: Specifies the maximum number of retry attempts the Hub Transport server should perform to immediately make a connection when it experiences a connection failure with a remote server. The default value is 6, and a setting of 0 means the next connection attempt is controlled by the Outbound Connection Failure Retry Interval.

Maximum Time Since Submission (Days): Specifies the timeout duration for messages. If a message is still in the queue to be delivered after the amount of time configured in this setting has passed, the message is returned to the sender as undeliverable. The default setting is 2 days.

Notify Sender When Message Is Delayed More Than (Hours): Specifies when the sender of a message should be notified that a message has not yet been delivered. The default value is 4 hours.

Maximum Concurrent Outbound Connections: Specifies the maximum number of outgoing connections that can be open at one time on the server. When the configured connection is reached, the server will open new connections until the current connections are closed. The default value is 1,000.

Maximum Concurrent Outbound Connections per Domain: Specifies how many connections should be allowed to a specific domain. The default value is 20.

FIGURE 3.22   The Limits tab of the Hub Transport server's Properties dialog box

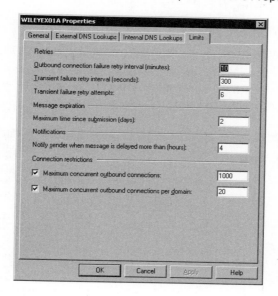

Configuring the Postmaster Mailbox

As we briefly discussed earlier in Chapter 2, there is no postmaster mailbox created by default when you install an Exchange Server 2007 organization. This is one of the most important mailboxes in your Exchange organization, and you should create one as soon as possible after installing the Hub Transport server role on a server. The postmaster mailbox is required in every messaging infrastructure per RFC 2822 and receives nondelivery reports and delivery status notifications. These reports and notifications will be useful to you over time as you troubleshoot and respond to reports of message delivery problems within your Exchange organization.

Many organizations will opt to add just the postmaster alias to an existing mailbox user, such as the default built-in Administrator, but it's almost always better to create and configure a separate mailbox user account just for this purpose. To create and configure the postmaster mailbox, we'll jump ahead just a bit and look at creating and configuring mailbox users from within the Exchange Management Console, a topic covered fully later in Chapter 5, "Working with Recipients, Groups, and Mailboxes." Exercise 3.4 outlines the steps for creating and configuring the postmaster mailbox.

EXERCISE 3.4

Creating and Configuring the Postmaster Mailbox

Follow these steps to create and configure the postmaster mailbox:

1. Click Start ➤ Programs ➤ Microsoft Exchange Server 2007 and then select Exchange Management Console.

2. Expand the Microsoft Exchange root object, expand the Recipient Configuration folder, and then click the Mailbox node, as shown here.

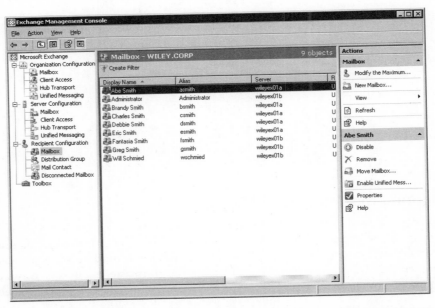

3. On the right side of the Exchange Management Console, click the New Mailbox link under the Mailbox group. The New Mailbox Wizard appears, as shown here.

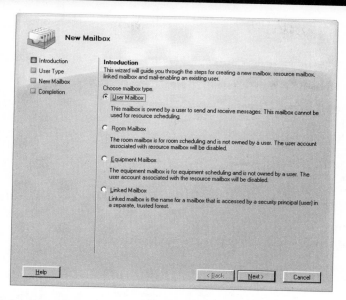

4. On the Introduction page, select User Mailbox and click Next.

5. On the User Type page, select New User and click Next.

6. On the User Information page, configure a new user appropriate for your environment, as shown here. Click Next to continue.

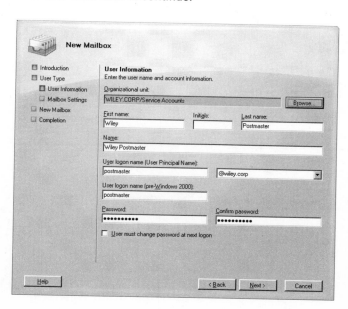

EXERCISE 3.4 *(continued)*

7. On the Mailbox Settings page, select the Mailbox server, storage group, and mailbox database that will contain the mailbox. Click Next to continue.

8. On the summary page, review the configuration, and click New to create the mailbox.

9. Click Finish to complete and close the wizard.

10. Now that the postmaster account and mailbox have been created, you will need to configure that mailbox as the postmaster address for the Exchange organization. You can do this via the Exchange Management Shell using the following command:

   ```
   Set-TransportServer servername
   -ExternalPostmasterAddress postmaster e-mail address
   ```

   So, for our organization example, the actual command might look like this:

   ```
   Set-TransportServer WILEYEX01A
   -ExternalPostmasterAddress postmaster@wiley.corp.
   ```

   The result of this command is shown here.

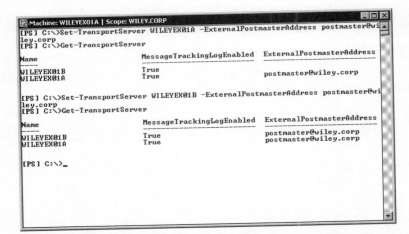

 You will need to perform the postmaster configuration once for every Hub Transport server in the organization. You can use the Get-TransportServer command to view the configuration and make sure that all Hub Transport servers have been correctly configured.

Configuring Domains

You can configure, and thus to some extent control, domains from which Exchange Server 2007 is allowed to accept and send mail. To configure the email domains from which mail is allowed to be sent, or to control how email is sent to a specific domain, you will need to create and configure remote domains. To configure the email domains for which inbound messages will be accepted, you will need to create and configure accepted domains.

Remote Domains

A *remote domain* is always outside your Exchange organization. You can create and configure remote domains to control mail flow more exactly, such as by specifying how delivery reports are handled and which character sets to use. Exercise 3.5 outlines the steps for creating a remote domain.

EXERCISE 3.5

Creating a Remote Domain

1. Click Start ➤ Programs ➤ Microsoft Exchange Server 2007 and then select Exchange Management Console.

2. Expand the Microsoft Exchange root object, expand the Organization Configuration folder, and then click the Hub Transport node, as shown here.

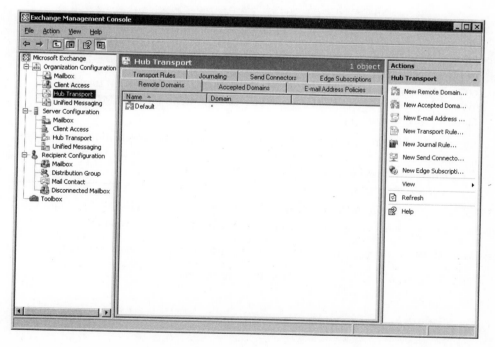

3. Click the New Remote Domain link under the Hub Transport options in the Actions pane on the right side of the Exchange Management Console. The New Remote Domain Wizard opens as shown here.

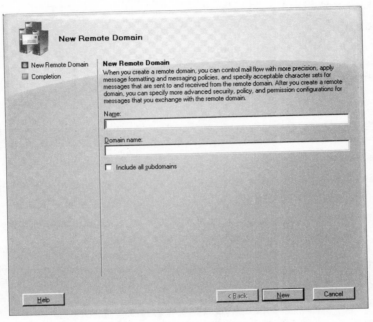

4. Enter a descriptive name and an SMTP domain name. You may want to check the Include All Subdomains box to allow global configuration for this SMTP domain. Click the New button to proceed.

5. As usual, you will be presented with a summary of what Exchange did and also given the chance to copy the actual PowerShell code used to perform the configuration. Click Finish to close the wizard.

You can create a remote domain, including all subdomains, from the Exchange Management Shell by using the following command for the Exchange Exchange SMTP domain:

```
new-RemoteDomain -Name "Exchange Exchange" -DomainName "*.exchangeexchange.com"
```

Figure 3.23 shows the results of this configuration action.

FIGURE 3.23   Creating a remote domain from the Exchange Management Shell

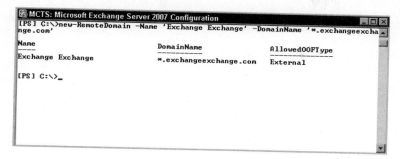

 The SMTP domain name field is limited to 256 characters in length.

You can see the results of your remote domain creation efforts by looking at the Exchange Management Console, shown in Figure 3.24.

FIGURE 3.24   Viewing remote domains in the Exchange Management Console

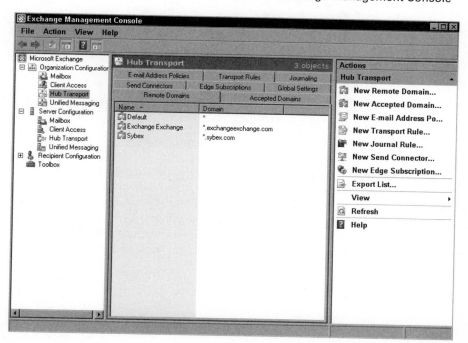

Regardless of how you create the remote domain object, two configuration tabs are available for you afterward. You can open the remote domain's Properties dialog box by right-clicking the remote domain and selecting Properties from the context menu or by clicking the Properties link under the remote domain options in the Actions pane on the right side of the Exchange Management Console.

The remote domain's Properties dialog box opens to the General tab, as shown in Figure 3.25. From the General tab, you can rename the remote domain object and configure how out-of-office (OOF) messages should be handled when senders from the remote SMTP domain send messages to an internal user who has OOF configured on their mailbox. The default setting is to allow external messages only.

FIGURE 3.25   The General tab of the remote domain's Properties dialog box

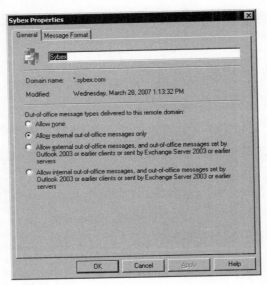

The Message Format tab of the remote domain's Properties dialog box, shown in Figure 3.26, allows you to configure several options that control how the messages sent to the remote domain are handled. You can enable or disable processes such as delivery and non-delivery reports, configure rich-text settings, and even configure a character set to be used for messages to the remote domain. These settings give you much more flexibility than in previous versions of Exchange as to which messages should leave your Exchange organization and also what they should look like.

FIGURE 3.26   The Message Format tab of the remote domain's Properties dialog box

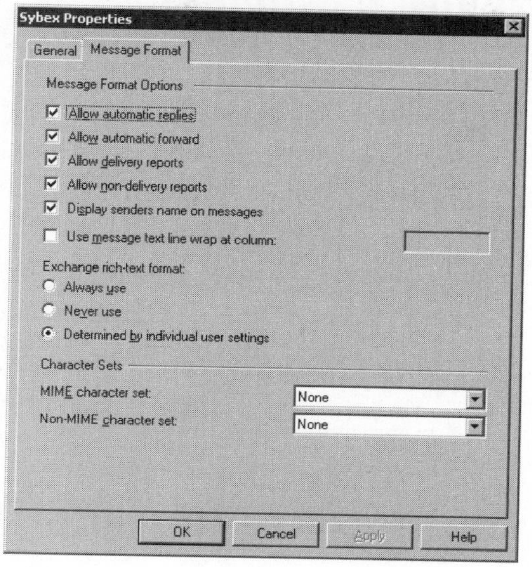

Accepted Domains

An *accepted domain* may or may not be within your Exchange organization or Active Directory forest, but it's almost certain to be a domain with which you have an administrative relationship, such as a partner domain or a domain within another Active Directory forest in your company or organization.

Accepted domains are used to specify the SMTP domains for which the Exchange server organization will accept and/or route messages. By default, the first accepted domain is created for you when the Exchange organization is created. You can create and configure additional accepted domains as needed or just make changes to the default accepted domain that was created automatically. Exercise 3.6 outlines the steps for creating an accepted domain.

EXERCISE 3.6

Creating an Accepted Domain

To create an accepted domain, follow these steps:

1.   Click Start ➢ Programs ➢ Microsoft Exchange Server 2007 and then select Exchange Management Console.

2.   Expand the Microsoft Exchange root object, expand the Organization Configuration folder, and then click the Hub Transport node.

EXERCISE 3.6   (continued)

3. Click the New Accepted Domain link under the Hub Transport options in the Actions pane on the right side of the Exchange Management Console. The New Accepted Domain Wizard opens, as shown here.

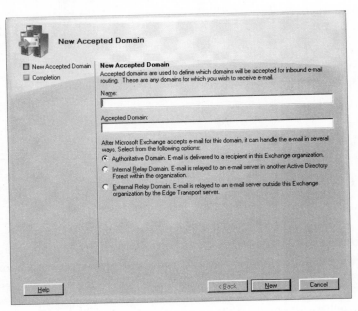

4. Enter a descriptive name and an SMTP domain name. You will also need to select how Exchange should route the messages that are received by this SMTP domain. If you have multiple external domain names but only a single Exchange organization, leave the default first option selected. If you have multiple Active Directory forests in your organization and they each have mail systems other than this Exchange organization, select the second option. If you are routing mail to a server outside your organization, then you may want to select the third option. Click New once you've made your selection.

5. As usual, you will be presented with a summary of what Exchange did and also given the chance to copy the actual PowerShell code used to perform the configuration. Click Finish to close the wizard.

You can create an accepted domain from the Exchange Management Shell by using the following command to create an accepted domain for the Wrox SMTP domain:

```
new-AcceptedDomain -Name Wrox -DomainName wrox.com
-DomainType Authoritative
```

Figure 3.27 shows the results of this configuration action.

FIGURE 3.27   Creating an accepted domain from the Exchange Management Shell

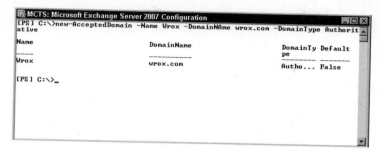

Regardless of how you go about creating the accepted domain object, there is just one configuration tab available for you to configure afterward. You can open the accepted domain's Properties dialog box either by right-clicking the accepted domain and selecting Properties from the context menu or by clicking the Properties link under the accepted domain options in the Actions pane on the right side of the Exchange Management Console.

On the General tab of the accepted domain's Properties dialog box, shown in Figure 3.28, you'll have the opportunity to change the friendly name of the accepted domain object and to change the type of accepted domain it is, as outlined in Exercise 3.6.

FIGURE 3.28   The General tab of the accepted domain's Properties dialog box

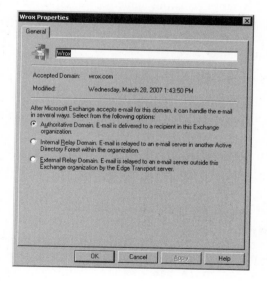

Once you configure accepted domains, you'll want to configure address policies. I'll cover address policies in Chapter 7.

Changing Roles and Removing Servers from the Exchange Organization

As your company or organization changes over time, your Exchange messaging needs are likely to change as well. Perhaps your company will implement a Voice over IP (VoIP) solution to replace an aging PBX system and you'll be asked to implement unified messaging. More commonly, the size of the company will change and the company will require more or fewer Exchange servers to be available. Sometimes servers need to be retired (and replaced) and thus removed from the Exchange organization. Whatever your situation, you're likely to need to change installed server roles or remove Exchange servers from the Exchange organization at some point.

Adding and Removing Server Roles

To add more server roles to an existing Exchange server, you need to make sure the server can support those roles and that the prerequisite software and conditions have been met on the server. For example, you can't add any other roles to a clustered Mailbox server, and you can't install the Edge Transport server with any other roles. Once you are ready to add the role, you can use either the Exchange setup GUI in "change" mode, which can be accessed from the Add/Remove Programs applet in the Control Panel, or the Exchange command-line setup process, by selecting just the roles in which you're interested. To add the Hub Transport role to a server that has the Client Access role installed, you can run the following from the command line:

```
Setup.com /mode:install /role:HT
```

To remove server roles already installed on an Exchange server, you can use the GUI in "change" mode or you can use the command line. To remove the Client Access server role from a server, you might use a command that looks like this:

```
Setup.com /mode:Uninstall /role:CA
```

Removing Exchange Servers from the Exchange Organization

If you want to remove an Exchange server from the Exchange organization completely, you can also perform this task from the Exchange setup GUI or from the command line. From the command line, be sure to specify all of the server's installed roles. If you use the setup GUI from the Add/Remove Programs applet of the Control Panel, select Remove as the mode and not Change. If a role is still in use, you may be required to make changes before you are able to install them. For example, if there are still mailboxes on the server, you will need to move them off before you are able to remove the Mailbox role successfully.

Summary

We've covered a lot of ground in this chapter, and all of it focused on the basic configuration and management of the two most common and critical Exchange Server 2007 roles: Mailbox and Hub Transport. Every organization that deploys Exchange Server 2007 will have Hub Transport and Mailbox servers. The two roles covered on the exam that we didn't examine in this chapter are the Client Access and Edge Transport roles. I'll discuss these roles in detail in the next chapter as I talk about client connectivity, routing, and connectors.

Exam Essentials

Understand the difference between a storage group and a database. Storage groups contain databases, plain and simple. In Exchange Server 2007 Enterprise Edition, you can have up to 50 storage groups and 50 databases. That one-to-one relationship leads you to design Exchange with one database per storage group. Recall that some items are configured at the storage group level, while others are configured at the database level. A storage group, regardless of how many databases it contains, uses only one set of transaction logs.

Understand the structure of the Exchange storage group and its files. The Exchange Server 2007 database structure is a fairly simple one, although it has many files that make up the entire database. Be sure to know each file type and its function in the overall operation of the storage group.

Learn the PowerShell commands. Almost every configuration or management action you perform from the Exchange Management Console will present you with the PowerShell code that was used to perform the action. Take advantage of this information and learn how to use the Exchange Management Shell to your advantage. Some of these commands are likely to make an appearance on your exam as well.

Know where to go to get the job done. Many times on the exam you are asked what configuration is needed to produce the required results. The Exchange Management Console has been completely redesigned to make it easier to navigate and to get to tasks, but that doesn't mean it will be easy to remember this later. Take the time as you review the material in this book to think about what types of configuration and management tasks you find yourself performing in each major node of the Exchange Management Console.

Review Questions

1. You have just installed a new drive on your Exchange server and want to move the transaction logs for one of your storage groups to that drive. Where would you go to do this?

   A. Click the Move Storage Group Path link under the storage group options in the Actions pane on the right side of the Exchange Management Console.

   B. Click the Change Transaction Logs Location link under the storage group options in the Actions pane on the right side of the Exchange Management Console.

   C. Open the storage group's Properties dialog box and change the path of the transaction logs from the General tab.

   D. You cannot do this. Once a transaction log is created, it cannot be moved.

2. Which of the following files is used to keep track of the information in a transaction log that has already been committed to the database?

   A. edb.log

   B. check.log

   C. edb.chk

   D. res1.log

3. One of your Exchange servers has unexpectedly shut down its Information Store service. You check the Event Log and discover that the disk containing the log files for the Information Store has run out of space. What has happened to any transactions that were outstanding when the problem occurred?

   A. The transactions are stored in memory and must be committed before shutting down the computer.

   B. The transactions are written to reserve logs and will be committed when the IS comes back online.

   C. Circular logging is turned on, and the oldest committed transaction log is overwritten.

   D. The transactions are lost.

4. What PowerShell command or commands would you use to mount each of the databases on SRV001?

   A. get-Mailbox | mount-Database

   B. get-MailboxDatabase | mount-Database

   C. get-MailboxDatabase -Server SRV001 | mount-Database

   D. get-Mailbox -Server SRV001 | mount-Database

5. What PowerShell command or commands would you use to create a new mailbox database that is immediately available for use? (Choose all that apply.)

   A. `new-Database`

   B. `start-Database`

   C. `mount-Database`

   D. `new-MailboxDatabase`

   E. `create-MailboxDatabase`

   F. `install-MailboxDatabase`

6. When a remote POP3 client has a session with a Client Access server and sends a message to be delivered, which server could receive the message for delivery? (Choose two.)

   A. A Mailbox server

   B. A Client Access server

   C. A Unified Messaging server

   D. A Hub Transport server

   E. An Edge Transport server

7. Which of the following PowerShell commands is the correct one to use if you want to move only the transaction logs for the Second Storage Group group on a server named SERVERA to a folder named Second Storage Group Logs?

   A. `move-StorageGroupPath -Identity 'SERVERA\Second Storage Group' -LogFolderPath 'L:\Program Files\Microsoft\Exchange Server\Mailbox\ Second Storage Group Logs' -SystemFolderPath 'L:\Program Files\ Microsoft\Exchange Server\Mailbox\Second Storage Group Logs'`

   B. `move-StorageGroupPath -Identity 'Second Storage Group' -LogFolderPath 'L:\Program Files\Microsoft\Exchange Server\Mailbox\Second Storage Group Logs'`

   C. `move-StorageGroupPath -Identity 'SERVERA\Second Storage Group' -SystemFolderPath 'L:\Program Files\Microsoft\Exchange Server\Mailbox\ Second Storage Group Logs'`

   D. `move-StorageGroupPath -Identity 'SERVERA\Second Storage Group' -LogFolderPath 'L:\Program Files\Microsoft\Exchange Server\Mailbox\ Second Storage Group Logs'`

8. What option do you need to change on a Hub Transport server to increase the length of time the server attempts to deliver a delayed message?

   A. Outbound Connection Failure Retry Interval (Minutes)

   B. Maximum Time Since Submission (Days)

   C. Transient Failure Retry Interval (Seconds)

   D. Transient Failure Retry Attempts

9. What purpose does it serve for you to configure additional accepted domains on the Hub Transport server?

   A. There is no need to configure additional accepted domains on the Hub Transport server.

   B. Configuring them allows you to send messages to these SMTP domains securely.

   C. Configuring them allows you to accept and route messages for these SMTP domains correctly.

   D. Configuring them allows you to enable journaling for messages received for these SMTP domains.

10. When a new transaction log is created in a storage group that contains a single mailbox database, how large is that transaction log initially?

    A. 0KB.

    B. 5,120KB.

    C. 1,024KB.

    D. The size is not fixed.

11. Where can you find the files for the First Storage Group group immediately after the Mailbox server is first installed on a server?

    A. `C:\Program Files\Microsoft\Exchange\Mailbox\First Storage Group`

    B. `C:\Program Files\Microsoft\ExchSvr\First Storage Group`

    C. `C:\Program Files\Microsoft\Exchange Server\First Storage Group`

    D. `C:\Program Files\Microsoft\Exchange Server\Mailbox\First Storage Group`

12. Which of the following are valid storage group configurations for an Exchange 2007 Server Standard Edition server that is not using local continuous replication? (Choose all that apply.)

    A. Five storage groups with a single database in each

    B. Ten storage groups with a single database in each

    C. One storage group with five databases

    D. One storage group with ten databases

13. Which of the following are valid storage group configurations for an Exchange 2007 Server Standard Edition server that is configured for local continuous replication?

    A. Five storage groups with a single database in each

    B. Ten storage groups with a single database in each

    C. One storage group with five databases

    D. One storage group with ten databases

14. You want to configure a postmaster mailbox for your new Exchange Server 2007 organization. Which of the following PowerShell commands must you use to perform the configuration for a server named SERVERA?

    A. `set-TransportServer SERVERA -ExternalPostmasterAddress postmaster@ mycompany.com`

    B. `put-TransportServer SERVERA -ExternalPostmasterAddress postmaster@ mycompany.com`

    C. `set-OrganizationPostmaster SERVERA -ExternalPostmasterAddress postmaster@ mycompany.com`

    D. `set-TransportServer SERVERA -PostmasterAddress postmaster@mycompany.com`

15. You have decided to use circular logging on a storage group that contains a single mailbox database with noncritical mailboxes. Which types of backups will you be able to perform on this storage group once circular logging is configured? (Choose all that apply.)

    A. Differential

    B. Incremental

    C. Normal

    D. Shadow

16. Your company does not want to send out-of-office messages to several SMTP domains outside the company. What can you create and configure in Exchange Server 2007 to allow this type of control?

    A. Accepted domains

    B. SMTP send connectors

    C. SMTP receive connectors

    D. Remote domains

17. Your company wants to exchange messages securely with an external partner company. What can you create and configure in Exchange Server 2007 to allow this type of control?

    A. Accepted domains

    B. SMTP send connectors

    C. SMTP receive connectors

    D. Remote domains

18. Your Exchange Server 2007 organization consists of four servers: ServerA is a Mailbox server, ServerB is a Client Access server, ServerC is a Hub Transport server, and ServerD is a Mailbox server. When a user with a mailbox on ServerA sends a message from Outlook to a user on ServerD, which servers are involved in the message transfer process?

    A. ServerA and ServerD only

    B. ServerA, ServerB, and ServerD only

    C. ServerA and ServerC only

    D. ServerA, ServerC, and ServerD only

    E. ServerA, ServerB, ServerC, and ServerD

19. Which of the following PowerShell commands will remove a storage group named Storage Group 2?

   A. `get-Storage group "Storage Group 2"`

   B. `remove-StorageGroup Storage Group 2`

   C. `remove-StorageGroup "Storage Group 2"`

   D. `remove-Storage -Group -Identity "Storage Group 2"`

20. By default, two SMTP receive connectors are configured during the installation of a Hub Transport server. What TCP ports are they listening on? (Choose two.)

   A. 25

   B. 3268

   C. 389

   D. 587

   E. 110

   F. 443

Answers to Review Questions

1. **A.** To change the transaction log path or the system file path for a storage group, simply click the Move Storage Group Path link under the storage group options in the Actions pane on the right side of the Exchange Management Console. Alternatively, you can right-click the storage group and select the Move Storage Group Path menu item from the context menu that appears. Either way, the Move Storage Group Path Wizard opens and allows you choose the new path for either or both items.

2. **C.** As transactions in transaction log files are committed to the database files, a check-point file (`edb.chk`) is updated. The checkpoint file keeps track of which transactions in the sequential list still need to be committed to a database by maintaining a pointer to the last information that was committed. This tells the engine that everything after that point still needs to be committed to a database.

3. **B.** Exchange creates two reserve log files (`Exxres00001.jrs` and `Exxres00002.jrs`) for each database. They are used if the system runs out of disk space. If that happens, Exchange shuts down the database service, logs an event to the Event Log, and writes any outstanding transaction information to these reserve log files. These two files reserve an area of disk space that can be used after the rest of the disk space is used.

4. **C.** Using `Get-MailboxDatabase` with the `-Server` switch returns a list of databases on the specified server. The results are then piped to the `mount-Database` command. Both of the commands that leverage the `Get-Mailbox` cmdlet return the mailboxes, not the databases, and thus will not properly mount the databases. Not specifying the `-Server` switch returns all databases on all servers, not just on the specific server.

5. **C,D.** You will need to use the `new-mailboxdatabase` command to create the new mailbox database and the `mount-database` command to mount the database, thus making it available for usage.

6. **D,E.** For POP3 and IMAP4 clients, submitted messages are sent directly to an SMTP server, which would be either a Hub Transport server accessible from the Internet or an Edge Transport server.

7. **D.** The PowerShell command `move-StorageGroupPath -Identity 'SERVERA\Second Storage Group' -LogFolderPath 'L:\Program Files\Microsoft\Exchange Server\ Mailbox\Second Storage Group Logs'` is the only one that will move the transaction logs for the Second Storage Group group correctly without moving any other files.

8. **B.** The Maximum Time Since Submission (Days) option specifies the timeout duration for messages. If a message is still in the queue to be delivered after the amount of time config-ured for this setting has passed, the message is returned to the sender as undeliverable. The default setting is 2 days, but can be set to any value from 1 to 90 days.

9. **C.** Accepted domains are used to specify the SMTP domains for which the Exchange Server organization will accept and/or route messages. Most commonly, an organization will have multiple SMTP domains if it accepts mail for multiple subsidiary companies or if it has multiple public domain names in use, such as microsoft.com and xbox.com.

10. C. The transaction logs used by Exchange Server 2007 are named E*xxhhhhhhhh*.log, which is the log prefix (such as E01) followed by an eight-character hexadecimal number, so you would have E0100000001.log as the first log file for the Second Storage Group on the server. The numbers 1 through 0 and the letters *A* through *F* are used in the hexadecimal numbering system. These files will always be 1,024KB in size.

11. D. By default, Exchange creates the storage groups on the system root, where Windows is installed. Therefore, on a typical server the location would be C:\Program Files\ Microsoft\Exchange Server\Mailbox\First Storage Group. You should move the transaction logs/system files and databases to their own separate physical volumes as soon as possible—definitely before putting the server into production use.

12. A,C. Standard Edition allows for up to five databases to be created and up to five storage groups. Since the server is not using continuous replication, multiple databases can exist in a single storage group.

13. A. Standard Edition allows for up to five databases and local continuous replication limits a storage group to having only one database in each. Any configuration that does not meet those requirements is not valid.

14. A. You will need to use the set-TransportServer SERVERA -ExternalPostmasterAddress postmaster@mycompany.com command to configure the postmaster address on SERVERA.

15. C. When you use circular logging, you must perform full (or normal) backups because the transaction logs will not be available if you need to recover the database. Therefore, incremental or differential backups are not suitable.

16. D. You need to create remote domain objects for the external SMTP namespaces to which you do not want out-of-office messages to be sent.

17. B. You need to create and configure an SMTP send connector that uses the Enable Domain Security (Mutual Auth TLS) option. Additional configuration will also be required beyond the creation of the SMTP send connector.

18. D. All messages go through the Hub Transport server for delivery, so the message would go from the user's Outbox on ServerA, go through the hub transport on ServerC, and be delivered to the Inbox of the user's mailbox on ServerD.

19. C. The Remove-StorageGroup cmdlet can be used to remove the storage group. Since the name of the storage group contains spaces, it must be enclosed in quotation marks. There is no get-Storage Exchange cmdlet, so neither of those commands would work.

20. A,D. The Client *servername* connector accepts messages on port 587, and the Default *servername* connector accepts messages on port 25.

Chapter

4

Configuring Connectors, Connectivity, and Routing

MICROSOFT EXAM OBJECTIVES COVERED IN THIS CHAPTER:

✓ **Installing and Configuring Microsoft Exchange Servers**

- Configure Exchange server roles.

✓ **Configuring the Exchange Infrastructure**

- Configure connectors.

- Configure client connectivity.

Now that I have discussed installing Exchange and configuring the Mailbox and Hub Transport servers, I will dive into configuring mail routing, the Edge Transport role, and Exchange's client connectivity. If you are an Exchange veteran, you might think that configuring client connectivity is as simple as enabling the POP3 or IMAP service. However, with the addition of Exchange Web Services and the Autodiscover service, it is a little more complicated.

The main topics of this chapter are as follows:

- Configuring connectors

- Configuring the Edge Transport role

- Configuring client connectivity

Configuring SMTP Connectors

Two types of SMTP connectors exist in Exchange Server 2007: send connectors and receive connectors. Hub Transport servers use the SMTP protocol to send and receive mail among themselves and also to transfer mail to and from Edge Transport servers. Hub Transport-to-Hub Transport routing is handled based on the Active Directory site topology, which I will discuss in greater detail later in this chapter. There is, however, no default configuration in place to ensure end-to-end mail from outside the organization to inside and vice versa. You will need to create and configure the appropriate implicit SMTP connectors to make this happen.

How you go about making these SMTP connectors, however, will depend on the installation and configuration of your Exchange organization. If you have the Microsoft-recommended configuration that has Edge Transport servers in the DMZ, you'll need to use the edge subscription service to subscribe an Edge Transport server to an Active Directory site, thus allowing replication of recipient and configuration data into an Active Directory Application Mode (ADAM) instance on the Edge Transport server. When you complete the subscription process for an Edge Transport server to an Active Directory site, the following default SMTP connectors are created by the Microsoft Exchange EdgeSync service:

- An implicit send connector from the Hub Transport servers to the Edge Transport server

- A send connector from the Edge Transport server to the Hub Transport servers in the Active Directory site to which the Edge Transport server is subscribed

- A wildcard (*) send connector from the Edge Transport server to the Internet

These SMTP connectors allow full end-to-end SMTP message routing in and out of the Exchange organization. Thus, having the Edge Transport servers correctly configured with the Edge Subscription service is the easiest way to create all of your default SMTP connectors. After the defaults are created, you can always create additional connectors and make additional configurations if needed.

In a scenario where you do not have an Edge Transport server or you have a third-party edge device or service that handles inbound filtering, you will need to create an SMTP send connector to get mail messages out of the Exchange organization and on their way to their final recipients. This SMTP send connector should be a wildcard (*) SMTP connector, allowing mail delivery to all SMTP domains.

Configuring SMTP Send Connectors

For the purposes of this section of the chapter and the specific discussion about Hub Transport servers, I'll assume your Exchange organization does not have yet have an Edge Transport server. Later on in this chapter, I will discuss the initial configuration that needs to be done for an Edge Transport server. Exercise 4.1 shows how to create a SMTP send connector.

EXERCISE 4.1

Creating an SMTP Send Connector

Follow these steps to create an SMTP send connector:

1. Click Start ➤ Programs ➤ Microsoft Exchange Server 2007 and then select Exchange Management Console.

2. Expand the Microsoft Exchange root object, expand the Organization Configuration folder, and then click the Hub Transport node.

3.   Click the New Send Connector link under the Hub Transport options in the Actions pane on the right side of the Exchange Management Console. The New SMTP Send Connector Wizard opens.

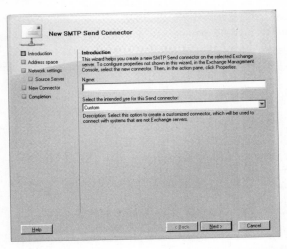

4.   Provide a descriptive name for the send connector, such as **Internet SMTP Connector**, and then select the Internet option from the drop-down menu. Click Next to continue to the Address Space page.

5.   On the Address Space page, configure the default wildcard address of * by clicking the Add button and entering an asterisk (*) in the Add Address Space dialog box. Click OK to close the dialog box and return to the Address Space page. Click Next to continue to the Network Settings page, shown here.

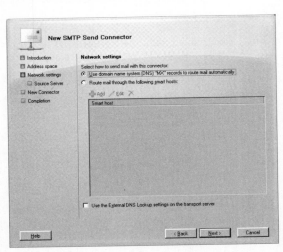

6. On the Network Settings page, you will need to either allow the connector to use DNS MX records to route mail or configure a smart host to route the mail. A smart host would be any SMTP device in your external network that can perform DNS queries and route SMTP traffic accordingly. Many organizations have existing devices or third-party applications that provide this function; thus, they won't be using an Edge Transport server. When you've made your selections, click Next to continue to the Source Server page.

7. On the Source Server page, you will be able to select which servers will be allowed to send SMTP messages through the send connector. Be careful not to select any server that you previously selected as a smart host on the Network Settings page. Add any other Exchange servers that should be allowed to send SMTP messages directly to the Internet (the fewer, the better for security's sake) or to your smart host. Then click Next to continue.

8. You'll be presented with a summary page allowing you to review your configuration. Click New to create the send connector.

9. As usual, you will be presented with a summary of what Exchange did and you will also be given the chance to copy the actual PowerShell code used to perform the configuration. Click Finish to close the wizard.

You can also create a send connector from the Exchange Management Shell by using a command similar to this one:

```
new-SendConnector -Name 'Internet SMTP Connector (WILEYEX01B)'
-Usage 'Internet' -AddressSpaces 'smtp:*;1' -DNSRoutingEnabled $true
-UseExternalDNSServersEnabled $false -SourceTransportServers 'WILEYEX01B'
```

Figure 4.1 shows the results of this configuration action.

FIGURE 4.1 Creating a send connector from the Exchange Management Shell

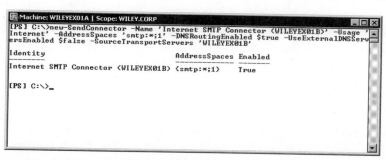

Regardless of how you create the send connector, four configuration tabs are available for you to configure afterward. You can open the send connector's Properties dialog box

either by right-clicking the send connector and selecting Properties from the context menu or by clicking the Properties link under the send connector options in the Actions pane on the right side of the Exchange Management Console.

General

On the General tab of the send connector's Properties dialog box, shown in Figure 4.2, you'll have the opportunity to change the friendly name of the send connector as well as to specify the protocol logging level and the fully qualified domain name (FQDN) that the send connector will return in reply to the HELO or EHLO queries. The logging level options are pretty simple: either none (logging off) or verbose (logging on). If no FQDN entry is made on the General tab, the connector will return the FQDN of the authoritative SMTP domain in the Exchange organization to which the Hub Transport server belongs.

FIGURE 4.2   The General tab of the send connector's Properties dialog box

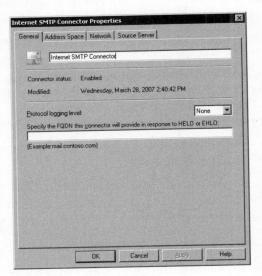

Address Space

On the Address Space tab of the send connector's Properties dialog box, shown in Figure 4.3, you'll be able to change, add, or delete the address spaces that are covered by this send connector.

Network

On the Network tab of the send connector's Properties dialog box, shown in Figure 4.4, you have several options to change the network configuration of the send connector. The only option that is not directly available during the creation process of the send connector is the Enable Domain Security (Mutual Auth TLS) option. This option will allow you to configure a send connector to a specific partner's SMTP address space and to attempt to make a connection with transport layer security (TLS) for all messages going out of that connector.

FIGURE 4.3   The Address Space tab of the send connector's Properties dialog box

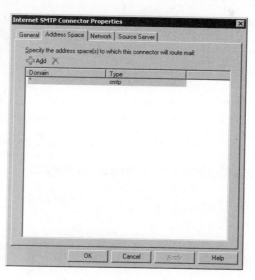

FIGURE 4.4   The Network tab of the send connector's Properties dialog box

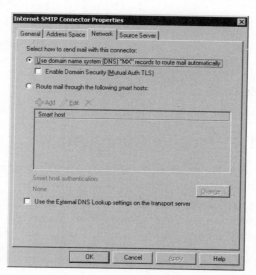

Unfortunately, it's not as easy as checking the box to enable TLS to a partner address space. To protect against man-in-the-middle attacks, you'll need to perform several other tasks if you're interested in using Partner TLS; those tasks are outside the scope of this exam. They include importing a trusted and valid TLS certificate into your Edge Transport servers, configuring inbound domain and outbound domain security, and testing proper mail flow and TLS protection.

Source Server

The Source Server tab of the send connector's Properties dialog box, shown in Figure 4.5, provides no new configuration options but does allow you to change, add, or delete the source servers that should be allowed to send SMTP messages across this send connector.

FIGURE 4.5   The Source Server tab of the send connector's Properties dialog box

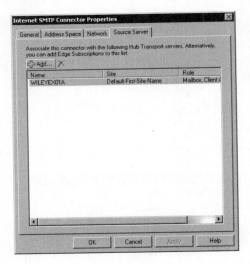

Configuring SMTP Receive Connectors

By default, the Exchange installation process creates two SMTP receive connectors on each Hub Transport server:

- The default SMTP receive connector Client *servername* accepts mail on TCP port 587, which is the default port for receiving messages from all non-MAPI clients (such as Outlook Express) for SMTP relay. The connector accepts mail on all installed network adapters in the Hub Transport server by default and also accepts the inbound messages from all IP addresses on the network by default and will accept mail from any client.

- The default SMTP receive connector Default *servername* accepts mail on TCP port 25, which is the default port for receiving messages from SMTP servers. The connector accepts mail on all installed network adapters in the Hub Transport server by default and also accepts the inbound messages from all IP addresses on the network by default, but only from Exchange servers. Additionally, this connector will not accept anonymous submissions.

The default SMTP receive connectors are visible for each Hub Transport server in the Exchange organization by examining the Server Configuration ➢ Hub Transport node of the Exchange Management Console, as shown in Figure 4.6.

FIGURE 4.6   The default SMTP receive connectors viewed in the Exchange Management Console

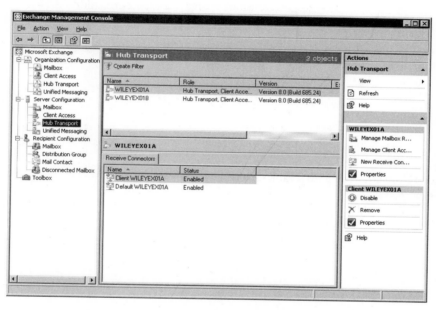

Exercise 4.2 outlines the steps for creating an SMTP receive connector.

EXERCISE 4.2

Creating an SMTP Receive Connector

Follow these steps to create an SMTP receive connector:

1. Click Start ➢ Programs ➢ Microsoft Exchange Server 2007 and then select Exchange Management Console.

2. Expand the Microsoft Exchange root object, expand the Server Configuration folder, and then click the Hub Transport node.

3. Select the server on which to configure the receive connector, and then click the New Receive Connector link under the server options in the Actions pane on the right side of the Exchange Management Console. The New SMTP Receive Connector Wizard opens.

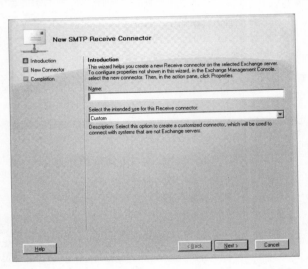

4. Provide a descriptive name for the receive connector, such as **Monitoring System Receive SMTP Connector**, and then select the appropriate option from the drop-down menu. In this example, select the Custom option to create a receive connector for receiving SMTP messages from an internal server monitoring application. Click Next to continue to the Local Network Settings page, shown here.

5.   On the Local Network Settings page, configure the IP addresses and TCP ports on which the receive connector should accept inbound messages. The default setting of (All Available) on port 25 will be suitable in most cases. Click Next to continue to the Remote Network Settings page, shown here.

6.   On the Remote Networks Settings page, you can leave the default selection of all IP addresses or edit the listing to specify just those servers from which you want to allow inbound mail using this receive connector. For an internal server monitoring application, you might want to configure this list to include just the IP addresses of the server hosting that monitoring application. Click Next to continue.

7.   You'll be presented with a summary page allowing you to review your configuration. Click New to create the send connector.

8.   As usual, you will be presented with a summary of what Exchange did and you will also be given the chance to copy the actual PowerShell code used to perform the configuration. Click Finish to close the wizard.

You can also create a receive connector from the Exchange Management Shell by using a command similar to this one, which creates a custom receive connector that accepts messages only from an internal pager server:

```
new-ReceiveConnector -Name 'Pager System Receive SMTP Connector'
-Usage Custom -Bindings 0.0.0.0:25
-RemoteIPRanges 192.168.0.242-192.168.0.242 -Server WILEYEX01A
```

Figure 4.7 shows the results of this configuration action.

FIGURE 4.7   Creating a receive connector from the Exchange Management Shell

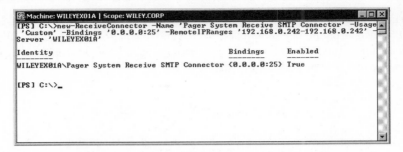

Regardless of how you create the receive connector, four configuration tabs are available for you to configure afterward. You can open the receive connector Properties dialog box either by right-clicking the receive connector and selecting Properties from the context menu or by clicking the Properties link under the receive connector options in the Actions pane on the right side of the Exchange Management Console.

General

On the General tab of the receive connector's Properties dialog box, shown in Figure 4.8, you'll have the opportunity to change the friendly name of the receive connector as well as to specify the protocol logging level and the fully qualified domain name (FQDN) that the receive connector will return in reply to the HELO or EHLO queries. The logging level options are pretty simple: either none (logging off) or verbose (logging on).

FIGURE 4.8   The General tab of the receive connector's Properties dialog box

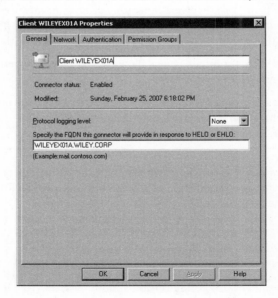

Network

On the Network tab of the receive connector's Properties dialog box, shown in Figure 4.9, you can change the local IP addresses and ports on which the connector will receive SMTP messages and the remote IP addresses that are allowed to send messages through the receive connector.

FIGURE 4.9   The Network tab of the receive connector's Properties dialog box

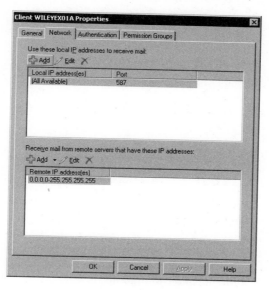

 On a Hub Transport server, the combination of the local IP address, local TCP port, and remote IP address range must be unique and cannot be duplicated by any other receive connector. You can, however, create the same receive connector on multiple Hub Transport servers.

Authentication

On the Authentication tab of the receive connector's Properties dialog box, shown in Figure 4.10, you can configure the authentication method to be used on the receive connector. Table 4.1 describes each method available.

FIGURE 4.10 The Authentication tab of the receive connector's Properties dialog box

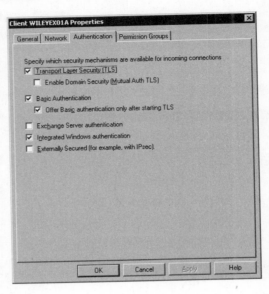

TABLE 4.1 Receive Connector Authentication Methods

Authentication Type	Description
None selected	No authentication configured.
Transport Layer Security (TLS)	Configures the server to advertise STARTTLS when connection attempts are made to remote systems. TLS requires that a server certificate be installed.
Basic Authentication	Uses standard authentication, which transmits credentials in clear text.
Exchange Server	Uses an Exchange authentication method, such as TLS or Kerberos through TLS.
Integrated Authentication	Uses Integrated Windows authentication, which includes NTLM (NT LAN Manager) and Kerberos. This is a good solution if both sides of the connection are Windows-based systems.
Externally Secured	Used when the other end of the connection is secured by some other external means, such as use of a private network or Internet Protocol Security (IPSec). Configuring this option tells Exchange that the connection is secured, even though the Exchange server cannot actually verify this fact. You must also select the Exchange server's permissions group on the Permission Groups tab when using this method.

Permission Groups

On the Permission Groups tab of the receive connector's Properties dialog box, shown in Figure 4.11, you can select the permission groups associated with this receive connector. Permission groups are predefined sets of permissions that are granted to well-known security principals such as users, computers, and security groups. A permission group defines the permissions that are then assigned to security principals. Table 4.2 outlines the permission groups, the corresponding security principals, and the specific Exchange permissions allowed to each.

FIGURE 4.11   The Permission Groups tab of the receive connector's Properties dialog box

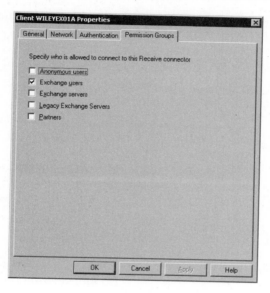

TABLE 4.2   Receive Connector Permission Groups

Permission Group	Member Security Principals	Exchange Permissions Granted
Anonymous Users	Anonymous user account	Ms-Exch-SMTP-Submit
		Ms-Exch-SMTP-Accept-Any-Sender
		Ms-Exch-SMTP-Accept-Authoritative-Domain-Sender
		Ms-Exch-Accept-Headers-Routing

TABLE 4.2 Receive Connector Permission Groups *(continued)*

Permission Group	Member Security Principals	Exchange Permissions Granted
Exchange Users	Authenticated user accounts	Ms-Exch-SMTP-Submit
		Ms-Exch-SMTP-Accept-Any-Recipient
		Ms-Exch-Bypass-Anti-Spam
		Ms-Exch-Accept-Headers-Routing
Exchange Servers	Hub Transport servers	
	Edge Transport servers	
	Exchange Servers security group (on the Hub Transport server only)	
Externally Secured servers	Ms-Exch-SMTP-Submit	Ms-Exch-SMTP-Accept-Any-Sender
		Ms-Exch-SMTP-Accept-Any-Recipient
		Ms-Exch-Accept-Authoritative-Domain-Sender
		Ms-Exch-Bypass-Anti-Spam
		Ms-Exch-SMTP-Accept-Authentication-Flag
		Ms-Exch-Bypass-Message-Size-Limit
		Ms-Exch-Accept-Headers-Routing
		Ms-Exch-Accept-Exch50
		Ms-Exch-Accept-Headers-Organization (Externally Secured servers only)
		Ms-Exch-Accept-Headers-Forest (not granted to Externally Secured servers)

TABLE 4.2   Receive Connector Permission Groups *(continued)*

Permission Group	Member Security Principals	Exchange Permissions Granted
Legacy Exchange Servers	Exchange Legacy Interop security group	Ms-Exch-SMTP-Submit
		Ms-Exch-SMTP-Accept-Any-Sender
		Ms-Exch-SMTP-Accept-Any-Recipient
		Ms-Exch-Accept-Authoritative-Domain-Sender
		Ms-Exch-Bypass-Anti-Spam
		Ms-Exch-SMTP-Accept-Authentication-Flag
		Ms-Exch-Bypass-Message-Size-Limit
		Ms-Exch-Accept-Headers-Routing
		Ms-Exch-Accept-Exch50
Partners	Partner server account	Ms-Exch-SMTP-Submit
		Ms-Exch-Accept-Headers-Routing

In the example where we created a receive connector to receive messages from our server monitoring application from the within PowerShell, we didn't select any permissions groups during the creation process. Therefore, the receive connector should receive messages from any source. If the messages are being submitted using a known service account, you could consider configuring the Exchange Users option to secure the receive connector somewhat. By comparison, the default receive connectors do have permissions groups configured on them. The Client *servername* receive connector is configured with only the Exchange Users permission group as being allowed to send messages through it. The Default *servername* connector is configured to allow the Exchange Users, Exchange Server, and Legacy Exchange Servers permission groups to send messages through it.

Deleting SMTP Connectors

The process of deleting SMTP connectors is much simpler than the creation and configuration process for the SMTP connector. Just select the send or receive SMTP connector in the Exchange Management Console, right-click it, and select Remove from the context menu.

Alternatively, you can click the Remove link under the connector options in the Actions pane on the right side of the Exchange Management Console.

If you're not certain whether you will any longer need the SMTP connector but you don't want it to be available for use, you can opt instead to disable it using the same process as discussed earlier, but this time select Disable instead of Remove.

Working with Active Directory Sites to Control Message Routing

Using SMTP connectors is especially important when providing coexistence and interoperability with SMTP-based services. However, as mentioned earlier, intra-Exchange 2007 mail is controlled by Active Directory sites. In larger environments, Active Directory configuration is controlled by a group that is separate from the messaging group. In that case, as a messaging professional you need to understand how the Active Directory sites are configured to see how they will affect mail flow and network traffic.

Rather than relaying a message to each Active Directory site, direct delivery from the local Hub Transport server to a Hub Transport server in the destination site is the default behavior, as shown in Figure 4.12.

FIGURE 4.12   Direct delivery of email is always attempted first.

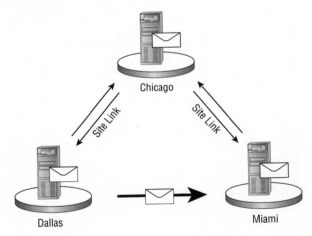

If direct delivery is not possible due to a network or server outage, a back-off occurs and the AD site link configuration is used to determine the closest site to the destination. Then the message is delivered there for later delivery, as shown in Figure 4.13

Often, no adjustments are needed to the standard AD site configuration. However, if you have dedicated AD sites for Exchange or you need to change the configuration without affecting Active Directory replication, you can set the Exchange cost on the Active Directory site links. This might be used if you wanted to favor one site for queuing over another. The lower the cost, the more likely the link will be used. An example of setting a lower Exchange cost for a site link is as follows:

```
set-AdSiteLink -Identity ChicagoToDallasSiteLink -ExchangeCost 5
```

FIGURE 4.13 When direct delivery is not possible, back-off occurs.

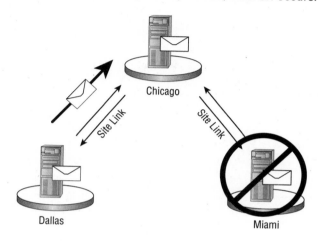

If the Exchange cost is not set, the Active Directory site link cost is used. To remove the Exchange cost and default back to the Active Directory cost, you can run the following:

```
set-AdSiteLink -Identity ChicagoToDallasSiteLink -ExchangeCost $null
```

If your network is configured in such a way that it requires all email to travel through a specific site, the hub site designation should be used. If a site is designated as a hub, all messages destined for a site on the opposite side of the hub site will first be delivered to a Hub Transport server and then sent to the destination site, if possible. In other words, after the least-cost route is chosen for a message, it is determined if a hub site exists along the path of the message. If it does, the message is first delivered to the hub site.

To set an AD site as a hub site, use the following command:

```
set-AdSite -Identity Chicago -HubSiteEnabled $true
```

After enabling the Chicago AD site as a hub site, the email delivery would look similar to the model shown in Figure 4.14.

FIGURE 4.14   Delivering email through a hub site

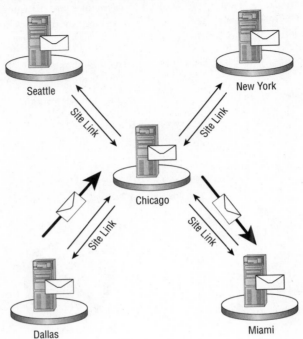

To disable a site as a hub site, use the following command:

```
set-AdSite -Identity Chicago -HubSiteEnabled $false
```

Configuring the Edge Transport Server

The Edge Transport server is one of the server roles introduced in Exchange Server 2007 that did not have a place in previous versions of Exchange Server. Many organizations used various solutions in the DMZ network to route and scan inbound and outbound Simple Mail Transfer Protocol (SMTP) mail, such as SMTP gateways and various third-party appliance and software-based applications. With the introduction of Exchange Server 2007, you have a choice to make: you can either continue to use the existing routing and scanning implementation you already have or implement one or more Edge Transport servers for your Exchange organization. Either choice is acceptable, and each will work as long as you ensure that the proper configuration is completed.

For our purposes here, I'll assume that an Edge Transport server is desired in your Exchange organization; thus, I'll show you how to install, configure, and manage one. Installing the Edge Transport server is really no different from the installations discussed in

Chapter 3, "Configuring the Mailbox and Hub Transport Roles." With this fact in mind, we'll jump right into the configuration and management tasks associated with a freshly installed Edge Transport server, as shown in Figure 4.15.

FIGURE 4.15   The Edge Transport role viewed from the Exchange Management Console

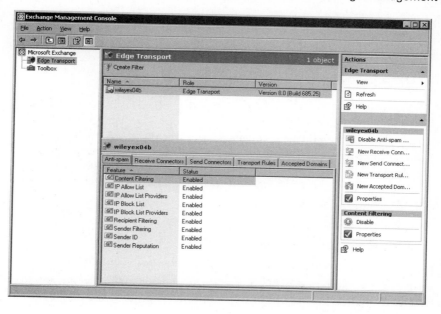

For the installation of the Edge Transport role to be completed successfully, you'll need to install the following components before starting the installation: .NET Framework 2.0 and PowerShell 1.0. On Windows Server 2003, you will also need to install Microsoft Management Console (MMC) 3.0 and Active Directory Application Mode (ADAM) with Service Pack 1. However, on Windows Server 2008, you need to install only Active Directory Lightweight Directory Services (AD LDS). Additionally, setup may prompt you to download and install some other updates. Lastly, you will need to configure a fully qualified domain name for your Edge Transport servers, which is not typically done with servers located in the DMZ. Exchange will refuse to install the Edge Transport role if these prerequisite items are not in place.

Configuring and Managing EdgeSync

The primary role of the Edge Transport server is to route inbound and outbound SMTP messages, checking them for spam and virus characteristics. Sometime after Exchange Server 2003 was released, Microsoft decided that running antispam and antivirus software on the same servers that hosted mailbox and public folder databases was not necessarily the best design, and thus the role-based implementation of Exchange Server 2007 was born. The Edge Transport server now assumes these roles in organizations where no other third-party software or hardware solution is in place. The following benefits are realized through the use of the Edge Transport server (or a similar solution):

- Reduces load on Mailbox servers because of filtering out unwanted messages, such as those containing spam or viruses
- Adds extra layer(s) of protection to the Exchange servers located on the internal network
- Prevents Internet connections directly to the Exchange servers located on the internal network

The first step you'll need to take to start realizing these benefits in your Exchange organization is to configure the EdgeSync service between your Edge Transport servers and your Hub Transport servers. By configuring EdgeSync, you'll enable the ADAM instance installed on the Edge Transport server to contain all the pertinent information needed to start filtering both inbound and outbound SMTP traffic. The following information is replicated to the ADAM database on the Edge Transport server once EdgeSync has been configured:

- A listing of all internal accepted domains
- A listing of all remote domains
- Any configured message classifications
- Information about internal send connectors that have been configured
- A listing of all valid internal SMTP addresses for the domain, which includes mailbox-enabled users, mail users, mail contacts, mail-enabled groups, and mail-enabled public folders
- The safe and blocked sender lists that have been configured for each of these users

The Edge Transport server is a powerful weapon against undesirable SMTP traffic entering your Exchange organization because of the information it has in the ADAM database plus the antispam and antivirus capabilities it provides. Even if you already have a third-party solution in place in your DMZ that provides some of these features, there might be a business justification for placing an Edge Transport server (or multiple Edge Transport servers) in the DMZ between the Exchange organization and the third-party solution so you can take advantage of the Edge Transport server's benefits.

The basic process to enable EdgeSync includes the following steps:

1. Ensure that the required ports on the Internet-to-DMZ and DMZ-to-internal-network firewalls are configured.

2. Ensure that accepted domains for which your Exchange organization will handle mail are configured on a Hub Transport server. Refer to Chapter 3 for a refresher if needed.

3. Ensure that DNS name resolution is functional between the Edge Transport servers in the DMZ and the Hub Transport servers on the internal network.

4. Define all internal Hub Transport servers so that Sender ID does not reject messages from them.

5. Create the edge subscription file on an Edge Transport server.

6. Copy the edge subscription file to a Hub Transport server.

7. Use the New Edge Subscription Wizard on the Hub Transport server to complete the process.

We will examine some of the pertinent steps in the following sections.

Firewall Ports Required for EdgeSync

Table 4.3 details the port configuration that needs to be in place (at a minimum) to allow your Edge Transport servers to function correctly in the DMZ.

TABLE 4.3   Edge Transport Firewall Ports

Firewall Location	Rule	Description
Internet to DMZ	Allow port 25 to and from all Internet hosts to and from the Edge Transport servers.	Port 25 is used for SMTP.
Internet to DMZ	Allow port 53 to all Internet hosts from the Edge Transport servers.	Port 53 is required for DNS resolution, which is required to route outbound SMTP messages to Internet hosts properly.
Internal to DMZ	Allow port 25 to and from specified Hub Transport servers to and from specified Edge Transport servers.	Port 25 is used for SMTP.
Internal to DMZ	Allow port 50636 from specified Hub Transport servers to specified Edge Transport servers.	Port 50636 is used for Secure Lightweight Directory Access Protocol (SLDAP) replication between Hub Transport servers and the ADAM database located on the Edge Transport servers.
Internal to DMZ	Allow port 3389 from the internal network to the specified Edge Transport servers.	Port 3389 is used for Remote Desktop Protocol (RDP) connections for managing servers remotely.
Internal to DMZ	Allow port 53 from the internal network to the specified Edge Transport servers.	Port 53 is required for DNS resolution, which is required to route messages properly.

Defining Internal SMTP Servers

Before you can enable EdgeSync, you need to define the list of internal SMTP servers (Hub Transport servers) that exist in your Exchange organization. This is required so that Sender ID on the Edge Transport server knows which servers are internal to your organization and so that connection filters know they should not reject connections from these internal SMTP servers. This required configuration is one of those tasks that you cannot perform from the Exchange Management Console, so you'll need to use the Set-TransportConfig cmdlet from the Exchange Management Shell. If your Hub Transport servers had IP addresses of 192.168.0.150 and 192.168.0.151, then the command to enter would look like this:

```
set-TransportConfig -InternalSMTPServers 192.168.0.150,192.168.0.151
```

As you can see in Figure 4.16, there is no feedback provided to let you know that you've done anything right or wrong. However, given that PowerShell is very good about alerting you to syntax errors, you can rest assured that you've probably gotten the task accomplished.

FIGURE 4.16   Setting the list of internal SMTP servers

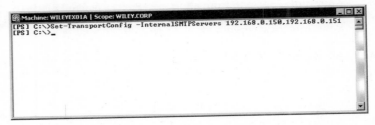

Creating the Edge Subscription File

In order to configure the Hub Transport servers to communicate with the Edge Transport servers, the Edge Transport servers must be subscribed to the Active Directory site. The subscription process consists of exporting an XML file from the Edge Transport server and then importing that file on one of the Hub Transport servers in the Active Directory site. You create an edge subscription file on the Edge Transport server that will be subscribed. When you create this file on the Edge Transport server it prepares the server to start synchronizing appropriate Active Directory information into the local ADAM database and provides the authentication information needed by the Hub Transport server to start the EdgeSync process. To create the XML-based subscription file you once again use an Exchange Management Shell cmdlet, New-EdgeSubscription. If you wanted to save the file to the F drive, your entry might look like this:

```
new-EdgeSubscription -FileName "F:\EdgeSubscription.xml"
```

As you can see in Figure 4.17, you are presented with a list of items to consider before completing the edge subscription file-creation process. Note the tasks that are disabled if you continue; you'll be performing them from the Hub Transport server only after EdgeSync is enabled.

FIGURE 4.17   Creating the edge subscription file

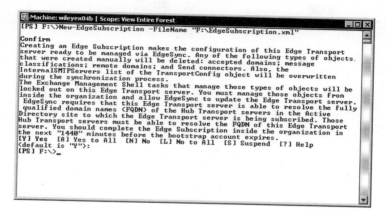

The full text presented for you to read is shown here for clarity because it is important to understand the implications of the decision to move forward with creating the edge subscription file:

```
Confirm

Creating an Edge Subscription makes the configuration of this Edge
Transport server ready to be managed via EdgeSync. Any of the following
types of objects that were created manually will be deleted: accepted
domains; message classifications; remote domains; and Send connectors.
 Also, the InternalSMTPServers list of the TransportConfig object will
be overwritten during the synchronization process.
The Exchange Management Shell tasks that manage those types of objects
will be locked out on this Edge Transport server. You must manage those
objects from inside the organization and allow EdgeSync to update the
Edge Transport server.  EdgeSync requires that this Edge Transport
server is able to resolve the fully qualified domain names (FQDN) of
the Hub Transport servers in the Active Directory site to which the
Edge Transport server is being subscribed. Those Hub Transport servers
must be able to resolve the FQDN of this Edge Transport server. You
should complete the Edge Subscription inside the organization in the
next "1440" minutes before the bootstrap account expires.

[Y] Yes  [A] Yes to All  [N] No  [L] No to All  [S] Suspend  [?] Help
(default is "Y"):
```

If you open the resulting XML file in Notepad, you can see what is inside it, as shown in Figure 4.18. Notice that the file contains both the short and fully qualified domain names of the Edge Transport server; the Hub Transport servers must be able to resolve this name via DNS queries.

FIGURE 4.18   Viewing the edge subscription file

Finishing the EdgeSync Process

Once you have the edge subscription file created, you will need to copy it to the Hub Transport server on which you'll be completing the EdgeSync process. With that task completed, you're ready to complete the EdgeSync process by running the New Edge Subscription Wizard, as detailed in Exercise 4.3.

EXERCISE 4.3

Creating a New Edge Subscription

To create a new edge subscription, follow these steps:

1. Click Start ➢ Programs ➢ Microsoft Exchange Server 2007 and then select Exchange Management Console.

2. Expand the Microsoft Exchange root object, expand the Organization Configuration folder, and then click the Hub Transport node.

3. In the Actions pane on the right side, click the New Edge Subscription link. The New Edge Subscription Wizard opens.

EXERCISE 4.3   *(continued)*

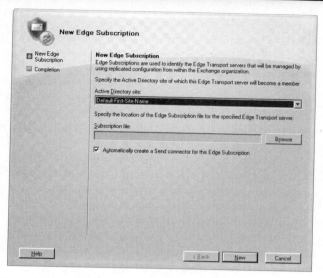

4. Select the Active Directory site that the edge subscription pertains to from the drop-down list provided, and then use the Browse button to locate the XML file you created previously. You should typically leave the default selection checked to create a send connector for this subscription. Click New when you're ready to proceed.

5. After a few seconds, the completion details will be presented. Note that once again you are informed that the Hub Transport servers must be able to resolve the name of the Edge Transport server in order for EdgeSync to work correctly.

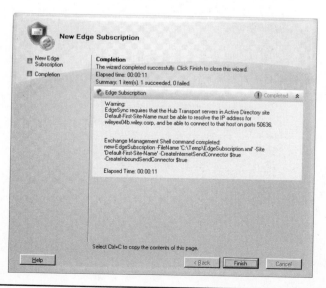

The corresponding Exchange Management Shell cmdlet you could have used to complete the EdgeSync process is New-EdgeSubscription. Assuming the filename is as we created it previously and the file was located in C:\Temp, your code might look like this:

```
new-EdgeSubscription -FileName 'C:\Temp\EdgeSubscription.xml'
-Site 'Default-First-Site-Name' -CreateInternetSendConnector $true
-CreateInboundSendConnector $true
```

After the wizard has completed, the edge synchronization process should start and begin to synchronize configuration data every hour. Recipient information will be synchronized every four hours. Should you need to force a synchronization, you can use the start-EdgeSynchronization cmdlet.

You can verify that edge synchronization is occurring properly by viewing the Application log on the Hub Transport server and looking for log entries from the MSExchange EdgeSyncsource. Figure 4.19 illustrates a successful configuration synchronization event, and Figure 4.20 illustrates a successful recipient configuration.

If you look closely at the Description field on both Event Log entries, you'll notice that the Exchange logs are shown in GMT times. Just keep that small (and not entirely trivial) fact in mind should you happen to be troubleshooting EdgeSync.

Moving back to the Edge Transport server, you can verify that synchronization has occurred by examining the accepted domains that are configured on the server, as shown in Figure 4.21.

FIGURE 4.19   Viewing a successful configuration synchronization Event Log entry

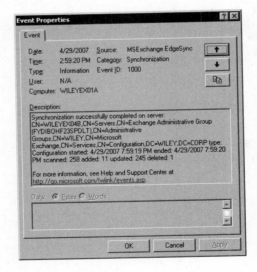

FIGURE 4.20   Viewing a successful recipient synchronization Event Log entry

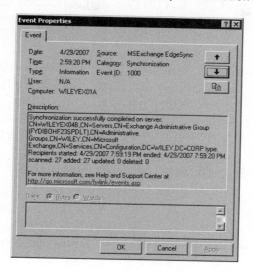

FIGURE 4.21   Viewing the list of accepted domains on the Edge Transport server

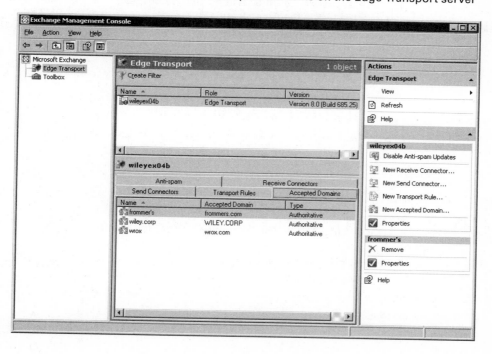

Configuring the Client Access Server

The Client Access server role will also always be present in any Exchange organization, especially given the prevalence of Outlook Web Access and mobile devices using ActiveSync now. Like Mailbox servers, Client Access servers can be configured for high availability, but not through clustering. Client Access servers can be, and should be, made highly available using network load balancing. Whatever your exact organization design calls for, the Client Access server will require that you perform some configuration and management actions before it is ready to perform its function in your organization.

Understanding the Client Access Process

The Client Access server does provide other functions besides just Office Outlook Web Access, such as Outlook Autodiscover and the Availability service, which you'll need in place if you are using Outlook 2007. Before we get into the configuration of the Client Access server, let's first examine how the Client Access server assists those non-MAPI client sessions in accessing a mailbox.

The Client Access server must be part of the Active Directory domain. Thus it needs to be inside the firewall and not directly exposed to the DMZ or the Internet. You need to open only the specific client access ports of concern to the Client Access server from outside the organization.

The following are some common non-MAPI client types you are likely to encounter:

- Outlook Web Access (OWA)
- Outlook Anywhere (replaces HTTP over RPC in Exchange Server 2003)
- Exchange ActiveSync (for Windows Mobile or third-party ActiveSync-compatible devices)
- POP3 or IMAP4 client applications

At least one Client Access server should also exist in every Active Directory site where a Mailbox server resides for best performance and reliability.

When a non-MAPI client needs to access a mailbox stored on an Exchange Server 2007 Mailbox server, the following basic steps occur:

1. The non-MAPI client contacts the Client Access server using whichever client access protocol is used, such as POP3 or HTTP.

2. The Client Access server connects to a domain controller using Kerberos to attempt to authenticate the user. The Internet Information Services (IIS) component on the Client Access server performs this authentication.

3. If the authentication was successful, the Client Access server next performs an LDAP query to an available global catalog server to locate the Mailbox server that houses the requested mailbox.

4. The Client Access server next connects to the required Mailbox server using MAPI over RPC. Messages can now be read from the mailbox or submitted to the database for routing. For POP3 and IMAP4 clients, submitted messages are sent directly to an SMTP server, which could be either a Hub Transport server accessible from the Internet or an Edge Transport server.

All communications between the Client Access server and the Mailbox server occur using MAPI. This is a major change from previous versions of Exchange, where the front-end Exchange server would contact the back-end Exchange server using whichever protocol the client itself was using.

Configuring Client Access

Now that we've briefly examined the client access process, let's discuss the more common Client Access server configuration and management items you'll need to perform. You'll examine Outlook Web Access, Outlook Anywhere, mobile device management, basic client security, and a few more advanced client access options.

Configuring and Managing Outlook Web Access

Outlook Web Access (OWA) in Exchange Server 2007 is a huge improvement over previous versions. The interface closely mimics that of Outlook 2007, and it works "out of the box" after an installation of the Client Access server. If you do no other configuration, your users could (and likely would) use OWA as is. However, there are some configuration options we will discuss that will customize and enhance the OWA experience for your users.

Configuring OWA for SharePoint and File Server Access

By default, SharePoint and file server access are enabled in OWA, but they are not likely to be configured the way you will need them to operate for your organization's environment. For example, you might want to allow access to some servers but block access to other servers on your network. Or maybe you want to allow OWA to access every server on your network except for a select few. Whatever your needs may be, Exchange Server 2007 has the tools you need to create your configuration. Exercise 4.4 outlines the steps for configuring allowed and blocked SharePoint and file servers for OWA access.

Configuring SharePoint and File Server Access

Follow these steps to configure SharePoint and file server access:

1. Click Start ≻ Programs ≻ Microsoft Exchange Server 2007 and then select Exchange Management Console.

2. Expand the Microsoft Exchange root object, expand the Server Configuration folder, and then click the Client Access node.

3. Select the server to configure in the top half of the middle pane, and then select the OWA (Default Web Site) item as shown here.

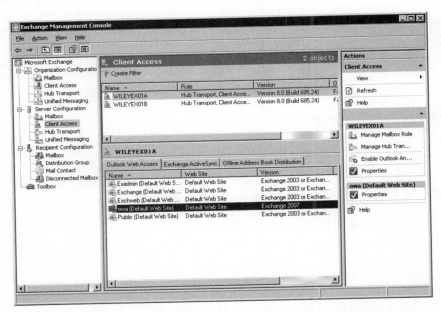

4. Open the OWA website properties by right-clicking the virtual directory and selecting Properties from the context menu. Alternatively, you can click the Properties link under the OWA (Default Web Site) options in the Actions pane on the right side of the Exchange Management Console. The OWA (Default Web Site) Properties dialog box opens to the General tab.

5. Select the Remote File Servers tab as shown here.

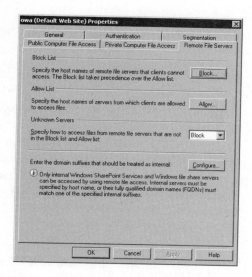

6. To block specific SharePoint or file servers from being accessed from OWA, click the Block button to open the Block List dialog box. Add, edit, or delete servers from the list as needed, and then click OK to return to the Remote File Servers tab.

7. To allow specific SharePoint or file servers explicitly to be accessed from OWA, click the Allow button to open the Allow List dialog box. Add, edit, or delete servers from the list as needed, and then click OK to return to the Remote File Servers tab.

8. For the Unknown Servers option, most organizations will likely leave the default selection of Block in place, thus allowing access only to those servers configured on the Allow list.

9. If you have multiple DNS suffixes in your organization, you can control or prevent access to certain suffixes by omitting them from the internal DNS suffix list. By default, no entries are configured here, allowing access to any internal server.

10. When you are finished making your configuration, click OK to save the changes, and close the OWA (Default Web Site) Properties dialog box.

By default, all computers accessing OWA (both public and private) can access SharePoint and file servers that you configured in Exercise 4.4. Exercise 4.5 outlines the steps for disabling SharePoint and file server access for OWA clients.

EXERCISE 4.5

Disabling SharePoint and File Server Integration with OWA

Follow these steps to disable SharePoint and file server access for OWA clients:

1. Click Start ≻ Programs ≻ Microsoft Exchange Server 2007 and then select Exchange Management Console.

2. Expand the Microsoft Exchange root object, expand the Server Configuration folder, and then click the Client Access node.

3. Select the server to configure in the top half of the middle pane, and then select the OWA (Default Web Site) item.

4. Open the OWA website properties by right-clicking the virtual directory and selecting Properties from the context menu. Alternatively, you can click the Properties link under the OWA (Default Web Site) options in the Actions pane on the right side of the Exchange Management Console. The OWA (Default Web Site) Properties dialog box opens to the General tab.

5. Select the Public Computer File Access tab, as shown here.

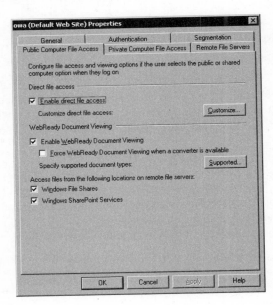

6. To disable access to file shares or SharePoint servers from public computers (determined by the user's selections on the OWA login page), remove the check from the appropriate option.

7. On the Private Computer File Access tab, shown here, you have the same options to disable access to file shares or SharePoint servers from private computers (determined by the user's selections on the OWA login page).

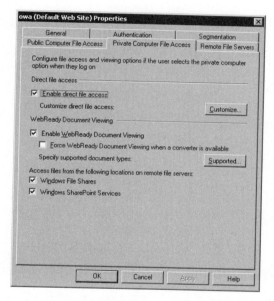

8. When you are done creating your configuration, click OK to save the changes and close the OWA (Default Web Site) Properties dialog box.

Unfortunately, there are no means to make certain file or SharePoint servers are available to OWA when the users log in. Users can, however, create and manage their own Favorites list of servers that they commonly access. To access a file server or SharePoint server from within OWA, click the Documents button at the bottom of the OWA screen, as shown in Figure 4.22.

FIGURE 4.22   The OWA interface

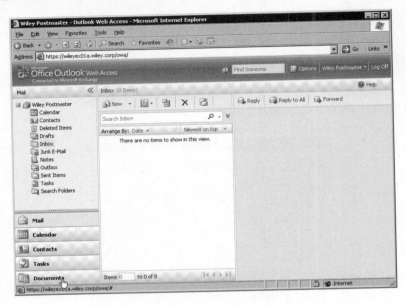

From the Documents page that loads, shown in Figure 4.23, click the Open Location link to open a dialog box that allows you to enter a UNC path such as \\MyServerA\ SalesDocs. As you can also see in Figure 4.23, the user has configured a favorite place that they can quickly access again later by clicking it in the Favorites list.

FIGURE 4.23   Working with file and SharePoint servers in OWA

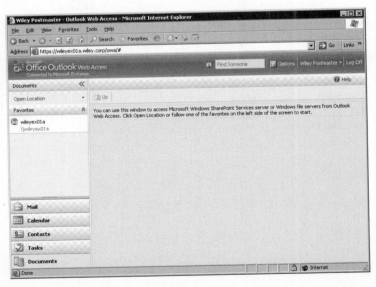

Configuring Other OWA Options

Several other OWA-related options are available to configure on the OWA (Default Web Site) virtual directory. Next, you'll briefly examine these items.

General

On the General tab of the OWA (Default Web Site) Properties dialog box, shown in Figure 4.24, the only real configuration you perform is changing the default value of the internal OWA URL and providing an external OWA URL.

FIGURE 4.24   The General tab of the OWA (Default Web Site) Properties dialog box

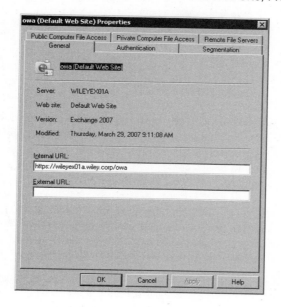

Authentication

On the Authentication tab of the OWA (Default Web Site) Properties dialog box, shown in Figure 4.25, you can change the authentication method used by the OWA website if you desire. By default, OWA in Exchange Server 2007 is configured for forms-based authentication using a self-issued SSL certificate. Replacing this certificate with one issued by a trusted third-party certificate authority such as Thawte or VeriSign should be a top priority when it comes to configuring OWA. You'll configure the SSL certificate, however, via the IIS console, which I will discuss later in this chapter.

FIGURE 4.25 The Authentication tab of the OWA (Default Web Site) Properties dialog box

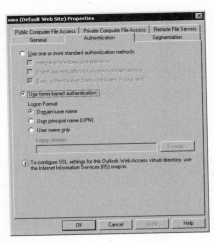

By default, the forms-based authentication is configured to use the domain\username format for OWA login. You can change this if desired to either UPN based (user@company. corp) or username based. If you select this method, you will need to select the default logon domain, of which only one can be selected.

Segmentation

On the Segmentation tab of the OWA (Default Web Site) Properties dialog box, shown in Figure 4.26, you can control which options will be available within OWA. Previously there was no easy way to configure these options in OWA—certainly no easy way within the standard Exchange management tools.

FIGURE 4.26 The Segmentation tab of the OWA (Default Web Site) Properties dialog box

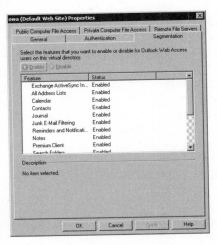

The following OWA options can be disabled or enabled from the Segmentation tab:

Exchange ActiveSync Integration: If disabled, it hides the Mobile Devices option in OWA.

All Address Lists: When this is disabled, only the global address list (GAL) is available.

Calendar: If disabled, it hides the user's Calendar folder in OWA. The Calendar folder is still available in Outlook sessions.

Contacts: If disabled, it hides the user's Contacts folder in OWA. The Contacts folder is still available in Outlook sessions.

Journal: If disabled, it hides the user's Journal folder in OWA. The Journal folder is still available in Outlook sessions.

Junk E-mail Filtering: When this is disabled, users are not able to control or change junk mail settings from OWA. These settings are still available to be changed from Outlook, and any settings in place will work but cannot be changed.

Reminders and Notifications: When this is disabled, users will not get reminders and notifications. Reminders and notifications are not available in OWA Light, which is a scaled-down version of OWA that was referred to as Basic in the version of OWA provided by Exchange Server 2003.

Notes: If disabled, it hides the user's Notes folder in OWA. The Notes folder is still available in Outlook sessions. Notes are read-only in OWA.

Premium Client: When disabled, it allows only OWA Light to be used.

Search Folders: When this is disabled, search folders are not available to the user in OWA.

E-mail Signature: When this is disabled, OWA users cannot manage message signatures.

Spelling Checker: When this is disabled, spell checking is not available to OWA users. Spell checking is not available in OWA Light.

Tasks: If disabled, it hides the user's Tasks folder in OWA. The Tasks folder is still available in Outlook sessions.

Public Computer File Access

On the Public Computer File Access tab of the OWA (Default Web Site) Properties dialog box, shown in Figure 4.27, you have options to control how different file types are handled when accessed via OWA or from file or SharePoint servers. The settings you make on this tab are applied to OWA sessions where the user selected "This is a public or shared computer" on the OWA login page.

FIGURE 4.27   The Public Computer File Access tab of the OWA (Default Web Site) Properties dialog box

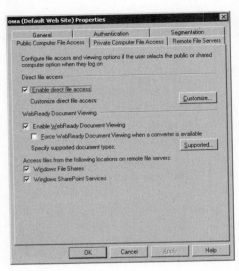

In the Direct File Access area, you can opt to enable or disable direct file access. Direct file access determines which file types can be opened directly within OWA, which file types can never be opened within OWA, and which file types must be saved first and then opened from the local computer's hard drive. By default, direct file access is enabled, and you'll almost certainly want to leave that setting in place. You may, however, want to customize the allow, block, and force save configurations by clicking the Customize button to open the Direct File Access Settings dialog box, shown in Figure 4.28.

FIGURE 4.28   The Direct File Access Settings dialog box

From the Direct File Access Settings dialog box, you can see which file types are always allowed to be opened within OWA, which file types are never allowed to be opened within OWA, which file types must be saved first before they can be opened, and what to do when a file type that hasn't been otherwise accounted for is encountered. Exchange provides many default entries in each section—take some time to look through them to make sure they make sense for your organization. When you're finished, click the OK button to save your changes and close the Direct File Access Settings dialog box.

Certain file types, such as Microsoft Word documents and Adobe Acrobat PDF documents, can be converted to HTML easily. These file types are known as WebReady file types. You can configure OWA to display these file types as HTML documents, thus allowing access to them even on computers that may not have the original applications used to create them installed. This can be a great benefit for computers in public places such as web cafes and public libraries. You can opt to force WebReady display if you like, but it is not enabled by default. Clicking the Supported button on the Public Computer File Access tab of the Properties dialog box opens the WebReady Document Viewing Settings dialog box, shown in Figure 4.29. From here you can change the default settings that Exchange provides.

The other options on the Public Computer File Access tab of the OWA (Default Web Site) Properties dialog box pertain to file server and SharePoint server access via OWA, which I've already discussed.

FIGURE 4.29   The WebReady Document Viewing Settings dialog box

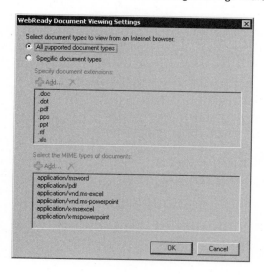

Private Computer File Access

On the Private Computer File Access tab of the OWA (Default Web Site) Properties dialog box, you have the same settings as those on the Public Computer File Access tab. The only difference is that these settings will be applied to OWA sessions that originate from "private" computers as selected by the user on the OWA login page.

Remote File Servers

On the Remote File Servers tab of the OWA (Default Web Site) Properties dialog box, you have options to configure remote file and SharePoint servers for OWA clients to access. We examined these settings previously in this section.

Configuring and Managing Outlook Anywhere

Outlook Anywhere is the new name for RPC over HTTPS, which was included in Exchange Server 2003, and it allows mailbox owners to work outside their network with their Outlook clients without needing to establish a VPN or another remote connection method. In a pure Exchange Server 2007 organization, Outlook Anywhere is fairly simple to configure and maintain. In organizations that still have mailboxes on Exchange Server 2003 servers, the configuration and management are more complex but still doable.

By default, Outlook Anywhere is not enabled on any Client Access server after installing the Client Access server role. You can enable Outlook Anywhere for a Client Access server by selecting the Client Access server in the Exchange Management Console (Microsoft Exchange ≻ Server Configuration ≻ Client Access) and clicking the Enable Outlook Anywhere link under the server options in the Actions pane on the right side of the Exchange Management Console. The Enable Outlook Anywhere Wizard opens (see Figure 4.30). Select your hostname, authentication, and SSL options, and then click Enable to complete the enabling process.

FIGURE 4.30   The Enable Outlook Anywhere Wizard

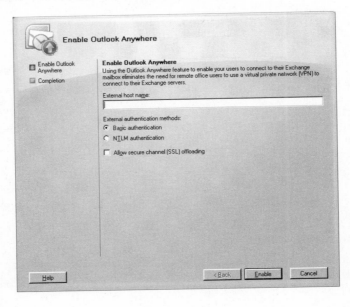

After the wizard completes, you can change the options you've configured by using the appropriate PowerShell command or by opening the Properties dialog box of the Client Access server. You can open the Client Access server's Properties dialog box by selecting the server, right-clicking, and selecting Properties from the context menu or by clicking the Properties link under the server options in the Actions pane on the right side of the Exchange Management Console. The General tab of the Client Access server Properties dialog box doesn't contain any settings you can edit, but the Outlook Anywhere tab, shown in Figure 4.31, will allow you to make changes to the configuration you entered for Outlook Anywhere.

FIGURE 4.31 Changing Outlook Anywhere options

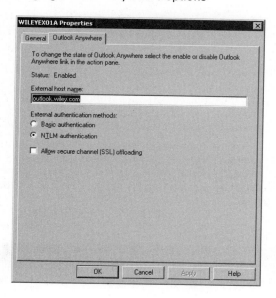

Configuring SSL on the Client Access Server

As discussed previously, Exchange Server 2007 actually issues its own self-signed SSL certificate for the Client Access server to use on all IIS virtual directories. This is good and bad. It's good because your clients can begin using OWA on Exchange Server 2007 with forms-based security the moment the installation of the Client Access server is complete. It's bad because your clients receive, and will continue to receive, certificate errors when they access OWA because there is no verification chain to follow to verify the validity of the certificate they're being given. Error feedback from Internet Explorer, like that shown in Figure 4.32, will likely confuse your users.

FIGURE 4.32 OWA certificate errors from the user's perspective

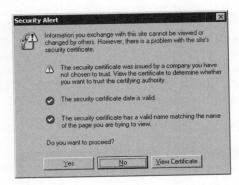

You can and should replace the default self-signed SSL certificate as soon as possible with one from a trusted third-party certificate authority such as Thawte or VeriSign. Exercise 4.6 details the process to request and subsequently install the certificate.

As you work through Exercise 4.6, you will be changing the behavior of the Client Access server in regard to OWA access. It's recommended that you perform the SSL certificate replacement as soon as possible after installing the Client Access server and before you make it available to users for OWA usage.

EXERCISE 4.6

Requesting and Installing a Third-Party SSL Certificate on Windows Server 2003

Follow these steps to request and install a third-party SSL certificate:

1. Click Start ➢ Programs ➢ Administrative Tools and then select Internet Information Services (IIS) Manager.

2. Expand the Internet Information Services root node, the *servername* node, and the Web Sites node.

3. Right-click the Default Web Site node, and select Properties from the context menu to open the Default Web Site Properties dialog box, shown here.

EXERCISE 4.6 *(continued)*

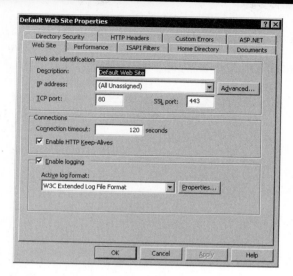

4. Select the Directory security tab, shown here.

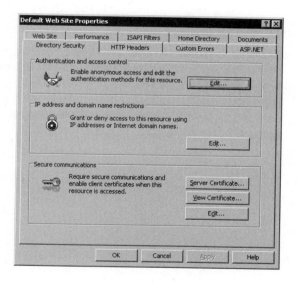

EXERCISE 4.6 *(continued)*

5. Remove the existing self-signed certificate from the Client Access server. To start this process, click the Server Certificate button to open the Web Server Certificate Wizard. Click Next to dismiss the first page of the wizard and then you'll see the Modify the Current Certificate Assignment page, shown here.

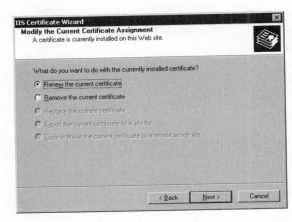

6. Select the Remove the Current Certificate option, and complete the remaining steps of the wizard to remove the self-signed certificate.

7. To start the process of requesting a third-party certificate, click the Server Certificate button again. Click Next to dismiss the first page of the wizard, and then you'll see the Server Certificate page, shown here.

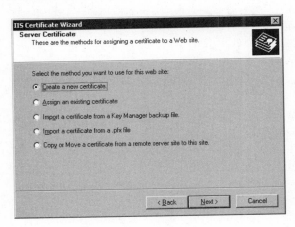

EXERCISE 4.6   *(continued)*

8. On the Server Certificate page, select the Create a New Certificate option and click Next to continue to the Delayed or Immediate Request page, shown here.

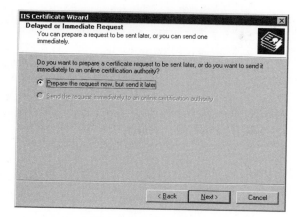

9. On the Delayed or Immediate Request page, select the option to create the request now and send it later, and click Next to continue to the Name and Security Settings page.

10. On the Name and Security Settings page, enter a friendly name and select the key length. It is usually best just to use the external OWA URL as the friendly name for simplicity. Click Next to continue to the Organization Information page, shown here.

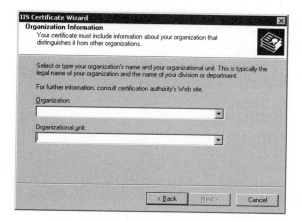

EXERCISE 4.6 *(continued)*

11. On the Organization Information page, enter the name of your company or organization and the organizational unit. Click Next to continue to the Your Site's Common Name page, shown here.

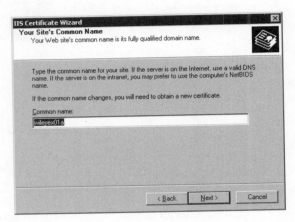

12. The Your Site's Common Name page is the most important part of the entire certificate request process. Many things will cause your request to be rejected by the issuing authority, but entering the wrong external URL on this page will render the certificate useless. Enter the external OWA URL, such as **owa.mycompany.com**, that clients will use to access OWA, and click Next to continue to the Geographical Information page, shown here.

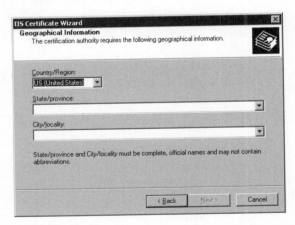

13. On the Geographical Information page, select your country and provide the complete (not abbreviated) state/province and city/locality information the page requests. Click Next to continue to the Certificate Request File Name page.

EXERCISE 4.6 *(continued)*

14. On the Certificate Request File Name page, enter the location and filename to use when saving the request and click Next to continue to the Request File Summary page.

15. On the Request File Summary page, verify that all the details are correct and click Next to create the request file.

16. Click Finish to close the wizard. You now have a certificate request file that can be submitted to your certificate authority of choice. Once you submit the request and pay the required fees, the certificate authority will send you a block of text or a text file that contains the actual certificate.

17. To import the certificate, return to the Directory Security tab once again and click the Server Certification button one more time. Click Next to dismiss the opening page of the wizard and go to the Pending Certificate Request page, shown here.

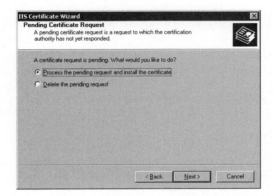

18. On the Pending Certificate Request page, select the Process the Pending Request and Install the Certificate option and click Next to process the text block you received from the certificate authority. If you made a mistake and the certificate authority rejects the certificate request, you can delete the pending request and then restart the process.

 Guidance on SSL certificates has changed slightly since Exchange Server 2007 was first introduced. You can read the latest information at the Microsoft Exchange team's blog by visiting http://msexchangeteam.com/archive/2007/02/19/435472.aspx

Configuring Client Connectivity

As the line from the movie *Field of Dreams* goes, "Build it, and they will come!" This is also true in terms of clients wanting to access the data contained within your Exchange organization. You must build it, by configuring it, before the users can come and connect. If your only concern is supporting Outlook MAPI clients and Outlook Web Access HTTP clients, then you really have nothing to worry about. In real life, that's almost certainly not the case. You're likely to have IMAP4 or even POP3 clients in your organization, especially if you support Apple computers on your network. Also, you can certainly expect to see Windows Mobile devices on your network as the push to make as much data as possible accessible all the time continues. Even if you don't end up supporting other client protocols, you'll still have a need to learn about the new features of Autodiscover and the Availability service, so read the following sections carefully!

Autodiscover

Exchange 2007 introduced Autodiscover, which allows Outlook 2007, Windows Mobile 6.1, and other clients to discover configuration information for a specific mailbox. Autodiscover is a web service that resides on the Exchange 2007 Client Access server role. The popular perception of Autodiscover is that it helps Outlook 2007 automatically locate an Exchange 2007 server, and that is correct in so far as it goes. However, Autodiscover actually helps Outlook locate a number of different types of Exchange resources, including the following:

▪ User's home Mailbox server

▪ Outlook Anywhere URL

▪ URL (internal or external) for the Offline Address Book

▪ URL (internal or external) for unified messaging

▪ URL (internal or external) for the Exchange Web Services, which empower the Availability service

When a user launches Outlook 2007 for the first time, they are prompted for some basic information (email address or domain/username and password). Outlook 2007 contacts the Autodiscover web service and looks up information such as the home Mailbox server, display name, and URLs for the Availability web service that provides free/busy information and where the Offline Address Book is stored. If this information is changed, then the Outlook client gets updated information (including the home Mailbox server name) from the Autodiscover service.

When users specify their email address, they should use their default SMTP address. Autodiscover may not work for additional SMTP addresses.

It is important to spend a few minutes talking about the Exchange Web Services. These services were created to access data in the Exchange store programmatically. Previously, many of these functions were spread out into multiple application programming interfaces (APIs) that complicated the task of developers creating software that accessed the Exchange store. What types of operations do the Exchange Web Services enable? Here is a short list:

- Create, copy, move, and delete items
- Create, copy, move, and delete folders
- Create, get, and delete attachments
- Subscribe to notifications
- Synchronize items
- Retrieve user availability and out-of-office information
- Manage delegates

One of the functions of the Exchange Web Services is what is called the *Availability service*. This service is leveraged both by Outlook Web Access and Outlook 2007 to retrieve live free/busy information from both Exchange 2007 and legacy mailboxes in not only the local Exchange forest but also in remote forests. Configuring the internal and external URL settings on the Exchange Web Services allows the Autodiscover service to configure clients to use the Availability service properly.

Internal vs. External Autodiscover

Outlook 2007 uses two approaches to locate the Autodiscover service and determine the necessary information. It uses the first approach when the Windows computer is a member of the Active Directory forest in which the Exchange server exists. Figure 4.33 shows the process that Outlook uses to locate resources. In this example, the computer on which Outlook 2007 is installed is a member of the Active Directory forest. This is considered the service process for internal clients.

In step 1 in Figure 4.33, Outlook is launched for the first time and there is no Outlook profile for the user account. Outlook contacts Active Directory to find a service connection point (SCP). A *service connection point* is an Active Directory object that can be used to publish and locate network services. The SCP object will provide Outlook with the fully qualified domain names of Client Access servers; Outlook then contacts a Client Access server in its local Active Directory site.

In step 2, the Outlook 2007 client queries the Client Access server to retrieve the user's home server. The username and domain name are used to locate the user's home Mailbox server. Outlook also retrieves information about the location of the Availability service and the distribution points for the OAB. From this information, the Outlook profile is created.

In step 3, Outlook connects to the user's home Exchange server.

FIGURE 4.33 The Autodiscover process when a client is in the same Active Directory forest

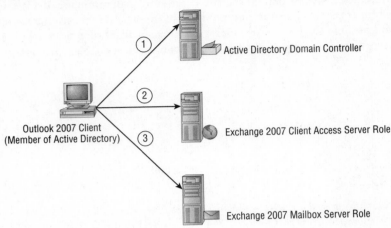

If the desktop client is not a member of the Active Directory or is outside the corporate network and cannot contact a domain controller, then Outlook 2007 uses a different approach. This is the Autodiscover service process for external access. In this approach, DNS is used to locate the Autodiscover service. Figure 4.34 shows an example of how the Autodiscover service is located for an external client. In this example, the user must provide their email address since it cannot be provided for them using their Active Directory user account.

FIGURE 4.34 The Autodiscover process when a client is not in the same Active Directory forest

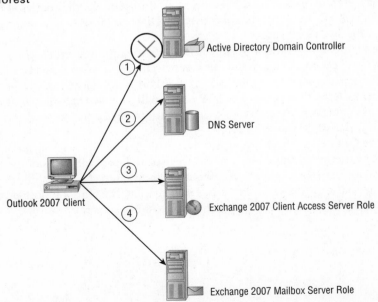

In step 1, Outlook tries to contact an Active Directory domain controller (if the client is a member of the Active Directory). If Active Directory cannot be located or the computer is not a member of the Active Directory, the user is presented with the Add New E-mail Account dialog box, shown in Figure 4.35. In this dialog box, the user must enter their primary SMTP address, their name, and their account password. The email address is important because the SMTP domain name is used in step 2.

FIGURE 4.35   Providing account information manually to Outlook

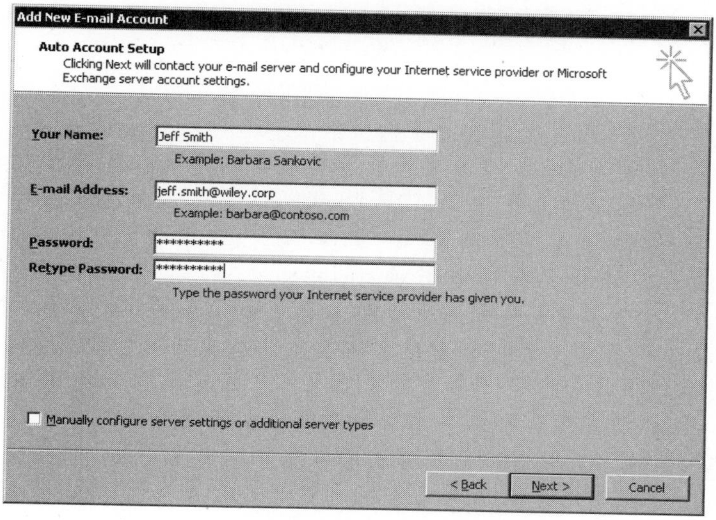

Add New E-mail Account	✕

Auto Account Setup
Clicking Next will contact your e-mail server and configure your Internet service provider or Microsoft Exchange server account settings.

Your Name: Jeff Smith
Example: Barbara Sankovic

E-mail Address: jeff.smith@wiley.corp
Example: barbara@contoso.com

Password: **********
Retype Password: **********
Type the password your Internet service provider has given you.

☐ Manually configure server settings or additional server types

< Back   Next >   Cancel

In step 2, the Outlook 2007 client performs a DNS query and uses the SMTP domain name. In our example, the domain name is wiley.corp. Outlook will use the following URLs to try to connect in order to locate the Autodiscover server:

```
https://wiley.corp/autodiscover/autodiscover.xml
https://autodiscover.wiley.corp/autodiscover/autodiscover.xml
```

An update was released for Outlook 2007 in which a DNS Service location (SRV) record can be created for Autodiscover to point to any hostname—even a host in a different domain. For more information about using a SRV record, see http://support.microsoft.com/kb/940881.

These URLs will need to be resolvable in DNS and accessible from outside your network for external clients. If you use the DNS approach for "external" clients on your inside network, you will want to make sure that one of these two URLs is resolvable using your internal DNS.

You can read more about Autodiscover in the Autodiscover service white paper that can be found at http://technet.microsoft.com/en-us/library/bb332063.aspx.

The Client Access server that hosts the Autodiscover URL will then return the Outlook Anywhere information necessary to configure Outlook 2007 as well as external URL locations for the Availability service and the Offline Address Book distribution point.

Configuring Autodiscover

When an Exchange 2007 Client Access server is installed, an SCP record is created in Active Directory for it. This includes the internal Outlook Anywhere settings, the internal URL for the OAB, and the internal URL for Exchange Web Services. However, depending on your environment, you may need to configure additional settings if, for example, you need to enable Outlook Anywhere (formerly RPC over HTTP) or define external URLs for other web services.

Configuring Autodiscover Virtual Directories

An Autodiscover virtual directory is automatically created on each Exchange 2007 Client Access server. The only way to configure this is through the Exchange Management Shell. The Get-AutoDiscoverVirtualDirectory cmdlet will let you view the Autodiscover virtual directories.

Configuring Outlook Anywhere and Autodiscover

By default, Outlook Anywhere is not enabled on the Client Access servers. To enable Outlook Anywhere, locate each Client Access server in the Server Configuration work center in the Exchange Management Console and select the Enable Outlook Anywhere task in the Actions pane. This launches a wizard that prompts you for the external hostname and the type of authentication, and it gives you the option to use SSL offloading, as shown in Figure 4.36.

If you are using network load balancing, the external hostname will be the fully qualified domain name that the clients will use externally. When you have completed the information required by the wizard, you can click the Enable Outlook Anywhere button in the upper-left corner.

Optionally, you could enable Outlook Anywhere using the Enable-OutlookAnywhere cmdlet. Here is an example:

```
enable-OutlookAnywhere -Server "WILEYEX02A"
-ExternalHostname "outlook.wiley.com"
-ExternalAuthenticationMethod "Basic" -SSLOffloading $false
```

Once Outlook Anywhere is enabled, you can select the properties of the Client Access server and view the Outlook Anywhere properties of that particular Client Access server. Figure 4.37 shows an example.

FIGURE 4.36 Enabling Outlook Anywhere

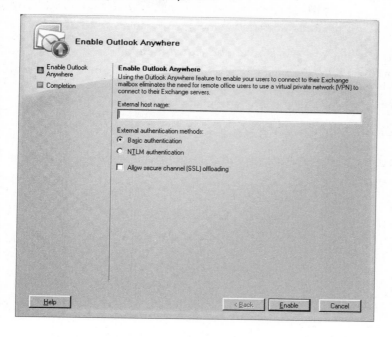

FIGURE 4.37 Configuring the external hostname for Outlook Anywhere

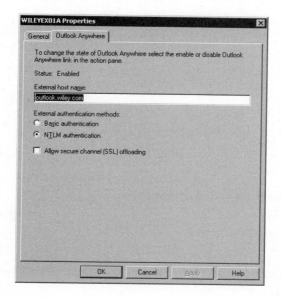

You can retrieve the same information (and more) using the `Get-OutlookAnywhere` cmdlet. When configuring the external hostname for Outlook Anywhere, remember that this is the URL that will be referred to external Outlook 2007 clients when Autodiscover is used.

Configuring Offline Address Books and Autodiscover

The Offline Address Book distribution points by default contain only the internal URL used to locate them. You can set these using the graphical user interface by selecting the properties of the Offline Address Book virtual directory in the Exchange Management Console. Figure 4.38 shows the URLs tab of the OAB (Default Web Site) virtual directory's Properties dialog box for a Client Access server.

FIGURE 4.38   Setting the external URL for Offline Address Book distribution

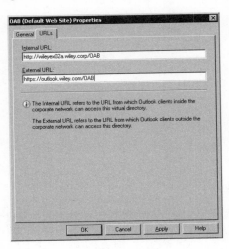

You can also set this parameter using the cmdlet `Set-OABVirtualDirectory`. Here is an example:

```
set-OABVirtualDirectory "WILEYEX02A\OAB (Default Web Site)"
-ExternalURL https://outlook.wiley.com/OAB -RequireSSL:$True
```

You can view the configuration of the Offline Address Book virtual directory using the `get-OABVirtualDirectory` cmdlet.

Configuring Web Services and Autodiscover

If remote or external clients need access to custom web services, you should configure the external URL for web services. You can do this only via the Exchange Management Shell. The following cmdlet is an example for setting the external URL for a Client Access server:

```
set-WebServicesVirtualDirectory "WILEYEX02A\EWS (Default web site)"
-ExternalUrl "https://outlook.wiley.com/EWS/Exchange.asmx"
-BasicAuthentication:$True
```

To check the configuration of the Web Services virtual directory, you can use the `Get-WebServicesVirtualDirectory` cmdlet.

Configuring Autodiscover and Secure Sockets Layer

If you have tried to deploy both internal and external URLs already, then by now you are wondering how Secure Sockets Layer is supposed to work if the FQDN of the internal location is different from the external FQDN. After all, if certificates are requested, you usually provide only one name in the certificate-signing request. There is a workaround, however, that allows you to have more than one common name for a Client Access server. This feature is called Subject Alternative Name (SAN) certificates in the Exchange documentation; however, many providers refer to these certificates as Unified Communication Certificates (UCCs). To use the workaround you have to create the certificate using the `New-ExchangeCertificate` cmdlet. The command line can be fairly involved. Here is an example:

```
new-ExchangeCertificate -GenerateRequest
-SubjectName "dc=com,dc=wiley,o=Wiley Publishing, cn=outlook.wiley.com"
-DomainName WILEYEX02A, WILEYEX02A.wiley.corp, outlook.wiley.com,
autodiscover.wiley.com -path c:\certrequest-WILEYEX02A.txt
```

This cmdlet creates a certificate request with multiple hostnames. In this case, the hostnames include outlook.wiley.com, autodiscover.wiley.com, WILEYEX02A, and WILEYEX02A.wiley.corp.

When requesting a Subject Alternative Name certificate, be sure to check with your SSL provider to see how many alternative names are allowed and if there are any restrictions on the number of servers on which the certificate can be installed.

You can take the contents of this file and get a certificate signed and issued by a trusted certificate authority, or you could sign it yourself using Windows Certificate Server. The result will be a file that is returned to you from the certification authority (in this case, `certnew.cer`). Here is an example using the `Import-ExchangeCertificate` cmdlet to import the signed certificate into the certificate store:

```
Import-ExchangeCertificate -path c:\certnew.cer -FriendlyName "WILEYEX02A Cert"
```

If you are used to creating certificate requests using the Internet Information Services Manager console, then there is a new step with which you may not be familiar. The `Import-ExchangeCertificate` cmdlet imports the certificate into the computer's personal certificate store, but it does not assign it to the default website. You will need to perform the steps in Exercise 4.7 to associate the certificate with the default website.

EXERCISE 4.7

Installing an SSL Certificate

Follow these steps to install an SSL certificate:

1. Click Start ≻ Programs ≻ Administrative Tools ≻ Internet Information Services (IIS) Manager.

2. Open the Web Sites container, right-click Default Web Site, and select Properties.

3. Select the Directory Security tab.

4. Click the Server Certificate button and then click Next.

5. Select the Assign an Existing Certificate radio button and click Next.

6. In the Select a Certificate list, select the certificate you have just imported using the Import-ExchangeCertificate cmdlet. When you have selected the certificate, click Next.

7. Confirm that port 443 is the SSL port, which is usually the case. Click Next.

8. On the Certificate Summary page, you can see some of the details of the certificate. When you are ready, click Next and then click Finish.

Congratulations! The certificate is now installed and associated with the default website. On the Directory Security tab, you can click the View Certificate button to see more details about the certificate.

Supporting POP3 and IMAP4 Clients

POP3 and IMAP4 are one of the most basic email protocols in use. With SMTP, they are the most straightforward of the email delivery mechanisms, and virtually every email server available supports them. However, they do have their drawbacks, particularly when used with Exchange.

For example, if you collect your email with POP3 from your Exchange mailbox, all email in the mailbox will be marked as read whether or not the message has actually been read on the client.

The other major issue with POP3 is that it is designed to remove the email from the server and store it locally. It is easy to make an error in configuration and remove all the email from the server. Although there are options to leave email on the server, it's easy to overlook them.

Things are a little better with IMAP4 because the email is actually stored on the server. However, you still are limited on the functionality from Exchange compared to the full Outlook client or Outlook Web Access.

Given that, POP3/IMAP4 access should be the last access protocol of choice. However, in some settings, such as academic environments, POP3 and IMAP4 clients are popular and must still be supported.

POP3 and IMAP4 are disabled by default in Exchange 2007. You can configure SMTP for use by POP3/IMAP4 clients using the Management Console. However, you may want to look at deploying TLS/SMTP because the standard port 25 is often blocked for accessing remote SMTP servers from home-user-type connections, meaning the POP3/IMAP4 clients will be unable to send email through your server.

Either way, because of the nature of the protocols, keeping a copy of the messages for compliance reasons is almost impossible. The user could send the message through another SMTP server, so there will be no trace of the message on your server.

If you need to track email messages for compliance reasons, you should look at using a MAPI connection such as Outlook Web Access or Outlook Anywhere.

Configuring Exchange to Support POP3 and IMAP4 Clients

Configuring Exchange Server 2007 to support POP3 or IMAP4 clients requires a couple of steps. These include enabling the services and configuring the Client Access servers to support these protocols.

Enabling the Services

Before clients can connect to the POP3 or IMAP4 services, the services must be enabled and started because they are set to start manually. You can enable POP3 and IMAP4 in two ways. As with Exchange 2003, you can change the service in the Services console, shown in Figure 4.39, to Automatic and then start the service.

FIGURE 4.39 Configuring POP3 and IMAP4 services

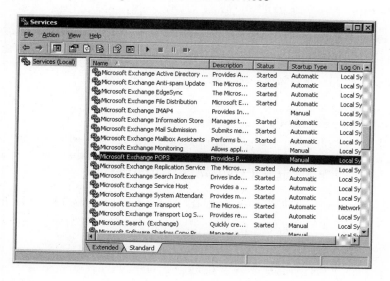

You can also enable the services through the Exchange Management Shell. To enable POP3, use the following command:

```
Set-Service msExchangePOP3 -startuptype automatic
```

Once it's enabled, you need to start the service by using the following command:

```
Start-Service -service msExchangePOP3
```

For IMAP4, the procedure is almost identical:

```
Set-Service msExchangeIMAP4 -startuptype automatic
```

To start the service, use the following command:

```
Start-Service msExchangeIMAP4
```

Configuring POP3 and IMAP4 Servers

Once you have enabled the services, you can configure them using either the Management Console or the Management Shell if you have Service Pack 1 installed. The default settings may be suitable for you. You can check the current settings using the following commands:

- For POP3, use `Get-PopSettings`.
- For IMAP4, use `Get-ImapSettings`.

The only additional configuration you may want to review is enabling TLS/SSL support, but we won't be discussing it here.

 You can find more information about securing POP3 and IMAP4 at the following TechNet location: http://technet.microsoft.com/en-us/library/bb430779.aspx.

Configuring POP3 and IMAP4 Mailboxes

By default, all user accounts are enabled for POP3 and IMAP4 access. Therefore, you may want to review the accounts and disable that functionality for those users who will not be accessing Exchange using POP3 or IMAP4. You do this using the `Set-CASMailbox` command.

For example, to disable POP3 for user robert.jones@wiley.com, use the following command:

```
Set-CASMailbox -identity robert.jones@wiley.com -POPEnabled:$false
```

You can view the status of the mailboxes simply by entering the command `Get-CASMailbox`, which will display all mailboxes in the Exchange organization and whether or not they are enabled.

Configuring a Receive Connector for Use with POP3 and IMAP4

POP3/IMAP4 clients need to have an SMTP connector through which to send their outbound email. For Exchange 2007, that means a receive connector must be configured to accept their messages and allow them to be relayed through the server to the clients.

There should already be a connector configured that is suitable for use; it is called Client *servername*. You can see this using the Exchange Management Console or by using the Management Shell command `Get-ReceiveConnector`.

This default connector should require little configuration. Note that this connector is configured to use port 587, which is the client SMTP submission port, and is also set to use TLS. It uses the certificate that is installed on the Exchange server during installation. If you intend to have clients relay email through the server on this port, then you need to either import the certificate to their machine so that it is trusted or replace the certificate with one from a trusted CA.

If you want to use the standard TCP port 25 to relay email, you need to review the configuration of the server connector. In all cases, basic authentication needs to be enabled on the connector because it is the only type of authentication that SMTP clients support. You can also use basic authentication requiring TLS.

Configuring a POP3 or IMAP4 Client

You will no doubt be familiar with the configuration of POP3/IMAP4 clients and SMTP. For Exchange, it is almost the same as any Internet email account you may have configured. For the server address of the POP3, IMAP4, and SMTP servers, you should use a hostname.

Although you can use an IP address, if you ever need to change the IP address of the server, it is far easier to change a single DNS entry than to try to get many users to update their email client configurations.

What you use for your hostnames is up to you—as long as they resolve correctly on the Internet. You may already have a hostname configured that points to your Exchange server used for MX records. If so, you could use the same hostname in the account settings. Alternatively, if you think you might change the configuration in the future so that the servers are different, you may want to use pop3.domain.com, imap4.domain.com, and smtp.domain. com, with all of them pointing at the same IP address. If you need to change them later, simply adjust the DNS records.

If you are using TLS/SSL for account access, ensure that you change the port setting in the email client to use the alternative port. This is often found in the advanced settings.

Finally, you need to enter credentials. For Exchange, these credentials need to be in a specific format:

- For POP3 and IMAP4 access, it is in the format of *domain\username*.

- For SMTP access, it is in the format of *domain\username*.

- In both cases, you can also use the UPN, *username@domain.local*.

The choice of authentication format is up to you and what you think will be easiest to support. It is best to decide on one format and then stick to it so it is easier to write documentation and maintain consistency.

Configuring Windows Mobile Devices and ActiveSync

Along with Exchange 2003, Microsoft introduced Exchange ActiveSync (EAS), which allows synchronization directly to the Exchange server over a network or Internet connection. This was initially on-demand sync, but Exchange 2003 Service Pack 2 enabled the "push mail" feature using HTTP or HTTPS. Push email enables email to be synchronized with the device as new messages arrive; when a message arrives in the user's Inbox, the Exchange server notifies connected mobile devices that a new message must be synchronized to the device.

Exchange 2007 enhanced EAS further; however, to take full advantage of the new features in EAS, you need to be using Windows Mobile 6.0 or higher.

Exchange ActiveSync was available with Windows Mobile 2003 but really became popular only with Windows Mobile 5. To use the push technology, you need to have a device with the Messaging and Security Feature Pack (MSFP) installed. This is not available as a separate download but will be part of a software update from the handset supplier.

 You must obtain Microsoft Messaging and Security Feature Pack updates for mobile devices or Windows Mobile 6 updates from the device vendor or the cell phone provider, not Microsoft.

If you have purchased a new device after June 2006, it almost certainly will come with a version of Windows Mobile 5.0 with MSFP. Also, many devices that run Windows Mobile 5 can be upgraded to the MSFP version.

How Can You Tell Whether Your Device Has the MSFP?

You can identify whether your handset has the MSFP update in two ways. In both cases, you need to look at the version information. You can find this by selecting Settings ➢ System in the About applet.

In the version information, you will see a string similar to OS 5.1.195 (Build 14847.2.0.0), as shown in Figure 4.40. With some handsets, the build number says Messaging and Security Feature Pack. If that is the case, you know for sure. If yours does not, then you need to look at the build number. The key element is the last three digits. To have the MSFP installed, it needs to be 2.0.0 or higher. Build 2.0.0 was the first build to have the MSFP update.

Configuring Exchange to Support ActiveSync

Exchange ActiveSync is enabled by default. This can confirmed by checking for the presence of a number of elements in the Internet Information Services (IIS) Manager. In the IIS Manager under Default website, as shown in Figure 4.41, check to see whether the virtual directory Microsoft-Server-ActiveSync exists.

FIGURE 4.40   Viewing the Windows Mobile version information

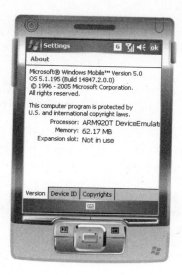

FIGURE 4.41   Viewing the Exchange virtual directories and application pools

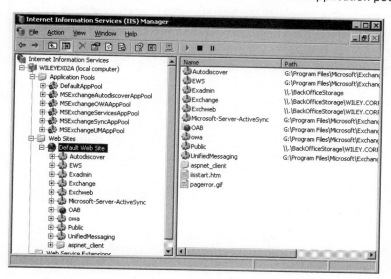

As an administrator, you will want to test Windows Mobile for yourself; however, getting hold of a device with the relevant software may be difficult. Microsoft has released an emulator for Windows Mobile; it was originally designed for developer use but is now available as a stand-alone product. You can install this on your workstation and connect to the Exchange server over your network. At the time of this writing, you can download the emulator from the Microsoft downloads site by searching for "Microsoft Device Emulator 3.0 Standalone Release" at www.microsoft.com/downloads/.

You can also check the Exchange-related application pools by right-clicking an application pool, such as the MSExchangeSyncAppPool application pool. If Start is available, then EAS is not running. Choose Start to enable the application pool.

You can do additional configuration of ActiveSync through the Exchange Management Console. Under Server Configuration, choose the Exchange ActiveSync tab. Right-click the virtual directory listed, and choose Properties. You'll see three tabs. The first tab, General, allows you to set the internal and external URL for ActiveSync. The second tab, Authentication, allows you to control authentication, including whether to use client certificates. The third tab allows you to control remote file server access. This is identical in operation to remote file server access through Outlook Web Access but is not available with the current versions of Windows Mobile.

For Exchange Management Shell configuration, you use two cmdlets:

- The cmdlet New-ActiveSyncVirtualDirectory will allow you to create a new virtual directory for another website on the same server.

- The cmdlet Set-ActiveSyncVirtualDirectory allows you to change settings for the ActiveSync virtual directory. This includes settings not available to you through the Exchange Management Console. This command will enable basic authentication on a server named WILEYEX02A:

```
Set-ActiveSyncVirtualDirectory
-Identity "EXCHANGE01\microsoft-server-activesync"
-BasicAuthEnabled:$true
```

Defining an ActiveSync Policy

An ActiveSync policy allows you to define certain settings for the devices. With Exchange 2003, the policy was applied to all devices and exceptions could be created for specific users. The level of control was very low. You can now have different settings for different users, allowing you more control over the devices—possibly depending on each user's job function.

 Exchange Server 2007 Service Pack 1 introduced the ability to set a default ActiveSync Policy. The policy that is set as the default is applied to all new mailboxes created.

ActiveSync policies are Exchange organization–wide, so you set them in the Organization Configuration ➤ Client Access node of the Exchange System Manager, as shown in Figure 4.42.

FIGURE 4.42   Viewing ActiveSync policies

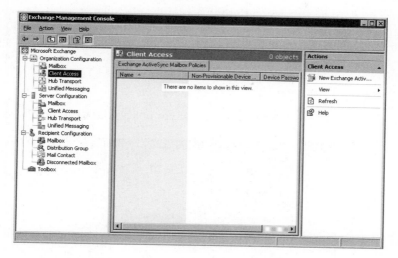

The policy is divided into two main areas: access and password.

The General tab of the ActiveSync policy's Properties dialog box, as shown in Figure 4.43, is for access-related settings. You can define whether attachments are downloaded to the device, configure access to Universal Naming Convention (UNC) and Windows SharePoint Services (WSS) servers, and choose whether non-provisionable devices can be configured.

FIGURE 4.43   The General tab of the ActiveSync policy's Properties dialog box

Non-provisionable devices are devices that do not support the Autodiscover service. Most sites will need to enable non-provisionable devices, at least initially until their devices or all users are using a version of Windows Mobile that supports provisioning via Autodiscover.

The Password tab of the ActiveSync policy Properties dialog box, as shown in Figure 4.44, is for password policy. The settings on this tab are fairly self-explanatory. If you want to take advantage of the remote wipe features, you need to require a device password. If you do not, when you attempt to remotely wipe the device, you will be asked to allow enforcement of a password policy. By saying no, you can maintain access to the device. Allow Simple Password is a policy that allows the user to set a password such as 1234. If you have policies regarding passwords, you may not want to enable that option.

FIGURE 4.44   The Password tab of the ActiveSync policy's Properties dialog box

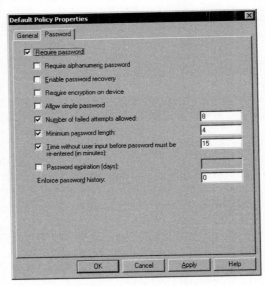

You can have more than one ActiveSync policy. To create another one, select New ActiveSync Policy from the Actions pane in the Exchange Management Console, or run the cmdlet New-ActiveSyncPolicy with the required parameters.

The following command will create a new policy called Sales, with Device Password enabled:

```
New-ActiveSyncMailboxPolicy -Name:"Sales" -DevicePasswordEnabled:$true
```

You can assign a policy to each user as required. To set a policy to a user through the Exchange Management Console, follow the steps in Exercise 4.8.

EXERCISE 4.8

Assigning an ActiveSync Policy to a User

To assign an ActiveSync policy to a user, follow these steps:

1. Click Start ➤ Programs ➤ Microsoft Exchange Server 2007 and then select Exchange Management Console.

2. Expand the Microsoft Exchange root object, expand the Recipient Configuration folder, and then click the Mailbox node.

3. In the Actions pane on the right side, click the Properties link to open the mailbox user's Properties dialog box.

4. Click the Mailbox Features tab, shown here.

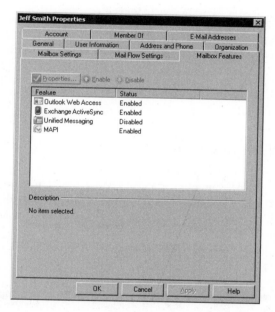

5. Click the Exchange ActiveSync item, and then click the Properties button. The Exchange ActiveSync Properties dialog box opens.

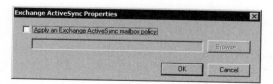

6. Click the Apply an Exchange ActiveSync Mailbox Policy option, and then click Browse to locate a policy to apply.

7. Click OK to close the Exchange ActiveSync Properties dialog box.

8. Click OK to close the mailbox user Properties dialog box.

If you want to set multiple users at the same time, you need to use the Exchange Management Shell. To set the policy through the Exchange Management Shell, use the Set-CASMailbox command. For example, to set the policy Sales on user rick.jones, run the following:

```
Set-CASMailbox Rick.Jones -ActiveSyncMailboxPolicy
(Get-ActiveSyncMailboxPolicy "Sales").Identity
```

If you want to set a policy to all users, which may be a good way to start off, you have to use a combination of commands. The following command will set the Default policy on all users:

```
Get-Mailbox | Set-CASMailbox -ActiveSyncMailboxPolicy
(Get-ActiveSyncMailboxPolicy "Default").Identity
```

Configuring a Windows Mobile Device

This section guides you through configuring a Windows Mobile device. These instructions and screen shots were created using the Windows Mobile 5.0 emulator, which is running build 2.0.0. Therefore, you may find that a few screens look slightly different from what is shown here. The entries are identical, so it should be easy enough to adapt to versions of Windows Mobile that are released after this book is published.

To configure your device to sync with Exchange, follow the steps outlined in Exercise 4.9.

Configuring ActiveSync on a Mobile Device

Follow these steps to configure ActiveSync on a mobile device:

1. Select ActiveSync from Programs. If this is the first time you have configured ActiveSync, you should simply select the text Set Up Your Device to Sync with It, as shown here. If you already have ActiveSync configured to synchronize with a desktop, then you can change the settings from the menu or use ActiveSync on the desktop to configure synchronization with a server.

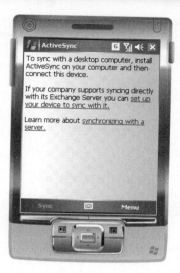

2. You will be asked for the server address as shown here. This needs to be the exter-
    nal name of the Exchange server, such as, for example, mail.domain.com. If you are
    going to use SSL, then the name needs to match what is on the certificate. The certif-
    icate also needs to be trusted by the device (either because you are using a commer-
    cial certificate that has a root certificate in the device or because you have imported
    the root or client certificate into the device in advance).

EXERCISE 4.9 *(continued)*

3. Enter the username, password, and domain for the account that is being used, as shown here. If you want to sync automatically, you will need to save the password.

4. Whether you want to set the advanced settings, as shown here, is up to you. Advanced settings deal with item conflict (the default is Replace the Item on My Device) and event logging (the default is None).

5.   On the last screen shown here, you can set what is synchronized over the server connection. Most users will be configuring all four options (Contacts, Calendar, E-mail,
and Tasks). You cannot sync the Notes folder over the air, so if you are using the Notes
feature in Outlook, you will need to continue to use the desktop ActiveSync as well.

6.   You can adjust how much is synchronized for some of the types, such as Calendar
and E-mail. Select the type, and then select Settings to adjust. Calendar allows you to
change how much of your calendar is synchronized. E-mail, shown here, allows you to
change how much old email is synchronized and whether attachments come across.

7. After you select Finish, the device will attempt to sync for the first time, as shown here. If there is a lot of email to come across, then you should have the device connected to the network via USB ActiveSync for that first sync.

 Exchange ActiveSync will sync over a wireless network connection. However, the push technology for email does not operate over wireless as it requires a mobile phone connection. Furthermore, if you have ActiveSync set to push, you will need to initiate a manual sync to sync over the wireless network.

Managing a Windows Mobile Device

At some point, one of your users will lose their device or you will need to wipe it. The management of Windows Mobile devices is now built in to Exchange. You can manage the devices in three ways.

First, the end user can manage it through Outlook Web Access. The administrator can turn off this option if they want. However, if you have lots of remote users, you may want to enable this feature so the users can wipe the devices as soon as they realize they have lost it. Mobile device management is within the options of OWA, as shown in Figure 4.45, once the user has logged in.

FIGURE 4.45 Managing a mobile device via OWA

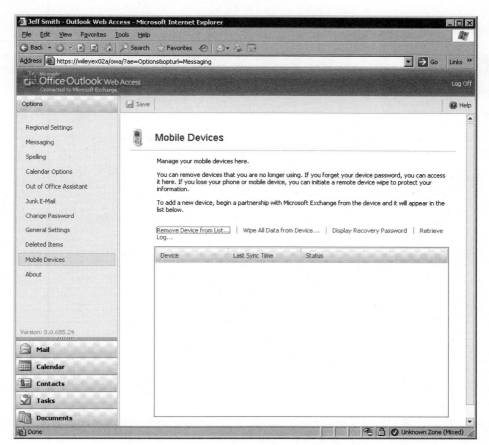

Second, you can manage the device through the Exchange Management Console. You can manage the device by right-clicking the user in the Recipients Configuration ➤ Mailbox node center and choosing Manage Mobile Device. This runs the Manage Mobile Device Wizard.

> The Manage Mobile Device task option appears only if there is a mobile device associated with a mailbox.

On the bottom of the Manage Mobile Device Wizard page, click Perform a Remote Wipe to Clear Mobile Device Data and then click the Clear button. You can return to this page to confirm that the wipe has taken place.

Finally, you can manage the device through the Exchange Management Shell. A series of commands will allow you to wipe the device. To wipe the device through the Exchange Management Shell, you need to perform the steps outlined in Exercise 4.10.

EXERCISE 4.10

Wiping a Mobile Device

To wipe a mobile device through the Exchange Management Shell, follow these steps:

1. Get the identity of the device. To get the identity of the device that is used by user Jeff Smith, run the following command:

    ```
    Get-ActiveSyncDeviceStatistics-Mailbox "Jeff Smith"
    | FL Identity
    ```

2. After you have the device ID, you can send the wipe command. To wipe a device with the ID of WM Jeff.Smith11, use this command:

    ```
    Clear-ActiveSyncDevice -Identity WM "Jeff Smith11"
    ```

3. To confirm that the wipe was successful, use the following command:

    ```
    Get-ActiveSyncDeviceStatistics -Mailbox "Jeff Smith"
    ```

Summary

In this chapter, you examined the role of the Edge Transport server in your Exchange organization. The Edge Transport server, a new dedicated Exchange Server 2007 role, is responsible for routing and scanning all inbound and outbound SMTP messages to and from your Exchange organization. Although they cannot be made highly available through network load balancing or Microsoft Clustering Services, multiple Edge Transport servers should be deployed for redundancy with the required DNS entries made in your external DNS zones.

When configured for EdgeSync, Edge Transport servers will obtain all connector information and domain information from Hub Transport servers. Additionally, a specialized ADAM installation on the Edge Transport server will be used to contain all recipient information for your Exchange organization in a protected format, thereby increasing the security of your internal network resources. When EdgeSync is configured, you don't need to perform the otherwise time-consuming edge cloning process to keep Edge Transport servers configured identically.

Outlook 2007 is a pretty user-friendly electronic-messaging client with lots of bells and whistles, such as task and calendaring capabilities and contacts. When Exchange Server 2007 is installed properly on a server, a user can easily install Outlook on a workstation and begin using it without having to respond to a single installation query. The Exchange service Autodiscover should reduce the support burden for Outlook 2007 users by reducing the number of calls to the help desk and the confusion surrounding getting an initial Outlook profile configured when they first start using a new desktop computer.

Access to email away from the desktop is now important to most users. Exchange 2007 provides more options than ever before for that access. Users now have full access to their email wherever and whenever they need it, and the security of the network is maintained. Windows Mobile and ActiveSync users can be provided with access to their mailboxes from their mobile devices. They can synchronize their mailboxes from anywhere they can get cell phone or Wi-Fi signals.

Finally, although in some organizations POP3 and IMAP4 clients have been replaced completely by web-browser-based clients or Outlook, many organizations still use POP3 and IMAP4. Exchange continues to support these clients.

Exam Essentials

Understand routing.   Routing is significantly changed in Exchange Server 2007. Know how mail flow is affected by AD site configuration and how to change delivery behavior. Also, know how and when to create implicit SMTP connectors.

Understand EdgeSync.   The EdgeSync process is a huge benefit to any messaging administrator. By taking the time to configure the Hub Transport servers with the desired settings and going through the EdgeSync process, you can greatly increase the performance and security of your Exchange organization. Be sure to understand the steps and reasons for each step involved in the EdgeSync process.

Know where to go.   Many times on the exam, you will likely to be asked what configuration is needed to produce the required results. The Exchange Management Console has been completely redesigned to make it easier to navigate and get to tasks, but that doesn't mean it won't be difficult to remember later. Take the time as you review the material in this book to think about what types of configuration and management tasks you find yourself performing in each major node of the Exchange Management Console.

Review Questions

1. By default, what type of authentication mechanism does Outlook Web Access use on an Exchange Server 2007 Client Access server?

   A. Integrated Windows authentication

   B. Forms-based authentication with a self-signed SSL certificate

   C. Forms-based authentication with a third-party SSL certificate

   D. Digest authentication

2. You've recently completed the installation of a new Client Access server, and you now have users running Outlook Web Access on it. You've gotten a few complaints about users being unable to open any file or SharePoint servers from their OWA sessions. What are the most likely reasons for this problem? (Choose two.)

   A. The users do not have the proper credentials to access the locations.

   B. You did not configure any Allowed file or SharePoint servers for that OWA virtual directory.

   C. You configured the servers the users want to access as Blocked on that OWA virtual directory.

   D. You did not enable remote file and SharePoint server access on that OWA virtual directory.

   E. You did not change the default setting for unknown servers on that OWA virtual directory.

3. Your organization is not sure it needs to deploy a Client Access server in its new Exchange Server 2007 organization. Prior to having Exchange, all email was hosted by a third party and accessed using a variety of methods. Which of the following access methods would require that you have a Client Access server installed? (Choose all that apply.)

   A. Outlook 2007

   B. IMAP4 clients

   C. Outlook Web Access

   D. POP3 clients

   E. Outlook 2003

   F. Windows Mobile devices using ActiveSync

4. What problem is caused by the SSL certificate that Exchange uses by default for Outlook Web Access?

   A. The certificate cannot be validated against a trusted root; thus, users will receive warning messages.

   B. The certificate does not provide true SSL security and should be used only for testing forms-based authentication.

   C. The certificate expires 30 days after the Client Access server role is installed, thus rendering OWA inaccessible after that time.

   D. The certificate is valid only in North America, so clients in other locations will not be able to use OWA on that server.

5. To set the Default ActiveSync policy for all recipients, which of the following commands would you need to use?

   A. `get-Mailbox | put-CASMailbox -ActiveSyncMailboxPolicy (Get-ActiveSyncMailboxPolicy "Default").Identity`

   B. `get-Mailbox | set-CASMailbox -ActiveSyncMailboxPolicy (Get-ActiveSyncMailboxPolicy "Default").Identity`

   C. `get-Mailbox | set-ActiveSyncMailboxPolicy (Get-ActiveSyncMailboxPolicy "Default").Identity`

   D. `get-Mailbox | set-Mailbox -ActiveSyncMailboxPolicy (Get-ActiveSyncMailboxPolicy "Default").Identity`

6. Which of the following things does Autodiscover help to configure? (Choose all that apply.)

   A. The internal URL for the Availability service

   B. The external URL for the Offline Address Book (OAB)

   C. A user's home Mailbox server

   D. The Outlook Anywhere URL

7. What two actions must be completed before an IMAP4 client can connect to an Exchange Client Access server?

   A. The service must be set to automatic start.

   B. The service must be set to manual start.

   C. The service must be installed.

   D. The service must be started.

8. You have several Edge Transport servers for which you need to use edge cloning. Your Edge Transport servers are not configured to use EdgeSync. Which of the following commands would you need to use from the Exchange Management Shell to configure the answer file for the import process?

   A. `ImportEdgeConfig -CloneConfigData:"F:\CloneConfigData.xml" -IsImport $true -CloneConfigAnswer:"F:\CloneConfigAnswer.xml"`

   B. `ImportEdgeConfig -CloneConfigData:"F:\CloneConfigData.xml" -IsImport $false -CloneConfigAnswer:"F:\CloneConfigAnswer.xml"`

   C. `ExportEdgeConfig -CloneConfigData:"F:\CloneConfigData.xml"`

   D. `ExportEdgeConfig -CloneConfigData:"F:\CloneConfigData.xml" -IsImport $false -CloneConfigAnswer:"F:\CloneConfigAnswer.xml"`

9. Before installing Edge Transport servers in the DMZ and configuring EdgeSync on them, what ports should you ensure are open between the DMZ and the internal network? (Choose all that apply.)

   A. 50636

   B. 3389

   C. 25

   D. 50389

   E. 110

   F. 443

10. What PowerShell cmdlet will you need to use to create the edge subscription file?

    A. New-EdgeSubscription

    B. Configure-EdgeSubscription

    C. create-EdgeSubscription

    D. enable-EdgeSubscription

11. What software components must be installed on the server before the Edge Transport server role can be installed? (Choose all that apply.)

    A. PowerShell 1.0

    B. .NET Framework

    C. Internet Information Server (IIS)

    D. ADAM with SP1/Active Directory Lightweight Directory Services (AD LDS)

12. You have recently used a custom PowerShell script to create 2,500 new mailbox-enabled users for a special project your company is launching. You need these mailboxes to begin accepting SMTP messages from Internet hosts immediately. What should you do to make this happen?

    A. Use the start-EdgeSynchronization cmdlet.

    B. Right-click a Hub Transport server in the Exchange Management Console, and select the Synchronize Now item from the context menu.

    C. Use the refresh-EdgeSynchronization cmdlet.

    D. Select a Hub Transport server from the listing in the Exchange Management Console, and click the Refresh link.

13. You've recently completed the installation of a new Client Access server, and you now have users running Outlook Web Access on it. You've gotten a few complaints about users being unable to open any file or SharePoint servers from their OWA sessions. What are the most likely reasons for this problem? (Choose two.)

A. The users do not have the proper credentials to access the locations.

B. You did not configure any Allowed file or SharePoint servers for that OWA virtual directory.

C. You configured the servers the users want to access as Blocked on that OWA virtual directory.

D. You did not enable remote file and SharePoint server access on that OWA virtual directory.

E. You did not change the default setting for unknown servers on that OWA virtual directory.

14. Your Exchange Server 2007 organization consists of four servers in a single AD site: ServerA is a Mailbox server, ServerB is a Client Access server, ServerC is a Hub Transport server, and ServerD is a Mailbox server. When a user with a mailbox on ServerA sends a message from Outlook to a user on ServerD, which servers are involved in the message transfer process?

A. ServerA and ServerD only

B. ServerA, ServerB, and ServerD only

C. ServerA and ServerC only

D. ServerA, ServerC, and ServerD only

E. ServerA, ServerB, ServerC, and ServerD

15. When a remote POP3 client is connected to a Client Access server and sends an email message, which server roles could receive that sent message from the client? (Choose two).

A. Mailbox server

B. Client Access server

C. Unified Messaging server

D. Hub Transport server

E. Edge Transport server

16. What option do you need to change on a Hub Transport server to increase the length of time Exchange attempts to deliver a delayed message?

A. Outbound Connection Failure Retry Interval (Minutes)

B. Maximum Time Since Submission (Days)

C. Transient Failure Retry Interval (Seconds)

D. Transient Failure Retry Attempts

17. Once EdgeSnyc has been completely configured, how often will recipient data be synchronized?

    A.   Every 120 minutes

    B.   Every 240 minutes

    C.   Every 60 minutes

    D.   Every 180 minutes

18. Once you create the edge subscription file on an Edge Transport server, within what time frame must you complete the process on a Hub Transport server?

    A.   24 hours

    B.   12 hours

    C.   6 hours

    D.   1 hour

19. You have several Edge Transport servers for which you need to use edge cloning. Your Edge Transport servers are not configured to use EdgeSync. When you configure the edge subscription file, what file format will it be in?

    A.   Compiled HTML

    B.   Comma-Separated Values

    C.   Text

    D.   XML

    E.   Binary

20. What network protocol does the ADAM (AD LDS on Windows Server 2008) instance on an Edge Transport server use to perform replication with Active Directory after the EdgeSync process has been completely configured?

    A.   SMTP

    B.   LDAP

    C.   SNTP

    D.   IMAP4

    E.   RPC

Answers to Review Questions

1. B. By default, Outlook Web Access in Exchange Server 2007 uses forms-based authentication with a self-signed SSL certificate. You should procure and install a trusted third-party SSL certificate as soon as possible after installing a Client Access server.

2. B, E. By default, there are no file or SharePoint servers configured in the Allow or Block lists on the OWA virtual directory. Also, the default behavior is to block all unknown servers, so you have a situation where no file or SharePoint servers can be accessed by users on that OWA server.

3. B, C, D, F. All non-MAPI clients require the Client Access server in order to access mailboxes on an Exchange Server 2007 Mailbox server. Only Outlook MAPI over RPC can directly access the Mailbox server without needing a Client Access server.

4. A. The SSL certificate that OWA uses by default after the installation of the Client Access server role is self-issued and self-signed, and thus it has no validation chain that leads up to a trusted root authority. Users connecting to the OWA site will receive a warning of such, which will ultimately lead to confusion. You should replace this certificate as soon as possible, preferably before putting the Client Access server into production.

5. B. To apply the Default ActiveSync policy to all recipients in your organization, you would need to use the following command:

```
Get-Mailbox | Set-CASMailbox -ActiveSyncMailboxPolicy
(Get-ActiveSyncMailboxPolicy "Default").Identity
```

6. A, B, C, D. Autodiscover actually helps Outlook locate a number of different types of Exchange resources, including these:
   - User's home Mailbox server
   - Outlook Anywhere URL
   - URL (internal or external) for the Offline Address Book
   - URL (internal or external) for unified messaging
   - URL (internal or external) for the Availability service

7. A, D. You need to configure the IMAP4 server for automatic start so that it will start every time the Client Access server is rebooted. After that, you need to start the IMAP4 service manually for the first time before clients will be able to connect to the Client Access server via IMAP4.

8. B. The `ImportEdgeConfig -CloneConfigData:"F:\CloneConfigData.xml" -IsImport $false -CloneConfigAnswer:"F:\CloneConfigAnswer.xml"` command would be the correct one to use to create the XML answer file. The `-CloneConfigAnswer` item specifies that an answer file is to be used/created, while the `-IsImport $false` item specifies that this action is not an actual import and is thus an answer file creation process.

9. A, B, C. You will need to ensure that ports 25 (SMTP), 3389 (RDP), and 50636 (S-LDAP) are open on the firewall between the DMZ and the internal network. Port 25 is required for SMTP traffic, port 3389 is required for Remote Desktop connections for remote management, and port 50636 is required for secure LDAP replication between Active Directory and the ADAM instance running on the Edge Transport server.

10. A. To create the edge subscription file, you will need to use the Exchange Management Shell cmdlet `New-EdgeSubscription`. If you wanted to save the file to the F drive, your entry might look like this: `New-EdgeSubscription -FileName "F:\EdgeSubscription.xml"`.

11. A, B, D. As with all the other Exchange Server 2007 roles, you must have the .NET Framework and PowerShell 1.0 installed before you can install the Edge Transport server role. Additionally, you must have ADAM with SP1 or AD LDS for Windows Server 2008 installed for Edge Transport servers. The Exchange setup routine will prompt you to install any missing components it detects before allowing you to install the Edge Transport server.

12. A. You can use the `Start-EdgeSynchronization` cmdlet to force EdgeSync synchronization to happen outside its regular schedule.

13. B, E. By default, there are no file or SharePoint servers configured in the Allow or Block lists on the OWA virtual directory. Also, the default behavior is to block all unknown servers, so you have a situation where no file or SharePoint servers can be accessed by users on that OWA server.

14. D. All messages go through the Hub Transport server for delivery, so the message would go from the user's Outbox on ServerA, go through the Hub Transport on ServerC, and be delivered to the Inbox of the user's mailbox on ServerD.

15. D, E. POP3 client use the POP3 protocol to receive mail from the Client Access servers. POP3 clients send email messages with the SMTP protocol. The only two server roles that can accept SMTP-based messages are the Hub Transport and Edge Transport roles.

16. B. The Maximum Time Since Submission (Days) option specifies the timeout duration for messages. If a message is still in the queue to be delivered after the time configured for this setting has expired, the message is returned to the sender as undeliverable. The default setting is 2 days, but it can be set to any value from 1 to 90 days.

17. B. Recipient data will be synchronized every 240 minutes (every four hours) once EdgeSync has been completely configured.

18. A. You need to complete the EdgeSync process within 1,440 minutes (24 hours) of creating the edge subscription file on the Edge Transport server.

19. D. The edge subscription file is an XML file that can be easily opened in Notepad for inspection. You must manually transfer the resulting XML file to a Hub Transport server to complete the EdgeSync configuration process.

20. B. ADAM/AD LDS uses Lightweight Directory Access Protocol (LDAP) to communicate with Active Directory for replication. The LDAP session is SSL secured as it passes through the internal firewall for security.

Working with Recipients, Groups, and Mailboxes

MICROSOFT EXAM OBJECTIVE COVERED IN THIS CHAPTER:

✓ **Configuring Recipients and Public Folders**

- Configure recipients.

- Configure mail-enabled groups.

- Configure resource mailboxes.

- Configure public folders.

Among an administrator's most important tasks are creating and configuring Exchange recipients. A *recipient* is an object in Active Directory that references a resource that can receive a message. The resource might be a mailbox in a mailbox database, as in the case of a user, or a public folder in the public folder database that is shared by many users. No matter where an actual resource exists, a recipient object is always created in Active Directory and configured within Exchange.

In this chapter, we will discuss the types of Exchange recipients, their creation, and their properties. The main topics of this chapter are as follows:

- Configuring mailbox-enabled and mail-enabled user accounts

- Configuring mail-enabled groups

- Configuring mail contacts

- Configuring resource mailboxes

Configuring User Accounts and Mailboxes

Exchange has four basic types of recipients:

Users   A *user* is an Active Directory object that typically represents a person who uses the network. Once Exchange is installed and updates the schema, each user in the Active Directory can be mailbox-enabled, mail-enabled, or neither. A *mailbox-enabled user* has an associated mailbox in a mailbox database on an Exchange server. Each user's *mailbox* is a private storage area that allows an individual user to send, receive, and store messages. A *mail-enabled user* is one who has an email address but does not have a mailbox on an Exchange server. These users send and receive email by using an external ISP.

Groups   A *group* in Active Directory is like a container to which you can assign certain permissions and rights. You can then place users (and other groups) into that group and they automatically inherit the group's permissions and rights. Exchange uses the concept of mail-enabled groups to form distribution groups. Messages sent to a group are redirected and sent to each member of the group. Groups allow users to send messages to multiple recipients without having to address each recipient individually.

Contacts   A *contact* is a pointer object that refers to an email address for a non-Exchange recipient. Contacts are most often used for connecting your organization to foreign messaging systems such as the Internet. As an administrator, you would create contacts so that frequently used email addresses are available in the global address list (GAL) as real names. This makes it easier to send mail because users do not need to guess at cryptic email addresses.

Public folders   A *public folder* is like a public mailbox. It is a container for information to be shared among a group of people. Public folders can contain email messages, forms, word-processing documents, spreadsheet files, and files in many other formats. Public folders can also be configured to send information to other recipients.

In short, an Exchange recipient is any object that has an email address, whether it's a mailbox user, a public folder, a distribution group, or a contact. In this chapter, I'll examine all of those items except for public folders, which I'll discuss in Chapter 6, "Configuring and Managing Public Folders."

User mailboxes are the most common type of Exchange recipient object you'll be working with, so naturally it makes sense to begin our discussion of recipient management there. As you know by now, some drastic changes were made to user account and mailbox creation, configuration, and management processes with the release of Exchange Server 2007. In Exchange Server 2003, you could create user accounts and mailbox-enable them all within the Active Directory Users and Computers console. Those days are no more because many organizations asked for a wider separation of permissions between the administrators who take care of Active Directory and those who take care of Exchange. In smaller organizations, they are often the same person or group of people, but in other organizations they are completely separate groups of administrative staff. The end result is that you now have a disjointed user account and mailbox management processes with Exchange Server 2007. In the following sections, we will dive deep into user account creation and mailbox configuration.

Mailbox-Enabled vs. Mail-Enabled

Every user in an organization needs access to an Exchange-based mailbox in order to send and receive messages using the Exchange server. Two of the principal administrative tasks in Exchange are creating and managing these mailboxes. In Exchange Server 2007, a user with an associated mailbox is called a *mailbox-enabled user*. Mailbox-enabled users are able to send and receive messages as well as store messages on an Exchange server.

A *mail-enabled user* is simply a user who has an email address but who does not have a mailbox on an Exchange server. This means the user can receive email through their custom address but cannot send mail using the Exchange system. You cannot mail-enable a user during account creation. The only way to create a mail-enabled user is first to create a new user that is not mailbox-enabled and then to enable mail for that user.

Managing User Accounts and Mailboxes

Before you can have an Exchange mailbox, you must have an Active Directory user account. The mailbox is just an extension of the properties and attributes of the user account object. That fact is not new, having been the case since the introduction of Exchange Server 2000, but the means by which you create and manage mailboxes is new in Exchange Server 2007. Although you can still create and manage user accounts from the Active Directory Users and Computers console, which you'll explore in a bit, you must now create and manage all messaging-related options and functionality from within the Exchange Management Console (EMC) or Exchange Management Shell (EMS).

Creating Accounts and Mailboxes with the Exchange Management Console

In the Exchange Management Console, you will find mailboxes and their corresponding management options listed in the Microsoft Exchange ≻ Recipient Configuration ≻ Mailbox node, as shown in Figure 5.1.

FIGURE 5.1   Viewing Exchange mailboxes

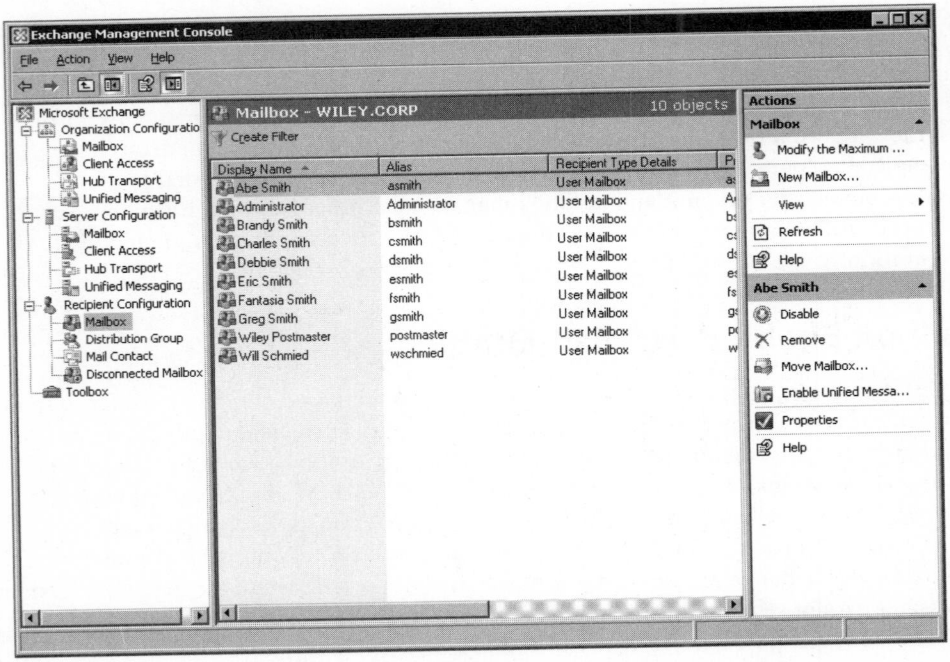

The default view is to list all recipients within the organization, although your initial view may not display them all, depending on how many mailboxes you've configured to be displayed. The default setting is 1,000 mailboxes, and it can be changed by clicking the Modify the Maximum Number of Recipients to Display link under the Mailbox options in the Actions pane on the right side of the Exchange Management Console.

You also have the option in the Actions pane to create a new mailbox. If you've selected a mailbox, then you have the following additional options: Disable, Remove, Move Mailbox, Enable Unified Messaging, and Properties. I'll examine all these options in the following sections.

Exercise 5.1 outlines the steps for creating a new user account that will be mailbox-enabled.

EXERCISE 5.1

Creating a New Mailbox-Enabled User

Follow these steps to create a mailbox-enabled user:

1. Click Start ➤ Programs ➤ Microsoft Exchange Server 2007 and then select Exchange Management Console.

2. Expand the Microsoft Exchange root object, expand the Recipient Configuration folder, and then click the Mailbox node.

3. In the Actions pane on the right, click the New Mailbox link. The New Mailbox Wizard starts.

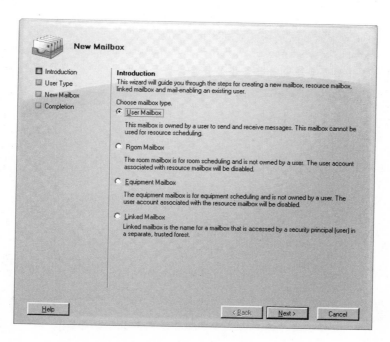

4. For the time being, you're going to be working only with user mailboxes—a mailbox that is assigned to an actual user. You'll examine resource mailboxes later in this chapter. Select the User Mailbox option, and click Next to continue to the User Type page, shown here.

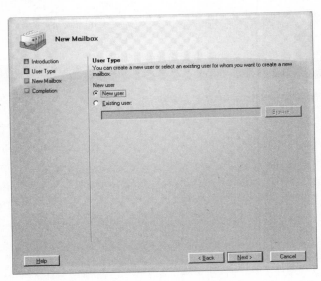

5. Since you want to create a new user account and mailbox-enable it in this exercise, select the New User option and click Next. The User Information page, shown here, appears.

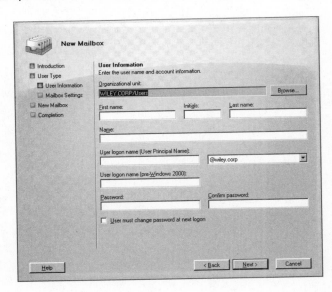

EXERCISE 5.1 *(continued)*

6. Enter all the required information: first name and last name, full (display) name, logon name, and password. If you do not want to create the user object in the default Users container of Active Directory, click the Browse button to open the Select Organizational Unit dialog box, shown here.

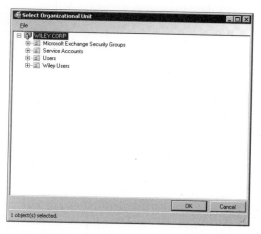

7. After you've correctly entered all the required information in the User Information page, click Next to continue to the Mailbox Settings page, shown here.

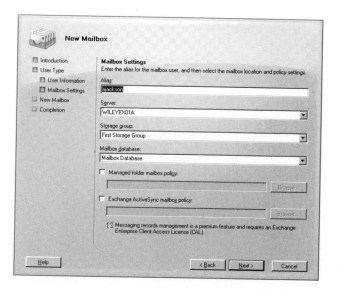

8. On the Mailbox Settings page, you will need to select the Mailbox server, storage group, and mailbox database in which the user's mailbox should be created. After making your selections, click Next to proceed to the New Mailbox page.

9. On the New Mailbox page, review all your configuration entries, and click New if you are satisfied. You can click Back to change any of the entries you made.

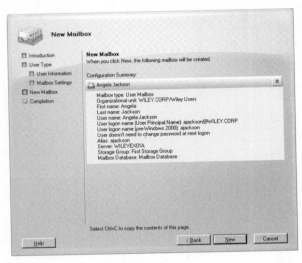

10. When you click New, the Completion page appears. As always, Exchange displays the PowerShell code it used to perform the user account and mailbox creation. Click Finish to close the wizard.

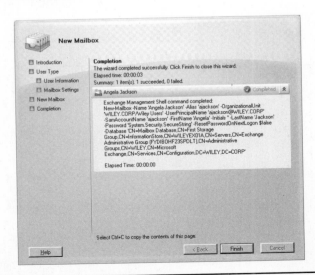

If you have user accounts that already exist in Active Directory but are not mailbox-enabled, you can perform the steps detailed in Exercise 5.2 to create a mailbox for those accounts.

Mailbox-Enabling an Existing User

Follow these step to mailbox-enable an existing user:

1. Click Start ➤ Programs ➤ Microsoft Exchange Server 2007 and then select Exchange Management Console.

2. Expand the Microsoft Exchange root object, expand the Recipient Configuration folder, and then click the Mailbox node.

3. In the Actions pane on the right, click the New Mailbox link. The New Mailbox Wizard starts.

4. Select the User Mailbox option, and click Next to continue to the User Type page.

5. On the User Type page, select Existing User and then click the Browse button to open the Select User dialog box, shown here.

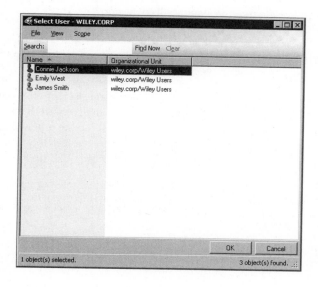

6. From the Select User dialog box, you will be able to select from a list of the user accounts in Active Directory that are not disabled and do not already have a mailbox assigned. Select a user account, and click OK to return to the User Type page. Click Next to go to the Mailbox Settings page.

7. On the Mailbox Settings page, you will need to select the Mailbox server, storage group, and mailbox database in which the user's mailbox should be created. After making your selections, click Next to proceed to the New Mailbox page.

8. On the New Mailbox page, review all your configuration entries and click New if you are satisfied. You can click Back to change any of the entries you made. When you click New, the Completion page appears.

9. As always, Exchange displays for you the PowerShell code it used to perform the user account and mailbox creation. Click Finish to close the wizard.

Remember that disabled Active Directory user accounts will not be displayed when you try to mailbox-enable an existing user account and you've selected the User Mailbox option.

Creating Accounts and Mailboxes with the Exchange Management Shell

Of course, anything you can do within the Exchange Management Console, you can do in the Exchange Management Shell as well. Creating mailbox-enabled user accounts and mailbox-enabling existing users are no exceptions. To create a new Active Directory user account that is mailbox-enabled, you need to use the new-Mailbox cmdlet within the Exchange Management Shell; the code would look something like this:

```
New-Mailbox -Name 'Erik Gustafson' -UserPrincipalName 'egustafson@wiley.corp' ↵
-SamAccountName 'egustafson' -FirstName 'Erik' -Initials 'ERG' -LastName ↵
'Gustafson' -ResetPasswordOnNextLogon $false -Database 'EX07SRV001\First ↵
Storage Group\Mailbox Database'
```

Figure 5.2 displays the output of this command.

FIGURE 5.2 Creating a new mailbox-enabled user account with the Exchange Management Shell

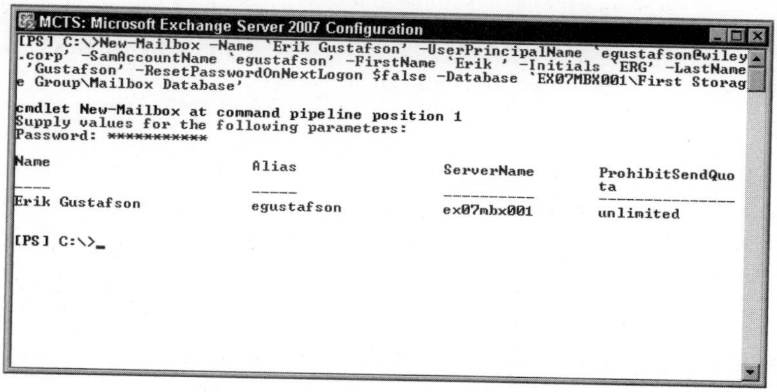

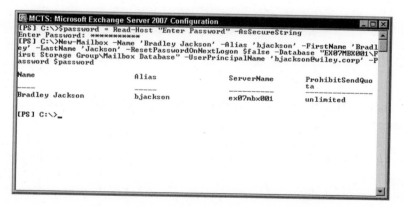

You cannot directly provide a string-based password using the -Password parameter. You have two options available to you in this scenario:

- Enter the password manually, as shown in Figure 5.2.

- Use a variable before entering the command(s) to create your mailbox-enabled user account(s), as illustrated in Figure 5.3. If you go this route, you could write a new PowerShell script that contains the line with the $password variable, thus prompting for the password to be used, and another line that uses the Import-CSV cmdlet to import a list of entries such as the password that should be passed to the new-Mailbox cmdlet.

FIGURE 5.3 Using a password variable to create mailbox-enabled user accounts with the Exchange Management Shell

For an example of how to create mailbox-enabled user accounts in Exchange Server 2007 using a CSV import file, see "Managing mailboxes in Exchange Server 2007," located at http://www.msexchange.org/tutorials/Managing-mailboxes-Exchange-Server-2007-Part1.html. Be sure to also check out the TechNet reference for the New-Mailbox cmdlet, located at http://technet.microsoft.com/en-us/library/aa997663.aspx.

If you need to mailbox-enable an existing Active Directory user account object, the code and process are much simpler because you don't need to worry about passwords and other account information. You'll use the Enable-Mailbox cmdlet, and the code would look something like this:

```
Enable-Mailbox -Identity HRadditz@wiley.corp
-Database 'EX07SRV001\First Storage Group\Mailbox Database'
```

Figure 5.4 displays the output of this command.

FIGURE 5.4   Mailbox-enabling an existing user account with the Exchange Management Shell

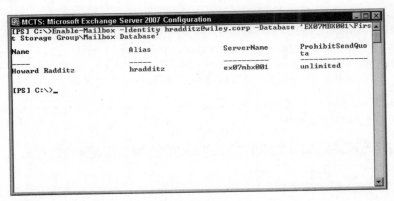

Creating Accounts with the Active Directory Users and Computers Console

Of course, you can still (and you will) create and manage user accounts from the Active Directory Users and Computers console. That's one of the main reasons for moving the messaging-specific functions back into the Exchange management tools, where they were in Exchange Server 5.5 and older versions. In larger organizations, some administrators will manage only Active Directory, and other administrators will manage only Exchange. In that case, the first group would be responsible for creating user accounts according to the organizational standards in place, and the second group would be responsible only for managing the messaging attributes of those user accounts. You might find it easier, however, if you manage both Active Directory and Exchange, to continue using whatever method you currently have in place for creating user accounts, such as using the dsadd command or VBScript, and then mailbox-enabling the accounts later using the PowerShell Enable-Mailbox cmdlet. You can call other commands from within a PowerShell script, and you could actually wrap the whole process into a single PowerShell script that uses some of the old and new methods available to you.

When you use the dsadd command, you can actually specify the initial password to be used by using the -pwd switch—something that can make scripting account creation easier than what the Exchange Management Shell currently offers with the new-Mailbox cmdlet.

As an example of what a typical dsadd command to create a new Active Directory user account might look like, consider the following example, which not only creates the new user account object but also assigns group memberships, a logon script, and a home folder:

```
dsadd user "CN=Smith\, Albert,OU=Sales,OU=Departments,DC=mycompany,DC=local"
-samid "amsith" -pwd *asmith042* -mustchpwd yes -fn "Albert" -ln "Smith"
-display "Smith, Albert" -desc "Sales"
-memberof "CN=Sales Group,OU=User Groups,DC=mycompany,DC=local"
-hmdrv "H:" -loscr "script.bat" -hmdir "\\SERVER42\SALES$\ASMITH"
-empid "42042" -dept "Sales" -company "My Company"
```

However, if you want to create and configure a new user account using the Active Directory Users and Computers console, then Exercise 5.3 has the steps you'll need to follow.

EXERCISE 5.3

Creating a New User Account in Active Directory Users and Computers

Create a new user by following these steps:

1. Log in to a domain controller or a computer that has the Windows Server 2003 SP1 or SP2 Administrative Tools installed. You will need the version that corresponds to the service pack level of your domain controllers, which must be at least Windows Server 2003 SP1 to install Exchange Server 2007 in the domain.

EXERCISE 5.3   *(continued)*

2.   Click Start ➢ Programs ➢ Control Panel ➢ Administrative Tools, and then select Active Directory Users and Computers. The Active Directory Users and Computers console opens.

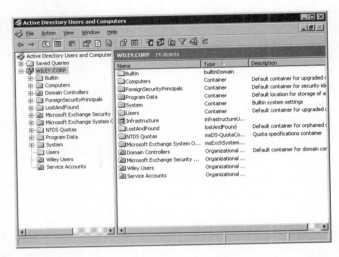

3.   Navigate to the organizational unit where you want the new user account to be created, and then click the New User button at the top of the console, as shown here.

4.   The New Object – User dialog box opens.

5. Enter all the required information: first name and last name, full (display) name, and logon name. Click Next to continue to the password page, shown here.

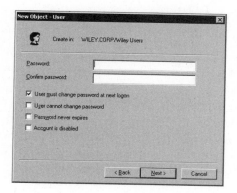

6. Enter the password for the user, and select any password-related options that are required. Click Next to go to the summary page.

7. On the summary page, click Finish to create the user if all the details displayed are correct. If you need to make any changes, click the Back button.

Of course, after the user account has been created, you can then mailbox-enable it from either the Exchange Management Console or the Exchange Management Shell as you learned earlier.

Modifying Mailbox-Enabled User Accounts

It only stands to reason that once you have mailbox-enabled users in your Exchange organization, eventually you're going to have to manage or modify their configurations. I'll discuss just that in the following sections.

Performing Basic Management from the Exchange Management Console

You do all mailbox management from the Exchange Management Console from the Microsoft Exchange ➤ Recipient Configuration ➤ Mailbox node, as shown previously in Figure 5.1. When a mailbox is selected in the middle of the console, you'll have mailbox-specific options that become available on the right side of the console, as shown in Figure 5.5. Of course, all these options are also available by right-clicking the appropriate mailbox and selecting them from the context menu.

FIGURE 5.5 Mailbox management options in the Exchange Management Console

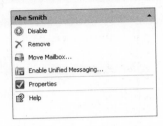

The Disable option is actually used to remove all messaging attributes from the user account object, not to disable the account itself. To disable the user account, and thus make it unable to be used for login, you'll need to visit the Active Directory Users and Computers console. If you click the Disable link in the Exchange Management Console, you'll be prompted to consider your action and whether you want to continue. You can accomplish the same effect using the Disable-Mailbox cmdlet.

The Remove option actually causes the Active Directory user account object to be deleted from Active Directory along with the corresponding mailbox. If you click the Remove link in the Exchange Management Console, you'll be prompted to consider your action and whether you want to continue. You can accomplish the same effect using the Remove-Mailbox cmdlet.

The Move Mailbox option allows you to move the selected mailbox to a different mailbox database on the same server or a different server within the Exchange organization. I'll talk in depth about moving mailboxes later in this chapter. Since I don't discuss unified messaging in this book, I won't look at the Enable Unified Messaging option.

Managing Mailbox Properties

When you click the last item available for a mailbox—that is, Properties—the mailbox's Properties dialog box opens to the General tab. I'll examine each tab and the configurable items found on each in the following sections.

General

The General tab of the mailbox's Properties dialog box, shown in Figure 5.6, contains all the basic identifying information about the mailbox. However, you can change only the display name field at the top of the tab and the Alias field at the bottom of the tab. You can also opt to have the mailbox hidden from view in the GAL, a common configuration for certain types of resource mailboxes or when an employee has been terminated from the organization but the mailbox has not yet been deleted.

FIGURE 5.6   The General tab of the mailbox's Properties dialog box

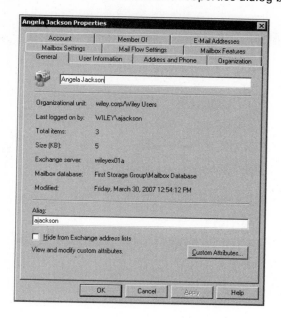

Other useful information you'll find on the General tab includes the following:

- The organizational unit in which the Active Directory user account is located

- The last user to log in to the mailbox

- How many items are contained within the mailbox and how large the entire mailbox is

- The Exchange Mailbox server, storage group, and database in which the mailbox is located

- The last time the mailbox properties were modified

By clicking the Custom Attributes button, you can access the Custom Attributes dialog box. Custom attributes are beyond the scope of the exam and will not be covered in this book.

User Information

The User Information tab of the mailbox's Properties dialog box, shown in Figure 5.7, allows you to configure basic information about the user who owns the mailbox. You can configure the following information on this tab:

- The user's first name, last name, and initials.

- A name that is displayed within Active Directory. (This setting does not impact the display name in the GAL.)

- A simple display name for the GAL that contains only ASCII characters and no Unicode characters.

- The user's web page.
- Notes about the mailbox and user that are not displayed anywhere else.

FIGURE 5.7   The User Information tab of the mailbox's Properties dialog box

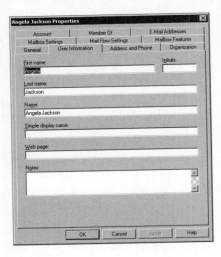

Address and Phone

The Address and Phone tab of the mailbox's Properties dialog box, shown in Figure 5.8, contains various information fields that you can configure with the user's address and contact information, such as their office, home, and mobile phone numbers.

FIGURE 5.8   The Address and Phone tab of the mailbox's Properties dialog box

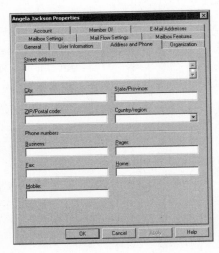

Organization

The Organization tab of the mailbox's Properties dialog box, shown in Figure 5.9, contains organizational information fields that you can configure about a user, such as title, company, and manager. The Direct Reports field is not directly configurable but is populated using reverse links from those Active Directory user account objects that have the Manager field configured.

FIGURE 5.9   The Organization tab of the mailbox's Properties dialog box

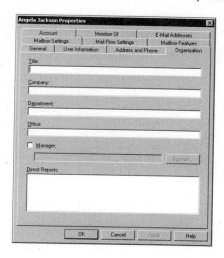

Mailbox Settings

The Mailbox Settings tab of the mailbox's Properties dialog box, shown in Figure 5.10, contains two items to configure: Messaging Records Management and Storage Quotas.

FIGURE 5.10   The Mailbox Settings tab of the mailbox's Properties dialog box

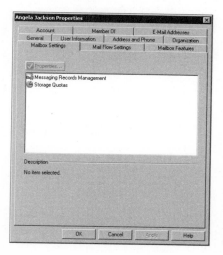

When you select the Messaging Records Management option and click the Properties button, the Messaging Records Management dialog box opens (see Figure 5.11). I will discuss these settings in Chapter 7, "Configuring Security, Compliance, and Policies."

FIGURE 5.11   The Messaging Records Management dialog box

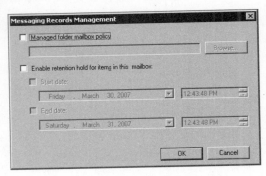

Back on the Mailbox Settings tab, you can select the Storage Quotas option and click the Properties button to open the Storage Quotas dialog box, shown in Figure 5.12. From here you can override the default storage quota limits put in place on the mailbox store that contains the user's mailbox. You might do this if a user is out of the office for an extended period of time and has no means to archive or delete messages. Alternatively, you might configure special storage quotas for certain users in your company, such as the chief information officer (CIO).

FIGURE 5.12   The Storage Quotas dialog box

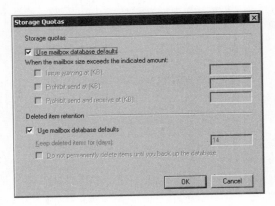

Mail Flow Settings

The Mail Flow Settings tab of the mailbox's Properties dialog box, shown in Figure 5.13, allows you to configure specific settings that determine how messages to or from this mailbox-enabled user are handled.

FIGURE 5.13   The Mail Flow Settings tab of the mailbox's Properties dialog box

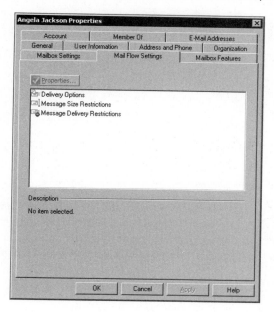

When you select the Delivery Options option and click the Properties button, the Delivery Options dialog box opens (see Figure 5.14). From here you can delegate the rights to send on behalf of this user to other mailbox-enabled users in Active Directory. This is commonly done to let administrative assistants send replies on behalf of their managers. Additionally, you can configure a forwarding location for the mailbox so that all messages received in the mailbox are delivered to another location, which can be another mailbox or a mail-enabled contact. You have the option of keeping a copy of the message in both mailboxes or just in the mailbox to which you are forwarding. Last, you have the option to limit how many recipients can be included in any message the user tries to send—this might be helpful if you have a user who keeps sending messages to large numbers of users; that is, spam.

FIGURE 5.14   The Delivery Options dialog box

You can select the Message Size Restrictions option (on the Mail Flow Settings tab) and click the Properties button to open the Message Size Restrictions dialog box, shown in Figure 5.15. From here you can configure mailbox-specific send and receive size limits that are applied only to the mailbox and that override those applied at the organizational or SMTP connector level.

FIGURE 5.15   The Message Size Restrictions dialog box

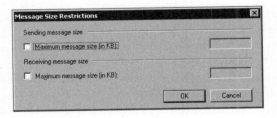

In the initial release of Exchange Server 2007, there was no location within the Exchange Management Console where you could view and/or configure message size restrictions. The default values for send and receive size for messages were unlimited, meaning that there was no limit in place and that it had to be set by using the Set-TransportConfig cmdlet. Service Pack 1 introduced a default 10MB limit and the ability to configure the setting in the Management Console.

> If you want to configure message size limits on a specific SMTP connector, you'll need to use either the Set-SendConnector cmdlet to change the limit on a send connector from its default value of 10MB or the Set-ReceiveConnector cmdlet to change the limit on a receive connector from its default value of 10MB. You can find out more information about using these cmdlets at http://technet.microsoft.com/en-us/library/aa998294.aspx and http://technet.microsoft.com/en-us/library/bb125140.aspx, respectively.

Select the Message Delivery Restrictions option (on the Mail Flow Settings tab) and click the Properties button to open the Message Delivery Restrictions dialog box, shown in Figure 5.16. From here you can configure which senders are allowed and which are not allowed to send messages to this mailbox. By default, there are no restrictions configured on the Message Delivery Restrictions dialog box.

FIGURE 5.16 The Message Delivery Restrictions dialog box

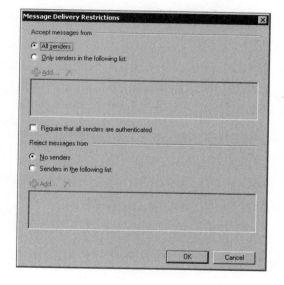

Mailbox Features

The Mailbox Features tab of the mailbox's Properties dialog box, shown in Figure 5.17, allows you to enable or disable specific Exchange features at the mailbox level. These options are similar to the Outlook Web Access segmentation options discussed in Chapter 4, "Configuring Connectors, Connectivity and Routing," except that they impact only the specific mailbox being configured. If an item has any other configurable properties, the Properties button will become available when the item is selected.

FIGURE 5.17 The Mailbox Features tab of the mailbox's Properties dialog box

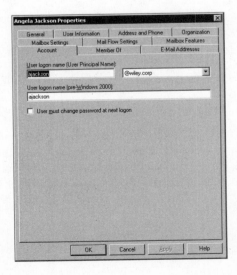

Account

The Account tab of the mailbox's Properties dialog box, shown in Figure 5.18, allows you to configure basic account information about the user. Items you can configure here include the User Principal Name logon name, the pre–Windows 2000 logon name, and whether the user must change their password at the next login attempt. Notice the inability to reset a user's password—that's still an action you'll definitely be performing from the Active Directory Users and Computers console.

FIGURE 5.18 The Account tab of the mailbox's Properties dialog box

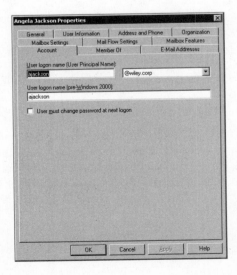

Member Of

The Member Of tab of the mailbox's Properties dialog box, shown in Figure 5.19, provides a read-only listing of all security and distribution groups of which the user is a member. Not listed on this tab is the built-in Domain Users group membership that all user accounts in the domain have by default. If you examined the user account from Active Directory Users and Computers, you'd see that group membership as well. To add a user to a distribution group, you'll need to work from the Distribution Group node of the Recipient Configuration node in the Exchange Management Console or use the Active Directory Users and Computers console. Non-mail-enabled security groups can be added only via the Active Directory Users and Computers console.

FIGURE 5.19   The Member Of tab of the mailbox's Properties dialog box

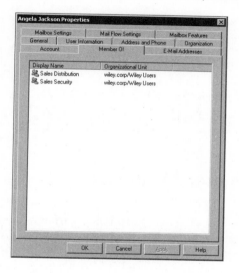

 Adding user accounts can also be accomplished by using scripting techniques such as the dsmod group command, VBScript, or the Add -DistributionGroupMember cmdlet.

E-Mail Addresses

The E-Mail Addresses tab of the mailbox's Properties dialog box, shown in Figure 5.20, allows you to add, remove, and edit email addresses assigned to the mailbox. The only type of email address that Exchange Server 2007 supports by default is SMTP, but you can configure custom types, if needed in your organization, by clicking the down arrow next to the Add button.

FIGURE 5.20   The E-Mail Addresses tab of the mailbox's Properties dialog box

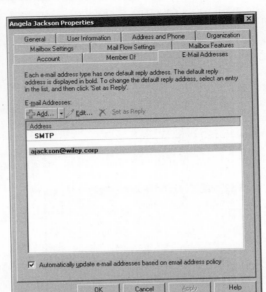

Working with Deleted Mailboxes

When you delete a user account that was mailbox-enabled or you disable a mailbox-enabled user account (which just removes the mailbox attributes from it), by default the mailbox itself is not deleted immediately. Deleted mailboxes are known as *disconnected* mailboxes until they are actually purged from the mailbox database. How long a mailbox remains disconnected from its user account is determined by the settings configured on the Limits tab of the mailbox database's Properties dialog box, as shown in Figure 5.21. By default, the value is 30 days to retain deleted (disconnected) mailboxes.

Refer to Chapter 2, "Installing Exchange Server 2007," if you want to review mailbox database configuration.

FIGURE 5.21   The Limits tab of the mailbox database's Properties dialog box

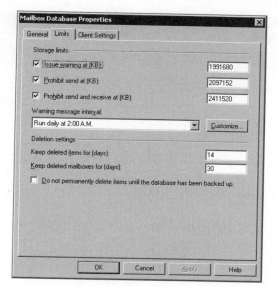

So, then, where do these disconnected mailboxes go and what can you do with them? The mailboxes are not visible under the Recipient Configuration ➢ Mailbox node of the Exchange Management Console, but they are visible in Recipient Configuration ➢ Disconnected Mailbox in the Exchange Management Console, as shown in Figure 5.22.

If you want to remove the mailbox permanently—to *purge* the mailbox, in Exchange-speak—you have two options: either wait for the 30-day default retention period to pass or use the Remove-Mailbox cmdlet. This is a two-step process, however, since you need some information about the disconnected mailbox that is not immediately available to you: the globally unique ID (GUID) of the mailbox. To get that information, you can use the Get-MailboxStatistics cmdlet to load a variable and then use the Remove-Mailbox cmdlet to purge the mailbox. Your code might look like the following:

```
$Temp = Get-MailboxStatistics | Where {$_.DisplayName -eq 'Connie Jackson'}
Remove-Mailbox -Database 'WILEYEX01A\First Storage Group\Mailbox Database'
-StoreMailboxIdentity $Temp.MailboxGuid
```

FIGURE 5.22 Viewing disconnected mailboxes

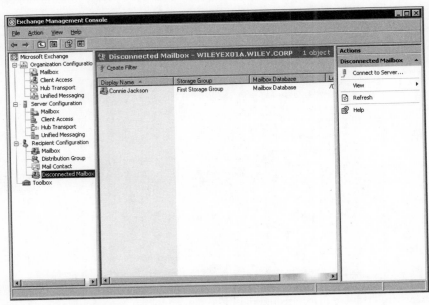

Figure 5.23 displays the output of this command. Of course, once you purge a mailbox, the only way to recover it is to restore a backup of the mailbox database that was created before the mailbox was purged.

FIGURE 5.23 Permanently deleting a disconnected mailbox with the Exchange Management Shell

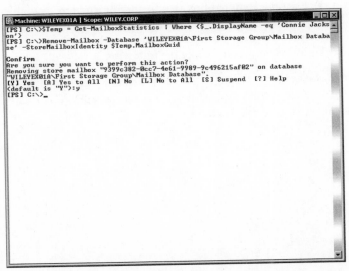

However, if you really did want to recover the mailbox—that is, to reconnect it to an existing Active Directory user account—you can easily do that from the Disconnected Mailbox node. Exercise 5.4 outlines the steps for reconnecting a disconnected mailbox.

> You won't be able to perform the steps in Exercise 5.4 unless you have previously removed or disabled a mailbox as just discussed. If you removed a mailbox and it is not yet shown as being disconnected, you may need to run Clean-Mailbox for the appropriate mailbox database to update the mailbox status.

EXERCISE 5.4

Reconnecting a Disconnected Mailbox

Follow these steps to reconnect a disconnected mailbox:

1. Click Start ➤ Programs ➤ Microsoft Exchange Server 2007 and then select Exchange Management Console.

2. Expand the Microsoft Exchange root object, expand the Recipient Configuration folder, and then click the Disconnected Mailbox node.

3. Select the disconnected mailbox and either right-click it and select Connect from the context menu or click the Connect link found in the Actions menu on the right. Either way, the Connect Mailbox Wizard starts.

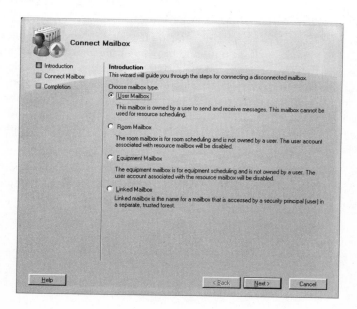

4. On the User Type page, select the type of mailbox you are reconnecting. For this exercise, click User Mailbox. Click Next to continue to the Mailbox Settings page, shown here.

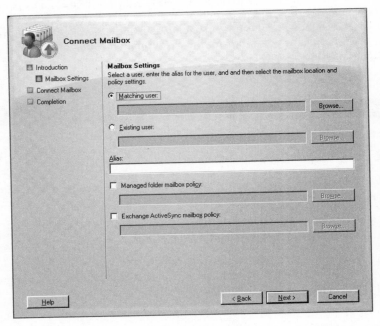

5. On the Mailbox Settings page, you will be able to select how to reconnect the mailbox. Use the Matching User option to browse to the user account to which the mailbox originally belonged, assuming that user account was not deleted. Use the Existing User option to browse to a list of all eligible Active Directory user accounts; that is, those that are not currently mailbox-enabled. You'll also need to configure an alias for the mailbox and select any policies that may need to be applied to the mailbox. After entering your selections, click Next to continue to the Connect Mailbox page.

6. On the Connect Mailbox page, you'll have the chance to review the configuration. If everything is correct, click the Connect button. If you need to make changes, use the Back button.

7. As always, Exchange displays the PowerShell code it used to perform the user account and mailbox creation. Click Finish to close the wizard.

If you look at the PowerShell code that Exchange uses to perform the reconnection action, you'll see the GUID and you'll notice how it would be difficult for you to remember it if you could find it in the first place. That code will be similar to the following:

```
Connect-Mailbox -Identity '39e169b0-5d41-4244-82e5-cb91152f505d'
-Database 'EX07MBX001 \First Storage Group\Mailbox Database'
-User 'bjackson' -Alias 'bjackson'
```

Managing Mail-Enabled User Accounts

As I discussed earlier, mail-enabled user accounts are those user accounts that have an email address configured but do not have a mailbox on an Exchange server. You might typically use a mail-enabled user account when you have a contractor coming into your organization for a period of time, and that contractor needs an Active Directory account but wants to receive all messages using their normal email account.

Creating Mail Users with the Exchange Management Console

Exercise 5.5 outlines the steps for creating a new user account that will be mail-enabled.

EXERCISE 5.5

Creating a New Mail-Enabled User

Follow these steps to create a new mail-enabled user:

1. Click Start ➢ Programs ➢ Microsoft Exchange Server 2007 and then select Exchange Management Console.

2. Expand the Microsoft Exchange root object, expand the Recipient Configuration folder, and then click the Mail Contact node.

3. In the Actions pane on the right, click the New Mail User link. The New Mail User Wizard starts.

4. Since you want to create a new user account and mail-enable it in this exercise, select the New User option and click Next. The User Information page appears.

5. Enter all the required information: first name and last name, full (display) name, logon name, and password. If you do not want to create the user object in the default Users container of Active Directory, click the Browse button to open the Select Organizational Unit dialog box.

6. After you've correctly entered all the required information on the User Information page, click Next to continue to the Mail Settings page.

EXERCISE 5.5 *(continued)*

7. On the Mail Settings page, you will need to select the mail alias, which is provided by default, and then create an external email address to be assigned to the mail-enabled user. Click the Edit button to open the SMTP Address dialog box. Enter the correct external SMTP email address and then click OK. Click Next to proceed to the summary page.

8. On the summary page, review all your configuration entries and click New if you are satisfied. You can click Back to change any of the entries you made. When you click New, the Completion page appears.

9. As always, Exchange displays the PowerShell code it used to perform the user account and mailbox creation. Click Finish to close the wizard.

If you have user accounts that already exist in Active Directory but are not mailbox-enabled or mail-enabled, you can perform the steps detailed in Exercise 5.6 to mail-enable those accounts.

EXERCISE 5.6

Mail-Enabling an Existing User

Follow these steps to mail-enable an existing user account:

1. Click Start ≻ Programs ≻ Microsoft Exchange Server 2007 and then select Exchange Management Console.

2. Expand the Microsoft Exchange root object, expand the Recipient Configuration folder, and then click the Mail Contact node.

3. In the Actions pane on the right, click the New Mail User link. The New Mail User Wizard starts.

4. Select the User Mailbox option, and click Next to continue to the User Type page.

5. On the User Type page, select Existing User and then click the Browse button to open the Select User dialog box.

6. From the Select User dialog box, you will be able to select from a list of the user accounts in Active Directory that are not disabled and do not already have a mailbox assigned. Select a user account, and click OK to return to the User Type page. Click Next to go to the Mail Settings page.

7. On the Mail Settings page, you will need to select the mail alias, which is provided by default, and then create an external email address to be assigned to the mail-enabled user. Click the Edit button to open the SMTP Address dialog box. Enter the correct external SMTP email address and then click OK. Click Next to proceed to the summary page.

8. On the summary page, review all your configuration entries and click New if you are satisfied. You can click Back to change any of the entries you made. When you click New, the Completion page appears.

9. As always, Exchange displays the PowerShell code it used to perform the user account and mailbox creation. Click Finish to close the wizard.

Creating Mail Users with the Exchange Management Shell

As you've seen countless times by now, anything you can do within the Exchange Management Console, you can do in the Exchange Management Shell as well. Creating mail-enabled user accounts and mail-enabling existing users are no exceptions. To create a new Active Directory user account that is mail-enabled, you need to use the new-MailUser cmdlet within the Exchange Management Shell. The code would look something like this:

```
New-MailUser -Name 'Alisha Smith' -Alias 'asmith1'
-OrganizationalUnit 'WILEY.CORP/Users'
-UserPrincipalName 'asmith1@WILEY.CORP'
-SamAccountName 'amsith1' -FirstName ' Alisha' -Initials '' -LastName 'Smith'
-ResetPasswordOnNextLogon $false
-ExternalEmailAddress 'SMTP:alisha.smith@externalcompany.com'
```

Figure 5.24 displays the output of this command.

FIGURE 5.24   Creating a new mail-enabled user account with the Exchange Management Shell

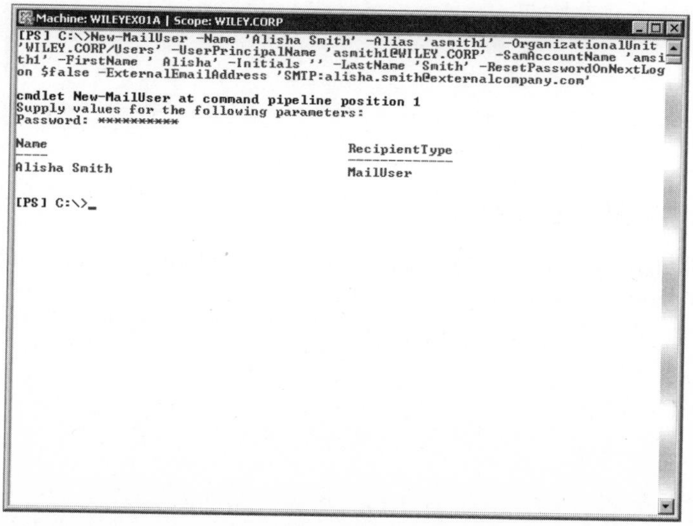

Of course, the same issue with passwords that you saw previously when creating mailbox-enabled user accounts from the PowerShell is still evident when creating mail-enabled user accounts.

If you need to mail-enable only an existing Active Directory user account object, the code and process is much simpler because you don't need to worry about messing with passwords. You'll use the `Enable-MailUser` cmdlet, and the code will look something like this:

```
Enable-MailUser -Identity 'WILEY.CORP/Wiley Users/Susan West' -Alias 'swest'
 -ExternalEmailAddress 'SMTP:susan.west@externalcompany.com'
```

Figure 5.25 displays the output of this command.

FIGURE 5.25   Mail-enabling an existing user account with the Exchange Management Shell

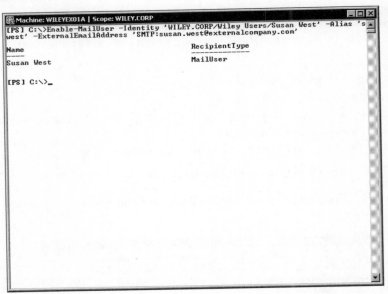

Managing Mail Users

If you have mail-enabled user accounts, or *mail users* as Exchange Server 2007 refers to them, then you're going to need to manage or change the configuration of some of them at some point in time. You'll examine the configuration options you have in the following sections.

Performing Basic Management from the Exchange Management Console

All mail user management is done from the Exchange Management Console from the Microsoft Exchange ➤ Recipient Configuration ➤ Mail Contact node, as shown in Figure 5.26. When a mail user is selected in the middle of the console, you'll have mailbox-specific options that become available on the right side of the console. Of course, all of these options are also available by right-clicking the appropriate mailbox and selecting them from the context menu.

FIGURE 5.26 Mail user management options in the Exchange Management Console

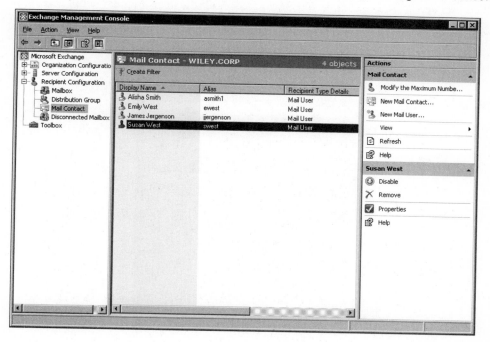

The Disable option is actually used to remove all messaging attributes from the user account object, not to disable the account itself. To disable the user account and thus make it unable to be used for login, you'll need to visit the Active Directory Users and Computers console. If you click the Disable link in the Exchange Management Console, you'll be prompted to consider your action and whether you want to continue. You can accomplish the same effect using the Disable-MailUser cmdlet.

The Remove option causes the Active Directory user account object to be deleted from Active Directory along with the corresponding mailbox. You can accomplish the same using the Remove-MailUser cmdlet.

The Move Mailbox option allows you to move the selected mailbox to a different mailbox database on the same server or a different server within the Exchange organization. I'll talk in depth about moving mailboxes in Chapter 9, "Monitoring and Reporting." Since we don't discuss unified messaging in this book, we won't look at the Enable Unified Messaging option.

Managing Mail Users' Properties

When you click the last item available for a mail user—that is, Properties—the mailbox Properties dialog box opens to the General tab, as shown in Figure 5.27. For the most part, these are the same tabs and options as discussed previously when working with mailbox-enabled user accounts. For that reason, I won't cover all the items in great detail here.

FIGURE 5.27 The General tab of the mail user's Properties dialog box

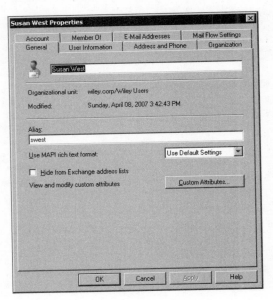

General

The General tab of the mailbox Properties dialog box contains all the basic identifying information about the mail user. However, you can change only the display name field at the top of the tab and the Alias field at the bottom of the tab. You can also opt to have the mail user hidden from view in the GAL if desired.

Other useful information you'll find on the General tab includes the following:

- The organizational unit in which the Active Directory user account is located

- The last time the mail user properties were modified

You can click the Custom Attributes button to open the Custom Attributes dialog box. Custom attributes are beyond the scope of the exam and will not be discussed in this book.

User Information

The User Information tab of the mailbox Properties dialog box allows you to configure basic information about the user account. You can configure the following information on this tab:

- The user's first and last name name, and initials
- A simple display name for the GAL that contains only ASCII characters and no Unicode characters
- The user's web page
- Notes about the mailbox and user that are not displayed anywhere else

Address and Phone

The Address and Phone tab of the mailbox Properties dialog box contains various information fields that you can configure with the user's address and contact information, such as their office, home, and mobile phone numbers.

Organization

The Organization tab of the mailbox Properties dialog box contains organizational information fields that you can configure about a user, such as title, company, and manager. The Direct Reports field is not directly configurable but is populated using reverse links from those Active Directory user account objects that have the Manager field configured.

Account

The Account tab of the mailbox Properties dialog box allows you to configure basic account information about the user. Items you can configure here include the user principal name logon name, the pre–Windows 2000 logon name, and whether the user must change their password at the next login attempt. Notice the inability to reset a user's password—that's still an action you'll definitely be performing from the Active Directory Users and Computers console.

Member Of

The Member Of tab of the mailbox Properties dialog box provides a read-only listing of all security and distribution groups of which the user is a member. Not listed on this tab is the built-in Domain Users group membership that all user accounts in the domain have by default. If you examined the user account from Active Directory Users and Computers, you'd see that group membership as well. To add a user to a distribution group, you'll need to work from the Distribution Group node of the Recipient Configuration node in the Exchange Management Console or use the Active Directory Users and Computers console. Security groups can be added only via the Active Directory Users and Computers console.

E-Mail Addresses

The E-Mail Addresses tab of the mailbox Properties dialog box allows you to add, remove, and edit email addresses assigned to the mailbox. The only type of email address that Exchange Server 2007 supports by default is SMTP, but you can configure custom types if needed in your organization by clicking the down arrow next to the Add button.

Mail Flow Settings

The Mail Flow Settings tab of the mailbox Properties dialog box allows you to configure specific settings that determine how messages to or from this mailbox-enabled user are handled. When you select the Message Size Restrictions option and click the Properties button, the Message Size Restrictions dialog box opens, allowing you to configure specific receive size limits that are applied only to this mail user and that override those applied at the organizational or SMTP connector level. You can select the Message Delivery Restrictions option and click the Properties button to open the Message Delivery Restrictions dialog box, allowing you to configure which senders are allowed and which are not allowed to send messages to this mail user. By default, there are no restrictions configured on the Message Delivery Restrictions tab.

Configuring Send As and Full Access Permissions

Many times the user account that is tied to a mailbox may not be the only one that needs to be able to send messages as that account (user). Some common examples of this scenario are departmental mailboxes, project mailboxes, and customer comment and suggestion mailboxes. Additionally, you might opt to configure Send As permissions instead of using the Outlook delegation process to allow a delegate to send as someone else, perhaps their supervisor. In these cases, no matter who is actually managing the messages within the mailbox, any replies or new messages from that mailbox appear to be from that mailbox and not the actual user sending the message. This requires a change to the Send As permission on the user account associated with the affected mailbox and can be performed from within the Active Directory Users and Computers console; however, most likely you will use the Exchange Management Console as outlined in Exercise 5.7.

EXERCISE 5.7

Configuring Send As Permissions on a Mailbox Using Exchange Management Console

Configure Send As permissions on a mailbox by following these steps:

1. Click Start ➤ Programs ➤ Microsoft Exchange Server 2007 and then select Exchange Management Console.

2. Expand the Microsoft Exchange root object, expand the Recipient Configuration folder, and then click the Mailbox node.

3. Right-click on the mailbox that you want to allow the user to send as, and choose Manage Send As Permission.

EXERCISE 5.7 *(continued)*

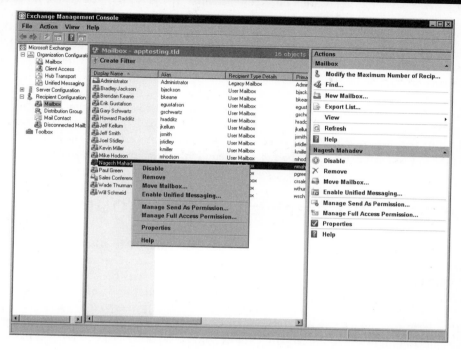

4. On the first page of the Manage Send As Permission Wizard, click Add and choose the user accounts that you want to assign the Send As permission to; then click Manage.

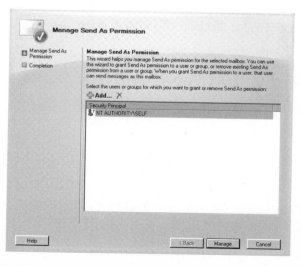

5. Review the changes made to the account and click Finish.

After you configure Send As permissions, it may take some time for them to become active because Active Directory replication must complete first. If you want to force the change to become effective immediately, you will need to stop and then restart the Microsoft Exchange Information Store service on the Mailbox server that houses the mailbox on which you configured the Send As permissions. Note that this action will interrupt all access to all mailboxes and public folders on that Mailbox server temporarily, so you'll likely not want to do that during production hours.

You may also need to provide full access to a mailbox to another user. You may do this for mailboxes shared for a department or perhaps an administrative assistant that needs access to their manager's mailbox. The steps to assign full access to a mailbox are identical to providing Send As permission, except that you choose Manage Full Access Permission rather than Manage Send As Permission from the Actions menu in the Exchange Management Console.

Configuring Mail-Enabled Groups

A group is an Active Directory object that can hold users and other groups. In the case of security groups, permissions can be assigned to a group and are inherited by all the objects in that group. This makes the group a valuable Windows security construct. Exchange Server 2007 also uses the group for another purpose. A group can be made mail-enabled and then populated with other mail- or mailbox-enabled recipients to make a *distribution group*, a term with which you may be familiar from earlier versions of Exchange Server. A group can contain users, contacts, public folders, and even other groups. When a message is sent to a mail-enabled group, the list of members is extracted and the message is sent to each member of the list individually. Groups are visible in the GAL if they are configured properly to be mail-enabled.

Windows Server 2003 supports two distinct types of groups. A security group can be assigned permissions and rights and be mail-enabled. A distribution group can be mail-enabled only.

Understanding Group Types and Scopes

Before we can begin any discussion on creating and managing groups, a discussion on group types and group scopes is necessary. You will need to have a good understanding of how the two different group types and three different group scopes work before you can effectively use groups in your Exchange organization.

Group Types

As mentioned previously, there are two types of groups within Active Directory: security groups and distribution groups. The names of these groups are fairly descriptive in regard to their usage.

Security Groups

Security groups, as the name implies, are used primarily to configure and assign security settings for those user and group objects placed within the group. An administrator can configure the desired rights and permissions of the group, and these settings will then automatically be applied to all group members without the administrator needing to configure the settings manually on the individual objects. As you can see, this is a benefit both from an administrative (less work to be done) and from an accuracy point of view (fewer chances of configuring individual object permissions incorrectly). Security groups can also be mail-enabled if desired, therefore allowing their mailbox-enabled and mail-enabled members to receive all messages that are sent to the security group.

Distribution Groups

Distribution groups, as their name implies, are used only for sending messages to a large number of objects without having to select each user, group, or contact manually. You can place all members of a specific department or geographical location into a distribution group and then send one message to the group that will be distributed to all members. Since distribution groups are not access control list (ACL)–enabled as security groups are, you cannot assign user rights or permissions to them.

You can change a distribution group into a security group at any time with no loss of functionality. However, changing a security group into a distribution group will result in the rights and permissions that have been configured on that group being lost. You will be warned of this when attempting to make the change.

Group Scopes

Within Active Directory, three different group scopes exist. The scope of the group determines who may be members of the group from an Active Directory standpoint. From an Exchange standpoint, the group scope determines who will be able to determine group membership when multiple domains exist within the organization.

Domain Local Groups

The membership of domain local groups is not published to the global catalog servers in the organization, thus preventing Exchange users from being able to determine the group membership of mail-enabled domain local groups outside the domain in which their user account is located. In most cases, if your organization consists of multiple domains, then you may opt not to use domain local groups for Exchange distribution purposes. The membership of domain local groups is dependent on the domain functional level of the domain but typically can include accounts from any domain in the forest.

Global Groups

Global groups are replicated to GCs. See the bottom of http://technet.microsoft.com/en-us/library/cc978012.aspx. The membership of global groups is dependent on the domain functional level of the domain but typically can include only those accounts from the same domain in the forest in which the group was created.

Universal Groups

Universal groups have their membership information published to the global catalog servers in the organization. This then allows Exchange users who are located in any domain in the forest to be able to determine the group membership of any group in the forest, regardless of the domain in which it has been created. The ability to create, and therefore use, universal groups is dependent on the domain functional level of the domain in that they can be created only when the domain functional level is at Windows 2000 native or Windows Server 2003. If your organization is capable of using universal groups, you'll want to consider their usage for Exchange distribution groups, especially when creating query-based distribution groups as discussed later in this chapter. Universal groups can contain members from any domain in the forest.

There is a lot more to be said about group scopes, including how the domain functional level impacts your ability to work with the different scopes. You can find more information about group scopes by searching the Windows Server 2003 help files for *group scopes* or by visiting this website: http://technet2.microsoft.com/windowsserver/en/library/79d93e46-ecab-4165-8001-7adc3c9f804e1033.mspx.

Managing Mail-Enabled Groups

Once you have mailbox-enabled and mail-enabled users (and perhaps mail contacts, as you'll examine later in this chapter), you'll likely want to start using mail-enabled groups to make messaging really work in your organization. Commonly, every department in an organization has at least one distribution group created for it, such as the Sales distribution group, which contains all members of the sales department. Although you can still create and manage groups from the Active Directory Users and Computers console as you'll explore here, you must now create and manage all messaging-related options and functionality from within the Exchange Management Console or Exchange Management Shell.

Creating Distribution Groups with the Exchange Management Console

In the Exchange Management Console, you will find distribution groups and their corresponding management options listed in the Microsoft Exchange ➤ Recipient Configuration ➤ Distribution Group node, as shown in Figure 5.28.

FIGURE 5.28   Viewing Exchange distribution groups

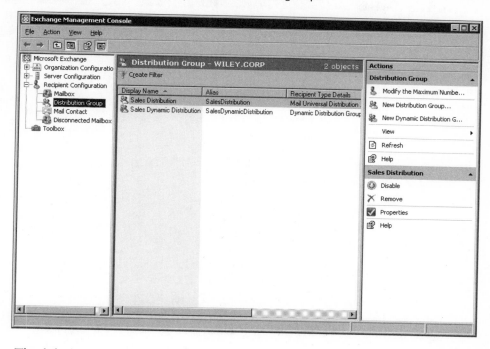

The default view is to list all distribution groups within the organization, although your initial view may not display them all, depending on how many mailboxes you've configured to be displayed. The default setting is 1,000 mailboxes and can be changed by clicking the Modify the Maximum Number of Recipients to Display link under the mailbox options in the Actions pane on the right side of the Exchange Management Console.

Other options you have in the Actions pane on the right side of the Exchange Management Console include creating a new distribution group and creating a new dynamic distribution group. If you've selected a distribution, then you have the following additional options: Disable, Remove, and Properties. I'll examine all these options in the following sections.

Exercise 5.8 outlines the steps for creating a new distribution group.

EXERCISE 5.8

Creating a New Distribution Group

To create a new distribution group, follow these steps:

1. Click Start ➢ Programs ➢ Microsoft Exchange Server 2007 and then select Exchange Management Console.

2. Expand the Microsoft Exchange root object, expand the Recipient Configuration folder, and then click the Distribution Group node.

3. In the Actions pane on the right, click the New Distribution Group link. The New Distribution Group Wizard starts.

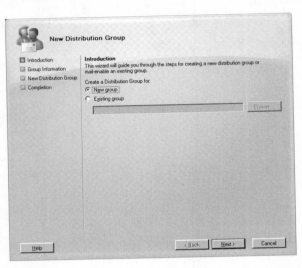

4. Select the New Group option, and click Next to continue to the Group Information page, shown here.

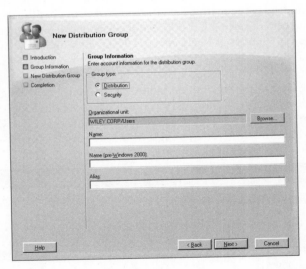

5. On the Group Information page, select Distribution and then select the location within Active Directory where the new group should be created by clicking the

EXERCISE 5.8 *(continued)*

Browse button. You'll also need to supply the group name from which the pre–Windows 2000 name and group alias will be automatically created, though you can change these values. Click Next to continue to the summary page.

6. On the summary page, review all your configuration entries and click New to create the new distribution group. If you need to change any entries, you can click the Back button.

7. As always, Exchange displays the PowerShell code it used to perform the preceding action. Click Finish to close the wizard.

If you have security groups that already exist in Active Directory but are not mail-enabled, you can perform the steps detailed in Exercise 5.9 to mail-enable those groups.

EXERCISE 5.9

Mail-Enabling an Existing Security Group

Follow these steps to mail-enable an existing security group:

1. Click Start ➤ Programs ➤ Microsoft Exchange Server 2007 and then select Exchange Management Console.

2. Expand the Microsoft Exchange root object, expand the Recipient Configuration folder, and then click the Distribution Group node.

3. In the Actions pane on the right, click the New Distribution Group link. The New Distribution Group Wizard starts.

4. On the Introduction page, select Existing Groups and then click the Browse button to open the Select Group dialog box, shown here. Note that the security group will need to be universal in scope in order to be displayed.

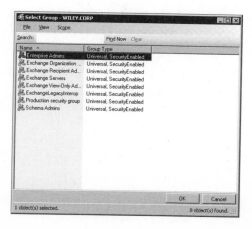

EXERCISE 5.9 *(continued)*

5. From the Select Group dialog box, you will be able to select from a list of the universal security groups in Active Directory that are not mail-enabled. Select a group, and click OK to return to the Introduction page. Click Next to go to the Group Information page.

6. On the Group Information page, the only value you'll be able to change is the alias. Click Next to continue to the summary page.

7. On the summary page, review all your configuration entries and click New if you are satisfied. You can click Back to change any of the entries you made. When you click New, the Completion page appears.

8. As always, Exchange displays the PowerShell code it used to perform the preceding action. Click Finish to close the wizard.

Even though every step of the process in Exercise 5.9 discusses distribution groups, by completing the wizard you are only mail-enabling the security group (adding an email address to it). You are not changing the group type from security to distribution, which is something that you can do from the Active Directory Users and Computers console if desired later.

Of course, you can create a new security group using the process outlined in Exercise 5.8 if you want. However, you'll need to manage the group membership of security groups from the Active Directory Users and Computers console.

Creating Distribution Groups with the Exchange Management Shell

Creating distribution groups from the Exchange Management Shell is a fairly simple task that you may want to undertake if a large number of groups must be created. To create a distribution group, you need to use the new-DistributionGroup cmdlet within the Exchange Management Shell. The code would look something like this:

```
New-DistributionGroup -Name 'Sales distribution group' -Type 'Distribution'
-OrganizationalUnit 'WILEY.CORP/Wiley Users'
-SamAccountName 'Sales distribution group' -Alias 'Salesdistributiongroup'
```

Figure 5.29 shows the output of this command.

FIGURE 5.29   Creating a distribution group with the Exchange Management Shell

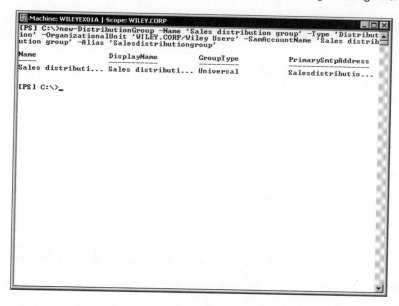

If you need to mail-enable only an existing universal group object, you'll use the `Enable-DistributionGroup` cmdlet and the code will look something like this:

```
Enable-DistributionGroup -Identity 'Sales security group'
```

Figure 5.30 shows the output of this command.

FIGURE 5.30   Mail-enabling an existing universal security group with the Exchange Management Shell

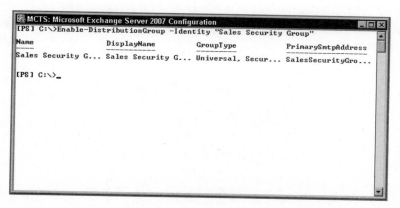

Creating Groups with the Active Directory Users and Computers Console

Of course, you can still (and you will) create and manage groups from Active Directory Users and Computers. That's the whole rationale behind moving the messaging-specific functions back into the Exchange management tools, where they were in Exchange Server 5.5 and older versions. In larger organizations, some administrators will manage only Active Directory while other administrators will manage only Exchange. In that case, the first group would be responsible for creating groups according to the organizational standards in place and the second group would be responsible only for managing the messaging attributes of those groups. You might find it easier, if you manage both Active Directory and Exchange, to continue whatever method you currently have in place for creating user accounts, such as using the dsadd command or VBScript, and then mail-enable the accounts later using the PowerShell Enable-DistributionGroup cmdlet.

Exercise 5.10 outlines the steps for creating a new group using Active Directory Users and Computers.

EXERCISE 5.10

Creating a New Group in Active Directory

Follow these steps to create a new group:

1. Log in to a domain controller or a computer that has the Windows Server 2003 Administrative Tools installed.

2. Click Start ➢ Programs ➢ Control Panel ➢ Administrative Tools, and then select Active Directory Users and Computers. The Active Directory Users and Computers console opens.

3. Navigate to the organizational unit in which you want the new group to be created, and then click the New Group button at the top of the console.

4. The New Object – Group dialog box, shown here, opens. In the Group Name field, type a name that represents the members of the group you are creating. Notice that Windows automatically fills in a group name that's compatible with pre–Windows 2000 versions.

5. Next you must choose a group scope. This determines at what level the group will be available in Active Directory—local, global, or universal. With Exchange Server 2007, it is usually best to make the group universal in scope so that it will be available throughout the organization. Otherwise, you may find that the group is limited by domain boundaries. Note that a domain must be running in the Windows 2000 native or Windows Server 2003 domain functional level to support universal groups.

6. Next you must define a group type. This determines whether the group is for security or distribution purposes. A *security group* can be made mail-enabled and used for distribution purposes. Recall that security groups can also be assigned permissions and made part of ACLs for resources. A *distribution group* is used for email purposes only and cannot be used for security purposes. Security groups can be converted later into distribution groups, with a loss of all configured ACL entries. Likewise, distribution groups can be converted later into security groups.

7. When you have entered all options, click OK to create the new group.

Even if you select distribution as the group type, no messaging configuration options are available in the group creation process. This is a direct result of the messaging attribute management being moved back to the Exchange Management Console in Exchange Server 2007.

Modifying Distribution Groups

It stands to reason that once you have distribution groups in your Exchange organization, you're eventually going to have to manage or modify their configurations. I'll discuss just that now.

Performing Basic Management from the Exchange Management Console

You do all distribution group management from the Exchange Management Console from the Microsoft Exchange ➤ Recipient Configuration ➤ Distribution Group node, as shown previously in Figure 5.28. When a distribution group is selected in the middle of the console, you'll have specific options that become available on the right side of the console. Of course, all these options are also available by right-clicking the appropriate mailbox and selecting them from the context menu.

The Disable option is actually used to remove all messaging attributes from the group object, not to disable the group itself since you can't disable a group in the same way that you would a user account. If you click the Disable link in the Exchange Management Console, you'll be prompted to consider your action and whether you want to continue. You can accomplish the same effect using the `Disable-DistributionGroup` cmdlet.

The Remove option causes the Active Directory group account object to be deleted from Active Directory along with the corresponding mail attributes. You can accomplish the same effect using the `Remove-DistributionGroup` cmdlet.

Managing Group Properties

When you click the last item available for a distribution—that is, Properties—the distribution group's Properties dialog box opens to the General tab. I'll examine each tab and the configurable items found on each in the following sections.

General

The General tab of the distribution group's Properties dialog box, shown in Figure 5.31, contains some the basic identifying information about the distribution. However, you can change only the display name field at the top of the tab and the Alias field at the bottom of the tab.

FIGURE 5.31   The General tab of the distribution group's Properties dialog box

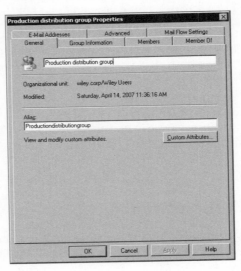

You can click the Custom Attributes button to open the Custom Attributes dialog box. Custom attributes are beyond the scope of the exam and will not be discussed in this book.

Group Information

The Group Information tab of the distribution group's Properties dialog box, shown in Figure 5.32, allows you to configure basic information about the distribution group. You can configure the following information on this tab:

- The group name, which is limited to 64 characters
- The pre–Windows 2000 group name, which is limited to 20 characters and cannot contain any of the following characters:

      ! # $ % ^ & - . _ { } | ~

- A user or security group who can manage the membership of this distribution group using Microsoft Outlook
- Notes about the distribution group that are not displayed anywhere else

FIGURE 5.32   The Group Information tab of the distribution group's Properties dialog box

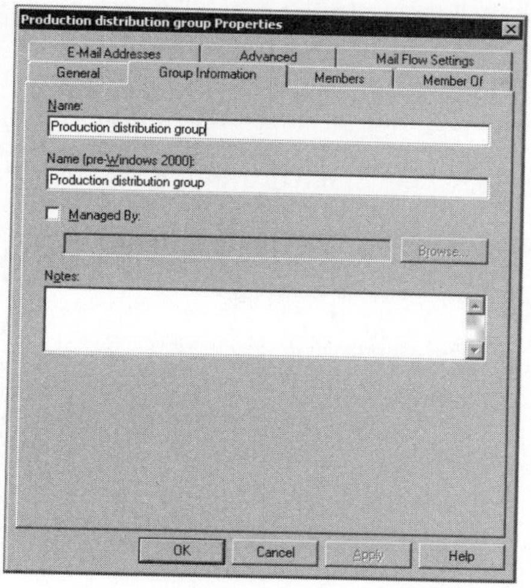

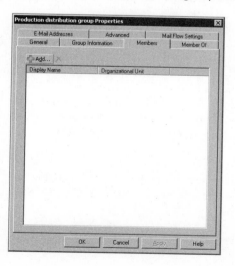

Members

The Members tab of the distribution group's Properties dialog box, shown in Figure 5.33, is likely where you'll spend the majority of your group configuration time. You can add new members by using the Add button. You can remove existing members by using the delete (X) button.

FIGURE 5.33   The Members tab of the distribution group's Properties dialog box

Member Of

The Member Of tab of the distribution group's Properties dialog box, shown in Figure 5.34, contains read-only information displaying a listing of any other groups of which this distribution group is a member. This information is automatically populated as you add this distribution to the Members tab of other distribution groups.

FIGURE 5.34   The Member Of tab of the distribution group's Properties dialog box

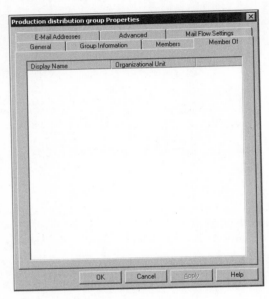

E-Mail Addresses

The E-Mail Addresses tab of the distribution group's Properties dialog box, shown in Figure 5.35, allows you to add, remove, and edit email addresses assigned to the distribution group. The only type of email address that Exchange Server 2007 supports by default is SMTP, but you can configure custom types, if needed in your organization, by clicking the down arrow next to the Add button. If multiple addresses exist, you can also configure one to be the default reply address using the Set as Reply button.

Advanced

The Advanced tab of the distribution group's Properties dialog box, shown in Figure 5.36, contains some useful configuration options that you'll likely find yourself using more than once for distribution groups.

FIGURE 5.35   The E-Mail Addresses tab of the distribution group's Properties dialog box

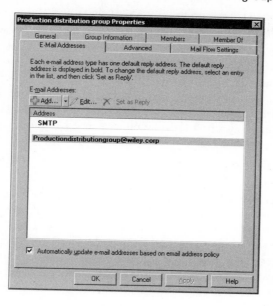

FIGURE 5.36   The Advanced tab of the distribution group's Properties dialog box

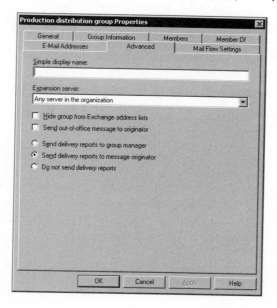

The following options can be configured on this tab:

Simple Display Name: This contains only ASCII characters and no Unicode characters.

Expansion Server: Whenever a message is sent to a group, the group must be expanded so that the message can be sent to each member of the group. A categorizer performs this expansion. The default choice is Any Server in the Organization. This choice means that the home server of the user sending the message always expands the group. You can also designate a specific server to handle the expansion of the group. The choice of a dedicated expansion server is a good one if you have a large group. In this case, expansion could consume a great amount of server resources, which can compromise performance of busy servers.

Hide Group from Exchange Address Lists: If you enable this option, the group is not visible in the GAL.

Send Out-of-Office Message to Originator: Users of Outlook clients can configure rules that enable the clients to reply to messages received automatically while the users are away from their office. When this option is enabled, users who send messages to groups can receive those automatic out-of-office messages from members of the list. For particularly large groups, the best practice is to not allow out-of-office messages to be delivered because of the excess network traffic they generate; however, it may be required in some situations to ensure that the sender of the email is aware when a group member is not going to respond to a request.

Send Delivery Reports to Group Manager: If you enable this option, notification is sent to the manager of the group whenever an error occurs during the delivery of a message to the group or to one of its members. Note that this option has no functionality if the group has not been assigned a manager.

Send Delivery Reports to Message Originator: If you enable this option, error notifications are also sent to the user who sent a message to the group.

Do Not Send Delivery Reports: If you enable this option, error notifications will not be sent.

Mail Flow Settings

The Mail Flow Settings tab of the distribution group's Properties dialog box, shown in Figure 5.37, allows you to configure specific settings that determine how messages to this distribution group are handled.

FIGURE 5.37   The Mail Flow Settings tab of the distribution group's Properties dialog box

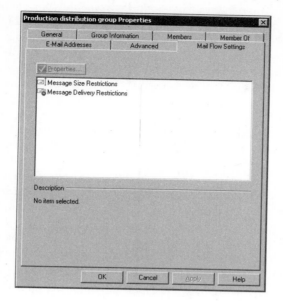

When you select the Message Size Restrictions option and click the Properties button, the Message Size Restrictions dialog box opens. From here you can configure distribution-group-specific receive size limits that are applied only to the distribution group and that override those applied at the organizational or SMTP connector level.

When you select the Message Delivery Restrictions option and click the Properties button, the Message Delivery Restrictions dialog box opens. From here you can configure which senders are allowed and which are not allowed to send messages to this distribution group. By default, there are no restrictions configured on the Message Delivery Restrictions dialog box.

Managing Dynamic Distribution Groups

Dynamic distribution groups were first introduced in Exchange Server 2003 as query-based distribution groups. One of the biggest problems with using static distribution groups in the past was the amount of work and time it took to maintain an accurate and up-to-date group membership. Dynamic distribution groups aim to correct that problem. As the name implies, a dynamic distribution group is a mail-enabled distribution group that has its membership defined by the results of an LDAP query that is made against the content of Active Directory.

The obvious advantage to using a dynamic distribution group is that it provides a way to configure the membership of a group dynamically from all Exchange recipients based on a configured LDAP query. You can create a query, for example, that might limit the membership of a group to those users who are part of the accounting department of your organization. By that same logic, you could also create a dynamic distribution group that specifies membership should be limited to those users, contacts, and distribution groups that are located in a specific building or in a specific geographical area (such as a state or city) within your organization. By being able to create, and change, the queries used to create these groups quickly, you save time and energy over maintaining larger standard distribution groups. Dynamic distribution groups are also much more accurate in their group membership because all the work is done by the results of the query you create.

As you might suspect by now, there is a trade-off to the power and flexibility that dynamic distribution groups provide. This trade-off comes in the form of increased loading on your global catalog servers. Each time an email is sent to a dynamic distribution group, the LDAP query you have configured must be run against the global catalog to determine the membership of the group.

Unlike query-based distributions in Exchange Server 2003, when you create a dynamic distribution group in Exchange Server 2007, you have a fairly small number of object attributes on which you can run queries. These attributes are as follows:

- State or province (from the Address and Phone tab of the object's Properties dialog box)
- Department (from the Organization tab of the object's Properties dialog box)
- Company (from the Organization tab of the object's Properties dialog box)
- Custom attributes 1–15 (from the General tab of the object's Properties dialog box)

Creating Dynamic Distribution Groups with the Exchange Management Console

In the Exchange Management Console, you will find dynamic distribution groups and their corresponding management options listed in the Microsoft Exchange ➤ Recipient Configuration ➤ Distribution Group node as shown previously in Figure 5.28.

Exercise 5.11 outlines the steps for creating a new dynamic distribution group.

EXERCISE 5.11

Creating a New Distribution Group

Follow these steps to create a new dynamic distribution group:

1. Click Start ➤ Programs ➤ Microsoft Exchange Server 2007 and then select Exchange Management Console.

2. Expand the Microsoft Exchange root object, expand the Recipient Configuration folder, and then click the Distribution Group node.

EXERCISE 5.11   *(continued)*

3. In the Actions pane on the right, click the New Dynamic Distribution Group link. The New Dynamic Distribution Group Wizard starts.

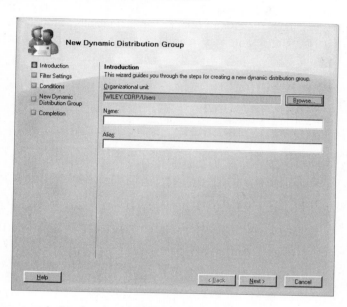

4. Enter the name and alias for the new dynamic distribution group, and click Next to continue to the Filter Settings page, shown here.

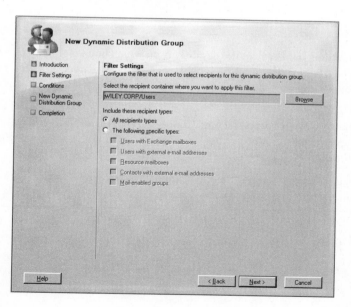

5. On the Filter Settings page, select the scope of the filter, such as a particular organizational unit or an entire Active Directory domain. You can also select which specific types of recipients you want to include, such as just user mailboxes or just mail contacts. Typically, you'll use the default selection to include all recipients. Click Next to continue to the Conditions page, shown here.

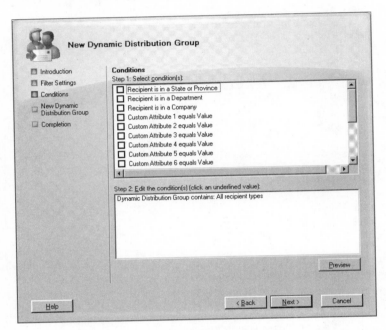

6. On the Conditions page, select the conditions on which you want to filter in the Step 1 area, such as State. Once you've selected a condition, you need to enter a value for this condition in the Step 2 area of the page. Once you've configured your desired conditions, click Next to continue to the summary page.

7. On the summary page, review all your configuration entries and click New to create the new dynamic distribution group. If you need to change any entries, you can click the Back button.

8. As always, Exchange displays the PowerShell code it used to perform the preceding actions. Click Finish to close the wizard.

Creating Dynamic Distribution Groups with the Exchange Management Shell

Creating dynamic distribution groups from the Exchange Management Shell is a fairly simple task, as you saw in Exercise 5.11. To create a new dynamic distribution group that uses the State condition you saw in Exercise 5.11, you need to use the New-DynamicDistributionGroup cmdlet within the Exchange Management Shell. The code will look something like this:

```
New-DynamicDistributionGroup -Name 'Sales dynamic distribution group'
-IncludedRecipients 'AllRecipients' -ConditionalDepartment 'Sales'
-OrganizationalUnit 'WILEY.CORP' -Alias 'Salesdynamicdistributiongroup'
-RecipientContainer 'WILEY.CORP/Wiley Users'
```

Figure 5.38 displays the output of this command.

FIGURE 5.38   Creating a dynamic distribution with the Exchange Management Shell

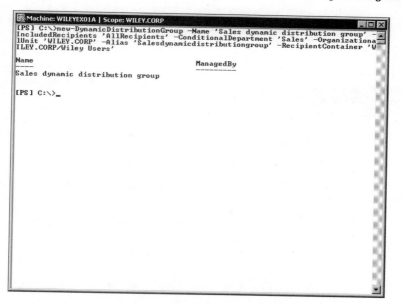

Modifying Dynamic Distribution Groups

It only stands to reason that once you have dynamic distribution groups in your Exchange organization, you're eventually going to have to manage or modify their configurations. I'll discuss just that now.

Performing Basic Management from the Exchange Management Console

You do all dynamic distribution group management from the Exchange Management Console from the Microsoft Exchange ➤ Recipient Configuration ➤ Distribution Group node, shown previously in Figure 5.28. When a dynamic distribution group is selected in the middle of the console, you'll have specific options that become available on the right side of the console. Of course, all these options are also available by right-clicking the appropriate mailbox and selecting them from the context menu.

Selecting the Remove option causes the Active Directory group object to be deleted from Active Directory along with the corresponding mail attributes. You can accomplish the same effect using the `Remove-DynamicDistributionGroup` cmdlet.

Managing Group Properties

When you click the only other item available for a distribution—that is, Properties—the distribution group's Properties dialog box opens to the General tab. I'll examine the tabs specific to dynamic distribution groups and the configurable items found on each in the following sections.

Filter

The Filter tab of the dynamic distribution group's Properties dialog box, shown in Figure 5.39, allows you to change the scope of the filter that defines the dynamic distribution group.

FIGURE 5.39   The Filter tab of the dynamic distribution group's Properties dialog box

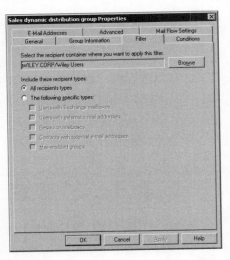

Conditions

The Conditions tab of the distribution group's Properties dialog box, shown in Figure 5.40, allows you to change the filter conditions that define the membership of the dynamic distribution group.

FIGURE 5.40   The Conditions tab of the distribution group's Properties dialog box

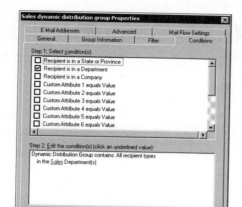

Once you've configured a filter scope and the conditions, you'll want to use the Preview button to open the Dynamic Distribution Group Preview dialog box, shown in Figure 5.41. From here, you'll be able to determine how effective your filter and conditions were at getting the recipients you wanted. It's at this time that the importance of maintaining accurate information in Active Directory for all Exchange recipients starts to become very clear to most administrators.

FIGURE 5.41   Previewing the membership of a dynamic distribution group

Configuring Mail Contacts

Mail-enabled contacts are commonly created to represent people outside your organization with whom users inside your organization commonly communicate via email. Another common implementation of mail contacts is to provide a means to route messages to mobile phones and pagers from monitoring programs via the Exchange infrastructure. Although you can still create and manage contacts from the Active Directory Users and Computers console, which you'll explore next, you must now create and manage all messaging-related options and functionality from within the Exchange Management Console or Exchange Management Shell.

Creating Contacts with the Exchange Management Console

In the Exchange Management Console, you will find contacts and their corresponding management options listed in the Microsoft Exchange ≻ Recipient Configuration ≻ Mail Contact node, as shown in Figure 5.42.

FIGURE 5.42   Viewing Exchange contacts

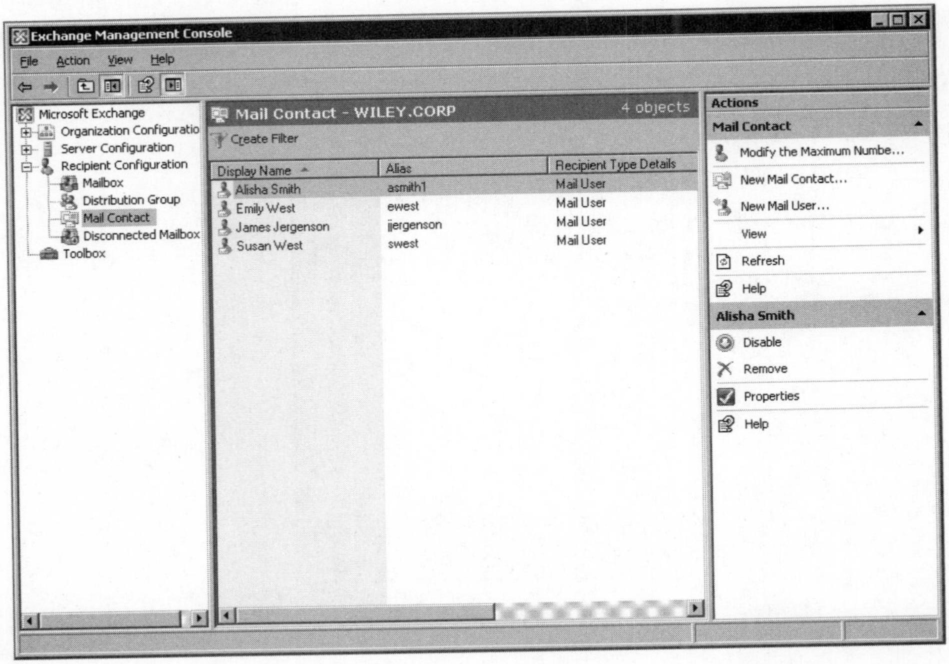

The default view is to list all contacts within the organization, although your initial view may not display them all, depending on how many mailboxes you've configured to be displayed. The default setting is 1,000 contacts, and it can be changed by clicking the Modify the Maximum Number of Recipients to Display link under the mailbox options in the Actions pane on the right side of the Exchange Management Console.

Other options you have in the Actions pane on the right side of the Exchange Management Console include creating a new mail contact and creating a new mail user (which we've already examined). If you've selected a contact, then you have the following additional options: Disable, Remove, and Properties. I'll examine all these options in the following sections.

Exercise 5.12 outlines the steps for creating a mail contact.

EXERCISE 5.12

Creating a New Mail Contact

To create a new mail contact, follow these steps:

1. Click Start ➢ Programs ➢ Microsoft Exchange Server 2007 and then select Exchange Management Console.

2. Expand the Microsoft Exchange root object, expand the Recipient Configuration folder, and then click the Mail Contact node.

3. In the Actions pane on the right, click the New Mail Contact link. The New Mail Contact Wizard starts.

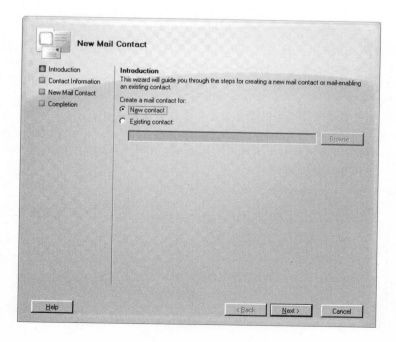

EXERCISE 5.12 *(continued)*

4. Since you want to create a mail contact in this exercise, select the New Contact option and click Next to go to the Contact Information page, shown here.

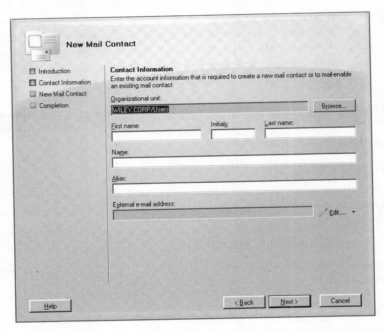

5. Enter all the required information: first name and last name, display name, alias, and external address. If you do not want to create the user object in the default Users container of Active Directory, click the Browse button to open the Select Organizational Unit dialog box. After you've correctly entered all the required information, click Next to continue to the summary page.

6. On the summary page, review all your configuration entries and click New if you are satisfied. You can click Back to change any of the entries you made. When you click New, the Completion page appears.

7. As always, Exchange displays the PowerShell code it used to perform the user account and mailbox creation. Click Finish to close the wizard.

If you have contact objects that already exist in Active Directory but are not mail-enabled, you can perform the steps detailed in Exercise 5.13 to mail-enable those contacts.

EXERCISE 5.13

Mail-Enabling an Existing Contact

Follow these steps to mail-enable an existing contact:

1. Click Start ➤ Programs ➤ Microsoft Exchange Server 2007 and then select Exchange Management Console.

2. Expand the Microsoft Exchange root object, expand the Recipient Configuration folder, and then click the Mail Contact node.

3. In the Actions pane on the right, click the New Mail Contact link. The New Mail Contact Wizard starts.

4. Select the User Mailbox option, and click Next to continue to the User Type page.

5. On the Introduction page, select Existing Contact and then click the Browse button to open the Select Contact dialog box.

6. From the Select Contact dialog box you will be able to select from a list of the contact objects in Active Directory that are not currently mail-enabled. Select a contact, and click OK to return to the Introduction page. Click Next to go to the Contact Information page.

7. On the Contact Information page you will be able to change only the alias and configure an external address. After you've correctly entered all the required information, click Next to continue to the summary page.

8. On the summary page, review all your configuration entries and click New if you are satisfied. You can click Back to change any of the entries you made. When you click New, the Completion page appears.

9. As always, Exchange displays the PowerShell code it used to perform the preceding action. Click Finish to close the wizard.

Creating Contacts with the Exchange Management Shell

To create a new mail contact using PowerShell, you need to use the New-MailContact cmdlet within the Exchange Management Shell. The code would look something like this:

```
New-MailContact -ExternalEmailAddress 'SMTP:rickjones@ exchangeexchange.com'
-Name 'Rick Jones'
-OrganizationalUnit 'WILEY.CORP/Wiley Users'
-FirstName 'Rick' -Initials 'RJ' -LastName 'Jones'
```

If you need to mail-enable only an existing Active Directory contact object, you'll use the Enable-MailContact cmdlet and the code would look something like this:

```
Enable-MailContact -Identity 'Danny Jones'
-ExternalEmailAddress 'SMTP:dannyjones@exchangeexchange.com'
```

Creating Contacts with the Active Directory Users and Computers Console

Of course, you can still (and you will) create and manage contacts from Active Directory Users and Computers. If you want to create and configure a new user account using the Active Directory Users and Computers console, then Exercise 5.14 has the steps you'll need to follow.

EXERCISE 5.14

Creating a New Contact in Active Directory Users and Computers

To create a new contact in Active Directory Users and Computers, follow these steps:

1. Log in to a domain controller or a computer that has the Windows Server 2003 Administrative Tools installed.

2. Click Start ➤ Programs ➤ Control Panel ➤ Administrative Tools, and then select Active Directory Users and Computers. The Active Directory Users and Computers console opens.

3. Navigate to the organizational unit in which you want the new user account to be created. Right-click the desired organizational unit, and select New ➤ Contact from the context menu. The New Object – Contact dialog box opens.

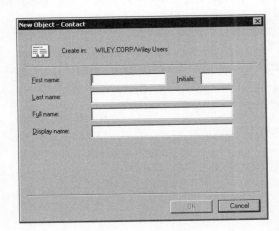

4. Enter all the required information: first name and last name, full name, and display name.

5. When you have entered all the information, click OK to create the new contact.

Of course, after the contact has been created, you can then mail-enable it from either the Exchange Management Console or the Exchange Management Shell, as you've learned previously.

Modifying Mail Contacts

It only stands to reason that once you have mailbox-enabled users in your Exchange organization, you're eventually going to have to manage or modify their configurations. I'll discuss just that now.

Performing Basic Management from the Exchange Management Console

You do all mail contact management from the Exchange Management Console from the Microsoft Exchange ➤ Recipient Configuration ➤ Mail Contact node, shown previously in Figure 5.42. When a mailbox is selected in the middle of the console, you'll have mailbox-specific options that become available on the right side of the console. Of course, all of these options are also available by right-clicking the appropriate mailbox and selecting them from the context menu.

The Disable option is actually used to remove all messaging attributes from the mail contact. If you click the Disable link in the Exchange Management Console, you'll be prompted to consider your action and whether you want to continue. You can accomplish the same effect using the `Disable-MailContact` cmdlet.

The Remove option causes the contact object to be deleted from Active Directory. You can accomplish the same effect using the `Remove-MailContact` cmdlet.

Managing Mailbox Properties

When you click the last item available for a mail contact, Properties, the mail contact's Properties dialog box opens to the General tab. I'll examine each tab and the configurable items found on each in the following sections.

General

The General tab of the mail contact's Properties dialog box, shown in Figure 5.43, contains all the information about the mail contact. You have the option to change the display name field at the top of the tab and the Alias field at the bottom of the tab. Additionally, you can opt to have the mailbox hidden from view in the GAL, change the MAPI settings, or configure the custom attributes.

FIGURE 5.43   The General tab of the mail contact's Properties dialog box

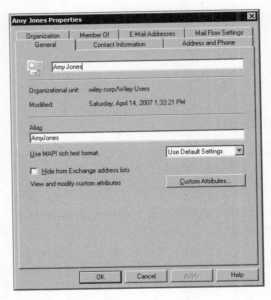

Contact Information

The Contact Information tab of the mail contact's Properties dialog box has the same basic configuration options for mailbox users as shown previously in Figure 5.7. You can configure the following information on this tab:

- The mail contact's first and last name, and initials.

- A name that is displayed within Active Directory. (This setting does not impact the display name in the GAL.)

- A simple display name for the GAL that contains only ASCII characters and no Unicode characters.

- The user's web page.

- Notes about the mailbox and user that are not displayed anywhere else.

Address and Phone

The Address and Phone tab of the mail contact's Properties dialog box has the same basic configuration options for mailbox users as shown previously in Figure 5.8. From here, you can configure the user's address and contact information, such as their office, home, and mobile phone numbers.

Organization

The Organization tab of the mail contact's Properties dialog box has the same basic configuration options for mailbox users as shown previously in Figure 5.9. From here you can configure organizational information fields about the mail contact, such as title, company, and manager. The Direct Reports field is not directly configurable but is populated using reverse links from those Active Directory user account objects that have the Manager field configured.

Member Of

The Member Of tab of the mail contact's Properties dialog box is a view-only listing of all groups that the mail contact is a member of, as shown previously for mailbox users in Figure 5.19.

E-Mail Addresses

The E-Mail Addresses tab of the mail contact's Properties dialog box, shown in Figure 5.44, allows you to add, remove, and edit internal and external email addresses assigned to the mail contact. The only type of email address that Exchange Server 2007 supports by default is SMTP, but you can configure custom types if needed in your organization by clicking the down arrow next to the Add button. Each mail contact must have at least one internal and one external email address associated with it to ensure proper mail flow.

FIGURE 5.44   The E-Mail Addresses tab of the mail contact's Properties dialog box

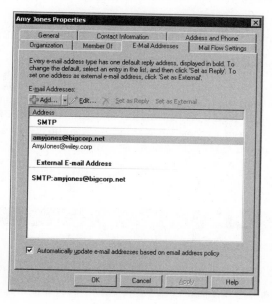

Mail Flow Settings

The Mail Flow Settings tab of the mail contact's Properties dialog box allows you to configure specific settings that determine how messages to this mail contact are handled, as shown previously for mailbox users in Figure 5.13.

When you select the Message Size Restrictions option and click the Properties button, the Message Size Restrictions dialog box opens. From here you can configure specific receive size limits that are applied only to the mail contact and that override those applied at the organizational or SMTP connector level.

When you select the Message Delivery Restrictions option and click the Properties button, the Message Delivery Restrictions dialog box opens. From here you can configure which senders are allowed and which are not allowed to send messages to this mail contact. By default, there are no restrictions configured on the Message Delivery Restrictions dialog box.

Configuring Resource Mailboxes

New in Exchange Server 2007 is the formal concept of a resource mailbox. Previously, many Active Directory and Exchange administrators had used resource mailboxes, but in reality they were no different from any other mailbox-enabled user account. In Exchange Server 2007, they have been designated as their own type of recipient and are handled slightly differently than normal users who have mailbox-enabled user accounts.

Creating Resource Mailboxes with the Exchange Management Console

In the Exchange Management Console, you will find mailboxes and their corresponding management options listed in the Microsoft Exchange ➤ Recipient Configuration ➤ Mailbox node, as shown previously in Figure 5.1. The basic management processes associated with resource mailboxes are the same as those for regular user mailboxes, so we'll examine only the differences in the remaining portion of this section.

Exercise 5.15 outlines the steps for creating a new user account that will be mailbox-enabled.

EXERCISE 5.15

Creating a New Resource Mailbox

To create a new resource mailbox, follow these steps:

1. Click Start ➤ Programs ➤ Microsoft Exchange Server 2007 and then select Exchange Management Console.

2. Expand the Microsoft Exchange root object, expand the Recipient Configuration folder, and then click the Mailbox node.

3. In the Actions pane on the right, click the New Resource Mailbox link. The New Mailbox Wizard starts.

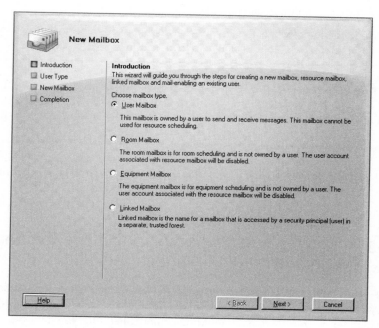

4. For this exercise, select the Room Mailbox option and click Next to continue to the User Type page.

5. Since you want to create a new user account and mailbox-enable it in this exercise, select the New User option and click Next. The User Information page appears.

6. Enter all the required information: first name and last name, full (display) name, logon name, and password. If you do not want to create the user object in the default Users container of Active Directory, click the Browse button to open the Select Organizational Unit dialog box.

7. After you've correctly entered all the required information, click Next to continue to the Mailbox Settings page.

8. On the Mailbox Settings page, you will need to select the Mailbox server, storage group, and mailbox database in which the user's mailbox should be created. After making your selections, click Next to proceed to the New Mailbox page.

9. On the New Mailbox page, review all your configuration entries and click New if you are satisfied. You can click Back to change any of the entries you made. When you click New, the Completion page appears.

10. As always, Exchange displays the PowerShell code it used to perform the user account and mailbox creation. Click Finish to close the wizard.

If you have disabled user accounts that already exist in Active Directory but are not mailbox-enabled, you can perform the steps detailed previously in Exercise 5.2 to create a mailbox for those accounts. You'll just need to select Room or Equipment for the mailbox type.

Remember that disabled Active Directory user accounts will not be displayed when you try to mailbox-enable an existing user account and you've selected the Room or Equipment option.

Creating Accounts and Mailboxes with the Exchange Management Shell

Creating resource mailboxes from the Exchange Management Shell is almost identical to the process you used previously to create mailbox-enabled users. You'll still need to use the new-Mailbox cmdlet within the Exchange Management Shell, but you'll need to configure an additional parameter: whether the mailbox is a room mailbox or whether it is an equipment mailbox. The code you would use would look something like this to create a room mailbox:

```
New-Mailbox -Name 'Sales Conference Room'
-UserPrincipalName 'crsales@WILEY.CORP'
-DisplayName 'Sales Conference Room'
-Database 'EX07MBX001\First Storage Group\Mailbox Database'
-Room
```

Figure 5.45 displays the output of this command. Notice that no password is required to be entered.

If you need to mailbox-enable only an existing disabled Active Directory user account object to be a resource mailbox, you'll use the Enable-Mailbox cmdlet. The code would look something like this for an equipment mailbox:

```
Enable-Mailbox -Identity 'Projector 1'
-Database 'EX07MBX001\First Storage Group\Mailbox Database' -Equipment
```

FIGURE 5.45 Creating a new resource mailbox with the Exchange Management Shell

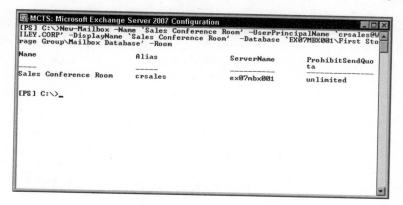

Modifying Resource Mailboxes

If you have resource mailboxes in your Exchange organization, then you're going to need to manage or modify their configurations at some point in time. I'll discuss just that now.

Performing Basic Management from the Exchange Management Console

You do all mailbox management from the Exchange Management Console from the Microsoft Exchange ➢ Recipient Configuration ➢ Mailbox node, shown previously in Figure 5.1. When a mailbox is selected in the middle of the console, you'll have mailbox-specific options that become available on the right side of the console. Of course, all these options are also available by right-clicking the appropriate mailbox and selecting them from the context menu.

The Disable option removes all messaging attributes from the user account object; it doesn't disable the account itself. To disable the user account and thus make it unable to be used for login, you'll need to visit the Active Directory Users and Computers console. If you click the Disable link in the Exchange Management Console, you'll be prompted to consider your action and whether you want to continue. You can accomplish the same effect using the Disable-Mailbox cmdlet.

The Remove option actually causes the Active Directory user account object to be deleted from Active Directory along with the corresponding mailbox. You can accomplish the same effect using the Remove-Mailbox cmdlet.

The Move Mailbox option allows you to move the selected mailbox to a different mailbox database on the same server or a different server within the Exchange organization. I'll talk in depth about moving mailboxes in Chapter 9. Since I don't discuss unified messaging in this book, we won't look at the Enable Unified Messaging option.

Managing Resource Mailbox Properties

When you click the last item available for a resource mailbox, Properties, the resource mailbox's Properties dialog box opens to the General tab. With the exception of a single new tab—the Resource Information tab—resource mailboxes have the same configuration properties available as any other mailbox-enabled account. To that end, I'll cover only the Resource Information tab here. If you need to review the other properties, refer to the section "Modifying Mailbox-Enabled User Accounts" earlier in this chapter.

Resource Information

The Resource Information tab of the mailbox's Properties dialog box, shown in Figure 5.46, contains configuration options that allow you to provide information to your users about the capabilities of the resource. The Resource Capacity field is used to specify how many people a room or resource can accommodate and accepts only numerical input ranging from 0 through 2,147,483,647.

FIGURE 5.46   The Resource Information tab of the mailbox's Properties dialog box

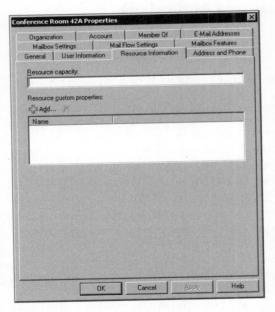

The Resource Custom Properties field allows you to select custom properties that have been defined in your Exchange organization and to indicate that this resource has those properties. Some examples might be selecting AV to indicate that the room has that capability or ConferenceCall to indicate that the room has a conference-call-quality phone. By default, there are no options configured to select from here, so you'll have to configure them yourself from the Exchange Management Shell by using the Set-ResourceConfig cmdlet. Unfortunately, if you simply use the cmdlet in its most basic format, you'll just end up setting the resource custom property to be the last entry you made. If you want to have multiple options available from which to select, you'll have to get more creative—perhaps using code similar to that displayed here, which reads in the current custom properties, adds some custom properties in an array, and then writes the array out:

```
$ResourceConfiguration = Get-ResourceConfig
$ResourceConfiguration.ResourcePropertySchema.Add("Room/AV")
$ResourceConfiguration.ResourcePropertySchema.Add("Room/TV")
$ResourceConfiguration.ResourcePropertySchema.Add("Room/Whiteboard")
$ResourceConfiguration.ResourcePropertySchema.Add("Room/ConferenceCall")
$ResourceConfiguration.ResourcePropertySchema.Add("Equipment/Projector")
$ResourceConfiguration.ResourcePropertySchema.Add("Equipment/Computer")
Set-ResourceConfig -Instance $ResourceConfiguration
```

Once you create resource custom properties, you'll be able to select them by clicking the Add button to open the Select Resource Custom Property dialog box, shown in Figure 5.47. Note that the custom properties will be shown only for the type of resource mailbox being configured, so you won't find the Projector option displayed when working with a conference room based on the PowerShell code used here. The configuration you end up with is limited only by your needs and imagination.

FIGURE 5.47   The Select Resource Custom Property dialog box

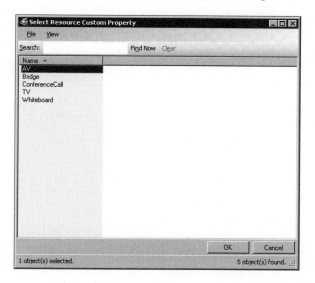

Once you've created and done basic configuration on your resource mailboxes, you should perform one additional step to enable their full functionality. To finish the configuration of the resource mailbox, you will need to log in to it via Outlook Web Access. Before you can do that, you'll need to change the password on the resource mailbox user account to one that meets your domain security policies and then enable it. You must perform these actions from the Active Directory Users and Computers console. Once you've done that, log in to the resource mailbox using Outlook Web Access and click the Options button. In the Options area, select the Resource Settings option on the left side of the window to display the advanced resource options you need to configure for the resource mailbox. Figure 5.48 and Figure 5.49 display these options.

FIGURE 5.48   First Section for Configuring resource mailbox properties via OWA

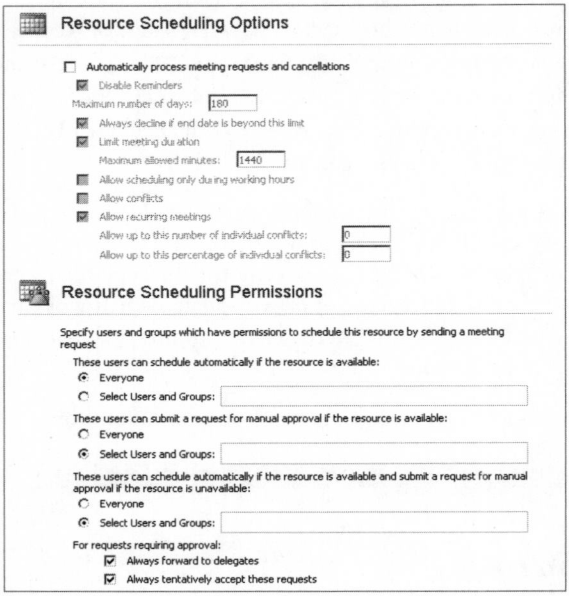

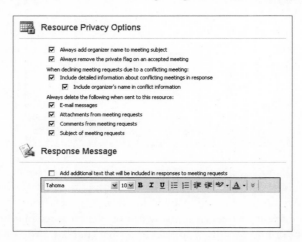

FIGURE 5.49   Second Section for Configuring resource mailbox properties via OWA

If you've ever used the Exchange Server 2003 Auto Accept Agent, many of these configuration settings will be familiar to you. If you haven't, they will still be useful to use as you configure how resources should behave when users send meeting requests to them. At the bare minimum, you need to enable the Automatically Process Meeting Requests and Cancellations option or else the resource won't accept any meetings. After making any changes, be sure to click the Save button at the top of the screen. Also, be sure to disable the associated user account once again after you've made your changes.

All of these settings are also available from the Exchange Management Shell by using the `Set-MailboxCalendarSettings` cmdlet. To do this from the EMS, you would just need to run the following cmdlet:

```
Set-MailboxCalendarSettings "Sales Conference Room"
-AutomateProcessing: AutoAccept
```

You can set AutomateProcessing to AutoAccept only on resource mailboxes.

There are over 30 available options to customize meeting processing using the `Set-MailboxCalendarSettings` cmdlet. Table 5.1 defines the parameters and when they would be used.

TABLE 5.1 Set-MailboxCalendarSettings Parameters

Parameter	Description
AddAdditionalResponse	If set to $true, it specifies that additional information would be sent when responding to meeting requests.
AdditionalResponse	Specifies the additional information to be included in responses to meeting requests.
AddNewRequestsTentatively	If set to $true, the Calendar Attendant puts the new calendar items tentatively on the calendar. If set to $false, only existing calendar items are updated by the Calendar Attendant.
AddOrganizerToSubject	If set to $true, specifies that the meeting organizer's name will be used as the subject of the meeting request.

TABLE 5.1   Set-MailboxCalendarSettings Parameters *(continued)*

Parameter	Description
AllBookInPolicy	If set to $true, specifies to automatically approve in-policy requests from all users. If it's set to $false, a resource delegate would need to approve all requests.
AllowConflicts	If set to $true, specifies to allow conflicting meeting requests.
AllowRecurringMeetings	Specifies whether to allow recurring meetings.
AllRequestInPolicy	If set to $true, specifies to allow all users to submit in-policy requests.
AllRequestOutOfPolicy	If set to $true, specifies to allow all users to submit out-of-policy requests.
BookingWindowInDays	Specifies the number of days in advance meetings are allowed to be booked.
BookInPolicy	Specifies a list of users who are allowed to submit in-policy meeting requests to the resource mailbox.
ConflictPercentageAllowed	Sets a conflict percentage threshold for recurring meetings. If the percentage of instances of a recurring meeting that conflict with other meetings exceeds this number, the recurring meeting request will be declined.
DefaultReminderTime	Specifies the default reminder time for the meeting requests.
DeleteAttachments	If set to $true, removes attachments from all incoming messages.
DeleteComments	If set to $true, removes any text in the message body of incoming meeting requests.
DeleteNonCalendarItems	If set to $true, removes all non-calendar items received by the mailbox.
DeleteSubject	If set to $true, removes the subject of incoming meeting requests.
DisableReminders	If set to $true, disables reminders for meetings in the mailbox.

TABLE 5.1   Set-MailboxCalendarSettings Parameters *(continued)*

Parameter	Description
EnableResponseDetails	If set to $true, includes the reasons for accepting or declining a meeting in the response email message.
EnforceSchedulingHorizon	If set to $true, recurring meetings that have an end date beyond the booking window will be rejected.
ForwardRequestsToDelegates	If set to $true, forwards incoming meeting requests to the delegates defined for the mailbox.
MaximumConflictInstances	Specifies the maximum number of conflicts allowed for recurring meetings.
MaximumDurationInMinutes	Specifies the maximum duration in minutes allowed for meeting requests.
OrganizerInfo	If set to $true, sends the organizer information when a meeting request is declined because of conflicts.
ProcessExternalMeetingMessages	If set to $true, processes meeting requests originating outside the Exchange organization.
RemoveForwardedMeetingNotifications	If set to $true, meeting forwarding notifications are moved to the Deleted Items folder after they are processed.
RemoveOldMeetingMessages	If set to $true, the Calendar Attendant removes old and redundant updates and responses.
RemovePrivateProperty	If set to $true, clears the private flag for incoming meeting requests.
RequestInPolicy	Specifies a list of users who are allowed to submit in-policy meeting requests to the resource mailbox. These meeting requests will still need to be approved by a delegate.
RequestOutOfPolicy	Specifies a list of users who are allowed to submit out-of-policy requests. These meeting requests will still need to be approved by a delegate.

TABLE 5.1   Set-MailboxCalendarSettings Parameters *(continued)*

Parameter	Description
ResourceDelegates	Specifies a list of users who are resource mailbox delegates.
ScheduleOnlyDuringWorkHours	If set to $true, allows meetings to be scheduled only inside work hours.
TentativePendingApproval	If set to $true, marks pending requests as tentative on the calendar. If set to $false, pending requests are marked as free.

 Real World Scenario

Using Resource Mailboxes

Although many administrators have been using the term *resource mailbox* for many years, why do you really need to go through the steps to create and configure one? In the past, before the Auto Accept Agent (or similar third-party methods), if you wanted to reserve a room or piece of equipment, you needed to make an entry on that item's calendar manually—assuming that it even had a mailbox.

By using resource mailboxes and taking the time to configure them fully and properly, you can empower users and resource managers to use and manage these resources as they need them. Do you need to book a conference room for a week that has AV and conference calling capabilities? It's no problem if the resource mailboxes that correspond to the conference rooms in your organization have been set up properly. Using resource mailboxes properly also ensures that there will be no conflicts for a resource—a conflicting meeting request that contains a resource will be denied by that resource mailbox. Since the scheduling information for a resource mailbox is available via free/busy, anyone trying to schedule a meeting or otherwise book any of these resources will be able to see when the desired resource is available before finalizing the meeting request, therefore ensuring that meetings won't have to be updated or rescheduled because the needed conference room or projector wasn't available at that time.

Take the time to implement and configure resource mailboxes properly for all your resources that can be reserved. When that's done, be sure to provide the user community with adequate instruction on how to leverage this functionality. When the dust settles, you'll have a happier, more productive user community, and your resource owners will be happy to be out of the business of scheduling resource usage.

Moving Mailboxes

Moving mailboxes is a constant process of adding servers and users, migrating users between databases, and maintaining Exchange database health; therefore, it is essential to understand how to move a mailbox or a group of mailboxes. Most likely you will come up with a plan or method for placing user mailboxes on Exchange servers. Some place them on a specific Mailbox server or in specific mailbox databases by department or geographical location. Others place them depending on job role or service level agreement (SLA) requirements. Regardless, moving mailboxes is simple enough that often entry-level Exchange administrators are tasked with completing the moves, either with the EMC or the EMS.

Using the Exchange Management Console

The most common, and familiar, method of moving mailboxes is to move them as needed using the GUI, in this case the Exchange Management Console. To move a mailbox from the Exchange Management Console, perform the steps outlined in Exercise 5.16.

EXERCISE 5.16

Moving a Mailbox with the Exchange Management Console

Follow these steps to move a mailbox using the Exchange Management Console:

1. In the Exchange Management Console, expand the Microsoft Exchange root object, expand the Recipient Configuration folder, and then click the Mailboxes node.

2. Select the mailbox to be moved in the center area of the window.

3. In the Actions pane on the right, click the Move Mailbox link. The Move Mailbox Wizard opens, as shown here.

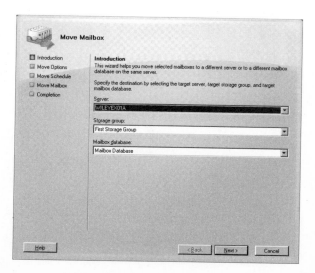

4. From the available options, select the destination Mailbox server, storage group, and mailbox database. After making your selections, click Next to continue to the Move Options page, shown here.

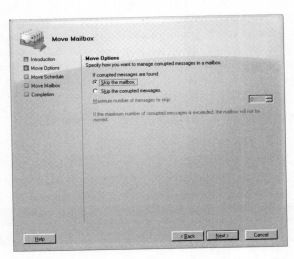

5. On the Move Options page, you'll be able to determine what to do if errors are encountered during the mailbox move process. Usually you'll want to leave the default selection of Skip the Mailbox selected, allowing you to return to the mailbox for a closer examination later if errors are encountered. After making your selection, click Next to continue to the Move Schedule page, shown here.

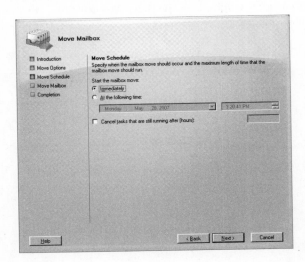

6. On the Move Schedule page, you will be able to start the move process immediately or schedule it for another time, such as off-peak hours when the user will likely not be using their mailbox. Selecting to move the mailbox at a later time is also commonly used when large groups of mailboxes are being moved. After making your selection, click Next to continue to the Move Mailbox page, shown here.

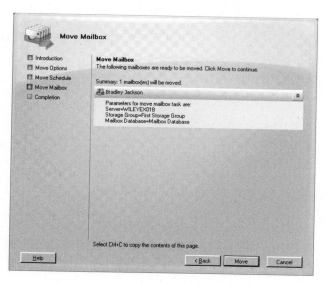

7. The Move Mailbox page summarizes your choices. Click Move to start or schedule the move process. Click Back if you need to make any changes to your selections.

8. If the move was set to occur immediately, you will be presented with the Completion page within a few minutes. Otherwise, the Completion page will appear after the scheduled move event. Click Finish to close the Move Mailbox Wizard.

Using the Exchange Management Shell

Of course, you can also perform the mailbox move process from the Exchange Management Shell, but the ease or difficulty of doing so depends on the number of mailboxes to be moved. If you are moving only a single mailbox, the process is simple and uses the Move-Mailbox cmdlet with no piped input, such as the following command to move the mailbox for James Smith (jsmith) to the default mailbox database on the server named wileyex01a:

```
Move-Mailbox jsmith
-TargetDatabase "WILEYEX01A\First Storage Group\Mailbox Database"
```

Figure 5.50 illustrates the output you'll see from this process.

FIGURE 5.50 Moving a mailbox from the Exchange Management Shell

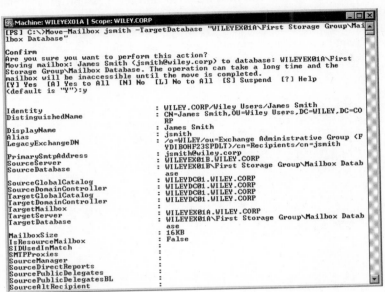

As you can see, all you needed to know was some identifying information about the mailbox to be moved, such as the alias, the user principal name or email address, and the destination location into which the mailbox should be moved. For the destination, you will need to specify at least the storage group name and the mailbox database name for same-server moves. If the move spans different servers, you'll need to provide the destination server name as well, as shown in the example.

This discussion of moving mailboxes from the Exchange Management Shell assumes the move is taking place within the same forest. For more advanced mailbox move operations, see the TechNet article at http://technet.microsoft.com/en-us/library/bb124797.aspx.

If you want to move multiple mailboxes from the Exchange Management Shell, you have a few different options available to you, depending on what you want to accomplish. If, for example, you wanted to move all the mailboxes for users with a last name of Jackson from one mailbox database to another, you could use a command similar to the following:

```
Get-Mailbox -Filter {alias -like "*jackson"} | Move-Mailbox
-TargetDatabase "WILEYEX01A\First Storage Group\Mailbox Database"
```

Figure 5.51 shows the output of this command. Notice how you were able to specify the mailboxes to be moved by using the Get-Mailbox cmdlet with a filter set on the alias. Once the list of mailboxes to move was available, the output was then piped to the Move-Mailbox cmdlet as input for the identity of the mailboxes to be moved.

FIGURE 5.51   Moving two mailboxes from the Exchange Command Shell

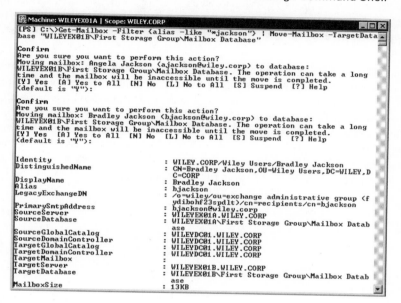

Moving mailboxes using the EMS is extremely powerful tool; the following are some of the common options used with the Get-Mailbox cmdlet:

- The -BadItemLimit parameter specifies how many failed items are allowed before the mailbox will be skipped for moving. An example of this is as follows: Move-Mailbox jsmith -TargetDatabase "WILEYEX01A\First Storage Group\Mailbox Database" -BadItemLimit 10.

- If the mailbox being moved is larger than allowed in the destination mailbox database, the move will fail unless you use the -MailboxSizeLimitOptions PreserveSource parameter. This will allow the move to succeed and the mailbox can be configured to have the same size limit as originally configured in the source mailbox database.

- To keep the recipient policies on the mailbox that existed in the source mailbox database, you'll need to use the -IgnorePolicyMatch $true option as part of the Move-Mailbox cmdlet.

- The SourceForestCredential <PSCredential> and SourceForestGlobalCatalog <Fqdn> parameters are used only when migrating mailboxes between Active Directory forests. A trust must exist between the forests and appropriate administrative permissions must be in place.

- The `SourceMailboxCleanupOptions` parameter is also used for cross-forest migrations and enables an administrator to delete the source account or mailbox or even associate a source account or contact with the destination mailbox.

- The `ConfigurationOnly` parameter is used to move a mailbox from one database to another database without attempting to copy the data in the mailbox. This is often used during a disaster recovery scenario when you are going to return service to the end users and at a later time restore mailbox data. When this is done, Office Outlook 2007 clients are able to use Autodiscover to reconfigure and connect to the new mailbox location.

- The `IgnoreRuleLimitErrors` switch should be specified when moving mailboxes from Exchange 2007 back to Exchange 2000 or 2003. In these previous versions of Exchange, mailboxes rules were limited to 32KB in each mailbox. Exchange 2007 by default allows for 64KB of rule storage in each mailbox; however, with additional configuration the limit can be set up to 256KB. Moving a mailbox to a previous version of Exchange will fail if the rules exceed the 32KB limit. In order to successfully move a mailbox without having the user manually delete rules, specifying this parameter will delete all rules to ensure a successful mailbox move.

Summary

Recipients are Active Directory objects that reference resources that can receive messages. In this chapter, I discussed three main types of recipients:

- Users
- Groups
- Contacts

A user is an Active Directory object that usually represents a person with an Exchange mailbox. A mailbox-enabled user has an associated mailbox in a mailbox database on an Exchange server. Each user mailbox is a private storage area that allows an individual user to send, receive, and store messages. A mail-enabled user is one who has an email address and can receive, but not send, messages.

A group is a container into which you can place other recipients. Recipients in a group automatically inherit that group's permissions and rights. Exchange uses mail-enabled groups to form distribution lists. Messages sent to a group are redirected and sent to each member of the group. Groups allow users to send messages to multiple recipients without having to address each recipient individually.

Dynamic distribution groups allow Exchange administrators to create distribution groups that maintain their group membership dynamically. Once the LDAP query has successfully been created for the query-based distribution group, the applicable objects (those that meet the filter query criteria) will automatically be members of the query-based distribution group. Every time an email message is sent to a query-based distribution group, the LDAP query is performed to determine the current group membership to which the message should be expanded.

A contact is a pointer to an email address for a non-Exchange recipient. Contacts are most often used for connecting your organization to recipients who exist outside your Exchange organization. As an administrator, you would create contacts so that frequently used email addresses are available in the global address list as real names.

Exam Essentials

Understand group types and scopes. It is important that you understand fully the different group types and group scopes that can exist within Active Directory. You should also understand how the use of a particular group scope can impact your Exchange organization by limiting who can determine group membership.

Know the difference between mailbox-enabled and mail-enabled. Although the concepts are simple in nature, many people get confused when it comes to remembering the difference between a mailbox-enabled object and a mail-enabled object. Mailbox-enabled objects can send and receive email messages using the Exchange organization and store their messages in an Exchange mailbox. Mail-enabled objects can send and receive email messages but do not have an associated Exchange mailbox. Some mail-enabled objects, such as contacts, send and receive email using an external ISP account. Other mail-enabled objects, such as distribution groups, use the Exchange organization to receive mail but have no mailbox themselves.

Learn the PowerShell commands. Almost every configuration or management action you perform from the Exchange Management Console will present you with the PowerShell code that was used to perform the action. Review this information carefully, and learn how to use the Exchange Management Shell to your advantage. Some of these commands are likely to make an appearance on your exam as well.

Know where to go for configuration and management tasks. Many times on the exam you are likely to be asked what configuration is needed to produce the required results. The Exchange Management Console has been completely redesigned to make it easier to navigate and get to tasks, but that doesn't mean it won't be difficult to remember later. Take the time as you review the material in this book to think about what types of configuration and management tasks you find yourself performing in each major node of the Exchange Management Console.

Review Questions

1. You need to create a new mailbox-enabled user account within your Exchange organization. What method would you need to use to perform this action with the fewest steps?

   A. Create the mailbox-enabled user account from the Active Directory Users and Computers console.

   B. Create the mailbox-enabled user account from the Exchange Management Shell using the `New-Mailbox` cmdlet.

   C. Create the mailbox-enabled user account from the Exchange Management Console.

   D. Create the mailbox-enabled user account from the command line using the `dsadd` command.

2. Your CIO has directed you to configure all user accounts belonging to management personnel in your organization to show correctly the employees they supervise. Every employee in your organization has an Active Directory account, but not all of them have mailboxes. How will you configure this information?

   A. Using the Exchange Management Console, select each manager's user account and enter the list of employees who work for that manager in the Direct Reports field.

   B. Using the Exchange Management Console, select each employee's user account and enter the user's manager in the Manager field.

   C. Using the Active Directory Users and Computers console, select each employee's user account and enter the user's manager in the Manager field.

   D. Using the Active Directory Users and Computers console, select each manager's user account and enter the list of employees who work for that manager in the Direct Reports field.

3. You are the Exchange administrator for your organization. During the summer months, your company hires several thousand temporary employees to help out as business increases. These temporary employees typically work for only two to four months and then are let go. Each employee has a mailbox-enabled user account. Your organization's default retention policy for deleted mailboxes is 90 days, but you don't want these mailboxes to be retained for this long. What is the best way to permanently and immediately delete these mailboxes that belonged to the temporary employees?

   A. Change the deleted mailbox retention period to one day, and let the regular Exchange maintenance routines delete them.

   B. Select them and delete them from the Disconnected Mailboxes node of the Exchange Management Console.

   C. Use the `Remove-Mailbox` cmdlet from the Exchange Management Shell.

   D. Use the `dsrm user` command from a command prompt.

4. Your organization has several resource mailboxes that multiple users need to be able send messages from. Where will you need to go to perform the required configuration to allow these users to send as the resource mailbox?

   A. The Exchange Management Shell

   B. The Exchange Management Console

   C. The Active Directory Users and Computers console

   D. Any of these locations

5. You are in the process of creating several new mail contacts in your Exchange organization that will represent external vendors with which users routinely communicate. When speaking of mail contacts, which of the following statements is true?

   A. A mail contact must have at least one internal email address and has no other requirements.

   B. A mail contact must have at least one internal email address and at least one external email address.

   C. A mail contact must have at least one external email address and has no other requirements.

   D. None of these statements is true.

6. What cmdlet will you use in the Exchange Management Shell to create a new user account with a mailbox?

   A. New-Mailbox

   B. Enable-MailUser

   C. Enable-Mailbox

   D. Connect-Mailbox

   E. New-MailUser

7. What cmdlet will you use in the Exchange Management Shell to mailbox-enable an existing Active Directory user account?

   A. New-MailUser

   B. Connect-Mailbox

   C. Enable-MailUser

   D. Enable-Mailbox

   E. New-Mailbox

8. You have recently created several universal distribution groups from the Active Directory Users and Computers console. After several days, the groups still do not have email addresses associated with them and do not show up in the global address list. What should you do to correct this problem? (Choose two; each answer presents a complete solution.)

   A. Use the `New-DistributionGroup` cmdlet from the Exchange Management Shell.

   B. Use the Exchange Management Shell to start the New Distribution Group Wizard.

   C. Locate the distribution group in the Exchange Management Console and mail-enable it.

   D. Use the `Enable-DistributionGroup` cmdlet from the Exchange Management Shell.

   E. Use the Exchange Management Console to start the New Distribution Group Wizard.

9. You are trying to create a new resource mailbox from the Exchange Management Shell by using the `New-Mailbox` cmdlet. When you create the resource mailbox, you are asked to supply a password. Later when you go to configure the calendar options for the resource mailbox in Outlook Web Access, those options are not available. What is the most likely problem?

   A. You must use the `New-ResourceMailbox` cmdlet to create resource mailboxes, not the `New-Mailbox` cmdlet.

   B. You cannot perform the initial creation of a resource mailbox from the Exchange Management Shell; you will need to use the Exchange Management Console.

   C. You did not specify that the mailbox was to be a resource mailbox by using the `-Resource` switch with the `New-Mailbox` cmdlet.

   D. You did not specify that the mailbox was to be a resource mailbox by using the `-Room` or `-Equipment` switch with the `New-Mailbox` cmdlet.

10. You are planning to create several dynamic distribution groups for use in your organization. What filter conditions are available to you by default and do not require any custom PowerShell code? (Choose all that apply.)

    A. Mailbox server

    B. Department

    C. Description

    D. Manager

    E. State or province

    F. Company

    G. Last name

    H. Mailbox database

11. You need to disable the user account of a salesperson who has left your organization. The salesperson had a mailbox on one of your Exchange Mailbox servers. You do not want to make any changes to the mailbox at this time. What method could you use to disable the user account?

    A. Use the `Disable-Mailbox` cmdlet from the Exchange Management Shell.

    B. Use the Disable link for the mailbox in the Exchange Management Console.

    C. Use the `Disable-MailUser` cmdlet from the Exchange Management Shell.

    D. Use the Active Directory Users and Computers console to disable the user account.

12. Your organization recently extended the contracts for three onsite contractors for an additional year. In the past, these contractors had mailboxes on one of your Exchange Mailbox servers. Going forward, the contractors will need only an Active Directory user account and will not need to have a mailbox. What should you do to remove the mailbox only, leaving the user account functional?

    A. Use the `Remove-Mailbox` cmdlet from the Exchange Management Shell.

    B. Use the `Disable-Mailbox` cmdlet from the Exchange Management Shell.

    C. Use the `Remove-MailUser` cmdlet from the Exchange Management Shell.

    D. Use the `Disable-MailUser` cmdlet from the Exchange Management Shell.

13. Which of the following types of objects can a distribution group contain? (Choose all that apply.)

    A. User

    B. Group

    C. Contact

    D. Public folder

14. Which of the following statements is true regarding security and distribution groups?

    A. Only a security group can be mail-enabled.

    B. Only a distribution group can be mail-enabled.

    C. Both types of groups can be mail-enabled.

    D. Neither type of group can be mail-enabled.

15. You are the Exchange administrator for your organization. During the summer months, your company hires several thousand temporary employees to help out as business increases. These temporary employees typically work for only two to four months and then are let go. Each of these employees needs to be able to receive company-wide email announcements that are sent on a fairly routine basis. These employees do not have any access to the network. What should you do to ensure that the temporary employees receive the required email messages? (Choose two; each answer is part of the overall solution.)

A. Create a mail-enabled user account for each one of them, and enter their external email address. Configure the user account to be a member of the temporary employees department.

B. Create a distribution group, and add each of the temporary employees to it.

C. Create a mail-enabled contact for each of them. Configure the contact to be a member of the temporary employees department.

D. Create a dynamic distribution group with a filter that adds each of the temporary employees to it by department.

16. Your company has hired an outside marketing agency to create marketing materials. Several of your employees will frequently need to email messages to people in this marketing agency. Since both the marketing agency and your network have Internet access, Internet email seems the best method. However, you want to set it up so that the people in the marketing agency appear in the Exchange global address list. What type of recipient object would you configure to achieve this?

A. Mailbox

B. Mail-enabled user

C. Contact

D. A mailbox with a foreign owner

17. You are the Exchange administrator for your organization. During the winter months, your company hires several hundred new employees to help out as business increases. A network administrator from the Active Directory group creates the user accounts for each new employee and configures them with all organizational information. A network administrator from the Exchange group then creates mailboxes for all the user accounts. You need to ensure that all new employees always receive email messages that are sent to their departments. What type of group should you create?

A. You should create a distribution group for each department. You should then place the members of the department in their respective distribution groups.

B. You should create a security group for each department. You should then place the members of the departments in their respective distribution groups.

C. You should create a dynamic security group for each department that filters group membership based on the Exchange object's Department attribute value.

D. You should create a dynamic distribution group for each department that filters group membership based on the Exchange object's Department attribute value.

18. You've just completed creating more than 200 resource mailboxes that represent various conference rooms and other equipment items your organization has that can be reserved. You've instructed the users in your organization to book these resources by including them as resources on all meeting requests. Users complain to you that when they book resources, they never get any notification of whether the booking was accepted or not and that sometimes when they go to use the resource they booked, someone else is already using it and saying that they also booked that resource for the same time period. What is the most likely cause of this problem?

    A. The user accounts associated with the resource mailboxes are not disabled.

    B. You did not perform any advanced configuration on the resource mailboxes using the `Set-MailboxCalendarSettings` cmdlet.

    C. You did not hide the mailboxes from the global address list.

    D. The Mailbox server that contains the resource mailboxes is not operating properly.

19. You have become aware that a few of your users have signed up for a daily newsletter that is published by a user in another department of your company and that often includes large file attachments. You would like to prevent all newsletter messages from this user from reaching these users' mailboxes. What is the best way to do this?

    A. Configure delivery restrictions for the users that allow all messages except those from the user sending the newsletter.

    B. Configure delivery restrictions for the users that allow only messages from within the Exchange system and from select originators outside the system.

    C. Configure a size limit on messages that can be sent to these users.

    D. Configure a storage limit on these users' mailboxes.

20. A user named Aaron leaves your company. Management would like a user named Bobbi to assume Aaron's responsibilities. What could you do so that Bobbi can receive Aaron's email messages? Select the best answer.

    A. Make Bobbi's mailbox an alternate recipient for Aaron's mailbox.

    B. Disable Aaron's user account, and give Bobbi profile permission to access Aaron's mailbox.

    C. Delete Aaron's mailbox, and forward all undeliverable messages to Bobbi.

    D. Create a rule in Aaron's mailbox so that all of Aaron's mail is forwarded to Bobbi.

Answers to Review Questions

1. B. By using the New-Mailbox cmdlet, you can create the new user account and mailbox-enable it all at once. No other method presented gives you that capability.

2. C. Since some employees do not have Exchange mailboxes, you will need to use the Active Directory Users and Computers console to configure all of them. The actual configuration change that must be performed is to enter the manager's name into the Manager field on the Organization tab of each user's account.

3. C. Although it is no small task when dealing with a number of disconnected mailboxes, the best way to delete them immediately is to use the Remove-Mailbox cmdlet. You cannot delete them using any other method except through the regular Exchange maintenance routines that depend on the deleted mailbox retention period. Changing the retention period to allow you quickly to delete the mailboxes belonging to the temporary employees will also likely cause you to delete other disconnected mailboxes you did not intend to delete.

4. D. Exchange 2007 with Service Pack 1 allows Send As permissions to be configured with Exchange Management Shell, Exchange Management Console or as done in previous versions by using Active Directory Users and Computers.

5. B. For email messages to be routed properly to a mail contact, the contact must have at least one internal email address and at least one external email address. You will configure the external email address manually when you create the mail contact, and Exchange will stamp the internal email address on the mail contact for you automatically after that.

6. A. You can use the New-Mailbox cmdlet to create and mailbox-enable a user account in one step.

7. D. You can use the Enable-Mailbox cmdlet to mailbox-enable an existing user account.

8. D, E. You can either use the Enable-DistributionGroup cmdlet from the Exchange Management Shell or use the Exchange Management Console to start the New Distribution Group Wizard. Either method will configure the messaging-related properties on the distribution group and resolve the issue you're experiencing.

9. D. In this scenario, given that you were prompted for a password and the resource calendar options do not show up in Outlook Web Access, the most likely problem is that you did not specify that the mailbox was to be a resource mailbox by using the -Room or -Equipment switch with the New-Mailbox cmdlet.

10. B, E, F. By default, you have the following filter conditions to select from when creating a new dynamic distribution group from either the Exchange Management Console or the Exchange Management Shell:

    - State or province
    - Department
    - Company
    - Custom attributes 1–15

If you need to create and sort conditions, you'll need to perform the configuration from the Exchange Management Shell using the parameter `-RecipientFilter` in the `New-DynamicDistributionGroup` or the `Set-DynamicDistributionGroup` cmdlet.

11. D. The only option listed that actually disables the user account and does not change any mail-related settings is to disable the user account from the Active Directory User and Computers console.

12. B. You should use the `Disable-Mailbox` cmdlet from the Exchange Management Shell. Using the `Remove-Mailbox` cmdlet from the Exchange Management Shell would cause the user account to be deleted as well.

13. A, B, C, D. A distribution group can contain any other type of recipient object, including other distribution groups.

14. C. Any type of group can be mail-enabled.

15. C, D. You should create a mail-enabled contact object for each of the temporary employees and configure the Department attribute to be Temporary Employees. You should then create a dynamic distribution group that uses a filter query based on the value of the Department attribute.

16. C. A contact is a pointer object that holds the address of a non-Exchange mail recipient. Contacts are made visible in the global address list and, therefore, permit Exchange clients to send messages to non-Exchange mail users.

17. D. The best solution is to create a dynamic distribution group that uses an LDAP filter query based on the value of the Department attribute to determine group membership. In this way, a dynamic group configured to filter all Exchange objects that belong to the marketing department will automatically include all matching objects. There is no such thing as a dynamic security group.

18. B. By default, a newly created resource mailbox will not automatically accept and schedule meeting requests that it receives. You will need to configure this behavior by using the `Set-MailboxCalendarSettings` cmdlet or by logging into the resource mailbox using Outlook Web Access.

19. A. The default delivery restrictions are to accept messages from everyone and reject messages from no one. You can enter specific originators from whom you want to block messages for individual users. You could configure a size limit on inbound messages to these users, but this would likely still allow some messages from the newsletter to be delivered.

20. A. Making Bobbi's mailbox an alternate recipient ensures that both mailboxes receive a copy of all messages sent to Aaron's mailbox. Creating a rule in Aaron's mailbox that forwards mail to Bobbi would also work but would require additional configuration on your part.

Chapter

6

Configuring and Managing Public Folders

MICROSOFT EXAM OBJECTIVE COVERED IN THIS CHAPTER:

✓ **Configuring the Exchange Infrastructure**

 ▪ Configure public folders.

Having easy access to essential business information is crucial to a successful business. Exchange Server 2007 with public folders fills this distinct need in today's business world as it provides a centralized location to store email, documentation, and calendaring information.

The main topics of this chapter are as follows:

- Understanding public folders

- Managing public folders

Understanding Public Folders

Public folders can be likened to a cross between a replicated file share and a mailbox. They are like a replicated file share in that files, email messages, and other content can be stored in them and other users have access to the local replica of the data. Public folders are also like mailboxes because they can be mail-enabled to allow them to send and receive email messages. With such a great fusion of features, there is no doubt why public folders have become so widely used by so many enterprises today. This would also point to why so many clamored to defend keeping public folders in the Exchange product when the Exchange product group hinted that they would be removed. Despite all of the hoopla around public folders being eliminated from Exchange Server, we still have them in Exchange 2007 and have been promised that they will be included in at least the next version of Exchange. Share-Point is touted as a replacement for public folders, but it has yet to fulfill all of the ways that public folders are being used today. However, the flip side of that is that SharePoint is an excellent tool in certain scenarios in which some people use public folders. Throughout this chapter, I will try to identify some of these scenarios so that you can recognize them when you come across them in your day-to-day work.

Just as you would access files on your computer using a drive letter and a file path, you access public folders using a structured naming system. There is only one MAPI-based public folder hierarchy or tree; therefore all user folders are included in it. This MAPI folder tree has two subtrees: Default public folders (IPM_Subtree) and System public folders (Non_IPM_Subtree). The Default public folders subtree contains all the user-created content. These folders are made by creating and then nesting folders under the root folder.

For instance, a folder named Marketing might be created in the root of the Default public folders' subtree for the marketing department. Nested within the Marketing folder might be other folders designed to store email received about special projects or perhaps a shared calendar for the department where everyone could post special events and vacation days pertinent to the group.

The System public folder subtree contains the content for legacy versions of Outlook, like the Offline Address Book (OAB) and Schedule+ Free Busy data, as well as the OWA ScratchPad, organization forms, store events, and other content inherent to the inner workings of Exchange.

Now that you understand the basic workings of public folders, it's going to get a little more complicated. It was mentioned previously that public folders are able to be replicated. Replication allows for a copy of the public folder's contents to exist on multiple Exchange mailbox servers. Replication is used to provide distributed Exchange environments with the ability to have copies of the data distributed throughout the Exchange environment, providing quick access to the end users. This also allows for data resilience: if a database failure occurs, other copies of the data are available. There is no locking mechanism to ensure that only one user is modifying an item at a time, nor is there any sophisticated way to arbitrate when multiple changes happen at the same time. This being the case, if you are doing any sort of document management, it might be good to look into Microsoft Office SharePoint Server as it offers those features.

Public folders have multimaster replication that is different from the Exchange 2007 high-availability replication options like cluster continuous replication (CCR), standby continuous replication (SCR), and local continuous replication (LCR). Therefore, if there are multiple active public folder databases in the Exchange organization, using any of the Exchange continuous replication technologies on a public folder database is not supported.

After creating a public folder and configuring permissions, you should also always configure any required replication settings for the public folder to ensure that replicas are available in each location that will access the database. The next section goes into doing all of those tasks.

Managing Public Folders

For many companies, public folders are a major part of their Exchange Server deployments. Public folders have been a staple of Exchange Server and using them is a powerful way to share knowledge and data throughout your organization. They are great for sharing content and information among many users, and since they can be mail-enabled, they can also be an easy way for third-party application developers to hook into Exchange. Just use the MAPI libraries to connect to Exchange as a user with permissions to the specified public folder comment and you have the ability to send and receive messages and share them with multiple users without doing a lot of coding.

At the same time, public folder management has been a weakness in previous versions of Exchange Server for the following reasons:

- There is a distinct lack of freely available command-line tools for managing public folders and public folder stores. Some tools were available from Product Support Services (PSS), but they weren't advertised or generally supported for versions of Exchange past 5.5.

- The public folder support in the legacy Exchange System Manager lacked effective bulk operation support; you could not, for example, easily add a new public folder store to the replica list of a given folder and its subfolders without visiting each folder in turn or without overwriting the replica lists of the subfolders with copies of the initial folder's list.

- The public folder replica and replication information displayed by the legacy System Manager was often incomplete, misleading, or just plain wrong.

- Recovering public folder data after deleted item retention requires third-party tools or complicated recovery procedures.

Unfortunately, Microsoft's announcement that it was de-emphasizing support for public folders in Exchange 2007 has caused a lot of worry and confusion. When you combine this with the lack of any GUI public folder management tools in the initial release of Exchange 2007, a lot of people concluded that you just can't use public folders anymore. If you have a large public folder deployment in your organization, this is obviously an area of concern. Be assured that public folders are alive and well, and in some ways, they're even better in Exchange 2007 than ever before. The new EMS cmdlets for handling public folders are a definite improvement. Even the lack of some of the built-in GUI functions offered in Exchange Server 2003 Service Pack 2 is offset by using a combination of the Public Folder Management Console added in Exchange Server 2007 Service Pack 1 and the Public Folder DAV Administrator (PFDAVAdmin) utility.

 The Exchange product group has posted important information on support for public folders at http://msexchangeteam.com/archive/2008/03/31/448537.aspx.

Creating the Public Folder Database

If you did not elect to install public folders on your Exchange Server 2007 Mailbox server during the initial installation, you can return later and create a public folder database. We'll examine that process briefly here because it is similar to the mailbox database creation process covered in detail in Chapter 3, "Configuring the Mailbox and Hub Transport Roles."

If you start with only Outlook 2007 clients, there is no requirement to have public folders in your Exchange organization. However, if you later add other clients, such as Outlook 2003, to your organization, you will need to create a public folder database and public folder tree to house the OAB and free/busy information. You might also just want to have public folders for other uses. If you're adding public folders for older clients, such as Outlook 2003, you'll need to restart the Microsoft Exchange Information Store service on the Mailbox server with the public folder database installed before these older clients will be able to see and connect to the public folder tree just created.

To create the storage group that will house your new public folder database, simply perform the steps outlined in Exercise 3.1 in Chapter 3. To create the new public folder database, perform the steps outlined in Exercise 6.1.

If you install Exchange Server 2007 Mailbox servers into an existing Exchange Server 2003 organization, a public folder database will be created automatically on the Mailbox server in a separate storage group. This ensures backward compatibility and cannot be changed or prevented.

EXERCISE 6.1

Creating a New Public Folder Database

To create a new public folder database, follow these steps:

1. Click Start ➤ Programs ➤ Microsoft Exchange Server 2007 and then select Exchange Management Console.

2. Expand the Microsoft Exchange root object, expand the Server Configuration folder, and then click the server containing the storage group in which you want to create a new database.

3. Right-click the storage group object in which you want to create the database, and select the New Public Folder Database option from the context menu. This opens the New Public Folder Database Wizard. Alternatively, you can click the New Public Folder Database link under the storage group options in the Actions pane on the right of the Exchange Management Console.

4. Type a name for the new public folder database, and select the database file path by clicking the Browse button. Remember, the database should be on a different physical volume than its storage group's transaction logs if possible. To ensure that the database is available for immediate use, leave the Mount This Database option checked. Click New to complete the database creation process.

5. As usual, Exchange displays a summary page showing the success or failure of the actions you instructed it to perform. Notice this time, however, that two actions are performed: creating the database and mounting the database.

6. Click Finish to close the wizard.

Exploring the Public Folder Management Options

Exchange Server 2007 is the first version to provide support for Microsoft Windows Share-Point Services integration as an alternative method of seamlessly sharing data within your organization and making it available to Outlook 2007 and Outlook Web Access (OWA) users. You can add these features while still using your public folder infrastructure. You can continue to use the Exchange 2003 System Manager console to create, manage, and delete public folders, or you can use the functionality built into Exchange 2007.

Understanding Native Exchange 2007 Support

Although the Public Folder Management Console offers support for public folders, Exchange 2007 provides the bulk of its built-in support via Exchange Management Shell (EMS) cmdlets. Don't worry; they're not difficult to use, even if you're not a script or command-line guru.

Using the Public Folder Management Console

Before I show you how to use the new public folder cmdlets, though, I'll cover exactly what you can do in the Public Folder Management Console (PFMC). You can view the public folder hierarchy, add or delete public folders, set folder properties, and view and manage replicas. To do other tasks, you'll need some other tool, such as Outlook to manage individual folders or the EMS to deal with public folders from the server. The Public Folder Management Console can be launched from within the toolbox section of the Exchange Management Console, as shown in Figure 6.1.

Once the Public Folder Management Console is launched and connected to a public folder server, you can perform these management functions:

- Update the public folder hierarchy.
- Add and remove public folders.
- Mail-enable and mail-disable public folders.
- View and modify public folder properties.
- View and modify public folder replicas.
- Manage Send As permissions for mail-enabled public folders.

Figure 6.2 illustrates using the console to view the public folder hierarchy.

FIGURE 6.1   Launching the Public Folder Management Console

FIGURE 6.2   Viewing the public folder hierarchy in the Public Folder Management Console

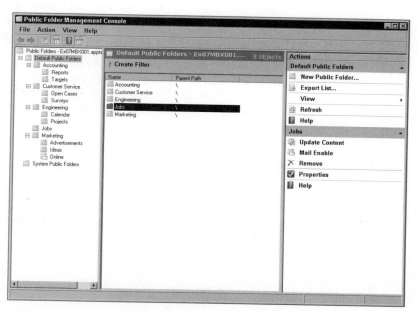

Using the Exchange Management Shell

Although the PFMC is good for many common tasks, you'll need to use the Exchange Management Shell (EMS) to manage the following tasks:

- Get statistics for public folders.
- Suspend and resume public folder replication.
- Configure public folder permissions for client users and administrators.
- Move public folder content from one public folder database to a new public folder database.

I am going to cover the aforementioned specialized functions of EMS as well as some other basic tasks. To begin, a review of some of the EMS basics is in order.

As you've seen many times up to this point, EMS is built on the Windows PowerShell technology. Because it's a specialized application of PowerShell, it uses the same format as standard PowerShell cmdlets. That format is as follows:

Verb-Noun

By combining the noun and verb in the name of the cmdlet, each cmdlet describes the type of operation it performs as well as the object it manipulates. Verbs produce a standard behavior regardless of the object to which they're applied. For example, the Get verb will always provide a read-only list of the object's properties, while the Set verb will always allow you to modify those properties—even when they vary from object to object.

In some of the PowerShell examples, you'll see lines terminated by a backtick (`` ` ``) character. PowerShell uses this character for line termination; it tells the shell that the logical line of input will be continued on the next physical line. This allows you to break up long lines for display and still ensure that they work correctly when you enter them. As a result, the same verbs and nouns tend to be used over and over again; this helps you learn your way around more quickly. Many of the properties are common across multiple objects, so you'll quickly get accustomed to how to use them. The help page for each cmdlet lists all parameters that can be used with that cmdlet.

Performing General Public Folder Tasks

These cmdlets apply to the entire public folder hierarchy at once and provide broad control of your public folder infrastructure:

Get-PublicFolderStatistics   This cmdlet provides a detailed set of statistics about the public folder hierarchy on a given server, such as Get-PublicFolderStatistics -Server "EX07MBX001".

Resume-PublicFolderReplication This cmdlet re-enables all public folder content replication when it has been suspended.

Suspend-PublicFolderReplication This cmdlet suspends all public folder content replication.

Update-PublicFolderHierarchy This cmdlet starts the content synchronization process for the public folder hierarchy on the specified server, as in `Update-PublicFolderHierarchy -Server "EX07MBX001"`.

Manipulating Individual Public Folders

These cmdlets are designed to work with a specific public folder:

Get-PublicFolder This cmdlet retrieves the properties for the specified public folder. If you don't name a public folder by specifying a value for the -Identity property, it will default to the root public folder. If you need to see system folders, you'll need to set the -Identity property to a value beginning with the string \NON IPM SUBTREE.

```
Get-PublicFolder-Identity "\Jobs\Posted" -Server "EX07MBX001"

Get-PublicFolder-Recurse

Get-PublicFolder -Identity \NON IPM SUBTREE -Recurse
```

By default, the Get-PublicFolder cmdlet returns the values for only a single folder. The -Recurse switch changes the behavior to report on all subfolders as well.

New-PublicFolder This cmdlet creates a new public folder. The -Path property is required and provides the name and location of the new public folder, as in `New-Public-Folder -Identity "\Jobs\New" -Server "EX07MBX001"`.

Remove-PublicFolder This cmdlet deletes a public folder. The -Path property is required and provides the name and location of the public folder to be deleted, as in `Remove-Public-Folder -Identity "\Jobs\Old" -Server "EX07MBX001"`.

By default, the Remove-PublicFolder cmdlet removes only the named public folder. The -Recurse switch will delete all subfolders as well, which is handy for removing an entire group of folders at once.

Set-PublicFolder This cmdlet allows you to set most of the properties (limits, replicas, replication schedules, and more) for the named public folder, as in `Set-PublicFolder -Identity "\Jobs\Posted" -Server "EX07MBX001"`.

You cannot use the Set-PublicFolder cmdlet to mail-enable a public folder or to change its mail-related attributes. See the next section, "Manipulating Public Folder Mail Attributes," for the cmdlets to use for these tasks.

Update-PublicFolder This cmdlet starts the content synchronization process for the named public folder. The -Identity property is required, as in Update-PublicFolder -Identity "\Jobs\Posted".

Manipulating Public Folder Mail Attributes

These cmdlets are designed to work with a specific public folder and modify the attributes it receives when it is mail-enabled:

Disable-MailPublicFolder This cmdlet takes an existing mail-enabled public folder and renders it mail-disabled, as in Disable-MailPublicFolder -Identity "\Jobs\New".

Enable-MailPublicFolder This cmdlet takes an existing public folder and renders it mail-enabled. The optional -HiddenFromAddressListsEnabled switch allows you to hide the folder from your address lists, as in Enable-MailPublicFolder-Identity "\Jobs\New" -HiddenFromAddressListsEnabled $true -Server "EX07MBX001".

You set the mail-related attributes separately using the Set-MailPublicFolder cmdlet.

Get-MailPublicFolder This cmdlet retrieves the mail-related properties for the specified public folder. If you don't name a public folder by specifying a value for the -Identity property, it will default to the root public folder, as in Get-MailPublicFolder -Identity "\Jobs\Old" -Server "EX07MBX001".

Set-MailPublicFolder This cmdlet allows you to set the mail-related properties for the named public folder, such as alias, email addresses, send and receive sizes, and permitted and prohibited senders, as in Set-PublicFolder-Identity "\Jobs\Posted" -Server "EX07MBX001" -Alias PostedJobs -PrimarySmtpAddress "postedjobs@exchangeexchange.com".

Once the mail-related attributes are configured for a public folder, it still must be mail-enabled using the Enable-MailPublicFolder cmdlet.

Managing Public Folder Databases

These cmdlets allow you to manage the public folder databases:

Get-PublicFolderDatabase This cmdlet provides the functionality used by the Exchange Management Console and allows you to view the properties of existing public folder databases, as in Get-PublicFolderDatabase -Server "EX07MBX001".

> The -Identity, -Server, and -StorageGroup parameters are not compatible with each other. Use only one of the three to narrow down your selection.

New-PublicFolderDatabase   This cmdlet allows you to create a new public folder database.

Remove-PublicFolderDatabase   This cmdlet deletes an existing public folder database from the active configuration of the server, as in Remove-PublicFolderDatabase -Identity "Public Folder Database".

> The corresponding EDB file is not deleted by the Remove-PublicFolderDatabase cmdlet; you have to remove it manually from the hard drive.

Set-PublicFolderDatabase   This cmdlet provides the underlying functionality used by the Exchange Management Console to update the properties of existing public folder databases, as in Set-PublicFolderDatabase -Identity "PublicFolderDatabase" -Name "New and Improved PF Database".

Managing Public Folder Permissions

These cmdlets allow you to modify and view the permissions on your public folders. Administrative and client permissions are handled through two separate sets of nouns. The Add-PublicFolderAdministrativePermission cmdlet allows you to add administrative permissions to a specified public folder. For example, adding rights for JSmith to the \Jobs\ Posted public folder might look like this:

```
Add-PublicFolderAdministrativePermission -User "JSmith"
-Identity "\Jobs\Posted" -AccessRights
"ViewInformationStore,AdministerInformationStore"
```

Single or multiple access rights can be specified; if multiple access rights are specified, they should be separated by commas. The valid administrative access rights are as follows:

None   Removes all rights to modify public folder attributes

ModifyPublicFolderACL   Adds the right to modify client access permissions for the specified folder

ModifyPublicFolderAdminACL   Adds the right to modify administrator permissions for the specified public folder

ModifyPublicFolderDeletedItemRetention   Adds the right to modify the Public Folder Deleted Item Retention attributes

ModifyPublicFolderExpiry   Adds the right to modify the Public Folder Expiration attributes

ModifyPublicFolderQuotas   Adds the right to modify the Public Folder Quota attributes

ModifyPublicFolderReplicaList   Adds the right to modify the replica list attribute

AdministerInformationStore   Adds the right to modify all other public folder properties included in the other rights

ViewInformationStore   Adds the right to view public folder properties

AllExtendedRights   Adds the right to modify all public folder properties

 You can specify a single access right or list multiple rights at once using the syntax shown in the example for the Add-PublicFolderAdministrativePermission cmdlet.

The following cmdlets also work with administrative permissions:

Get-PublicFolderAdministrativePermission   This cmdlet lets you view the administrative permission entries on a given public folder, as in Get-PublicFolderAdministrativePermission -Identity "\Jobs\Posted".

Remove-PublicFolderAdministrativePermission   This cmdlet lets you remove an administrative permission entry from a given public folder, as in Remove-PublicFolderAdministrativePermission -User "Fran.Jones" -Identity "\Jobs\Posted" -AccessRights "ViewInformationStore".

CLIENT PERMISSIONS

Once you've configured public folders using the cmdlets described in the preceding sections, users and groups can then work with a public folder using their Outlook clients. For emphasis, I'll restate what I just said in a somewhat different form: you grant public folder access permissions to Exchange recipients, not to Windows users and groups. Once access to a public folder is granted, Exchange recipients access the folder in their Outlook clients while connected to their mailboxes.

If you create a public folder logged in as a domain administrator, then that user account is given the role of Owner. The owner of a public folder has complete control over the folder.

If a user has the appropriate permissions on a public folder, that user can change access permissions on the folder for other users. You can modify them from within the Outlook client using the Permissions tab for a public folder, and you can modify them using the EMS.

Which of these you use depends on your security rights. If you are an Exchange user with no extraordinary permissions who is an owner of a public folder, you manage permissions for the folder in Outlook using the Permissions tab for the public folder. If you're an Exchange administrative user, you can use the EMS to modify a single public folder or create a PowerShell script to automate administration.

A group named Default includes all Exchange recipients not separately added to the Name list. When the folder is created, this group is automatically given the default role of Author. Note that Authors don't own the folder and can't create subfolders. Also note that Authors can edit and delete only their own folder items.

Microsoft has come up with several predefined roles— including Owner, Publishing Editor, Editor, Publishing Author, Author, Nonediting Author, Contributor, Reviewer, and Custom—each with a different combination of client permissions. Table 6.1 describes these permissions, descending from the permission with the most capabilities to the permission with the fewest. The word *items*, as used in this table, refers to the contents of the public folder, such as email messages, forms, documents, and other files. Table 6.2 lists the predefined groupings of permissions according to role. Several of the permissions set the ability to modify all items, only the users own items or none of the items in the public folder.

TABLE 6.1   Public Folder Client Permissions

Permission	Description
Create Items	Can create new items in a folder.
Read Items	Can open and view items in a folder.
Create Subfolders	Can create subfolders within a folder.
Folder Owner	Can change permissions in a folder and perform administrative tasks, such as adding rules and installing forms on a folder.
Folder Contact	Receives email notifications relating to a folder. Notifications include replication conflicts, folder design conflicts, and storage limit notifications.
Folder Visible	Determines whether the folder is visible to the user in the public folder hierarchy.
Edit Items	Can edit (modify) items in a folder.
Delete Items	Can delete items in a folder.

TABLE 6.2 Predefined Client Roles and Their Permissions

Role	Create Items	Read Items	Create Subfolders	Folder Owner	Folder Contact	Folder Visible	Edit Items	Delete Items
Owner	Yes	Yes	Yes	Yes	Yes	Yes	All	All
Publishing Editor	Yes	All	Yes	No	No	Yes	All	All
Editor	Yes	All	No	No	No	Yes	All	All
Publishing Author	Yes	Yes	Yes	No	No	Yes	Own	Own
Author	Yes	Yes	No	No	No	Yes	Own	Own
Nonediting Author	Yes	Yes	No	No	No	Yes	None	None
Contributor	Yes	No	No	No	No	Yes	None	None
Reviewer	No	Yes	No	No	No	Yes	None	None
None	No	No	No	No	No	Yes	None	None

Custom roles consisting of any combination of individual permissions may also be assigned. When a public folder is created, the following three users are included on the permissions list by default:

The user who created the public folder This user is automatically assigned the Owner role.

A special user named Default This user represents all users who have access to the public folder store but aren't explicitly listed in the permissions list. In top-level folders, the Default user is automatically granted the Author role (this can be modified). Below the top-level folders, the Default user automatically inherits the permissions it has at its parent folder.

A special user named Anonymous The Anonymous user represents all users logged on with Anonymous access. For example, an Exchange server could contain public folders holding promotional information for public viewing. People without user accounts could use a web browser or news reader program and the Anonymous account to access the Exchange server and read the promotional information. Any permissions assigned to the Anonymous account are applied to these users.

Exchange administrators can always designate themselves as the owners of public folders. This is especially important if the recipient who is the owner of a public folder (or all Active Directory accounts that are on the permissions list of that recipient) is deleted.

 Administrative rights are granted to Windows 2003 users and security groups, not to Exchange recipients and distribution groups, just as in versions of Exchange prior to Exchange 2000 Server.

Client permissions control how users can interact in with public folders and their contents. These rights are different from the administrative permissions. The client access rights are as follows:

ReadItems   Adds the right to read items within the specified public folder.

CreateItems   Adds the right to create items within the specified public folder.

EditOwnedItems   Adds the right to edit the items that the user owns in the specified public folder.

DeleteOwnedItems   Adds the right to delete items that the user owns in the specified public folder.

EditAllItems   Adds the right to edit all items in the specified public folder.

DeleteAllItems   Adds the right to delete all items in the specified public folder.

CreateSubfolders   Adds the right to create subfolders in the specified public folder.

FolderOwner   Sets the user as the owner of the specified public folder. This means the user has the right to view and move the public folder and create subfolders. This does not give the user rights to read, edit, delete, or create items. If the user needs any of these rights, they need to be assigned separately.

FolderContact   Sets the user as the contact for the specified public folder.

FolderVisible   Allows the user to view the specified public folder, but does not allow the user to read or edit items within the specified public folder.

Unfortunately, there isn't a graphical view of client permissions in EMC or in the PFMC; therefore, a number of cmdlets are used to manage client permissions from within the EMS. The cmdlets are as follows:

Add-PublicFolderClientPermission   This cmdlet lets you add a client permission entry to a given public folder, as in Add-PublicFolderClientPermission -User "JSmith" -Identity "\Jobs\Posted" -AccessRights "CreateItems".

Get-PublicFolderClientPermission   This cmdlet lets you view the client permission entries on a given public folder, as in Get-PublicFolderClientPermission -Identity "\Jobs\Posted".

Remove-PublicFolderClientPermission   This cmdlet lets you remove a client permission entry from a given public folder, as in `Remove-PublicFolderClientPermission -User "Nathan.Smith" -Identity "\Jobs\Posted" -AccessRights "CreateItems"`.

Using Additional Scripts for Complicated Tasks

Although the cmdlets described in the preceding sections are certainly great for single-folder operations, performing common operations on entire groups of folders starts getting sticky. Since most of us aren't scripting gurus, Exchange 2007 provides some sample Exchange Management Shell scripts that allow you to perform more complicated server and management tasks that affect groups of folders:

AddReplicaToPFRecursive.ps1   This script adds the specified server to the replica list for a given public folder and all folders underneath it.

AddUsersToPFRecursive.ps1   This script allows you to grant user permissions to a folder and all folders beneath it.

MoveAllReplicas.ps1   This script finds and replaces a server in the replica list of all public folders, including system folders for a given public folder database.

RemoveReplicaFromPFRecursive.ps1   This script removes the specified server from the replica list for a given public folder and all folders underneath it.

ReplaceReplicaOnPFRecursive.ps1   This script finds and replaces a server in the replica list of a given public folder as well as all subfolders.

ReplaceUserPermissionOnPFRecursive.ps1   This script finds and replaces one user in the permissions on a given public folder and all its subfolders with a second user; the original user permissions are not retained.

ReplaceUserWithUserOnPFRecursive.ps1   This script copies one user's access permissions on a given public folder and all its subfolders to a second user while retaining permissions for the first user.

RemoveReplicaFromPFRecursive.ps1   This script removes the given user's access permissions from the given public folder and all its subfolders.

You can find these scripts in the Scripts subfolder of the Exchange 2007 installation folder. Note that with the default Windows PowerShell configuration, you just can't click these scripts and run them; you must invoke them from within the Exchange Management Shell, usually by navigating to the folder and calling them explicitly.

Using Outlook

Just as in previous versions of Exchange, public folders can also be created by mailbox-enabled users in their email clients. I'll show you how to create a public folder using the Outlook client.

Open Outlook and make sure the folder list is displayed. Next, double-click Public Folders in the folder list, or click the plus icon just in front of Public Folders. Notice that the plus sign becomes a minus sign when a folder is expanded to show the folders within it.

You've now expanded the top-level folder for public folders, which contains two sub-folders: Favorites and All Public Folders. Expand the All Public Folders folder, and you'll see that it has at least one subfolder: Internet Newsgroups. If your organization uses public folders, you probably have at least one other subfolder here as well.

> If your Exchange organization has a large number of public folders, you can drag the ones you use often to your Favorites subfolder. This makes them easier to find. Folders in the Favorites folder are also the only ones that are available when you work offline without a connection to your Exchange server.

To create new public folders in the folder All Public Folders, follow the steps in Exercise 6.2.

EXERCISE 6.2

Creating New Public Folders with Outlook

Here's how to create new public folders in the All Public Folders folder:

1. Open the Outlook client.

2. Right-click the All Public Folders item, and then select New Folder from the context menu. The Create New Folder dialog opens.

3. Enter a name for the folder; I've given this one the somewhat unimaginative name Maintenance Team.

4. When you're done creating your folder, click OK.

Note that the folder I created in Exercise 6.2 holds email and posted items, which is the default selection. Email items are messages. Posted items contain a subject and text. You can post an item in a folder designed to hold posts without dealing with messaging attributes such as to whom the item is sent. To post an item, click the down arrow near the New icon on the main Outlook window and select Post in This Folder from the drop-down menu. If you wanted to create a public folder to house calendar items or contact items, you'd need to select the correct type of public folder contents from the Folder Contains drop-down list shown in Exercise 6.2.

If you're told you don't have sufficient permissions to create the folder, you need to assign those permissions using one of the other Exchange public folder management tools. If you have Exchange administrative permissions, you can make this change yourself.

The new public folder now shows up under the All Public Folders hierarchy. If you can't see the full name of your new folder, make the Folder List pane a little wider. Now right-click your new folder, and select the Properties option from the context menu. This opens the folder's Properties dialog box, shown in Figure 6.3.

FIGURE 6.3   Public folder properties

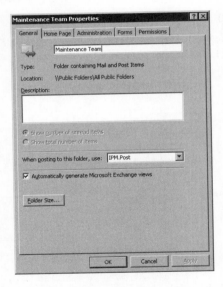

I'm not going to spend a lot of time with this dialog box. Among other things, mailbox owners use the public folder's Properties dialog box to do the following:

- Add a description for other mailbox owners who access the folder
- Make the folder available on the Internet
- Set up a default view of the folder, including grouping by such things as the subject or sender

- Set up some administrative rules on folder characteristics, access, and such
- Set permissions for using the folder

Go ahead and look around in the public folder's Properties dialog box. When you're done, click Cancel unless you've made some changes you want to keep. If you have, then click OK to save your changes.

> You create and manage private folders in mailboxes in the same way you create and manage public folders in the Public Folders hierarchy.

Using the Public Folder Management Console

In Exchange 5.5, you could create public folders using only an email client. You couldn't create one in the Administrator program. Exchange 2003 enabled you to create public folders in Exchange System Manager as an Exchange administrator. This functionality is carried over to the Public Folder Management Console.

Launch the PFMC, then right-click on the Default Public Folders node and select New Public Folder from the context menu to open the new public folder's Properties dialog box. This starts the New Public Folder Wizard, shown in Figure 6.4. In this wizard you are prompted to assign a name to the new public folder. Click New and then the Finish button.

FIGURE 6.4   The New Public Folder Wizard

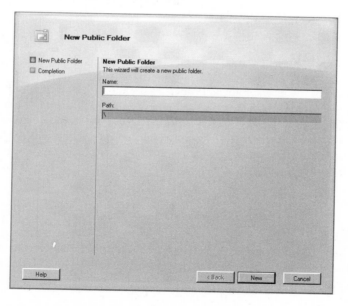

Once you have a public folder created, you can configure its properties. To view the properties of the public folder, just right-click on the folder and choose Properties from the context menu. Let's take a look at the key tabs in this dialog box.

General

You use the General tab of the public folder's Properties dialog box, as shown in Figure 6.5, to name your folder. The Path field shows where the folder is located in the Public Folder hierarchy after it has been created. If Maintain per-User Read and Unread Information for This Folder is selected, each user will see items in the folder they have read in non-bold text. If this option is not selected, all items, whether or not they have been read, will show in bold text for all users.

FIGURE 6.5 The General tab of the public folder's Properties dialog box

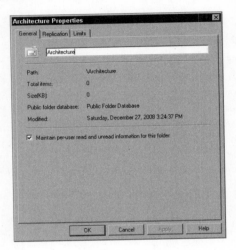

Replication

The Replication tab of the public folder's Properties dialog box, as shown in Figure 6.6, is an important property page because it is used to manage the replication of folders between this server and other Exchange servers. Replication enables you to put copies of the same folder on multiple Exchange servers. It is useful either for local load balancing or for limiting wide area network traffic and improving performance by placing copies of folders in routing groups at geographically distant sites.

Limits

The Limits tab, shown in Figure 6.7, allows three types of limits to be configured. Let's look at each of these limits:

- *Storage quotas*: As with mailboxes, you can set thresholds at which warnings are sent and specify that posting to the folder is prohibited. You can also set a maximum posted-item size. If you want, you can choose to use the default storage limits settings for the public folder store where the folder resides.

- *Deleted item retention*: As with mailboxes, you can set the maximum number of days that a deleted item will be kept for recovery before being totally deleted. If you deselect the Use Database Retention Defaults check box, you can enter a number of days that deleted items should be retained. If you don't want items retained at all, set the number of days to 0.

- *Age limits*: This is the number of days that an item in the folder lives before being deleted. This is a handy tool for controlling storage usage.

FIGURE 6.6   The Replication tab of the public folder's Properties dialog box

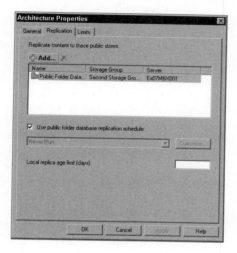

FIGURE 6.7   The Limits tab of the public folder's Properties dialog box

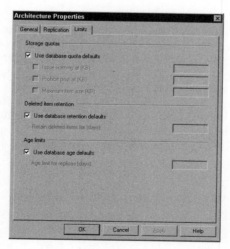

Using the Public Folder DAV Administration Tool

There is one more way to perform public folder management: by using an outstanding, freely available GUI tool, the Public Folder DAV Administrator (PFDAVAdmin). PFDAVAdmin is a .NET application that uses WebDAV instead of MAPI to access the public folder store.

PFDAVAdmin requires the .NET Framework version 1.1 to be installed, which means you must maintain multiple versions of the .NET Framework on your management servers and workstations.

You might now be wondering whether using PFDAVAdmin is a good idea, given its reliance on WebDAV. In Exchange 2007, support for the WebDAV protocol is "deemphasized," meaning that Microsoft doesn't promise it will be around for the next major version of Exchange. But it's still here in Exchange 2007, and it allows you to use this wonderful management tool. One caveat to this is if your public folder server is installed on Windows Server 2008, WebDAV support will need to be installed and configured separately for PFDAVAdmin to work.

PFDAVAdmin is a wonderfully flexible tool. At first glance, it seems to give you the ability to manage public folder permissions using a GUI that is close to the legacy Exchange System Manager. In addition to querying and setting permissions, you can add, replace, and remove individual access control entries (ACEs) across a set of folders without having to replace wholesale the access control lists (ACLs) in question. PFDAVAdmin will also notify you when an ACL is damaged or in noncanonical order (meaning that the ACEs aren't properly ordered) and allow you to fix them on more than one folder at once.

Administrators who used the installable file system (IFS)—otherwise known as the M drive—in Exchange 2000 Server and Exchange Server 2003 upgrades would often use the Windows Explorer permission tool to modify permissions on public folders. Unfortunately, this usually causes ACEs to get written in the wrong order, creating all sorts of subtle problems. PFDAVAdmin is the easy way to fix them if you've got to deal with them and you don't want to wait until you have Exchange 2007 in your organization to do it! Thankfully, Exchange 2007 makes the IFS go away, so once you fix the problems, they're not likely to return.

You can also use PFDAVAdmin to do the following:

- Perform bulk operations on folder properties. In addition, you can do bulk search and removal operations of per-item permissions.
- Apply changes to your list of replicas to a folder and all subfolders without overwriting each folder's replica list (that is, add or remove specific server entries without making each folder's replica list an exact copy of your starting point).

- Export folder permissions on folders, public folder stores, and mailbox stores.
- Export and import public folder replica lists.

Microsoft makes PFDAVAdmin freely available through the Microsoft Exchange tools download website. You can find the download link by searching for "PFDAVAdmin" at the following location: www.microsoft.com/downloads/.

Using Other Public Folder Tools

Exchange administrators have used a couple of other tools throughout the years. Although these tools work with legacy Exchange servers, many of them are not certified for use with Exchange 2003 (let alone Exchange 2007). However, you can still use them as long as you have legacy Exchange public folder servers in your organization. I'll mention two in particular:

- The PFAdmin tool (PFAdmin.exe) is a command-line tool for common administrative tasks. With it, you can manage ACLs, manage replicas, and re-home folders. If you happen to have some old product CDs, you can find a copy of this tool on the BackOffice Resource Kit (BORK) 4.5 CD.
- The PFInfo tool (PFInfo.exe) is a GUI tool that provides reporting on a server's folder replicas and associated permissions. You can even use the output of this tool as input to PFAdmin, allowing you to provide a level of consistency across multiple servers.

Although you might be tempted to use PFAdmin and PFInfo in your Exchange 2007 organization (especially if you're already using them), since these tools are no longer supported with Exchange 2007 it is recommended that you retire these tools before retiring your legacy Exchange public folder servers. The most compelling reason to use these tools with legacy Exchange servers was to provide the missing command-line and scripting capability for public folder management, and now that Exchange 2007 includes the EMS, you should really put the effort into mastering the public folder cmdlets it provides.

You might find one additional legacy tool of value. The Public Folder Migration Tool (PFMigrate.wsf) is a Visual Basic script that was introduced in the Exchange Server 2003 Deployment Tools (ExDeploy). This script was designed for one purpose: to provide a simple interface for performing bulk public folder replica transfers from Exchange Server 5.5 servers to Exchange Server 2003 servers. However, because it can handle cross-administrative group replica transfers, PFMigrate can move replicas to Exchange 2007 servers. The script is downloadable from the Microsoft website as part of the latest versions of the Exchange Server 2003 ExDeploy tools.

Working with the Public Folder Hierarchy

You can create public folders in any available public folder store on any Exchange Mailbox server. By default, public folder stores are not created on Exchange 2007 Mailbox servers unless you specify that the server will be used with clients running Outlook 2003 and earlier. When you create a new public folder store on an Exchange 2007 Mailbox server, you can create a new storage group for it or place it in a storage group that already has one or more mailbox stores in it.

A public folder hierarchy, or public folder tree, is a list of public folders and their sub-folders that are stored in the default public folder stores on the Exchange servers in an Exchange organization. The hierarchy also includes the name of the server on which a copy of each folder resides. Because the hierarchy exists in Active Directory as a separate object, it does not contain any of the actual items in your various public folders. There is one organization-wide public folder hierarchy object, although in previous versions of Exchange you could create additional public folder trees that were not visible through the Public Folder object in Outlook but could be accessed through other methods, such as NNTP.

You cannot create non-visible public folder trees using the management tools in Exchange Server 2007; you will need to continue using the Exchange Server 2003 System Manager if you want to create these objects.

Replicating Public Folders

In an environment with a single Exchange server, the hierarchy exists and is stored on the Exchange server. In an environment with multiple public folder stores, each Exchange server that has a public folder store has a copy of the public folder hierarchy. Exchange servers work together to ensure that each Exchange server in an administrative group has an up-to-date copy of the public folder hierarchy. This process, called *public folder hierarchy replication*, is automatic. In Exchange 2000 Server and Exchange Server 2003, there were certain limitations with this process when replication crossed administrative and routing group boundaries. Once you've fully migrated to Exchange Server 2007, these limitations will be a thing of the past; all Exchange Server 2007 servers are in a single separate administrative group that has been created for backward compatibility with Exchange 2000 Server and Exchange Server 2003 servers in the organization.

The Public Folder Management Console uses the public folder hierarchy to display appropriately public folder objects in various containers and to retrieve information about public folders, whether that information is stored in the hierarchy or on the server where the public folder physically resides. Email clients such as Outlook and OWA use the hierarchy to list public folders available on all servers in the organization and to access items in a specific folder. Security limits associated with a given public folder, of course, limit the actual access granted to administrators and users. Figure 6.8 shows the default public folder property that is on each mailbox database; it defines the public folder store that each client will attempt to connect to first.

The public folder hierarchy also includes *system folders*, such as the Schedule+ Free/Busy folder. I'll talk about it and the other system folders later in this chapter.

FIGURE 6.8   The default public folder store property of a mailbox database in Exchange Server 2007

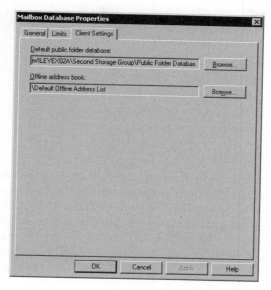

If a specific public folder doesn't exist in the default public folder store, the client is provided a list of servers where the public folder resides, sorted by distance, based on Active Directory cost. As you can imagine, when many public folders are accessed over a lower-bandwidth network, server and network loads can get pretty heavy as users access public folders on one or a limited number of Exchange servers. If you need to, you can replicate folders on one Exchange server to other Exchange servers.

When would you want to create replicas of public folders? There are five main circumstances, but perhaps you can think of additional ones:

- When you need to balance public folder access loads on your Exchange servers. Having all your users connect to a single server for all their public folder access can quickly result in an overwhelmed server if you have a large number of users or if you have heavy public folder usage.

- When you have an Exchange server or group of Exchange servers separated from other servers in your organization by low-bandwidth links. In that case, you may be better off having limited replication traffic over your links and allowing users to connect to local replicas, keeping their traffic on the LAN.

- When IMAP4 clients see folders only on the Exchange server to which they connect, including public folders. If you want an IMAP4 client to be able to see a specific public folder, you must create a replica of that folder on the IMAP4 user's Mailbox server.

- When public folder replication is essential when you're planning to remove an Exchange server from your organization (like all those Exchange 2003 servers you're migrating away from). If the server you're removing hosts the only replica for a set of public folders and you don't want to lose those folders, you must replicate them to another Exchange server in your organization.

- When you are coexisting with previous versions of Exchange, you must have a replica of the public folder on an Exchange 2007 server in order to provide access to the content from within the same Outlook Web Access browser window.

Now that I've whetted your appetite regarding public folder replication, I'll tackle the subject in further detail in the next section.

Managing Public Folders

All of what I said about public folders in single administrative group environments in the "Replicating Public Folders" section of this chapter applies to public folders in multi-administrative group environments. Again, remember that with Exchange Server 2007 you may have multiple administrative groups while you're in the process of upgrading your organization from an earlier version of Exchange, but you will end up with a single administrative group when you've finally switched completely to Exchange Server 2007. Until that day, though, you'll need to use the Exchange 2003 Exchange System Manager to manage fully some of the complications listed in this section.

Public folder management gets to be more complex as additional administrative groups are created and connected by routing groups. Two issues come to mind immediately.

First, an Exchange organization's one and only MAPI-based default public folder tree can remain in the administrative group where it was originally created or can be moved to another administrative group. In either case, when the default public folder tree has been moved to a new administrative group, control of its management can be delegated to a specially constituted Windows group.

 WARNING   Do not delete the administrative group where the Exchange public folder hierarchy is found. Public folders *will* stop working.

Second, as Exchange organizations grow in size and complexity, nothing becomes more important on the public folders side than the location of public folders and replicas of public folders. You can significantly reduce network traffic and decrease folder access times by replicating heavily accessed public folders to Exchange servers in different sites with relatively low-bandwidth links to the Exchange servers where the public folders currently reside.

Let's take a closer look at public folder tree management and public folder replication.

Performing Public Folder Replication

Technically, all copies of a public folder, including the one on the Exchange server where the folder was originally created, are called *replicas*. There's good reason for this. After a folder has been replicated, users will place items into it via the replica on their own default public folders server or on the nearest server as calculated using connector costs. So, no replica of the folder can be considered a master copy. The replicas of a folder update each other on a regular basis, reinforcing the idea that there is no master copy.

You can set up replication of a public folder on either the server that will provide the folder or the server that will hold the new replica of the public folder. To replicate a folder, follow the steps outlined in Exercise 6.3.

EXERCISE 6.3

Creating Public Folder Replicas

Follow these steps to replicate a public folder:

1. On an Exchange Server 2007 computer, click Start ➤ All Programs ➤ Microsoft Exchange Server 2007 ➤ Exchange Management Console.

2. Expand the Toolbox node, and click on the Public Folder Management Console.

3. Expand the Default Public Folders node in the Public Folder Management Console, then right-click the folder to be replicated, and select Properties from the context menu. This opens the Properties dialog box for the public folder.

4. Switch to the Replication tab, shown here.

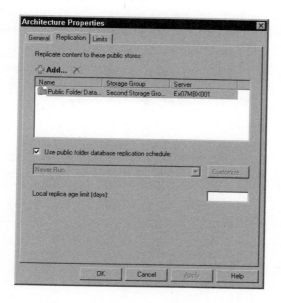

EXERCISE 6.3 *(continued)*

5. To add a replica of the public folder to another public folder database, click the Add button to open the Select Public Folder Databases dialog box, shown here.

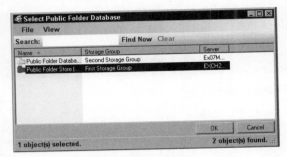

6. Select the server to which the replica is to be added and click OK.

7. Click OK to close the public folder's Properties dialog box.

Some of the other properties dealing with public folder replication you can configure include the schedule to replicate and the replication priority, as shown in Figure 6.9. The public folder replication interval is based on a schedule you can set. Depending on the importance of the contents of the folder and the available network bandwidth, you can accept the default Always Run, select other options from the drop-down list, or create your own custom schedule for replication of this folder.

FIGURE 6.9 The Replication tab of the public folder's Properties dialog box

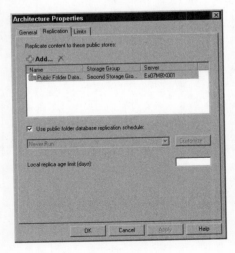

Verifying Public Folder Replication

You can verify the existence of a replica on the Exchange Server 2007 Mailbox server by using the Get-PublicFolderStatistics cmdlet. Alternatively, you can just use the Exchange Server 2003 System Manager to examine the Public Folders node of the public folder database. The replicated public folder will show up for viewing as well.

That's really all there is to public folder replication. Monitoring replication is a matter of attending to the replication status of your replicas and, of course, ensuring that the connectors between your routing groups are up and running.

Setting Public Folders Options

Although a good deal of public folder management has to do with replication and limits, there is more to public folders. Let's take a look at some of the public folder configuration options available to you. The tabs you'll see when you go to manage the properties of a public folder will depend on whether it has been mail-enabled. The General, Replication, and Limits tabs are available for all public folders, regardless of whether they've been mail-enabled. The Exchange General, E-Mail Addresses, Mail Flow Settings, and Member Of tabs exist only for mail-enabled public folders. The Member Of tab is only used for listing the distribution lists that the public folder is a member of, and cannot be used to manage these memberships. I covered the General, Replication, and Limits tabs earlier, so we will focus on just these additional tabs.

EXCHANGE GENERAL

The Exchange General tab, shown in Figure 6.10, has fields to define how the mail-enabled public folder is viewed in the global address list (GAL). The alias for the public folder can be set. Also the display name and the simple display name may be set. You may be wondering why you need a display name and a simple display name, and the answer is actually pretty simple. The display name is used to identify the public folder in the GAL and accepts Unicode characters. The simple display name is used for backward compatibility with older clients and third-party products since it supports only ASCII characters.

FIGURE 6.10 The Exchange General tab of the public folder's Properties dialog box

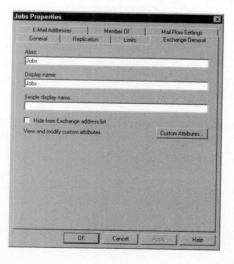

This tab also allows you to select the Hide from Exchange Address List property, which keeps the mail-enabled public folder from showing up in the address list. If you want users to be able to send mail that appears to be from the public folder, or to select the public folder from the GAL and send email to it, you would not want to hide it from the GAL.

The last option on this tab is the Custom Attributes button. This option opens the window shown in Figure 6.11, which will allow you to modify the custom attributes for the public folders. Custom attributes can be assigned to all mailboxes and public folders. These are additional properties that can be used for capturing information that does not fit into predefined properties. This could be project numbers, general ledger accounts, or an attribute that could be used to include this recipient in an address list or dynamic distribution group.

FIGURE 6.11   The Custom Attributes dialog box accessed through the public folder's Properties dialog box

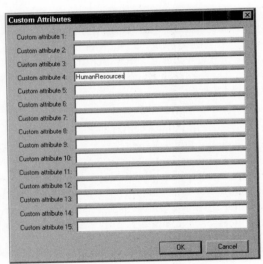

E-MAIL ADDRESSES

The E-Mail Addresses tab, shown in Figure 6.12, is similar to the same tab for a mailbox. You can use it to modify the assigned email addresses or to exempt the public folder from having its email addresses automatically assigned by the address policy.

MAIL FLOW SETTINGS

The Mail Flow Settings tab, shown in Figure 6.13, is used to configure a lot of the more advanced mail-enabled public folder settings, such as delivery options and message size and delivery restrictions.

FIGURE 6.12   The E-Mail Addresses tab of the public folder's Properties dialog box

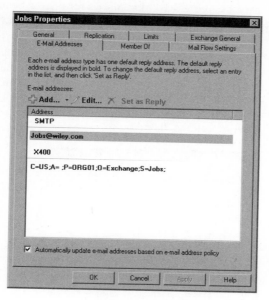

FIGURE 6.13   The Mail Flow Settings tab of the public folder's Properties dialog box

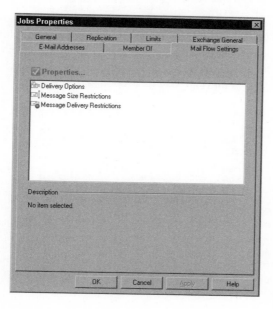

Selecting the Delivery Options property from the Mail Flow Settings tab brings up an additional dialog box, shown in Figure 6.14, that allows for setting Send on Behalf permissions and the ability to forward any email delivered to another mail-enabled object. You would grant the Send on Behalf permission if you want to allow a user to send an email that appears to have been sent from the public folder. This is often done when a public folder is used to receive email for an entire department, such as customer service, IT support, or a job posting queue, and the responses to the inbound email messages would come from the public folder.

FIGURE 6.14 The Delivery Options dialog box

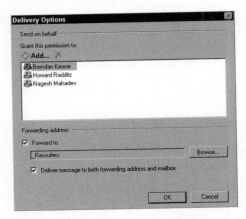

The Message Size Restrictions dialog box accessed from the Mail Flow Settings tab is shown in Figure 6.15 and is primarily used to limit the size of messages that can be sent or received by the public folder. This would usually be changed only if the limits for this public folder differed from the global message size restriction settings.

FIGURE 6.15 The Message Size Restrictions dialog box

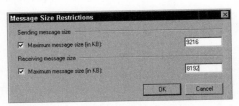

Lastly, the Message Delivery Restrictions settings, shown in Figure 6.16, by default allow anyone with appropriate client permissions to send email to the public folder. The options here allow a much more granular control of which security principles are able to send email to the public folder.

FIGURE 6.16 The Message Delivery Restrictions dialog box

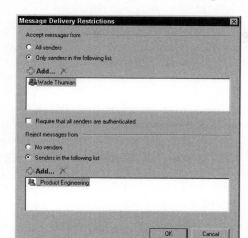

Summary

If you're new to Exchange 2007 or don't have a lot of investment in public folders in your current Exchange organization, then you probably haven't been too worried about the rumors of the demise of public folders in Exchange 2007. These rumors are, fortunately, not true; public folders are still supported in Exchange, even if the out-of-the box management options aren't all that we could want.

By concentrating its effort on providing solid support for public folder management in the Exchange Management Shell, Microsoft has finally provided the missing command-line management interface that can simplify dealing with one-off public folder management tasks. These cmdlets also make it easy to do large-scale scripted and bulk management operations.

The lack of all the features that were included in the Exchange 2003 GUI is offset by Microsoft's continued development and support of the PFDAVAdmin tool, which provides a familiar interface for those who are used to the legacy Exchange System Manager. However, it also gives you a lot more power, providing sophisticated bulk operations and import/export capabilities that make managing large public folder deployments smoother. While you still have legacy servers in your organization, you can continue using the legacy System Manager to manage your public folder replicas.

Exam Essentials

Know the different types of public folder permissions.   Public folders, like most other objects in Active Directory, can be configured with permissions to determine access to the public folders themselves. Public folders have three different sets of permissions that can be configured on them: client permissions, directory rights, and administrative rights. Permissions are configured from the Permissions tab of the public folder's Properties dialog box. Client permissions determine which users are allowed to perform specific tasks in the public folder, such as posting new items and creating new child folders. Directory rights are used to configure the NTFS permissions that determine who can perform modifications on the public folder object that is stored in Active Directory. Administrative rights allow you to assign NTFS permissions to users and groups that determine who is actually allowed to perform administrative tasks on the public folder.

Learn the PowerShell commands.   Almost every configuration or management action you perform from the Exchange Management Console will present you with the PowerShell code that was used to perform the action. Take advantage of this information, and learn how to use the Exchange Management Shell to your advantage. Some of these commands are likely to make an appearance on your exam as well.

Know where to go.   You will likely be asked many times on the exam what configuration is needed to produce the required results. The Exchange Management Console and other management tool have been completely redesigned to either make it easier to navigate or to work with new features in Exchange Server 2007. To more easily distinguish the correct answer on the exam it is important to remember how each tool works and how to use the tools for common administrative tasks. Take the time as you review the material in this book to think about what types of configuration and management tasks you find yourself performing in each of the Exchange Management tools.

Review Questions

1. A user named Perry is the owner of a public folder named Research. Perry leaves your company, and another administrator deletes Perry's user account. What would you do as an administrator to modify the permissions on the Research folder?

   A. Create a new account with the same user information as the deleted account.

   B. Restore a backup tape of the server that was created before Perry was deleted.

   C. Designate your account as the owner of the Research folder.

   D. Create a new public folder, and move the contents of the Research folder to it.

2. Which cmdlet can you use to get a complete listing of all public folders on a Mailbox server?

   A. `Get-PublicFolderStatistics`

   B. `Get-PublicFolder`

   C. `Get-PublicFolderStatus`

   D. `Get-PublicFolderListing`

3. What would be the proper command to issue to mail-enable the Activities public folder and have it be hidden from the global address list?

   A. `Enable-MailPublicFolder-Identity "\Activities" -HiddenFromAddressLists: $false`

   B. `Enable-MailPublicFolder-Identity "\Activities" -ShownInAddressLists: $true`

   C. `Enable-MailPublicFolder-Identity "\Activities" -HiddenFromAddressLists: $true`

   D. `Enable-MailPublicFolder-Identity "\Activities" -HiddenFromAddressListsEnabled`

4. Which of the following predefined public folder roles enable a user to delete items other than the items they created? (Choose all that apply.)

   A. Owner

   B. Reviewer

   C. Editor

   D. Publishing Author

5. Which cmdlet will you need to use to configure most of the properties of a public folder?

   A. `Put-PublicFolder`

   B. `Update-PublicFolder`

   C. `Configure-PublicFolder`

   D. `Set-PublicFolder`

6. From which of the following tools can you configure replicas for public folders?

   A. Exchange Management Console

   B. Active Directory Users and Computers

   C. Exchange System Manager

   D. PFDAVAdmin

7. What kind of permissions must you configure to give Exchange recipients the ability to manage and create content within public folders?

   A. Directory rights

   B. Recipient rights

   C. Administrative rights

   D. Client rights

8. Which cmdlet will you need to use to add client permissions to a public folder?

   A. Add-PublicFolderClientPermission

   B. Put-PublicFolderClientPermission

   C. Configure-PublicFolderClientPermission

   D. Set-PublicFolderClientPermission

9. Which three users are included by default on the permissions list of a new public folder?

   A. The user who created the folder

   B. The local Administrator account

   C. A special user account named Default

   D. A special user account named Anonymous

   E. The Exchange Administrator account

10. Which of the following tasks can the PFDAVAdmin tool be used for? (Choose all that apply.)

    A. Export and import public folder replica lists.

    B. Export folder permissions on folders, public folder stores, and mailbox stores.

    C. Perform bulk operations on folder properties. In addition, you can do bulk search and removal operations of per-item permissions.

    D. Apply changes to your list of replicas to a folder and all subfolders without overwriting each folder's replica list.

11. Your organization has a public folder named Safety Issues that employees use to post notices about safety hazards that have been located within your office buildings and warehouses. You want all employees in the company to be able to post new items into this folder and read any existing items but perform no other actions. What role do you need to configure for the Default user on this public folder?

    A. Contributor

    B. Author

    C. Nonediting Author

    D. Editor

12. Where in System Manager would you go to find out the current replication state of public folders on a server?

    A. The property pages for that server

    B. The property pages for the public folder

    C. The property pages for the public folder store

    D. The Replication Status subcontainer of the public folder store

    E. The Public Folders subcontainer of the public folder store

13. You recently created a public folder that employees of your company can use to post personal announcements, such as marriages and births. You have now become aware that a number of people are also posting large attachments to messages in the form of photos or other documents. This is causing the public folder to swell considerably in size. People enjoy the Announcements folder, and you want to keep it available. However, you want to keep users from posting large messages or attachments. What is your best option?

    A. Set a limit on the size of messages that each user may send by using the property pages for that user.

    B. Set a limit on the size of messages that can be posted in the public folder by using the folder's property pages.

    C. Set a limit on the maximum size that a public folder can reach before new posts are prohibited, and then manually delete large posts.

    D. Set a limit on the maximum size that a public folder can reach before new posts are prohibited, and then create a script that deletes large posts automatically.

14. The age limit on your public folders is set to 14 days. The deleted-item retention time is set to 7 days. A user deletes an item 12 days after it was created. That same user then recovers the deleted item 7 days later. How long will it be until the item expires?

    A. The item will expire immediately.

    B. The item will expire in 2 days.

    C. The item will expire in 5 days.

    D. The item will expire in 14 days.

15. What task would require using the Exchange Management Shell to manage? (Choose all that apply.)

    A. Get statistics for public folders.

    B. Suspend and resume public folder replication.

    C. Schedule backups.

    D. Configure OWA options.

16. The Exchange Management Shell is built on what Windows technology?

    A. Internet Information Services (IIS) 7.0

    B. Windows Shadow copy

    C. Windows PowerShell

    D. NTFS

17. What role is a user automatically assigned when they create an Exchange public folder?

    A. Author

    B. Editor

    C. Guest

    D. Owner

18. Where can you find additional scripts to perform complex Exchange 2007 tasks?

    A. \I386 folder

    B. Subfolder of the Exchange 2007 installation folder

    C. \Windows\System

    D. Windows Server 2008 installation CD

19. In Exchange 2007 public folders, the Publishing Editor has what permissions? (Choose all that apply.)

    A. Delete Items

    B. Folder Owner

    C. Folder Contact

    D. Create Subfolders

20. By default, public folder stores are not created on Exchange 2007 Mailbox servers unless you specify that the server will be used with clients running what version of Outlook?

    A. Outlook Express

    B. Microsoft Office Outlook 2007

    C. Microsoft Office Outlook 2003 and earlier

    D. Microsoft Entourage 2004 and earlier

Answers to Review Questions

1. **C.** An administrator has the permission to change the owner of a folder. Once the administrator takes ownership of the folder, they can perform administrative tasks, such as adding rules and installing forms.

2. **A.** You will use the `Get-PublicFolderStatistics` cmdlet to get a listing of all public folders on a server.

3. **D.** To mail-enable the Activities public folder and cause it to be hidden from the global address list, you would use the `Enable-MailPublicFolder-Identity "\Activities" -HiddenFromAddressListsEnabled` command.

4. **A, C.** Only the Owner, Editor, and Publishing Editor of a public folder can delete items other than their own. The Publishing Author, Author, and Nonediting Author can delete their own items only. All other roles cannot delete any items.

5. **D.** The `Set-PublicFolder` cmdlet allows you to set most of the properties for the named public folder, such as limits, replicas, replication schedules, and more, as in `Set-Public-Folder -Identity "\Jobs\Posted" -Server "WILEXEX01A"`.

6. **C.** Of the available tools, only the Exchange System Manager provides a means to configure public folder replication options.

7. **D.** Client permissions assign access rights to Exchange users and distribution groups, who can then work with a public folder using their Outlook clients.

8. **A.** To configure client permissions on a public folder, you will need to use the `Add-PublicFolderClientPermission` cmdlet.

9. **A, C, D.** When a public folder is created, the user who created the folder is given the role of folder owner. The Default user represents all users who have access to the public folder store and aren't explicitly listed in the permissions list. The Anonymous user represents all users logged on with anonymous access.

10. **A, B, C, D.** You can use the PFDAVAdmin tool to do the following:
    - Perform bulk operations on folder properties. In addition, you can do bulk search and removal operations of per-item permissions.
    - Apply changes to your list of replicas to a folder and all subfolders without overwriting each folder's replica list (that is, add or remove specific server entries without making each folder's replica list an exact copy of your starting point).
    - Export and import public folder replica lists.
    - Export folder permissions on folders, public folder stores, and mailbox stores.

11. C. The Nonediting Author role will allow users to read existing items in the public folder and create new items but will not allow them any other permissions on the public folder

12. D. The Replication Status subcontainer lists all folders and the number of servers that contain a replica of each folder. It also lists the current replication state and the time of the last replication.

13. B. The Limits tab for a public folder contains several settings that govern public folder limits. One setting allows you to specify the maximum size of messages that can be posted to the public folder. This is the best way to ensure that large posts are not made. Setting a limit on the size of the messages that users can send would also restrict the sending of regular email messages. Deleting posts, whether done manually or automatically, might be considered intrusive and arbitrary by users.

14. D. Since the item was recovered after the original expiration date, a new expiration date is set equal to the original expiration period. If the item had been recovered before the original expiration date, it would have then expired on the original expiration date.

15. A, B. Although the PFMC is good for many common tasks, there are a few things that you will need to use the EMS to manage, such as getting statistics for public folders and suspending and resuming public folder replication.

16. C. The EMS is built on Windows PowerShell technology.

17. D. When a user creates an Exchange public folder, they are automatically assigned the Owner role.

18. B. Additional scripts can be found in the subfolder of the Exchange 2007 installation folder.

19. A, D. Among the permissions the Publishing Editor has are Delete Items and Create Subfolders

20. C. By default, public folder stores are not created on Exchange 2007 Mailbox servers unless you specify that the server will be used with clients running Outlook 2003 and earlier.

Chapter

7

Configuring Security, Compliance, and Policies

MICROSOFT EXAM OBJECTIVE COVERED IN THIS CHAPTER:

✓ **Configuring the Exchange Infrastructure**

- Configure transport rules and message compliance.

- Configure policies.

- Configure the antivirus and antispam system.

Thanks to government regulations, companies such as Enron, and an overabundance of lawyers, we find ourselves in a world with a great many rules and compliance requirements. Exchange Server 2007 comes with marked improvements and added features to help you get started in this regulated world. The main focus of the Exchange Server 2007 compliance feature set is regulatory compliance, applied in business sectors such as publicly traded companies, financial services companies, and medical companies. The compliance feature set also focuses on protecting private information and providing solutions that ensure that corporate governance principles are being maintained.

The feature set is basically "compliance in transport." A design change in Exchange Server 2007 now forces every message in an Exchange organization to travel through a Hub Transport server. Even messages sent between mailboxes in the same database and on the same Mailbox server have to travel through a Hub Transport server. This was a deliberate design change in Exchange Server 2007 that allows actions to be done to every message in an Exchange organization. These actions are what enable you to ensure that your Exchange organization is meeting compliance requirements.

Other functionality, such as antivirus and antispam, is also extremely important for today's messaging systems. These features ensure that all messages are virus free and as few spam messages as possible are delivered to your users' mailboxes. This chapter goes over each of these topics.

The main topics of this chapter are as follows:

- Messaging records management

- Server-based rules

- Message classifications

- Server-based policies

- Configuring and managing antispam settings

Configuring Message Compliance and Record Management

Corporate compliance requirements are becoming increasingly important across business sectors and geographies. In the United States, the market focus has primarily been on regulatory compliance for publicly traded companies and companies operating in regulated sectors, such as healthcare and financial services. In addition to compliance requirements, attention is being focused on protecting private information and on providing solutions that ensure that corporate governance principles are being maintained.

Most compliance-based market attention is focused on the requirements to abide by regulations such as the Health Insurance Portability and Accountability Act (HIPAA), the Sarbanes-Oxley (SOX) Act, the EU Data Protection Act, and California SB 1386. However, the broader demand is driven by the need to maintain controlled access and show both information and process integrity for electronic communications. This section will cover the basic compliance feature concepts and how to configure the compliance features offered by Exchange Server 2007.

Message compliance in Exchange Server 2007 is facilitated by messaging records management (MRM). MRM is an Enterprise feature set that controls the contents of custom and default managed folders. Managed folders are folders that appear in users' mailboxes and are controlled by the administrator. You can create custom *managed folders* or work with the default folders. Folder contents are controlled by the *managed content settings* that control the life span of a message by moving, deleting, and archiving/journaling messages when you say so. Groups of managed folders can be conveniently assigned to users' mailboxes by means of *managed folder mailbox policies*. All the settings and tasks are then applied to the folders when you want them to be applied by the *managed folder assistant*.

Exchange MRM depends on users to classify their own messages. One of the keys to successful MRM deployment is coupling the right folder structure with effective retention limits so users can correctly designate messages that need to be retained. The other key is effective training and simplification of the categorization process so that users will not have issues determining how to classify a message.

When it comes to planning and deploying MRM, you should consider these key planning points:

- For MRM and messaging policies to be truly effective, you need to prohibit personal folders (.pst) on your network. You cannot control the messages in a personal folder. Because you cannot control them, they present a bit of a hole in any effort to conform to a compliance requirement or in any effort to control messages.

- Apply content settings and policies to default folders. This provides retention actions for message types stored in the default set of user folders. Everyone has these folders, and this is where you can make the most automated impact on messages. If you don't want to delete items from the default folders automatically, you may consider creating a Review and Then Delete folder into which Inbox mail is moved after a given period of time.

- Create any custom-managed folders that you might need in order to fulfill any corporate governing body's compliance requirements. With custom folders created, you should create content settings and apply them to the default and custom folders to ensure that needed items will be properly retained while still maintaining good storage management practices.

- Consider creating a custom self-service web page that uses Exchange web services to allow users to subscribe to their own managed custom folders. Eventually there will probably be prepackaged web pages for this, but for now, this will mean some custom development work.

- With all these settings and mail manipulations in place, how will you know whether they are working? To be best informed, you should develop a tracking plan that monitors how messages are being retained, moved, and dealt with.

- Before implementing any compliance, get buy-in from all of the required stakeholders, like your auditors and legal staff. This way you can make sure you meet the compliance requirements.

Configuring Managed Folders

The Exchange Server 2007 managed folders feature enables you to create message retention folders that better organize and manage email messages. Managed email folders are automatically created in target users' mailboxes. An automated process scans the Inbox and these folders in order to retain, expire, or journal messages based on managed content settings. Once you've created the managed folders, users choose in which retention folder a given item should be placed. This is why it is important to preplan the folder names and structure of your managed folders.

Two types of managed folders are available in Exchange Server 2007:

Managed custom folders   Managed custom folders are folders you can create in user mailboxes. They are controlled by the administrator and cannot be renamed, moved, or deleted by the user. They should be given names that reflect their intended purpose—remember that users will decide what goes in these folders. Think like a user, and make the names as short and descriptive as possible.

Managed default folders   Managed default folders are the folders that Exchange creates by default, such as the Sent Items, Deleted Items, and Inbox folders. The administrator and the users can't create new managed default folders or rename managed default folders.

Although you cannot change the name of the default folders, you can create a custom folder with a folder of the same name. For example, you could apply a content setting of Delete After 30 Days to the Inbox of a specific group of users and then create another custom Inbox called Year Inbox. The Year Inbox folder would be created as a type that corresponds to the folder you want to replace. An example would be an Inbox type, and it could be given to users based on a managed mailbox policy. The policy would determine which Inbox folder the users would see: the 30-day one or Year Inbox. The Year Inbox folder would replace the default Inbox folder but would still be named Inbox to the users. In this example, users would always see the standard default folder name Inbox in their mailboxes, regardless of whether the mailbox policy specified the 30-day Inbox or Year Inbox folder. In addition, you can specify only one Inbox; you cannot have two instances of any default folders in a user's mailbox.

To create a managed folder, perform the steps outlined in Exercise 7.1 and Exercise 7.2.

 Real World Scenario

Rules and MRM Used for International Biotech's Compliance

It has been noticed that certain business sectors have more requirements placed upon them than others. One example of this is an international biotech company that works in the medical field and on classified projects with many different agencies. This company therefore has some complex message retention needs. For example, one agency wants all messages to be secure, another agency wants all project data to be retained for seven years, and another organization requires that certain messages are to have limited distribution. Prior to deploying Exchange Server 2007, this company used a number of third-party tools and manual employee systems to attempt to comply.

This company was excited to have Exchange Server 2007 and Outlook 2007 because it allowed the company's employees simply to classify messages based on project and compliance needs from within Outlook. They were also able to leverage transport rules to classify some of the messages automatically, to reduce further the probability of error and frustration. Once the messages were classified, MRM moved the messages where they needed to be to have the right content setting applied and thus be retained in the proper manner. Transport rules also helped the company limit the locations to which messages can be sent and from which they can be received.

MRM, message classification, and transport rules allowed this company to free up resources from its compliance effort so it could focus on efforts that have a more positive effect on the company's bottom line.

EXERCISE 7.1

Creating a Managed Folder Using the Exchange Management Console

To create a managed folder using the Exchange Management Console, follow these steps:

1. Open the Exchange Management Console, and click the Mailbox node in the Organization Configuration section. In the Actions pane to the right, select New Managed Custom Folder or New Managed Default Folder. This will launch the wizard to create a new managed folder.

2. On the first page of the New Managed Folder Wizard, fill out the Name field and then select the default folder type of the folder you plan on replacing with the new managed folder. For some folder types, you will be able to add a message that will be displayed in Outlook or OWA. Once you've filled out this page, click New and you will create the managed folder.

3. On the first page of the New Managed Custom Folder Wizard, fill in the name and the Outlook display name, set a storage limit if you need one, and then add the Outlook or OWA message if needed. Once you've filled out this page, click New and you will create the new custom managed folder.

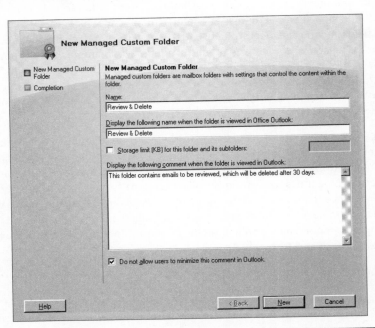

EXERCISE 7.2

Creating a Managed Folder Using the Exchange Management Shell

Follow these steps to create a managed folder using the Exchange Management Shell:

1. Open the Exchange Management Shell, and run the following command to create a managed custom folder (make sure to change the parameters enclosed in brackets):

    ```
    New-ManagedFolder -Name <Folder_Name>
    -FolderName <Folder_Display_Name>
    ```

2. To create a new managed default folder run the following command:

    ```
    New-ManagedFolder -Name <Folder_Name>
    -DefaultFolderType <Default_Folder_Type>
    ```

Configuring Managed Content Settings

The Exchange Server 2007 MRM message content settings allow you to control the life span of messages. You can control a message's life span in two ways:

- By controlling how long a message is retained in a folder before it is moved or deleted.
- By controlling the journaling or archiving of a message to an archival location. Message content settings can be applied to both default and user-created custom managed folders.

Each managed folder should have a managed content setting applied to it that defines what should be done with the messages in the folder. Managed content settings can apply to all items in a folder or to specific message types (message type examples are voicemail messages, email messages, and task items). The managed content settings for a folder specify three retention settings:

- The period of time a message should be retained in the folder.
- When the retention period starts. Does it start once a message is placed in x folder, when the message is created, or after the message has been in a folder for x days?
- What action should be taken at the end of the retention period? Should the message be deleted or moved or placed somewhere else, possibly in an archival system?

As an example, you could create a managed content setting that moves all messages in everyone's Sent Items folder to a custom managed folder called Review & Delete. You could then specify that everything in the Review & Delete folder be deleted after 30 days. To create a new managed content setting, follow the steps outlined in Exercise 7.3 and Exercise 7.4.

EXERCISE 7.3

Creating a Managed Content Setting Using the Exchange Management Console

Follow these steps to manage content settings using the Exchange Management Console:

1. Open the Exchange Management Console, and click the Mailbox node in the Organization Configuration section. Select the Default or Custom Managed Folder tab, and then select the folder to which you want to apply the setting. In the Actions pane to the right, select New Managed Content Setting. This will launch the New Managed Content Settings Wizard.

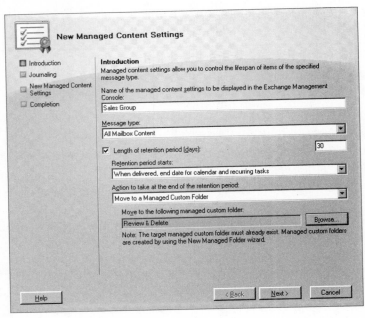

2. On the first page of the New Managed Content Settings Wizard, enter the name of the content setting, select the type of messages you want to change in the folder, and then configure the retention periods and actions. Click Next.

3. On the second page of the wizard, you can configure journaling by selecting a message format for a journaling mailbox. Click Next.

4. On the summary page, verify that all the settings are correct and then click New to create the custom content setting.

EXERCISE 7.4

Creating a Managed Content Setting Using the Exchange Management Shell

Open the Exchange Management Shell, and run one of the following commands (make sure to change the parameters enclosed in brackets):

```
New-ManagedContentSettings -FolderName <Folder_To_Apply_Setting_TO>
-MessageClass <Item_Type> -Name <Setting_Name> -RetentionEnabled $true
-RetentionAction <Action>
-AgeLimitForRetention    <Age_Of_Item_Before_Action_Is_Taken>
```

Configuring Managed Folder Mailbox Policies

You can use managed folder mailbox policies to create a group of folders that you can then apply to single user or groups of users. Say you have salespeople that all need the same folders: 100 Days to Delete, Keep Forever, and Keep for X Years. If you created a policy that had each folder in it, you could simply apply that policy to the sales group and then the salespeople would all have the folders. Otherwise, you would have to add each folder one at a time for every sales user. In this section, first I will cover how to create a managed folder mailbox policy and then I will cover how to apply the policy to a user. To create and apply a managed folder mailbox policy, follow the steps outlined in Exercise 7.5, Exercise 7.6, Exercise 7.7, and Exercise 7.8.

EXERCISE 7.5

Creating a Managed Folder Mailbox Policy Using the Exchange Management Console

Create a managed folder mailbox policy using the Exchange Management Console, using these steps:

1.   Open the Exchange Management Console, and click the Mailbox node in the Organization Configuration section. In the Actions pane to the right, select New Managed Folder Mailbox Policy. This will launch the New Managed Folder Mailbox Policy Wizard.

2. On the first page of the New Managed Folder Mailbox Policy Wizard, enter the name for the policy, click the Add button, and add the folders you want in the policy. Once everything is filled out, click the New button to create the managed folder mailbox policy.

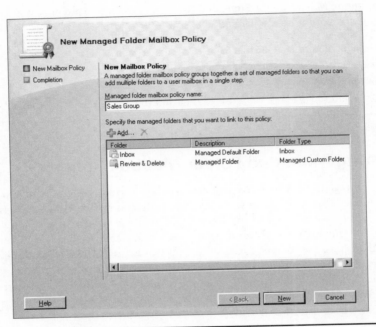

EXERCISE 7.6

Creating a Managed Folder Mailbox Policy Using the Exchange Management Shell

Open the Exchange Management Shell, and run one of the following commands (make sure to change the parameters enclosed in brackets):

```
New-ManagedFolderMailboxPolicy -Name <Policy_Name>
-ManagedFolderLinks <Folder_Names>
```

EXERCISE 7.7

Applying a Managed Folder Mailbox Policy Using the Exchange Management Console

Use the Exchange Management Console to apply a managed folder mailbox policy, by following these steps:

1. Open the Exchange Management Console, and click the Recipients node in the Recipients Configuration section. In the Actions pane, right-click a user and select Properties. Select the Mailbox Settings tab.

2. On the Mailbox Settings tab, select Managed Records Management and in the Messaging Records Management dialog box, check the Managed Folder Mailbox Policy box.

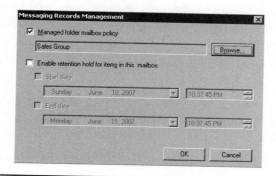

EXERCISE 7.8

Applying a Managed Folder Mailbox Policy Using Exchange Management Shell

Open the Exchange Management Shell, and run one of the following commands (make sure to change the parameters enclosed in brackets):

```
Set-Mailbox -Identity <Mailbox_Name>
-ManagedFolderMailboxPolicy <Managed_folder_Mailbox_Policy_Name>
```

Configuring the Managed Folder Assistant

The managed folder assistant is the Exchange Server 2007 function that creates managed folders in mailboxes and then applies managed content settings. When the managed folder assistant is run, it will process every mailbox on the server. The assistant can be scheduled to run with a start time and an end time. If it does not complete processing all of the mail-boxes on a server in the allotted time, the next time it starts it will continue where it left off. Keep in mind that the assistant is not scheduled by default; you must manually enable it or the managed content settings won't ever be applied.

Be aware that running the managed folder assistant is a resource-intensive process. The process has to read the date on every object in a mailbox, calculate how that date relates to the managed content settings, and then act on the actions in the settings. The managed folder assistant should be run only when the server can tolerate the extra load. It doesn't have to run every night; you should run the assistant just enough to satisfy your compliance obligations. To schedule the managed folder assistant, perform the steps outlined in Exercise 7.9 and Exercise 7.10.

EXERCISE 7.9

Scheduling the Managed Folder Assistant Using the Exchange Management Console

Use the Exchange Management Console to schedule the managed folder assistant, by following these steps:

1. Open the Exchange Management Console, and click the Mailbox node in the Server Configuration section. Right-click a server on which you want to schedule the assistant to run, and select Properties. Select the Messaging Records Management tab.

2. On the Messaging Records Management tab, click the Customize button and schedule when you want to run the assistant.

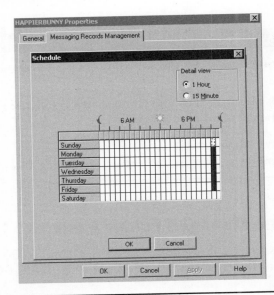

EXERCISE 7.10

Scheduling the Managed Folder Assistant Using the Exchange Management Shell

Open the Exchange Management Shell, and run one of the following commands (make sure to change the parameters enclosed in brackets):

```
Set-MailboxServer -Identity <Mailbox__Server_Name>
-ManagedFolderAssistantSchedule <Day_StartTime_Day_StopTime>
```

Configuring Message Classifications

The Exchange Server 2007 message classification feature allows administrators to create classifications for users to apply to messages. This allows users to classify messages according to their content or intended purpose. When a user applies a classification in Outlook 2007 or OWA 2007, metadata is added to the message. This metadata gives instructions to the recipients and/or to the transport server to help them make decisions about what to do with the messages.

When the recipient opens the message in Outlook or OWA, the classification metadata is used to retrieve and then display a classification message to the recipient. The classification message helps the recipient determine how to treat the message. One of the default classifications is Company Confidential. The Company Confidential classification has a classification message that says, "This message contains sensitive information, the distribution of which should be limited." This will remind the user to not send the message to competitors or people who should not see it in general. Figure 7.1 is an example of what a client would see when viewing a classified message.

FIGURE 7.1 Viewing a classified message in Outlook

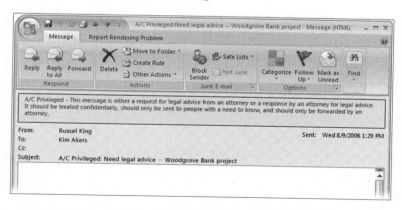

Message classifications can also be applied or acted upon by server-based transport rules. For example, you could have a rule that removes attachments from messages that were deemed inappropriate. After the rule removed the attachment, it could apply another rule that would then tell the user what happened to the message attachment. You could also have a rule that looks for messages with a Company Confidential classification on them, keeps those messages from leaving the company, and then forwards the message to a compliance officer. The compliance officer could then perform any additional steps to remedy the incident.

Exchange Server 2007 ships with a default set of five classifications, as outlined in Table 7.1.

TABLE 7.1 Exchange Server 2007 Default Classifications

Default Classification	Default Classification Message
A/C Privileged	This message contains legally sensitive information that is privileged between an attorney and a client.
Attachment Removed	This message had one or more attachments that were removed for security purposes.
Company Confidential	This message contains sensitive information, the distribution of which should be limited.
Company Internal	This message contains information that should not be forwarded or disseminated outside the company.
Partner Mail	This message contains content from or to business partners.

You can modify classifications and the classification messages based on your company needs, and you can create new classifications using the Exchange Management Shell command New-MessageClassification. Here is an example of an Exchange Management Shell command that can be used to create a new message classification:

```
New-MessageClassification -Name ContractReview -DisplayName "Contract Review"
-SenderDescription "This message has been classified as relating to
  contract reviews" -RecipientDescription "This message has been
classified as being related to contract review and must be treated
  in accordance with company policy"
```

You should be aware of several key attributes that each message classification has.

Display name   This attribute defines how the message classification will appear in Outlook and OWA when a user is selecting the classification to apply.

Sender description   This attribute should explain to the sender what this classification is used for.

Recipient description   This attribute should explain to the recipient what the message classification is used for.

Locale   This attribute specifies a culture code to create a locale-specific version of the message classification. If you have a number of locales, you may need to create a number of different classifications to meet the varied needs of these locations.

If you do not want the recipient to know that a message has been classified, you can set the EnableUserDisplay parameter to $false. You can also assign precedence to classifications to help determine in which order classifications should be applied in the event that a message has more than one classification; to do so, use the DisplayPrecedence parameter when using the Set-MessageClassification cmdlet.

Configuring Message Classifications in Outlook 2007

You must add classifications manually to Outlook 2007 by creating an XML-based file on the server and making it available to the client's computers. The XML file can be generated manually with an Exchange Management Shell script. The script is in a subfolder (named Scripts) of where Exchange is installed on your server. From the folder that has the script, run the following command to create the XML file:

```
.\Export-OutlookClassification.ps1 > c:\exports\Classifications.xml
```

Now that you have the XML file, Classifications.xml, you need to make it available to the client machines. Before Outlook can see this XML-based file, you need to add a Registry key to the computer to turn on this functionality and tell Outlook where the file is stored. But wait, there's more—the Registry key is in the HKEY_Current_User hive, so this has to be added for each user on a given computer. The Registry keys are as follows:

```
[HKEY_CURRENT_USER\Software\Microsoft\Office\12.0\Common\Policy]
"AdminClassificationPath"="c:\Exchange\Classifications.xml"
"EnableClassifications"=dword:00000001
"TrustClassifications"=dword:00000001
```

The AdminClassificationPath key specifies the path from which the client can read the Classifications.xml file. Once the Registry key and the XML-based file are in place on the client computer, Outlook needs to be restarted in order to read the XML file. One last bit of information about classifications: Exchange Server 2007 is a localized server product; almost everything in Exchange can be localized, including the message classification messages. You do this by using the -Locale switch when you create a new classification with the New-MessageClassification Exchange Management Shell command.

Configuring Rights Management Service (RMS) Exchange Agents

Information rights management (IRM) is a useful collateral technology that can be used to protect email messages and documents against improper disclosure. IRM embeds usage information in the document so that access restrictions, expiration information, and policy controls travel with the document. Microsoft's implementation of IRM is based on the Windows Rights Management Server plus, on the client-side, support built into Office 2003, Office 2007, and SharePoint Server 2007. IRM is particularly useful for protecting sensitive content from being improperly forwarded or copied. It also allows for expiration of documents and messages so that they cannot be accessed past a specified date.

Exchange 2007 is the first version of Exchange that is RMS-aware; however, there is no requirement to configure Exchange Server to support Windows Rights Management Server (known as Active Directory Rights Management Services—AD RMS—in Windows Server 2008). The only configuration that can be done is enabling the AD RMS Prelicensing agent. This agent is used to fetch the user licenses on behalf of the client.

Enabling the AD RMS Prelicensing agent is as simple as running the following cmdlet:

```
Enable-TransportAgent "AD RMS Prelicensing Agent"
```

After running this cmdlet you will need to restart the Exchange transport service.

Configuring Transport Rules

Transport rules function similarly to Outlook rules, but they are applied to messages during transport by the Hub and Edge Transport server roles, and they are under complete control of the administrator. As previously mentioned, every message in an Exchange organization must travel through a Hub Transport server. Even messages sent to another mailbox on the same server travel through a Hub Transport server before they are sent right back to the same Mailbox server. Since this is always the case, this puts the Hub Transport server in a position to perform actions on messages consistently as they pass through.

There is one uniform rule applied throughout the organization with which every Hub Transport server has to work. Transport rules are stored in the Configuration container of Active Directory; therefore, all Hub Transport servers share the same set of transport roles.

Transport rules are a great tool for compliance, and as administrators, we can also use them to have some control over users. The following is a list of some actions you can use rules to accomplish:

- You can create ethical walls to limit the interaction of certain groups of users.
- You can filter personal information in emails (SSNs, account numbers, and so on) from being sent.
- You can set up message classifications that can be acted upon by transport rules.

- You can use transport rules to add items such as legal disclaimers, notes, or subjects to messages.

- You can forward, copy, and blind copy messages to additional recipients.

- You can create mail flow rules for enforcing encryption and routing policies.

- You can perform message hygiene functions on an Edge Transport server.

You can do a lot more with rules; they are a flexible tool for controlling email. The Exchange Management Console transport rule GUI is similar to the interface used to create rules in Outlook. You can also work with rules in the Exchange Management Shell.

Transport Predicates

Each transport rule contains two components: a predicate and an action. There are two types of *predicates*:

- Conditions specify which email message attributes, headers, recipients, senders, or other parts of the message are used in identifying which messages a rule should act upon. If no condition is applied to a transport rule, the transport rule applies the configured action unless the message matches a configured exception.

- Exceptions specify messages that should be exempt from a transport rule, even if the message matches a transport rule condition. Exceptions are optional.

Table 7.2 lists all the conditions and exceptions available on a Hub Transport server.

TABLE 7.2   Predicates Available on a Hub Transport Server

Predicate name (EMC)	Predicate name (EMS)	Description
Between members of distribution list and distribution list	BetweenMemberOf	Matches email messages that are sent between members of two distribution groups.
From a member of distribution list	FromMemberOf	Matches the email senders that are members of the specified distribution group.
From people	From	Matches the email senders that are mail-enabled Active Directory objects like mailboxes, mail-enabled users, and contacts. If the From address is from outside the Exchange organization, a contact should be created.

TABLE 7.2 Predicates Available on a Hub Transport Server *(continued)*

Predicate name (EMC)	Predicate name (EMS)	Description
From users inside or outside the organization	FromScope	Matches email messages that are sent from either inside the Exchange organization or outside the Exchange organization.
Marked with classification	HasClassification	Matches messages that are classified with the specified classification.
Marked with importance	WithImportance	Matches messages that are set to the specified importance.
Sent to a member of distribution list	SentToMemberOf	Matches email messages that that are sent to members of the specified distribution group. These recipients can be specified anywhere in the To, carbon copy (Cc), or blind carbon copy (Bcc) fields of the message.
Sent to people	SentTo	Matches email messages that are sent to mailboxes, mail-enabled users, or contacts. These recipients can be specified anywhere in the To, Cc, or Bcc field of the message.
Sent to users inside or outside the organization	SentToScope	Matches email messages that are sent to either inside the Exchange organization or outside the Exchange organization.
When a message header contains specific words	HeaderContains	Matches messages where the specified message header field contains the specified value.

TABLE 7.2 Predicates Available on a Hub Transport Server *(continued)*

Predicate name (EMC)	Predicate name (EMS)	Description
When any attachment file name contains text patterns	`AttachmentNameMatches`	Matches messages that contain text patterns in attachment filenames that match a specified regular expression.
When any of the recipients in the Cc field is a member of distribution list	`AnyOfCcHeaderMemberOf`	Matches messages that are sent to members of a specified distribution group where they are listed in the Cc field of the message.
When any of the recipients in the Cc field is people	`AnyOfCcHeader`	Matches email messages that are sent to mailboxes, mail-enabled users, or contacts. These recipients must be listed in the Cc field of the message.
When any of the recipients in the To field is a member of distribution list	`AnyOfToHeaderMemberOf`	Matches messages that are sent to members of a specified distribution group where they are listed in the To field of the message.
When any of the recipients in the To field is people	`AnyOfToHeader`	Matches email messages that are sent to mailboxes, mail-enabled users, or contacts. These recipients must be listed in the To field of the message.
When any of the recipients in the To or Cc fields are people	`AnyOfToCcHeader`	Matches email messages that are sent to mailboxes, mail-enabled users, or contacts. These recipients must be listed in the To or Cc field of the message.
When any of the recipients in the To or Cc fields is a member of distribution list	`AnyOfToCcHeaderMemberOf`	Matches messages that are sent to members of a specified distribution group where they are listed in either the To or Cc field of the message.

TABLE 7.2 Predicates Available on a Hub Transport Server *(continued)*

Predicate name (EMC)	Predicate name (EMS)	Description
When the From address contains specific words	FromAddressContains	Matches messages that contain the specified words in the From field.
When the From address contains text patterns	FromAddressMatches	Matches messages that contain text patterns in the From field that match a specified regular expression.
When the message header contains text patterns	HeaderMatches	Matches messages with a header field that contains text patterns that match a specified regular expression.
When the size of any attachment is greater than or equal to limit	AttachmentSizeOver	Matches messages that contain attachments that are larger than the specified value.
When the Subject field contains specific words	SubjectContains	Matches messages that contain the specified words in the subject field.
When the Subject field contains text patterns	SubjectMatches	Matches messages where text patterns in the Subject field match a specified regular expression.
When the Subject field or the body of the message contains specific words	SubjectOrBodyContains	Matches messages that contain the specified words in the Subject field or in the body.
When the Subject field or the body of the message contains text patterns	SubjectOrBodyMatches	Matches messages where text patterns in the Subject field or body match a specified regular expression.
With a spam confidence level (SCL) rating that is greater or equal to limit	SclOver	Matches messages that have a specified SCL or higher.

Since the Edge Transport server does not have direct access to Active Directory and serves a different purpose, it also has a different predicates available for Transport rules. Table 7.3 lists these predicates.

TABLE 7.3 Predicates Available on an Edge Transport Server

Predicate name (EMC)	Predicate name (EMS)	Description
From users inside or outside the organization	FromScope	Matches email messages that are sent from either inside the Exchange organization or outside the Exchange organization.
When a message header contains specific words	HeaderContains	Matches messages where the specified message header field contains the specified header field value.
When any recipient address contains specific words	AnyOfRecipientAddressContains	Matches messages that contain the specified words in the To, carbon copy (Cc), or blind carbon copy (Bcc) field.
When text patterns in any of recipient address	AnyOfRecipientAddressMatches	Matches messages where text patterns in the To, Cc, or Bcc field match a specified regular expression.
When the From address contains specific words	FromAddressContains	Matches messages that contain the specified words in the From field.
When the From address contains text patterns	FromAddressMatches	Matches messages that contain text patterns in the From field that match a specified regular expression.
When the message header contains text patterns	HeaderMatches	Matches messages where the specified message header field contains text patterns that match a specified regular expression.

TABLE 7.3   Predicates Available on an Edge Transport Server *(continued)*

Predicate name (EMC)	Predicate name (EMS)	Description
When the size of any attachment is greater than limit	AttachmentSizeOver	Matches messages that contain attachments that are larger than the specified value.
When the Subject field contains specific words	SubjectContains	Matches messages that contain the specified words in the Subject field.
When the Subject field contains text patterns	SubjectMatches	Matches messages where text patterns in the Subject field match a specified regular expression.
When the Subject field or the body of the message contains specific words	SubjectOrBodyContains	Matches messages that contain the specified words in the Subject field or body.
When the Subject field or the body of the message contains text patterns	SubjectOrBodyMatches	Matches messages where text patterns in the Subject field or body contain a specified regular expression.
With a spam confidence level (SCL) rating that is greater than or equal to limit	SclOver	Matches messages that are configured by using the specified SCL.

Transport Actions

The *action* portion of the transport rule *s*pecifies what should happen to email messages that match all the predicates defined on the transport rule. Actions modify some aspect of the message or the message's delivery. Every transport rule must have at least one action configured. Actions include the ability to modify the message header or body, add or remove recipients, apply classifications, add disclaimers, bounce the message with an NDR, or silently drop the message.

Hub Transport servers have the actions listed in Table 7.4.

TABLE 7.4   Available Actions on Hub Transport Servers

Action name (EMS)	Action name (EMS)	Description
Add a recipient in the To field addresses	AddToRecipient	Adds one or more recipients to the To address list of the e-mail message.
Append disclaimer text using font, size, color, with separator, and fall-back to action if unable to apply	ApplyDisclaimer	Applies a disclaimer to the message.
Apply message classification	ApplyClassification	Applies a message classification to the message.
Blind copy (Bcc) the message to addresses	BlindCopyTo	Adds one or more recipients to the Bcc address list. The original recipients cannot see the additional addresses.
Copy message to addresses	CopyTo	Adds one or more recipients to the Cc field of the message.
Log an event with message	LogEvent	Adds an event into the Application log of the local computer.
Prepend the subject with string	PrependSubject	Prepends a string to the start of the message's subject field.
Redirect message to addresses	RedirectMessage	Redirects the message to one or more recipients that are specified.
Remove header	RemoveHeader	Removes the specified message header field.
Send bounce message to sender with enhanced status code	RejectMessage	Deletes the message and sends a non-delivery receipt to the sender.
Set header with value	SetHeader	Creates a new or modifies an existing message header field.
Set the spam confidence level to value	SetScl	Sets the spam confidence level (SCL) on a message.
Silently drop the message	DeleteMessage	Deletes the message without sending a notification.

Again, since the Edge Transport role has a different purpose, there are also different actions that can be done on an Edge Transport server, as shown in Table 7.5.

TABLE 7.5 Available Actions on Edge Transport Servers

Action name (EMC)	Action name (EMS)	Description
Add a recipient in the To field addresses	AddToRecipient	Adds one or more recipients to the To address list of the e-mail message.
Blind carbon copy (Bcc) the message to addresses	BlindCopyTo	Adds one or more recipients to the Bcc address list. The original recipients cannot see the additional addresses.
Copy the message to addresses	CopyTo	Adds one or more recipients to the Cc field of the message.
Drop connection	Disconnect	Drops the connection between the sending server and the Edge Transport server. This does not generate a nondelivery report (NDR) message.
Log an event with message	LogEvent	Adds an event into the Application log of the local computer.
Prepend the subject with string	PrependSubject	Prepends a string to the start of the message's subject field.
Put message in quarantine	Quarantine	Quarantine redirects the message to the spam quarantine mailbox that is configured by using the Set-ContentFilterConfig cmdlet.
Redirect the message to addresses	RedirectMessage	Redirects the message to one or more recipients that are specified.
Remove header	RemoveHeader	Removes the specified message header field.
Set header with value	SetHeader	Creates a new or modifies an existing message header field.
Set the spam confidence level to value	SetScl	Sets the spam confidence level (SCL) on a message.

TABLE 7.5   Available Actions on Edge Transport Servers *(continued)*

Action name (EMC)	Action name (EMS)	Description
Reject the message with status code and response	`SmtpRejectMessage`	Deletes the message and sends a notification to the sender with a specified delivery status notification (DSN) code.
Silently drop the message	`DeleteMessage`	Deletes the message without sending a notification.

Working with Transport Rules

You can specify conditions and exceptions using a large number of criteria that allow the rule to match messages according to specific AD objects (such as sender or addressee), patterns of text (either literal or using regular expressions), or other conditions.

Before configuring transport rules, you should consider these few design and planning tips:

- Every Hub Transport server will have to evaluate every rule on every message that passes through it. Rules are cached in RAM. Larger numbers of rules will therefore require larger allocations of RAM on each of the Hub Transport servers.

- The official limit to rules is 1,000 per forest. Note that this rule was based on performance testing and is more a recommendation than a hard limit. You should monitor server performance and message delivery times to determine the appropriate number of rules for your organization.

- Using regular expressions in rules is very powerful and yet it's easy to make a mistake that causes unexpected behavior. Regular expressions can add to the processing requirements of a rule.

- Transport rules must use universal security groups. This is required because transport rules apply to all Hub Transport servers in the forest; therefore, they need to be accessible in the entire forest. Because Hub Transport uses a recipient cache that refreshes only every four hours, changes to members of a group may take several hours to take effect across the organization.

- Test all transport rules in a lab before deploying them into production.

To create a new Hub Transport rule, follow the steps outlined in Exercise 7.11 and Exercise 7.12.

EXERCISE 7.11

Creating a New Transport Rule Using the Exchange Management Console

To create a new Hub Transport rule using the Exchange Management Console, follow these steps:

1. Open the Exchange Management Console, and click the Hub Transport node in the Organization Configuration section. Select the Transport Rules tab.

2. In the Actions pane to the right, click New Transport Rule, and the New Transport Rule Wizard will guide you through creating a rule

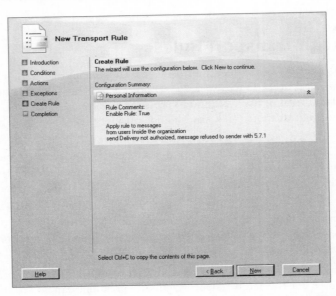

3. When you create the rule, you have the option of enabling it. A rule will not do anything until it is enabled, so if you do not enable the rule at the end of the wizard, you can do so later by right-clicking the rule and selecting Enable Rule.

EXERCISE 7.12

Creating a New Transport Rule Using the Exchange Management Shell

Open the Exchange Management Shell, and run the following commands (make sure to change the parameters enclosed in brackets):

```
New-TransportRule -Name <Rule_Name> -Condition <Conditions>
-Exception <Exceptions> -Action <Actions>
```

Real World Scenario

A Real-Life Rule Story

One small office deployment had a local administrator who was instructed to prepend *[Contracts]* to the Subject field of every message sent between two specific people. Although the reasoning behind the rule wasn't quite clear, she thought she had it figured out until later in the day when these two people could no longer reply to any messages. All of the messages were being NDRed, saying the Subject field was too long. After looking more closely at the message, she determined the rule was doing exactly what it was configured to do, prepend the text to all messages include ones that already had the text. This wasn't what she had expected the rule to do. Her quick fix was to add an exception to the rule telling it to not add the text if it was already there.

These types of stories demonstrate the power of transport rules and encourage you to plan for all your rules and how they will work. Rules will do what you tell them to do regardless of consequences. With every rule you create, spend some time to figure out what might go wrong and what exceptions you might need.

Configuring Policies and Address Lists

The functionality available for controlling and managing a messaging environment is one of the standout features of Exchange 2007. How is it that you are able to customize how email addresses are assigned or how the address lists are laid out? Also, how is it that you can maintain control over content that mobile devices are accessing? In this section I will tackle these questions.

Configuring Email Address Policies

Email address policies assign email addresses to mailboxes and mail-enabled users, contacts, groups, and public folders based on a set of conditions. You can create email policies to assign specific email addresses using criteria such as departments or business units. For instance, your company may want an address of user@exchangeexchange.com assigned to your corporate users; however, your consulting division may require user@namedpipes.net email addresses. This and a lot more can be configured through email policies.

One major change in Exchange Server 2007 vs. Exchange 2000 and Exchange 2003 is that the Recipient Update Service (RUS) no longer exists. For anyone who worked with previous versions in large environments, this is a somewhat welcome change. The RUS applied address policies in the background. The RUS had to modify (also referred to as "stamp") each user account before the user could receive email. The process was scheduled to run every 15 minutes by default. The benefit of this was that you could create users any way you wanted to and the RUS would come along and stamp them with the appropriate attributes. The problem was that it could be difficult to troubleshoot and control, especially in larger, more complex organizations.

In Exchange Server 2007, the process that creates or modifies a mail-enabled object applies the email address policy. Also, when you make a change to an email policy, you can allow it to run immediately or schedule it to run at a later time. You can also update the email address with the `Update-EmailAdressPolicy` command.

Email address policies are not limited to just assigning basic SMTP email addresses. The following types of addresses are available by default in Exchange 2007:

- Precanned and Custom SMTP
- cc:Mail
- Exchange Unified Messaging Proxy Address
- Legacy Exchange DN
- Lotus Notes
- Microsoft Mail
- Novell GroupWise
- X.400
- X.500

Most likely, you will modify the SMTP-based email address policies to create email addresses for users in your company. There are a number of precanned, or premade, SMTP addresses available, as shown in Figure 7.2.

FIGURE 7.2   Adding a precanned SMTP email address

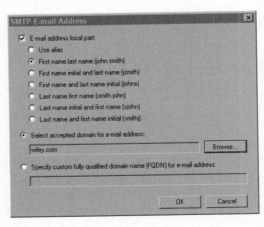

If these precanned options don't meet your needs, you can use variables to create a custom SMTP address policy. Perhaps you want to create an email address based on the first two letters of someone's first name and their last name. In that case, you would enter %2g%s@exchangeeexchange.com as the custom SMTP address. There are a number of options available for these custom SMTP addresses; Table 7.6 shows the available variables.

TABLE 7.6 Available Variables for Custom SMTP addresses

Variable	Value
%g	First name (given name)
%i	Middle initial
%s	Last name (surname)
%d	Display name
%m	Exchange alias
%xs	Uses the *x* number of letters of the first name.
%xg	Uses the *x* number of letters of the last name.

To create a new email address policy, follow the steps outlined in Exercise 7.13 and Exercise 7.14.

EXERCISE 7.13

Creating a New Email Address Policy Using the Exchange Management Console

Follow these steps to create a new email address policy using the Exchange Management Console:

1. Open the Exchange Management Console, and click the Hub Transport node in the Organization Configuration section. Select the E-Mail Address Policy tab.

2. In the Actions pane to the right, click New E-Mail Address Policy, and the New E-Mail Address Policy Wizard will guide you through creating a policy.

3. On the first page of the New E-Mail Address Policy Wizard, choose the name of the policy and the recipient types that will be affected by the policy, such as Exchange Mailboxes, Resource Mailboxes, External Accounts, and more. Once you fill out this page, click Next.

4. On the second page, select the conditions that must be met by the objects that the policy will apply to. You can apply policies based on state, company, department, and custom attributes 1 through 15. Clicking the Preview button will display of list of objects that will be affected by the conditions. Click Next when you are satisfied with the conditions.

5. On the third page, enter the email address that will be applied to the objects that meet the conditions set on the last page. Click the Add button to add addresses. Select how the email address will be formatted. When all the desired email addresses are entered, click Next.

6. On the next page, you are presented with the option of applying the policy immediately or scheduling it to be applied later. Once you have configured when the policy will be applied, click New and the policy will be created.

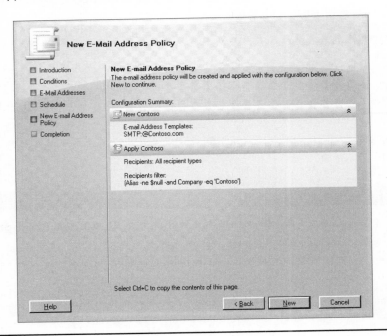

EXERCISE 7.14

Creating a New Email Address Policy Using the Exchange Management Shell

Open the Exchange Management Shell, and run one of the following commands (make sure to change the parameters enclosed in brackets):

```
New-EmailAddressPolicy -Name <Policy_Name> -IncludedRecipients
<Who_To_Apply_Policy_To> -EnabledPrimarySMTPAddressTemplate
<Email_Address_To_Apply>
```

Configuring Address Lists

An *address list* is a collection of recipient and other AD objects such as groups, contacts, users, and rooms. You can use address lists to organize recipients and resources, making it easier for users to find the recipients and resources they want. Address lists are updated dynamically based on LDAP queries. This is beneficial because objects don't have to be added manually to the lists when they are created in your organizations. The default address list for an organization is called the global address list (GAL). The GAL should contain all the objects in your organization that are Exchange-enabled and not set to be hidden from address lists. There are a number of other default address lists, but none has its own acronym like the GAL. These lists are for the most part self-explanatory:

The All Contacts list   All the Exchange-enabled nonhidden contacts in the Exchange organization

The All Groups list   All the Exchange-enabled nonhidden groups in the Exchange organization

The All Rooms list   All the Exchange-enabled nonhidden rooms in the Exchange organization

The All Users list   All the Exchange-enabled nonhidden users in the Exchange organization

The Public Folders list   All the Exchange-enabled nonhidden public folders in the Exchange organization

The default global address list   All the Exchange-enabled objects in the Exchange organization

In larger environments, the GAL can become unwieldy and difficult to navigate for end users. To alleviate some of this confusion, you can create additional address lists that provide a subset of the objects in it. For example, in a company that has two major divisions that primarily communicate intra-division, you can create an address list for each, allowing the end users to search the local address list for contacts. Of course, end users can also still use the GAL if they need to communicate with others outside of their division.

Address lists are stored on the server and accessed from the server. When Outlook is either disconnected or in cached mode, it does not have access to the server to perform lookups in the GAL. To facilitate this, Exchange also creates an Offline Address Book (OAB). The OAB is downloaded to the Outlook client and so that it can use it as a local query source for address book lookups.

Outlook cached mode uses the OAB by default to cut down on network requests over the wire. This has both advantages and disadvantages. The OAB is by default only generated once a night. This means that those who are using the OAB will see address list changes only once a day after they have downloaded the new version. This could lead to users not being able to see any of the changes made to the address lists until they download a new OAB copy. To rectify this problem, you can modify how often the OAB is generated by changing the update schedule properties of the OAB. The default offline address list automatically includes the default global address list; if additional address lists are created, they must also be added to the OAB.

To create a new address list, follow the steps in Exercise 7.15 and Exercise 7.16.

EXERCISE 7.15

Creating a New Address List Using the Exchange Management Console

To create a new address list using the Exchange Management Console, follow these steps:

1. Open the Exchange Management Console, and click the Mailbox node in the Organization Configuration section. Select the Address Lists tab.

2. In the Actions pane to the right, click New Address List, and the New Address List Wizard will guide you in creating an address list.

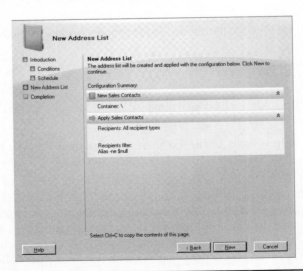

EXERCISE 7.16

Creating a New Address List Using the Exchange Management Shell

Open the Exchange Management Shell, and run one of the following commands (make sure to change the parameters enclosed in brackets):

```
New-AddressList -Name <Address_List_Name>
-Container <Where_To_Place_The_Address_List>
-ConditionalCustomAttribute1 <Query>
```

Configuring Mobile Device Policies

Experts agree that mobile devices pose one of the highest risks for divulging confidential information. Since mobile devices are able to synchronize your email and contacts and access SharePoint documents, care needs to be taken to protect your company data. This need has not gone unnoticed. Exchange ActiveSync mailbox policies let you apply a number of settings to a user's or group of users' ActiveSync-capable mobile devices. The settings are there to allow you to have some control over the phones that attach to your organization and how secure they are.

 Not all ActiveSync-capable devices support all of the available policy settings. The policies available can also vary in each version of the device software. Be sure to understand the settings that are available for your user devices and how those devices behave when policies are applied.

Table 7.7 lists some of the available ActiveSync settings.

TABLE 7.7   Common ActiveSync Settings

Setting	Description
Allow Nonprovisionable Devices	This allows older Windows mobile devices that do not fully support ActiveSync policies to connect via ActiveSync.
Allow Simple Password	This enables or disables the ability to use passwords based on simple patterns, such as sequential numbers like 5678 (numbers in order) or 0852 (patterns on the phone dial pad).
Alphanumeric Password Required	This requires that a password be more complex and contain at least one nonnumeric character.

TABLE 7.7   Common ActiveSync Settings   *(continued)*

Setting	Description
Attachments Enabled	If enabled, this setting allows attachments to be downloaded to the mobile device. If your phones are on pay-for-bit data plans, it might be good to disable this setting to help reduce bandwidth costs on the phones.
Device Encryption Enabled	If this setting is enabled, it forces the device to use encryption when communicating with the Exchange servers.
Password Enabled	If this setting is enabled, it forces the device to have a password.
Password Expiration	This setting sets the length of time after which a device password will expire and must be changed.
Password History	This sets how many passwords are saved in order to limit the user from reusing a previous password.
Policy Refresh Interval	This setting defines how frequently the device will connect to the Exchange server and update mobile device policy information.
Maximum Attachment Size	This setting specifies the maximum size of attachments that will be automatically downloaded to the device.
Maximum Failed Password Attempts	This setting specifies how many times an incorrect password can be entered before a device wipe is performed.
Maximum Inactivity Time Lock	This setting specifies the length of time a device can go without user input before the device will be locked and require a password to unlock it.
Minimum Password Length	This setting specifies the minimum required length of a password.
Password Recovery	This enables the device password to be recovered from the server.
UNC File Access	This setting, if enabled, allows the device to access files stored on Universal Naming Convention (UNC) shares on the company network.
WSS File Access	This setting, if enabled, allows the device to access files stored on Microsoft Windows SharePoint Services sites on the company network.

For a list of the available ActiveSync policy settings, please see http://
technet.microsoft.com/en-us/library/bb123484.aspx.

To create an ActiveSync mailbox policy, follow the steps outlined in Exercise 7.17 and Exercise 7.18.

EXERCISE 7.17

Creating an ActiveSync Mailbox Policy Using the Exchange Management Console

Follow these steps to create an ActiveSync mailbox policy using the Exchange Management Console:

1. Open the Exchange Management Console, and click the Client Access node in the Organization Configuration section. Select the Exchange ActiveSync Mailbox Policy tab.

2. In the Actions pane to the right, click New Exchange ActiveSync Mailbox Policy to open the New Exchange ActiveSync Mailbox Policy Wizard.

3. On the first page of the wizard, set the name of the policy and then set all the settings listed in Table 7.7. Once all settings have been configured, click New to create the policy.

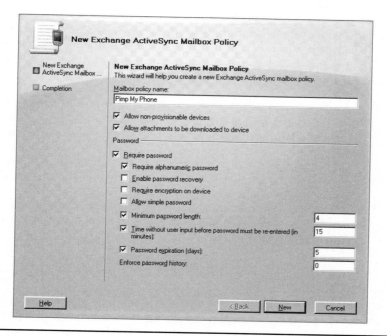

Creating an ActiveSync Mailbox Policy Using the Exchange Management Shell

Open the Exchange Management Shell, and run one of the following commands (make sure to change the parameters enclosed in brackets):

```
New-ActiveSyncMaiboxPolicy -Name <Policy_Name>
-DevicePasswordEnabled:$false
-AlphanumericDevicePasswordRequired:$false
```

Configuring Antivirus and Antispam

The critical components of any email system today always include a comprehensive antivirus and antispam solution. In this section, I will focus on these two functions of Exchange and how they can be configured.

When Exchange is deployed in an enterprise environment, Microsoft recommends using an Edge Transport server to provide the bulk of the antispam and inbound antivirus functions. All of the antispam features are available by default on an Edge Transport server, and therefore most of the antispam documentation you read from Microsoft will be specific to the Edge Transport role.

It is possible to enable all of the antispam features except for the attachment filtering agent on a Hub Transport server; however, this not considered best practice. To enable the antispam features on a single Hub Transport server, you need to run the Install-AntispamAgents.ps1 PowerShell script from the Scripts subfolder of where Exchange has been installed, restart the Transport service, and manually exempt all of the internal SMTP servers from connection filtering. You can find more information about this process and its limitations at http://technet.microsoft.com/en-us/library/bb201691.aspx.

Content Filtering

Content filtering in Exchange Server 2007 is really the third generation of the intelligent message filter (IMF) that was introduced in Exchange Server 2003. The content filter works by examining the content of each message passing through the Edge Transport server based on keyword analysis, message size, and other factors. When the analysis has been completed, the message is then assigned a spam confidence level (SCL) value from 0 to 9. A value of 0 means the message has been determined almost certainly *not* to be spam, whereas a value of 9 means the message has been determined almost certainly to be spam.

To configure the Content Filtering options, select the Content Filtering item from the Antispam tab of the Edge Transport options. You can either right-click the Content Filtering item and select Properties from the context menu or click the Properties link in the Actions pane on the right side for the Content Filtering item. Either way, the Content Filtering Properties dialog box opens to the General tab, shown in Figure 7.3. The General tab provides no configurable options but does provide information about the status of content filtering and the last modification date.

FIGURE 7.3 The General tab of the Content Filtering Properties dialog box

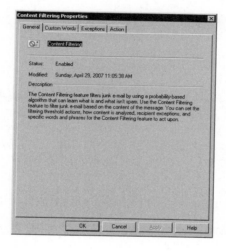

Custom Words

The Custom Words tab, shown in Figure 7.4, allows you to enter a list of words that will modify the default behavior of the content filter. In the top area of this tab, you can enter words that will never be blocked, such as those that might otherwise typically be blocked by the content filter. The bottom half of the tab allows you to enter words that will always be blocked, except if they are also contained in the "always allowed" list.

FIGURE 7.4   The Custom Words tab of the Content Filtering Properties dialog box

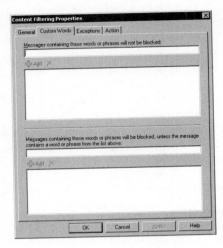

Exceptions

The Exceptions tab, shown in Figure 7.5, allows you to enter a list of email addresses that should always receive messages, even if those messages would have ordinarily been blocked by the content filter. You might want to enter a generic spam email address here to collect these messages, such as spamcollection@mycompany.com. Also, there will likely be one or more users who want to opt out completely of the content filter, so you'll need to enter their email addresses here.

FIGURE 7.5   The Exceptions tab of the Content Filtering Properties dialog box

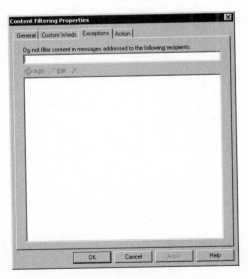

Action

The Action tab, shown in Figure 7.6, allows you to configure what the content filter will do when a message has been classified at a certain SCL. You have three options: delete the message (with no NDR), reject the message (with an NDR), or quarantine the message to an internal mailbox. By default, only message rejection is enabled and it has an SCL value of 7. You will want to configure these options to suit your organization's needs and tolerance of spam.

FIGURE 7.6   The Action tab of the Content Filtering Properties dialog box

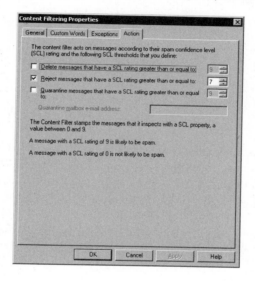

IP Allow Lists

Sometimes you may just need to configure one or more IP addresses that are always allowed to send messages without being treated as spam, as long as you know those senders are authentic. A common implementation of this might be to configure the IP addresses of internal servers that need to send notification email messages, thereby allowing their messages always to be delivered even if they trigger an SCL rating as they pass through the Edge Transport server.

You can manually configure IP addresses to be allowed by opening the Properties dialog box for the IP Allow List item. On the Allowed Addresses tab, shown in Figure 7.7, you'll be able to add IP addresses that are to be allowed or to remove existing entries if they should no longer be allowed to be sent with the content filter taking action.

FIGURE 7.7   The Allowed Addresses tab of the IP Allow List Properties dialog box

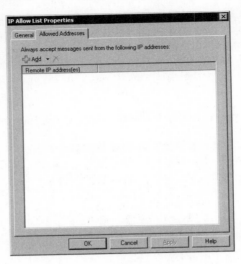

If you've subscribed to an external service that maintains a verified list of "safe" IP addresses that are known not to send spam, you can configure the IP Allow List Providers item to allow the Edge Transport server to do lookups against that provider upon the receipt of inbound messages. On the Providers tab of the IP Allow List Providers Properties dialog box, shown in Figure 7.8, you can add or remove providers. You can disable or enable providers on the list at any time and change the order as well. You should always put the best or fastest providers highest on the list because Exchange will stop querying other providers once it has matched the IP address of the sending system against an allow provider's list.

FIGURE 7.8   The Providers tab of the IP Allow List Providers Properties dialog box

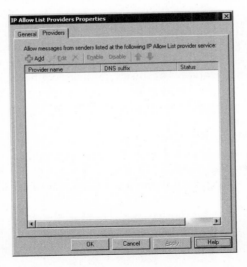

IP Block Lists

Configuring IP addresses to be blocked works the same way as configuring an IP address to be allowed. You can either enter addresses manually from the Blocked Address tab of the IP Block List Properties dialog box, shown in Figure 7.9, or configure one or more external services to provide this information to you.

Configuring the IP block list providers options will almost immediately cause a difference in the amount of spam your users receive, so treat this area with the importance it deserves. On the Providers tab of the IP Block List Providers Properties dialog box, shown in Figure 7.10, you can configure one or more providers that the Edge Transport server should consult to determine whether the sending IP address of a received message is a known spammer. Just as with the IP Allow List Providers item, you can add or remove providers as you want, as well as disable, enable, or reorder the providers in the list. Using the best or fastest provider here, as your experience dictates, will provide the best results since the Edge Transport server will stop looking to see whether the IP address belongs to a known spammer once it finds a match.

Some of the most popular block list providers include the following, although you can use any provider you trust:

- Spamhaus, www.spamhaus.org
- SpamCop, www.spamcop.net
- ABUSEAT CBL, http://cbl.abuseat.org
- SORBS, www.sorbs.net

Because sometimes you or your users will want or need to get every message sent to them, regardless of its SCL rating, you can configure a list of email addresses on the Exceptions tab of the IP Block List Providers Properties dialog box, as shown in Figure 7.11; the email addresses you configure here will always get messages addressed to them.

FIGURE 7.9   The Blocked Addresses tab of the IP Block List Properties dialog box

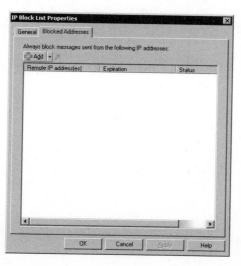

FIGURE 7.10 The Providers tab of the IP Block List Providers Properties dialog box

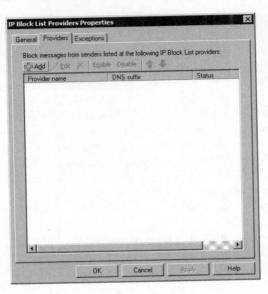

FIGURE 7.11 The Exceptions tab of the IP Block List Providers Properties dialog box

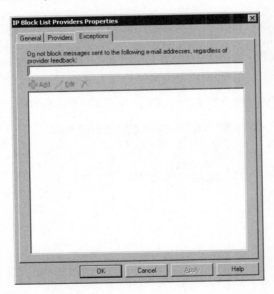

Recipient Filtering

Another powerful spam reduction tool you have available by default in Exchange Server 2007 is recipient filtering. Considering how much email is misaddressed and eventually winds up in the postmaster mailbox, using recipient filtering to block inbound messages to recipients who don't exist in the global address list (GAL) is a powerful tool. The Blocked Recipients tab of the Recipient Filtering Properties dialog box, shown in Figure 7.12, allows you to block messages sent to recipients of your choosing and/or those not in the GAL. Take the time at least to enable the GAL-based filtering, and you'll save your organization a lot of spam that might otherwise be delivered.

You can use the option to block additional recipients in situations where you might have some internal email addresses that should never receive mail from the Internet. Typical scenarios for this include compliance reporting, spam and virus reporting, and mail-enabled public folders used for workflow applications.

FIGURE 7.12   The Blocked Recipients tab of the Recipient Filtering Properties dialog box

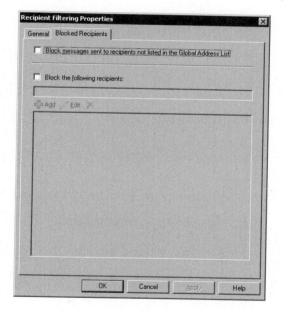

Sender Filtering

Sometimes using an IP block list provider isn't good enough if you need to block certain senders. This can happen when a new IP address starts sending you mail that isn't in the block list provider's database yet but is obviously sending you spam. Alternatively, you might need to block messages from IP addresses that are not sending spam but are otherwise sending messages that your organization has deemed it does not want to receive, such as job offers sent to employees from competing businesses in the area. You can add a list of sender IP addresses to block from the Blocked Senders tab of the Sender Filtering Properties dialog box, as shown in Figure 7.13. Note the option at the bottom of the dialog box to block messages from blank senders; using blank senders is a common tactic of spammers.

On the Action tab, shown in Figure 7.14, you can configure the desired action to occur if the IP address of the sending system is found in the Blocked Senders listing. Either you can block the message entirely, which is the default setting, or you can opt to adjust the SCL rating and continue processing the message. Most organizations will likely opt to block the message entirely.

FIGURE 7.13   The Blocked Senders tab of the Sender Filtering Properties dialog box

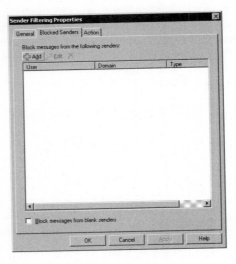

FIGURE 7.14   The Action tab of the Sender Filtering Properties dialog box

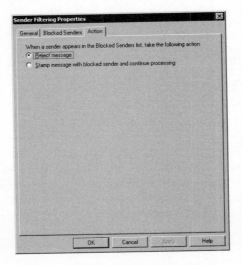

Sender ID

Sender ID is a relatively new method being used to fight both spam and phishing email messages. Since it relies on legitimate senders registering their email servers, it cannot be counted on 100 percent of the time in identifying unsolicited email. Many sending systems are not participating in Sender ID yet, even though they are legitimate and valid senders; thus, you should not use Sender ID as an absolute just yet. To that end, the default configuration is to simply note the Sender ID status in the message headers for SCL evaluation and pass the message along for further analysis. You can configure the action that the Edge Transport server should take when a Sender ID check fails on an inbound message from the Action tab of the Sender ID Properties dialog box, as shown in Figure 7.15.

FIGURE 7.15   The Action tab of the Sender ID Properties dialog box

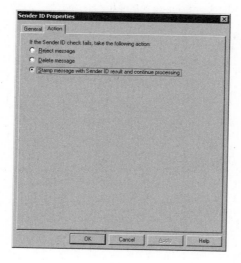

To find out more about Sender ID and how to publish your Sender ID Sender Policy Framework (SPF) record, visit the Microsoft Sender ID resource center at www.microsoft.com/mscorp/safety/technologies/senderid/default.mspx.

Sender Reputation

The Sender Reputation item is a dynamic method Exchange Server 2007 uses to add (and subsequently remove) sending IP addresses to the IP block list depending on their recent behavior patterns. If a certain IP address does not otherwise appear in any IP block list but has sent a large amount of spam as classified by your Edge Transport servers, then it can be dynamically added to the IP block list for a certain amount of time. Assuming that the IP address does not continue to send spam messages above your SCL ratings, it will automatically be removed from the IP block list after this period of time. Because of its dynamic nature, Sender Reputation can be both a powerful tool and a complex one to use. You could end up putting an IP address on the block list that you did not want to end up there, although if the rest of the settings are working correctly (per your organization's needs), then any IP address that the Sender Reputation item adds to the block list is almost certainly there for a good reason.

By default, the Edge Transport server is configured to detect open ports and relays on sending systems. The Sender Confidence tab of the Sender Reputation Properties dialog box, shown in Figure 7.16, allows you to turn off this option, although there is no reason why you would ordinarily do this.

FIGURE 7.16   The Sender Confidence tab of the Sender Reputation Properties dialog box

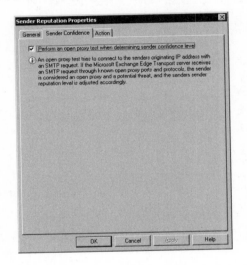

The Action tab, shown in Figure 7.17, allows you to configure the sender reputation level (SRL) value that will result in the sender being added to the IP block list for the number of hours configured. A setting of 0 on the slider indicates that the sender is almost certainly not a spammer, with a less than 1 percent probability of being a spam source. Conversely, a setting of 9 on the slider indicates that sender is almost certainly a spammer, with a greater than 99 percent probability of being a spam source. The default setting is an SRL of 7, which most organizations will find acceptable. If anything, you will most likely move the slider up to a setting of 8 to decrease the chances of inadvertently adding an acceptable sender to the IP block list.

FIGURE 7.17   The Action tab of the Sender Reputation Properties dialog box

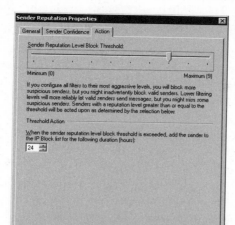

Attachment Filtering

The last antispam agent I'll examine here is the attachment filtering agent. Unlike the previous items I've covered, no Exchange Management Console configuration is available for attachment filtering, so warm up your Exchange Management Shell! By default, the attachment filtering agent is enabled on a newly installed Edge Transport server, but you can check to be sure by issuing the `Get-TransportAgent` cmdlet from the Exchange Management Shell, as shown in Figure 7.18.

FIGURE 7.18   Checking the status of antispam transport agents

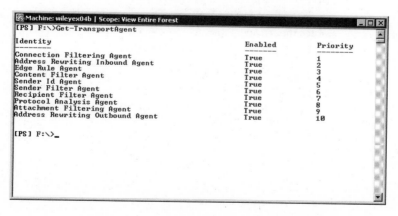

To see the default configuration of the attachment filtering agent, you will need to use the `Get-AttachmentFilterListConfig` cmdlet. This should return the following result on a newly installed Edge Transport server:

```
Name                 : Transport Settings
RejectResponse       : Message rejected due to unacceptable attachments
AdminMessage         : This attachment was removed.
Action               : Strip
ExceptionConnectors  : {}
AttachmentNames      : {ContentType:application/x-msdownload,
ContentType:message/partial, ContentType:text/scriptlet,
ContentType:application/prg, ContentType:application/msaccess,
ContentType:text/javascript, ContentType:application/x-javascript,
ContentType:application/javascript, ContentType:x-internet-signup,
ContentType:application/hta, FileName:*.xnk, FileName:*.wsh,
FileName:*.wsf, FileName:*.wsc, FileName:*.vbs, FileName:*.vbe...}


AdminDisplayName     :
ExchangeVersion      : 0.1 (8.0.535.0)
DistinguishedName    : CN=Transport Settings,
CN=First Organization,CN=MicrosoftExchange,CN=Services,CN=Configuration,
CN={67E9AD9B-2D4C-4E33-BAEA-28295AE49B99}
Identity             : Transport Settings
Guid                 : 07e65d0f-206b-45ee-9d7e-cd935eed2aaa
ObjectCategory       : CN=ms-Exch-Transport-Settings,
CN=Schema,CN=Configuration,CN={67E9AD9B-2D4C-4E33-BAEA-28295AE49B99}
ObjectClass          : {top, container, msExchTransportSettings}
WhenChanged          : 4/29/2007 2:28:17 PM
WhenCreated          : 4/29/2007 11:03:48 AM
OriginatingServer    : localhost
IsValid              : True
```

As you can see, a few file types, such as Access databases, JavaScript files, and VBScript files, are going to be stripped from messages by default. You will likely want to add and/or remove file types of your own. To add new file types to the attachment filtering agent, you will need to use the `Add-AttachmentFilterEntry` cmdlet. If you wanted to add all attachments with the filename extension of .pdf, you would use a command like this:

```
Add-AttachmentFilterEntry -name *.pdf -type FileName
```

Since filename extensions can be spoofed, it is advisable also to use a MIME type value to block attachments. To do this, you would use the following command to strip all MPEG audio/video files:

```
Add-AttachmentFilterEntry -name audio/mpeg -type ContentType
```

> You can get a listing of all registered MIME types by visiting the following website: www.iana.org/assignments/media-types/.

You can see the results of the commands in Figure 7.19.

FIGURE 7.19   Adding file types to the Attachment Filter Agent

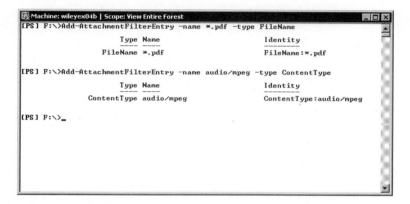

Conversely, you can remove a file type from the Attachment Filter Agent by using the Remove-AttachmentFilterEntry cmdlet. If you wanted to remove the previously added entry for MPEG files, your command would look like this:

```
Remove-AttachmentFilterEntry -Identity contenttype:audio/mpeg
```

You'll be prompted to confirm your intention, however, as shown in Figure 7.20, when you remove an entry from the list.

FIGURE 7.20   Removing file types from the Attachment Filter Agent

If you want an easier way to view the full and current list of file types that are covered by the Attachment Filter Agent, you can use the Get-AttachmentFilterEntry cmdlet, as shown in Figure 7.21. The information provided here is much easier to read than that provided by the Get-AttachmentFilterListConfig cmdlet you saw earlier.

FIGURE 7.21 Viewing file types configured for the Attachment Filter Agent

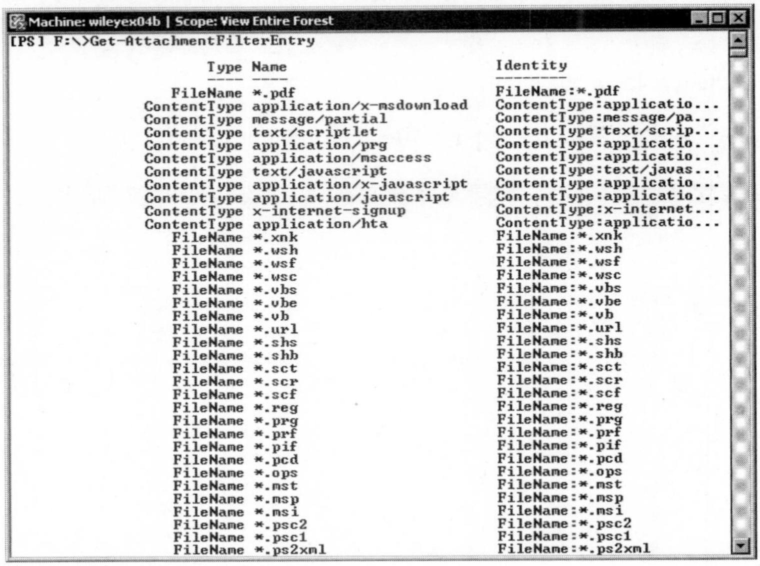

```
Machine: wileyex04b | Scope: View Entire Forest                        _ □ X
[PS] F:\>Get-AttachmentFilterEntry

          Type Name                        Identity

      FileName *.pdf                       FileName:*.pdf
   ContentType application/x-msdownload    ContentType:applicatio...
   ContentType message/partial             ContentType:message/pa...
   ContentType text/scriptlet              ContentType:text/scrip...
   ContentType application/prg             ContentType:applicatio...
   ContentType application/msaccess        ContentType:applicatio...
   ContentType text/javascript             ContentType:text/javas...
   ContentType application/x-javascript    ContentType:applicatio...
   ContentType application/javascript      ContentType:applicatio...
   ContentType x-internet-signup           ContentType:x-internet...
   ContentType application/hta             ContentType:applicatio...
      FileName *.xnk                       FileName:*.xnk
      FileName *.wsh                       FileName:*.wsh
      FileName *.wsf                       FileName:*.wsf
      FileName *.wsc                       FileName:*.wsc
      FileName *.vbs                       FileName:*.vbs
      FileName *.vbe                       FileName:*.vbe
      FileName *.vb                        FileName:*.vb
      FileName *.url                       FileName:*.url
      FileName *.shs                       FileName:*.shs
      FileName *.shb                       FileName:*.shb
      FileName *.sct                       FileName:*.sct
      FileName *.scr                       FileName:*.scr
      FileName *.scf                       FileName:*.scf
      FileName *.reg                       FileName:*.reg
      FileName *.prg                       FileName:*.prg
      FileName *.prf                       FileName:*.prf
      FileName *.pif                       FileName:*.pif
      FileName *.pcd                       FileName:*.pcd
      FileName *.ops                       FileName:*.ops
      FileName *.mst                       FileName:*.mst
      FileName *.msp                       FileName:*.msp
      FileName *.msi                       FileName:*.msi
      FileName *.psc2                      FileName:*.psc2
      FileName *.psc1                      FileName:*.psc1
      FileName *.ps2xml                    FileName:*.ps2xml
```

If you want to change the default behavior or message when attachment stripping occurs, you will need to use the `Set-AttachmentFilterListConfig` cmdlet, which has the following syntax:

```
Set-AttachmentFilterListConfig [-Action <Reject | Strip | SilentDelete>]
[-AdminMessage <String>] [-DomainController <Fqdn>]
[-ExceptionConnectors <MultiValuedProperty>]
[-Instance <AttachmentFilteringConfig>] [-RejectResponse <String>]
```

You can set the `Action` behavior to one of the following options:

`Reject`, which issues an NDR to the sender and prevents the message and attachment from passing

`Strip`, which removes the attachment but allows the message to pass through with text indicating an attachment was stripped

`SilentDelete`, which deletes the message and sends no NDR to the sender

The `AdminMessage` value specifies the contents of a text file that will be attached to messages to replace a stripped attachment. The default value is "This attachment was removed." However, you might want to customize it to include a contact email address or phone number for the help desk in your organization so that a recipient can get more information about attachment filtering policies. The `RejectResponse` value specifies the message body of NDR messages sent to senders whose attachments have been rejected. The default value of "Message rejected due to unacceptable attachments" is fairly useful, but you might want also to customize it with an externally available contact phone number or email address if a sender needs help determining what attachment types are allowed through your email system. The `RejectResponse` value has a limit of 240 characters, so be sure to check your text before changing the value. You can configure connectors that the Attachment Filter Agent should not function on by using the `ExceptionConnectors` value.

The following example command will change the default `Action` behavior to `Reject` and will change the `RejectResponse` value to be more informative:

```
Set-AttachmentFilterListConfig -Action Reject
-RejectResponse "Your message and attachment(s) have not been delivered
to the intended recipient.  Please contact the Wiley Publishing Help
Desk at 1-877-555-1234 for more information."
```

Figure 7.22 shows the changes and the verification of the changes using the `Get-AttachmentFilterListConfig` cmdlet.

FIGURE 7.22   Modifying the Attachment Filter Agent behavior

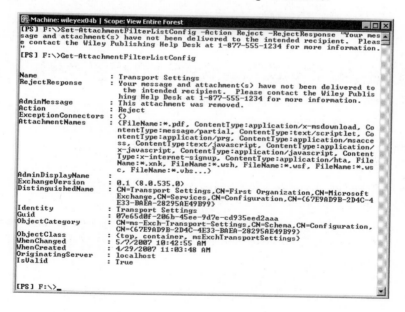

Configuring Microsoft Forefront Security for Exchange Server

The obvious choice for antivirus is Microsoft's own Forefront Security for Exchange Server, a product previously known as Antigen by Sybari but now part of Microsoft through acquisition. There are many other viable alternatives for Exchange-based antivirus; however, any questions regarding antivirus on the exam will no doubt be based on Forefront.

Installing Forefront Security for Exchange Server

The installation process for Forefront is fairly straightforward and can be initiated from one of two places: either by using the Exchange Server DVD from which you installed Exchange Server or by using a separate Forefront for Exchange Server CD. In Exercise 7.19, I'll show how to install Forefront via the Exchange Server DVD for simplicity.

You can find and download the Forefront Security for Exchange Server user's guide at the following location: http://go.microsoft.com/fwlink/?LinkID=106018

EXERCISE 7.19

Installing Forefront Security for Exchange Server

Follow these steps to install Forefront from the Exchange Server DVD:

1. Open Windows Explorer or My Computer on the server containing the Exchange Server 2007 DVD and navigate to the Forefront directory on the DVD.

2. Double-click the Setup.exe item to start the installation process. Click Next to dismiss the opening page of the installation wizard.

3. On the License Agreement page, click Yes to accept the EULA after reading and/or printing it. You will not be able to continue with the installation without clicking Yes.

4. On the Customer Information page, shown here, enter the pertinent information and click Next to continue to the Installation Location page.

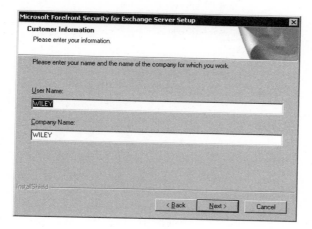

5. On the Installation Location page, shown here, select the Local Installation option to install the relevant Forefront product on the local Edge Transport Exchange server. Click Next to continue to the Installation Type page.

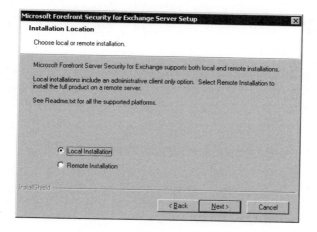

6. On the Installation Type page, shown here, select Full Installation to install the relevant Forefront application files and the administrative console on the Edge Transport server. Click Next to continue to the Quarantine Security Settings page.

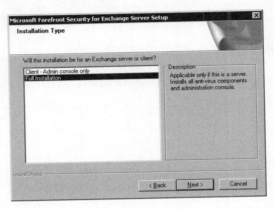

7. On the Quarantine Security Settings page, shown here, you will need to select how you want messages in the quarantine to be handled when you attempt to deliver them manually. You have the following two options:

    ▪ *Secure Mode*: The default setting causes all messages and their attachments that are delivered from the quarantine to be scanned again at that time for viruses and spam filter matches. This setting will often result in items not being deliverable from the quarantine.

    ▪ *Compatibility Mode*: This option will allow messages and attachments to be delivered from the quarantine without being scanned for spam filter matches. Virus scanning always occurs, however, on messages and attachments that are delivered from the quarantine.

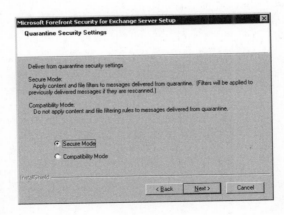

8. For the purpose of this installation, select the Compatibility Mode option and then click Next to continue to the Engines page.

9. On the Engines page, shown here, you can either accept the engines that Forefront has randomly configured or choose your own scan engines up to a maximum of five, including the always-selected Microsoft Antimalware Engine. You can select fewer than five engines, but you cannot select more than five. Click Next to continue to the Engine Updates Required page.

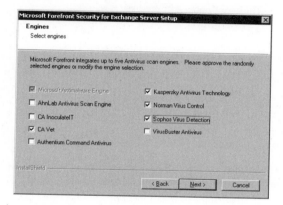

10. On the Engine Updates Required page, shown here, you will be notified that the scan engines you've selected will need to be updated at the completion of the Forefront installation. Click Next to continue to the Enable Anti-Spam Updates page.

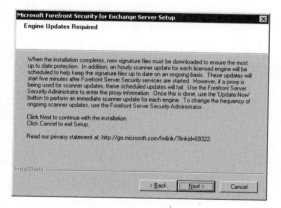

EXERCISE 7.19 *(continued)*

11. On the Enable Anti-Spam Updates page, shown here, you will have the option to enable antispam updates to occur automatically via Microsoft Update. Leave this option selected, and click Next to continue to the Choose Destination Location page.

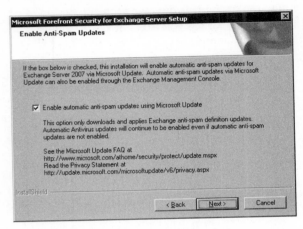

12. On the Choose Destination Location page, shown here, you will be able to change the install location for the Forefront files. In most cases, you should just leave the default selection. Click Next to continue to the Select Program Folder page.

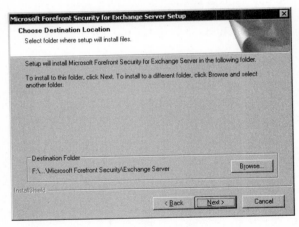

13. On the Select Program Folder page, you have the option to change the name of the folder created on the Start menu from its default value. Leave the default selection intact, and click Next to continue to the Start Copying Files page.

14. On the Start Copying Files page, you will have a chance to review your settings. Click Next to allow Forefront to start installing onto your Edge Transport server.

15. After some time, the Restart Exchange Transport Service page, shown here, will appear. Click Next to allow the Exchange Transport Service to be restarted. You must restart this service to allow the Forefront installation to complete.

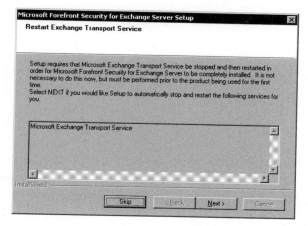

16. When the service has been restarted, click Next to continue.

17. When the installation has completed, click the Finish button to close the wizard.

Now that the installation is completed, you can move on to configuring Forefront.

Configuring Forefront for Exchange Server

Administrators familiar with Sybari's Antigen product for Exchange Server 2003 will have little trouble adjusting to the new version, Microsoft Forefront Security for Exchange Server. For those administrators who've never worked with Antigen or Forefront, the adjustment can be a bit overwhelming at first. Fortunately, all tasks within Forefront are organized into one of four areas of the Forefront administrative console. We'll examine each area of the administrative console in the following sections of this chapter.

Settings

The default view of the Forefront administrative console is of the Settings area, as shown in Figure 7.23. The Settings area is divided into five smaller areas of administration:

- Scan Job
- Antivirus
- Scanner Updates
- Templates
- General Options

FIGURE 7.23 The Forefront administrative console

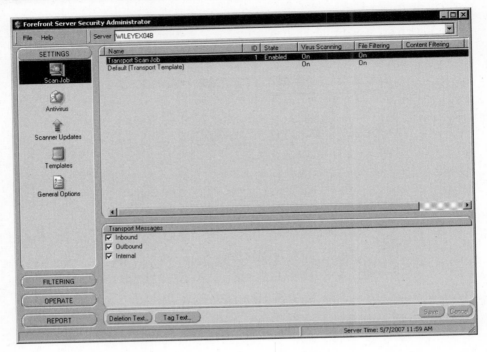

 For the purpose of this exam, I'll cover only the antivirus functionality of the Forefront Security for Exchange Server product, which is actually a small portion of the overall functionality. Most of the spam-filtering tasks designed to manage and maintain a Forefront installation are beyond the scope of the exam and require a significant investment of time or training to understand and perform correctly. Also, I'll cover the default Transport Scan Job only.

Scan Job

The configuration options in the Scan Job section are pretty simple; the job is on for any combination of inbound messages, outbound messages, or internal-only messages. The Internal messages option has little consequence on an Edge Transport server, but the Inbound and Outbound options do. In addition to configuring to which messages the template will apply, you can also change the deletion text or tag text by clicking the appropriate buttons at the bottom of the console.

Clicking the Deletion Text button opens the File Deletion Text dialog box, shown in Figure 7.24. From here you can change the default text from its current value if desired. This text is used to create a replacement file when an infected file is deleted from a message. You might customize this text with information about how to contact the help desk for assistance.

FIGURE 7.24 Changing the deletion text for viruses in messages

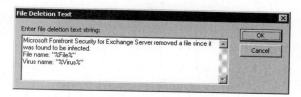

Clicking the Tag Text button opens the Tag Text dialog box, shown in Figure 7.25. From here you can configure options to tag the subject line or MIME header of a message when a filter action has been set to Identify: Tag Message.

FIGURE 7.25 Changing the tag text for messages

Antivirus

In the Antivirus area, shown in Figure 7.26, you can configure how the template or job scans messages, including which scan engines to use, how the engines should be used, and what action to perform when a virus is found.

To change the scan engines in use by a template, select the template in the top section of the administrative console and then change the scan engines by deselecting or selecting scan engines in the bottom portion of the console. Recall that you can have a maximum of five scan engines configured at any one time.

FIGURE 7.26   The Antivirus area of the administrative console

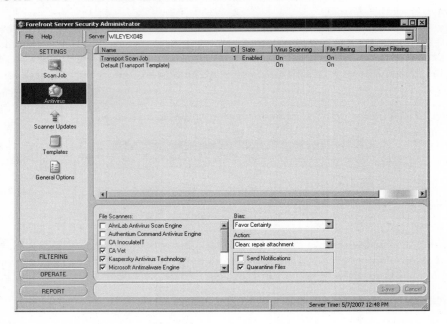

The Bias setting determines how many scan engines will be used on each attachment when checking for infected items. The following options are available:

Maximum Performance: Each item is scanned using only one of the selected scan engines. This option provides the fastest performance but offers the least protection.

Favor Performance: Each item is randomly scanned with either one of the selected scan engines or half of the selected scan engines. This option provides slightly better protection and slightly lower performance.

Neutral: Each item is scanned with at least half of the selected scan engines.

Favor Certainty: Each item is randomly scanned with either all of the selected scan engines or at least half of the selected scan engines. This is the default option.

Maximum Certainty: Each item is scanned with all the selected scan items. This option provides the best protection but will result in the slowest performance.

You can configure the action to be performed by Forefront when a virus is detected from the following options:

Skip: Detect Only: This option configures Forefront to only detect and report on infected files. No attempt to clean or delete the infected files is made. You should not ordinarily use this option on any production installation of Forefront because of the significant decrease in functionality when selected.

Clean: Repair Document: The default action of Forefront is to attempt to clean the virus from the infected file. If the cleaning action is successful, the previously infected attachment will be replaced with a clean version. Should the cleaning attempt fail, the attachment is deleted from the message and replaced with a text file indicating the action taken. The message body remains in place, and the message is delivered to the recipient in this state.

Delete: The infected attachment is deleted from the message without any attempt being made to clean it first. A text file is then attached to the message, indicating an infected attachment was deleted by Forefront. The message is then delivered to the recipient.

In addition, you can elect to have notifications generated as a result of infected files. I'll discuss the configuration of notifications later in the section "Report." The option to save messages and their infected attachments to the quarantine is enabled by default and should not ordinarily be turned off. Leaving this option on will allow you to review the quarantine and attempt message delivery at a later time.

Scanner Updates

The Scanner Updates area, shown in Figure 7.27, is possibly the first place you'll actually want to come to after a new installation of Forefront. As indicated in the installation process, the scan engines need to be updated to the most current definitions available to provide the best level of protection.

FIGURE 7.27 The Scanner Updates area of the administrative console

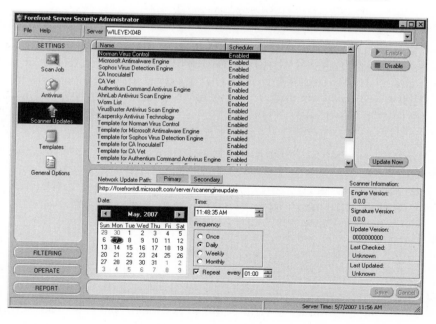

The options you have in this area are fairly straightforward. To manage a particular scan engine, select it from the list in the center part of the administrative console. On the right side of the console, you have options to enable, disable, or update the selected engine. To get your engines up-to-date, you should select each one displayed and click the Update Now button. You can monitor the status of the update, as shown in Figure 7.28. In addition, once the update has been applied, the version information will be updated appropriately in the lower-right side of the administrative console; the Scanner Information area is shown in Figure 7.29.

FIGURE 7.28   Updating scan engines

FIGURE 7.29   Viewing scan engine version information

In the bottom middle section of the Scanner Updates area, you can configure a custom update schedule for each engine as well as a secondary download location should the primary location be unavailable. By default, each engine is configured to check for updates hourly, with each engine separated from the previous engine by a five-minute interval. Templates that are shown in this location are also configured to check automatically for updates hourly, in five-minute intervals. You cannot manually check for template updates, though, as you can with scan engine updates.

Templates

The entire Forefront system revolves around using templates. By default, the installation of Forefront on an Edge Transport server uses one scan job and one template: the transport scan job (which is enabled by default with a priority setting of 1) and the default transport template. The transport scan job uses the default transport template for its settings. In older installations of Antigen, there would typically be many more templates depending on the number of storage groups on the server.

General Options

The General Options area, shown in Figure 7.30, allows you to configure many other settings that control how Forefront works. Here you can find items such as email notifications on service startup, event logging, and update notification, among many others.

FIGURE 7.30   The General Options area of the administrative console

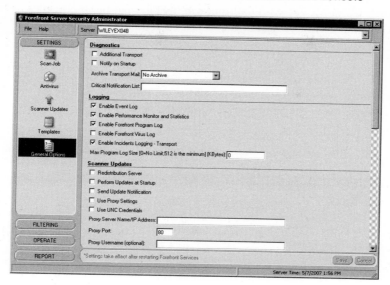

Operate

The Operate area of the Forefront administrative console allows you to manage configured jobs. By default, the only area available within the Operate area is the Run Job area, as shown in Figure 7.31.

FIGURE 7.31   The Run Job area of the administrative console

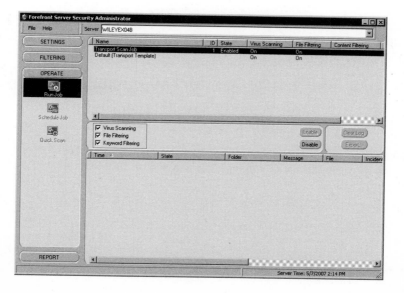

From here, you can disable or enable a job or change the particular areas that a job covers, such as virus scanning, keyword filtering, and file filtering. Be sure to click Save after making any changes, or click Cancel to cancel any changes without saving them.

Report

As with any antivirus application, Forefront has a quarantine area that you'll want to examine and manage periodically. You can find the quarantine as well as other important items in the Report area of the administrative console, as shown in Figure 7.32, which shows the Notification area.

FIGURE 7.32 The Notification area of the administrative console

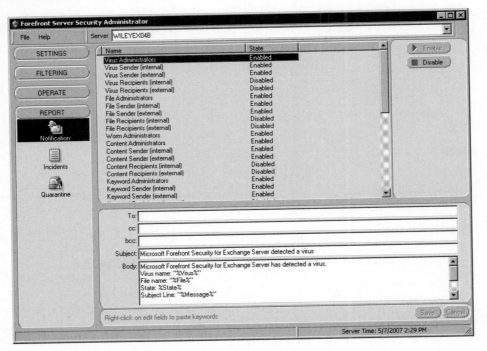

Notification

In the Notification area, shown in Figure 7.32, you have the ability to configure options associated with various notifications that can be enabled or disabled for various events that might occur with Forefront. For each notification, you can also configure the following email-related fields:

- The To address(es) to send notifications to
- The Cc address(es) to send notifications to
- The Bcc address(es) to send notifications to
- The Subject text of the notification
- The Body text of the notification

> **NOTE** Often, virus-laden messages are not sent with a valid return address; it is now common practice not to send notification messages to the sender of antivirus messages, as they would most likely not be delivered to the originator of the virus.

As they pertain to viruses, the following notifications are available to configure:

Virus Administrators: Sends alert messages to administrators for all viruses detected on the server. Typically these alerts will be sent to a distribution group containing the mailboxes of all messaging administrators.

Virus Sender (Internal): Sends alert messages to the sender of the message, if the sender is located in your Exchange organization, when a virus has been detected in a message they have sent. The body text of this notification might be customized with information about how to get help with the virus problem.

Virus Sender (External): Sends alert messages to the sender of the message if the sender is not located in your Exchange organization.

Virus Recipients (Internal): Sends alert messages to the recipient of the message, if the recipient is located in your Exchange organization, that the message contained an infected attachment. The body text of this notification might be customized with information about how to contact the help desk for further assistance.

Virus Recipients (External): Sends alert messages to the recipient of the message if the recipient is not located in your Exchange organization.

Incidents

The Incidents area, shown in Figure 7.33, lists virus detections or filter operations for the server. The incidents are logged into the Incidents database, `Incidents.mdb`, and stored indefinitely by default. You will likely want to enable the automatic purging of incidents to occur every 30 days or so to keep the size of the database from growing too large. You can also filter the view for items between specific dates and export the information to a text file for archiving or later viewing.

FIGURE 7.33 The Incidents area of the administrative console

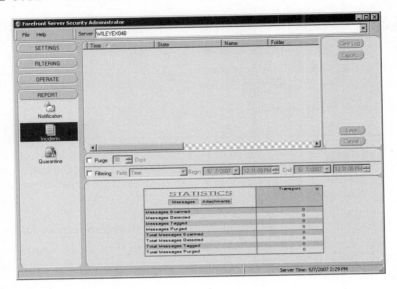

Quarantine

The Quarantine area, shown in Figure 7.34, lists all detected files. A copy of the detected file is placed here before a clean, delete, or skip action occurs within Forefront. Over time, the number of items in the Quarantine folder will build up, so you might want to enable automatic purging after 30 days or so.

FIGURE 7.34 The Quarantine area of the administrative console

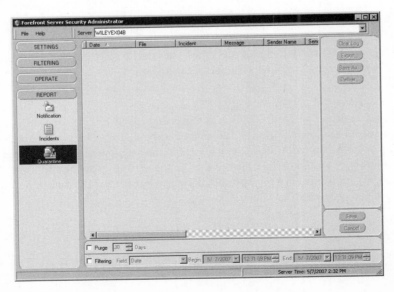

Depending on the Quarantine security option you selected while installing Forefront, you will be able to release items from the quarantine by selecting them and clicking the Deliver button without filter matching occurring (Compatibility Mode) or with filter matching occurring (Secure Mode). Either way, all items that are attempted for delivery from the quarantine will always be rescanned for viruses. Should you not be able to deliver a message and its attachment from the quarantine, you can save the attachment using the Save As button—a task you will likely find yourself performing often for files that wouldn't ordinarily be allowed through but higher-level users will want anyway.

You can also filter the view of the quarantine or export a list of quarantine items as desired.

 Real World Scenario

Using Exchange's Built-in Power

As you have seen throughout the course of this chapter, the Edge Transport server provides you with a powerful antispam solution right out of the box. How powerful and effective that solution is, however, will depend on how much time you spend assessing the available options and configuring them in a way that makes the most sense for your organization. If you take the time to evaluate and document your needs thoroughly and then take the time to plan your required configuration, you could get away without even needing to purchase or install an additional antispam product for your Exchange organization. Of particular note are the IP Block List and Attachment Filtering options. You can use these two areas to block the majority of all spam entering your organization. Whatever path you decide to choose when it comes to spam control, do your organization a favor and take your time. The spam problem will not be going away anytime soon, but you can definitely make a difference to your users if you understand the powerful options Exchange Server 2007 gives you, and configure them to their maximum potential.

Summary

I covered a decent amount of ground in this chapter, focusing on the basic configuration and management of MRM, rules, and server policies. Every organization that deploys Exchange Server 2007 will have Hub Transport, CAS, and Mailbox servers. This chapter also covered some of the tools available to you to control messages as they travel through an organization and while they are stored in an organization.

For additional security, you should install some antivirus and antispam product on your Edge Transport servers. Forefront Security for Exchange Server is a perfect fit and is fully supported by Microsoft, but you may find other third-party applications that meet your needs as well. You might not even end up using Edge Transport servers at all if your organization already has a functional virus- and spam-control solution in place today.

Exam Essentials

Understand all of the parts of MRM.   Messaging records management (MRM) consists of default and custom managed folders, content settings, and managed folder policies. All these components are important tools for managing the life span of a message in an Exchange organization. Understand what all of these components are and how they fit together.

Know the parts of a rule action, exception, and condition.   Transport rules have three different configurable parts: the condition triggers the rule, the exception specifies what part of the condition to exclude, and the action says what to do with the email message if it fits the condition and is not excluded from the rule.

Know your antispam options.   One of the best features of the Edge Transport server is the wealth and variety of antispam options it provides you. Be sure to investigate thoroughly each one and understand the pros and cons of using each. You'll want to be able to differentiate between the options as well when given an exam question asking which option would be best to perform a specific task.

Review Questions

1. How do you rename the Inbox folder and apply a different retention policy to it?

    A. You have to reformat the server because you can select the folder names only when you install Exchange.

    B. You create a new managed folder, specify Inbox as the folder, and then apply your settings to it as desired.

    C. You can change the settings on the Inbox folder, but you cannot rename it.

    D. None of the above.

2. When should the MRM mailbox assistant be run?

    A. It should be run after you have deleted or moved a number of mailboxes as part of a mailbox cleanup operation.

    B. It should be run every Monday morning when you have the biggest load on the Mailbox server, because MRM functions better where there is extra server load.

    C. It is automatically run when it needs to be run; you shouldn't have to worry about when it runs.

    D. You should run it when the server has the least load, because it is a resource-intensive operation.

3. What is a managed folder mailbox policy used for?

    A. It allows you to apply a grouping of folders to users all at once instead of one at a time.

    B. It allows you to group folders and then apply a single mailbox content setting to them. This eliminates having to create the same set of content settings over and over again.

    C. It applies settings to new folders as they are created to make sure the new folders all have uniform settings.

    D. It allows you to create a group of default settings that are applied to all newly created custom managed folders.

4. Your server has issues with the network time servers due to an error at the Navy time sources, and somehow it jumps forward a few hours during the time that the managed folder assistant is running. This time shift causes the server to stop the assistant before it has a chance to complete. What will happen the next time the managed folder assistant runs?

    A. The assistant will not start, and an error with event ID 1299 will be entered in the Application log stating that the assistant failed to start because of a failure.

    B. The assistant will start up right where it left off.

    C. The assistant will start back from the beginning because things might have changed since last time.

    D. The assistant will simply restart after it failed.

5. If an enabled transport rule has no condition, what will it do when it runs?

   A. Currently a message that has no condition will cause the transport service to stop responding; this is a known issue and will be fixed in Exchange Server 2007 SP1.

   B. The rule will do nothing at all.

   C. The rule will act on every message.

   D. An event log entry with event ID 1966 will be entered in the event log stating the rule has no condition and that it has been disabled.

6. Email address policies are applied by what?

   A. The RUS

   B. The address policy service

   C. The `Update-EmailAddress` command

   D. None of the above

7. GAL stands for what?

   A. Global address locator

   B. Group attribute locale

   C. Group address book

   D. Global address list

8. What is the recommended limit to the number of rules in an organization?

   A. 1,000 per server

   B. 10,000 per AD domain

   C. 500 per Exchange organization

   D. 1,000 per AD forest

9. You have two groups of users to which you want to apply different Inbox content settings. One group wants items in their Inbox to be maintained for only 30 days, and the other group wants to maintain their email for 392 days. How would you do this?

   A. Create a separate managed content setting for each group of people, and apply those settings to the managed mailbox policy for each group.

   B. Create a new default managed folder, and apply the content settings to each default folder as needed.

   C. Create new custom managed folders, replace the Inbox folders with the custom folders, and then apply the content settings to each custom folder as needed.

   D. None of the above.

10. When you delete a custom managed folder in the Exchange management console, what happens to the folders in the user's mailbox?

   A. The folders are deleted along with all the messages in them.

   B. Nothing happens to the folder.

   C. When you delete a custom managed folder, you are prompted to enter an expiration date for the folder.

   D. When you delete a custom managed folder, you have the option to pick what happens.

11. Managed content settings can do all of the following except which action?

   A. Delete mail items

   B. Move mail items

   C. Mark mail items as read

   D. Send mail items to a journaling location

12. The Maximum Inactivity Time Lock setting performs what action when applied on an Exchange server policy?

   A. Allows you to monitor and then disable mailboxes that are not accessed by anyone for a given amount of time

   B. Logs users out of OWA if there has been no activity for a given amount of time

   C. Locks a mobile device if it has no activity for a given amount of time

   D. Disconnects an SMTP session if there has been no activity for a given amount of time

13. What's an OAB good for?

   A. The Object Attribute Block list stores all of the junk email blocked addresses and domains that are configured on every Outlook client in an Exchange organization. The list is used on the Edge Transport server to block spam messages.

   B. The Offline Address Book is used as a local copy of the Exchange address lists by Outlook clients to cut down on network requests to Exchange and global catalog servers.

   C. The Offline Address Book gives offline users access to email address and company contact information stored in their online contacts folder.

   D. None of the above.

14. Which of the following is not an available method to classify a message?

   A. The user can use the Exchange Management Shell command `Classify-Message`.

   B. The user can manually classify a message via OWA 2007.

   C. The user can manually classify a message using Outlook 2007.

   D. Administrators can classify messages using server transport rules.

15. Yesterday you created a new rule on your Hub Transport server located in Hawaii, and the rule does not seem to be working on your Hub Transport server in Cape Town. You know that your connections are all good and that mail is being routed between the two locations. You can log in to both servers from your location. What could be keeping your Cape Town server from running the rule that you made on the Hawaii server?

    A. The RUS.

    B. The HubSync service might not be running on both servers. Without this service, rules do not replicate.

    C. You should check AD replication to be sure that the GC that Cape Town is talking to has replicated from the server that Hawaii is connected to.

    D. None of the above.

16. You've created a transport rule that adds the text *[CONFIDENTIAL]* to the subject line of every message sent between the R&D department and the marketing department. About a week goes by, and you start to get complaints that users in both departments are not able to send messages to each other. What is most likely the cause of messages not being sent?

    A. A routing error must be taking place on the transport server.

    B. The subject line has exceeded the maximum allowed size.

    C. The antispam agents on the Edge Transport server must be blocking the messages.

    D. There is not enough information given in the question to answer it.

17. Your boss comes into your office and says, "I want you to delete all messages in everyone's Sent Items folder older than 43 days." He then leaves your office. What MRM feature would you use to make this happen?

    A. Custom managed folders

    B. Custom mailbox policy

    C. Managed content settings

    D. Both A and C

18. Your boss comes back into your office, and he is excited after you completed your last task so quickly. He now says, "I don't want anyone but my assistant and my daughter to be able to send email to me. I want all the rest of the emails to me to be sent to my assistant instead." What should you do?

    A. Use mailbox security settings.

    B. Assign your boss a secret email address, and give it only to his assistant and his daughter.

    C. Use a Hub Transport server transport rule or two.

    D. Apologize to your boss and say you cannot do that.

19. To create a new custom managed folder using the Exchange Management Shell, which command would you use?

    A. `Create-NewCustomManagedFolder`

    B. `New-CustomManagedFolder`

    C. `New-ManagedFolder -Type Custom`

    D. None of the above

20. Your manager is concerned about the impact a stolen mobile device might have on company information. If a phone is stolen, she wants to make sure that the thief can't access any information on it. What ActiveSync setting could you use to make your manager more comfortable?

    A. You could set Device Encryption Enabled to Enabled, which would make the data on the mobile device secure.

    B. You could set the maximum failed password attempts to three, which would erase all the information on the device if the incorrect password were typed more than three times.

    C. You could set the Password Inactivity setting to three days, which would make the phone reformat itself if it has not correctly logged into Exchange in more than 72 hours.

    D. None of the above.

Answers to Review Questions

1. **D.** You cannot rename the default folders, but you can replace them with custom managed folders.

2. **D.** You should run the MRM mailbox assistant when there is the least load on the server, because it is a resource-intensive operation. It is best to run it during nonpeak business hours.

3. **A.** A managed folder mailbox policy makes it simpler to push folders to users' mailboxes.

4. **B.** The assistant will restart where it left off.

5. **C.** Setting a condition is optional. Without a condition, a rule will act on every message unless the exception expects the message.

6. **D.** The correct Exchange Management Shell command to apply an email address policy is the `update-emailaddresspolicy` command.

7. **D.** The correct answer is the global address list, which is the address that contains all the nonhidden Exchange-enabled objects in the organization.

8. **D.** The correct answer is 1,000 rules per forest. Rules are forestwide and applied to each and every Hub Transport server in the forest. This is a recommended limit, and you should base your limit on this and the performance testing of your Hub Transport servers.

9. **B.** The correct answer is to replace the Inbox of each group with a new default managed folder that has the content settings needed.

10. **B.** When the custom folder is deleted, the folders in the user's Inbox will stay there until you manually delete them.

11. **C.** Managed content settings cannot mark items as read. Content settings can be used to move, delete, and journal messages.

12. **C.** The Maximum Inactivity Time Lock setting is an ActiveSync policy and allows you to force mobile devices to become locked after a given amount of time with no activity and requires a password before they can be used again.

13. **B.** The Offline Address Books contain offline copies of address lists that can be used by Outlook. OABs are customizable on the server and can contain whatever address lists they need to contain. The OAB allows offline clients access to the address lists, and they allow online clients to access the address lists locally, cutting down on network traffic.

14. **A.** There is no Exchange Management Shell command to classify a message.

15. **C.** Hub Transport servers store their rules in the AD configuration container and are replicated to Exchange servers based on AD site replication.

16. B. The rule you created is missing an exception that tells it to not add the text to the subject line if the text is already there. This has caused the subject lines to become larger than Exchange will allow you to send.

17. C. Managed content settings allow you to perform actions on messages in folders based on criteria such as the age of a message.

18. C. You could configure a Hub Transport rule to redirect all of your boss's email to his assistant. To allow email from his daughter and his assistant to reach him, you could place an exception on the rule so that the rule is not executed when his daughter or his assistant is listed in the From line.

19. D. The correct Exchange Management Shell command to create a new managed custom folder is `New-ManagedFolder`.

20. B. Setting the maximum failed password attempts is the best way to secure the data on a mobile device, because it deletes all the information on the device if the password is not typed correctly. You should also set the Maximum Inactivity Time Lock setting so that the phone will lock itself if it is inactive.

Chapter

8

Configuring Highly Available Exchange Server Solutions

MICROSOFT EXAM OBJECTIVES COVERED IN THIS CHAPTER:

✓ **Installing and Configuring Microsoft Exchange Servers**

  ▪ Install Exchange.

✓ **Configuring Disaster Recovery**

  ▪ Configure high availability.

The term *high availability (HA)* is often thrown into conversations, but few administrators take the time to understand what it really means. Administrators have been conditioned by article after article to think that high availability means the same thing as clustering. Although Microsoft server clustering and network load balancing are highly available platforms for applications, they do not provide high availability by themselves. Every administrator should understand that clustering is only a piece of high availability.

High availability requires strong management processes, proper testing procedures, and well-planned implementation and change control processes. An organization cannot achieve high availability just by implementing clustering technologies. The most important requirement in achieving high availability is implementing a high-availability philosophy or spirit within the organization, where administrators stop, think, evaluate, collaborate, and then decide what to do in the event of a major failure or when changing the configuration of an application or server. Proper change control, for example, is part of that spirit.

The main topics of this chapter are as follows:

- High availability for Mailbox servers

- High availability for Hub Transport, Client Access, and Edge Transport servers

NOTE Information Technology Infrastructure Library (ITIL) and the Microsoft Operations Framework (MOF) are methodologies that promote proper IT management and thus are considered part of a holistic high-availability approach.

High Availability Overview

Many organizations go through a process called *risk management* or *risk identification* where they list everything that could possibly go wrong or that would cause Exchange Server 2007 services to be unavailable. For example, an organization may list disk failure as a possible risk and then take steps to mitigate that risk by using redundant array of inexpensive disks (RAID) controllers and configuring all disks in fault-tolerant arrays. Another example would be where an organization lists main board failure as a risk and then decides to implement a server clustering solution to mitigate that risk.

In a nutshell, *high availability* is the combination of well-designed, -planned, -tested, and -implemented processes, software, and fault-tolerant hardware focused on supplying and maintaining application availability.

As a high-level example, consider messaging in an organization. A poor implementation of Exchange is usually slapped together by purchasing a server that the administrator thinks is about the right size and installing Exchange Server 2007 on it. Messaging clients are installed on network-connected desktops, and profiles are created. The Exchange server might even be configured successfully to connect to the Internet. It is possible to install an Exchange messaging environment over a week or even overnight in some cases. It is easy to do it fast and get it done, but lots of important details are missed.

By contrast, in a high-availability environment, the deployment of messaging is well designed. Administrators research organizational messaging requirements. Users are brought into discussions with administrators and managers. Messaging is considered a possible solution for many company ills. Research may go on for an extended period while consultants are brought in to help build a design and review the design of others. Vendors are brought in to discuss how their products (antivirus and content management solutions, for example) will keep the messaging environment available and not waste messaging resources processing spam and spreading viruses. Potential third-party software is tested and approved after a large investment of administrator and end-user time. Hardware is sized and evaluated based on performance requirements and expected loads. Hardware is also sized and tested for disaster recovery and to meet service-level agreements for both performance and time for recovery in the event of a disaster. Hardware that's selected will often contain fault-tolerant components such as redundant memory, drives, network connections, cooling fans, power supplies, and so on. A high-availability environment will incorporate a significant amount of design, planning, and testing. A high-availability environment will often, but not always, include additional features, such as server clustering, which decreases downtime by enabling rolling upgrades and allowing for a preplanned response to failures. A top-notch high-availability messaging environment will also consider the messaging client software and its potential configurations that lead to increased availability for users. For example, Outlook 2003 and later offers a cache mode configuration that allows users to create new messages, respond to existing mail in their Inboxes, and manage their calendars (among many other tasks) without having to maintain a constant connection to the Exchange server. Cache mode allows users to continue working even though the Exchange server might be down for a short time, and it also allows for the more efficient use of bandwidth.

All critical business systems have to be analyzed to understand the cost incurred when they are unavailable. If there is a significant cost, then the organization should take steps to minimize downtime. Taking this view to the extreme, the goal is really to provide ***continuous availability (CA)*** of applications and resources for the organization. Doesn't everyone want email always to be available for processing messaging traffic and helping the people in the organization collaborate? Of course, we want applications and their entire environment to continue running forever. We strive for continuous availability, and we often settle for high availability.

Unfortunately, hardware will always fail; it is just a matter of when. Software also becomes obsolete over time. Don't forget that high availability includes not just the hardware and software solution but also the backup/restore solution and failover processing. Most high-availability experts will also add that a true high-availability environment includes a well-documented development, test, and production-migration process for any changes made in production environments. All in all, there is much to take into account to achieve high availability, but you can achieve high levels of application availability through well-designed, -planned, -tested, and -implemented processes, software, and hardware.

Another example is if you use *network load balancing (NLB)* to provide application availability to your users. In Exchange Server 2007, you can use NLB for the Edge Transport server role and for the Client Access server role. NLB helps keep the applications available to your users. The same can be said for failover clustering; however, you need to take into account the unavailability during the actual failover of your application in the event of hardware or software failures. Sometimes, failover is a matter of seconds; in other cases, it can be several minutes. In all cases, a clustering solution will drive down unavailability significantly and increase the uptime of applications run on your servers. For any application or system to be highly available, the parts need to be designed around availability, and the individual parts need to be tested before being put into production. As an example, if you are using third-party products with your Exchange environment, you may find that they are a weak link that results in the loss of availability. Implementing a cluster will not necessarily result in high availability if there are problems with other portions of the entire solution.

This bit of background should not detract from the great features provided for high availability in Exchange 2007; rather, the purpose of this discussion is to provide a frame of reference as the Exchange-specific high-availability features are discussed. High availability is so much more than just slapping a couple of servers together in a cluster.

Exchange Server 2007 includes many new features that enhance availability. *Local continuous replication (LCR), cluster continuous replication (CCR), single copy clustering (SCC),* and *standby continuous replication (SCR)* are all designed to increase the reliability and the availability of Exchange Server 2007 services.

Failover clustering and NLB are fairly complicated topics and explaining them fully would require more room than is available in this book. Rest assured, I will cover the basics of failover clustering and NLB so that you will be well equipped to pass the exam. In this chapter, you'll learn the availability options for each of the server roles.

High Availability for Mailbox Servers

There are four options for mailbox availability that combine clustering and replication in different blends. As mentioned in the previous section, they are *local continuous replication* (LCR), *single copy cluster* (SCC), *cluster continuous replication* (CCR), and *standby continuous replication (SCR)*. I will be covering each of these options individually. With so many options, it's kind of difficult to keep them straight. To start, let's review a list of the types and the key features of each:

LCR: Single server, data redundancy, manual failover

SCC: Failover cluster, no data redundancy, automatic failover

CCR: Failover cluster, data redundancy, automatic failover

SCR: Multiple servers, data redundancy, manual failover

As you study for the exam, or just try to get these straight, here are a couple ways to help determine which one is which:

- Ones that end in *R* use replication and thus have data redundancy.
- Ones that contain *CC* use failover clustering.

Configuring Local Continuous Replication (LCR)

LCR is not an enterprise-class high-availability solution. It does, however, provide mitigation against several possible failures. LCR provides mitigation against database disk failure and database corruption, and it is usually a good fit for small and remote offices that may not have the facilities or expertise to manage a failover cluster.

LCR uses a process called *log shipping* to send logs of completed transactions from the disk where the production storage group exists to another disk that holds a copy. The copy is updated by replaying the logs to maintain an exact copy of the production storage group and to keep it updated, as shown in Figure 8.1.

FIGURE 8.1 LCR overview

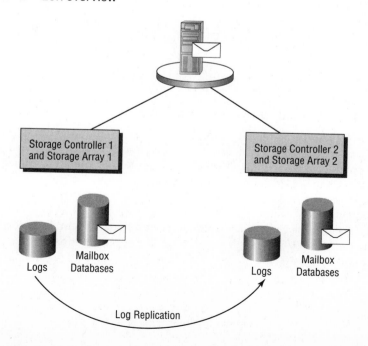

Storage Controller 1 and Storage Array 1

Storage Controller 2 and Storage Array 2

Logs

Mailbox Databases

Logs

Mailbox Databases

Log Replication

In the event of a disk failure or problems with database corruption, you can simply use the second copy of the data to resume service. This is a significant reduction in time compared to how long it would take to restore the storage group from backup, either from tape or from disk. The LCR failover and recovery processes may be manual, but they are not complex. LCR improves availability and reduces total cost of ownership by doing the following:

- It reduces the time it takes to recover from a failed disk or corrupted database.

- It reduces the number of backups of the storage group that must be made, although it still requires regular backups.

- With the proper hardware and software, it can improve performance during the backup process by using VSS-enabled backups on the passive instead of the active copy so the active copy is not affected by the backup process (VSS stands for Volume Shadow Copy Service).

Streaming backups can be done only on the active database. VSS backups can be done using either the active database or the passive copies. The VSS backups done using the passive database will truncate all of the log files on both nodes that have been committed to the passive database.

Overall, LCR is an excellent feature for organizations requiring quick recovery of disk and database failures. However, because moving the passive database copy into production requires downtime, the service-level agreement must allow for this process. Compared to other availability options, LCR is an inexpensive solution. Also, in most cases it's highly recommended when you're not using a server clustering solution, because of the following:

- Recovery to the passive copy storage is a simple and quick process.

- It is possible to run backups against the copy and not impact the production storage group at all during the backup process.

- Users requiring the additional protection can be grouped in the same storage group.

Preparing for Local Continuous Replication

Preparing for LCR requires building the proper storage group and database structure. To detect disk or database failures, a monitoring solution should be in place. Microsoft System Center Operations Manager (SCOM), NetIQ AppManger, HP Operations Manager, and other monitoring and management tools can provide monitoring services. Proper disk, memory, and CPU resources should be provided to meet the performance service-level agreements for Exchange services.

Disk subsystems must be capable of handling the additional input/output for LCR. Since LCR generates more I/O through the copy of the log information and the writing and application of the log information on the target, keeping the databases a reasonable size is important. Also, since the copy is often used to capture backups, the disks used for the copy should be similar to the disks used for the production storage group. Any supported type of storage can be used with LCR, including direct-attached storage, serially attached SCSI, and iSCSI. You can also use volume mount points instead of using drive letters. Using mount points may be a better solution for LCR because you can then just take the disk used for the copy and mount it to the same point as the production storage group after it is removed.

Disk recommendations and restrictions exist for LCR and include the following:

- Each storage group can contain only one database. This is also a limitation for both CCR and SCR. However, it should not be a real constraint as you can have up to 50 storage groups when the Enterprise Edition of Exchange is installed.

- If you have more than one public folder database in the Exchange organization, you will not be able to use LCR for that the public folder database because if you have two or more public folder databases, then the public folders use public folder replication. Replication is always occurring even if the public folders are not configured to replicate.

- Use RAID with redundancy so that the partitions are spread over multiple disks. This will increase performance for I/O, which should always be considered with Exchange Server 2007. It is also considered a best practice to separate the log files from the database by putting them on separate sets of physical disks. To make troubleshooting easier, you should spread out your data so it is located on separate disks as follows:

    - The operating system files should be on RAID-1.
    - The Exchange binaries should be on either RAID-5 or RAID-1.
    - The database files for the active storage group should be on their own set of disks.
    - The transaction logs for the active storage group should be on another set of disks.
    - The database files for the passive database should be on another set of disks.
    - The transaction logs for the passive database should also be on another set of disks.

- Size the copy disks so that they are approximately the same size as the active storage group disks. Both the active database copy disks and the passive database copy disks should be sized to allow for defragmentation and to allow for growth of the databases. The maximum recommended size is 100 gigabytes (GB) for databases without continuous replication and a maximum of 200GB for databases with replication.

An additional gigabyte of memory over the base requirement is suggested for an LCR-enabled server because both the active and passive databases are running on the same server. The CPU requirements for Exchange Server 2007 with LCR are also higher than without LCR.

Enabling Local Continuous Replication

There are two main scenarios you could have when implementing LCR:

- Existing storage group
- New storage group

In each scenario, the account used must have the appropriate Exchange Server 2007 permissions, and the account must be an Exchange Server administrator as well as a local administrator for the Exchange server that will be enabled for LCR.

Existing Storage Group

You can configure LCR for an existing storage group using the Exchange Management Console or the Exchange Management Shell. In Exercise 8.1, you'll use the Exchange Management Console to configure an existing Exchange Server 2007 server with an existing storage group to start using LCR and to generate the copy in the location entered.

EXERCISE 8.1

Using the Exchange Management Console to Configure LCR for an Existing Storage Group

To use the Exchange Management Console to configure LCR for an existing storage group, follow these steps:

1. Start the Exchange Management Console.

2. Expand Microsoft Exchange ➢ Server Configuration and select Mailbox.

3. Select the Mailbox server containing the target storage group for LCR.

4. Right-click the target storage group, and select Enable Local Continuous Replication to start the Enable Storage Group Local Continuous Replication Wizard.

5. Click Next on the Introduction page.

6. On the Set Paths page, set the locations for the LCR log files and LCR system files by clicking Browse. Click Next.

7. On the database page, use Browse to set the path for the LCR database file. Click Next.

8. Verify the information in the Configuration Summary area on the Enable page. Click Enable.

9. Click Finish to close the wizard upon completion.

In Exercise 8.2, you'll configure an existing Exchange Server 2007 server with an existing storage group to start using LCR and generate the copy in the location entered by using the Exchange Management Shell.

EXERCISE 8.2

Using the Exchange Management Shell (PowerShell) to Configure LCR for an Existing Storage Group

To use the Exchange Management Shell to configure LCR for an existing storage group, follow these steps:

1. Configure the database copy:

    ```
    Enable-DatabaseCopy -Identity<Server>\<StorageGroup>\<Database>
    -CopyEDBFilePath:<FullPathWithDatabaseFileNameAndExtension>
    ```

2. Configure the storage group copy:

    ```
    Enable-StorageGroupCopy -Identity <Server>\<StorageGroup>
    -CopyLogFolderPath:<FullPath
    -CopySystemFolderPath:<FullPath>
    ```

New Storage Group

You can configure LCR for a new storage group using either the Exchange Management Console or the Exchange Management Shell. In Exercise 8.3, you'll configure an existing Exchange Server 2007 server to create a new storage group, to configure it for LCR, and to generate the copy in the location entered by using the Exchange Management Console.

EXERCISE 8.3

Using the Exchange Management Console to Create a Storage Group and Enable It for LCR

To use the Exchange Management Console to create a storage group and enable it for LCR, follow these steps:

1. Open the Exchange Management Console.

2. Expand Microsoft Exchange ➢ Server Configuration and select Mailbox.

3. Right-click the target server for the new storage group, and select New Storage Group to start the New Storage Group Wizard.

4. On the New Storage Group page, enter the name for the new storage group in the Storage Group Name box.

5. Select the location for the log files and system files using the Browse buttons.

6. Select the Enable Local Continuous Replication for This Storage Group check box.

7. Set the locations for the copy of the log files and system files using the Browse buttons, and click New.

8. Click Finish to close the wizard.

In Exercise 8.4, you'll configure an existing Exchange Server 2007 server to create a new storage group, to configure it for LCR, and to generate the copy in the location entered by using the Exchange Management Shell.

EXERCISE 8.4

Using the Exchange Management Shell to Create a Storage Group and Enable It for LCR

To use the Exchange Management Shell to create a storage group and enable it for LCR, run the following command:

```
New-StorageGroup -Server <Server>
-Name <StorageGroupName> -HasLocalCopy:$True
-
CopyLogFolderPath <PathforLCRLogFiles>
-CopySystemFolderPath <PathforLCRSystemFiles>
```

Disabling Local Continuous Replication

Sometimes it is necessary to disable replication. In some cases, it is necessary for maintenance purposes or so that the production database can be replaced with the copy. The account must be an Exchange Server administrator and must be a local administrator for the Exchange server that is currently enabled for LCR.

After disabling LCR, you have to delete the files in the copy storage group and all the databases manually, as shown in Exercise 8.5.

EXERCISE 8.5

Using the Exchange Management Console to Disable LCR

Follow these steps to use the Exchange Management Console to disable LCR:

1.   Open the Exchange Management Console.

2.   Expand Microsoft Exchange ➢ Server Configuration and select Mailbox.

3.   Select the Mailbox server that contains the production storage group you want to disable for LCR.

4.   Right-click the target storage group, and then click Disable Local Continuous Replication.

5.   Click Yes to confirm.

6.   Click OK to acknowledge the Microsoft Exchange warning.

7.   Manually delete the LCR storage group and database files.

You can also use the Exchange Management Shell to disable LCR on an Exchange Server 2007 server, as shown in Exercise 8.6. In many cases, using the Exchange Management Shell is preferred once administrators become familiar with it.

EXERCISE 8.6

Using the Exchange Management Shell to Disable LCR

Here's how to use the Exchange Management Shell to disable LCR:

1. Run the following command:

   `Disable-StorageGroupCopy -Identity <StorageGroup>`

2. Manually delete the LCR storage group and database files.

Seeding a Local Continuous Replication Copy

The process of log shipping includes shipping closed log files to a passive copy of the database. These logs are then played into the copy of the database to maintain the database change and growth that occurs on the active copy of the database. This passive copy of the database needs first to be made available on the passive node. This can occur through a variety of methods, including manually copying the files, with a backup and restore, or even disk-based replication. This process is generally referred to as "seeding" the database. When you're configuring LCR initially, seeding is typically done automatically. Sometimes the seeding process has to be done again; that is, the database needs to be reseeded. Reseeding is required in the following situations:

- When Exchange Server 2007 has discovered corrupted log files that cannot be replayed into the passive database copy
- When an offline defragmentation of the active database has been completed.

The time needed to seed the copy depends on the size of the production database, the available bandwidth, and the overall load on the server. You can seed the copy using any of these methods:

- Run `Update-StorageGroupCopy` to make a copy backup of the storage group. After the copy process is done, it can be moved to the LCR database folder.
- Using `Enable-StorageGroupCopy` on the server will seed the passive copy database by default. You can use the `-SeedingPostponed` parameter to stop the automatic seeding. The `Enable-StorageGroupCopy` cmdlet includes the steps of the `Update-StorageGroupCopy` command. When the `Enable-StorageGroupCopy` cmdlet is run on a Mailbox server, it seeds the database by default, unless the `-SeedingPostponed` option is used.
- The passive copy database can also be manually copied from the production database by taking the database offline or by stopping all Exchange services. Of course, by using this process, the Exchange server will not be able to process messages until the production database is brought back online.

In Exercise 8.7, you'll use the Exchange Management Console to dismount the passive database copy, suspend replication, delete the copy information, copy the active database to the passive location, and resume replication.

EXERCISE 8.7

Seeding the LCR Database Using the Exchange Management Console

Follow these steps to use the Exchange Management Console to seed the LCR database:

1. Open the Exchange Management Console.

2. Expand Microsoft Exchange ➤ Server Configuration and select Mailbox.

3. Select the server containing the LCR copy, right-click the storage group containing the LCR copy, and select Dismount Database.

4. Suspend the replication process by right-clicking the storage group containing the LCR copy, selecting Suspend Local Continuous Replication, and then selecting Yes to confirm.

5. Remove the database files, log files, and checkpoint files from the copy, and delete the files with filename extensions of *.log, *.jrs, and *.chk files, as well as .edb, from the LCR database folder.

6. After dismounting the database and deleting the files in the LCR database folder, copy the database file from the production storage group to the copy location.

7. Once the copy process is complete, right-click the database and select Mount Database.

8. Right-click the copy database and select Resume Local Continuous Replication.

In Exercise 8.8, you'll use the Exchange Management Shell to suspend the copy process, clean up files in the copy location, seed the copy location, and then restart the replication process.

EXERCISE 8.8

Seeding the LCR Database Using the Exchange Management Shell

Here's how to seed the LCR database using the Exchange Management Shell:

1. Open the Exchange Management Shell.

2. Run Suspend-StorageGroupCopy -Identity <Server>\<StorageGroupName> -SuspendComment:"Seeding" to suspend replication.

3. Delete all the database and log files as well as all the checkpoint files from the LCR location. Delete all files with the filename extensions *.log, *.jrs, and *.chk, as well as .edb, from the LCR folder.

4. Run Update-StorageGroupCopy -Identity:<Server>\<StorageGroupName> to seed the LCR location. This command will automatically restart replication. Use the -ManualResume parameter to stop the copy from starting automatically.

5. If the replication was not resumed automatically, run Resume-StorageGroupCopy -Identity:<Server>\<StorageGroupName>.

6. After the Update-StorageGroupCopy command is complete and the storage group copy is resumed, verify that replication is working correctly by using the Get-StorageGroupCopyStatus cmdlet.

Once you've completed Exercise 8.8, the replication process should start up. Log shipping and replay will start automatically.

Testing the Health of the Local Continuous Copy Process

A standard practice for general maintenance should be to test the health of the LCR process. After all, if the passive copy isn't healthy, then it becomes less useful or even useless. In Exercise 8.9, you'll test the health of LCR.

Testing the Health of LCR Using the Exchange Management Console

Here's how to use the Exchange Management Console to test the heath of LCR:

1. Open the Exchange Management Console.

2. Expand Microsoft Exchange ➢ Server Configuration and select Mailbox.

3. Select the Mailbox server containing the passive database copy that you setup previously.

4. Right-click the storage group and select Properties.

5. Click the Local Continuous Replication tab to view the status of LCR.

Getting the same information using the Exchange Management Shell is pretty simple. From the shell, enter the command **Get-StorageGroupCopyStatus -Identity <Server>\<StorageGroup>**, and then view the resulting information.

They key information for the copy status includes the following:

- Summary status
- Copy queue length
- Replay queue length

It is important to capture this information on a regular basis. Administrators can use this information to establish baselines for times of the day, for weeks, and for months. With solid baseline information, administrators can easily tell whether processes are possibly problematic and need additional attention.

For another way to see how replication is performing, you can use the Test -ReplicationHealth cmdlet. This cmdlet should be run on the Mailbox server about which you are interested in obtaining information. It returns information about replication, services, and the replay queue.

Switching to the Passive Database Copy

The whole point of implementing LCR is to mitigate failure or corruption of the production database. Once failure of the database has been identified through monitoring or through user reports, it is up to administrators to run a manual process to switch the Exchange server to the copy database and make it the production database.

With quick notification and rapid response, it is possible to recover using the copy database in a few short minutes. The Restore-StorageGroupCopy command includes a -ReplaceLocations parameter. Instead of using this process and changing the location that Exchange uses for the database, the recommendation is that the database be changed to the old location by resetting the letter (or mount point) of the drive so that it equals the old production drive letter.

Exercise 8.10 covers the steps required to switch to the copy database and make it the production database.

EXERCISE 8.10

Recovering from a Corrupted Database to the Passive Database Copy

Follow these steps to recover from a corrupt database:

1. Identify the source of the corruption if possible. Some simple things to check include making sure the log and database drives are online. If the log drive is not available at the time of failure, it is possible that data might be lost. If the log files are still available, and they should be if they were properly deployed on a separate disk from the actual database, then there should be no loss of data.

2. Dismount the corrupt active database either by using the Dismount-Database cmdlet in the Exchange Management Shell or by using the Dismount option from the context menu for the database in the Exchange Management Console.

EXERCISE 8.10 *(continued)*

3. Use the Exchange Management Shell to activate the passive copy. An Exchange administrator can run the `Restore-StorageGroupCopy -Identity <Server>\` `<StorageGroupName>` cmdlet. This command will disable LCR for the production storage group.

4. Use the disk management tool, or other tools, to change the drive letter and possibly the folder structure so that the passive database is in the same logical location as the previously active database.

5. Once everything is properly placed, mount the database, and it will become active.

The steps to recover from a failed production disk or corrupt database take only a few minutes to run. Since there is no need to copy data, the process is not constrained by the size of the database.

Installing Failover Clustering

Failover clustering is a technology that allows an instance of software to run on a single server, with the ability to move that instance of an application between nodes in the cluster without having to restart the application. A controlled failover process maintains the application state in order to reduce the impact on the end users. Failover clustering is the foundation of both SCC and CCR Exchange functionality.

Without a properly built and configured server cluster, it is not possible to properly install Exchange Server 2007 in the cluster and have it be reliable. Installing server clustering requires several steps:

1. Installing and configuring the hardware, which includes installing and configuring the server nodes, configuring the network, setting up the disk structure, and making sure all the firmware is up-to-date.

2. Installing and configuring the operating system. This step includes some basics of server hardening as well as other steps to prepare for clustering.

3. Configuring the *cluster service*. This step is where you find out whether your hardware and operating system will work for you. Once this step is complete, you will have a cluster, but nothing will be running on it.

4. Installing and configuring applications. This step will be covered in detail when configuring both SCC and CCR clusters are considered later in this chapter.

For more detailed information about Windows Server failover clustering and network load balancing, please see *MCTS: Windows Server 2008 Applications Infrastructure Configuration Study Guide: Exam 70-643* (Sybex, 2008) or the instructor-lead course 6423: Implementing and Managing Windows Server 2008 Clustering by Microsoft Learning.

Configuring Single Copy Clustering (SCC)

A *single copy cluster* is very similar to the cluster functionality used for Exchange Server 2003 server clustering, with a few minor exceptions. One exception is that with Exchange Server 2007, it is possible to have a larger number of databases. Exchange Server 2007 allows for 50 storage groups of up to 5 stores per storage group. Also, Exchange 2007 SCC clusters are much easier to configure and manage because the setup process and management tools were created with clustering in mind.

In Exchange Server 2003, it was possible to use server clustering for everything except for the front-end role, which used NLB to provide scalability and high availability. In Exchange Server 2007, there are now five roles: Mailbox Server, Client Access, Hub Transport, Unified Messaging, and Edge Transport. The only role that can be used for failover clustering in Exchange Server 2007 is the Mailbox role. To install the clustered mailbox environment, you need to have a server with both the Hub Transport role and Client Access server role in the same site.

The basic architecture of an SCC looks like Figure 8.2. In a typical SCC there are two nodes, but there can be as many as eight. In between each node is a private network that handles the heartbeat traffic and a public network used by clients to access the nodes and the virtual server(s) running in the cluster. In the case of Figure 8.2, there is only one virtual server. Client machines connect to the cluster using the virtual server's name and IP address.

FIGURE 8.2 SCC overview

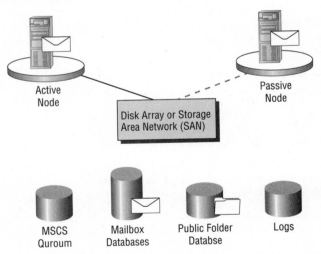

Another one of the differences between clustering in Exchange Server 2003 and Exchange Server 2007 is that Exchange Server 2007 no longer supports active/active clustering where there are two virtual servers with one running on each node. In Exchange Server 2007, there must be a passive node, whether it is a two-node cluster or whether it is an eight-node cluster.

Meeting Basic Requirements for Single Copy Clustering

The following are the basic requirements for SCC:

Domain   You can install SCC only in a domain that supports Exchange Server 2007. All nodes of SCC must belong to the same Active Directory domain. SCC nodes cannot be members of a workgroup or belong to different domains. Exchange Server 2007 is not supported if the nodes for SCC are domain controllers. The nodes must be member servers.

Compatibility   Although you can install Exchange Server 2007 in an Exchange Server 2003 environment, the cluster cannot contain both versions of Exchange and it cannot contain Exchange 2000. It must solely be Exchange Server 2007. Also, an Exchange Server 2007 cluster cannot contain any version of Microsoft SQL Server.

> Exchange Server 2007 requires 64-bit hardware and 64-bit operating system versions. Exchange Server 2003 and Exchange 2000 both use 32-bit hardware and operating systems. It is not possible to mix 32-bit and 64-bit versions of Windows in the same cluster.

Software   The SCC cluster must be installed on a 64-bit version of Windows Server 2003 Enterprise, Windows Server 2003 Enterprise R2, or Windows Server 2008 Enterprise. The operating system files need to be installed in the same locations. The boot and system files need to be in the same locations on all nodes. The Exchange binaries must be installed on the same locations on all nodes.

Network and disk   I covered the network and disk requirements for server clustering earlier in this chapter. You must follow the basic requirements for server clustering.

Installing SCC

You can install SCC via the command line or the graphical interface. I'll show both here.

In Exercise 8.11, you'll install SCC using the setup command and using the graphical setup interface on Windows Server 2003. The process is a little more complex; however, it is important to go through the entire process to see the individual steps taken when using the GUI.

> If Exchange Server 2007 needs to be installed in another location on each node, make sure to specify the location. To change the location, run setup /mode:install /role:mailbox /targetdir:<filepath>, and make sure the same file path is used on all nodes.

EXERCISE 8.11

Installing SCC on Active Node and on Passive Node Computers Using the Exchange Management Console on Windows Server 2003

To install SCC using the Exchange Management Console, follow these steps:

1. Connect to the installation media, and run setup from a command line to start the Exchange install on the active node of the cluster. In the Exchange Server 2007 Setup Wizard, click Next on the Introduction page, click Next to accept the license agreement, click Next on the Error Reporting page, select the Custom Exchange Server Installation option, and click Next, as shown here.

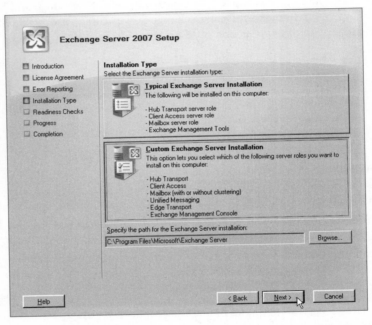

2. On the Server Role Selection page, select Active Clustered Mailbox Role, select the file installation path, and click Next. The file installation path needs to point to the drive letter of one of the shared disks in the cluster that already exists or that will be created later.

3. Select the Single Copy Cluster option on the Cluster Setting Selection page, and enter the following information for the virtual server for the SCC installation:

   - Clustered mailbox server name

   - IP address

   - Shared storage location for the database files

4.   On the Client Settings page, click Yes or No depending on whether your organization will have Outlook 2003 or Entourage clients. Click Next to start the checks and the installation.

5.   Click Install once all the checks are completed on the Readiness Checks page.

6.   The Progress page will show the steps being performed, and once they are completed, click Finish.

7.   The next step will be to click Step 5: Get Critical Updates for Microsoft Exchange, which must be run to download any updates. Once all updates are completed, click Close to complete the installation.

8.   Create the physical disk resources for the new Exchange cluster group, or move the disks from another location in the Cluster Administrator. Make sure the Affect the Group check box is cleared while setting up the disk resources.

9.   Install the passive node using steps 1 through 7 of this exercise, but in step 2, select Passive Clustered Mailbox Role during installation, as shown here.

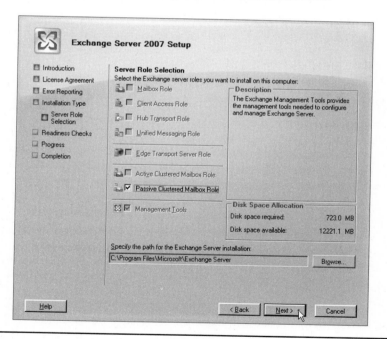

In Exercise 8.12, you'll install SCC on an existing Windows Server 2003 server cluster.

EXERCISE 8.12

Installing SCC on Active Node and on Passive Node Computers Using the Exchange Management Shell on Windows Server 2003

To install SCC using the Exchange Management Shell on Windows Server 2003, follow these steps:

1. Log onto the first node of the cluster.

2. Open a command prompt, navigate to the source code for Exchange Server 2007, and run setup /mode:install /role:mailbox to make sure the Active Directory schema is updated and all the proper Exchange server files for the Mailbox role are copied onto the first node.

3. At the command prompt, change to the location of the bin folder on the first node's hard Exchange Server\bin. From this location, run the following (all on one line):

   Setup /newcms /CMSname:<NameofClusteredMailboxServer>
   /CMSIPAddress:<ClusteredMailboxServerIPAddress>
   /CMSSharedStorage /CMSDataPath:<PathToSharedStorageForDatabase>

4. In Cluster Administrator, create the proper physical disks inside the new SCC group or move them from another location if they were previously created.

5. Log onto the second node of the cluster.

6. Open a command prompt, navigate to the source code for Exchange Server 2007, and run setup /mode:install /role:mailbox to make sure the Active Directory schema is updated and all the proper Exchange server files for the mailbox role are copied onto the second node. If there are multiple nodes, perform the same step on each.

It is important that the information in step 3 in Exercise 8.12 be correct. It is easy to mistakenly give the information for the default cluster group that was created when the cluster was built. This information must be unique because it will be used for the new virtual server that will be created for the SCC installation.

To install the passive node, you will follow the same steps you used to install the active node. Once it is complete, the end result will be two nodes in an SCC. You can see the results of the work in the Windows Server 2003 Cluster Administrator MMC, as shown in Figure 8.3.

FIGURE 8.3   Windows Server 2003 Cluster Administrator MMC

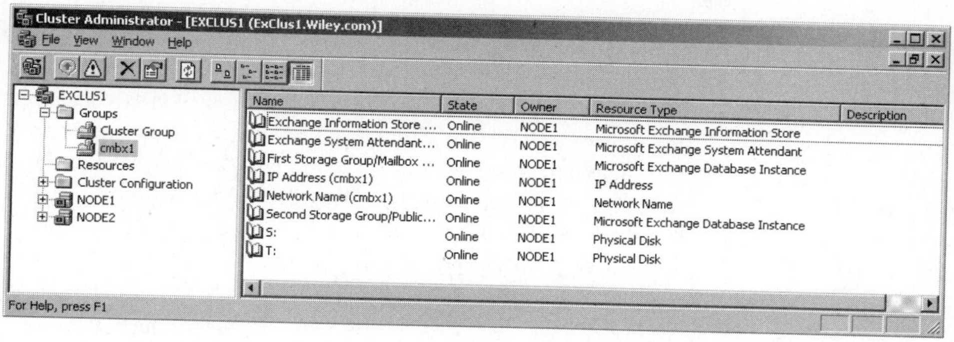

After installation, use the Exchange Server 2007 command shell and use the following command to move the Mailbox role from the active node to the passive node: `Move -Clustered MailboxServer`.

It is possible to use the Cluster Administrator console to perform the move, or *handoff*, as it is called for Exchange Server 2007; however, the Cluster Administrator console is not Exchange 2007–aware. As a best practice, you should always move the Mailbox role in as SCC using the command shell or the Managed Cluster Mailbox Server Wizard available in EMC.

Configuring Cluster Continuous Replication (CCR)

Many organizations in the past tended to shy away from failover clustering for a number reasons. One concerned a single point of failure potential around the SAN environment and the disks provided by the SAN, which include the quorum and the cluster disks used for database and transaction log storage. Another major concern is related to geographically dispersed clustering, also called *geoclustering*.

CCR is capable of providing high availability in a single data center or in two data centers by using geographically dispersed clustering. In either case, CCR provides a solution with the following attributes:

- CCR has no single point of failure. With a majority node set quorum and the replication capability provided in Exchange Server 2007, the cluster has no single point of failure. CCR has no special disk infrastructure requirements, such as a SAN or multiple SANs with replication capabilities. The biggest change is that with log shipping capabilities, CCR does not require a SAN to provide shared disks and doesn't need multiple SANs for a geocluster.

- CCR can be used to reduce backup times, the load on production during backup times, and the recovery time to return to full production. The copy location (the passive node) can be used to perform backups. This takes the load off of the production environment and increases the performance of backups. Volume Shadow Copy Service backups are supported for the passive node, but streaming backups will not work.

Configuring Majority Node Set

Microsoft implemented *majority node set (MNS)* quorums in Windows Server 2003, called Node and File Share Majority quorum in Windows Server 2008, to address the first two issues. For simplicity, I will refer to this as an MNS cluster. Instead of selecting a shared physical disk to host the quorum, it is possible to select the MNS option to create a server cluster. In an MNS cluster, the quorum data is actually stored on multiple disks across the cluster and a file share is used to help determine cluster quorum. MNS is designed and built so that it ensures that the cluster data stored remains consistent across the different disks. Since MNS clusters can use locally attached disks, nodes do not require expensive shared disks to maintain clustering information in the quorum. MNS has several unique issues, including the following:

- MNS covers only quorum. It provides a nice geographically dispersed method to handle the quorum. It doesn't provide a method for replicating data that would normally be shared by nodes; it is up to the application or storage vendor to provide this functionality.
- MNS requires a minimum of two nodes and a *file share witness (FSW)*.

The unique features of MNS dovetail nicely with the new capabilities that Exchange Server 2007 CCR brings to the table.

Building an MNS cluster is similar to building a standard cluster with a shared disk quorum. To install CCR properly, the cluster must first be configured using an MNS quorum (or Node and File Share Majority in Windows Server 2008). After the cluster is established using the first node, the second node must be installed and then the cluster will be ready to install CCR for Exchange Server 2007.

Once the cluster is built and configured, then it is possible to install CCR with Exchange Server 2007. However, if there is a node failure at this point, there will not be a majority, or quorum, so the cluster service will fail. After all, one out of two is not greater than 50 percent. This is where the FSW comes in.

File Share Witness

To allow for the failure of a node in a majority node set cluster, there must be enough nodes (or votes) online and communicating to constitute more than one half of the number of available votes in order to maintain a quorum. In a two-node implementation, there aren't any extra votes available to allow for failure. The file share provides the third vote in the cluster to allow for a failure of one of the three while still allowing the cluster to maintain a quorum.

Microsoft recommends using a Hub Transport server for the FSW, but other types of servers will work just fine as long as they are running the server service. In order to maintain a quorum in the event of a single site failure in a geocluster, it is recommended that the FSW be in a different site than either of the two CCR nodes.

Introducing CCR

In a CCR implementation, such as the one shown in Figure 8.4, there is no requirement for a SAN to provide shared disk access. The active node uses its own local disks to provide Exchange mailbox services, and it uses log shipping to send updated transactions from the active to the passive server. The passive server then receives the logs and replays them into the passive copy of the database. The process is very similar to how LCR functions; however, now the log files are being sent to a second server in a cluster.

FIGURE 8.4 Typical CCR cluster implementation

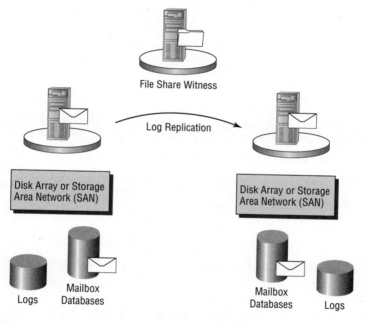

The replication process is asynchronous. This means it is possible that the failure of the active node could result in loss of messages if all of the transaction logs are not able to be transmitted to the passive node. This potential for lost messages led to another technology designed to overcome any lost message. The transport dumpster is a feature of the Hub Transport service.

Transport Dumpster

Since all messages are handled by the Hub Transport role, this is a logical place to do message caching. The transport dumpster is a required component for CCR implementations. The queue size in the Hub Transport role is controlled by time/space limitations set by the Exchange administrator. When a uncontrolled failover is experienced in CCR, the surviving clustered mailbox server automatically requests every Hub Transport server in the Active Directory site to resubmit mail from the transport dumpster cache/queue. As the messages are received by the Mailbox server, the information store deletes any duplicates and redelivers only the mail that was lost.

The transport dumpster is used for CCR and LCR (with Service Pack 1) implementations; however, unlike the manual process used in LCR, redelivery is automatically requested during CCR recovery. The transport dumpster is configured to be used automatically in CCR implementations, and its default settings are a MaxDumpsterSizePerStorageGroup setting of 18MB and a MaxDumpsterTime setting of seven days. These settings are typically sufficient for the majority of organizations, but you can modify them to meet the specific needs of your organization in the EMC in the global transport settings or by using the Set-TransportConfig cmdlet.

Microsoft recommends that you set the default size limit to 1.5 times the maximum message size. For example, if your organization sets a limit on message size at 5MB, then you should set the transport dumpster to a maximum of 7.5MB. Exercise 8.13 shows how to identify the current settings.

EXERCISE 8.13

Identifying Current Transport Dumpster Settings

Follow these steps to identify current transport dumpster settings:

1. Open the Exchange Management Shell.

2. Run Get-Transportconfig.

Exercise 8.14 shows how to set the transport dumpster configuration using the Exchange Management Shell.

EXERCISE 8.14

Configuring Transport Dumpster Settings

To configure the transport dumpster settings, follow these steps:

1. Open the Exchange Management Shell.

2. Run Set-TransportConfig -MaxDumpsterSizePerStorageGroup <size> -MaxDumpsterTime <time>.

The size should be listed as number of megabytes, as in 20MB. The duration should be listed as days.hours:minutes:seconds, with days being a two-digit number, such as 07.00:00:00.

Other Issues and Limitations of CCR

It is important to note that there are several limitations when deploying CCR:

- Just like LCR, there can be only a single database in each storage group so that there is a direct mapping from the database to the transaction logs for the database. However, since Exchange Server 2007 is now capable of handling 50 storage groups, the limitations are not drastic.

- There are several limitations of public folders in a CCR implementation because of conflicts between CCR replication and standard public folder replication:

  - If there is only one mailbox server (the CCR cluster in the Exchange organization), then it can host a public folder store because public folder replication is disabled.

  - If there are multiple mailbox servers and only one hosts a public folder store (the CCR cluster), then it can host it because public folder replication is disabled.

  - If there are multiple mailbox servers and there are multiple public folder stores, then no public folders can be hosted on the CCR cluster.

- Mailbox server names are limited to 15 characters or fewer to provide down-level support for email clients.

- CCR cannot be hosted in the same cluster as Exchange Server 2003, Exchange 2000, or any version of SQL Server.

- CCR nodes are not supported on nodes that are also domain controllers or global catalog servers.

- The same version of Exchange Server 2007 must be installed on all nodes, and all nodes must use the same drives and paths for the Exchange binary files, the databases, and the transaction logs.

- The performance of the network will be important when configuring the disk structures. Microsoft recommends using Gigabit Ethernet for connections between nodes. However, this is not always possible, especially when configuring CCR for geoclustering. The network speed is extremely important if there is a failure of the production server such that its drive must be replaced. In this case, the new production server must reseed the new passive server. The faster the network, the faster the reseeding process.

Installing a CCR Cluster

Now that the biggest steps have been completed, installing the cluster service using MNS and configuring the FSW, it is time to create the CCR cluster.

Exercise 8.15 will walk through the steps to configure the CCR cluster.

EXERCISE 8.15

Installing a CCR Cluster

Here's how to install a CCR cluster:

1. Install the prerequisite components for the selected operating system.

2. Connect to the installation media, and run setup from a command line to start the Exchange install on the active node of the cluster. In the Exchange setup wizard, click Next on the Introduction page, click Next to accept the license agreement, click Next on the Error Reporting page, select the Custom Exchange Server Installation option, and then click Next, as shown here.

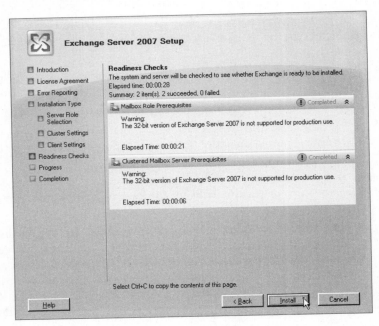

3. On the Server Role Selection page, select Active Clustered Mailbox Role, select the file installation path, and click Next. The file installation path needs to point to the drive letter and path where the Exchange binaries will be installed.

4. On the Cluster Settings page, select the Continuous Copy Replication option and enter the following information for the virtual server for the CCR installation:

- Clustered mailbox server name
- IP address
- Storage location for the database files, which will be a local hard drive

EXERCISE 8.15 *(continued)*

5. On the Client Settings page, click Yes or No depending on whether the organization will have Outlook 2003 or Entourage clients. Click Next to start the checks and the installation.

6. Click Install once all the checks are completed on the Readiness Checks page.

7. The Progress page will show the steps being performed. Once they are completed, click Finish.

8. The next step will be to click Step 5: Get Critical Updates for Microsoft Exchange, which must be run to download any updates. Once all updates are completed, click Close to complete the installation.

9. Install the passive node using steps 1 through 7 of this exercise, but in step 2, select Passive Clustered Mailbox Role during installation, as shown here.

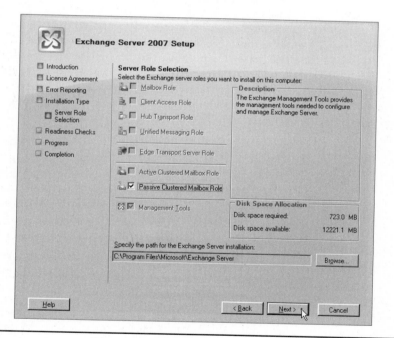

 Exchange Server 2007 does not support placing the databases or the transaction logs at the root of a drive. A directory must be created to hold these files.

Dealing with CCR Outages

There are basically two types of outages regarding CCR, and the behaviors are a bit different for each type of outage. The two main types of outages are scheduled and unscheduled.

Scheduled Outage

The architecture of CCR allows for extended scheduled outages of a specific node without an extended outage of the clustered mailbox server. Because one node can be offline, the other node is capable of providing mailbox services while the offline node is repaired or undergoes ordinary maintenance. Scheduled outages make sure that all log data on the active node is successfully copied to the passive node before the active node is allowed to take itself offline. Scheduled outages should never result in the loss of data, even though the replication is asynchronous.

In a two-node CCR solution, only one node can be taken offline at a time. A second node being taken offline or failing will cause the mailbox services provided by the cluster to stop, and clients will no longer be able to access their email. With the redundancy built into MNS with the file share witness, either the file share witness or the passive node can be taken offline for maintenance, updates, and repairs without the entire cluster failing. Of the two nodes and the file share witness, only one can be down at a time for maintenance. If two of the three are brought down, then the entire cluster will fail. It is a best practice to move the clustered mailbox to the passive node before doing maintenance on the active node. It is easy to identify the active node using the Cluster Administrator MMC. It is also easy to check using the Exchange Management Shell by running the `Get-ClusteredMailboxServerStatus` cmdlet.

 The standard process of shutting down a Windows server node in a CCR cluster does not automatically handle moving the clustered mailbox from an active CCR mailbox node to the passive node. It is important to move the clustered mailbox manually before shutting down the active server node.

SETTING *AUTODATABASEMOUNTDIAL*

Microsoft has implemented controls to handle the behavior in the case of an active mailbox server failing. CCR has an attribute that can be used to control unscheduled failures. The attribute, `AutoDatabaseMountDial`, has three possible values:

- *Lossless*: When `AutoDatabaseMountDial` is set to Lossless, the passive node waits for the failed node to come back online before its databases are mounted. In this mode, it is vital that there is no loss of messages. For the process to succeed, the failed node must come back online with all logs available. When the unscheduled outage occurs, the passive node becomes the active node, and the Information Store is brought online using standard clustering technologies. The new active node then checks to see whether all the databases can be mounted without any lost data. If it is possible to mount the databases without any lost data, then the information store will mount the databases and make sure the clustered mailbox is available to clients. If the databases cannot be mounted without lost data, then the active node of the CCR cluster will look to the other node and try to copy logs from it to bring itself fully up-to-date. If the failed server comes back online with all its logs available, then this process will eventually update the active node. If the failed node comes back online and its logs are not available, then the database will not mount. In this environment, it is possible for the Exchange administrator to mount the databases manually.

- *Good Availability*: When `AutoDatabaseMountDial` is set to Good Availability, the cluster provides fully automatic recovery if replication is working properly and the logs are replicating as fast as they are being created.

- *Best Availability*: Best Availability is the default setting. It allows automatic recovery even if replication has some latency. In case of a failure, the new active node might be slightly behind the state of the old active node after the failover and some data loss is experienced.

The `Move-ClusteredMailboxServer` cmdlet checks and verifies the health of the passive node to make sure it has a good copy of the database and it is relatively current. If for some reason the passive node is missing a significant amount of data, the time for the move is increased to allow the rest of the replication that is out of sync to catch up.

Scheduled moves are sometimes used to force the update of the passive copy and to move to the passive copy to perform maintenance on a corrupted database.

The `Move-ClusteredMailboxServer` cmdlet prompts the Exchange administrator for information regarding the move. This information is then copied to the event logs. The cmdlet requires the Exchange administrator to specify the server node for the new location. This step is used to prevent the clustered mailbox from being moved when it is already running in the correct location.

Do not use the Windows Failover Cluster Administration tools to move Exchange Server 2007 clustered mailbox servers. These tools can cause serious problems with replication.

RESTORING REPLICATION ACTIVITY AFTER A SCHEDULED OUTAGE

Once the scheduled outage is complete, moving the clustered mailbox to its original location is often part of testing the changes made. After you make all the changes and perform the scheduled maintenance, the node should be restarted. There are two scenarios:

- *Successful outage*: The scheduled outage was completely successful, no problems were found during the move of the clustered mailboxes, and the database came online and mounted without any problems. In this situation, both nodes had consistent storage groups and databases. Once the outage is complete and the old passive node has become active, it will begin replicating to the old active node, which is now passive. Once replication is caught up, then the clustered mailbox can be moved to its original location and maintenance can be performed on the other node if necessary.

- *Partially successful outage*: In this case, the scheduled outage was not completely successful. It is possible that there was database corruption prior to the outage. During the failover process, Exchange could not verify that all logs on the source were made available to the target before mounting the database on the passive cluster node. CCR can automatically recover from some inconsistencies. Replication will start and process any available logs. If replication cannot recover automatically, the copy is marked as broken and creates an event in the event log identifying the issue. If the database can be used, then reseeding might be required.

Unscheduled Outage

Unscheduled outages happen because of failures of the dependent services or the resources. CCR minimizes failures based on items that are not likely to be real issues that would normally have caused a failover in Exchange Server 2003 server clustering. CCR focuses its automatic recovery on situations where there is a high degree of confidence that the clustered mailbox would experience improved performance and reliability. In an unscheduled outage, the clustered mailbox is moved to the passive node, and the database is mounted. After mounting, the clustered mailbox becomes the active database, and all updates and new information are processed. The formerly active node becomes the passive node, and all updates are sent to the new passive node and read into its database.

Since CCR uses asynchronous replication, unscheduled outages result in some data loss. The lost data will include, at a minimum, the active logs being written to by the active server. To address this lost information, CCR controls the failover behavior and provides the ability to recapture the transactions that would most likely be lost. The process evaluates whether databases on the passive node will be mounted and used.

The default configuration is Good Availability. When `AutoDatabaseMountDial` is set to Good Availability, the node will mount all databases that are synchronized. In most cases, Good Availability will bring a database online if, during the time it took to generate a new log, the last generated log was replicated. This means Good Availability will mount the database if changes are being applied as fast as they are being generated on the production server before the failure. Best Availability allows for more variation in the inconsistency between the two copies. Lossless guarantees the copy is not brought online unless it can be confirmed that there will be no data loss. If Lossless is used, automatic recovery will occur only when the original server is operational again and all log data is available and not corrupted.

The Lossless AutoDatabaseMountDial setting can result in long outages. In some cases, it does not make sense to use Lossless because the downtime will cause major impacts on organizational production.

As in the scheduled outage, if the databases are not automatically mounted in a failover, an Exchange administrator can still mount the databases manually. The administrator must check the state of the copy and then issue two commands.

The same rules for streaming and VSS backups that apply for LCR as discussed earlier also apply to a CCR solution. More information about backup and restore procedures can be found in Chapter 10, "Disaster Recovery Operations for Exchange Server."

Configuring Standby Continuous Replication (SCR)

A new high-availability option was introduced in Exchange Server 2007 Service Pack 1, called standby continuous replication (SCR). Since clustering is not used, the failover process is manual; hence the reason for calling it "standby." It works similar to how LCR works but can span multiple servers like CCR. Basically this feature allows multiple copies of a database to be created on multiple Exchange servers, without the need for clustering.

Rather than designating a single active and a single passive copy, SCR employs sources and targets. Sources are the active copy of the data and targets are the destinations of the copies.

The following are valid sources:

- A CCR mailbox server
- An SCC mailbox server
- A stand-alone mailbox server

And the valid targets are as follows:

- A stand-alone mailbox server without LCR enabled
- A failover cluster where the Passive Clustered Mailbox role is installed but no clustered mailbox servers are installed

Here are some key points to remember about SCR:

- SCR supports multiple replication targets per storage group source. There is no hard limit imposed for the number of targets a source may have; however, four targets is the recommended maximum.

- SCR provides a default delay of 24 hours before the log files are played into the target copy; however, an administrator can adjust this from no delay to up to 7 days. Changing the delay to a shorter time is done to reduce the recovery time required to play logs into the target. Changing the delay to a longer period may be necessary to allow for a more customized recovery point.

- SCR is managed using the Exchange Management Shell.

- A storage group can have only one database to be SCR-enabled.

- The source and target servers must store the storage group files in the same location.

- Both the source and target must be running the same operating system version; however, the same operating system edition is not required.

- SCR targets cannot be backed up, either with streaming or VSS backups.

Enabling SCR

With Exchange Server 2007 Service Pack 1 installed, you must enable SCR from the EMS, as demonstrated in Exercise 8.16.

EXERCISE 8.16

Enabling SCR

Follow these steps to enable SCR:

1. Open the Exchange Management Shell.

2. To enable SCR for SG01 with a source of MBX001 and a target of MBX002, type:

```
Enable-StorageGroupCopy
-Identity MBX001\SG01\MB01 -StandbyMachine MBX002
-ReplayLagTime 0.1:0:0.
```

Since SCR is similar to LCR and CCR, there may be times when automatic seeding of the database does not work or a reseed is required after replication is interrupted. The seeding process for the SCR database is the same as in LCR and CCR, but it cannot be done from the EMC. This is because the `Suspend-StorageGroupCopy`, `Update-StorgeGroupCopy`, and `Resume-StorageGroupCopy` functions are not exposed for SCR-enabled storage groups in the EMC. The steps for reseeding an SCR copy were covered previously in Exercise 8.7, as they are the same as reseeding an LCR copy.

Activating SCR Targets

The process of making a target the primary database is called *activation*. There are three ways to activate an SCR target, depending on the type of failover and the type of target. The three options are using database portability, using server recovery, and using clustered server recovery.

Using Database Portability

Database portability is a feature introduced in Exchange 2007 that allows a mailbox database to be moved between servers in the same organization. One benefit of using database portability is that just a single database can be recovered, leaving the remaining databases intact on the source server. In order to use database portability, the target database cannot just be mounted on the target server. Rather, a new storage group and database needs to be created with the Allow Restore to Overwrite option enabled so that the target database files can be placed into the newly created storage group and database folders can be mounted and recovered. Last, the `Move-Mailbox` cmdlet can be run with the `ConfigurationOnly` parameter to rehome the mailboxes to the new location. Since all of these steps are done from the EMS, they can be scripted so that, in event of a failure, each step can be done accurately and quickly.

Exchange Server 2007 Service Pack 1 introduced the Test-ReplicationHealth cmdlet, which provides an overall health check on how LCR, CCR, and SCR replication tasks are performing.

The process for using database portability with SCR targets is captured in Exercise 8.17.

EXERCISE 8.17

Activating an SCR target with Database Portability

To use database portability to activate an SCR target, follow these steps:

1. Open EMS on the target server.

2. Dismount the source database, if it's not already offline, using the following command:

    `Dismount-Database EXMBX001\SG01\MBX01`

3. To allow the target database to be mountable, run this command:

    `Restore-StorageGroupCopy EXMBX001\SG01 -StandbyMachine EXMBX002`

4. Verify that the target database is consistent by running this command:

    `eseutil /mh D:\MDBDATA\SG01\MB01.edb | findstr state`

5. Create a new storage group and the database into which you'll mount the target database by running the following commands:

    ```
    New-StorageGroup -Server MBX002 -name SG01DP
    -LogFolderPath D:\MDBDATA\SG01DP
    -SystemFolder D:\MDBDATA\SG01DP
    New-MailboxDatabase -StorageGroup MBX002\SG01DP
    -Name MB01DP -EdbFilePath F:\MDBDATA\SG01DP\MB01DP.edb
    Mount-Database MBX002\SG01DP\MB01DP
    Dismount-Database MBX002\SG01DP\MB01DP
    Set-MailboxDatabase MBX002\SG01DP -AllowFileRestore:$true
    ```

6. Set the location of the target database files to be the location of the files for the newly created storage group and database by using the –ConfigurationOnly parameter:

    ```
    Move-StorageGroupPath MBX002\SG01DP
    -LogFolderPath D:\MDBDATA\SG01
    -SystemFolderPath D:\MDBDATA\SG01 -ConfigurationOnly
    Move-DatabasePath MBX002\SG01DP\MB01DP
    -EdbFilePath E:\MDBDATA\SG01\MB01.Edb -ConfigurationOnly
    ```

EXERCISE 8.17 *(continued)*

7. Mount the target database files in the database portability storage group using this command:

   ```
   Mount-Database MBX002\SG01DP\MB01DP
   ```

8. Update the mailbox information in Active Directory to point to the new database without moving system mailboxes:

   ```
   Get-Mailbox -Database MBX001\SG01\MB01 | where
   {$_.ObjectClass -NotMatch '(SystemAttendantMailbox|ExOleDbSystemMailbox)'}|
    Move-Mailbox -ConfigurationOnly
   -TargetDatabase MBX002\SG01DP\MB01DP
   ```

Using Server Recovery and Clustered Server Recovery

The recover server (`setup.com /m:RecoverServer`) and the recover clustered mailbox server (`setup.com /RecoverCMS`) options can be use to recover all of the storage groups on a source server to a target server. The process for recovering is as follows:

1. Prepare the SCR target for mounting.
2. Disable SCR.
3. Run setup recovery.
4. Mount the databases.

 A complete SCR recovery scenario can be found at on TechNet at `http://technet.microsoft.com/en-us/library/bb738150.aspx`.

Configuring High Availability for Client Access, Hub Transport, and Edge Transport Roles

Failover clustering is not an option for the other Exchange server roles. To provide your Exchange organization with Hub Transport services, you need a single Hub Transport in each Active Directory site with a Mailbox server. To provide for redundancy, two or more Hub Transport servers should be configured in each site. There is no additional configuration required. When you are providing highly available Client Access services, there are two options, and really only one if you want true redundancy: network load balancing (NLB).

For inbound email delivery with Edge or Hub Transport servers, the typical way to provide redundancy is to use an MX record for each of the email servers accessible for email delivery. MX records are weighted records in DNS that point to the email servers responsible for receiving mail for a domain. The MX records with a lower weighting will be attempted before higher-weighted records. Records that have the same weight will be load-balanced. Since using MX records to provide this redundancy is part of the way SMTP was designed, this configuration is often sufficient. In some instances, however, NLB is also leveraged. The next section discusses using NLB for CAS and SMTP servers.

More information about MX records and how they are used can be found in RFC 2821.

Installing and Configuring Network Load Balancing

Many organizations have applications that are critical to daily operations, such as databases, messaging systems, and file/print services. There are some places where technologies such as NLB are more appropriate than using server clustering to achieve high availability for those applications.

Email is often considered a mission-critical application, and it must be running 24 hours a day, 7 days a week. In addition, network email services need the ability to scale performance to handle large volumes of traffic without creating unwanted delays. Network load-balanced clusters enable you to manage a group of independent servers as a single system for higher availability, easier manageability, and greater scalability.

Windows includes NLB functionality that is a fully distributed, software-based solution and does not require any specialized hardware or network components. Even better, there aren't any additional licensing costs associated with using NLB. All members of the Windows Server family have NLB built into their operating systems at no additional cost.

NLB is also available from third parties and, in some cases, provides additional features such as the ability to ensure that a specific server is functioning properly before allowing access to it. The principles are the same for all sorts of NLB solutions.

Exchange Server 2007 is somewhat limited in where NLB can be used. The Edge Transport server role and the Client Access server role can both use NLB and are fully supported for NLB.

As the name suggests, an NLB cluster uses the network to provide load balancing and redundancy. It is able to accomplish this using a virtual IP address and a virtual media access control (MAC) address that is shared between all of the nodes in the cluster. Client connections are all made to this virtual IP address, as shown in Figure 8.5. When an incoming packet is addressed to the virtual IP address, all of the NLB nodes receive it, but only the appropriate node responds.

FIGURE 8.5 NLB architecture

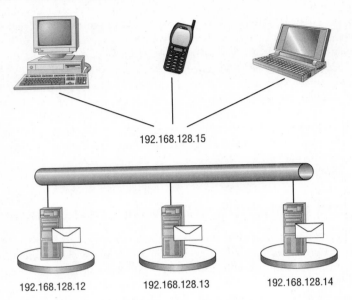

192.168.128.15

192.168.128.12   192.168.128.13   192.168.128.14

When a client request arrives, all hosts simultaneously perform a calculation in order to determine which node should handle the request. The chosen node then accepts and responds to the client request and the other cluster nodes discard it. If the NLB driver decides it is supposed to process the packet and the packet meets the port rules for the NLB cluster, then it passes the packet to the TCP/IP layer and through the rest of the network model. If all nodes are configured identically, the same percentage of client requests will be load-balanced to each node; however, this can be customized to match server capabilities. All nodes synchronize their data about which node should respond to each request and which nodes are active members of the cluster.

One of the features of NLB that you need to know about when working with Exchange 2007 is creating port rules. Port rules specify how requests to a specific port range are sent to the NLB cluster. This allows customization for you to specify which nodes will receive traffic for specific TCP/IP ports. For an example of how this might be used, suppose that you have an NLB cluster consisting of four servers and it needs to load-balance the OWA and POP3 connections. OWA, which runs on TCP ports 80 and 443, can be limited to use only three of the NLB nodes, and POP3 can be set to run only on two nodes of the NLB cluster. This will help reduce the number of nodes the POP3 services will impact when under load.

One drawback with Windows Server NLB is that it is not natively capable of looking into the individual nodes and testing to see whether an application or service is running properly. If an application or service (such as the World Wide Web Publishing Service) fails, NLB will continue to include the node in the NLB cluster and some connections will fail.

Using DNS Round-Robin

DNS round-robin may sound like something complicated, but in reality it is very simple to set up. When you create multiple DNS host record entries with the same name, the DNS server will alternate responding to queries with each of the different IP addresses. For example, you could create a host record entry for owa.exchangeexchange.com with an IP address of 192.168.2.50 and another host record entry for owa.exchangeexchange .com with an IP address of 192.168.2.51. Each time owa.exchangeexchange.com is requested from DNS, the response would alternate between the two IP addresses and thus load-balance between the two addresses. If the two servers providing services for owa .exchangeexchange.com were overloaded, another server could be configured and another owa.exchangeexchange.com host record with an IP of 192.168.2.52 could be added. What happens is that the first client receives the first address; the second client, the second address; the third client, the third address; the fourth client receives the first address, and they continue to loop in this manner. Thus by using DNS round-robin, it is possible to spread the load among multiple servers.

Can you spot a problem with using round-robin DNS for high availability? There are several. One is that it is completely unable to handle a down server. In the event that one of the servers fails, the address will continue to be given to clients (unless DNS is modified), and a portion of the clients will use the address of the unavailable server and will fail to connect. Another problem is that, if multiple clients share the same local DNS server as in a LAN environment, all of those clients will use the same IP address that is cached by the local DNS server; if most of the clients are from the same location, the load will be very balanced across the servers.

Summary

Exchange Server 2007 has taken some great strides toward filling in some of the holes that previous versions of Exchange failed to address adequately for high availability. In particular, several different levels of high availability are provided for in Exchange Server 2007, including local continuous replication and cluster continuous replication.

Local continuous replication provides the protection from database corruption that administrators have been looking for since the release of Exchange. Previous high-availability solutions did not address the concerns of administrators when it came to database corruption. Now, it is fairly inexpensive to protect an organization against database corruption or against a complete drive failure of the messaging database.

Single copy clustering is a fine solution and meets most organizations' needs for high availability. However, like the legacy server cluster solution for Exchange Server 2003, this solution also has problems related to the corruption of the database and the clustered disk architecture providing single points of failure for the solution. SCC provides for clusters of two to eight nodes with up to seven virtual servers hosting clustered mailboxes.

Cluster continuous replication is a definite step in the right direction. With CCR, there are no longer single points of failure around the disk architecture like those found in a typical server clustering configuration. Combining the file share witness with the capabilities of the transport dumpster, CCR is a fairly inexpensive and extremely trustworthy solution.

Standby continuous replication allows for some additional flexibility in configuring highly available solutions. With SCR, additional time-lagged copies of the databases can be kept on a number of servers in multiple locations without requiring complex failover clustering.

Exchange Server 2007 has definitely taken some large steps forward in helping to keep messaging up and running so it is available for users around the clock.

Exam Essentials

Understand the differences between LCR, SCC, SCR, and CCR.   While all these are considered high-availability components when talking about Exchange Server 2007, each one fits a particular need.

Know how to implement LCR, SCC, SCR, and CCR.   Knowing how to install these components is only part of the process. It is also important to understand how to recover from a failure in each situation. You should also understand how server clustering works in general with Windows Server.

Know which roles can be used in LCR, SCC, SCR, and CCR.   It is important to understand how the different roles are supported or not supported when it comes to high availability.

Review Questions

1. You are planning to upgrade your current Exchange Server 2003 organization to Exchange Server 2007. Your company uses public folders extensively and is not ready to move them into Microsoft Office SharePoint Server (MOSS) just yet. What are your options regarding creating a CCR cluster of mailbox servers in Exchange Server 2007? (Choose all that apply; each answer presents a complete solution.)

   A. Create one or more Exchange Server 2007 mailbox servers that house public folders only, without any mailbox databases. Create a CCR cluster with additional Exchange Server 2007 mailbox servers that have only mailbox databases.

   B. Leave the public folders on Exchange Server 2003 servers. Create a CCR cluster with additional Exchange Server 2007 mailbox servers that have only mailbox databases.

   C. Move all public folders to an Exchange Server 2007 mailbox server, configuring no replicas for the public folders. Create a CCR cluster that includes this server.

   D. Move all public folders to an Exchange Server 2007 mailbox server, configuring multiple replicas for the public folders. Create a CCR cluster with additional Exchange Server 2007 mailbox servers that have only mailbox databases.

2. You moved your file server from its switch to another switch that also hosts network load-balanced Client Access servers. Users report that the file server is extremely slow. What should you do?

   A. Move the file server to another switch.

   B. Add another NIC to the file server, and implement network teaming.

   C. Create a special VLAN for all file server clients.

   D. Defragment the hard drives on the file server.

3. Your company has had problems with Exchange databases becoming corrupted. In each case, the lost data has caused management to become very upset. What technology should you implement to mitigate against corruption of mailbox data?

   A. Single copy clustering

   B. Local continuous replication

   C. Network load balancing

   D. RAID-5 drives for databases

4. Your company has two identical servers. You have installed Windows Server 2003 Enterprise Edition on the first one and installed Exchange Server 2007 on it as well. You install Windows Server 2003 Enterprise on the second server, but you are unable to configure single copy clustering. What should you do?

    A. Select the Custom installation method on the second node, select the Passive Cluster Mailbox role, select Single Copy Cluster, and run the installation to completion.

    B. Rerun the Exchange install on top of the existing server, select the role for Active Cluster Mailbox, install the second node, select the Passive Cluster Mailbox role, then select Single Copy Cluster and run the installation to completion.

    C. Uninstall all roles other than the Mailbox role on the first computer, then rerun the installation, select the role for Active Cluster Mailbox, then install the second node, select the Passive Cluster Mailbox role, select Single Copy Cluster, and run the installation to completion.

    D. Reformat and rebuild the first server so that it has just the operating system on it, configure clustering, and then install Exchange Server 2007 using SCC.

5. You need to provide high availability for an Edge Transport server. What technology should you use?

    A. Network load balancing

    B. Local continuous replication

    C. DNS round-robin

    D. Single copy clustering

6. You intend to configure two server nodes into a single copy cluster for Exchange Server 2007. Which of the following are required? (Choose all that apply.)

    A. A minimum of two network adapters

    B. A minimum of two identical nodes

    C. An Enterprise edition of Windows Server

    D. Shared disk architecture, such as a storage area network

7. You are configuring the network for a two-node continuous copy replication cluster on Windows 2003 servers. You configure the public network for Node1 with 192.168.2.20/24, and you configure the public network for Node2 with 192.168.3.35/24 in a remote site. You configure the private network for Node1 with 10.10.10.1/24 and the private network for Node2 with 10.10.10.2/24. When you try to create the cluster, you are unable to make it work. What should you do to make it work properly? (Choose all that apply.)

    A. Put the two public adapters in the same network segment.

    B. Configure the public network with a VLAN.

    C. Configure the private network with a VLAN.

    D. Implement a shared disk quorum using the letter Q.

8. You need to patch the current single copy cluster that you have running. What should you do?

   A. Apply the patch to the active node, and restart the active node. Then apply the patch to the other node, and restart it.

   B. Apply the patch to both nodes, and restart them at the same time.

   C. Apply the patch to both nodes, and restart them by restarting the active node first and waiting for it to restart fully before restarting the other node.

   D. Patch the passive node, use the PowerShell command to move the clustered mailbox, then patch the other node, and use the PowerShell command to move the clustered mailbox to its original location.

9. You need to move the clustered mailbox from Node1 to Node2 for maintenance. What should you do?

   A. Use the Cluster Administrator MMC, right-click the clustered mailbox cluster group, and select Move.

   B. Use the Cluster Administrator MMC, right-click the clustered mailbox cluster group, and select Take Offline.

   C. Use PowerShell, and run `Move-ClusteredMailboxServer`.

   D. Use `cluster.exe`, and run `Cluster Group <groupname> /Move`.

10. You are designing a two-node single copy cluster for Exchange Server 2007. How many IP addresses do you need for the public network?

   A. 2

   B. 3

   C. 4

   D. 5

11. You are configuring a Windows Server 2003 cluster for Exchange Server 2007 CCR. You must create a service account for the cluster service. Which of the following should you do? (Choose all that apply.)

   A. Create a standard domain user account.

   B. Make the account a local administrator on all cluster nodes.

   C. Configure the account so it can log onto the cluster nodes only.

   D. Let the cluster installation set the rest of the rights during configuration.

12. You have configured your cluster, but you find that there is not enough bandwidth between the cluster nodes and the storage area network. What should you do? (Choose all that apply.)

   A. Add another storage adapter to each server node, and use multipathing software.

   B. Add another network adapter to each server node, and implement load-balanced network adapter teaming.

   C. Add another HBA to the SAN device itself, and configure multipathing.

   D. Implement RAID-1+0 instead of RAID-5 for databases.

13. What are the different control levels that can be implemented in Exchange Server 2007 for CCR to manage potential data loss during a failover? (Choose all that apply.)

    A. Lossless

    B. Good Availability

    C. Best Availability

    D. Fast Failover

14. Under which situations can you install public folders on a clustered mailbox? (Choose all that apply.)

    A. If there is only one mailbox server (the CCR cluster)

    B. If there are multiple mailbox servers and only one hosts a public folder store (the CCR cluster)

    C. If there are multiple mailbox servers and there are multiple public folder stores

    D. If there is one mailbox server other than the CCR cluster

15. Which of the following HA options can be used across two different data centers?

    A. LCR

    B. CCR

    C. SCC

    D. SCR

16. Which of the following is recommended to host the file share witness?

    A. On the active node of the cluster

    B. On the passive node of the cluster

    C. Local Hub Transport server

    D. On the domain controller

17. You have just run the command in PowerShell to view the status of LCR. Which of the following are available to view? (Choose all that apply.)

    A. Data copied in the last hour

    B. Summary status

    C. Copy queue length

    D. Replay queue length

18. You have implemented network load balancing for your Edge Transport servers in the perimeter network. You need to limit the port flooding so that it does not impact other servers. What should you do? (Choose all that apply.)

   A. Configure a VLAN on a switch, and put all the NLB cluster nodes in that VLAN only.

   B. Set up a hub and connect all NLB cluster nodes to the hub; then connect the hub to the switch environment.

   C. Implement port mirroring on the switch device.

   D. Manually change the MAC addresses on the NLB cluster nodes.

19. Which of the following HA Mailbox configurations leverage failover clustering?

   A. LCR

   B. CCR

   C. SCR

   D. SCC

20. Which of the following server roles can be load balanced?

   A. Edge Transport

   B. Mailbox

   C. Hub Transport

   D. Client Access

Answers to Review Questions

1. A, B, C. There are several limitations related to public folders in a CCR implementation because of conflicts between CCR replication and standard public folder replication, including the following:

    -   If there is only one mailbox server (the CCR cluster), then it can host a public folder store because public folder replication is disabled.

    -   If there are multiple mailbox servers and only one hosts a public folder store (the CCR cluster), then it can host it because public folder replication is disabled.

    -   If there are multiple mailbox servers and multiple public folder stores, then no public folders can be hosted on the CCR cluster.

2. A. NLB clusters cause port flooding that can cause other devices on the same switch as NLB nodes to degrade in performance as they try to process all the packets sent to them.

3. B. Local continuous replication (LCR) copies the database to another physical disk using log shipping. Since it is not using block-level replication, the corruption itself should never be copied to the LCR location.

4. D. You cannot install an application in a cluster until clustering has been installed.

5. A. Network load balancing or DNS round-robin will work for Edge Transport. However, DNS round-robin does not provide high availability.

6. A, B, C, D. All of the options are required for a single copy cluster.

7. A, B, C. A requirement for all Windows Server 2003 clusters is that all public network connections be in the same network segment, and the only way to get that to work is to use VLANs. The same is true of the private network.

8. D. It is always a best practice to patch the passive node first; that way, if for some reason the clustered mailbox does not start up properly on the patched node, it can be restarted in its original location until troubleshooting reveals the problem.

9. C. The way to successfully move the clustered Exchange mailbox server from one node to the other is by using either the `Move-ClusteredMailboxServer` cmdlet or the Exchange Management Console.

10. C. You need a minimum of four IP addresses for the public network. You need one for each server node, for a total of two. You also need one for the cluster itself, and then you need one more during the setup of Exchange Server 2007 for clustering. That's a total of four.

11. A, B, C, D. All the options are considered to be best practices for configuring the cluster service account.

12. A, C. The only way to increase bandwidth to the disk structure is to add more paths and configure multipathing.

13. A, B, C. Lossless, Good Availability, and Best Availability are the three levels for controlling potential data loss during a failover of a CCR cluster.

14. A, B, C. The clustered mailbox can host a public folder only in situations where public folder replication is not run.

15. B, D. Both CCR and SCR can be used across computers and datacenters when properly configured. Niether SCC nor LCR are supported in a multi-site configurations.

16. C. A local Hub Transport server is recommended to be a file share witness. Although it is possible for a domain controller to be a file share witness it is not the recommendation. Also, neither of the cluster nodes can act as the file share witness.

17. B, C, D. `Get-StorageGroupCopyStatus` retrieves the summary status, copy queue length, and replay queue length.

18. A, B, C. Manually changing the MAC address would actually break NLB. It also is not an option through the GUI; you would have to do it through the `netsh` command.

19. B, D. Both CCR and SCC rely on failover clustering to provide HA services. Neither LCR and SCR provide automatic failover nor do they rely on failover clustering for services.

20. A, C, D. Only the Mailbox and Unified Messaging roles are not able to be load balanced. The Edge Transports, Hub Transport and Client Access server roles can be load balanced using network load balancing and DNS round balancing.

Chapter

9

Monitoring and Reporting

MICROSOFT EXAM OBJECTIVE COVERED IN THIS CHAPTER:

✓ **Monitoring and Reporting**

- Monitor mail queues.
- Perform message tracking.
- Monitor system performance.
- Create server reports.
- Create usage reports.
- Monitor client connectivity.

"If your Exchange environment fails and no one is around to monitor it, does it make a sound?" The answer is yes, it does—users will cry out! This being the case, you'll most likely do more monitoring and reporting than deploying of new servers or other tasks. You'll want to monitor your Exchange servers to keep track of healthy or unhealthy trends. In addition, you will likely be required to produce data for reports on the status of the Exchange infrastructure and to determine when problems occur and how to remedy them quickly. Whatever your circumstances, you'll need to have some monitoring and reporting skills in your toolset. The main topics of this chapter are as follows:

- Monitoring the system performance of the Exchange organization and its servers

- Creating reports about Exchange servers, performance, databases, and queues

- Creating reports about Exchange recipients

Monitoring System Performance

The most common monitoring that Exchange administrators perform is typically performance monitoring. With that in mind, you should know that performance monitoring includes both hardware (servers) and software (operating system and Exchange itself), and it is no longer limited to just using the Windows Performance Monitor. Exchange Server 2007 builds on the tools available in Windows Server and brings several of its own to the table. We'll examine common monitoring tasks and tools in the following sections.

Monitoring Server Services

At the heart of Exchange are several key services that run on the Exchange servers and provide the functionality of Exchange. We examined these services in Chapter 2, "Installing Exchange Server 2007," and Table 9.1 reviews them.

TABLE 9.1 Exchange Server 2007 Services

Service	Server Role Where Found
Microsoft Exchange Active Directory Topology	Mailbox, Client Access, Hub Transport, Unified Messaging
Microsoft Exchange ADAM	Edge Transport
Microsoft Exchange Antispam Update	Hub Transport, Edge Transport
Microsoft Exchange Credential Service	Edge Transport
Microsoft Exchange EdgeSync	Hub Transport
Microsoft Exchange File Distribution Service	Client Access, Unified Messaging
Microsoft Exchange IMAP4	Client Access
Microsoft Exchange Information Store	Mailbox
Microsoft Exchange Mail Submission Service	Mailbox
Microsoft Exchange Mailbox Assistants	Mailbox
Microsoft Exchange Monitoring	Mailbox, Client Access, Hub Transport, Unified Messaging, Edge Transport
Microsoft Exchange POP3	Client Access
Microsoft Exchange Replication Service	Mailbox
Microsoft Exchange Search Indexer	Mailbox
Microsoft Exchange Service Host	Mailbox, Client Access
Microsoft Exchange Speech Engine	Unified Messaging
Microsoft Exchange System Attendant	Mailbox
Microsoft Exchange Transport	Hub Transport, Edge Transport
Microsoft Exchange Transport Log Search	Mailbox, Hub Transport, Edge Transport
Microsoft Exchange Unified Messaging	Unified Messaging
Microsoft Search (Exchange Server)	Mailbox

More often than not, when a key Exchange service fails, the problem will surface quickly. However, in some cases a service might fail and you would not know about it without either having an automated health-monitoring application in place, such as System Center Operations Manager (SCOM) 2007, or by manually checking the health of your server services. Since SCOM is outside of the scope of this exam, I'll focus here instead on some methods you can, and should, use to monitor the Exchange services on your Exchange servers.

Using the Services Console

If you only have to troubleshoot a specific problem, or you just like to monitor Exchange manually, then a visit to the Services console can give you some insight into the status of the services on the server. You can find the Services console in the Administrative Tools folder or as a node within the Computer Management console. Use the location that makes the most sense for you. Figure 9.1 shows the Services node of the Computer Management console. You can see that the Exchange services on the server are up and running as expected.

FIGURE 9.1 Viewing the Exchange services in the Services node of the Computer Management console

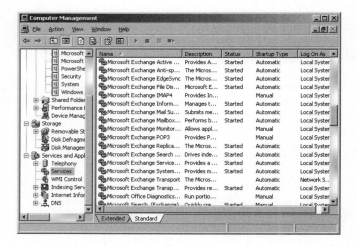

 You can quickly open the Computer Management console by right-clicking the My Computer icon on the Desktop and selecting Manage from the context menu.

Using Event Viewer

Should you identify a service that is not running, you will most often want to do two things: find out why it stopped, and then restart it. You can restart the service from the Services console shown in Figure 9.1, but if you want to get more information about what's going on with the service, you will need to visit the Event Viewer, shown in Figure 9.2. The Event Viewer is also conveniently located in the Computer Management console and is available as a stand-alone viewer in the Administrative Tools folder.

FIGURE 9.2   Exploring the Event Viewer node of the Computer Management console

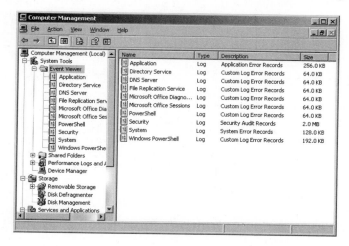

Typically, you'll find the most useful information about service status changes in the System log. The Application log will also often yield useful information. Figure 9.3 illustrates a sample Event Log entry you might find in the System log for a service that has stopped. By going forward and backward in the Event Viewer logs from a specific time of interest, you can find out what happened before and after an event in which you're interested occurred, such as the failure of a critical Exchange service.

FIGURE 9.3   Viewing an Event Log entry

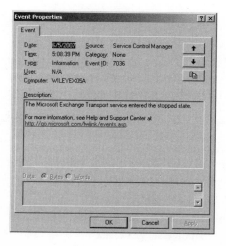

Using PowerShell

As with most other aspects of Exchange Server 2007 management, you can quickly and easily get service status information from the Exchange Management Shell using one or two PowerShell cmdlets. By just using the `Get-Service` cmdlet, you can view the information on all of the services installed on the server, including their status, short name, and display name. Figure 9.4 shows some sample output.

FIGURE 9.4   Viewing services from the Exchange Management Shell

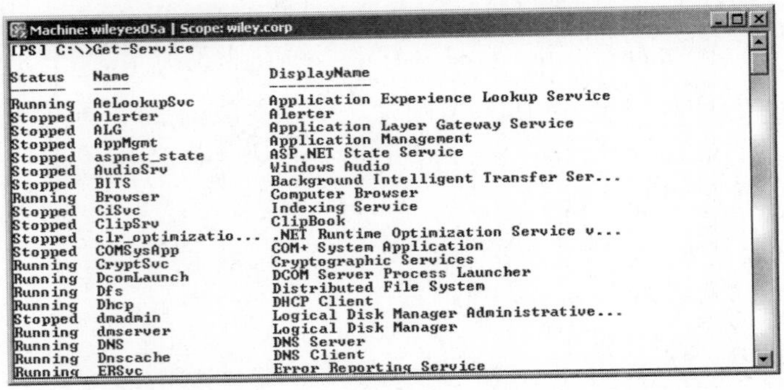

If you just want to view the Exchange-specific services, you can use the `Get-Service *Exchange*` cmdlet to return just a list of those services whose short names include the string "Exchange" in them, as shown in Figure 9.5.

FIGURE 9.5   Viewing only Exchange services from the Exchange Management Shell

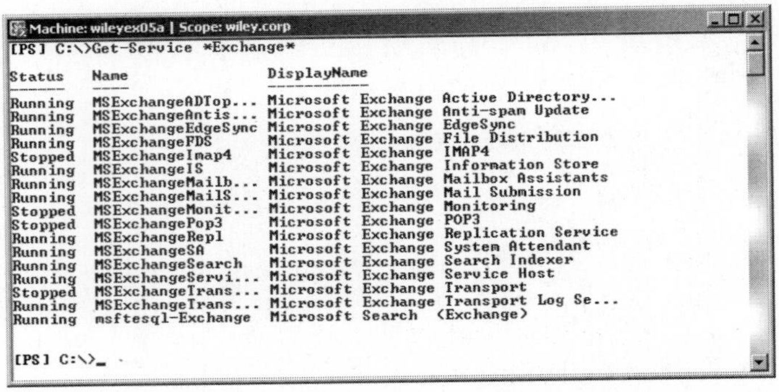

To narrow down the status further, because it is normal for some Exchange services to be in a stopped state, you can use the following cmdlets to return a listing of those Exchange-related services that are or are not currently running:

- To get a list of running Exchange services, use `Get-Service *Exchange* | Where-Object {$_.status -eq "Running"}`.

- To get a list of stopped Exchange services, use `Get-Service *Exchange* | Where-Object {$_.status -eq "Stopped"}`.

By using these filtered cmdlets, you might notice that the Microsoft Exchange Transport service wasn't running on the server, as shown in Figure 9.5. You could go a step further and use the `Start-Service MSExchangeTransport` cmdlet to start the stopped service and resume mail flow on your Hub Transport server.

In addition to working with services, PowerShell can be used to parse the Event Log by using the `Get-EventLog` cmdlet. To obtain the last five events from the Application log, you could use `Get-EventLog -LogName Application -Newest 5`.

Running this will return something similar to the following:

```
Index Time          Type Source          EventID Message
----- ----          ---- ------          ------- -------
 2513 Aug 04 18:00  Info MSExchange ADAccess    2080 Process MSEXCHANGEADT...
 2512 Aug 04 17:45  Info MSExchange ADAccess    2080 Process MSEXCHANGEADT...
 2511 Aug 04 17:30  Info MSExchange ADAccess    2080 Process MSEXCHANGEADT...
 2510 Aug 04 17:15  Info MSExchange ADAccess    2080 Process MSEXCHANGEADT...
 2509 Aug 04 17:00  Info MSExchange ADAccess    2080 Process MSEXCHANGEADT...
```

More-complicated tasks can also be done with this cmdlet. For example, if you wanted to filter for only errors with a source of MSExchange ADAccess, you could use the `where -object` cmdlet to filter the results, as illustrated in the following example:

```
Get-EventLog -LogName Application -Newest 2000 | where-object
{($_.entrytype -eq "Error") -and $_.Source -eq "MSExchange ADAccess"}
```

Running this command will produce a result similar to the following:

```
Index Time          Type Source          EventID Message
----- ----          ---- ------          ------- -------
 2191 Jul 22 21:02  Erro MSExchange ADAccess    2102 Process MAD.EXE (PID=...
  863 Jul 14 14:06  Warn MSExchange ADAccess    2121 Process STORE.EXE (PI...
  862 Jul 14 14:06  Erro MSExchange ADAccess    2104 Process STORE.EXE (PI...
  861 Jul 14 14:06  Erro MSExchange ADAccess    2102 Process MAD.EXE (PID=...
```

As you become more familiar with using PowerShell and the Exchange Management Shell, you will be able to create more elegant scripts that will pinpoint specific problems in your Exchange environment.

Monitoring Performance

Although the Performance console has always been available to you in Windows Server, Exchange Server 2007 gives you a customized Performance console called the Exchange Server Performance Monitor that you can access from the Toolbox node of the Exchange Management Console, as shown in Figure 9.6.

FIGURE 9.6 Using the performance and troubleshooting tools in the Toolbox node

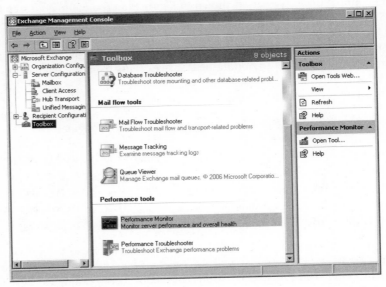

Double-clicking the Performance Monitor item opens the Exchange Server Performance Monitor, shown in Figure 9.7. Several key Exchange performance counters are already loaded for you in the console, making it ready to use immediately.

FIGURE 9.7 Using the Exchange Server Performance Monitor

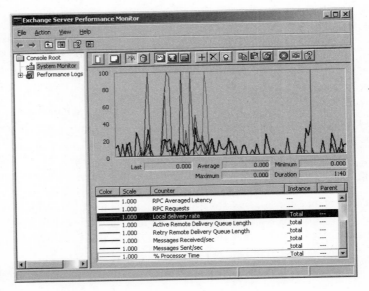

The counters listed in Table 9.2 are prepopulated in the Exchange Server Performance Monitor.

TABLE 9.2 Exchange Server Performance Monitor Counters

Counter	Description
LogicalDisk – Avg. Disk sec/Read	Displays the average time, in seconds, of a data read action from the disk. Typically, the average value of this counter should be less than 10 milliseconds. The value of this counter should never exceed 50 milliseconds.
LogicalDisk – Avg. Disk sec/Write	Displays the average time, in seconds, of a data write action to the disk. Typically, the average value of this counter should be less than 10 milliseconds. The value of this counter should never exceed 50 milliseconds.
Memory – Pages/sec	Displays the rate at which pages are read from or written to disk to resolve hard page faults. The value of this counter should never be more than 1,000.
MSExchange Store Interface – RPC Latency average (msec)	Displays the average latency of RPC requests in milliseconds.
MSExchange Store Interface – RPC Requests outstanding	Displays the current number of RPC requests that are outstanding (not serviced) on the server.
MSExchangeIS – RPC Requests	Displays the current number of client requests that are being processed by the Information Store on the Exchange server.
MSExchangeIS – RPC Averaged Latency	Displays the latency, in milliseconds, of the last 1,024 RPC packets on the server.
MSExchangeIS Mailbox – Local delivery rate	Displays the rate at which messages are being delivered locally.
MSExchangeTransport Queues – Active Remote Delivery Queue Length	Displays the number of active items in the remote delivery queues on the server.
MSExchangeTransport Queues – Retry Remote Delivery Queue Length	Displays the number of items in a retry status on the remote delivery queues on the server.

TABLE 9.2   Exchange Server Performance Monitor Counters *(continued)*

Counter	Description
MSExchangeTransport SmtpRecieve – Messages Received/sec	Displays the number of messages that are being received by the SMTP server each second.
MSExchangeTransport SmtpSend – Messages Sent/sec	Displays the number of messages that are being sent by the SMTP send connectors each second.
Processor – % Processor Time	Displays the percentage of time the processor(s) in the server spend executing threads that are not in an idle state.

To get some historical insight into server performance, you should monitor these counters for comparison monthly at the same time on the same day of the week for a two-hour (or longer) period of time.

Using the Exchange Performance Troubleshooter

Should the time come when you get that dreaded complaint from your users, "The email server is so slow today," you'll be well equipped to deal with the issue by using the Performance Troubleshooter found in the Toolbox node of the Exchange Management Console. The Performance Troubleshooter is focused on only one thing: RPC-related issues within the Exchange organization. To perform a troubleshooting scan, follow the steps outlined in Exercise 9.1.

EXERCISE 9.1

Using the Exchange Performance Troubleshooter

Follow these steps to perform a troubleshooting scan:

1.   Click Start ➤ Programs ➤ Microsoft Exchange Server 2007, and then select Exchange Management Console.

2.   Expand the Microsoft Exchange root object, and click the Toolbox node.

3.   Scroll down to the bottom of the list, and double-click Performance Troubleshooter. The Exchange Performance Troubleshooter opens.

EXERCISE 9.1 *(continued)*

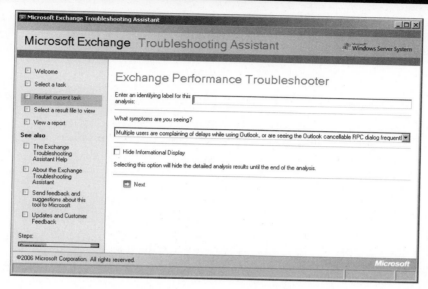

4. For easy identification later, enter some sort of descriptive name. From the symptoms drop-down list, select the symptom that most closely matches the problem you're having. For this exercise, select the default option of Multiple Users Are Complaining of Delays While Using Outlook, or Are Seeing the Outlook Cancellable RPC Dialog Frequently. Click the Next link to continue to the page shown here.

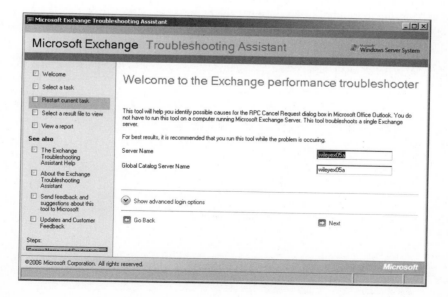

5. On this page, enter the name of the Exchange server you want to troubleshoot and the name of a global catalog server. After entering the server names, click the Next link.

6. The Performance Troubleshooter will perform some connectivity tests and then return a results page, shown here.

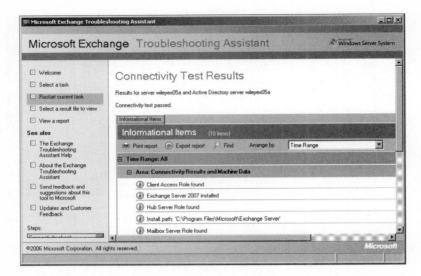

7. After reviewing the information presented, click the Next link at the bottom of the page to continue to the Configure Data Collection page, shown here.

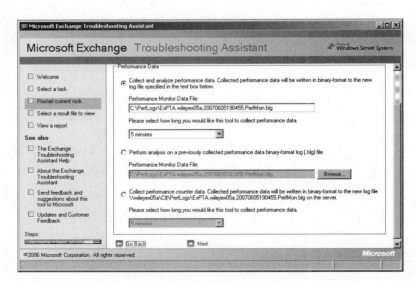

8. In most cases you will want to collect and analyze performance data, which is the default selection. For this exercise, you'll do just that. Leave the default selection enabled, and click the Next link at the bottom of the page.

9. The Performance Troubleshooter will perform some additional counter and data path verification before starting the performance data collection process. After some time, the results page will appear, as shown here.

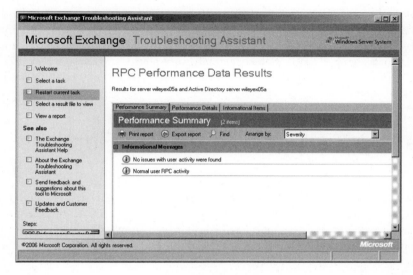

10. On the Performance Summary tab, you will be able to determine quickly whether any performance issues were found on the Exchange server. On the Performance Details tab, you can view more detailed information about each of the counter objects that were monitored. The Informational Items tab provides additional amplifying information to view.

11. When you're done viewing the report, you can either print it or export it to HTML or CSV. Be aware that these actions print or export only the currently viewed tab, so you'll need to print or export three times to save all the available information.

Monitoring Hardware

Hardware monitoring of your Exchange servers is every bit as important as monitoring services and performance. As it stands, though, it's not something that is included in

Exchange Server 2007. Each major hardware vendor has an enterprise-quality monitoring and management application available for its hardware:

- Dell offers Dell OpenManage; see www.dell.com/content/topics/global.aspx/sitelets/solutions/management/openmanage?.

- HP offers HP Systems Insight Manager (SIM); see http://h18013.www1.hp.com/products/servers/management/hpsim/index.html.

- IBM offers IBM Systems Director; see www-03.ibm.com/systems/management/director/index.html.

Several third-party platform-independent monitoring applications are available that use imported Simple Network Management Protocol (SNMP) management information base files (MIBs). Also, you can often import a vendor's hardware-specific MIBs into another vendor's monitoring application. Whichever hardware platform you use for your Exchange Server 2007 infrastructure, you should seriously consider acquiring, installing, and configuring the corresponding management application.

Creating Server and Usage Reports

In order to get a good handle on what is going on in your Exchange environment, you will need to be able to report overall usage. This information will allow you to trend how the environment is changing in response to company needs and equip you with the information required to identify changes that may be necessary to implement in response to those changing needs. In the following sections, I'll cover some of the common types of server and usage reports you might be asked to prepare.

Creating Health Reports

Creating a server health report in Exchange Server 2007 is an easy task thanks to the Exchange Best Practices Analyzer (ExBPA), now a built-in tool. You can find the ExBPA in the Toolbox node of the Exchange Management Console. To create a health report using the ExBPA, follow the steps outlined in Exercise 9.2.

EXERCISE 9.2

Creating a Health Report

Here's how to use the ExBPA to create a health report:

1. Click Start ➢ Programs ➢ Microsoft Exchange Server 2007, and then select Exchange Management Console.

2. Expand the Microsoft Exchange root object, and click the Toolbox node.

3. At the top of the list, double-click the Best Practices Analyzer item. The Exchange Best Practices Analyzer opens, as shown here.

EXERCISE 9.2 *(continued)*

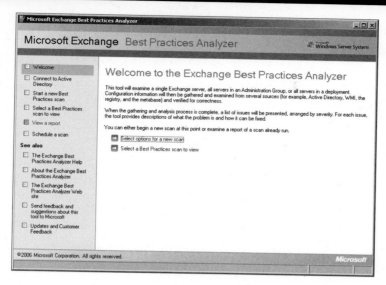

4. To get started, click the Select Options for a New Scan link. The Connect to Active Directory page opens.

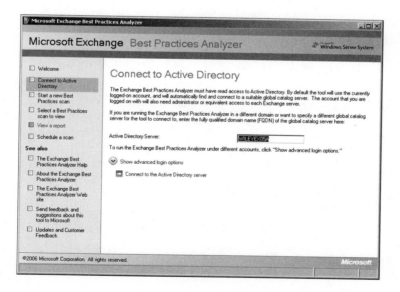

5. Enter the name of a global catalog server that the ExBPA should connect to, and then click the Connect to the Active Directory Server link. After a brief connectivity check, the Start a New Best Practices Scan page will appear, as shown here.

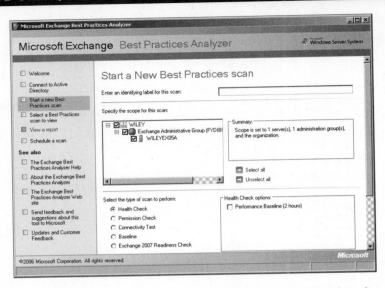

6. On the Start a New Best Practices Scan page, select the Health Check option and choose one or more Exchange servers on which to perform the health check. To make it easier to locate this ExBPA report later, you can give it a friendly label. After entering all selections, click the Start Scanning link at the bottom of the page.

7. A health check takes about two minutes per server to complete. After the check is completed, you will be presented with the option to view the report. Click the View a Report of This Best Practices Scan link to open the report, shown here.

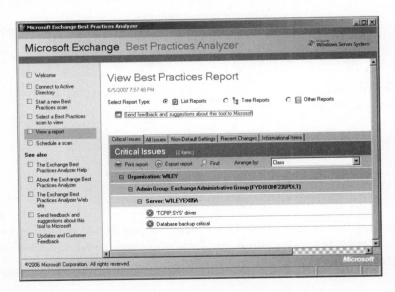

8. The first tab you'll see is the Critical Issues tab, and that's where you'll want to start focusing your efforts, if anything is listed there.

9. You can also print or export the ExBPA report to HTML, CSV, or XML. Exporting to HTML or CSV will export only the currently selected tab; exporting to XML will result in the entire scan report being exported.

10. Alternatively, you will have the ability to revisit scans later by returning to the Welcome page of the ExBPA and clicking the Select a Best Practices Scan to View link. A listing of all past scans will be made available, as shown here.

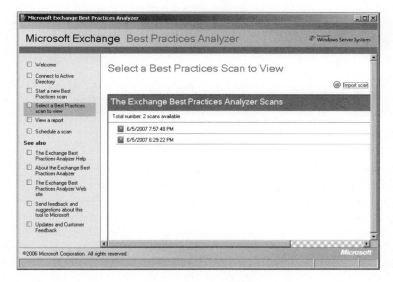

11. To view a previous scan report, click it to expand a list of options. You can view a report from the scan, export the scan as an XML file, delete the scan, or label it to make it easily identifiable.

Creating Availability Reports

To get true, usable availability reports on Exchange Server 2007, you'll need to use another application, such as Systems Center Operations Manager (SCOM) 2007 with the Exchange Server 2007 Management Pack (MP). SCOM includes many reports on the Exchange environment. Table 9.3 lists the available reports in SCOM with the Exchange Server 2007 MP. The reports are divided into three columns; the first column lists the service availability reports, the second column list metrics reports, and the third column lists antispam reports.

TABLE 9.3 Systems Center Operations Manager Reports for Exchange Server 2007

Service Availability	Metrics	Antispam
Service Availability Summary	Client Performance	Attached File Filter
Mailbox Service Availability	Mailbox Count	Connection Filter
Mailflow Local Service Availability	RPC and Database Performance	Recipient Filter
Mailflow Remote Service Availability	Unified Messaging Call Summary	Sender ID
Outlook Web Access External Service Availability	Unified Messaging Message Summary	Sender Filter
Outlook Web Access Internal Service Availability		Content Filter
ActiveSync Internal Availability		Protocol Analysis
Unified Messaging Local Voice Service Availability		
Unified Messaging Local Fax Service Availability		
Unified Messaging Remote Voice Service Availability		

As mentioned earlier, working with SCOM is beyond the scope of the 70-236 exam, but if your organization has more than two or three Exchange servers, you should take the time to explore how SCOM or another third-party monitoring tool could help you monitor Exchange, Active Directory, and many other key Microsoft products and services.

You can get more information about SCOM at www.microsoft.com/systemcenter/operationsmanager/en/us/default.aspx. You can get more information about implementing SCOM for Exchange Server 2007 monitoring at http://technet.microsoft.com/en-us/library/bb201735.aspx.

Creating Database and Message Queue Reports

You can create quick, useful reports on the status of all Exchange databases and queues on a server by using the Exchange Management Shell. To create a report showing all the information about all mailbox databases on a server, use the Get-MailboxDatabase | Export-CSV *c:\mailboxdb.csv* cmdlet, specifying your own location and name for the output file. Figure 9.8 shows an example of this report. The following information is available.

AdminDisplayName	MaintenanceSchedule
AdministrativeGroup	MinAdminVersion
AllowFileRestore	MountAtStartup
BackupInProgress	Mounted
CopyEdbFilePath	Name
DatabaseCreated	ObjectCategory
DeletedItemRetention	ObjectClass
Description	OfflineAddressBook
DistinguishedName	Organization
EdbFilePath	OriginalDatabase
EventHistoryRetentionPeriod	OriginatingServer
ExchangeLegacyDN	ProhibitSendQuota
ExchangeVersion	ProhibitSendReceiveQuota
Guid	PublicFolderDatabase
HasLocalCopy	QuotaNotificationSchedule
Identity	Recovery
IndexEnabled	RetainDeletedItemsUntilBackup
IssueWarningQuota	Server
IsValid	ServerName
JournalRecipient	StorageGroup
LastFullBackup	StorageGroupName
LastIncrementalBackup	WhenChanged
MailboxRetention	WhenCreated

More than likely, however, this much information is more than you'll really need to create the report you want. To create a report that contains just the specific fields of data in which you're interested, you can use a cmdlet similar to the following: Get-MailboxDatabase | Select-Object Name,Server,StorageGroup,Mounted,*Quota* | Export-CSV *c:\mailboxdb .csv*. The output from this more structured cmdlet will be much less and will be easier to work with. You can use any of the available fields listed for the Select-Object cmdlet.

FIGURE 9.8 Viewing a mailbox database report for a server

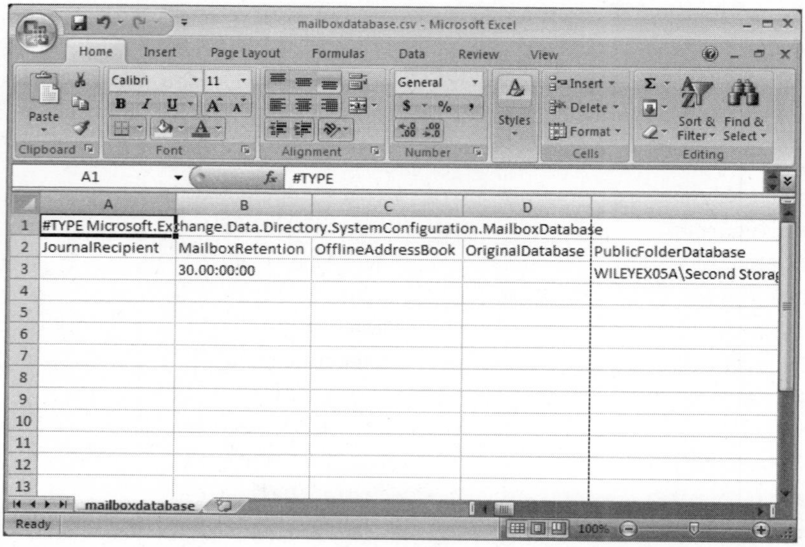

To create a report showing all the public folder databases on a server, you can use the `Get-PublicFolderDatabase` | `Export-CSV` *c:\publicfolderdb.csv* cmdlet, specifying your own location and name for the output file. The following list shows the properties available from the `Get-PublicFolderDatabase` cmdlet.

AdminDisplayName	Guid
AdministrativeGroup	HasLocalCopy
Alias	Identity
AllowFileRestore	IssueWarningQuota
BackupInProgress	IsValid
CopyEdbFilePath	ItemRetentionPeriod
DatabaseCreated	LastFullBackup
DeletedItemRetention	LastIncrementalBackup
Description	MaintenanceSchedule
DistinguishedName	MaxItemSize
EdbFilePath	MinAdminVersion
EventHistoryRetentionPeriod	MountAtStartup
ExchangeLegacyDN	Mounted
ExchangeVersion	Name
FirstInstance	ObjectCategory

ObjectClass	ReplicationSchedule
Organization	RetainDeletedItemsUntilBackup
OriginatingServer	Server
ProhibitPostQuota	ServerName
PublicFolderHierarchy	StorageGroup
PublicFolderReferralServerList	StorageGroupName
QuotaNotificationSchedule	UseCustomReferralServerList
ReplicationMessageSize	WhenChanged
ReplicationPeriod	WhenCreated

To create a report detailing the current status of all the queues on the server, you can use the Get-Queue | Export-CSV *c:\queues.csv* cmdlet. The following list shows the report fields available.

DeliveryType	NextHopConnector
Identity	NextHopDomain
IsValid	NextRetryTime
LastError	ObjectState
LastRetryTime	Status
MessageCount	

Creating Mailbox and User Usage Reports

Of the usage reports, most of them will involve users and/or mailboxes. You'll want to know how many mailboxes are located in a certain database, storage group, or server. You'll want to know which users are using the most space in the mailbox database so that you ensure that the appropriate quotas are set. This type of information will also be helpful when it comes to planning for server migrations or decommissioning.

The general cmdlet you can use to get information about mailboxes is the Get-Mailbox cmdlet. When run from the Exchange Management Console just like that, the cmdlet will return a small subset of data fields from what's really available to you. Figure 9.9 illustrates the feedback you'll get when using the Get-Mailbox cmdlet with no modification.

FIGURE 9.9 Viewing the output of the Get-Mailbox cmdlet

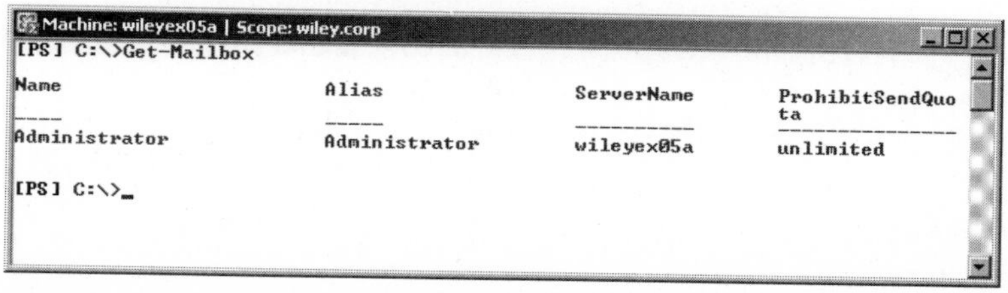

If you use the cmdlet Get-Mailbox | Export-CSV *c:\mailboxes.csv*, you'll get a CSV file that looks vaguely similar to the one shown earlier, in Figure 9.8, in that there will likely be more information than you'll need or want. Again, by using the Select-Object cmdlet to filter the information that is exported to the CSV file, you can get a much more usable report. The following is a list of the properties available for reporting.

AcceptMessagesOnlyFrom	GrantSendOnBehalfTo
AcceptMessagesOnlyFromDLMembers	Guid
AddressListMembership	HiddenFromAddressListsEnabled
Alias	Identity
AntispamBypassEnabled	IsLinked
CustomAttribute1	IsMailboxEnabled
CustomAttribute2	IsResource
CustomAttribute3	IsShared
CustomAttribute4	IssueWarningQuota
CustomAttribute5	IsValid
CustomAttribute6	Languages
CustomAttribute7	LegacyExchangeDN
CustomAttribute8	LinkedMasterAccount
CustomAttribute9	ManagedFolderMailboxPolicy
CustomAttribute10	MaxBlockedSenders
CustomAttribute11	MaxReceiveSize
CustomAttribute12	MaxSafeSenders
CustomAttribute13	MaxSendSize
CustomAttribute14	Name
CustomAttribute15	ObjectCategory
Database	ObjectClass
DeletedItemFlags	Office
DeliverToMailboxAndForward	OfflineAddressBook
DisplayName	OrganizationalUnit
DistinguishedName	OriginatingServer
EmailAddresses	PoliciesExcluded
EmailAddressPolicyEnabled	PoliciesIncluded
EndDateForRetentionHold	PrimarySmtpAddress
ExchangeGuid	ProhibitSendQuota
ExchangeSecurityDescriptor	ProhibitSendReceiveQuota
ExchangeUserAccountControl	ProtocolSettings
ExchangeVersion	RecipientLimits
Extensions	RecipientType
ExternalOofOptions	RecipientTypeDetail
ForwardingAddress	RejectMessagesFrom

RejectMessagesFromDL-Members	SCLRejectEnabled
RequireSenderAuthenticationEnabled	SCLRejectThreshold
ResourceCapacity	ServerLegacyDN
ResourceCustom	ServerName
ResourceType	SimpleDisplayName
RetainDeletedItemsFor	StartDateForRetentionHold
RetainDeletedItemsUntilBackup	UMDtmfMap
RetentionHoldEnabled	UMEnabled
RulesQuota	UseDatabaseQuotaDefaults
SamAccountName	UseDatabaseRetentionDefaults
SCLDeleteEnabled	UserAccountControl
SCLDeleteThreshold	UserPrincipalName
SCLJunkEnabled	WhenChanged
SCLJunkThreshold	WhenCreated
SCLQuarantineEnabled	WindowsEmailAddress
SCLQuarantineThreshold	

A useful report on mailboxes might use the following cmdlet: `Get-Mailbox | Select-Object Name,SamAccountName,*Quota*,Database | Export-CSV c:\mailboxes.csv`. You may have noticed that this report does not include the size of the mailboxes. For that information, you'll have to leverage the `Get-MailboxStatistics` cmdlet. Here is one example of using this:

```
Get-Mailbox | Get-MailboxStatistics | Select-Object
DisplayName,TotalItemSize,ItemCount,StorageLimitStatus
| Export-CSV c:\mailboxes.csv
```

The following list shows the report fields available when you use the `Get-MailboxStatistics` cmdlet.

AssociatedItemCount	LastLogonTime
Database	LegacyDN
DatabaseName	MailboxGuid
DeletedItemCount	ObjectClass
DisconnectDate	OriginatingServer
DisplayName	ServerName
Identity	StorageGroupName
IsValid	StorageLimitStatus
ItemCount	TotalDeletedItemSize
LastLoggedOnUserAccount	TotalItemSize
LastLogoffTime	

Real World Scenario

Using SCOM to Achieve a Higher Class of Service

Although Exchange Server 2007 offers a good number of monitoring and reporting tools and capabilities, it doesn't offer enough tools to meet the needs of many larger organizations. In addition, many organizations want automated monitoring and alerting because of the critical role that Exchange has in most organizations. To meet these requirements, you should consider implementing SCOM.

It's not just an Exchange-only benefit, because SCOM can monitor and report on almost any current Microsoft product as well as many non-Microsoft products. SCOM offers management packs for Exchange, SQL Server, Windows, network load balancing, Active Directory, HP storage arrays, Windows Software Update Services (WSUS), SharePoint Services, Forefront for Exchange, File Replication Service (FRS), and many others.

SCOM is not necessarily inexpensive, and it does require some training to be able to implement and manage it properly, but if you spend the time and effort to deploy and customize it to your organization's needs, it will pay off over time with quicker failure recovery, detailed performance reporting, and improved application availability. So if you're looking for better monitoring and reporting, get to know SCOM to see the benefits it can bring your organization.

Managing Mail Queues and Message Tracking

Eventually it will happen—message flow in your Exchange organization will stop working correctly. It might be due to a dismounted database, a problem with DNS, a problem with the network, or a variety of other possibilities. Regardless of what the problem is, examining the Exchange message queues will most likely be the first step in troubleshooting the problem. In the following sections of this chapter, we'll examine the queues found on an Exchange Server 2007 Hub Transport server and I'll show how you can interact with them. We'll also spend some time examining how to configure and use the message tracking functionality of Exchange Server 2007.

Introducing the Exchange Queues

A *queue* is a temporary staging location for those messages in transit that are between processing steps. There are multiple queues found on each Hub Transport server, and each one represents a set of messages to be processed in a specific way. Queues can be managed from both the Exchange Management Console and the Exchange Management Shell, as you'd expect. The queues are Extensible Storage Engine (ESE) databases—the same as the mailbox and public folder databases within Exchange Server 2007, thus allowing Exchange Server to interact with them at a very low level.

> There are also queues on the Edge Transport servers for messages that are coming inbound from the Internet or going outbound to the Internet. For all intents, the management of the queues on the Edge Transport server is the same as for the Hub Transport server. We'll be working with Hub Transport servers only for this chapter.

On the Hub Transport server, you can find the following types of queues:

- *Submission queue*: This is a persistent (always present) queue that is used by the categorizer to group all messages that have just been submitted for transport. The categorizer is an Exchange component that processes these messages and determines what to do with them and where they need to be routed, such as expanding the membership of a distribution group for messages queued on the Hub Transport server. Once the categorizer has determined the information it needs about the message, including recipients, it can then apply any transport policies and route the message properly.

- *Mailbox delivery queue*: This queue holds the messages that are being attempted for delivery to a Mailbox server. Multiple Mailbox server queues can exist on a Hub Transport server; however, they will exist only for Mailbox servers located in the same Active Directory site as the Hub Transport server. The next hop for messages located in a mailbox delivery queue is to the Mailbox server to which they are destined.

- *Remote delivery queue*: This queue holds messages that are being routed to remote SMTP destinations, such as servers that are located outside the Active Directory site containing the Hub Transport server. Remote delivery queues are dynamically created and removed as needed, depending on the messages that are being routed on the server. The next hop for messages located in a remote delivery queue is a remote Active Directory site or SMTP domain or smart host.

- *Poison message queue*: This queue holds messages that have been determined to be potentially harmful to the Exchange organization after a server failure has occurred, such as messages that contain fatal errors. When no messages meeting this condition are found, this queue does not exist on the Hub Transport server, although it is in a ready state should it be needed. There is no attempt to deliver messages placed into the poison message queue, and their status is set to suspended, allowing the messages to be examined and deleted or released by the administrator after further review. The next hop for messages located in the poison message queue that have been released is the submission queue.

- *Unreachable queue*: This queue holds messages that cannot be routed to their destinations for any reason, such as changes in the routing path that block message transport.

Managing Exchange Queues and Queued Items

You have many options available to you as to how to manage the queues as a whole or how to manage individual messages in the queues. Which action you take will depend largely on the scenario you are facing and, to a smaller degree, the queue with which you are working. In the following sections, we'll examine queue and queued item management in depth.

You can access the Queue Viewer from the Exchange Management Console by navigating to the Toolbox node, as shown in Figure 9.10. Once you've located the Queue Viewer tool, simply double-click it to open the Queue Viewer, shown in Figure 9.11.

FIGURE 9.10   Locating the Queue Viewer in the Exchange Management Console

FIGURE 9.11   Examining the Queue Viewer window

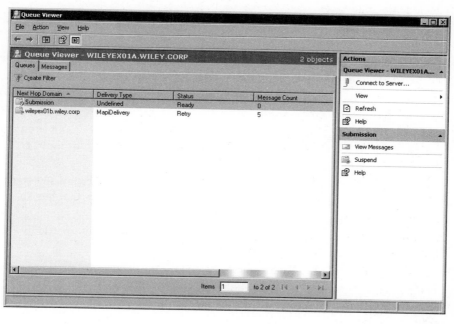

By default, the Queue Viewer opens to display the queues on that Hub Transport server, but you can change this view by clicking the Connect to Server link in the Actions pane on the right side of the Queue Viewer window.

Managing Queues

Once in the Queue Viewer, you can quickly determine the status of each queue that exists on that Hub Transport server. The main display of the Queue Viewer provides a wealth of information about the status of each queue on the server, which will be important knowledge in your monitoring and troubleshooting efforts. The following data fields are available in the Queue Viewer for each queue present:

- *Next Hop Domain*: Provides information about the destination of messages in the selected delivery queue. Possible values here include the following:
  - An Active Directory site name
  - The fully qualified domain name (FQDN) of an Exchange Mailbox server
  - A connector name
  - A routing group name
  - A remote SMTP domain name
  - An Exchange server name

- *Delivery Type*: Provides information about the next hop destination. Possible values here include the following:
  - *MapiDelivery*: Messages are queued for delivery to recipients with mailboxes in the local Active Directory site.
  - *DNSConnectorDelivery*: Messages are queued for delivery to an external recipient via an SMTP connector configured to use DNS for message routing.
- *NonSmtpGatewayDelivery*: Messages are queued for delivery to an external recipient using a non-SMTP connector.
  - *SmartHostConnectorDelivery*: Messages are queued for delivery to an external recipient via an SMTP connector configured to use a smart host for message routing.
  - *SmtpRelayWithinAdSitetoEdge*: Messages are queued for delivery to an external recipient using an SMTP connector on an Edge Transport server that has an EdgeSync subscription to Active Directory.
  - *SmtpRelayWithinAdSite*: Messages are queued for delivery to another Hub Transport server in the same Active Directory site.
  - *SmtpRelaytoRemoteAdSite*: Messages are queued for delivery to another Exchange server in a remote Active Directory site.
  - *SmtpRelaytoTiRg*: Messages are queued for delivery to an Exchange Server 2003 routing group.
  - *Undefined*: Messages are located in the submission queue, and the next hop has not yet been determined.
  - *Unreachable*: Messages are located in the unreachable queue, where a route to the recipient could not be determined.
- *Status*: Provides the current status of the queue. Possible values here include Active, Suspended, Ready, and Retry.
- *Message Count*: Provides the number of message items currently in the queue.
- *Next Retry Time*: Provides the date and time of the next connection attempt for a queue in a retry status.
- *Last Error*: Provides the last recorded error for the queue.
- *Last Retry Time*: Provides the date and time of the last connection attempt for a queue in a retry status.

To drill down into a specific queue and see the messages contained within, you can double-click it, or you can click once to select it and then click the View Messages link in the Actions pane on the right side of the window. Either way, a new tab opens for the selected queue and displays information about the items contained within that queue, as shown for the mailbox delivery queue for server wileyex01a.wiley.corp in Figure 9.12.

FIGURE 9.12   Examining messages in a specific queue

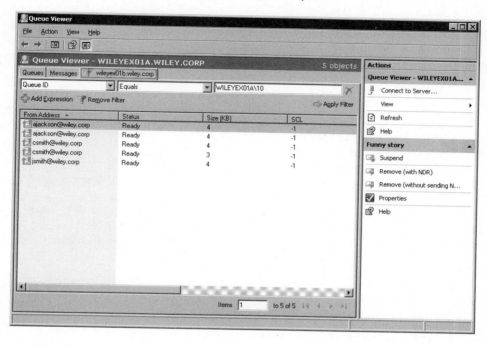

I'll discuss message-level management tasks in the next section of this chapter, so for now let's backtrack to the Queue Viewer's main window, shown previously in Figure 9.11. When you select a specific queue of interest, a number of queue management tasks become available in the Actions pane on the right side of the Queue Viewer, as shown in Figure 9.13.

FIGURE 9.13   Exploring the message queue tasks

These tasks are as follows:

- *View Messages*: Clicking this link will open the selected queue in another tab, shown previously in Figure 9.13.

- *Suspend*: Clicking this link will temporarily prevent any messages in the selected queue from being delivered. New messages can enter the queue, but no messages can leave the queue while in a suspended state.

- *Resume*: Clicking this link enables messages in the selected suspended queue to be delivered and routed as required.

- *Retry*: Clicking this link will cause messages in a queue with a retry status to have delivery attempted before the next regularly scheduled retry event. If delivery is successful, the messages will be routed. If delivery is not successful, the retry timer will be reset for the next retry time.

- *Remove Messages (with NDR)*: Clicking this link will cause all messages in the selected queue to be deleted, and it sends a nondelivery report (NDR) for each message. NDR messages are not sent for messages that are in the queue at the time of deletion.

- *Remove Messages (without Sending NDR)*: Clicking this link causes all messages in the selected queue to be deleted silently, without sending an NDR.

Of course, you can perform all these tasks from the Exchange Management Shell as well.

To get a detailed listing of all queues on the local server, you will use the `Get-Queue | format-list` cmdlet, which produces output like that shown in Figure 9.14.

You can accomplish the remaining tasks using the following PowerShell cmdlets:

- To suspend a queue, use the `Suspend-Queue` cmdlet.

  - To suspend a queue with a next hop domain of wiley.com that is in a retry status, you would use the following cmdlet: `Suspend-Queue -Filter {NextHopDomain -eq "wiley.com" -and Status -eq "retry"}`.

  - To suspend all queues on the server wileyex01a.wiley.corp that have more than 2,000 messages in them, you would use the following cmdlet: `Suspend-Queue -Server wileyex01a.wiley.corp -Filter {MessageCount -gt 2000}`.

- To resume a suspended queue, use the `Resume-Queue` cmdlet.

  - To resume a suspended queue on the server wileyex01a.wiley.corp that contains messages destined for the wrox.com domain, you would use the following cmdlet: `Resume-Queue -Server wileyex01a.wiley.corp -Filter {NextHopDomain -eq "wrox.com"}`.

- To retry a queue, use the `Retry-Queue` cmdlet.

  - To force a retry attempt on a queue that contains messages destined for the wrox.com domain, you would use the following cmdlet: `Retry-Queue -Filter {NextHopDomain -eq "wrox.com" -and Status -eq "retry"}`.

- To remove messages from a queue, with or without sending an NDR, use the `Remove-Message` cmdlet. The value of the `withNDR` parameter determines whether an NDR is sent and can be either `$true` or `$false`.

  - To remove messages from a queue on the server wileyex01a that contains messages destined for the wileyex01b.wiley.corp Mailbox server, use the following cmdlet: `Remove-Message -Filter {Queue -eq "wileyex01a\wileyex01b.wiley.corp"} -withNDR $false`.

FIGURE 9.14   Viewing message queues from the Exchange Management Shell

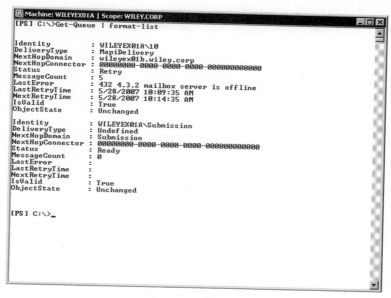

Managing Queued Messages

Of course, you may need or want to manage only specific messages in a selected queue and not the entire queue itself. Once you select the tab belonging to a specific queue of concern in the Queue Viewer, you'll have a listing of messages that are currently in the queue, as shown previously in Figure 9.12. Each queue in the Queue Viewer has the following data fields available:

- *Date Received*: This is the date and time the message was received on the server.
- *Expiration Time*: This is the data and time the message will be deleted from the queue if it is not delivered first.
- *From Address*: This is the SMTP address of the sender of the message.
- *Internet Message ID*: The message GUID and SMTP address of the sending server are combined to make a unique ID that you can find in the message header.
- *Last Error*: This is the value of the last error that was recorded for the message.
- *Message Source Name*: This is the value of the component that submitted the message to the queue.
- *Queue ID*: This is the identity of the queue where the message is located.
- *SCL*: This is the value from 0 to 9 that specifies how likely it is that the message is spam.

- *Size (KB)*: This is the size of the message in kilobytes (KB).
- *Source IP*: This is the IP address of the originating server that submitted the message.
- *Status*: This is the current status of the message. Possible values here include the following:
    - *Active*: The message is currently being delivered to its destination or being processed by the categorizer.
    - *Suspended*: The message is currently suspended.
    - *PendingRemove*: The message was selected for deletion, but it was already in a delivery status. If the message delivery attempt fails, the message will be deleted.
    - *PendingSuspend*: The message was selected for suspension of delivery, but it was already in a delivery status. If the message delivery attempt fails, the message will be suspended.
    - *Ready*: The message is waiting to be processed.
    - *Retry*: The message was not successfully delivered on the last attempt and is awaiting the next queue retry.
- *Subject*: This is the subject value of the message.

When a message (or group of messages) is selected, management tasks become available in the Actions pane on the right side of the Queue Viewer, as shown in Figure 9.15.

FIGURE 9.15   Queued message tasks

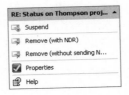

These tasks are as follows:

- *Suspend*: Clicking this link temporarily prevents the selected message(s) from being delivered out of the queue.
- *Resume*: Clicking this link enables the delivery of the selected suspended messages. You can resume only a queue that has been previously suspended.
- *Remove (with NDR)*: Clicking this link causes all selected messages to be deleted and sends an NDR for each message.
- *Remove (without Sending NDR)*: Clicking this link causes all selected messages to be deleted silently, without sending an NDR.
- *Properties*: Clicking this link opens a new dialog box, shown in Figure 9.16, which displays header and recipient information for the selected message. This can be useful when trying to determine to whom the message is addressed.

FIGURE 9.16   Viewing queued message properties

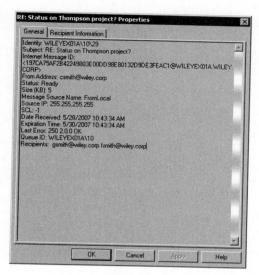

As you'd expect, you can perform all these tasks from the Exchange Management Shell as well:

- To suspend a message, use the `Suspend-Message` cmdlet.

  - To suspend all messages in all queues that are from the SMTP sender loanstoday@moremoney.biz, use the following cmdlet: `Suspend-Message -filter {FromAddress -eq "loanstoday@moremoney.biz"}`.

- To resume suspended messages, use the `Resume-Message` cmdlet.

  - To resume all messages in all queues that are from the SMTP sender ceo@wiley .corp, use the following cmdlet: `Resume-Message -filter {FromAddress -eq "ceo@wiley.corp"}`.

- To remove messages, with or without sending an NDR, use the `Remove-Message` cmdlet.

  - To remove all messages with the subject of "Make Mon3y Fast!!" from all queues, use the following cmdlet: `Remove-Message -filter {Subject -eq "Make Mon3y Fast!!"} -WithNDR $false`.

- To view the properties of one or more messages, use the `Get-Message` cmdlet.

  - To view the properties of all messages in all queues that were sent from the wiley .corp SMTP domain, use the following cmdlet to produce the results shown in Figure 9.17: `Get-Message -Filter {FromAddress -like "*@wiley.corp"} | format-list`.

  - To view the properties of a specific message in any queue that has a subject of "RE: Lunch with vendor?" use the following cmdlet: `Get-Message -Filter {Subject -eq "RE: Lunch with vendor?"} | format-list`.

FIGURE 9.17 Viewing queued message properties in the Exchange Management Shell

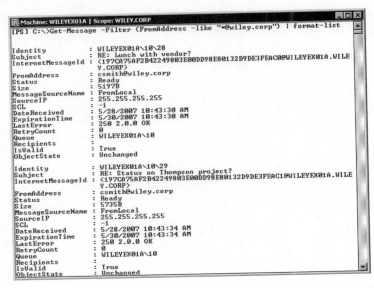

You can also export a suspended message from a queue using the Exchange Management Shell; this is a task you cannot perform from the Exchange Management Console. By using the Export-Message cmdlet, you can save a copy of a queued message to an .EML file that can be examined in its entirety or passed along to a user to be opened in Outlook. To export a specific message in any queue that has a message identity of WILEYEX01A\10\28, use the following cmdlet: Export-Message -Identity WILEYEX01A\10\28 -Path "c:\mymessage.eml".

You can determine the message identity of a specific message by using the output of the Get-Message | format-list cmdlet.

Configuring Queue Viewer Properties

You can configure only two properties within the Exchange Management Console that control the behavior of the Queue Viewer. You can access these items once the Queue Viewer is open by selecting Tools ➤ Options. The Queue Viewer Options dialog box opens. As shown in Figure 9.18, you can change the refresh interval and the number of messages that are displayed per page from here.

You can find the actual queue database files (in a default installation) in the location shown in Figure 9.19.

FIGURE 9.18   Setting Queue Viewer options

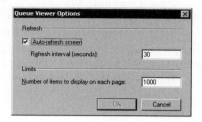

FIGURE 9.19   Viewing the queue database files

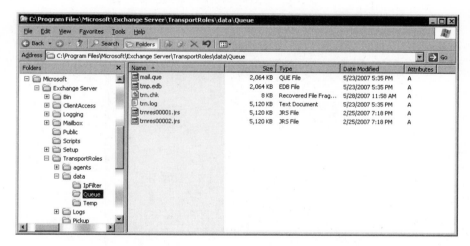

The files that make up the queue database are similar to those that make up mailbox and public folder databases; they include the following:

- `Mail.que`: The actual queue database file.

- `Tmp.edb`: A temporary database file used to verify the queue database schema during service start-up on the Exchange server.

- `Trn.log`: The active transaction log file.

- `Trntmp.log`: An empty transaction log file that has been provisioned to be the next `Trn.log` file.

- `Trnnnnn.log`: An old transaction log file that has reached its maximum capacity.

- `Trn.chk`: The checkpoint file that keeps track of all transaction log entries that have already been committed to the queue database file.

- `Trnres00001.jrs` and `Trnres00002.jrs`: Reserve transaction logs that act as place-holders to ensure adequate space exists to shut down the queue database cleanly should the drive containing it run out of free space.

The behavior of the queue database cannot be configured by either the Exchange Management Shell or the Exchange Management Console but instead is configured via an XML file named `EdgeTransport.exe.config` that is located in `C:\Program Files\Microsoft\Exchange Server\Bin` by default. Figure 9.20 displays some of the contents of this XML file.

Common changes that you might make to the `EdgeTransport.exe.config` file would be to change the retry, resubmit, and expiration intervals of messages. The TechNet article at the following URL provides guidance on these tasks: `http://technet.microsoft.com/en-us/library/aa998043.aspx`.

FIGURE 9.20 Viewing the queue database configuration file

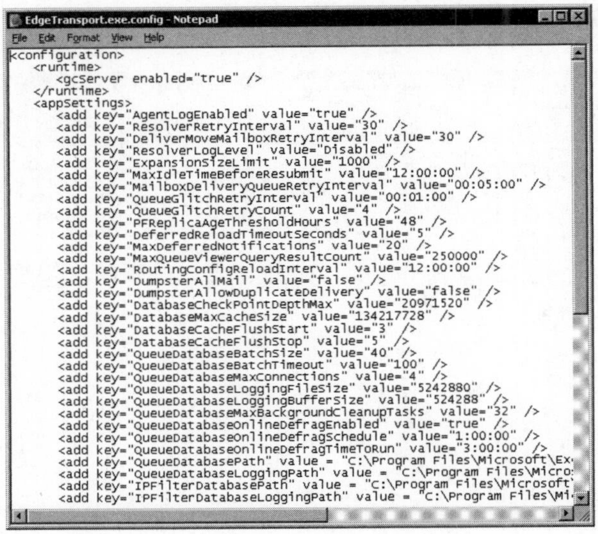

EdgeTransport.exe.config - Notepad

File Edit Format View Help

```
<configuration>
   <runtime>
      <gcServer enabled="true" />
   </runtime>
   <appSettings>
      <add key="AgentLogEnabled" value="true" />
      <add key="ResolverRetryInterval" value="30" />
      <add key="DeliverMoveMailboxRetryInterval" value="30" />
      <add key="ResolverLogLevel" value="Disabled" />
      <add key="ExpansionSizeLimit" value="1000" />
      <add key="MaxIdleTimeBeforeResubmit" value="12:00:00" />
      <add key="MailboxDeliveryQueueRetryInterval" value="00:05:00" />
      <add key="QueueGlitchRetryInterval" value="00:01:00" />
      <add key="QueueGlitchRetryCount" value="4" />
      <add key="PFReplicaAgeThresholdHours" value="48" />
      <add key="DeferredReloadTimeoutSeconds" value="5" />
      <add key="MaxDeferredNotifications" value="20" />
      <add key="MaxQueueViewerQueryResultCount" value="250000" />
      <add key="RoutingConfigReloadInterval" value="12:00:00" />
      <add key="DumpsterAllMail" value="false" />
      <add key="DumpsterAllowDuplicateDelivery" value="false" />
      <add key="DatabaseCheckPointDepthMax" value="20971520" />
      <add key="DatabaseMaxCacheSize" value="134217728" />
      <add key="DatabaseCacheFlushStart" value="3" />
      <add key="DatabaseCacheFlushStop" value="5" />
      <add key="QueueDatabaseBatchSize" value="40" />
      <add key="QueueDatabaseBatchTimeout" value="100" />
      <add key="QueueDatabaseMaxConnections" value="4" />
      <add key="QueueDatabaseLoggingFileSize" value="5242880" />
      <add key="QueueDatabaseLoggingBufferSize" value="524288" />
      <add key="QueueDatabaseMaxBackgroundCleanupTasks" value="32" />
      <add key="QueueDatabaseOnlineDefragEnabled" value="true" />
      <add key="QueueDatabaseOnlineDefragSchedule" value="1:00:00" />
      <add key="QueueDatabaseOnlineDefragTimeToRun" value="3:00:00" />
      <add key="QueueDatabasePath" value = "C:\Program Files\Microsoft\Ex
      <add key="QueueDatabaseLoggingPath" value = "C:\Program Files\Micro
      <add key="IPFilterDatabasePath" value = "C:\Program Files\Microsoft
      <add key="IPFilterDatabaseLoggingPath" value = "C:\Program Files\Mi
```

WARNING

Editing the `EdgeTransport.exe.config` file should be undertaken by only the most advanced Exchange administrators. If you choose to edit this file, take care to check the correct syntax and spelling of your changes. You can get more information about the available parameters and options by visiting the TechNet article at: `http://technet.microsoft.com/en-us/library/aa996006.aspx`. After you make any changes to the `EdgeTransport.exe.config` file, you'll need to restart the Microsoft Exchange Transport service to make the changes active on the server.

Another common change you might want to make is to move the queue database to a different location. You should reference the TechNet article at the following URL for more information about that task: `http://technet.microsoft.com/en-us/library/bb125177.aspx`.

Managing Message Tracking

The message tracking tool has been a staple for Exchange administrators for some time, and its usefulness is not likely to change anytime soon. To access the message tracking interface, simply go back to the Toolbox shown previously in Figure 9.10 and double-click the Message Tracking item. The first time you run the message tracking tool, you'll be prompted to check for updates. Once you've done this and you are in the tool itself, you'll have an interface to work with like that shown in Figure 9.21. Note how the actual Get-MessageTrackingLog cmdlet that will be used to perform the tracking action is already displayed and changes as you select parameters.

FIGURE 9.21   Viewing the message tracking interface

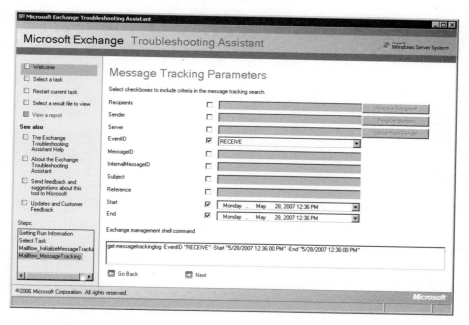

Performing Message Tracking

The actual process to use message tracking hasn't really changed much from Exchange Server 2003, so administrators with experience using it there should be able to jump right into it in Exchange Server 2007. Even if you haven't had a lot of experience with tracking messages, the interface is simple and purpose-built, so you can get right to work.

As an example, if you wanted to check the delivery status of all messages sent from Angela Jackson (ajackson@wiley.corp) to Will Schmied (wschmied@wiley.corp) during the time frame of 1:30 p.m. on May 21, 2007, to 1:30 p.m. on May 28, 2007, you might configure the message tracking parameters as shown in Figure 9.22.

FIGURE 9.22   Configuring message tracking parameters

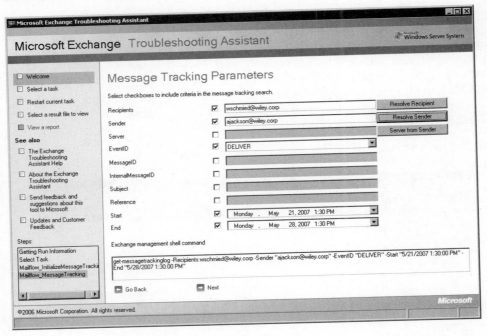

The resulting output is a bit difficult to work with at first, but eventually you will get used to the more detailed and less user-friendly display that Exchange Server 2007 provides, as shown in Figure 9.23.

FIGURE 9.23   Viewing message tracking output

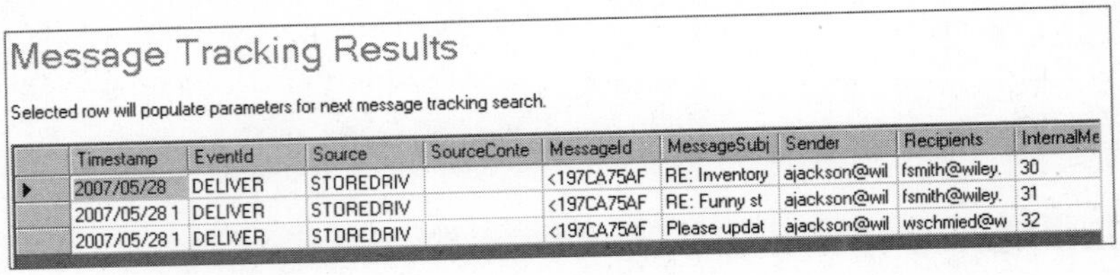

The corresponding cmdlet to execute this search is `Get-MessageTrackingLog -Recipients:wschmied@wiley.corp -Sender "ajackson@wiley.corp" -EventID "DELIVERY" -Start "5/21/2007 1:30:00 PM" -End "5/28/2007 1:30:00 PM" | format-list`, which produces the result shown in Figure 9.24.

FIGURE 9.24 Viewing message tracking output from the Exchange Management Shell

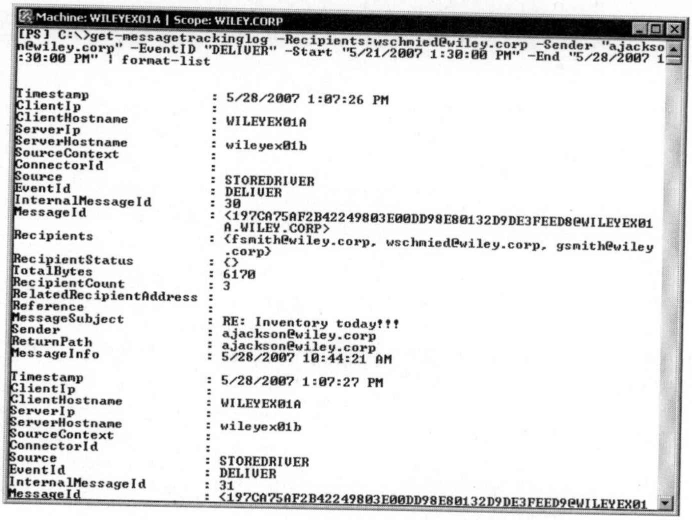

The EventID field is searchable and is oftentimes the piece of information you're looking for when it comes to determining the final status of a specific message. Was the message that Jim claimed to never have received really delivered? You can answer that question and many others through message tracking. The EventID field has the following values, each of which will tell you the exact status of that particular line in the tracking logs:

- *BADMAIL*: The message could not be delivered or returned to sender.

- *DELIVER*: The message was delivered to the recipient's mailbox.

- *DEFER*: The delivery of the message was delayed.

- *DSN*: A delivery status notification was generated for the message.

- *EXPAND*: The membership of a distribution was expanded to determine the final recipients of the message.

- *FAIL*: Delivery of the message has failed permanently.

- *POISONMESSAGE*: The message was put into or removed from the poison message queue.

- *RECEIVE*: The message was received and committed to the database.

- *REDIRECT*: The message was redirected to another recipient.

- *RESOLVE*: The message's recipient was resolved to a different email address.

- *SEND*: The message was sent using SMTP to a different server.

- *SUBMIT*: The message was submitted to the Hub Transport server from a Mailbox server or Edge Transport server.

- *TRANSFER*: The recipients of the message were moved to a forked message because of recipient limits or conversion of the message content.

Note that the DELIVER status in the EventID field is your confirmation that a message was actually delivered to a recipient's mailbox—no matter what they try to tell you!

Configuring Message Tracking

The actual message tracking logs are located (in a default installation) at the following location, as shown in Figure 9.25: C:\Program Files\Microsoft\Exchange Server\ TransportRoles\Logs\MessageTracking.

FIGURE 9.25 Locating the message tracking logs

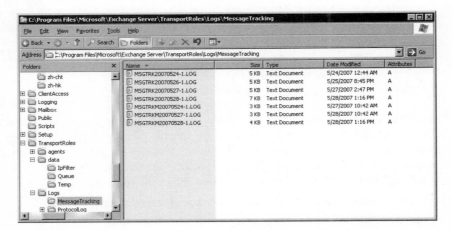

The logs are formatted as comma-separated-value (CSV) files, so you can open them in any text editor, as shown in Figure 9.26, or you can even import them into Microsoft Excel for advanced sorting and grouping if you want, although you'll most commonly access the logs using the message tracking interface.

FIGURE 9.26 Examining a message tracking log

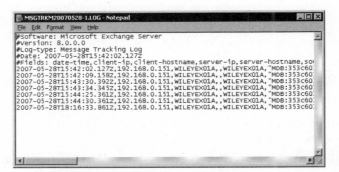

You may want to perform a few configuration actions for tracking logs (I'll discuss these in the following sections):

- Disabling or enabling message tracking on a server
- Changing the tracking log location
- Changing the tracking log maximum size
- Changing the tracking log directory maximum size
- Changing the tracking log maximum age
- Disabling or enabling message subject logging

Disabling or Enabling Message Tracking on a Server

By default, message tracking is enabled on all Edge Transport, Hub Transport, and Mailbox servers. You can disable (or enable) message tracking by using the following commands for Edge Transport and Hub Transport servers:

- To disable message tracking, use `Set-TransportServer` *servername* `-MessageTrackingLogEnabled:$false`.
- To enable message tracking, use `Set-TransportServer` *servername* `-MessageTrackingLogEnabled:$true`.

You can disable (or enable) message tracking by using the following commands for Mailbox servers:

- To disable message tracking, use `Set-MailboxServer` *servername* `-MessageTrackingLogEnabled:$false`.
- To enable message tracking, use `Set-MailboxServer` *servername* `-MessageTrackingLogEnabled:$true`.

Changing the Tracking Log Location

To change the location of the tracking logs from their default location, you can use the following commands:

- For Hub Transport or Edge Transport servers, use `Set-TransportServer` *servername* `-MessageTrackingLogPath "T:\Message Tracking"`.
- For Mailbox servers, use `Set-MailboxServer` *servername* `-MessageTrackingLogPath "T:\Message Tracking"`.

Changing the Tracking Log Maximum Size

To change the maximum size of each individual tracking log, you can use the following commands:

- For Hub Transport or Edge Transport servers, use `Set-TransportServer` *servername* `-MessageTrackingLogMaxFileSize 15MB`.
- For Mailbox servers, use `Set-MailboxServer` *servername* `-MessageTrackingLogMaxFileSize 15MB`.

By default, each message tracking log created has a maximum size of 10MB. You can use values in bytes (B), kilobytes (KB), megabytes (MB), gigabytes (GB), or terabytes (TB) when configuring the maximum size of each message tracking log.

Changing the Tracking Log Directory Maximum Size

To change the maximum size of the folder containing the message tracking logs, you can use the following commands:

- For Hub Transport or Edge Transport servers, use Set-TransportServer *servername* -MessageTrackingLogMaxDirectorySize 5GB.

- For Mailbox servers, use Set-TransportServer *servername* -MessageTrackingLogMaxDirectorySize 5GB.

Changing the Tracking Log Maximum Age

To change the message tracking log age, you can use the following commands:

- For Hub Transport or Edge Transport servers, use Set-TransportServer *servername* -MessageTrackingLogMaxAge 45.00:00:00.

- For Mailbox servers, use Set-MailboxServer *servername* -MessageTrackingLogMaxAge 45.00:00:00.

The value entered has a format of dd.hh:mm:ss, where d = days, h = hours, m = minutes, and s = seconds. If the value is set to 00:00:00, Exchange will not automatically prune tracking logs because of age.

Disabling or Enabling Message Subject Logging

By default, message subject logging is enabled, but you can disable or enable it if you want. You can disable (or enable) subject logging by using the following commands for Edge Transport and Hub Transport servers:

- To disable subject logging, use Set-TransportServer *servername* -MessageTrackingLogSubjectLoggingEnabled $false.

- To enable message tracking, use Set-TransportServer *servername* -MessageTrackingLogSubjectLoggingEnabled $true.

You can disable (or enable) message tracking by using the following commands for Mailbox servers:

- To disable message tracking, use Set-MailboxServer *servername* -MessageTrackingLogSubjectLoggingEnabled $false.

- To enable message tracking, use Set-MailboxServer *servername* -MessageTrackingLogSubjectLoggingEnabled $true.

Routing Log Viewer

As mentioned previously, Exchange 2007 does not rely on link-state routing as in previous versions. Therefore, the tools used to troubleshoot message routing no longer work. A new utility, the Routing Log Viewer, designed to view routing information, was added into the Exchange Management Console Toolbox in Service Pack 1.

The Routing Log Viewer allows the administrator to open routing logs to view how the local Hub Transport server has identified message routing information from Active Directory. This is useful for a few very important reasons. First, an administrator can use this information to determine what path a message will take and determine if any routing adjustments need to be made. The second benefit is that previous versions of the log files can also be parsed to see how, or if, routing has changed over time. Last, log files from multiple servers can be opened to establish any differences existing between servers.

The Routing Log Viewer is launched through the Toolbox in the Exchange Management Console just like the other mail flow tools. After you launch the Routing Log Viewer, the first step is to open a log file. As shown in Figure 9.27, the dialog provides for opening local or remote log files.

FIGURE 9.27   Opening routing table log files

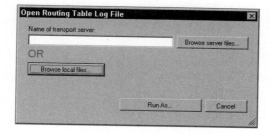

Once the log file has been opened, you will be presented with a window with four tabs: Active Directory Sites & Routing Groups, Servers, Send Connectors, and Address Spaces. The Active Directory Sites & Routing Groups tab, as shown in Figure 9.28, shows what the Hub Transport server has discovered about Active Directory sites and any routing group connectors. The Servers tab lists of all the Exchange servers in the organization, in what site they are located, the cost to send to the servers from the local server, databases hosted on the server, and other details. The Send Connectors tab lists all of the connectors in the Exchange organization along with details about each connector, including costs and address spaces. The last tab, the Address Spaces tab, lists all of the address spaces in the Exchange organization as well as details about their cost and an ordered list of each of the address space connectors.

FIGURE 9.28   Viewing the Active Directory Sites & Routing Groups tab

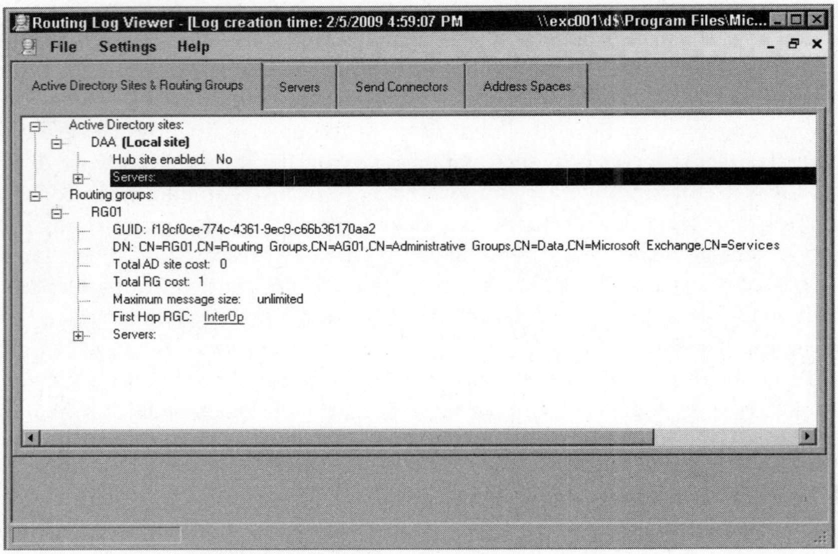

Using the Test cmdlets

Rather than leave it to your own devices to come up with tests, Microsoft has developed 17 cmdlets to provide a wide range of tests. Many of these cmdlets are used by products like SCOM to gather information on the health of the Exchange environment. Understanding these powerful tools will allow you to get the information you need to pinpoint potential issues.

The cmdlets are as follows:

- **Test-ActiveSyncConnectivity**: Tests a full simulated synchronization using Exchange ActiveSync.

- **Test-EdgeSynchronization**: This is run against a Hub Transport server to test its ability to synchronize with an Edge Transport server.

- **Test-ExchangeSearch**: Tests whether search indexes are being updated.

- **Test-ImapConnectivity**: Tests connectivity to a Client Access server via the IMAP4 protocol and returns the results.

- **Test-IPAllowListProvider**: Tests an IP address to determine if it is listed on a configured safe list provider.

- **Test-IPBlockListProvider**: Tests the configuration of the specified IP Block List provider.

- **Test-Mailflow**: Tests email transportation to a specific server, between two servers, or to external addresses.

- **Test-MAPIConnectivity**: Tests connectivity to Active Directory and to a mailbox. If the server parameter is specified, connectivity to the system mailbox on the server specified.

- **Test-OutlookWebServices**: Performs a series of tests against a Client Access Server role to verify that the Autodiscover settings are properly configured.

- **Test-OwaConnectivity**: Tests the configuration of the Exchange virutal directories.

- **Test-PopConnectivity**: Tests connectivity to a Client Access server via the POP3 protocol and returns the results.

- **Test-ReplicationHealth**: Tests the health of all replication types, status of cluster services, and replay status to provide a comprehensive status.

- **Test-SenderId**: Tests an IP address to determine if it is valid for a given SMTP domain.

- **Test-ServiceHealth**: Tests to determine whether the required services that are also set to start automatically are started.

- **Test-SystemHealth**: Tests to see how the current Exchange configuration adheres to best practices.

- **Test-UMConnectivity**: Tests basic unified messaging connectivity or full end-to-end unified messaging connectivity.

- **Test-WebServicesConnectivity**: Tests to determine if OutlookAnywhere is functioning properly.

 Although testing internally is extremely important, testing from outside the network is also a good tool to aid in troubleshooting. The Exchange support team has set up www.testexchangeconnectivity.com which can perform a wide variety of client connectivity tests.

Summary

In this chapter, I briefly covered some of the most common monitoring and reporting functionality that Exchange Server 2007 offers you. As is often said in management circles, you can't manage what you can't measure. That axiom holds true for every aspect of system administration—if you don't know what's going on with your servers or applications, you can't effectively manage or troubleshoot them.

Exam Essentials

Practice performance monitoring. Using the performance counters effectively is not something you can just start doing on your first try. To get effective results out of your performance monitoring, you need to do it often and you need to take the time to understand what each counter is telling you. I covered some of the more specific counters relevant to Exchange Server 2007, but dozens of other counters are important to the Windows Server operating system as well. After all, if your server is not performing well, it stands to reason that Exchange won't be performing well. Take some time to learn which counters are pertinent to your organization, and make it a point to take performance measurements on a schedule to get an accurate indication of how your servers are performing.

Learn the PowerShell commands. Almost every configuration or management action you perform from the Exchange Management Console will present you with the PowerShell code that was used to perform the action. Take advantage of this information and learn how to use the Exchange Management Shell to your advantage. Some of these commands are likely to make an appearance on the exam.

Know where to go. You will often be asked on the exam what configuration is needed to produce the required results. The Exchange Management Console has been completely redesigned to make it easier to navigate and get to tasks, but that doesn't mean it won't be difficult to remember later. Take the time as you review the material in this book to think about what types of configuration and management tasks you find yourself performing in each major node of the Exchange Management Console.

Review Questions

1. What performance counter would you most likely want to monitor to determine whether your Exchange Mailbox server has a problem with excessive paging?

   A. Processor – % Processor Time

   B. LogicalDisk – Avg. Disk sec/Write

   C. Memory – Pages/sec

   D. LogicalDisk – Avg. Disk sec/Read

2. What PowerShell cmdlet should you use to determine the status of services on a server?

   A. Show-Service

   B. Get-Service

   C. List-Service

   D. Display-Service

3. Which of the following PowerShell cmdlets will you need to use to create a CSV report that contains information about mailboxes, including the number of items and size of each mailbox? (Choose all correct answers.)

   A. Get-Mailbox

   B. Get-MailboxStatistics

   C. Select-Object

   D. Export-CSV

4. Which of the following tools in the Toolbox node of the Exchange Management Console would you use to create a health report on your Exchange Server 2007 servers?

   A. Performance Monitor

   B. Performance Troubleshooter

   C. Best Practices Analyzer

   D. Database Troubleshooter

5. To export the results of an ExBPA scan to a single file containing all the results, which file format must you use?

   A. CSV

   B. XML

   C. HTTP

   D. PDF

6. Which of the following would be the best choice for monitoring the status of hardware components in your Exchange servers?

   A. Microsoft System Center Operations Manager (SCOM)

   B. An application from the hardware vendor

   C. Exchange Server Performance Monitor

   D. A custom PowerShell script that creates CSV reports

7. Which logs in the Event Viewer will typically contain useful information for troubleshooting Exchange service issues? (Choose two.)

   A. Application

   B. PowerShell

   C. Security

   D. System

   E. Windows PowerShell

8. Which of the following tools in the Toolbox node of the Exchange Management Console would you use to determine whether there are RPC problems on your Exchange Server 2007 servers?

   A. Performance Monitor

   B. Performance Troubleshooter

   C. Best Practices Analyzer

   D. Database Troubleshooter

9. Given that most of the installed Exchange services on an Exchange Mailbox server should normally be running, you want to determine quickly using the PowerShell which Exchange services are not running. Which of the following cmdlets would you need to use to perform this task?

   A. `List-Service *Exchange* | Where-Status {-eq "Stopped"}`

   B. `Get-Service *Exchange* | Where-Status {-eq "Stopped"}`

   C. `List-Service *Exchange* | Where-Object {$_.status -eq "Stopped"}`

   D. `Get-Service *Exchange* | Where-Object {$_.status -eq "Stopped"}`

10. When monitoring performance of your Exchange Mailbox server using the Exchange Server Performance Monitor, you see a lot of fluctuation in the values of the LogicalDisk – Avg. Disk sec/Write counter. This counter should typically be less than which value?

    A. 10 milliseconds

    B. 20 milliseconds

    C. 50 milliseconds

    D. 75 milliseconds

11. You're looking at the queues on one of your Hub Transport servers and need to find the one corresponding to a particular Mailbox server. The Mailbox server and Hub Transport server are located in the same Active Directory site. What pieces of information in the main window of the Queue Viewer can help you determine which queue is the correct one? (Choose all that apply.)

   A. The Next Hop Domain value should indicate the fully qualified domain name of the Mailbox server.

   B. The Next Hop Domain value should indicate the Active Directory site name.

   C. Delivery Type should indicate DNSConnectorDelivery.

   D. Status should indicate Suspended.

   E. Delivery Type should indicate MapiDelivery.

   F. Message Count should indicate that no messages are in the queue.

12. By default, what size will each message tracking log be limited to in Exchange Server 2007?

   A. 5MB

   B. 1MB

   C. 10MB

   D. 20MB

13. To view the sizes of all mailboxes in your Exchange organization, what three Exchange Management Shell cmdlets must you use? (Choose three correct answers.)

   A. Show-Information

   B. Get-MailboxStatistics

   C. Get-MailboxInformation

   D. Get-Mailbox

   E. Show-MailboxStatistics

   F. Select-Object

   G. List-Mailbox

14. What EventID in the message tracking log indicates that a message was originally sent to an SMTP address that belongs to a distribution group?

   A. Explode

   B. Receive

   C. Committed

   D. Expand

15. What EventID in the message tracking log indicates that a message was committed to the database on the destination Mailbox server?

   A. Deliver

   B. Receive

   C. Committed

   D. Written

16. When looking at the status of a queue for messages being delivered to a Mailbox server, which one of the following status messages would not be seen?

   A. Retry

   B. Resumed

   C. Suspended

   D. Ready

   E. Active

17. What EventID in the message tracking log indicates that a message was placed in the recipient's mailbox on the database on the destination Mailbox server?

   A. Deliver

   B. Receive

   C. Committed

   D. Written

18. A queue that contains messages that are destined for delivery to a different Hub Transport server in the same Active Directory site will have what delivery type associated with it?

   A. MapiDelivery

   B. SmtpRelayWithinAdSite

   C. SmtpRelaytoRemoteAdSite

   D. SmtpRelaytoHubTransport

   E. SmtpRelaytoTiRg

19. What cmdlet would you need to use to prevent all messages in a selected queue from being attempted for delivery?

   A. Resume-Queue

   B. Freeze-Queue

   C. Hold-Queue

   D. Suspend-Queue

   E. Stop-Queue

20. If messages are placed into a specific queue, they are not attempted for delivery. These messages are available for administrative review and can be released manually by an administrator. Which of the listed queues is this?

A. Mailbox delivery queue

B. Remote delivery queue

C. Submission queue

D. Unreachable queue

E. Suspect queue

F. Poison message queue

Answers to Review Questions

1. **C.** The Memory – Pages/sec counter displays the rate at which pages are read from or written to disk to resolve hard page faults. The value of this counter should never be more than 1,000.

2. **B.** By using the `Get-Service` cmdlet with no modification, you can view the status of all services installed on the server, including each one's status, short name, and display name.

3. **A, B, C, D.** You'll actually need to use all four cmdlets to create the required report. For example, if you created the report and listed the name, item count, mailbox size, and over/under quota status, your cmdlet might look like this:

   ```
   Get-Mailbox | Get-MailboxStatistics | Select-Object
   DisplayName,TotalItemSize,ItemCount,
   StorageLimitStatus | Export-CSV c:\mailboxes.csv
   ```

4. **C.** You can quickly and easily create a server health report using the Exchange Best Practices Analyzer (ExBPA), which is located in the Toolbox node of the Exchange Management Console.

5. **B.** Only the XML export format will result in the entire ExBPA scan report being saved in a single file. Unfortunately, XML does not lend itself to printing, so if your intent is to save the report and then print it later, you'll want to save each tab of the report using the HTML format. The XML format is intended for exporting the report from one location and later importing it into another location for viewing and action.

6. **B.** Hardware monitoring of your Exchange servers is every bit as important as monitoring services and performance. As it stands, though, it's not something that is included within Exchange Server 2007. Each major hardware vendor has an enterprise-quality monitoring and management application available for its hardware. It's usually best to use the corresponding monitoring application from the vendor that supplied the hardware on which your Exchange servers are running.

7. **A, D.** Typically, you'll find the most useful information about service status changes in the System log. The Application log will also often yield useful information.

8. **B.** The Performance Troubleshooter is focused on only one thing: RPC-related issues within the Exchange organization.

9. **D.** By using the `Get-Service *Exchange* | Where-Object {$_.status -eq "Stopped"}` cmdlet, you can quickly get a listing of all the Exchange-related services that are not currently running. From this list, you can determine which ones should and should not be in a stopped state.

10. **A.** The LogicalDisk – Avg. Disk sec/Write counter displays the average time, in seconds, of a data write action to the disk. Typically, the average value of this counter should be less than 10 milliseconds. The maximum value of this counter should never exceed 50 milliseconds.

11. A, E. Since this is delivery from a Hub Transport server to a Mailbox server in the same Active Directory domain, you can look for two key pieces of information about the queues to determine which one is for delivery to that Mailbox server. The Next Hop Domain value should indicate the fully qualified domain name of the Mailbox server, and the Delivery Type value should indicate MapiDelivery.

12. C. The default size of the message tracking logs in Exchange Server 2007 is 10MB. You can change that value by using the `Set-TransportServer servername -MessageTrackingLogMaxFileSize` cmdlet.

13. B, D, F. To get the size information on each mailbox in your Exchange organization, you need to use the `Get-Mailbox` cmdlet to pipe input to the `Get-MailboxStatistics` cmdlet. The output of the `Get-Mailbox` cmdlet should then be piped to the `Select-Object` cmdlet to display the specific information in which you're interested, such as `TotalSize`, `DisplayName`, or `LastLogonTime`.

14. D. The EventID of Expand indicates that the membership of a distribution was expanded to determine the final recipients of the message.

15. B. The Receive status in the message tracking log indicates that the message was received and committed to the database.

16. B. The status of a queue can be only one of the following four values: Active, Suspended, Ready, Retry.

17. A. The Delivery status in the message tracking log indicates that the message was delivered to the recipient's mailbox.

18. B. A queue that contains messages that are being routed to a different Hub Transport server in the same Active Directory site will have a delivery type of SmtpRelayWithinAdSite. If the queue contained messages for delivery to a Hub Transport server in a different Active Directory site, it would have a delivery type of SmtpRelaytoRemoteAdSite. The delivery type of SmtpRelaytoTiRg is used when the queue contains messages queued for delivery to an Exchange Server 2003 routing group.

19. D. You would need to use the `Suspend-Queue` cmdlet. As an example, to suspend a queue with a next hop domain of wiley.com that is in a retry status, you would use the following cmdlet: `Suspend-Queue -Filter {NextHopDomain -eq "wiley.com" -and Status -eq "retry"}`.

20. F. The poison message queue holds messages that have been determined to be potentially harmful to the Exchange organization after a server failure has occurred, such as messages that contain fatal errors. When no messages meeting this condition are found, this queue does not exist on the Hub Transport server, although it is in a ready state should it be needed. There is no attempt to deliver messages placed into the poison message queue, and their status is set to Suspended, allowing the messages to be examined and deleted or released by the administrator after further review. The next hop for messages located in the poison message queue that have been released is the submission queue.

Chapter 10

Disaster Recovery Operations for Exchange Server

MICROSOFT EXAM OBJECTIVE COVERED IN THIS CHAPTER:

✓ **Configuring Disaster Recovery**

- Recover server roles.
- Recover messaging data.
- Configure backups.

For many organizations, messaging services are critical to the operation of the business. The failure of such a business-critical service could result in the loss of productivity and earnings. Even if a small part of the Exchange organization is not available, it could significantly impact your company. Once the Exchange Server 2007 infrastructure is installed and configured, the disaster recovery plan designed along with the infrastructure should be validated. A proper basic disaster recovery plan should cover how to back up the data, servers, and configuration and how to restore these items.

Once that foundation is in place, the plan can be broadened to encompass what to do if there is a loss of an entire data center or the offices from which users connect. This planning should be well documented and practiced so that, in the event of a disaster, you will be able to make the best decisions in a limited time frame. To be able to create and execute a disaster recovery plan, you need to understand and practice backup and recovery. Although the 70-236 exam does not include any design aspects, it is still essential to understand the concepts around creating a design in order to execute the individual tasks.

In this chapter, we will examine the Windows Server backup application. The main topics of this chapter are as follows:

- Understanding disaster recovery, how it applies to Exchange Server 2007, and how Exchange Server 2007 fits into an overall company disaster recovery plan

- Configuring backups, including how to create, modify, perform, and monitor backup jobs

- Recovering messaging data, including how to recover messages and mailboxes, reconnect mailboxes, recover mailbox and messaging queue Extensible Storage Engine (ESE) databases, and repair a damaged database

- Backing up and recovering different server roles, including how to recover a Client Access server (CAS), a Hub Transport server, and an Edge Transport server

What Is Disaster Recovery?

Disaster recovery means different things to different people, and it is applied differently at different companies, depending on experience and company requirements. For the purpose of the Exchange Server 2007 certification exams, *disaster recovery* means having enough data to recover from the loss of any Exchange server data or Exchange server. This can be limited to the loss of a single email message or it can encompass the loss of an entire data center. To create a disaster recovery plan properly, you need to plan for any possible disaster situation and protect against that eventuality.

You need to keep backups for a number of reasons, such as data loss, hardware failure, site loss, and compliance. Data seems to have a way of becoming corrupted, lost, or needed after it has been deleted. Although you may never experience one of these situations, it is best to be prepared for them just in case.

To plan properly for a disaster in Exchange Server 2007, you need to consider the following:

- You should understand the kinds of disasters from which you might need to recover, including the loss of a single mail item, a mailbox, a server, a data center, or your only office location.

- You should understand how Exchange relies on Active Directory and whether there is a plan in place to protect Active Directory.

- You should understand how Exchange relies on Active Directory's directory service for both server configuration and user setting and configuration data.

- You should know how to establish a service-level agreement (SLA). If you are proposing no more than five hours of downtime a year, you will plan differently than if you were offering guaranteed uptime only during business hours.

- You should understand the ESE database technology that Exchange uses to store data. The ESE's database is a transaction-based database that writes data to a log file before the data is committed to the database.

- You should know what backup technology is available to your organization and how your choices will affect your backup implementations. Different companies have different budgets, requirements, and needs for backup that will affect what you use to back up your system.

- You should understand the backup technologies in Exchange and how they can solve some of your backup needs.

Basically, you need to have backups of your Exchange server's configuration, the Exchange databases, and Active Directory recipient information. You then need to have a plan to rebuild your servers and recover your Exchange databases. This chapter will cover how to use Exchange Server 2007, Windows backup technologies, and the Exchange Management Shell to back up everything you need. It will also cover how to restore those backups.

Avoiding Disasters and Reacting to Them

The best way of dealing with something that you fear, or with which you might be uncomfortable, is to prepare adequately with the right knowledge and tools. Fear tends to subside as knowledge and experience grow. This chapter will empower you to understand the tools and features available in Exchange Server 2007 to deal with disasters. Exchange Server 2007 offers a number of technologies that help you avoid data obstacles or easily overcome them quickly.

Avoiding Data Loss

The first step to avoiding data loss is to design your Exchange server hardware and disk systems to be as redundant as possible. You have many different choices and methods for accomplishing a good redundancy plan. The absolute best hardware configuration varies with budget and usage but also changes over time as new technology becomes available. Also, choosing the latest technology can often result in a steep learning curve, causing undue frustration and the possibility of data loss while you learn how to use it. The following are some recommendations for designing highly redundant hardware solutions:

- Purchase the highest-quality hardware your budget will allow and as much redundancy as you can afford. This includes hardware with more than one processor, separate memory buses, dual network connections, and hardware that has the ability to auto-correct or to run even with hardware errors.

- Consider the support agreement that comes with the hardware. Find out how soon parts can be shipped or whether parts can be stored on-site to fix a problem. Find out within how many hours (4, 8, 24, 38, 72, or more) a support issue will be fixed after it is reported.

- Know how quickly the hardware can be replaced. With blade server technology and servers booting and running entirely from a SAN, you could install your Exchange server on blade hardware and have a hot-swappable spare blade available that, in the event of a hardware failure, automatically replaces the entire server minus the disk subsystem.

- Make sure your operating system is always stored on redundant disks and that it has the proper I/O performance.

- Make sure your database and transaction logs are on a redundant disk solution. This might be a RAID solution where the loss of a disk does not mean the loss of all your data. It could also mean that your data is stored on a SAN or NAS solution where the entire disk subsystem replicates to another site. However you design it, there should always be redundancy in your Exchange Server 2007 disk subsystem.

- Even the best hardware can fail. It is important to monitor your hardware for any signs of failure. You should react quickly to any sign that there might be a failure on the horizon.

Exchange Server 2007 has a number of new and improved availability technologies that can help you almost completely avoid the need to recover your data in the event of a hardware failure or data loss situation. Local continuous replication (LCR), cluster continuous replication (CCR), and standby continuous replication (SCR) allow you to have a near-real-time replica of your Exchange database on separate hardware. For more information about LCR and CCR, see Chapter 8, "Configuring Highly Available Exchange Server Solutions."

Reacting to Disasters

How you react to a disaster can affect the amount of downtime and the loss of productivity your organization could experience. Reacting effectively and efficiently is possible when you know and practice your disaster recovery procedure. Exchange Server 2007 offers a number of new and improved tools to help you react to a disaster quickly and efficiently:

- *Dial-tone recovery*: This recovery method was an option in previous versions of Exchange and continues to be an excellent tool for recovery. Dial-tone recovery can be likened to restoring the "dial tone" of your email service—the ability to send and receive email without historical email data. This allows quick recovery from a lost Exchange database by mounting an empty database. This will allow the users to be able to send and receive email. It will further allow users to get back up and running while you work to recover and/or restore the Exchange database. After the data is recovered or restored, it can be migrated back into the users' mailboxes in the background.

- *Database portability*: Databases can be moved to or mounted on any Exchange Server 2007 server in an organization. If one Mailbox server fails but you still have access to your Exchange databases, you could quickly mount the databases on a new server and run the `Move-Mailbox -ConfigurationOnly` Exchange Management Shell command to point your users to the new location.

- *Deleted item retention*: When a user deletes an item, it appears deleted to the user. However, a copy of the deleted item is kept in the mailbox database for a specified period of time, which allows the item to be recovered quickly and easily if it was deleted unintentionally.

- *Deleted mailbox retention*: When a mailbox is deleted, it appears deleted to the user. However, the mailbox is kept in the mailbox database in a disconnected state for a specified period of time, which allows the mailbox to be recovered if it was deleted unintentionally.

- `Setup.com /Mode:RecoverServer`: Almost all the configuration information for your Exchange Server 2007 servers is stored in Active Directory. In the event of a server loss, you can quickly reinstall Exchange on a server with the same settings by running `Setup.com /Mode:RecoverServer` and applying all the configuration information stored in Active Directory to the new server. The equivalent command for recovering a clustered mailbox server is `Setup.com /RecoverCMS`.

Setup.com /Mode:RecoverServer will not work on an Edge Transport server because the Edge Transport server is not attached to Active Directory. It will also not recover any of the modifications made to IIS on a Client Access server. In addition, any local configuration settings applied to any server role in areas such as the Registry or XML configuration files will not be recovered.

- *Database technology*: The Exchange database is designed to alert you to problems and recover from failure. For example, before a disk fails, you will receive -1018 error messages that indicate possible errors in the disk subsystem. After a database has failed, you can use Exchange-provided tools, such as the Disaster Recovery Analyzer, ISInteg, and ESEUtil, that can repair most errors in the database. If you need to recover from a point-in-time backup, you can apply all the transaction logs since that backup and recover almost to the point of failure.

Understanding these tools and knowing which one is best for any given situation will allow you to react quickly, correctly, and efficiently in the event that a disaster does happen. That being said, sometimes you might not have enough experience to judge properly what needs to be done. To assist, numerous consulting companies specialize in dealing with disasters. I mention this only to give you all the tools you need to deal most effectively with a disaster.

Configuring Backups

By far the most important information to back up is your Exchange database. The Exchange database holds all of the email, calendaring, contact, and task data associated with the users' mailboxes stored in that database. The importance of the database makes it the focus of most disaster recovery plans. Exchange Server 2007 offers two different backup technologies to back up your Exchange database:

- *Legacy streaming backups*: A legacy streaming backup runs while the database is mounted and in use by making a copy of the EDB file. A streaming backup reads every page of the Exchange database and checks the database for consistency in the process. Streaming backups are being de-emphasized in Exchange going forward, partly because it takes a long time to stream the database to a backup. They are considered a legacy technology with a mature feature set. Legacy streaming backups are the only supported Exchange-aware backup type offered by Windows Server Backup on Windows Server 2003; however, native support is unavailable in Windows Server 2008.

- *Volume Shadow Copy Service (VSS)*: VSS was introduced in Exchange 2003, and a great deal of development time has been invested and improvements have been implemented with Exchange Server 2007. The VSS backup engine pauses all write operations to the Exchange database and log files, prepares the backup for the snapshot, and then takes a snapshot of the database. It takes only a few seconds to take a snapshot, and then the database resumes normal operations. Windows Server Backup does not support Exchange-aware VSS backups. Because of this lack of support, native Windows Server VSS backups are not the recommended method to back up Exchange Server 2007.

In addition to choosing a backup technology and software product, you need to consider a number of variables when designing your backup process. A proper backup plan needs to provide for backing up all needed information and data without having much noticeable impact on your users. When needed, those backups are then used to return your systems to full working order or to get data that is not available online. When creating your backup plan, be sure to do the following:

- Consider the duration of time that your backups will take to complete and the time allocated to restore them. You should have an established expectation with your company of how long a database can be down—20 minutes, 2 hours, 2 days, or something else. Once you know that, you should then determine how much data you could restore in that given time. That size should be your maximum database size.

- Consider the required resources needed for a backup and what you will need to accomplish with those resources. Exchange runs an online maintenance process by default at night that checks the database for errors and fragments. You should be aware of when this process runs and how it might compete with your backups if they happen to run at the same time, because this can overburden a server. A backup can be a very CPU- and I/O-intensive operation, so it is not recommended that you run it during times of user load on the server. Watch the system CPU, I/O load, and network bandwidth to determine the best window of time to perform your Exchange backups.

- Define recovery point objectives. Recovery point objectives should cover the expected and minimum data losses that your company can tolerate, including how much data you must recover and how much you are expected to recover. If the loss of more than one day's worth of data is not acceptable, you will need a different backup scheme than if the loss of no more than one hour of data is acceptable.

- Consider the backup hardware you have and how it helps you support the recovery requirements. Older, slower tape technology might limit what you can offer in the form of recovery point objectives. Newer disk- or optical-based backup technology might allow faster and more regular backup and restore operations. LCR might enable faster recovery times by offering a near-real-time replica of your database.

- Consider the backup applications you are using. Different software can support different backup types and media, which might allow for faster or more efficient backups and restores.

- You should have a copy of your data off-site in some format; you need to determine what the mandated business requirements are and do your best to satisfy those needs. In addition to business requirements, you need to determine whether any government or regulatory agency policy might require a specific data retention policy for your company. With this information in mind, you then need to create a media rotation policy. A typical media rotation schedule will be based on tape devices and will require a number of tapes. Table 10.1 shows an example of a tape rotation schedule for a company that makes a log file backup every day of the week and then a full backup every week, month, and year. The full backups are rotated as needed. This is only an example; the needs of your organization might be very different.

TABLE 10.1   Tape Rotation Schedule

Tape Name	Tape Usage
Weekly Even	This tape is used every day except Friday of an even week to back up the log files.
Weekly Odd	This tape is used every day except Friday of an odd week to back up the log files.
Friday 1–5	These tapes are Friday full-backup tapes numbered 1 through 5 to cover every week of a month.
Monthly 1–12	These tapes are monthly month-end tapes numbered 1 through 12, so you will have one for each month of the year.
Yearly 1–7	These tapes are yearly year-end tapes numbered 1 through 7, so you will have one for the end of each year for seven years.

After considering the previous points, you then need to determine the best backup type to use to back up your Exchange databases. Each backup type has inherent advantages and disadvantages that you should consider. Exchange Server 2007 supports four backup types that have different backup and recovery times, require different amounts of backup space, and allow you to customize your backups to fit your needs better:

- *Full backup*: A full backup is a complete backup that captures all the data in a given database. This includes the EDB file and all necessary log files. Log files older than the checkpoint at the time of the backup are deleted after the backup completes. Perform a full backup on a daily basis to ensure that log files do not build up and consume all the space in the log file drive. The full backup is the simplest backup with which to work because it requires only a single backup set for both backup and restore. It takes the longest to complete because it captures all the data.

The Windows Server Backup application terms a full backup as a *normal* backup.

- *Copy backup*: A copy backup is the same as a full backup except that log files are not deleted at the completion of the backup. You can perform a copy backup to capture a specific point in time. Copy backups should be used before performing maintenance on the database.

- *Incremental backup*: An incremental backup is a change-only backup that archives the transaction log files only since the last full or incremental backup. Log files older than the checkpoint are deleted after the backup is complete. You cannot perform an incremental backup when circular logging is enabled because circular logging limits and reuses log files. An incremental backup can be used to support a short data loss window by allowing you to perform backups on an hourly or more frequent basis, and these backups do not take very long to complete or have major user impact. The downside is that you need to have the last full backup and all the incremental backups since that full backup to restore the database fully.

- *Differential backup*: A differential backup is a change-only backup that archives only the transaction log files since the last full or incremental backup. The difference between an incremental and a differential backup is that the differential backup does not delete the log files after it completes a backup. Incremental and differential backups are the smallest backup files and take the shortest time to complete.

You now know what technologies are available for backup, what types of backups are available, the performance impacts, and your backup and restore needs. Now that you know this, you can map out your backup and recovery plan and then move on to configuring your backup jobs.

Ideally, your backups should be run in a given window of time at night when your servers have the fewest users connected. You should capture all your Exchange databases and any server data you might need to restore your servers.

Generally, streaming backup solutions are only suitable for small to medium configurations. VSS-based snapshot backups are usually leveraged for larger implementations because it is possible to have backup windows that are measured in minutes instead of hours. Larger organizations lean toward VSS-based backups because of the need and resulting cost of the VSS-enabled third-party software and hardware along with the added complexity of management. Snapshot backup sizes are limited only by Exchange database, backup hardware, and software constraints. Even with snapshot backups, there still may be a need to make full backups or to back up the snapshots to tape in order to store the data off-site.

Creating, Modifying, and Performing Backup Jobs

At the core of any Exchange backup plan is backing up the mailbox database. You can rebuild any server role if it comes down to it, but you cannot rebuild your mailbox data without a proper mailbox.

The Windows Server 2003 backup utility only provides legacy streaming backup capabilities. With the addition of third-party backup software, however, you can use the Windows built-in VSS engine and perform the more time-efficient VSS snapshot backup.

 Microsoft generally does not provide exam questions that reference third-party software; therefore, for this exam, backup questions that relate to an application will be based on Windows Server Backup. All the backup technologies and types discussed here are Microsoft supported, so you should expect to see questions about VSS and legacy streaming backups.

To use Windows Server Backup on Windows Server 2003 to back up an Exchange server, you need to install the Exchange Management Console on the server on which you are going to run backups. Installing the Exchange Management Console installs the Windows Server Backup APIs, which allows Windows Server to back up an Exchange database.

The Windows Server 2008 Server Backup utility does not include the ability to perform Exchange-aware backups. Microsoft is releasing a VSS-based plug-in for Windows Server Backup. You can read more information about this plug-in on the Exchange Team blog at http://msexchangeteam.com/archive/2008/06/18/449031.aspx.

Exercise 10.1 outlines the basic steps to create, modify, and schedule a backup job using Windows Server Backup on a Windows Server 2003 computer.

EXERCISE 10.1

Backing Up the Exchange Server Mailbox Database with Windows Server Backup on Windows Server 2003

Follow these steps to back up the mailbox database:

1. Open Windows Server Backup in Advanced mode. (The Wizard mode does not allow you to select an Exchange database.)

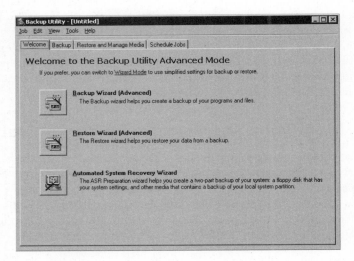

2. Select the Backup tab, expand Microsoft Exchange Server, and then expand the Exchange database you want to back up. Select an entire storage group, or expand a storage group and select a database within the storage group.

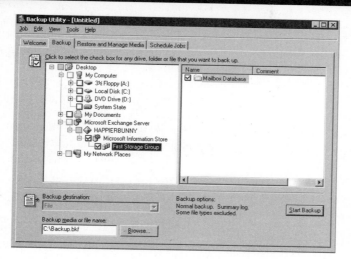

3. Once you have selected what you want to back up, choose the type of media and then the media destination. In the Backup Destination drop-down box, choose the media type to which you want to back up. Your options are generally Tape or Disk. In the Backup Media or File Name box, select the tape or file to which you want to back up.

4. After you have selected what to back up and where to back it up, you can save the job and schedule or launch it later. Alternatively, you can click Start Backup to start the backup job, or you can schedule it to run right now.

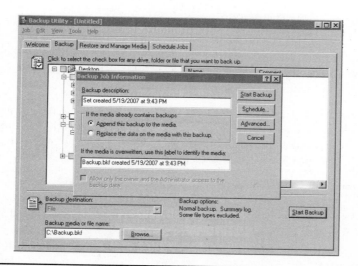

Monitoring and Validating Backup Jobs

You should never consider a backup valid unless you have tested it and verified that there is restorable data in it. It is good practice to schedule time to restore a random backup regularly, at least once a month. In the meantime, you can perform a number of tasks to feel more confident that your backups are running properly.

The Windows Server Backup utility writes backup confirmations and errors to a backup log file and to the Windows Server Event log. You should check both the backup log file and the server event logs on a daily basis. Almost every backup application should have some sort of logging, regardless of whether you are using Windows Server Backup or a third-party application; you should still expect to see a backup log file in addition to the event log entries. When monitoring and validating your backup job, you should do the following:

- Make sure there are no error messages in the log indicating that there was an error in the backup process. Any error messages should give you enough information to begin to determine what went wrong.

- Make sure the backup that completed was the backup you had configured to run. If you back up the wrong data, it is as useless as though you had not run a backup at all.

- Verify that the size of the backup is close to the size of the data you are backing up.

 Real World Scenario

Test Your Backups

An Exchange Expert shares his story:

"I worked with a school district that would faithfully back up all its student records. The IT staff scheduled a full backup every night, and the backup operator would take a copy home with her at night and rotate the copy at home into the backup schedule. There were three backup sets in rotation.

"Then one day, one of the drives in the server died and we needed to recover from backup. Up until that failure, the backups had never been tested. When we went to restore the backups, it became apparent that over the course of time the backup media had become worn out. Therefore, the backups were useless; there was nothing to restore.

"We had to send the backup media away to a data recovery company that was able to extract data in a clean room with special tools. Thankfully, they were successful and returned the data to us. The recovery process took three days and cost about $3,000. This story underscores how important it is to monitor that your backups are complete and valid. It is also shows how important it is to test the restore process to ensure that the backups contain restorable data. Had we ever tested a restore, we would have realized the media was damaged and would have been able to replace it with fresh media, and we could have avoided learning this costly lesson."

The Exchange backup engine writes a number of events to the Application event log. These indicate when a backup started, when it completed, the log files that successfully purged, the backup type used, and more. Look for events from source ESE and ESE backup. You need to research ESE and ESE backup errors or warning events to determine whether a problem has occurred. If a problem has occurred, then you need to fix it.

Repairing a Damaged Exchange Database

Repairing an Exchange database can be a complex, frustrating, and time-consuming process. The Exchange database repair process begins by determining the problem with the database. You can usually find an error message in the Application event log that will be generated when you try to mount the database. Armed with the error message, you can then follow one of two paths. You can search the Microsoft support site and the Internet to find more information about the problem, or you can contact someone who is experienced in disaster recovery. At the time of this writing, a call to Microsoft Customer Support Services (CSS) costs $259. However, this can be a very small price to pay to have a trained Microsoft professional walk you through the database repair process.

After determining which path to take, whether you are contacting Microsoft or going it alone, your next step is to start the database repair process. After the database has been repaired, you then get to see whether the repair was successful by attempting to mount the database. At this point, you are presented with either success or another error in the Application event log, and you get to continue the repair process. Knowing which commands and utilities to run and how long they will take to run is a key to having a successful database repair.

Although it is possible to repair a database, when a recent backup is available it is sometimes preferred over the repair process. This is because when you recover from a backup, you get a known good database at the end of the recovery process. When you repair a database, you are unsure what, if any, data was lost, and there is a chance that other errors will crop up later.

Understanding the Exchange Database Structure

The Exchange database is referred to as the ESE database, and it stores all the user data and almost all the configuration data used by Exchange Server 2007. There are databases on the Edge Transport server, the Hub Transport server, and the Mailbox server.

At one time the ESE database, also known as the Joint Engine Technology (JET) database, was a single B-tree database product inside Microsoft. It then diverged into a number of different databases as different product groups wanted to use the JET database. These product groups had different needs and requirements and wanted to do different things with the JET code. The JET database we use now was once called JET Blue and JET Red. Simplistically put, Blue was for Exchange and Red was for Microsoft Access. When Active Directory came about, the Windows Server Active Directory team borrowed some resources from the Exchange team, who had already implemented an x.400 directory structure in Exchange. Windows NT Server had already used the JET database for a number of features, such as DHCP and WINS, and the Exchange team was very comfortable with the JET database, so it was decided that JET would be the database for Active Directory.

Figure 10.1 illustrates the files that make up the Exchange database.

FIGURE 10.1 The Exchange database

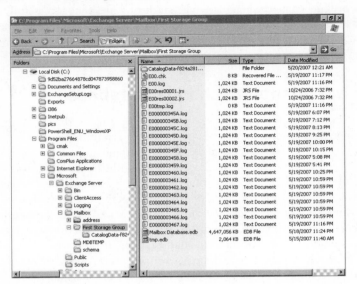

The ESE Exchange databases on the Edge Transport, Hub Transport, and Mailbox servers consist of the same database with a few minor configuration differences. Regardless of the server roles, databases consist of a number of files. The main files are as follows:

- *The EDB file* (.edb): The EDB file is *the* file where all the data is stored. It has a size limit of 16TB based on the ESE database design, but the actual database size limit that you enforce should be much smaller. This allows time for backups and restores to complete without disrupting business and within time limits specified in your SLAs.

- *The temporary database* (Tmp.edb): The temporary database is used to process transactions as they are being committed to the EDB database file.

- *The checkpoint file* (Exx.chk): The E00.chk file maintains the checkpoint for the storage group. This checkpoint file keeps track of the last-committed transaction log file. If you are ever forced to perform a recovery, this file contains the point at which the replaying of transaction logs must start. The 00 after the E is the designation for the storage group.

- *Transaction log files*: All changes made to the Exchange database are first committed to memory and then to transaction log files. Once the server has time, the log files are applied to the EDB file. The total number of transaction log files created depends on the transaction load on the server. There are three types of transaction logs:

  - *Working log file* (Exx.log): This is the current transaction log being written for the storage group. Once the log file reaches 1MB in size, it is renamed and a new E00.log file is created. The 00 after the E is the designation for the storage group.

  - *Transaction log* (Exxhhhhhhhh.log): These are the main transaction logs. They are numbered sequentially starting with E0000000001. Transaction log files are created and named based on an E, followed by a two-character sequence, followed by a hexadecimal number from 1 to 0x7FFFFFFF, allowing for a total of 2,147,483,647 log files in the log stream. Transaction files are 1MB in size with Exchange Server 2007 to support log shipping technology in LCR and CCR better. (Previous versions used 5MB log files.) The 00 after the E is the designation for the storage group.

- *Reserved log files (Exxres00001.jrs* and *Exres00002.jrs)*: These are the reserved log files. In the event that the disk runs out of space, then the last transactions are written to these log files while the database dismounts. The 00 after the E is the designation for the storage group.

Using the Recovery Tools

Exchange Server 2007 includes two main command-line tools and two GUI wrappers for those tools to repair and work with your Exchange databases. The two tools, ESEUtil and Isintag, are the main tools for working with the Exchange database.

ESEUtil   The Exchange Server Database Utility (ESEUtil.exe) is a command-line tool that you can use to repair, view, and modify an Exchange database at the page level. ESEUtil is located in the Bin directory under your Exchange installation. In the past, ESEUtil could be used to work only with mailbox and public folder databases. To perform most of the operations that it performs, ESEUtil will create a new temporary database and write all the fixed information to that new database. It is recommended that you have 1.2 times as much free space as there is data in your Exchange database before performing ESEUtil operations. You can determine the size of your database by looking for event IDs 1221 and 1224 in your event log and subtracting the whitespace reported from the total file size. For example, if your database is 45GB and the 1221 event for the database says that you have 12GB of whitespace in the database, then your database is 33GB and you should be sure that you have approximately 40GB of free space to perform ESEUtil operations on the Exchange database.

You can load ESEUtil with a number of switches; you can see them by running eseutil /? from a command prompt as shown in Figure 10.2. The following is a brief explanation of the switches:

- /D Defragmentation: Defragments the database offline. This mode reduces the size on the disk of the EDB file by discarding the whitespace in the database and then rebuilding the indexes. It is not recommended that you run defragmentation as a regular maintenance operation. An online defrag is run every night, and the only difference between the online and offline defrag is that the offline defrag recovers whitespace. To recover whitespace in a database, it is better to create a new database and then move users to it.

- /P Repair: Repairs a corrupt offline database by discarding any pages that cannot be fixed. In repair mode, the ESEUtil tool fixes individual tables but does not maintain the relationships between tables. Use the ISInteg tool to check and fix links between tables in the repaired database.

- /R Recovery: Replays transaction log files to restore a database to internal consistency.

- **/G Integrity:** Verifies the page-level and ESE-level logical integrity of the database. Does not verify the integrity at the application level. You can verify application-level logical integrity with the ISInteg tool.

- **/M File Dump:** Displays headers of database files, transaction log files, and checkpoint files. Also displays database page header information and database space allocation and metadata.

- **/K Checksum:** Verifies checksums on all pages in the database, log files, and checkpoint files.

- **/C Restore:** Allows you to run hard recovery on a database restored from a streaming backup. It also allows you to view some of the Restore.env file.

- **/Y Copy File:** Copies large files much faster on the same volume than the normal Windows copy routine. It copies larger blocks at a time to accomplish the greater speed. You can use this switch to copy more than just Exchange files.

FIGURE 10.2   Running ESEUtil.exe

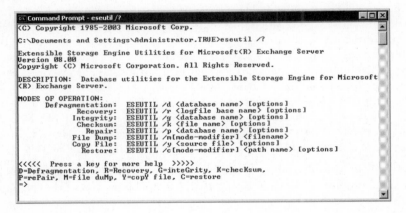

ISInteg   The Information Store Integrity Checker (ISInteg.exe) finds and eliminates errors from the Exchange database at the application level. The ISInteg tool works at the logical schema level, and it can recover data that ESEUtil cannot. This is because data that is valid for the ESEUtil tool at the physical schema level can be invalid at the logical schema level. ISInteg is most often used after running the ESEUtil repair operation. The ISInteg tool, as shown in Figure 10.3, repairs information, relationships, and index tables between pages in the database at the application level.

The two GUI utilities—Exchange Database Recovery Management and Exchange Database Troubleshooting Assistant—are tools in their own rights. They are based on the Exchange Best Practice Analyzer (ExBPA) engine, which has grown into the Exchange Analyzer family of tools that troubleshoot mail flow, performance, databases, and more. The two database tools in the toolbox analyze the current state of the server by reading Event Log files, database headers, user-added information, and log files. Once a problem has been identified, the tools react to the problem based on best practices established by Microsoft CSS, the Exchange team, and the Exchange communities. On occasion, the tools do not have the prescriptive advice or steps to repair your Exchange database, in which case you are again presented with the option of calling Microsoft CSS or working on the problem yourself.

You can find the Exchange troubleshooting tools in the Exchange Management Console in the Toolbox section, as shown in Figure 10.4.

FIGURE 10.3   The ISInteg utility

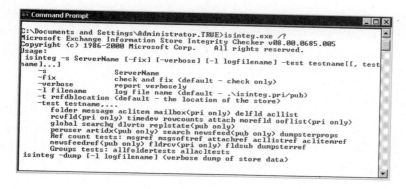

FIGURE 10.4   Starting the Ex Database Troubleshooter

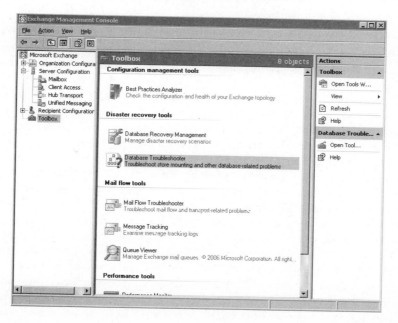

Features are always being added based on CSS-reported issues; this helps relieve the number of calls by automating the most common or most simple restore and repair situations. You should download the latest version of the tools before starting any restore or repair operation. Here's what the two tools do at the time of this writing:

- *Exchange Database Recovery Management*: This tool assists working with recovery storage groups and restoring databases. It can also perform a dial-tone database swap and merge for you, creating a dial-tone database, recovering a database to a recovery storage group (RSG), swapping the two, and finally merging the dial-tone database information into the recovered database.

- *Exchange Database Troubleshooting Assistant*: This tool is the tool you would use to help repair a damaged Exchange database. The troubleshooter can analyze the event logs for you and help determine the error. It can read the database and checkpoint files to determine the current state of the database and how best to deal with the database and transaction log files.

With the large number of possible issues that might cause you to need to repair a database, it is not really possible to cover everything about the Exchange Database Troubleshooting Assistant tool in this chapter of the book. Armed with this tool, Internet searching skills, and the understanding of the ESE database laid out in this section, you should be able to repair most database problems you may encounter.

Recovering Messaging Data

The simplest way to recover deleted messaging data is with Exchange Server 2007's message retention and mailbox retention features. These features basically provide a repository that retains every deleted message and mailbox for a given period of time. At the end of that period, the repository will be emptied—but not until an Exchange-aware backup has completed. You can turn off this feature by checking the Do Not Permanently Delete Items Until This Database Has Been Backed Up setting on the storage group; however, that is not a recommended configuration. By default, message data retention is configured to 14 and mailbox retention is configured to 30 days, with a minimum of 0 days (although not recommended) and a maximum of 24,855 (69 years).

Message and mailbox retention settings can be configured on a per-database basis as well as a per-user basis, the latter of which is useful if, for example, your board of directors has different retention requirements than your sales force. Per-user mailbox retention settings will always override per-database settings, which makes it simple to mix and match settings to serve your end users better. If a message or mailbox is deleted and it is no longer in the retention dumpster, then the recovery process becomes much more involved. Figure 10.5 shows the dialog box where you can set the mailbox and item retention settings.

Recovering messages or mailboxes that are no longer in the retention dumpster involves first restoring the database to an RSG or a test server. Once you have done that, you can export the message or mailbox to a Personal Folder file (PST), or in the case of mounting to an RSG, you can attach the mailbox to a user account. Although performing this process may provide you with needed practice performing restore operations, it can be time-consuming and just plain annoying.

FIGURE 10.5   Dialog box to set mailbox and item retention settings

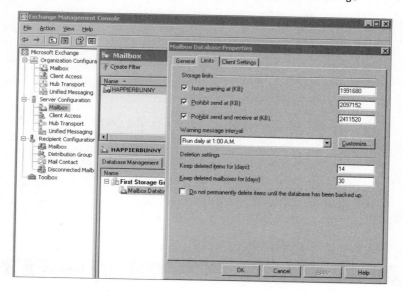

Recovering Messages with Deleted Items Retention

To a user, an email message appears to be gone once it's deleted and emptied from the Deleted Items folder. Similarly, when a user deletes an item while holding down the Shift key, the item instantly appears to be gone from the folder from which it was deleted. Although both actions will place the message in the server retention dumpster, a Shift+Delete will bypass the Deleted Items folder.

By default, Outlook enables deleted item recovery from the Deleted Items folder only. If you press Shift+Delete on a message in your Inbox, the message does not go to the Deleted Items folder; instead, it is deleted directly from the folder. That doesn't mean the item is completely lost; the item is still captured in the Deleted Items dumpster. You can use the DumpsterAlwaysOn Registry value on the client computer to enable recovery of items deleted this way from any mailbox folder. The instructions in Microsoft Knowledge Base article 246153 at http://support.microsoft.com/kb/246153 cover this procedure. In Outlook Web Access (OWA), deleted items recovery is available only in the Deleted Items folder.

Exercises 10.2 and 10.3 illustrate how to recover deleted items from the OWA and Outlook clients.

EXERCISE 10.2

Recovering Deleted Items in Outlook Web Access

Follow these steps to recover a deleted item from within Outlook Web Access:

1. In Outlook Web Access (Premium Edition), click the Options button next to your mailbox name in the top-right corner of the screen.

2. Select Deleted Items in the options pane to the left.

3. You are now presented with a list of deleted items. Select the items you want to recover, and click Recover to Deleted Items folder.

Deleted item recovery in OWA is available only in the Premium Edition.

EXERCISE 10.3

Recovering Deleted Items in Outlook

Follow these steps to recover a deleted item from within Outlook:

1. In Outlook, select Tools ➢ Recover Deleted Items.

2. You are now presented with a list of deleted items. Select the items you want to recover, and click the Recover Selected Items button.

Recovering Deleted Mailboxes with Deleted Mailbox Retention

Exchange Server 2007's deleted mailbox retention feature is meant to safeguard primarily against accidentally deleting a mailbox that is still needed. This can happen when someone is let go from the company and it is determined that some content is still needed from the mailbox afterward. Deleted mailbox retention will hold a mailbox until the mailbox retention period for that mailbox database has lapsed and a full Exchange backup has completed, assuming the Do Not Permanently Delete Items Until This Database Has Been Backed Up setting is enabled. If you need to remove a deleted mailbox immediately, you can purge the mailbox from the database.

Exercises 10.4 and 10.5 illustrate how to recover a deleted mailbox using the Exchange Management Console and the Exchange Management Shell.

EXERCISE 10.4

Recovering a Deleted Mailbox Using the Exchange Management Console

Follow these steps to recover a deleted mailbox using the Exchange Management Console:

1. In the Exchange Management Console tree, expand Recipient Configuration and then click Disconnected Mailboxes.

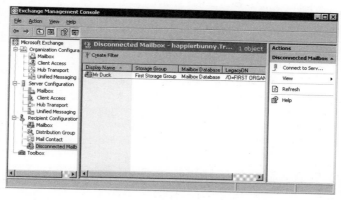

2. In the Actions pane, you will now see all the disconnected mailboxes on the current selected server.

3. Select the mailbox you want to recover and then, in the Actions pane, click Connect Mailbox to start the Connect Mailbox Wizard.

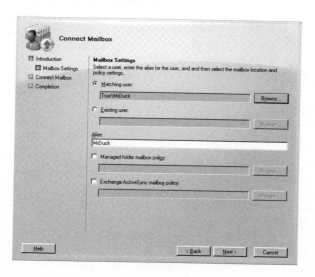

4. Follow the instructions to reconnect the disconnected mailbox in the Connect Mailbox Wizard.

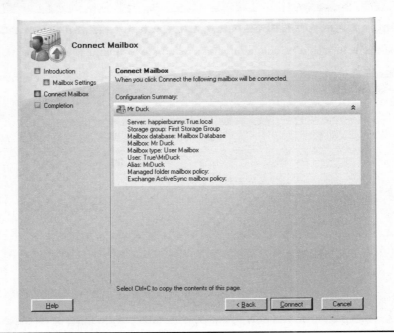

Recovering a Deleted Mailbox Using the Exchange Management Shell

Follow these steps to recover a deleted mailbox using the Exchange Management Shell:

1. To find all the disconnected mailboxes on a given server, you need to run the Get-MailboxStatistics command piped to an SQL where statement that searches for mailboxes that don't have DisconnectDate set to null. To do this, run the following Exchange Management Shell command:

```
Get-MailboxStatistics -Server <server> |
where { $_.DisconnectDate -ne $null } |
  select DisplayName,DisconnectDate
```

EXERCISE 10.5´ *(continued)*

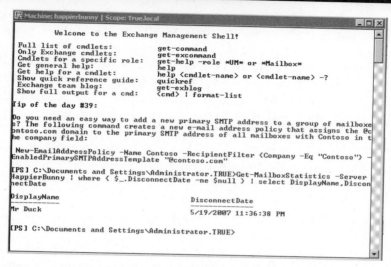

2. To reconnect a disconnected mailbox where the user object is still in Active Directory directory service, run the following Exchange Management Shell command:

```
Connect-Mailbox -Database <Mailbox_Database>
-Identity <Deleted_Mailbox>
```

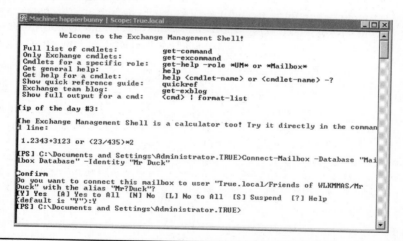

Recovering Mailbox Databases

Recovering an Exchange Server 2007 mailbox database is a somewhat simple process; it is by no means as complicated as attempting to repair an Exchange database. Before you start to restore a database, it helps to understand why you are restoring it. Different restoration needs will require a different restoration process and will be approached differently. Here are some reasons that might motivate you to restore an Exchange database from backup:

- A hardware or site failure to the point that your Exchange server needs to be rebuilt. Once the server is rebuilt, mailbox databases are restored to the server so that it can serve data to users and receive email.

- A minor system failure—including power, hard disk, software, or hardware—that caused the Exchange database to be corrupted. It is usually simpler in this case to restore from backup and replay the log files into the restored database than it is to attempt to repair the database.

- Something was deleted from the mailbox database after the point of time where it might be in the retention dumpsters.

Once you've determined the business requirements for the backup, then you can determine the best approach to restoring the data. You will approach recovering a single mailbox or mail item differently than you would approach restoring 10 servers in a data center that was down for a number of days because of some failure. The following are some situations and some different approaches you might take:

- A request was accepted by your manager to provide an employee that left the company in good standing two months ago with a copy of her contacts. In this case, you would need to find a backup taken before this employee left the company and restore it to an RSG. Once the restore is complete, you could export the mailbox contents to a PST using the `export-mailbox` cmdlet.

- A SAN failure during business hours caused a loss of one of the five databases on the Exchange server and only streaming tape backups are available. In this situation, the first step is to create a dial-tone database so users can resume sending and receiving email. Then recovery from the most recent backup can begin to the RSG. That backup might be in the form of a full backup or in the form of a full backup plus a number of incremental backups. After the restored database is mounted to the RSG and all recovered log files have been played into the database, the Database Recovery Management tool can be used to swap the dial-tone and restored databases and then merge the two databases.

- An Exchange server in your organization has failed, and a restore process will take longer than the business mandates. In this situation, a dial-tone database can be created on another Exchange server in the organization and the `Move-Mailbox -ConfigurationOnly` cmdlet can be used to redirect all your users to the new databases. This process allows users to send and receive email and continue working. In the background, all of the data can be restored into an RSG on the new server. Then the Database Recovery Manager can be used to complete the swap and merge of the recovered and dial-tone databases.

As these examples illustrate, you need to approach each situation a little bit differently. Although the approaches might have been slightly different, a few key concepts and technologies stand out. Understanding these concepts will allow you to create better disaster recovery plans and to deal skillfully with the situations that confront you. The key concepts and technologies that will help you the most with an Exchange database restore revolve around having as little noticeable impact on users as possible. The goal is to create a manual level of functionality quickly for the users in order to give you the time to deal with the overall situation properly. Although most of these have been mentioned briefly already, the technologies and concepts that make this possible are as follows:

- *Recovery storage group*: The RSG is a special storage group on an Exchange server that allows you to mount a database that is not connected to any user accounts or that might have come from another Exchange server in the same organization. Once a database is mounted in an RSG, mailboxes can be linked to users and moved to a production database or extracted and merged into an existing user's mailbox.

> You cannot restore an Exchange database from a different Exchange organization or a different version of Exchange to an RSG. You can, however, mount Exchange Server 2007 databases from the same Exchange Server 2007 organization to an RSG.

- *Dial tone*: The goal in any disaster situation is to recover as much functionality as possible as quickly as possible. The dial tone allows you to recover quickly from the loss of an Exchange database by mounting an empty database that will allow users to send and receive email.

- *The Move-Mailbox -ConfigurationOnly cmdlet*: If you don't have room on the server or the server is missing, you can create a dial-tone database on an alternative server and then point users to that alternate server with the `Move-Mailbox -ConfigurationOnly` cmdlet. In the past, this was a complicated process that required ADSIEdit to resolve. In Exchange Server 2007, it is much simpler.

The basics of a mailbox recovery are to restore mail service using a dial tone as quickly as possible, recover as much previously stored mail data as possible, and make that data available to your users. Before you can start your recovery, you should have the following in place:

- A server in position with enough disk space to hold the restored database and all the log files that you might need to restore.

- A copy of a database and transaction files ready prior to attempting to repair or restore over them, just in case they are needed later to recover.

- The most recent backups that are relevant to the situation.

Now let's look at one of the situations shown earlier, where you lose a single database on a server; here I'll walk you through the steps to restore it. In Exercise 10.6, you will see how to recover an Exchange database.

EXERCISE 10.6

Recovering an Exchange Database

Follow these steps to recover an Exchange database:

1. Mount an empty database as a dial-tone database in place of the failed database. To do this, you must move the old database to a new location. Therefore, to mount an empty database in the Exchange Management Console, in the navigation pane, expand Server Configuration and then select Mailbox in the results pane. Select the server and then the mailbox database that failed. In the Actions pane, select Mount Database. You will be warned that you are creating an empty database, which is OK because you know what you are doing and you indeed want to do that.

2. With a dial-tone database mounted, your users will not be able to send and receive email. They might complain that they cannot see their old email. Before you can start the backup recovery, you need to create the recovery storage group. You can create an RSG either by using the Exchange Management Shell or by using the Database Recovery Management tool in the Toolbox section of the Exchange Management Console. To recover a mailbox database using the Exchange Management Shell, use the following steps:

   a. To create an RSG via the Exchange Management Shell, you need to first create a new recovery storage group by running the following commands:

   ```
   New-StorageGroup -Name <RSG_Name> -Server <Server_Name>
   -LogFilePath <Log_File_Path>
   -SystemFolderPath <Storage_Group_Path>
   ```

   b. In the storage group that you just created, you need to create a database to which you will recover the corrupted database. This database should be named the same as the database you are restoring. Do this by running the following command:

   ```
   New-MailboxDatabase -MailboxDatabaseToRecover
   ```

   c. Once the database is created, you need to allow for database recovery:

   ```
   Set-MailboxDatabase <RSG_Name\Recovery_Database_Name>
   -AllowFileRestore $true
   ```

   d. Next, restore your database using Windows Server Backup.

   e. Once the database has been restored, mount it using the following Exchange Management Shell command:

   ```
   Mount-Database <RSG_Name\Recovery_Database_Name>
   ```

3. To recover a mailbox database using the Database Recovery Management tool, open the Database Recovery Management tool and follow the wizard's steps. The tool is constantly being updated, so it's not useful to document it step-by-step here because the steps might have changed by the time you read this book.

Backing Up and Recovering a Mailbox Server Configuration

Mailbox server recovery is a two-part process. Part one is recovering the server back to a usable state. Part two is recovering the mailbox database. Now that I've covered recovering mailboxes, we can address the mailbox configuration.

Almost all configuration data for the Mailbox server is stored in Active Directory. As long as Active Directory is present and properly backed up, the Mailbox server configuration will also be backed up. To restore the Mailbox server, all that needs to be done is to build a new server with the same name and then run Setup /Mode:RecoverServer or, in the case of a clustered mailbox server, build a cluster and then run Setup /RecoverCMS /CMSName:<*Original Cluster Name*>. Once that is done, the Mailbox server is configured for use. As discussed previously, the mailbox and public folder data will still need to be recovered.

Backing Up and Recovering Server Roles

Disaster recovery planning has become more complicated and involved in Exchange Server 2007 with the introduction of different server roles. It is no longer just about backing up your Exchange database and being able to restore it and its mailboxes. You must now deal with a variety of other concerns:

-   The Client Access server IIS Metabase is no longer synced with Active Directory, so you have to back up the IIS Metabase along with the system state on a Client Access server.

-   Edge Transport server configuration is not stored in Active Directory but can be backed up into XML files with included PowerShell scripts.

-   Transport queue databases are not stored in EML files anymore but are now stored in an ESE database.

-   The unified messaging custom audio files do not even have to be stored on an Exchange server. They just have to be accessible to the Unified Messaging server via a UNC path.

-   Local configuration information on each server role is stored in the Registry and in local files.

Backing Up and Recovering a Client Access Server

The Client Access server has a very basic backup process, unless you've done any customization. Modifications to a Client Access server, such as changes to the `Web.config`, `Microsoft.Exchange.Imap4.Exe.Config`, `Microsoft.Exchange.Pop3.Exe.Config`, or Outlook Web Access files, constitute customizations that will need to be captured in order to be restored.

> More information on creating a script to back up and restore Client Access customizations can be found in the article "How to Back Up and Recover a Client Access Server," available at `http://technet.microsoft.com/en-us/library/bb124359.aspx`.

If the Client Access server was not modified, then all of the essential information needed to recover it is stored in Active Directory. If this the case, the restore procedure is first to build a new server with the same name and OS configuration as the previous server and then to run `Setup /Mode:RecoverServer`. All settings stored in Active Directory will be applied to the server.

If there are modifications applied to your Client Access server, you should be aware of what they are and what kind of backup will be required for each modification. The following list includes some of the modifications on the Client Access server that will need to be backed up:

- *IIS settings*: The IIS Metabase stores configuration data for all the websites and web services on the Client Access server. Changes made to the IIS Metabase are not synchronized with Active Directory; they are stored locally only on the CAS sever where the changes were made. To back up the IIS Metabase, you should perform a system state backup of the Exchange server.

- *web.config*: The web.config file holds settings for the websites and web services on the Client Access server. If these are modified, you need to document the modifications so they can be reapplied to a server, or you should back them up with a file-level backup application.

- *Web pages*: For any web pages (for example, ASP or HTML files) that were modified, you need to document the modifications so they can be reapplied to a server, or you should back them up with a file-level backup application.

> Installing an Exchange service pack or rollup hotfix might change the web pages, requiring that you reapply your web page modifications. If you have modified web pages, you should apply them to a test machine before applying them in production to see what is modified and how it affects any customizations you might have made.

- *POP3 and IMAP4 settings*: You can modify POP3 and IMAP4 configurations by modifying settings in XML files. You need to document these XML file modifications so they can be reapplied to a server, or you should back them up with a file-level backup application.

- *Windows Registry settings*: You can set some custom Registry settings on a Client Access server. You need to document these settings so they can be reapplied to a server, or you should back them up with a system state backup.

If your Client Access server has been modified, you can recover it as shown earlier by running `Setup /Mode:RecoverServer`. Once you've done that, you will need to reapply all the modifications. How you reapply those will depend on how you backed up the modifications.

Included in the Exchange Server 2007 online help and in the application help files is an example script that you can use to back up a Client Access server easily, as well as all CAS custom modifications. The script functions much like the Edge Transport server export and import scripts. It does not make sense to include the Client Access server script here because, with the release of Service Pack 1, the backup methods of a Client Access server will change. The help file will have the most up-to-date example of the script because the Exchange Server 2007 help files are updated on a regular basis. You should look at the example script to help plan your Client Access server disaster recovery.

Backing Up and Recovering a Hub Transport server

The Hub Transport server is the easiest role to recover because almost all of the configuration settings for the Hub Transport server are stored in Active Directory. As long as your Active Directory is present and backed up, then your Hub Transport server is also backed up. To restore your Hub Transport server, all you have to do is build a new server with the same name and then run `Setup /Mode:RecoverServer`. Once you've done that, your Hub Transport server is set up and ready to go again.

A few things are not captured and restored in a recovery scenario, but for the most part they are not key to a Hub Transport server's functioning. These items and how they might impact the Hub Transport server are as follows:

- *The message queue database*: Data in the message queue database is transient information that exists in the database only while a message is in transport on that server or while messages are in a retry queue. A salvaged queue database can be mounted on any Hub Transport server in the organization, or messages can be extracted from the database via the Exchange Management Shell by using the command `Export-Message`. Keep in mind that the data you might recover could be minimal. You can find the message queue database in the `\Exchange server\TransportRoles\data\Queue` folder.

- *Windows Registry settings*: You could set custom Registry settings on a Hub Transport server. You need to document these settings so they can be reapplied to a server, or you can back them up so they can be reapplied.

- *The message tracking logs*: Each Hub Transport server has message tracking logs that hold a record of all the actions taken for every message that the server touched. The message tracking logs can be useful for performing diagnostic and forensic operations in an Exchange organization. If this data is valuable, then you should back it up on a regular basis with a file-level backup utility. You can find the message tracking logs in the \Exchange Server\TransportRoles\Logs folder.

Backing Up and Recovering an Edge Transport server

Unlike all the other Exchange Server 2007 server roles, the Edge Transport server role does not store configuration data in Active Directory. The Edge Transport server role uses Active Directory Application Mode (ADAM) or Active Directory Lightweight Domain Services (AD LDS) in Windows Server 2008 to store configuration data. This database is a static copy of Active Directory and is not replicated to any other server. This means you cannot recover an Edge Transport server as simply as running the Setup /M:RecoverServer command. This also means that if you have more than one Edge Transport server, you must back up the configuration data for each server.

To recover the Edge Transport server, Microsoft included with Exchange Server 2007 two Exchange Management Shell scripts that back up and restore all of the Edge Transport server configuration data using XML files. You can back up and restore the Edge Transport server configuration by using the following scripts in the Exchange Management Shell:

- ExportEdgeConfig.ps1: This script exports all configuration data from an Edge Transport server and stores that data in an XML file.

- ImportEdgeConfig.ps1: This script imports all configuration data stored in the XML file that is created by the ExportEdgeConfig.ps1 script and applies those settings to a new Edge Transport server.

The default location of the folder where you can find these scripts is C:\Program Files\ Microsoft\Exchange Server\Scripts. The script exports the critical configuration information stored on an Edge Transport server out to an XML file. Once this XML file is created, it should be copied off the server and backed up.

An added benefit of this XML file backup process is what is called the *cloned configuration process*. It allows you to configure one Edge Transport server and then clone the configuration to other Edge Transport servers.

 For more detailed information about the ExportEdgeConfig.ps1 script, see the topic "Using Cloned Configuration Tasks for Edge Transport Server Disaster Recovery" at http://technet.microsoft.com/en-us/library/ bb125150.aspx.

To capture the configuration of an Edge Transport server, run the `ExportEdgeConfig.ps1` script. Running this script extracts the Edge Transport server configuration and places it in an XML file that can be backed up for later use. To reapply the XML backup to a newly installed Edge Transport server with the same server name, run the `ImportEdgeConfig.ps1` script. Running this script will apply all the settings in the XML file to your Edge Transport server. After the settings have been applied, you need to initiate EdgeSync to populate the local configuration database. Your Edge Transport server should now be restored and ready to go. Exercise 10.7 covers these steps in more detail. Exercises 10.7 and 10.8 provide a basic outline of the steps that you would take to back up and restore an Edge Transport server.

EXERCISE 10.7

Backing Up an Edge Transport Server

To back up an Edge Transport server, use the following steps:

1. On the Edge Transport server that you want to back up, run the following Exchange Management Shell command:

   `.\ExportEdgeConfig -cloneConfigData:"<Path_and_FileName_Of_XML_File>"`

2. Place the XML file on a secure server in a location that is backed up.

EXERCISE 10.8

Restoring an Edge Transport Server

To restore the configuration on an Edge Transport server, follow these steps:

1. Install a fresh install of an Exchange Server 2007 Edge Transport server, giving the server the same name as the server you are replacing.

2. Place the XML backup file on the Edge Transport server that you want to restore.

3. On the Edge Transport server you want to restore, run the following Exchange Management Shell command:

   `.\ImportEdgeConfig.ps1 -cloneConfigData`
   `"C:\CloneConfigData.xml" -isImport:$true`

4. Once your server has been configured with the restored settings, you need to repopulate the ADAM database by running the EdgeSync process to import all the user objects from Active Directory.

Summary

Disaster recovery for Exchange Server 2007 is an involved and complex concept that includes numerous levels of protection and different methods for recovery and restoration. With new server roles in Exchange Server 2007, disaster recovery has become more complex than in previous versions. Each server role requires different considerations to protect it properly in the event of a disaster.

The best way to deal with a disaster is to prevent it before it happens, with redundant and reliable hardware, diligent monitoring, excellent planning, and knowledge. If a disaster cannot be prevented and you must cope with one, the best way to deal with it is to have well-documented and well-practiced procedures in place. Even with the best disaster prevention plans, you still need to have good, verified backups.

Exam Essentials

Know your Exchange Server roles.   Each server role stores valuable data differently, including the IIS Metabase and web pages for the Client Access server roles, the queue database on the Edge and Hub Transport servers, everything in an XML file on the Edge Transport server, and the Exchange 2003 databases on the Mailbox server.

Know how to use Windows Server Backup.   Windows Server Backup can back up and restore your Exchange server's databases, files, and system state. You need to know how Exchange Server makes backups and from where it can back up data, and then you need to know how to restore items and where Windows Server 2003 Backup can restore items. You should be aware of all the options available to you for backups, including streaming, VSS, full, incremental, and differential.

Understand Exchange's disaster recovery features.   Know the new and updated disaster recovery features, including dial-tone recovery, database portability, the recovery storage group, the disaster recovery analyzer wizards, deleted items retention, deleted mailbox retention, Setup /Mode:RecoverServer, /RecoverCMS, the Edge Transport server scripts, LCR, SCR, and CCR.

Plan for and verify everything.   You should never consider a backup to be an actual backup unless it is restorable. You need to test your backups to prove that they are usable backups. You should test your backups and use that as an opportunity to test and refine your disaster recovery plans.

Review Questions

1. A database on your Exchange Server 2007 Mailbox server becomes dismounted. The error in the Application log reports that your database was taken offline because it ran out of disk space. Searching for items to delete, you find a folder with thousands of 1MB files with names like E0000FA344.log. Which of the following is true?

   A. They are just logs of things that have been done to the Exchange database and can all be deleted.

   B. The files are all locked and in use by the Information Store service. You need to stop that service before you can delete the files.

   C. You should run an Exchange-aware backup. That backup will deal with the log files for you.

   D. Both B and C are correct.

2. You should always use an Exchange-aware backup solution to back up your Exchange databases. With Windows Server 2003 Backup, what are the available backup methods for Exchange Server 2007?

   A. Volume Shadow Copy Service (VSS) backups.

   B. The Streaming Backup API.

   C. Full and incremental, but not differential backups.

   D. All these methods support Exchange-aware backup solutions.

3. For Exchange Server 2007 storage groups and databases to show up in Windows Server 2003 Backup, what application needs to be installed?

   A. You need to install the Exchange Server 2007 backup drivers by running ExBackup. exe, found on the Exchange Server 2007 installation DVD.

   B. You need to install Exchange backup support for Windows Server by opening Control Panel, selecting Add or Remove Programs, selecting Add/Remove Windows Components, and then adding Exchange Backup Support for Windows Server Backup.

   C. You have to install the Exchange Management Console API by running Exchange Server 2007 setup and selecting only the Management Console.

   D. You have to install the Exchange Server 2007 Mailbox server role on the backup server to allow Windows Server Backup to back up an Exchange database.

4. If your Mailbox server is configured with 3 storage groups and 18 mailbox databases, how many sets of transaction log files would it have?

   A. 3

   B. 15

   C. 54

   D. 18

5. You come to work and find that one of your Mailbox servers has crashed. After further inspection, you determine that nothing is recoverable from the Mailbox server. To provide dial tone to the users whose mailboxes are on the failed server, you've decided to create new dial-tone databases on an existing Mailbox server in your Exchange organization. To do this, what Exchange Management Shell command would you run?

    A. `Move-Mailbox -Identity` *Mailbox_Name* `-DialToneMove -MailboxDatabase` *Destination_database*

    B. `Get-MailboxStatistics -Database` *Missing_Database_Name* `| Move-Mailbox -ConfigurationOnly -TargetDatabase` *New_Database_Name*

    C. `Move-Mailbox -Database` *Missing_Database_Name* `-TargetDatabase` *New_Database_Name*

    D. `Move-Mailbox -ConfigurationOnly -Database` *Missing_Database_Name* `-TargetDatabase` *New_Database_Name*

6. The CEO of your company accidentally deleted an important message while holding down the Shift key. Deleted item retention has been configured for his mailbox for 60 days. He calls the help desk and is instructed to select Tools ➤ Recover Deleted Items in Outlook 2003. He is unable to find the message. What should you do?

    A. Your CEO is using the wrong version of Outlook. Exchange Server 2007 supports deleted item recovery only from Outlook 2007. You should tell your CEO to use OWA to recover his message.

    B. The local deleted items cache on your CEO's computer is out-of-date and needs to be refreshed. You should instruct your CEO to reboot his computer and try again.

    C. If the message is not there, then it is gone and cannot be recovered. You should ask your CEO to call his wife and ask what was in the email.

    D. You need to add the DumpsterAlwaysOn Registry key to your CEO's computer and then restart Outlook. Then his deleted item will be recoverable.

7. A power failure causes one of your Mailbox servers to power down. After you restore power, one of the Exchange databases does not mount and the error leads you to believe that your database has become corrupted. To repair the database, which would be the best tool to use?

    A. `ESEUtil /D`

    B. `ISInteg -patch`

    C. Exchange Database Troubleshooter

    D. Both A and B

8. Where does the Edge Transport server store configuration information that should be backed up?

    A. The ADAM database on the Edge Transport server.

    B. XML files on the Edge Transport server.

    C. The Windows Server Registry.

    D. All the above places hold configuration information that should be backed up on an Edge Transport server.

9. Once the Edge Transport server configuration information has been restored, what else needs to be reestablished on an Edge Transport server?

   A. You need to reconfigure your SMTP connectors to receive email from the Internet.

   B. You need to run EdgeSync to repopulate the ADAM database.

   C. You need to reinitialize the Hub Transport and Edge Transport server transport connectors so that your Edge Transport server can send messages to your Hub Transport servers.

   D. You need to rebuild your Edge Transport server's real-time IP block list cache manually.

10. You have a single Hub Transport server that failed with a considerable amount of email in the outbound message queue. You need to recover the queued mail. What should you do?

    A. Rebuild the Hub Transport server by creating a new server OS with the same name and then install Exchange by running `Setup /Mode:RecoverServer`.

    B. Instruct the users to send the messages again.

    C. Repair the queue database, copy the file to another Hub Transport server, and mount the database.

    D. None of the answers are correct.

11. Which of the following is not true for a recovery storage group?

    A. Users can access all their email once a database is mounted in the recovery storage group.

    B. You can mount a database created on any Exchange Server 2007 server in an organization.

    C. You cannot manage a recovery storage group from inside the Exchange Management Shell.

    D. You can have only one recovery storage group on a server at a time.

12. To restore an Edge Transport server, you could do any of the following except what?

    A. Copy your backup XML files, and run the `ImportConfig.ps1` script.

    B. Create a server with the same server name, and set up Exchange by running `Setup /Mode:RecoverServer`.

    C. Keep a detailed log of all the modifications made to your server. Rebuild the server, and then apply all the modifications in the log to the server.

    D. All the options are valid Edge Transport server restore scenarios.

13. A single disk shelf failure caused the loss of several databases on one of your Exchange servers. You are now missing 300GB of mailbox data. Which of the following technologies would help you quickly recovery from this situation?

    A. CCR

    B. Windows Server Backup

    C. ESEUtil

    D. Exchange Database Troubleshooter

14. The last Exchange 2003 Mailbox server in your Exchange Server 2007 organization is missing from the server room. You suspect foul play because someone on the server team had motive. The executive management team does not really care. All the executives care about is retrieving their mailboxes that were on the missing Exchange 2003 server. Which of the following approaches would be a viable solution to recover their mailboxes?

A. Restore the databases to an Exchange Server 2007 storage group, and merge them with the executive team's databases.

B. Build a server with the same name, reinstall Exchange Server 2007 with `Setup /Mode:RecoverServer`, and then restore the databases to that server.

C. Build an Exchange 2003 server with the same name, and then restore the database to that server.

D. Create new databases on one of your Exchange Server 2007 servers with the same name as the missing databases, mark those databases so that they can be overwritten, and then restore the databases to that server.

15. On a Client Access server, which of the following items should be backed up but isn't critical for restoring basic functionality?

A. The message tracking logs

B. The transport queue database

C. The SMTP tracking logs

D. None of the above

16. You suspect the Exchange databases have been tampered with and subsequently cannot be mounted. You need to determine the status of the database files to determine the next steps to take for recovery. Which of the following would you run to read the database header information on your databases?

A. `ESEUtil /M`

B. `ISINteg -header`

C. `Get-MailboxDatabase -name <Database_Name> -DatabaseHeader`

D. Both A and C

17. ESE is short for what?

A. Exchange Storage Engine

B. Enterprise Storage Extension

C. Extreme Storage Engineers

D. Extensible Storage Engine

18. You have heavily modified IIS on your Client Access server. You know that CAS does not store everything in Active Directory. Which of the following places might the Client Access server use to store your modifications?

    A. The IIS XML configuration files

    B. The IIS Metabase

    C. The ADAM database

    D. The Client Access server mailbox on the Mailbox server

19. Setup /Mode:RecoverServer is a great tool to rebuild your Exchange servers. Which of the following statements is not true about this tool?

    A. Setup /Mode:RecoverServer extracts server configuration information from the Configuration node of Active Directory and applies it to your Exchange servers.

    B. For Setup /Mode:RecoverServer to recover a server, you need to build the server with the same server name as the server you are recovering.

    C. To run Setup /Mode:RecoverServer, you need to have the Exchange Server 2007 server installation files.

    D. Setup /Mode:RecoverServer can rebuild the following server roles: CAS, Edge Transport, and Mailbox. It cannot be used to recover a Hub Transport server.

20. You work for an email sales–based company. Missing any email is a horrible problem for your company, so you've been asked to support a backup solution where no more than five minutes of email data can be lost in the worst-case scenario. Which of the following backup methods would be the best fit to support this request?

    A. Volume shadow copy backups every five minutes taken with Windows Server Backup

    B. Local continuous replication

    C. Streaming full backups every five minutes taken with Windows Server Backup

    D. Copy backups taken every five minutes with Windows Server Backup

Answers to Review Questions

1. C. You should never delete the transaction log files unless you've been directed to do so by CSS or you fully understand what the ramifications are. The best way to delete the log files is to run an Exchange-aware backup utility that will fully commit all the files to the database and then delete them.

2. B. The Windows Server 2003 Backup application supports both VSS and streaming backups; however, it does not support VSS as an Exchange-aware backup method. The only Exchange-aware backup solution supported by Windows Server 2003 Backup is the Exchange steaming backup method.

3. C. Installing the Exchange Management Console is all you need to do to be able to see your Exchange storage groups and Exchange databases in Windows Server 2003 Backup.

4. A. Transaction log sets are associated with storage groups. If your server has three storage groups, then it would have three sets of transaction logs.

5. D. The correct command is `Move-Mailbox -ConfigurationOnly`. You can use the `Get-MailboxStatistics` command to list all the mailboxes in a database and then send those mailbox names to the `Move-Mailbox` command by using the following command: `Get-MailboxStatistics -Database Missing_Database_Name | Move-Mailbox -ConfigurationOnly -TargetDatabase New_Database_Name`.

6. D. By default, deleted items are recoverable only from the Deleted Items folder. By holding down Shift while deleting his message, the CEO deleted it without first placing it in the Deleted Items folder. To see deleted items in folders other than the Deleted Items folder, you need to set the DumpsterAlwaysOn Registry key on the client computer.

7. C. The Exchange Database Troubleshooter would be the best tool to use when confronted with a corrupted Exchange database. The troubleshooter will evaluate the problem and then choose the best course of action to fix the database.

8. D. The Edge Transport server configuration information is stored in ADAM, in XML files, and in the Registry. If you are going to back up an Edge Transport server properly, you should capture the data in all these locations.

9. B. After a failed Edge Transport server has been reconfigured, you need to run EdgeSync to populate the ADAM database with all the attributes that are needed from Active Directory.

10. C. Exchange Server 2007 Hub Transport servers store messages in an ESE database. That database can be mounted on any Hub Transport server in your Exchange organization. To recover the messages, copy the queue database to another Hub Transport server, perform recovery on the database, and then mount that queue database.

11. A. Users cannot access any data in a recovery storage group. To access data in a recovery storage group, you need to merge that data into another user's mailbox or move the mailbox from the recovery storage group and place it in a live database attached to a user account.

12. B. `Setup /Mode:RecoverServer` extracts setup information from Active Directory and applies the setup information to the server on which you are running it. The Edge Transport server does not store any configuration information in Active Directory.

13. A. CCR is the correct answer. Had the Mailbox server been configured as a CCR cluster, it would be able to fail over to the other node in the cluster. That other node would be attached to a second disk array with a replica of your Exchange database.

14. C. Currently you have to restore the databases to an Exchange 2003 server because you cannot mount an Exchange 2003 database in an Exchange Server 2007 recovery or normal storage group.

15. D. All the listed items are items you should back up on a Hub Transport server, but not on a Client Access server.

16. A. `ESEUtil /M` would, when run with the right information, be able to display the database header for you.

17. D. ESE is short for Extensible Storage Engine.

18. B. IIS stores its configuration information in the IIS Metabase. This database is not replicated and should be backed up if settings are changed that might need to be restored in the event of a server failure.

19. D. `Setup /Mode:RecoverServer` cannot be run on an Edge Transport server. It can be run on a Hub Transport server.

20. B. LCR would give you the most up-to-date backup of your Exchange databases.

Appendix

About the Companion CD

✓ **In this appendix:**

- What you'll find on the CD
- System requirements
- Using the CD
- Troubleshooting

What You'll Find on the CD

The following sections are arranged by category and summarize the software and other goodies you'll find on the CD. If you need help with installing the items provided on the CD, refer to the installation instructions in the "Using the CD" section of this appendix.

Some programs on the CD might fall into one of these categories:

Shareware programs are fully functional, free, trial versions of copyrighted programs. If you like particular programs, register with their authors for a nominal fee and receive licenses, enhanced versions, and technical support.

Freeware programs are free, copyrighted games, applications, and utilities. You can copy them to as many computers as you like—for free—but they offer no technical support.

GNU software is governed by its own license, which is included inside the folder of the GNU software. There are no restrictions on distribution of GNU software. See the GNU license at the root of the CD for more details.

Trial, *demo*, or *evaluation* versions of software are usually limited either by time or by functionality (such as not letting you save a project after you create it).

Sybex Test Engine

For Windows

The CD contains the Sybex test engine, which includes two bonus exams located only on the CD.

PDF of Glossary of Terms

For Windows

We have included an electronic version of the Glossary in .pdf format. You can view the electronic version of the Glossary with Adobe Reader.

Adobe Reader

For Windows

We've also included a copy of Adobe Reader so you can view PDF files that accompany the book's content. For more information on Adobe Reader or to check for a newer version, visit Adobe's website at www.adobe.com/products/reader/.

Electronic Flashcards

For PC, Pocket PC, and Palm

These handy electronic flashcards are just what they sound like. One side contains a question or fill-in-the-blank question, and the other side shows the answer.

System Requirements

Make sure your computer meets the minimum system requirements shown in the following list. If your computer doesn't match up to most of these requirements, you may have problems using the software and files on the companion CD. For the latest and greatest information, please refer to the ReadMe file located at the root of the CD-ROM.

- A PC running Microsoft Windows 98, Windows 2000, Windows NT4 (with SP4 or later), Windows Me, Windows XP, or Windows Vista
- An Internet connection
- A CD-ROM drive

Using the CD

To install the items from the CD to your hard drive, follow these steps:

1. Insert the CD into your computer's CD-ROM drive. The license agreement appears.

> *Windows users*: The interface won't launch if you have autorun disabled. In that case, click Start ➤ Run (for Windows Vista, Start ➤ All Programs ➤ Accessories ➤ Run). In the dialog box that appears, type **D:\Start.exe**. (Replace *D* with the proper letter if your CD drive uses a different letter. If you don't know the letter, see how your CD drive is listed under My Computer.) Click OK.

2. Read the license agreement, and then click the Accept button if you want to use the CD.

The CD interface appears. The interface allows you to access the content with just one or two clicks.

Troubleshooting

Wiley has attempted to provide programs that work on most computers with the minimum system requirements. Alas, your computer may differ, and some programs may not work properly for some reason.

The two likeliest problems are that you don't have enough memory (RAM) for the programs you want to use or you have other programs running that are affecting installation or running of a program. If you get an error message such as "Not enough memory" or "Setup cannot continue," try one or more of the following suggestions and then try using the software again:

Turn off any antivirus software running on your computer. Installation programs sometimes mimic virus activity and may make your computer incorrectly believe that it's being infected by a virus.

Close all running programs. The more programs you have running, the less memory is available to other programs. Installation programs typically update files and programs; so if you keep other programs running, installation may not work properly.

Have your local computer store add more RAM to your computer. This is, admittedly, a drastic and somewhat expensive step. However, adding more memory can really help the speed of your computer and allow more programs to run at the same time.

Customer Care

If you have trouble with the book's companion CD-ROM, please call the Wiley Product Technical Support phone number at (800) 762-2974. Outside the United States, call +1(317) 572-3994. You can also contact Wiley Product Technical Support at `http://sybex.custhelp.com`. John Wiley & Sons will provide technical support only for installation and other general quality-control items. For technical support on the applications themselves, consult the program's vendor or author.

To place additional orders or to request information about other Wiley products, please call (877) 762-2974.

Glossary

A

accepted domain   An email domain for which your Exchange servers accept inbound mail.

access control entries (ACEs)   Entries on an access control list (ACL) that define a user's permission for an object.

access control list (ACL)   A list of users and groups allowed to access a resource and the particular permissions each user has been granted or denied.

Active Directory   Stores information objects and information about users, computers, services and other information for a Windows Server network and serves this information out for administrators, users, and applications to find and use.

address space   The set of remote addresses that can be reached through a particular connector. Each connector must have at least one entry in its address space.

administrative group   Used to define administrative boundaries within an Exchange 2000/2003 environment.

administrative rights   NTFS permissions that determine what administrative tasks a user or group is permitted to perform on a public folder.

age limit   A property that specifies the length of time a unit of data may remain in its container (for example, a public folder).

alias   An alternative name for an object. In Exchange, an alias is usually generated for a user based on the user's name.

All Public Folders   The name for the default public folder tree in an Exchange organization. This tree is accessible by all clients that can access public folders.

anonymous access   Accessing a server by logging in using a Windows account set up for general access.

anonymous authentication   See *anonymous access*.

application programming interface (API)   A collection of programming classes and interfaces that provide services used by a program. Other programs can use a program's API to request services or communicate with that program.

architecture   The description of the components of a product or system, what they are, what they do, and how they relate to each other.

archive   A location and collection of data (messages) that needs to be preserved for a given time. An archive is generally not online and immediately accessible, but it is searchable and accessible if needed.

attribute   A characteristic of an object. For example, attributes of a mailbox-enabled user include the display name and storage limits. The terms *attribute* and *property* are synonymous.

auditing   Windows Server can be configured to monitor and record certain events. This can help diagnose security events. The audit information is written to the Windows Security Event Log.

authentication   A process whereby the credentials of an object, such as a user, must be validated before the object is allowed to access or use another object, such as a server or a protocol. For instance, the Microsoft Exchange Server POP3 protocol can be configured to allow access only to POP3 clients that use the Integrated Windows authentication method.

B

backfill   The process used in public folder replication to fill in messaging data that is missing from a replica.

backup   Typically a hard drive or backup tape that stores copies of files.

Bad Mail folder   The folder in which SMTP stores undeliverable messages that cannot be returned to the sender.

Basic (clear-text) authentication   Requires the user to submit a valid Windows username and password. The username and password are sent across the network as unencrypted clear text.

Basic over Secure Sockets Layer (SSL) authentication   Extends the Basic (clear-text) authentication method by allowing an SSL server to encrypt the username and password before they are sent across the network.

C

cache mode   A feature in Outlook 2003 and Outlook 2007 that allows clients to work disconnected from the Exchange server. Outlook will periodically reconnect to the Exchange server and synchronize any changes to the user's mailbox.

categorizer   A component of the Exchange Server 2007 routing engine used to resolve the sender and recipient for a message, expanding any distribution groups as needed. In previous versions of Exchange Server, this task was performed by the message transfer agent.

centralized model   An administrative model in which one administrator or group of administrators maintains complete control over an entire Exchange organization.

certificate   Allows verification of the claim that a given public key actually belongs to a given individual. This helps prevent someone from using a phony key to impersonate someone else. A certificate is similar to a token.

certificate authority (CA)   The central authority that distributes, publishes, and validates security keys. The Windows Server 2003 Certificate Services component performs this role. See also *public key* and *private key.*

certificate revocation list (CRL)   A list containing all certificates in an organization that have been revoked.

certificate store   A database created during the installation of a certificate authority (CA) that is a repository of certificates issued by the CA.

certificate template   Stored in Active Directory; defines the attributes for certificates.

certificate trust list (CTL)   Holds the set of root CAs whose certificates can be trusted. You can designate CTLs for groups, users, or an entire domain.

challenge/response   A general term for a class of security mechanisms, including Microsoft authentication methods that use Windows Server 2003 network security and an encrypted password.

change number   One of the constructs used to keep track of public folder replication throughout an organization and to determine whether a public folder is synchronized. The change number consists of a globally unique identifier for the Information Store and a change counter that is specific to the server on which a public folder resides.

checkpoint file   The file (EDB.chk) that contains the point in a transaction log that is the boundary between data that has been committed and data that has not yet been committed to an Exchange database.

child domain   Any domain configured underneath another domain in a domain tree.

circular logging   The process of writing new information in transaction log files over information that has already been committed. Instead of repeatedly creating new transaction logs, the Exchange database engine "circles back" and reuses log files that have been fully committed to the database. Circular logging keeps down the number of transaction logs on the disk. These logs cannot be used to re-create a database because the logs do not have a complete set of data. The logs contain only the most recent data not yet committed to a database. Circular logging is disabled by default.

client access license (CAL)   Gives a user the legal right to access an Exchange server. Any client software that has the ability to be a client to Microsoft Exchange Server is legally required to have a CAL purchased for it.

Client Access server   Non-MAPI clients, such as POP3, IMAP4, mobile, and web-based clients, must connect to the Mailbox servers via a Client Access server. In this way, the Client Access server is most like the front-end servers utilized in previous versions of Exchange Server. All requests from these non-MAPI clients are received by the Client Access server and then forwarded to the applicable Mailbox server for action.

cluster   A group of servers (also called *nodes*) that function together as a single unit.

cluster continuous replication (CCR)   This is a new cluster implementation that removes the requirement for a shared disk implementation such as a SAN. This configuration uses a majority node set quorum and log shipping to keep the data synced between the active and passive nodes.

cluster resource   A service or property, such as a storage device, an IP address, or the Exchange System Attendant service, that is defined, monitored, and managed by the cluster service.

cluster service   The software service used to manage all the cluster activity. The cluster service controls access to resources by the individual nodes of the cluster.

clustering   A Windows service that enables multiple physical servers to be grouped logically for reasons of high availability.

committed   When a transaction is transferred from a transaction log to an Exchange database, it has been committed.

compliance   For the purpose of Exchange, compliance is the act of complying with government, agency, or corporate policies that dictate how communications and information should be handled.

Computer Management snap-in   An administrative tool holding a variety of utilities, including Event Viewer and disk management tools.

contact   A recipient object that represents a foreign message recipient. Contacts appear in the global address list (GAL) and allow Exchange clients to address messages to foreign mail users. Also referred to as a *mail contact*.

container object   An object in the Exchange or Active Directory hierarchy that contains and groups other objects. For example, the organization object in System Manager is a container object that contains all other objects in the organization.

contiguous namespace   When multiple entities share a common namespace. For example, Windows Server 2003 domain trees share a contiguous namespace; domain forests do not.

continuous availability (CA)   The unattainable desire never to have applications unavailable.

convergence   The process during which the active nodes in a cluster calculate a new, stable state among themselves after the failure of one or more cluster nodes.

copy backup   During a copy backup, all selected files are backed up, regardless of how their archive bit is set. After the backup, the archive bit is not changed in any file.

D

daily backup   During this backup, all files that changed on the day of the backup are backed up, and the archive bit is not changed in any file.

Data Encryption Standard (DES)   A secret-key encryption method that uses a 56-bit key.

database   There are two types of databases in Exchange Server 2007: public databases that hold public folders meant to be accessed by groups of users, and mailbox databases that hold user mailboxes.

DAVEx   An IIS component that passes client requests between W3svc and the Information Store.

dcdiag   A command-line utility that can be used to analyze the state of all domain controllers in a forest and report problems that were found.

decentralized model   Typically used to define administrative boundaries along real geographical or departmental boundaries. Each location would have its own administrators and its own administrative group.

decryption   Translating encrypted data back to plain text.

dedicated public folder server   An Exchange server whose primary purpose is to hold public folder databases and from which the mailbox databases have been removed.

deleted-item retention time   The period that items in a public or private database deleted by users are actually retained on the Exchange server.

demilitarized zone (DMZ)   See *perimeter network*.

dial-tone recovery   A basic recovery that provides the ability to send and receive email but does not provide any historical email data. A dial-tone recovery is used as a go-between to provide basic services and allow users to continue to work while a database restore takes place.

differential backup   A method in which all files that have been changed since the last full backup are backed up. See also *incremental backup*.

digital signature   A process of digitally signing data using public and private keys so that the recipient of the data can verify the authenticity of both the sender and the data.

directory   A hierarchy that stores information about objects in a system. A directory service (DS) manages the directory and makes it available to users on the network.

directory replication   Transferring directory information from one server to another. In Active Directory, directory information is replicated between domain controllers. In previous versions of Exchange, directory information is replicated between Exchange servers.

directory rights   Used to configure the NTFS permissions that determine who can perform modifications on the public folder object that is stored in Active Directory.

disaster recovery   The act of recovering from the loss of any Exchange Server data or Exchange Server. This would require having enough data in a recoverable format and can be limited to the loss of a single email message or can encompass the loss of an entire data center.

Disaster Recovery mode   An Exchange Server 2007 setup mode that lets you recover an Exchange installation after a failure.

discovery   The actions that are taken when records are requested to comply with a given policy or form of governance.

discretionary access control list (DACL)   A list of access control entries (ACEs) that gives users and groups specific permissions on an object.

dismounting   The process of taking a public or mailbox database offline.

distribution group   An Active Directory group formed so that a single email message can be sent to the group and then sent automatically to all members of the group. Unlike security groups, distribution groups don't provide any security function.

DMZ   See *perimeter network*.

DNS   See *Domain Name Service (DNS)*.

domain   A group of computers and other resources that are part of a Windows Server 2003 network and share a common directory database.

domain controller   A computer running Windows Server 2003 that validates user network access and manages Active Directory.

domain forest   A group of one or more domain trees that do not necessarily form a contiguous namespace but may share a common schema and global catalog.

Domain Name Service (DNS)   The primary provider of name resolution within an organization.

domain tree   A hierarchical arrangement of one or more Windows Active Directory domains that share a common namespace.

dynamic distribution group   An email-enabled distribution group whose group membership is determined by the results of an LDAP query created when the group is configured.

E

Edge Transport server   Designed to be deployed in the DMZ of your network, the Edge Transport server is used to provide a secure SMTP gateway for all messages entering or leaving your Exchange organization. As such, the Edge Transport server is responsible for antivirus and antispam controls as well as protecting the recipient data held within Active Directory.

EHLO   The SMTP command used by one host to initiate communications with another host.

encryption   The process of scrambling data to make it unreadable. The intended recipient will decrypt the data into plain text in order to read it.

enterprise CA   Acts as a certificate authority for an enterprise and requires access to the Active Directory. See also *certificate authority (CA)*.

Enterprise Edition   The premier version of Exchange Server 2007, with support for up to 50 storage groups and 50 databases.

ethical walls   A rule or system that prevents communication between specific groups in an organization.

Event Log   A set of three logs (Application, Security, and System) maintained by Windows Server. The operating system and many applications, such as Exchange Server 2007, write software events to the Event Log.

Exchange Management Console   A snap-in for the Microsoft Management Console used to manage an Exchange Server 2007 organization.

expanding a distribution group   The process of determining the individual addresses contained within a distribution group. This process is performed by the home server of the user sending the message to the group unless an expansion server is specified for the group.

extended permissions   Permissions added to the standard Windows Server 2003 permissions when Exchange Server 2007 is installed.

Extensible Storage Engine (ESE)   The database engine used by Exchange Server 2007.

F

failback   The process of cluster resources moving back to their preferred node after the preferred node has resumed active membership in the cluster.

failover   The process of moving resources off a cluster node that has failed to another cluster node. If any of the cluster resources on an active node become unresponsive or unavailable for a period of time exceeding the configured threshold, failover will occur.

file share witness (FSW)   The FSW is a file share on another computer that is not part of the cluster but can be used to maintain a majority for MNS. The file share witness feature allows for the creation of another quorum resource that will work with MNS quorum resources to provide more redundancy of the quorum. This new change allows the use of two nodes for the cluster and a third server of some kind someplace on the network to provide another quorum resource to work with MNS. The file share witness is perfect for clusters that have no need for shared storage for their data, or it can be provided via other methods. Now you can have two nodes and still have a majority available in the case of a single node failure.

firewall   A set of mechanisms that separate and protect your internal network from unauthorized external users and networks. Firewalls can restrict inbound and outbound traffic as well as analyze all traffic between your network and the outside.

foreign system   A non-Exchange messaging system.

forest root domain   The first domain installed in a domain forest and the basis for the naming of all domains in the forest.

forms registry   Stores the Outlook Web Access (OWA) forms rendered by Internet Information Services (IIS) and passed to the client.

free/busy   Terminology used in the Microsoft Schedule+ application to denote an unscheduled period of time (free) or a scheduled period of time (busy).

full-text indexing   A feature that can be enabled for a database. With full-text indexing, every word in the database (including those in attachments) is indexed for much faster search results.

fully qualified domain name (FQDN)   The full DNS path of an Internet host. An example is `sales.dept4.widget.com`.

function call   An instruction in a program that calls (invokes) a function. For example, MAPIReadMail is a MAPI function call.

G

GAL   See *global address list (GAL)*.

general-purpose trees   Public folder trees added to an Exchange organization beyond the default public folder tree. General-purpose trees are not accessible by MAPI clients such as Microsoft Outlook.

global address list (GAL)   A database of all the recipients in an Exchange organization, such as mailboxes, distribution lists, custom recipients, and public folders.

global catalog   Used to hold information about all objects in a forest. The global catalog enables users and applications to find objects in an Active Directory domain tree if the user or application knows one or more attributes of the target object.

group   A collection of users and other groups that may be assigned permissions or made part of an email distribution list.

groupware   Any application that allows groups of people to store and share information.

H

heartbeat   A special communication among members of a cluster that keeps all members aware of one another's existence (and thus their operational states).

HELO The SMTP command used by one host to initiate communications with another host.

hierarchy Any structure or organization that uses class, grade, or rank to arrange objects.

high availability (HA) The combination of well-defined, -planned, -tested, and -implemented processes, software, and fault-tolerant hardware focused on supplying and maintaining application availability.

host bus adapter (HBA) This adapter connects the server node to the storage area network using fiber or, potentially, an iSCSI SAN.

HTML See *Hypertext Markup Language (HTML)*.

HTTP See *Hypertext Transfer Protocol (HTTP)*.

HTTP Digest authentication An Internet standard that allows the authentication of clients to occur using a series of challenges and responses over HTTP.

Hub Transport server The server that routes messages for delivery within the Exchange organization. When message routing is moved to another server (other than the Mailbox server), many new and needed features and functions become available in Exchange Server 2007. As an example, while messages are being routed through the Hub Transport server, they can have transport rules and filtering policies applied to them that determine where they'll wind up, such as being delivered to a compliance mailbox in addition to the recipient's mailbox, or what they'll look like, such as every outbound message being stamped with a disclaimer.

Hypertext Markup Language (HTML) The script language used to create content for the World Wide Web (WWW). HTML can create hyperlinks between objects on the Web.

Hypertext Transfer Protocol (HTTP) The Internet protocol used to transfer information on the World Wide Web (WWW).

I

IIS metabase The database of configuration information maintained by Internet Information Services.

Inbox The storage folder that receives new incoming messages.

Inbox repair tool A utility (Scanpst.exe) used to repair corrupt personal folder (.pst) files.

incremental backup The method in which all files that have changed since the last normal or incremental backup are backed up. The archive bit is cleared after an incremental backup is performed.

Information Store See *Store.exe*.

infrastructure master   The operations master role that is responsible for updating references from objects in its domain to objects in other domains.

inheritance   The process through which permissions are passed down from a parent container to objects inside that container (child objects).

installer package (MSI file)   One of the files generated by Windows Installer; used to control configuration information during installation. The installer package contains a database that describes the configuration information. See also *installer transform (MST file)*.

installer transform (MST file)   One of the files generated by Windows Installer; used to control configuration information during installation. The transform file contains modifications that are to be made as Windows Installer installs Outlook. See also *installer package (MSI file)*.

Integrated Windows authentication   Requires the user to provide a valid Windows username and password. However, the user's credentials are never sent across the network. At the Windows 2000 native domain functional level or the Windows Server 2003 domain functional level, this method uses Kerberos v5.

Internet Information Services (IIS)   A built-in component of Windows Server 2003 that allows access to resources on the server through various Internet protocols, such as POP3, IMAP4, and HTTP.

Internet Message Access Protocol version 4 (IMAP4)   An Internet retrieval protocol that enables clients to access and manipulate messages in their mailbox on a remote server. IMAP4 provides additional functions over POP3, such as access to subfolders (not merely the Inbox folder) and selective downloading of messages.

ipconfig   A command-line utility that can be used to display and modify TCP/IP information about all installed network adapters. Common uses include flushing the local DNS resolver cache and releasing and renewing DHCP leases.

K

Kerberos version 5 (v5)   The primary form of user authentication used by Windows Server 2003.

key   A randomly generated number used to implement advanced security, such as encryption or digital signatures. See also *key pair*, *public key*, and *private key*.

key pair   A key that is divided into two mathematically related halves. One half (the public key) is made public; the other half (the private key) is known by only one user.

L

leaf object   An object in a Microsoft Management Console window that does not contain any other objects.

Lightweight Directory Access Protocol (LDAP)   An Internet protocol used for client access to an X.500-based directory, such as Active Directory.

local continuous replication (LCR)   This is a single-server environment where the active storage group is copied to another physical disk on the same server using log shipping.

local procedure call (LPC)   An instruction that is issued by a program and executed on the same computer as the program executing the instruction.

lockbox   The process of using a secret key to encrypt a message and its attachments and then using a public key pair to encrypt and decrypt the secret key.

log file replay   A process in which Exchange examines the transaction log files for a storage group to identify transactions that have been logged and that have not been incorporated into a database. This process, also known as *playing back log files*, brings the databases up-to-date with the available transaction log files.

logical unit number (LUN)   The logical unit number is the disk structure as defined on the SAN or NAS device used to provide disk resources to a cluster. On the SAN, for example, there may be 10 physical disks combined in a RAID format. These disks are exposed from the SAN to the computer as one unit. The Windows computer then sees one large physical disk connected to it.

M

Mail and Directory Management (MADMAN) MIB   A specialized version of the base management information base that was created for monitoring messaging systems. See also *management information base (MIB)*.

mail-enabled user   A user who has been given an email address but no mailbox.

mail exchanger (MX) record   A record in a DNS database that indicates the SMTP mail host for an organization.

mailbox   The generic term referring to a container that holds messages, such as incoming and outgoing messages.

mailbox-enabled user   A user who has been assigned an Exchange Server mailbox.

mailbox database   A database on an Exchange server that holds mailboxes. See also *database*.

mailbox server   The primary function of the Mailbox server role is to provide users with mailboxes that can be accessed directly from the Outlook client. The Mailbox server also contains the databases that hold public folders, if you are still using them in your organization. Thus, as a point of comparison, the Mailbox server is most like the back-end server from previous versions of Exchange.

majority node set (MNS) cluster   In Windows Server 2003 Enterprise Edition, Microsoft presented another option to the shared disk environment for the quorum. Instead of selecting a shared physical disk to host the quorum, it is possible to select the majority node set (MNS) option to create a server cluster. From the perspective of Windows, MNS looks just like a single quorum disk, but the quorum data is actually stored on multiple disks across the cluster. MNS is designed and built so it ensures that the stored cluster data is kept consistent across the different disks on different computers.

management information base (MIB)   A set of configurable objects defined for management by SNMP.

MAPI   See *Messaging Application Programming Interface (MAPI)*.

MAPI client   A messaging client that uses the Messaging Application Programming Interface (MAPI) to connect to a messaging server. See also *Messaging Application Programming Interface (MAPI)*.

MAPI subsystem   The second layer of the MAPI architecture; this component is shared by all applications that require its services and is therefore considered a *subsystem* of the operating system.

message state information   Information that identifies the state of a message in a public folder. Message state information consists of a change number, a time stamp, and a predecessor change list.

Messaging Application Programming Interface (MAPI)   An object-oriented programming interface for messaging services, developed by Microsoft.

Microsoft Clustering Service (MSCS)   A Windows service that provides for highly available server solutions through a process known as *failover*. An MSCS cluster consists of two or more nodes (members) that are configured such that, upon the failure of one node, any of the remaining cluster nodes can transfer the failed node's resources to itself, thus keeping the resources available for client access.

Microsoft Management Console (MMC)   A framework application in which snap-ins are loaded to provide the management of various network resources. System Manager is an example of a snap-in.

Microsoft Office Outlook 2007   The premier client application for use with Exchange Server 2007.

Microsoft Search Service   The service that performs full-text indexing of mailbox and public databases.

migration   Moving resources, such as mailboxes, messages, and so on, from one messaging system to another.

mounting   The process of bringing a mailbox or public database online. See also *dismounting*.

multimaster replication model   A model in which every replica of a public folder is considered a master copy.

multipathing   Multipathing is commonly used in Fiber SAN designs. Nodes will have two HBAs (remember, high availability requires redundancy) that are then joined using software. Some common products include PowerPath (EMC) and SecurePath (HP). The two HBAs can be bound together and load balanced to improve throughput from 2GB to 4GB for a particular node. It is also fairly common, though, that the fiber array will also use two HBAs bound together to provide 4GB of throughput, which is then shared among all the servers that attach to the array for storage; 4GB may not be enough. In some cases, organizations will invest and provide four fiber connections from the SAN to the fabric, thus providing 8GB of throughput.

Multipurpose Internet Mail Extensions (MIME)   An Internet protocol that enables the encoding of binary content within mail messages. For example, MIME could be used to encode a graphics file or word processing document as an attachment to a text-based mail message. The recipient of the message would have to be using MIME also to decode the attachment. MIME is newer than UUENCODE and in many systems has replaced it. See also *Secure/Multipurpose Internet Mail Extensions (S/MIME)* and *UUENCODE*.

MX   See *mail exchanger (MX) record*.

N

name resolution   The DNS process of mapping a domain name to its IP address.

namespace   Any bounded area in which a given name can be resolved.

nbtstat   A command-line utility that is used to give statistics, view cache information, resolve NetBIOS names to IP addresses, and register with NetBIOS.

netdiag   A command-line utility that is used to troubleshoot and isolate network connectivity problems by performing a number of tests to determine the exact state of a server.

netstat   A command-line utility that is used to display TCP/IP connection information and protocol statistics for a computer.

network load balancing (NLB)   Provides horizontal scalability as well as high availability. Horizontal scaling is achieved by the servers sharing the load between them. If the application becomes oversubscribed, new servers can be built and added into the NLB web farm to spread the load out even more. High availability is achieved through the NLB web farm in that if a single server fails (or even multiple servers), NLB will redistribute the load among the remaining servers.

Network News Transfer Protocol (NNTP)   An Internet protocol used to transfer newsgroup information between newsgroup servers and clients (newsreaders) and between newsgroup servers.

NNTP   See *Network News Transfer Protocol (NNTP)*.

node   In a Microsoft Management Console window, a node is any object that can be configured. In clustering, a node is one of the computers that is part of a cluster.

normal backup   During this backup, all selected files are backed up, regardless of how their archive bit is set. After the backup, the archive bit is set to off for all files, indicating that those files have been backed up.

notification   Defines the event that is triggered when a service or resource being watched by a server or link monitor fails. Notifications can send email and alerts and even run custom scripts.

nslookup   A command-line utility that can be used to gather information about the DNS infrastructure inside and outside an organization and to troubleshoot DNS-related problems.

O

object   The representation, or abstraction, of an entity. As an object, it contains properties, also called *attributes*, that can be configured.

Object Linking and Embedding version 2 (OLE 2)   The Microsoft protocol that specifies how programs can share objects and therefore create compound documents.

Offline Address Book (OAB)   A copy stored on a client's computer of part or all of the server-based global address list (GAL). An OAB allows a client to address messages while not connected to their server.

offline backup   A backup made while the Exchange services are stopped. When you perform an offline backup, users do not have access to their mailboxes while the backup takes place.

offline folder   See *Offline Storage (OST) folder*.

Offline Storage (OST) folder   Folders located on a client's computer that contain replicas of server-based folders. An OST allows a client to access and manipulate copies of server data while not connected to their server. When the client reconnects to their server, they can have their OST resynchronized with the master folders on the server.

OLE 2 See *Object Linking and Embedding version 2 (OLE 2).*

Open Shortest Path First (OSPF) A routing protocol developed for IP networks based on the shortest path first or link-state algorithm.

organization The highest-level object in the Microsoft Exchange hierarchy.

organizational unit (OU) An Active Directory container into which objects can be grouped for permissions management.

Outlook Anywhere A new mode of connecting remote Outlook 2007 clients to an Exchange Server 2007 organization without requiring the use of a virtual private network (VPN) or Outlook Web Access (OWA). RPCs are passed over the HTTP connection and secured with SSL encryption. Basic authentication is used to authenticate the user and is also protected by the SSL. Outlook Anywhere was first introduced in Exchange Server 2003 as RPC over HTTP.

Outlook Web Access (OWA)
A service that allows users to connect to Exchange Server and access mailboxes and public folders using a web browser.

OWA Light A scaled-down version of Outlook Web Access that was referred to as Basic in the Exchange Server 2003 version of OWA.

P

patch files Temporary logs that store transactions while a backup is taking place. Transactions in these logs are committed when the backup is finished.

pathping A new command that is a mix of both `ping` and `tracert`. The `pathping` command provides the ability to determine the packet loss along each link in the path and at each router in the path to the destination. This can be particularly helpful when troubleshooting problems where multiple routers and links are involved.

Performance Monitor See *Performance snap-in.*

Performance snap-in A utility used to log and chart the performance of various hardware and software components of a system. The Performance snap-in is also referred to as Performance Monitor, Performance tool, and System Monitor in various manuals.

perimeter network A network formed by using two firewalls to separate an internal network from the Internet and then placing certain servers, such as an Exchange front-end server, between the two firewalls. This is also referred to as a *demilitarized zone (DMZ).*

permission Provides specific authorization or denial to a user to perform an action on an object.

Personal Address Book (PAB)   An address book created by a user and stored on that user's computer or a server.

Personal Store (PST) folder   Folder created by a user and used for message storage instead of their mailbox in the mailbox database. PSTs can be located on a user's computer or on a server, although they are not supported when accessed from a server over the network.

Pickup folder   Used for outbound messages on some SMTP hosts. Exchange Server 2007 creates but does not ordinarily use this folder.

ping   Stands for Packet Internet Groper, the basic network connectivity troubleshooting tool that works by sending a series of ICMP Echo Request datagrams to a destination and waiting for the corresponding ICMP Echo Reply datagrams to come back. The return packets are then used to determine how many datagrams are getting through, the response time, and the time to live (TTL).

plain text   Unencrypted data. Synonymous with *clear text*.

Point-to-Point Protocol (PPP)   An Internet protocol used for the direct communication between two nodes. Commonly utilized by Internet users and their Internet service providers on the serial line point-to-point connection over a modem.

polling   A process that queries a server-based mailbox for new mail.

POP3   See *Post Office Protocol version 3 (POP3)*.

port number   A numeric identifier assigned to an application. Transport protocols such as TCP and UDP use the port number to identify to which application a packet is delivered.

Post Office Protocol version 3 (POP3)   An Internet protocol used for client retrieval of mail from a server-based mailbox.

postmaster mailbox   The postmaster mailbox is required in every messaging infrastructure per RFC 2822 and receives nondelivery reports and delivery status notifications.

primary domain controller (PDC) emulator   An operations master role server that is responsible for authenticating non–Active Directory clients, such as Windows 95 or Windows 98 clients. The PDC emulator is responsible for processing password changes from these clients and is also the responsible server for time synchronization within the domain.

private folder   See *mailbox*.

private key   The half of a key pair that is known by only the pair's user and is used to decrypt data and digitally sign messages.

property   A characteristic of an object. Properties of a mailbox include display name and storage limits. The terms *property* and *attribute* are synonymous.

public database   A database that holds public folders on an Exchange server. See also *database*.

public folder   A folder stored in a public store on an Exchange server and accessible to multiple users.

public folder hierarchy   The relative position of all the folders in a public folder tree.

public folder referral   The process by which a client can locate a requested public folder outside their home Exchange server.

public folder replication   The transferring of public folder data to replicas of that folder on other servers.

public folder tree   A hierarchy of public folders associated with a particular public database.

public key   The half of a key pair that is published for anyone to read and is used when encrypting data and verifying digital signatures.

public key infrastructure (PKI)   A system of components working together to verify the identity of users who transfer data on a system and to encrypt that data if needed.

public-key encryption   An encryption method that employs a key pair consisting of a public and a private key.

Q

queue folder   A folder in which messages that have yet to be delivered are stored.

Queue Viewer   A part of the Exchange System Manager that lets you view and manipulate the messages in a queue.

quorum disk   The disk set that contains definitive cluster configuration data. All members of an MSCS cluster must have continuous, reliable access to the data that is contained on a quorum disk. Information contained on the quorum disk includes data about the nodes that are participating in the cluster, the applications and resources that are defined within the cluster, and the current status of each member, application, and resource.

R

recipient   An object that can receive a message. Recipient objects include users, contacts, groups, and public folders.

recovery   When it refers to Exchange databases, *recovery* means to replay transaction log files into a restored database. This action brings the database up-to-date. There are two distinct forms of recovery: soft recovery and hard recovery. *Soft recovery* occurs with a database that failed and has been repaired or is just being remounted. A soft recovery is an automatic transaction log file replay process that occurs when a database is remounted after an unexpected failure. Soft recovery uses the log files that are currently in the log file location, using the checkpoint file to determine which log files to start with during the sequential replay process. A *hard recovery* occurs after a restore of a database. The hard recovery process plays the transaction log files into a restored database to bring the database back to a consistent state. The hard recovery process uses a RESTORE.env file that is generated during recovery to determine which transaction log files must be replayed from the temporary directory to which the backup was restored. The hard recovery process then continues to replay any additional transaction log files that it finds in the current transaction log file directory of the restored database.

recovery server   A server separate from the organization that is used as a dummy server for recovering individual mailboxes or messages from a backup.

recovery storage group   A feature first introduced in Exchange Server 2003 that provides a special storage group on a server to be used for performing restorations without needing to use an alternative recovery forest or take the database offline for an extended period of time.

regular expression   A string or set of symbols used to describe patterns of text. Regular expressions can be used in transport rules as a condition or exception. For example, you could use a regular expression to search message bodies for Social Security numbers and then perform an action on those messages if they had a Social Security number.

relative identifier (RID) master   An operations master role server that is responsible for maintaining the uniqueness of every object within its domain. When a new Active Directory object is created, it is assigned a unique security identifier (SID). The SID consists of a domain-specific SID that is the same for all objects created in that domain, and a relative identifier (RID) that is unique among all objects within that domain.

remote delivery   The delivery of a message to a recipient that does not reside on the same server as the sender.

remote domain   An email domain outside your Exchange organization.

remote procedure call (RPC)   A set of protocols for issuing instructions that can be sent over a network for execution. A client computer makes a request to a server computer, and the results are sent to the client computer. The computer issuing the request and the computer performing the request are separated remotely over a network. RPCs are a key ingredient in distributed processing and client/server computing. See also *local procedure call (LPC)*.

replica   A copy of a public folder located on an Exchange server.

replication   The transferring of a copy of data to another location, such as another server or site. See also *directory replication* and *public folder replication*.

reserve log files   Two transaction log files created by Exchange Server that are reserved for use when the server runs out of disk space.

resolving an address   The process of determining where (on which physical server) an object with a particular address resides.

resource group   Functions in a cluster that is not bound to a specific computer and can fail over to another node.

restore   To return the original files that were previously stored in a backup to their location on a server. For Exchange, this generally means restoring a database backup to a recovery storage group.

Rich Text format (RTF)   A Microsoft format protocol that includes bolding, highlighting, italics, underlining, and many other format types.

role   A group of permissions that define which activities a user or group can perform with regard to an object.

root CA   Resides at the top of a certificate authority hierarchy and is trusted unconditionally by a client. All certificate chains terminate at a root CA. See also *certificate authority (CA)*.

root domain   The top domain in a domain tree.

routing group   A collection of Exchange servers that have full-time, full-mesh, reliable connections between each and every server. Messages sent between any two servers within a routing group are delivered directly from the source server to the destination server.

routing group connector (RGC)   The primary connector used to connect routing groups in an organization. The RGC uses SMTP as its default transport mechanism.

routing group master   A server that maintains data about all the servers running Exchange Server 2000/2003 in a routing group.

rule   A set of instructions that defines how a message is handled when it reaches a folder.

S

S/MIME   See *Secure/Multipurpose Internet Mail Extensions (S/MIME)*.

scalable   The ability of a system to grow to handle greater traffic, volume, usage, and so on.

Schedule+ Free Busy public folder   A system folder that contains calendaring and synchronization information for Exchange users.

schema   The set of rules defining a directory's hierarchy, objects, attributes, and so on.

schema master   An operations master role that controls all updates and changes that are made to the schema.

secret key   A security key that can be used to encrypt data and that is known only by the sender and the recipients whom the sender informs.

Secure Sockets Layer (SSL)   An Internet protocol that provides secure and authenticated TCP/IP connections. A client and server establish a "handshake" whereby they agree on a level of security they will use, such as authentication requirements and encryption. SSL can be used to encrypt sensitive data for transmission.

Secure/Multipurpose Internet Mail Extensions (S/MIME)   An Internet protocol that enables mail messages to be digitally signed, encrypted, and decrypted.

security group   A group defined in Active Directory that can be assigned permissions and has an SID. All members of the group gain the permissions given to the group.

server license   Provides the legal right to install and operate Microsoft Exchange Server 2007 (or another server product) on a single-server machine.

service provider   A MAPI program that provides messaging-oriented services to a client. There are three main types of service providers: address book, message store, and message transport.

signing   The process of placing a digital signature on a message.

simple display name   An alternate name for the mailbox that appears when, for some reason, the full display name cannot.

Simple Mail Transfer Protocol (SMTP)   The Internet protocol used to transfer mail messages. It has been the default transport protocol since Exchange 2000 Server.

Simple Network Management Protocol (SNMP)   The Internet protocol used to manage heterogeneous computers, operating systems, and applications. Because of its wide acceptance and applicability, SNMP is well suited for enterprise-wide management.

single copy cluster (SCC)   This is a standard cluster much like previous server cluster implementations for Exchange. This implementation requires use of a shared disk implementation such as a SAN to host the quorum, the storage disks, and the transaction log disks.

single-instance storage   Storing only one copy. A message that is sent to multiple recipients homed in the same storage group has only one copy (that is, instance) stored on the server. Each recipient is given a pointer to that copy of the message.

site   A logical grouping of servers in previous versions of Exchange (prior to Exchange 2000 Server) that are connected by a full mesh (every server is directly connected to every other server) and communicate using high-bandwidth RPC. All servers in a site can authenticate one another either because they are homed in the same Windows domain or because of trust relationships configured between separate Windows domains. A site is also a group of Windows servers that are connected with full-time, reliable connections.

smart host   An SMTP host designated to receive all outgoing SMTP mail. The smart host then forwards the mail to the relevant destination.

SMTP   See *Simple Mail Transfer Protocol (SMTP)*.

SMTP connector   Using SMTP as its transport mechanism, the SMTP connector can be used to connect routing groups to one another and to connect Exchange to a foreign SMTP system.

SMTP virtual server   A logical representation of the SMTP protocol on a physical server.

SNMP   See *Simple Network Management Protocol (SNMP)*.

spooling   The process used by SMTP to temporarily store messages that cannot be delivered immediately.

stand-alone CA   Used to issue certificates to users who are outside the enterprise and who do not require access to the Active Directory. See also *certificate authority (CA)* and *enterprise CA*.

Standard Edition   The basic version of Exchange Server 2007 with support for up to five storage groups and five databases. There is no support for CCR or SCC clustering in this edition.

standard permissions   Permissions that are defined in a standard installation of Windows Server 2003. Extended permissions are created when Exchange Server 2007 is installed.

standby continuous replication (SCR)   A multiserver environment where the active storage group is copied to another server using log shipping. SCR was first introduced in Exchange Server 2007 SP1.

storage area network (SAN)   A set of connected devices (such as disks and tapes) and servers that are connected to a common infrastructure, such as Fibre Channel. The communication and data transfer channel for a given SAN environment is commonly called a *storage fabric*. The fabric of the SAN enables multiple servers to connect to a pool of storage devices that can include multiple arrays. In a SAN, any server can be configured to access any storage device or part of a storage device. In a SAN environment, management of the environment provides security for the storage units.

storage group   A collection of databases (up to five) that all share a common set of transaction logs. Exchange 2007 allows for five storage groups, and the Enterprise Edition allows for 50 storage groups per server.

Store.exe   The actual process that governs the use of stores on an Exchange server. Often referred to as the *Information Store service*.

store-and-forward   A delivery method that does not require the sender and recipient to have simultaneous interaction. Instead, when a message is sent, it is transferred to the next appropriate location in the network, which temporarily stores it, makes a routing decision, and forwards the message to the next appropriate network location. This process occurs until the message is ultimately delivered to the intended recipient or an error condition causes the message to be returned to the sender.

subordinate CA   A CA found underneath the root CA in the CA hierarchy and maybe even under other subordinate CAs. See also *certificate authority (CA)* and *root CA*.

subsystem   A software component that, when loaded, extends the operating system by providing additional services. The MAPI program, mapi32.dll, is an example of a subsystem. mapi32.dll loads on top of the Windows 98 or Windows XP operating system and provides messaging services.

System Monitor   See *Performance snap-in*.

system state backup   A form of backup that includes the Windows Registry, the IIS metabase, and the Active Directory (if run on a domain controller). Additionally, this may include the client access server configuration or cluster quorum for client access servers and clustered servers, respectively.

T

Task Manager   Displays the programs and processes running on a computer. It also displays various performance information, such as CPU and memory usage.

telnet client   A text-based command-line tool that allows you to communicate with a host remotely.

template   An object, such as a user or group, that contains configuration information that is applicable to multiple users. Objects for each user can be easily created by copying the template and filling in individual information.

TLS encryption   Transport Layer Security (TLS) encryption is a generic security protocol similar to Secure Sockets Layer encryption.

token   The packet of security information a certificate authority sends to a client during advanced security setup. Information in the packet includes the client's public key and its expiration. A token is similar to a certificate.

top-level folders   The folders found in the root level of a public folder tree.

tracert   A command-line utility that uses ICMP packets to determine the path that an IP datagram takes to reach its final destination.

transaction log   A file used to write data quickly. That data is later written to the relevant Exchange database file. It is quicker to write to a transaction log file because the writes are done sequentially (that is, one right after the other). Transaction log files can also be used to replay transactions from the log when rebuilding an Exchange database. All stores in a single storage group share the same set of transaction logs.

Triple Data Encryption Standard (3DES)   A newer, more secure variant of the DES standard that uses three 56-bit keys, one after another, to produce a 168-bit key.

Typical installation   This option installs the Exchange Server software, the basic Messaging and Collaboration components, and the System Manager snap-in program. It does not include the additional connectors.

U

Unified Messaging server   The Unified Messaging server role provides the following functionality to an Exchange Server 2007 organization:

- Fax reception and delivery to Exchange mailboxes
- Voice call answering and delivery of recorded voicemail files to Exchange mailboxes
- Voicemail access via a phone connection
- Message read-back via a phone connection, including replying to the message or forwarding it to another recipient
- Calendar access via a phone connection, including meeting request acceptance
- Out-of-office messages in voicemail via a phone connection

uniform resource identifier (URI)   A generic term for all types of addresses that refer to objects on the World Wide Web and private networks.

uniform resource locator (URL)   An addressing method used to identify Internet servers and documents.

URL   See *uniform resource locator (URL)*.

Usenet   A network within the Internet that is composed of numerous servers containing information on a variety of topics. Each organized topic is called a *newsgroup*.

user object   An object in Active Directory that is associated with a person on the network. Users can be mailbox-enabled or mail-enabled in Exchange Server 2007.

UUENCODE   Stands for Unix-to-Unix Encode and is a protocol used to encode binary information within mail messages. UUENCODE is older than MIME. See also *Multipurpose Internet Mail Extensions (MIME)*.

V

virtual local area network (VLAN)   A VLAN is an implementation where remote sites can be configured so that they appear to be on the same network segment.

virtual server   A group of resources that contains an IP address resource and a network name resource. The network name is then published to the network so that others can attach to its name to access resources included within the group. Clients access the resources of a virtual server exactly as they would access the resources of a physical server. Whether the server is a virtual server or a physical server doesn't matter to client computers on the network. They don't know the difference, and they just don't care, either.

volume shadow copy   A new feature in the Windows Server 2003 Backup Utility to back up open files as if they were closed at the moment of the backup event.

W

W3svc   The World Wide Web (WWW) publishing service of Internet Information Server (IIS).

Web   See *World Wide Web (WWW)*.

WebReady file types   Certain file types, such as Microsoft Word documents and Adobe Acrobat PDF documents, that can be converted to HTML easily. You can configure OWA to display these file types as HTML documents, thus allowing access to them even on computers that may not have the original applications they were created in installed.

well-known port numbers   Numbers that are commonly used as the TCP port numbers for popular applications, usually under 1,024.

Windows 2000 mixed domain functional level   The domain functional level that allows Windows NT 4.0 backup domain controllers to exist and function within a Windows 2003 domain.

Windows 2000 native domain functional level   The domain functional level that requires all domain controllers to be Windows 2000 Server or Windows Server 2003 and does not provide support for Windows NT 4.0 backup domain controllers.

Windows Event Log   See *Event Log*.

Windows Internet Naming System (WINS)   A name resolution service for resolving NetBIOS names on a Windows network.

Windows Server 2003 domain functional level   The highest domain functional level in Windows 2003, which implements all the new features of Windows 2003 Active Directory.

Windows site   A group of computers that exists on one or more IP subnets. Computers within a site must be connected by a fast, reliable network connection.

World Wide Web (WWW)   The collection of computers on the Internet using protocols such as HTML and HTTP.

WWW   See *World Wide Web (WWW)*.

X

X.400   An International Telecommunications Union (ITU) standard for message exchange.

X.500   An International Telecommunications Union (ITU) standard for directory services.

X.509 certificate   The most widely used format for certificates, X.509 certificates contain not only the public key but also information that identifies the user and the organization that issued the certificate.

Index

Note to the Reader: Throughout this index **boldfaced** page numbers indicate primary discussions of a topic. *Italicized* page numbers indicate illustrations.

O

S

Wiley Publishing, Inc.
End-User License Agreement

The Best MCTS: Configuring Microsoft Exchange Server 2007 Book/CD Package on the Market!

Get ready for the new MCTS: Microsoft Exchange Server 2007, Configuration exam (70-236) with the most comprehensive and challenging sample tests anywhere!

The Sybex Test Engine features:

- All the review questions, as covered in each chapter of the book.

- Challenging questions representative of those you'll find on the real exam.

- Two full-length bonus exams available only on the CD.

- An assessment test to narrow your focus to certain objective groups.

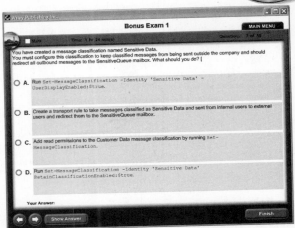

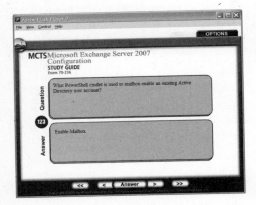

Use the electronic flashcards to jog your memory and prep last-minute for the exam!

- Reinforce your understanding of key concepts with these hardcore flashcard-style questions.

Search through the complete book in PDF!

- Access the entire *MCTS: Microsoft Exchange Server 2007 Configuration Study Guide, 2nd Edition* complete with figures and tables, in electronic format.

- Search the *MCTS: Microsoft Exchange Server 2007 Configuration Study Guide, 2nd Edition* chapters to find information on any topic in seconds.